INSIDE BACK FLAP: KEY TO SYMBOLS AND PAGE MARKER

Published by the Scottish Tourist Board
P.O. Box 705, Edinburgh EH4 3EU

ABOUT THIS BOOK

For more than thirty years **Where to Stay** has been the Scottish Tourist Board's official guide to holiday accommodation in Scotland. It is recognised as the most comprehensive of its kind and is revised annually. Hotels, guest houses and university accommodation in all parts of Scotland are listed here in alphabetical order by place-name.

CLASSIFICATION SCHEME

In 1975 voluntary registration of accommodation was introduced by the Scottish Tourist Board, and recommended minimum standards were established. These standards have now been extended to a much fuller classification which offers more detailed information about what facilities are available to the visitor.

The classification scheme is voluntary: establishments classify their facilities themselves, and are not normally inspected.

Bedrooms, **Services** and **Meals** are classified separately, on a scale of [1] to [6] for each facility. The larger the number, the greater the range of facilities. Thus, an establishment showing [1] in the Meals section offers only breakfast, while an establishment showing [4] offers breakfast, lunch and dinner, with a choice of dishes at all meals. The number refers only to **availability** of the facility, and is not an indication of quality.

Where an establishment has not agreed to supply the relevant information, or where it does not meet Category [1] requirements, a dash (—) appears.

In addition, each establishment agrees to comply with the Scottish Tourist Board's Code of Conduct.

Details of the categories for **Bedrooms**, **Services** and **Meals** are given on pages 298 to 301, along with the Code of Conduct.

Remember—the higher the number, the greater the range of facilities.

DISABLED VISITORS

Most of the places listed in this booklet welcome disabled visitors. However the suitability of these places does vary considerably and it is always advisable to check with an establishment before booking, that it provides the facilities or amenities which meet your particular needs. Blind people with a guide dog should inform the management about their circumstances.

The undernoted organisations may be able to provide further information and advice:—

Scottish Information Services for the Disabled
Princes House
5 Shandwick Place
EDINBURGH EH2 4RG
Tel: 031-229 8632

Holiday Care Service
2 Old Bank Chambers
Station Road
HORLEY
Surrey RH6 9HW
Tel: Horley (02934) 74535

BOOKING

It is always advisable to book accommodation in advance. This applies particularly during Easter and July and August.

Your travel agent will always be delighted to help you and to take care of your travel arrangements.

For those who have not booked in advance the accommodation booking services are very useful. More details on page xxiv.

There are about 150 Tourist Information Centres in Scotland, a list of which is given on page xviii. Not all operate the Book a Bed Ahead scheme; but whether they do or not, they are always glad to help with accommodation problems.

RESERVATIONS

Whilst the Scottish Tourist Board can give advice and information about any aspect of holidays in Scotland, it is **not** in a position to arrange accommodation or to make reservations; this should be done through a travel agent, a Tourist Information Centre which provides this service or directly to the hotel.

When you accept offered accommodation, on the telephone, or in writing, you are entering into a legally binding contract with the proprietor of the establishment. This means that if you cancel a reservation or fail to take up the accommodation (regardless of the reasons) the proprietor will be entitled to compensation if it cannot be relet for all or a good part of the booked period. If a deposit has been paid it is likely to be forfeited and an additional payment may be required.

COMPLAINTS

Any complaints or criticisms about individual hotels or guest houses should where possible be taken up immediately with the management. In most cases the problems can be dealt with satisfactorily, thus avoiding any prolonged unhappiness during your stay.

If this procedure fails to remedy the grievance to your satisfaction, and particularly where serious complaints are concerned, please write to the local Tourist Board (see p. xviii).

DOGS

Where dogs are permitted, owners are asked to take responsibility for pets' behaviour. In particular, please keep dogs under control in the presence of farm animals.

VALUE ADDED TAX (VAT)

Please note that VAT is calculated by establishments for this publication at a rate of 15%. Any subsequent changes in this rate will affect the price you will be charged.

PRICES

To make this guide available at the earliest possible and practical time for 1984, the information contained has had to be gathered far ahead of the 1984 holiday season. Accordingly, in these inflationary days, the prices given can only be forecasts of the likely range.

The prices and details of establishments quoted herein are as supplied by the respective operators and to the best of our knowledge were correct at the time of going to press.

Some establishments have not been able to supply advance information about prices for all of their facilities. Where this is the case, a dash (—) appears in the entry. This does not necessarily mean that the facility will not be available.

There may have been amendments subsequently and in your own interests you should check before making a booking.

The Scottish Tourist Board can accept no responsibility for any errors or omissions in prices or facilities.

The prices quoted are normally the minimum for the majority of rooms in the establishment and include service charges, if any, and Value Added Tax. In a few cases where normally breakfast is charged separately, the rates quoted include this charge; it may, however, be for Continental breakfast—if full breakfast is required, this charge should be checked. In many cases, double/twin bedded rooms can accommodate families: the availability of these and of family rooms is shown, along with other details.

September 1983

FRANÇAIS

OU SE LOGER EN ECOSSE

Bienvenue en Ecosse!

Voici le guide touristique officiel des hôtels et pensions de famille en Ecosse, publié par l'Office écossais du tourisme. Revu chaque année, ce guide est reconnu depuis trente ans comme le plus complet en son genre. Des hôtels, pensions de famille et résidences universitaires de toutes les régions de l'Ecosse y sont classés selon l'ordre alphabétique des localités. Sauf indication contraire, l'indicatif téléphonique est celui de la localité.

Au moment de mettre sous presse, il ne nous est pas possible de donner des prix définitifs; il est vivement conseillé aux visiteurs de demander confirmation des prix lorsqu'ils effectuent la réservation.

Nous avons signalé à l'attention des gourmets les hôtels qui offrent les spécialités de la cuisine écossaise (recettes écossaises traditionnelles à base de produits écossais de haute qualité).

NB. L'Office écossais du tourisme (Scottish Tourist Board) décline toute responsabilité en cas d'erreurs ou d'omissions.

AVERTISSEMENT: CHIENS ETC.

Il est rappelé aux visiteurs étrangers que l'introduction d'animaux domestiques en Grande-Bretagne est soumise à une réglementation très stricte, qui prévoit une longue période de quarantaine. Etant donné le danger de propagation du virus rabique, des peines très sévères sont prévues pour toute infraction aux réglements.

SUR LES ROUTES D'ECOSSE

Veillez à attacher votre ceinture de sécurité, si votre voiture en est munie. Le port de la ceinture est obligatoire en Grande Bretagne.

La légende des symboles se trouve au volet de la couverture, qui fait aussi office de signet.

Nom et Adresse		Prix		Chambres		Facilités
VILLE Comté — Réf. cartographique / Chambres / Services / Repas		Chambre et petit déjeuner (par nuit) — Chambre pour une personne / Chambre pour deux (grand lit ou lits jumeaux)	Demi-pension par personne — Par jour / Par semaine	Nombre de chambres — Pour une personne (grand lit/ lits jumeaux) / Familiale	Salles de bain/ douches — Privées (avec WC) / Publiques	Heure du dîner / Nombre de places de stationnement pour voitures / Mois d'ouverture (1-12) / Symboles
Etablissement Adresse Téléphone Télex						

DEUTSCH

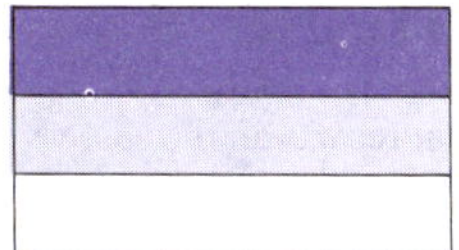

WO ÜBERNACHTET MAN IN SCHOTTLAND

Willkommen in Schottland!

Dieses Buch ist der offizielle Führer des Schottischen Touristenbüros für Ferienübernachtungen in Privatpensionen in Schottland. Seit dreißig Jahren wird dieses Buch als das umfassendste seiner Art anerkannt. Es wird jedes Jahr auf den neuesten Stand gebracht. Hotels, Gasthäuser und Unterbringung in den Universitäten in allen Teilen Schottlands sind hier nach Ortsnamen in alphabetischer Reihenfolge aufgeführt. Die jeweilige Vorwahlnummer ist unter dem Ortsnamen zu finden, außer, wenn sie extra angegeben ist.

Zu Beginn der Drucklegung dieses Buches ist es noch nicht möglich, feste Preise anzugeben, und Besuchern wird daher geraten, sich nach den Tarifen zu erkundigen, wenn sie Buchungen vornehmen.

Das Schottische Touristenbüro (Scottish Tourist Board) kann keine Verantwortung für eventuelle Fehler oder Auslassung von Preisen und Einrichtungen übernehmen.

Als weitere Hilfe haben wir die Privatpensionen gekennzeichnet, die echte schottische Küche—Taste of Scotland—anbieten. Das bedeutet, daß hier traditionell schottische Rezepte verwandt werden unter Benutzung schottischer Produkte von hoher Qualität.

HUNDE

Das Mitbringen von Tieren jeder Art aus dem Ausland ist wegen Tollwutgefahr strengstens untersagt. Die Übertretung dieses Gesetzes wird mit hohen Strafen belegt.

AUTOFAHREN IN SCHOTTLAND

Schnallen Sie sich immer an! Es witd nun zur Pflicht. (Vorausgesetzt, Ihr Auto ist mit Sicherheitsgurt ausgestattet.)

Die Zeichenerklärungen befinden sich im eingeklebten Faltblatt am Ende des Buches.

Name und Adresse			Preise				Zimmer		Einrichtungen
STADT Bezirk	Kartenkoordinaten Schlafzimmer		Übernachtung mit Frühstück		Halbpension		Anzahl der Schlafzi.	Anzahl Bad/ Dusche	
		Dienstleistungen							
		Mahlzeiten							
Name Adresse Telefon Telex			Einzelzimmer (pro Übernachtung)	Doppel-/Zweibettzimmer (pro Übernachtung)	pro Person (pro Tag)	pro Person (pro Woche)	Einzelzi. / Doppel-/Zweibettzi. / Familienzi. / Privat / Etagenbad.-dusche	Abendessen / Parkplätze / Monate geöffnet (1-12)	Symbole

YOUR HOLIDAY IN SCOTLAND

USEFUL INFORMATION ABOUT SCOTLAND

TRAVEL

Bookings for rail, sea and air travel to Scotland and within Scotland should be made through your travel agent, or directly to British Rail, airlines and ferry companies. The Scottish Tourist Board will be glad to give you information but cannot make your bookings for you.

Seats may be booked in advance on the main long-distance coaches, aircraft and for berths and cabins in the steamers to the islands. Sleeping berths on trains should always be booked well in advance. It is necessary to book seats for 'extended' coach tours and also for day coach outings operated from most holiday and touring centres.

Car hire bookings should also be made in advance wherever possible, especially for July and August, Taxis are readily available in Edinburgh, Glasgow, and other major centres at controlled charges. Taxis are generally available in most communities, but in smaller, less populous areas charges may vary considerably.

DRIVING

The 'Rules of the Road' are the same in Scotland as in the rest of the U.K. While there is limited motorway mileage in Scotland, the roads are uniformly good. In the remoter areas there is a considerable mileage of one-way roads, with frequent passing-places. Please, *never* use these passing-places as lay-bys — or for overnight parking of caravans. Slow-moving traffic (and motorists towing caravans), are asked to pull in to passing places, where appropriate, to let faster traffic through.

When touring in the far north and west particularly, remember that petrol stations are comparatively few, and distances between them may be considerable. Some petrol stations close on Sundays. Fill your tank in good time, and keep it as full as possible.

SCOTLAND'S WEATHER

Did you know that in June, places in the north of Scotland have an average of 18-20 hours of daylight each day, and that resorts on the east coast are particularly noted for their hours of sunshine?

June has those marvellous long evenings when it's light till very late, and the palm trees which grow on the west coast must say something about how warm it is.

Yes, we do have to admit, it does sometimes rain in Scotland; but rainfall is surprisingly low despite the age-old myths. The rainfall in the Edinburgh area, for example, is almost exactly the same as that around London — and Rome for that matter. And don't forget, even if you do get caught in a shower, that Scotland is well-endowed with a whole host of indoor attractions to keep you entertained till long after the sun has come out again.

PUBLIC HOLIDAYS

The Bank Holidays which are also general holidays in England do not apply in Scotland. Most Bank Holidays apply to banks and to some professional and commercial offices only, although Christmas Day and New Year's Day are usually taken as holidays by everyone. Scottish banks are closed in 1984 on 2 and 3 January, 20 April, 7 and 28 May, 6 August, 25 and 26 December. In place of the general holidays, Scottish cities and towns normally have a Spring Holiday and an Autumn Holiday. The dates of these holidays vary from place to place, but they are almost invariably on a Monday.

MONEY

Currency, coinage and postal rates in Scotland are the same as in the rest of the U.K. Scotland differs from England in that Scottish banks issue their own notes. These are acceptable in England, at face value, as are Bank of England notes in Scotland. Main banks are open during the following hours:

Monday, Tuesday, Wednesday: 0930-1230, 1330-1530

Thursday: 0930-1230; 1330-1530; 1630-1800

Friday: 0930-1530

Some city centre banks are open daily 0930-1530.

In rural areas, banks post their hours clearly outside and travelling banks call regularly.

SHOPPING

The normal shopping hours in Scotland are 0900-1800, although bakeries, dairies and newsagents open earlier. Many shops have an early closing day (1300) each week, but the actual day varies from place to place and in cities from district to district.

EATING

Lunch in restaurants and hotels outside the main centres is usually served between 1230 and 1400. Dinner usually starts at 1900 or 1930 and may not be served much after 2100. Where you know you may arrive late it is advisable to make arrangements for a meal in advance. An alternative to dinner is High Tea, usually served between 1630 and 1830.

A TASTE OF SCOTLAND 

When eating out, don't forget to sample a 'Taste of Scotland'. Look out for the 'Stockpot' sign at hotels and restaurants. This indicates that the establishment offers traditional Scottish recipes using the best of Scottish produce: Scottish soups with intriguing names like Powsowdie or Cullen Skink; Aberdeen Angus steaks or venison or game in season; salmon or trout from Scottish rivers, or herring or haddock cured in a variety of ways; and a choice of some 30 varieties of Scottish cheese — these are some of the 'Tastes of Scotland' which add to the enjoyment of a holiday.

LICENSING LAWS

Currently in Scotland, the hours that public houses and hotel bars are open to serve drinks are the same all over the country. 'Pubs' are open from 110 to 1430 and from 1700 to about 2300 hours, Monday to Saturday inclusive and some are now licensed to open on Sundays. In addition, some establishments may have obtained extended licences for afternoon or late night opening.

Hotel bars have the same hours as 'pubs', and are open on Sundays from 1230 to 1430 and 1830 to 2300. Residents in licensed hotels may have drinks served at any time. Some restaurants and hotels have extended licences allowing them to serve drinks with meals until 0100 in the morning. Persons under the age of 18 are not allowed to drink in licensed premises.

CHURCHES

The established Church of Scotland is Presbyterian, but the Roman Catholic and other denominations have very considerable numbers of adherents. The Episcopal Church of Scotland is in full communion with the Church of England, and uses a similar form of worship. In the far north and west of Scotland, particularly in the islands, many people belong to the Free Church of Scotland, and appreciate it when their views on the Sabbath as a day when there should be no recreational or other unnecessary activity, are respected by visitors. Times of services of the various denominations are usually intimated on hotel notice boards, as well as outside the churches and, of course, visitors are always welcome.

COMING FROM OVERSEAS?

Visitors to Scotland from overseas require to observe the same regulations as for other parts of the U.K. As a general rule they must have a valid passport and, in certain cases, visas issued by British Consular authorities overseas: check with a local Travel Agent, or where appropriate, the overseas offices of the British Tourist Authority.

Currency: Overseas visitors who require information about the import and export of currency, cars, or other goods, on personal purchases and belongings, shopping concessions, etc., should consult a Travel Agent or Bank or the overseas offices of the B.T.A.

Driving: Motorists coming from overseas who are members of a motoring organisation in their own country may obtain from them full details of the regulations for importing cars, motor cycles, etc., for holiday and touring purposes into the U.K. They can drive in Britain on a current Driving Licence from their own country, or with an international Driving Permit, for a maximum period of 12 months. Otherwise, a British Driving Licence must be obtained: until the Driving Test is passed it is essential to be accompanied by a driver with a British licence.

Seat belts: Drivers and front seat passengers **must** wear safety belts while driving in Britain, by law.

VAT: Value Added Tax, currently charged at 15% on many goods, can sometimes be reclaimed by overseas visitors who buy items for export. Visitors should ask the shopkeeper about the retail export schemes before making a purchase, and will be required to fill in special forms.

RABIES

Britain is *very* concerned to prevent the spread of rabies. Strict quarantine regulations apply to animals brought into Britain from abroad and severe penalties are enforced if they are broken or ignored. Dogs and cats are subject to 6 months quarantine in an approved quarantine centre. Full details from the Department of Agriculture and Fisheries for Scotland, Chesser House, 500 Gorgie Road, Edinburgh EH11 3AW. The restrictions do not apply to animals from Eire, Northern Ireland, the Isle of Man or the Channel Islands.

SCOTLAND'S TOURIST AREAS

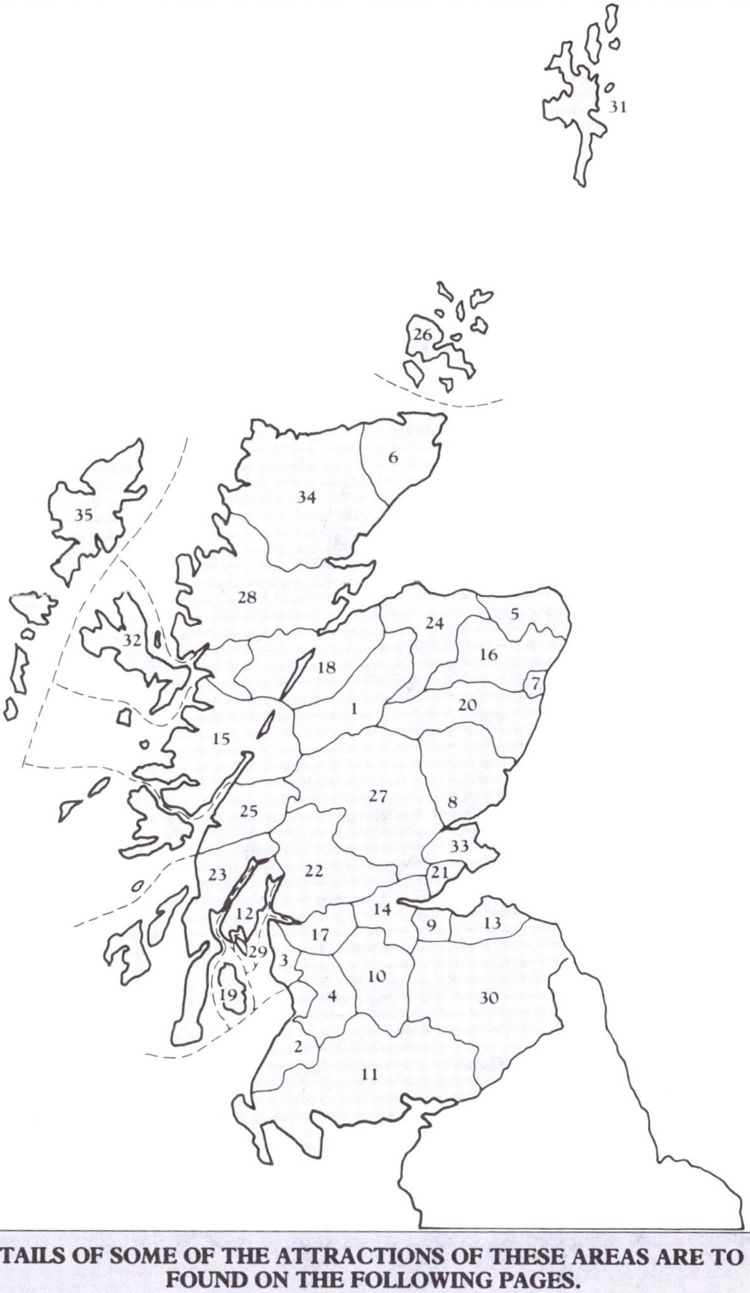

DETAILS OF SOME OF THE ATTRACTIONS OF THESE AREAS ARE TO BE FOUND ON THE FOLLOWING PAGES.

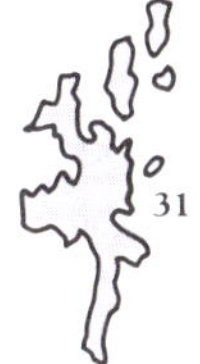

SCOTLAND'S TOURIST AREAS

— 1 —

Aviemore and Spey Valley

Dominated by tree-clad, craggy mountains, river, loch and stream, the Spey Valley offers a unique welcome. Come climbing and ski-ing in the mighty Cairngorms, sailing and canoeing on rivers and lochs and angling in the famous River Spey. History abounds with ruined castles and a relic of the Jacobite rebellion, the formidable Ruthven Barracks. Folk and clan museums, wildlife and nature parks, osprey, reindeer and breathtaking scenery provide a land of contrast. Accommodation in hotels, guest and farmhouses, caravan and campsites and the attractions of a modern holiday complex at the Aviemore Centre offer all the year round Highland hospitality.

— 2 —

Ayrshire and Burns Country

Ayrshire and Burns Country, situated on the south-west coast of Scotland, offers something for everyone. The area's rich and colourful heritage is depicted by the many castles, both ruined and otherwise, scattered throughout the district. Robert Burns, Scotland's National Poet, was born at Alloway, the starting point for the Burns Heritage Trail. With fifteen golf courses, including three championship ones, Turnberry, Troon and Prestwick, the area is aptly described as a paradise for any golfer. With no shortage of good accommodation and entertainment facilities, why not visit ABC Land and see for yourself that it's just too good to miss!

— 3 —

Ayrshire and Clyde Coast

On Scotland's west coast — encompassing north Ayrshire and the islands of Arran and Cumbrae, this area is rich in natural beauty. The mainland coastline has many fine beaches, with superb golf courses backing them. The islands have a magic of their own: peace, tranquillity, yet plenty to do from cycling to mountain climbing. Irvine has a beach park and leisure centre which ranks as one of the largest in Europe, and the coastal resorts of Saltcoats, Ardrossan and Largs have much to offer including Largs' world famous Viking Festival.

— 4 —

Ayrshire Valleys

The Ayrshire Valleys Tourist Area — Kilmarnock and Loudoun and Cumnock and Doon Valley — the very heart of Scotland. Every year more and more tourists discover the special appeal of the Ayrshire Valleys. Much of the history of Scotland is here in stone and in reputation. From this area came individuals who contributed massively to the progress of mankind, inventions bringing benefits world wide, industrial innovation and literature. This heritage together with the gentle scenic beauty and the warm hospitality of Ayrshire make the Ayrshire Valleys increasingly popular for the tourist who seeks the real Scotland.

— 5 —

Banff and Buchan

Banff and Buchan is the unspoiled north-east corner of Scotland, where majestic crags thrust out into the sea. Excellent uncrowded roads take you through the rolling fertile countryside contrasting with the picturesque harbours along the coast. Fisher villages, almost untouched by time, perch precariously between breakers and cliff. A host of activities for the whole family — boating, swimming, fishing, golf, riding and bowling as well as museums and craft centres. The friendly local folk will welcome you with a cheery smile to a wide range of comfortable and good value accommodation, ranging from snug hotels to beach-side caravans.

Tourist Information Centres in these areas and addresses to write for further information are on pages xviii to xxiii.

SCOTLAND'S TOURIST AREAS

6

Caithness

At the north-east corner of Scotland lies a land of contrasts, of the past and the future, of the rugged coastline and the hospitable people. From the deep past there are ancient standing stones, and from medieval times castles and ruins to remind us of our turbulent heritage; but for the future Caithness is home to Dounreay nuclear power station. The coastline juts out into the wild sea which has created many spectacular sights, like Dunnet Head and the Duncansby Stacks. But come and stay and you'll be won over by our hospitable ways.

7

City of Aberdeen

Come to Aberdeen when a myriad of purple, golden, scarlet and white flowers spell out the romantic magic of spring . . . come in summer when the air is full of the fragrance of millions of roses . . . come in autumn or winter when clear skies and 'Turner' sunsets enhance this lovely city. Come at Festival time . . . come at anytime . . . to enjoy walking on our unspoilt beach . . . to see our historic buildings . . . to visit the magnificent castle country that surrounds the Granite City. Just come. You'll fall in love — with a city and with an almost forgotten quality of life.

8

City of Dundee and Angus

Dundee is on the north bank of the Firth of Tay, the estuary of the River Tay, the longest river in Scotland, famed for both its salmon and sea trout fishing. Its setting provides beautiful vistas across the river to Fife, west over the fertile Carse of Gowrie and north to the Sidlaw Hills. Beyond, in Angus, are the historic towns of Arbroath, Montrose and Forfar, and delightful Highland glens. Many famous historical figures including William Wallace and Mary, Queen of Scots, have influenced the area's heritage and are reflected in the many castles and other ancient artefacts.

9

City of Edinburgh

Edinburgh, Scotland's beautiful capital and international Festival City, is full of historic and romantic interest. It is surrounded by hills, woodlands and rivers and also features an extensive coastline. The City is dominated by its ancient fortress towering over gardens which during the summer feature Highland and Scottish country dancing, interesting shopping and the treasures of the Royal Mile. For the young, and not so young, there is always something interesting to see or to do. A warm welcome awaits you.

10

Clyde Valley

The Clyde Valley links the districts of Clydesdale, Hamilton & Motherwell. It follows the course of the Clyde from Leadhills in the south to Uddingston in the north. This area has many attractions for the visitor: scenic beauty, urban parks, orchard country, pastoral valleys, purple hills and moorlands; a rich historical heritage including museums, castles and churches; many outdoor activities such as golf and watersports; a fine selection of facilities plus an exciting calendar of events. The main route between England and Scotland (A74) runs through the area — making it an ideal place to break your journey north or south.

11

Dumfries and Galloway

This is a relatively forgotten corner of Scotland, but for the discerning tourist looking for beaches and hills; castles and abbeys; museums and

Tourist Information Centres in these areas and addresses to write for further information are on pages xviii to xxiii.

SCOTLAND'S TOURIST AREAS

gardens; sea angling and salmon fishing; or a winter holiday away from the rigours of ski-ing: it is an area you are unlikely to forget. One of Scotland's principal highways, the A74, cuts through the area from south to north. So why don't you leave the headlong flight to others and take yourself off the dual carriageway into the quiet and meandering byways of Dumfries and Galloway.

12

Dunoon and Cowal

Holidaying on an island stirs the romantic blood. Cowal is an island — well almost! Most visitors travel on the short ferry crossing from Gourock to Dunoon, but you can 'Take the High Road' and be in Dunoon in under two hours from Glasgow. Being slightly off-the-beaten-track of the 'doing Scotland' tourist brigade, the Cowal Peninsula is a peaceful corner of Argyll where you can travel on quiet, uncluttered roads, where you can relax and enjoy our magnificent scenery, our mountains, our seascapes, our lochs and glens, and the steeply wooded hillsides of the Argyll Forest Park.

13

East Lothian

East Lothian is an area rich in contrast which provides just about everything for the family. You can be assured of a genuine welcome, good food, unspoilt scenery, historic sites, perfect stretches of golden sand, the opportunity for recreation or the relief of doing simply nothing. Hotels and guest houses, with 14 golf courses on their doorstep, specialise in catering for the golfer and his family. East Lothian — an experience you will treasure for a lifetime.

14

Forth Valley

Crowned by the magnificent Forth Bridges, Forth Valley has a wealth of history: neolithic Cairnpapple; the Antonine Wall in Falkirk; Scotland's ancient capital, Dunfermline; quaint 17th century burgh, Culross; picturesque Linlithgow Palace, birthplace of Mary Queen of Scots; elegant stately homes, The Binns, Dalmeny and Hopetoun Houses; and relics of the industrial age, the canals and Bo'ness Steam Railway. The attractive countryside may surprise you. Wander in peace in the country parks, Almondell, Beecraigs, Polkemmet, Lochore and Muiravonside. Forth Valley is easy to reach wherever you're heading. Start your holiday by leaving the motorways, to explore the Forth Valley.

15

Fort William and Lochaber

From the centre of Lochaber, Ben Nevis, Britain's highest mountain, oversees a vast area of beauty and history. Glencoe and the Stewart country of Appin together with the Road to the Isles encompass the history of Bonnie Prince Charlie and the Jacobite rebellion with its romance and intrigue. To the west lie Ardnamurchan and Morvern with their tranquillity and solitude. Mallaig and Morar, with the 'Local Hero' silversands overlook the Small Isles of Muck, Rhum, Eigg and Canna and to the north Glenspean and the Great Glen invite exploring, and in Fort William itself there is always something to see and do.

16

Gordon

You have to be prepared for enchantment if you choose to come to Gordon District. Gordon's countryside varies from the sandy beaches of Balmedie on the east coast to the upland terrain of the western part of Strathdon. Restored castles and romantic ruins abound. Age-old crafts are being revived and visitors are welcome. But Gordon is not just for the spectator — it is a paradise for anglers, golfers, skiers, hillwalkers, railway enthusiasts and malt

Tourist Information Centres in these areas and addresses to write for further information are on pages xviii to xxiii.

SCOTLAND'S TOURIST AREAS

whisky drinkers. Your holiday in Gordon District can be as quiet and relaxing or as energetic and lively as you care to make it.

—17—

Greater Glasgow

Glasgow, Scotland's largest city, is the cultural capital of Scotland. It is home to Scottish Opera, Scottish Ballet, Scottish National Orchestra, Scottish Theatre Company and a priceless collection of art treasures housed in a number of museums, the newest being Pollok House which is the home of the magnificent Burrell Collection. Entertainment of all kinds is a particular feature of the area as are the excellent shopping facilities. With its many first-class hotels and excellent connections by road, rail and air the Greater Glasgow Area is an ideal touring base from which to explore Scotland.

—18—

Inverness, Loch Ness and Nairn

In Inverness's glorious river salmon can be caught near the city centre. Shopping is excellent, while entertainment sparkles more brightly each year. The Caledonian Canal sees more craft making use of its lovely passage. Nairn, a longtime favourite with famous visitors for its generous servings of sunshine, its beaches and golf, has an updated caravan park and new small intimate theatre. At Culloden Moor the excellent visitor facilities have been enlarged and the battlefield is being returned to how it was in 1746. Visit this hub of the Highlands for a combination of the best of the past and today.

—19—

Isle of Arran

A Hebridean refugee sheltering in the Firth of Clyde, the Isle of Arran is only an hour's sail from the mainland port of Ardrossan, which connects with rail and road traffic. Towering mountains in the north, soft rolling lands in the south, sixty miles of glorious coastline with sub-tropical palms, glens, inland lochs and waterfalls — a veritable photographer's paradise. Past and present merge when you gaze across the Firth once scoured by the Vikings and crossed by Bruce and his 300. The energetic will appreciate the Island's sporting facilities and the numerous beaches — the only problem is where to start.

—20—

Kincardine and Deeside

Kincardine and Deeside extends a heartfelt welcome and invites you to a feast of ever changing spectacle and colour — from the regal splendour of Balmoral Castle, the Scottish summer residence of the Royal Family to the thrilling sights and sounds of the world famous Braemar Gathering, to the homeland of the sparkling Dee famous for its salmon fishing. Lush pine-clad hillsides rise from its banks, while along its length a wonderland of romantic castles speaks of the sometimes turbulent past. Our coastline is as varied as it is beautiful. Kincardine and Deeside is an experience you will never forget.

—21—

Kirkcaldy

Kirkcaldy and District is an area rich in heritage which has been preserved to ensure you will remember your stay. In Kirkcaldy, with its fine views across the Firth of Forth, you can trace the lives of Adam Smith, the philosopher, or Robert Adam, the architect; or admire the skill of the local Wemyss Ware pottery. There are many picturesque seaside villages in the area, while inland there is plenty of scope for walks and golf. If you want to travel further afield, the attractions of the East Neuk of Fife, Perth, Falkland Palace and Loch Leven are just a short drive away.

Tourist Information Centres in these areas and addresses to write for further information are on pages xviii to xxiii.

SCOTLAND'S TOURIST AREAS

22

Loch Lomond, Stirling and the Trossachs

Bridging the gap between highlands and lowlands lies the scenic splendour of Loch Lomond and the Trossachs combining with the excitement of historic Stirling. Underlying the visual impact, feel the brooding atmosphere of the area's heritage; the land of folk hero Rob Roy McGregor, the stirring site of Bannockburn, and the castle homes of Scotland's royalty and aristocracy. Couple this with some of today's fascinating visitor attractions; lose yourself in the tranquillity of a boat trip on one of the lochs; or walk the unspoilt country paths, all before coming home to Scottish hospitality within a superb choice of accommodation.

23

Mid Argyll, Kintyre and Islay

Situated in the South West Highlands, this holiday area has over 1,000 miles of coastline, heavily indented with attractive sea lochs and natural harbours — a yachtsman's paradise. Hillwalking and loch fishing, golf and archaeology, sub-tropical gardens and bird watching — a gentle countryside to enjoy these varied pursuits. Blessed with a temperate climate the Atlantic seaboard on Kintyre and Islay provides a habitat for many species of wintering birds, especially geese. Enjoy the colourful sub-tropical gardens which flourish on Gigha and at Crarae, all year round golf, the ultimate seclusion of exploration on Jura — holidays to suit everyone.

24

Moray

Moray District lies on the sunny southern shores of the Moray Firth, midway between Aberdeen and Inverness, embracing the ancient bishopric whose symbol is the magnificent ruined Cathedral of Elgin. Along the coast sandy beaches alternate with villages whose traditional architecture is a link with the prosperous times of the fishing industry. Inland the fertile farmlands of Moray rise gently through extensive forest and beyond the River Spey — famed among salmon fishermen — to the high Cairngorm Mountains. Moray is the heart of the whisky industry, with almost half of Scotland's distilleries within its borders, many of them open to visitors.

25

Oban, Mull and District

Oban is the gateway to a world of tranquillity — to the enchantment of the highlands and the Hebrides. Sail away to the dreaming isles of Mull, Coll, Tiree, Staffa and the Holy Isle of Iona — or escape to the naturalists' paradise of Colonsay. Explore the land of Lorne — the grandeur of its mountains, winding lochs, whispering forests — villages, castles, gardens — and, of course, the town of Oban itself. Wherever you go you will find traditional hospitality in the friendly shops, the Highland Games and Ceilidhs — and, from country house to country cottage, holiday accommodation to suit all tastes.

26

Orkney

Separated by a mere six miles from mainland Scotland, the low lying fertile islands that comprise Orkney have an abundance of treasures. Here is the richest historic area in Scotland which is home to over one million seabirds. The lochs of Orkney provide wild brown trout and no permits are required. The surrounding waters provide good sea angling with record-breaking Skate and Halibut. Scapa Flow and its sunken German warships is Europe's best dive site. Add to this the genuine friendliness and hospitality of the people and

---

Tourist Information Centres in these areas and addresses to write for further information are on pages xviii to xxiii.

SCOTLAND'S TOURIST AREAS

you can be assured of an island adventure in Britain's Treasure Islands.

27

Perthshire

Break away to the heartland of Scotland, to Perthshire's heather hills and hidden lochs. Come by rail, air or road — and you'll come back again. To find peace if you wish, and space, or action if you choose. Here, in one of Europe's most beautiful holiday regions, covering over 2,000 square miles in the heartland of Scotland is where a nation's story was written. Sir Walter Scott once wrote: 'If an intelligent stranger were asked to describe the most varied and most beautiful province in Scotland, it is probable that he would name the county of Perthshire'. Our visitors all agree.

28

Ross and Cromarty

Explore the coast of Wester Ross and you'll discover breathtaking mountains and great cliffs. Wander through East Ross and the Black Isle, and you'll be amid gentle hills, woods and charming Highland villages. Coast to coast — there's plenty to surprise and interest you. The incredible sub-tropical Inverewe Gardens, Torridon's mighty peaks and Hugh Miller's Cottage in Cromarty. Visit Strathpeffer, the Victorian spa village or Ullapool and enjoy a pleasure cruise to the Summer Isles. Golfers, walkers and fishers can always find new experiences or alternatively just laze on sandy beaches such as the Golden Sands at Gairloch.

29

Rothesay and Isle of Bute

The Isle of Bute has long been one of Scotland's favourite holiday retreats, set in the heart of the glorious Firth of Clyde. Safe, sandy beaches adorn the coastline. There are enough entertainments and facilities in Rothesay alone to amuse the whole family. There's golf on three courses, each enjoying spectacular views; sailing and cruising; walking and cycling. Delve into Bute's rich history at the ancient Castle and the Bute Museum. All this just 30 minutes by ferry from Wemyss Bay (serving Central Scotland and the motorways) or only 5 minutes across the Kyles of Bute from Colintraive (Argyll).

30

Scottish Borders

In Scotland's south-eastern corner, the Scottish Borders is a land of rolling hills, wooded river valleys, prosperous farmland and rugged castles. A link with the region's turbulent past is evidenced by the hilltop ruins of castles and keeps, while the ruined abbeys remind the visitor of a more peaceful era, and there are houses from various times. The thriving woollen textile industry produces quality knitwear and tweeds. The River Tweed, famous for its salmon fishing, threads its way through the region, and provides a superb setting for many of the towns and villages of the region.

31

Shetland

The enchanting Shetland islands lie almost as close to Norway as to Scotland and the Viking heritage lives on in culture, dialect and place names. A scattered mosaic of 100 islands or skerries, there is so much to see and explore. Nature abounds — the cliffs are teeming with birds, the lochs are filled with trout, ponies roam the hills, and seals and otters frequent the bays. Transport to Shetland is easy with frequent daily flights and drive-on drive-off ferries. For a holiday abroad in Britain, visit Shetland — the natural holiday choice.

Tourist Information Centres in these areas and addresses to write for further information are on pages xviii to xxiii.

SCOTLAND'S TOURIST AREAS

32

South West Ross and The Isle of Skye

A short ferry trip from South West Ross, Skye has over 900 miles of coastline rich in bays and towering cliffs, dominated by the great ridge of the Cuillin Mountains. Rich in Bonnie Prince Charlie's history it has a romantic but awe-inspiring atmosphere which can only be felt by visiting this remarkable island. The old way of life is reflected in the Black House Museums, contemporary crafts are plentiful and unusual, from candle-making to hand-weaving. With South West Ross so close on the main land, rich too in its own history — the whole area 'comes well recommended'.

33

St Andrews and North East Fife

North East Fife, approximately one hour from Edinburgh by road or rail, lies between the Firth of Forth and the River Tay. The coastline from Lundin Links to Crail — 'The East Neuk' — is a chain of delightful fishing villages and forms part of Scotland's Fishing Heritage Trail. Inland, the many places of interest to visitors are linked by a network of quiet country roads centred on the market town of Cupar. The university town and holiday resort of St Andrews is famous too as the 'Home of Golf' and the Old Course is the venue for many international tournaments.

34

Sutherland

Sutherland is a scenic area of great beauty, with mystical sea-lochs, magnificent mountains, crystal-clear streams, rugged coastline, picturesque villages and vibrant moorlands laced with quiet meandering roads. Visit Dunrobin Castle with its fairytale turrets, marvel at our range of peaks and discover the huge sea cliffs near Cape Wrath and awesome Smoo Cave. You simply won't believe our clean and extensive beaches and don't forget to visit the Strathnaver Museum which depicts the tragedy of the Highland 'Clearances'. So come north and visit us soon. Getting to Sutherland couldn't be easier.

35

Western Isles

Due to their separation from the mainland of Scotland the Western Isles have a unique character all of their own. This splintered sweep of islands, stretching 130 miles from the Butt of Lewis to Barra Head incorporates six immensely beautiful holiday islands. On the west coasts there are long stretches of pasture land with wild flowers and miles of clean sandy beaches. The eastern coasts are rugged with cliffs and small bays which have an atmosphere all their own. The islands are ideal for ornithology, for fishing and sea angling, for the photographer, or the holidaymaker seeking peace and tranquillity.

Tourist Information Centres in these areas and addresses to write for further information are on pages xviii to xxiii.

TOURIST INFORMATION CENTRES

Scotland has about 150 local Tourist Information Centres dispersed throughout many towns and villages. These Centres offer you a friendly welcome, information and help with:

* places to stay
* places to see
* things to do
* routes to take
* local events
* detailed literature

PLACES TO STAY

Almost all Centres have accommodation booking services offering both LOCAL BED-BOOKING and the BOOK-A-BED-AHEAD scheme for hotels, guest houses, and bed and breakfast.

Even at short notice, many Centres can also help you book a self catering holiday in their areas, using up-to-date lists of available accommodation. Centres marked with an asterisk * in the next few pages offer this service.

PLACES TO SEE

All Centres have friendly and well-informed staff ready to tell you about castles and abbeys, museums, walks and trails and all the special delights in the area. Many Centres have displays of local attractions and posters giving details of opening times and charges.

THINGS TO DO

Local bus, rail, ferry and air time-tables are usually available for consultation and staff will be delighted to offer their suggestions on the best way to get you to your destination. They may, too, offer you suggestions of ways you'd never thought of, like the Postbus service.

ROUTES TO TAKE

There are always maps and advice available to ensure that you discover all the delights of the local countryside for yourself. Staff will help you plan your day trips to see the sights and to take the most attractive routes in the area.

LOCAL EVENTS

Tourist Information Centres are always the best place to find out what's on in the area, particularly special events, festivals and important happenings. They get detailed day-to-day information to make sure you don't miss something which would make your stay in the area a memorable one.

DETAILED LITERATURE

All the information services of these Centres are backed up by a wide range of publications, some free, some saleable, which are available to you. Many Centres produce their own publications and all can offer you the local regional booklets and those published by the Scottish Tourist Board.

✉ **Shows that you can write to the Centre for information during its normal months of opening. In some cases an alternative Centre is shown for written enquiries.**

* **Self Catering Late Booking Service operated.**

Local Bed-booking and Book-a-bed Ahead.

TOURIST INFORMATION CENTRES

1

Aviemore and Spey Valley

AVIEMORE * ✉ 🛏
Aviemore and Spey Valley
Tourist Board
Grampian Road
Tel: Aviemore (0479) 810363
Jan-Dec

CARRBRIDGE * 🛏
Information Centre
Inverness Road
Tel: Carrbridge (047 984) 630
May-Sept
✉ Aviemore

GRANTOWN-ON-SPEY * 🛏
Information Centre
54 High Street
Tel: Grantown-on-Spey (0479)
2773
May-Sept
✉ Aviemore

KINGUSSIE * 🛏
Information Centre
King Street
Tel: Kingussie (054 02) 297
May-Sept
✉ Aviemore

NEWTONMORE *
Information Centre
Tel: Newtonmore (054 03) 274
May-Sept
✉ Aviemore

RALIA 🛏
Nr. Newtonmore
Tel: Newtonmore (054 03) 253
May-Sept
✉ Aviemore

2

Ayrshire and Burns Country

AYR ✉ 🛏
Information Bureau
30 Miller Road
Tel: Ayr (0292) 284196
Jan-Dec

CULZEAN CASTLE (NTS)
Tel: Kirkoswald (065 56) 269
Apr-Oct

GIRVAN ✉ 🛏
Information Centre
Bridge Street
Tel: Girvan (0465) 2056/7
Jan-Dec

PRESTWICK ✉ 🛏
Information Centre
2 The Cross
Tel: Prestwick (0292) 79234
Jan-Dec

British Airports Authority
Information Desk
Prestwick Airport
Tel: Prestwick (0292) 77309
Jan-Dec

TROON ✉ 🛏
Information Centre
Municipal Buildings
South Beach
Tel: Troon (0292) 315131
Jan-Dec

3

Ayrshire and Clyde Coast

LARGS ✉ 🛏
Information Centre
Promenade KA30 8BE
Tel: Largs (0475) 673765
Jan-Dec

MILLPORT 
Information Centre
Guildford Street
Tel: Millport (047553) 753
✉ Largs
June-Sep

4

Ayrshire Valleys

CUMNOCK 🛏
Information Office
Glaisnock Street
Tel: Cumnock (0290) 23058
April-Sept
✉ Kilmarnock

NEW CUMNOCK ✉ 🛏
Information Centre
Town Hall
Tel: New Cumnock (029 04) 581
April-Sept

DALMELLINGTON 🛏
Tourist Information Centre
April-Sept
✉ Kilmarnock

DARVEL 🛏
Tourist Information Centre
April-Sept
✉ Kilmarnock

FENWICK (A77) 🛏
Tourist Information Centre
Fenwick Hotel
April-Sept
✉ Kilmarnock

KILMARNOCK ✉ 🛏
Tourist Information Centre
Civic Centre
Tel: Kilmarnock (0563) 21140
Jan-Dec

5

Banff and Buchan

BANFF ✉ 🛏
Information Centre
Collie Lodge
Tel: Banff (026 12) 2419
Mid May-Sept

FRASERBURGH 
Information Centre
Saltoun Square
Tel: Fraserburgh (034 62) 28315
Mid May-Sept
✉ Banff

6

Caithness

JOHN O' GROATS ✉ 🛏
Information Centre
Tel: John o' Groats (095 581) 373
May-Sept

THURSO ✉ 🛏
Information Centre
Car Park
Riverside
Tel: Thurso (0847) 2371
May-Sept

WICK 🛏
Caithness Tourist Board
Whitechapel Road
off High Street
Tel: Wick (0955) 2596
Jan-Dec

7

City of Aberdeen

ABERDEEN ✉ 🛏
City of Aberdeen,
Tourist Board,
St. Nicholas House,
Broad Street.
Tel: Aberdeen (0224) 632727
Telex: 73366
Jan.-Dec.

Information Caravan 🛏
Stonehaven Road
Tel: Aberdeen (0224) 873030
May-Sept

Tourist Information Desk 🛏
British Rail Travel Centre
Railway Station
Guild Street
May-Sept

8

City of Dundee and Angus

ARBROATH 
Angus District Council
Parks, Recreation & Tourism
Service
Information Centre
Market Place
Tel: Arbroath (0241) 72609/76680
Jan-Dec

CARNOUSTIE
Angus District Council
Parks, Recreation & Tourism
Service
Information Centre
24 High Street
Tel: Carnoustie (0241) 52258
Jan-Dec
✉ Arbroath

DUNDEE
Information Centre
Nethergate Centre
Tel: Dundee (0382) 27723
Jan-Dec

MONTROSE
Angus District Council
Parks, Recreation and Tourism
Service
Information Centre
212 High Street
Tel: Montrose (0674) 72000
Jan-Dec
✉ Arbroath

9

City of Edinburgh

EDINBURGH
City of Edinburgh Tourist
Information and Accommodation
Service
5 Waverley Bridge
(Waverley Market from Summer 1984)
Tel: 031-226 6591/031-225 8821
Telex 727143 (Mon-Fri only)
Jan-Dec
✉ 9 Cockburn Street
Edinburgh EH1 1BP

10

Clyde Valley

ABINGTON 
'Little Chef'
Tel: Crawford (086 42) 436
May-Sept

BIGGAR
Information Centre
Main Street
Tel: Biggar (0899) 21066
May-Sept

HAMILTON
District Museum
Muir Street
Tel: Hamilton (0698) 422291
May-October

Nr HAMILTON (M74)
Roadchef Service Area
Tel: Hamilton (0698) 285590
May-October

LANARK
Clyde Valley Tourist Board
South Vennel
Tel: Lanark (0555) 61331 ext. 88
Jan-Dec

Tourist Information Caravan
Hyndford Place
Tel: Lanark (0555) 61661
May-Oct

LEADHILLS
Ramsay Library
Main Street
Tel: Leadhills (06594) 243
May-Oct

LESMAHAGOW
The Resource Centre
New Trows Road
Tel: Lesmahagow (0555) 894449
May-Oct

MOTHERWELL
The Library
Hamilton Road
Tel: Motherwell (0698) 64414
May-Oct

NEW LANARK
Scottish Wildlife Trust Visitor
Centre
Nursery Buildings
Tel: Lanark (0555) 61662
May-Oct

STRATHCLYDE PARK
Visitor Centre
Tel: Motherwell (0698) 63034
May-Oct

11

Dumfries and Galloway

CASTLE DOUGLAS
Information Centre
Markethill
Tel: Castle Douglas (0556) 2611
Easter-Oct

DALBEATTIE
Information Centre
Car Park
Tel: Dalbeattie (0556) 610117
Easter-Oct

DUMFRIES
Information Centre
Whitesands
Tel: Dumfries (0387) 53862
Easter-Oct

GATEHOUSE OF FLEET
Information Centre
Car Park
Tel: Gatehouse of Fleet
(05574) 212
Easter-Oct

GRETNA
Information Centre
Annan Road
Tel: Gretna (046 13) 834
Easter-Oct

KIRKCUDBRIGHT
Information Centre
Harbour Square
Tel: Kirkcudbright (0557) 30494
May-Sept

LANGHOLM
Town Hall
Tel: Langholm (0541) 80581
Easter-Oct

MOFFAT
Information Centre
Church Gate
Tel: Moffat (0683) 20620
Easter-Oct

NEWTON STEWART
Information Centre
Dashwood Square
Tel: Newton Stewart (0671) 2431
Easter-Oct

STRANRAER
Information Bureau
Port Rodie
Tel: Stranraer (0776) 2595
Easter-Oct

THREAVE GARDEN (NTS)
nr Castle Douglas
Tel: Castle Douglas (0556) 2575
Apr-Oct

12

Dunoon and Cowal

DUNOON
Dunoon & Cowal
Tourist Board
Pier Esplanade
Tel: Dunoon (0369) 3785
Jan-Dec

---

* Self Catering Late Booking Service operated.   Local Bed-booking and Book-a-bed Ahead.

TOURIST INFORMATION CENTRES

13
East Lothian

DUNBAR * ✉ 📢
Information Centre
Town House
High Street
Tel: Dunbar (0368) 63353
Jan-Dec

MUSSELBURGH ✉ 📢
Brunton Hall
East Lothian
Tel: 031-665 6597
Mid June-mid Sept

NORTH BERWICK * ✉ 📢
Information Centre
Quality Street
Tel: North Berwick (0620) 2197
Jan-Dec

PENCRAIG
A1
East Linton
June-Aug

14
Forth Valley

CULROSS (NTS)
Tel: Newmills (0383) 880 359
Jan-Dec

DUNFERMLINE ✉ 📢
Information Centre
Glen Bridge Car Park
Tel: Dunfermline (0383) 20999
Easter-Sept

FORTH ROAD BRIDGE 📢
Information Centre
Tel: Inverkeithing (0383) 417759
April-Sept
✉ Linlithgow

KINCARDINE BRIDGE 📢
Tourist Information Centre
Pine 'n' Oak
Kincardine Bridge Road
Airth, Falkirk
Tel: Airth (032 483) 422
Easter-Sept
✉ Linlithgow

LINLITHGOW ✉ 📢
Burgh Halls
The Cross
Tel: (050 684) 4600
Apr-Oct

15
Fort William and Lochaber

BALLACHULISH 📢
Tourist Office
Tel: Ballachulish (085 52) 296
May-Sept
✉ Fort William

FORT WILLIAM ✉ 📢
Fort William and Lochaber
Tourist Board
Tel: Fort William (0397) 3781 Jan-Dec

GLENCOE
Visitor Centre (NTS)
Tel: Ballachulish (085 52) 307
Apr-mid Oct

GLENFINNAN MONUMENT
(NTS)
by Fort William
Tel: Kinlocheil (039 783) 250
Apr-mid Oct

MALLAIG ✉ 📢
Information Centre
Tel: Mallaig (0687) 2170
May-Sept

16
Gordon

ALFORD 📢
The Station
May-Sept
✉ Aberdeen

ELLON 📢
Information Caravan
Market Street Car Park
Tel: Ellon (0358) 20730
Mid May-Sept
✉ Aberdeen

HADDO HOUSE (NTS)
Nr. Ellon
Tel: Tarves (06515) 440
May-Sept

HUNTLY 📢
Information Centre
Tel: Huntly (0466) 2255
Mid May-Sept
✉ Aberdeen

INVERURIE 📢
Information Centre
Town Hall, The Square
Tel: Inverurie (0467) 20600
Mid May-Sept
✉ Aberdeen

PITMEDDEN GARDEN (NTS)
Nr. Ellon
Tel: Udny (0651) 2445
May-Sept

17
Greater Glasgow

GLASGOW ✉ 📢
Information Bureau
George Square
Glasgow G2 1ES
Tel: 041-221 7371/2 and
041-221 6136/7
Telex: 779504
Jan-Dec

GOUROCK ✉
Information Centre
Municipal Buildings
Shore Street
PA19 1QY
Tel: Gourock (0475) 31126
Jan-Dec

GREENOCK ✉ 📢
Information Centre
Municipal Buildings
23 Clyde Square
PA15 1NB
Tel: Greenock (0475) 24400
Jan-Dec

PAISLEY 📢
Town Hall
Abbey Close
Tel: 041-889 0711
Jan-Dec
✉ Glasgow

18
Inverness, Loch Ness and Nairn

FORT AUGUSTUS 📢
Information Centre
Car Park
Tel: Fort Augustus (0320) 6367
April-mid Oct
✉ Inverness

CULLODEN BATTLEFIELD
(NTS)
by Inverness
Tel: Culloden Moor (046 372) 607
Apr-mid Oct.

DAVIOT
Daviot Wood
by Inverness
April-mid Oct
✉ Inverness

INVERNESS * ✉ 🛏
Inverness, Loch Ness and
Nairn Tourist Board
23 Church Street
Tel: Inverness (0463) 234353
Telex: 75114
Jan-Dec

NAIRN 🛏
Information Centre
62 King Street
Tel: Nairn (0667) 52753
April-mid Oct
✉ Inverness

19
Isle of Arran

BRODICK, Isle of Arran * ✉ 🛏
Tourist Information Centre
The Pier
Tel: Brodick (0770) 2140/2401
Jan-Dec.

Brodick Castle (NTS)
Tel: Brodick (0770) 2202
2 Apr-30 Sept

20
Kincardine and Deeside

BALLATER ✉ 🛏
Information Centre
Station Square
Tel: Ballater (033 82) 55306
Easter: May-Oct

BANCHORY ✉ 🛏
Information Caravan
Dee Street Car Park
Tel: Banchory (033 02) 2000
May-Sept

BRAEMAR ✉ 🛏
Information Centre
Kindrochit Castle
Tel: Braemar (033 83) 600
May-mid Oct.

CRATHES CASTLE (NTS)
Nr. Banchory
Tel: Crathes (033 84) 651
Apr-Mid Oct

STONEHAVEN ✉ 🛏
Information Centre
The Square
Tel: Stonehaven (0569) 62806
May-Sept

21
Kirkcaldy

BURNTISLAND ✉ 🛏
96 High Street
Tel: Burntisland (0592) 872667
Jan-Dec

LEVEN ✉ 🛏
Information Centre
South Street
Tel: Leven (0333) 29464
Jan-Dec

22
Loch Lomond, Stirling and The Trossachs

ABERFOYLE ✉ 🛏
Information Centre
Main Street
Tel: Aberfoyle (087 72) 352
May-Sept

BALLOCH ✉ 🛏
Information Centre
Tel: Alexandria (0389) 53533
May-Sept

BANNOCKBURN (NTS) 🛏
Bannockburn
by Stirling
Tel: Bannockburn (0786) 812664
Apr-Oct

CALLANDER ✉ 🛏
Tourist Information Centre
Leny Road
Tel: Callander (0877) 30342
Easter-Sept

DUNBLANE ✉ 🛏
Tourist Information Centre
Stirling Road
Tel: Dunblane (0786) 824428
May-Sept

HELENSBURGH ✉ 🛏
Pier Head Car Park
Tel: Helensburgh (0436) 2642
May-Sept

KILLIN ✉ 🛏
Tourist Information Centre
Main Street
Tel: Killin (056 72) 254
May-Sept

STIRLING 🛏
Tourist Information Centre
Dumbarton Road
Tel: Stirling (0786) 5019
Jan-Dec

TARBET, Loch Lomond 🛏
Information Caravan
May-Sept
✉ Stirling

TILLICOULTRY ✉ 🛏
Information Centre
Clock Mill
Upper Mill Street
May-Sept

TYNDRUM ✉ 🛏
Information Centre Car Park
Tel: Tyndrum (083 84) 246
May-Sept

23
Mid Argyll, Kintyre and Islay

BOWMORE, Isle of Islay 🛏
Information Centre
Tel: (049 681) 254
Apr-Sept
✉ Campbeltown

CAMPBELTOWN ✉ 🛏
Mid Argyll, Kintyre & Islay
Tourist Board
Tel: Campbeltown (0586) 52056
Jan-Dec

INVERARAY 🛏
Information Centre
Tel: Inveraray (0499) 2063
Apr-Sept
✉ Campbeltown

LOCHGILPHEAD 🛏
Information Centre
Tel: Lochgilphead (0546) 2344
Apr-Sept
✉ Campbeltown

TARBERT, Loch Fyne 🛏
Information Centre
Tel: Tarbert (088 02) 429
Apr-Sept
✉ Campbeltown

24
Moray

CULLEN 🛏
Information Centre
20 Seafield Street
Tel: Cullen (0542) 40757
June-Sept
✉ Elgin

DUFFTOWN 🛏
Information Centre
The Square
Tel: Dufftown (0340) 20501
Mid May-Sept
✉ Elgin

ELGIN * ✉ 🛏
Information Centre
17 High Street
Tel: Elgin (0343) 3388/2666
Jan-Dec

---

* **Self Catering Late Booking Service operated.**   🛏 **Local Bed-booking and Book-a-bed Ahead.**

TOURIST INFORMATION CENTRES

FORRES 🛏
Information Centre
Falconer Museum
Tolbooth Street
Tel: Forres (0309) 72938
Easter: Mid May-Sept
✉ Elgin

KEITH 🛏
Information Centre
Church Road
Tel: (054 22) 2634
Mid May-Sept
✉ Elgin

TOMINTOUL 🛏
Information Centre
Tel: Tomintoul (080 74) 285
Easter: Mid May-Sept
✉ Elgin

25
Oban, Mull and District

OBAN ✉ 🛏
Oban, Mull and District
Tourist Board
Argyll Square
Tel: Oban (0631) 63122/63551
Telex: 778866
Jan-Dec

TOBERMORY, Isle of Mull
✉ 🛏 all year
Information Centre
48 Main Street
Tel: Tobermory (0688) 2182
Apr-Sept

26
Orkney

KIRKWALL ✉ 🛏
Orkney Tourist Board
Information Centre
Broad Street KW15 1NX
Tel: Kirkwall (0856) 2856
Jan-Dec

STROMNESS 🛏
Information Centre
Ferry Terminal Building
Pierhead
Tel: Stromness (0856) 850716
June-Sept
✉ Kirkwall

27
Perthshire

ABERFELDY * ✉ all year 🛏
Aberfeldy and District Tourist
Association
8 Dunkeld Street
Tel: Aberfeldy (0887) 20276
May-Sept

AUCHTERARDER * ✉ all
year 🛏
Auchterarder and District
Tourist Association
Crown Wynd
High Street
Tel: Auchterarder (076 46) 3450
May-Sept

BEN LAWERS (NTS)
Tel: Killin (056 72) 397
Apr-Sept

BLAIRGOWRIE * ✉ all year 🛏
Blairgowrie and District Tourist
Association
Wellmeadow
Tel: Blairgowrie (0250) 2960 (2258
when closed)
Easter-mid Oct

CRIEFF * ✉ all year 🛏
Crieff & Strathearn Tourist
Association
James Square
Tel: Crieff (0764) 2578
Easter-Oct

DUNKELD * ✉ all year 🛏
Dunkeld and Birnam Mercantile
& Tourist Association
The Cross
Tel: Dunkeld (035 02) 688
Apr-Oct

GLENSHEE ✉ all year
Information Officer
Glenshee Tourist Association
Newton Terrace
Blairgowrie
Tel: Blairgowrie (0250) 2785

KILLIECRANKIE (NTS)
Tel: Killiecrankie (079 684) 3233
Apr-mid Oct

KINROSS ✉ all year 🛏
Kinross-shire Tourist Association

Information Centre
Turfhills
Tel: Kinross (0577) 63680
Apr-Oct

PERTH * ✉ 🛏
Perth Tourist Association
The Round House
Marshall Place
Tel: Perth (0738) 22900/27108
Jan-Dec

PITLOCHRY * ✉ 🛏 all year
Pitlochry and District
Tourist Association
22 Atholl Road
Tel: Pitlochry (0796) 2215/2751
Jan-Dec

28
Ross and Cromarty

GAIRLOCH ✉ 🛏
Ross & Cromarty
Tourist Board
Information Office
Achtercairn
Gairloch IV21 2DN
Tel: Gairloch (0445) 2130
Jan-Dec

INVEREWE (NTS)
by Poolewe
Tel: Poolewe (044 586) 229
Apr-Oct

NORTH KESSOCK ✉ 🛏
Ross & Cromarty Tourist Board
Tourist Office
Tel: Kessock (046 373) 505
Jan-Dec

STRATHPEFFER 🛏
Ross & Cromarty
Tourist Board
Information Centre
Visitors Centre
Tel: Strathpeffer (099 72) 415
Easter, May-Sept
✉ North Kessock

TORRIDON (NTS)
Countryside Centre at Junction of
A896 and Diabeg Road
Tel: Torridon (044 587) 221
June-Sept

ULLAPOOL 🛏
Ross & Cromarty Tourist Board,
Information Centre
Tel: Ullapool (0854) 2135
Easter & May-Sept
✉ Gairloch

29
Rothesay and Isle of Bute

ROTHESAY, Isle of Bute ✉ 🛏
Rothesay & Isle of Bute Tourist
Board
The Pier
Tel: Rothesay (0700) 2151
Jan-Dec

30
Scottish Borders

COLDSTREAM * ✉ 🛏
Henderson Park
Tel: Coldstream (0890) 2607
Easter: May-Sept

EYEMOUTH * ✉ 🛏
Auld Kirk
Tel: Eyemouth (0390) 50678
Easter: May-October

✉ Shows that you can write to the Centre for information during its normal months of opening. In some cases an alternative Centre is shown for written enquiries.   NTS—National Trust for Scotland.

GALASHIELS * ✉ 🛏
Bank Street
Tel: Galashiels (0896) 55551
Easter: May-Sept

HAWICK * ✉ 🛏
Common Haugh
Tel: Hawick (0450) 72547
Easter: May-Sept

JEDBURGH * ✉ 🛏
Information Centre
Murray's Green
Tel: Jedburgh (0835) 63435/63688
Jan-Dec

KELSO * ✉ 🛏
66 Woodmarket
Tel: Kelso (0573) 23464
Easter: May-Sept

MELROSE * ✉ 🛏
(joint with NTS)
Priorwood Gardens, nr. Abbey
Tel: Melrose (089 682) 2555
Easter-Oct.

PEEBLES * ✉ 🛏
Chambers Institute
High Street
Tel: Peebles (0721) 20138
Easter: May-October

SELKIRK * ✉ 🛏
Halliwell's House
Tel: Selkirk (0750) 20054
Easter: May-October

31
Shetland

LERWICK, Shetland ✉ 🛏
Shetland Tourist Board
Information Centre
Tel: Lerwick (0595) 3434
Telex: 75119
Jan-Dec

32
South West Ross and The Isle of Skye

BROADFORD, Isle of Skye * 🛏
South West Ross & The Isle of Skye
Tourist Board
Tel: (047 12) 361/463
Easter-Sept
✉ Portree

KINTAIL (NTS)
Morvich Camping Site (off A87)
Information Point, Morvich Farm,
Inverinate by Kyle
Tel: Glenshiel (059 981) 219
Apr-Sept

KYLE OF LOCHALSH * 🛏
South West Ross and
Isle of Skye Tourist Board
Tel: Kyle (0599) 4276
Easter-Sept
✉ Portree

PORTREE, Isle of Skye * ✉
South West Ross & Isle of Skye
Tourist Board
Tourist Information Centre
Tel: Portree (0478) 2137
Jan-Dec

SHIEL BRIDGE 🛏
Information Caravan
Tel: Glenshiel (0599) 81264
Easter-Sept
✉ Portree

33
St. Andrews and North East Fife

ANSTRUTHER 🛏
East Neuk Information Centre
Scottish Fisheries Museum
Tel: (0333) 310368/310628
Jan-Dec
✉ St Andrews

CUPAR 🛏
Information Centre
Fluthers Car Park
Tel: Cupar (0334) 53722
May-Sept
✉ St Andrews

FALKLAND PALACE (NTS) *
Tel: (033 75) 397
1 Apr-Oct

ST. ANDREWS ✉ 🛏
Information Centre
South Street
Tel: St. Andrews (0334) 72021
Jan-Dec

34
Sutherland

BETTYHILL 🛏
Information Centre
Tel: Bettyhill (064 12) 342
June-Sept
✉ Dornoch

BONAR BRIDGE 🛏
Information Centre
Tel: Ardgay (08632) 333
June-Sept
✉ Dornoch

DORNOCH ✉ 🛏
Sutherland Tourist Board
The Square
Tel: Dornoch (0862) 810400
Jan-Dec

DURNESS 🛏
Information Centre
Tel: Durness (097 181) 259
June-Sept
✉ Dornoch

GOLSPIE
Information Centre
Tel: Golspie (04083) 3835
June-Sept
✉ Dornoch

HELMSDALE 🛏
Information Centre
Tel: Helmsdale (043 12) 640
June-Sept
✉ Dornoch

LAIRG 🛏
Information Centre
Tel: Lairg (0549) 2160
June-end Sept
✉ Dornoch

LOCHINVER 🛏
Information Centre
Tel: Lochinver (057 14) 330
June-Sept
✉ Dornoch

35
Western Isles

CASTLEBAY, Isle of Barra 🛏
Information Centre
Tel: Castlebay (087 14) 336
May-Sept
✉ Stornoway

LOCHBOISDALE 🛏
Isle of South Uist
Information Centre
Tel: Lochboisdale (087 84) 286
May-Sept
✉ Stornoway

LOCHMADDY 🛏
Isle of North Uist
Information Centre
Tel: Lochmaddy (08763) 321
May-Sept
✉ Stornoway

STORNOWAY, Isle of Lewis ✉ 🛏
Western Isles Tourist Board
Administration and Information
Centre
4 South Beach Street
Tel: Stornoway (0851) 3088/2941
Jan-Dec

TARBERT, Isle of Harris 🛏
Information Centre
Tel: Harris (0859) 2011
May-Sept
✉ Stornoway

*** Self Catering Late Booking Service operated.** 　　**🛏 Local Bed-booking and Book-a-bed Ahead.**

BOOK-A-BED-AHEAD

The Scottish Tourist Board's *Book A Bed Ahead* scheme, which operates throughout Scotland, is available at all the Tourist Information Centres where the 'bed' symbol is displayed.

You can book your accommodation ahead for the coming night and subsequent nights at any of these Centres, even if your destination is many miles away. It is a guaranteed booking. Hotels, guest houses and bed and breakfast places may all be reserved by means of the scheme.

By using this scheme, the holidaymaker may save hours which would otherwise have been spent in trying to find accommodation —and the motorist can also save petrol— and knows exactly where he is going and that a welcome awaits him.

Full details of the *Book A Bed Ahead* scheme are available at all Tourist Information Centres.

RESERVATION A L'AVANCE

Vous pouvez utiliser la formule de réservation à l'avance lancée par l'Office écossais du tourisme dans tous les bureaux d'information touristique affichant l'enseigne du lit illustrée ci-dessus.

Moyennant le paiement d'une somme modique, vous pouvez retenir votre chambre pour le soir même dans un hôtel ou une pension de n'importe quelle région de l'Ecosse.

Rien n'est plus simple, et cette formule de réservation vous permet d'économiser de précieuses heures de vacances, qui seraient sinon passées à la recherche d'un logement, sans parler de l'économie d'essence, pour les vacanciers motorisés!

Renseignez-vous donc dans un bureau d'information touristique. Faites votre réservation, et partez profiter de votre journée en toute quiétude!

VORAUSBUCHUNG

Das Schottische Touristenbüro hat ein System entwickelt, wonach Sie ein Zimmer für die kommende Nacht im voraus buchen können. Buchungen können bei jedem Touristen-Informationszentrum vorgenommen werden, an dem das ''Betten-Symbol'' ausgestellt ist.

Gegen eine geringe Gebühr reserviert man Ihnen dort ein Zimmer in einem Hotel, Gasthaus oder in einer Privatpension überall in Schottland.

So einfach ist das.

Durch diesen Dienst sparen Sie wertvolle Urlaubsstunden, die Sie dann nicht mit Zimmersuche verbringen müssen. Und für den Autofahrer ergibt sich auch eine erhebliche Benzinersparnis.

Sie genießen Ihren Urlaub ohne Sorgen um die nächste Unterkunft.

Erkundigen Sie sich nach dem System der ''Vorausbuchung'' bei jedem beliebigen Touristen-Informationszentrum, buchen Sie Ihr Zimmer im voraus und lassen Sie sich gleich beraten, wie Sie den Rest des Tages am besten verbringen.

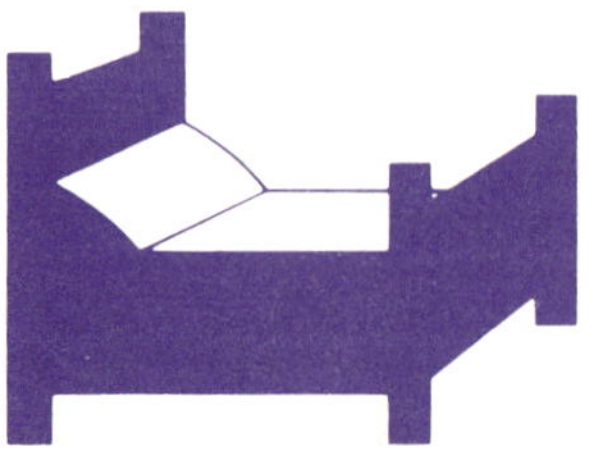

BOOKS TO HELP YOU

SCOTLAND: WHERE TO STAY HOTELS AND GUEST HOUSES £1.90

A detailed list of over 2,000 hotels and guest houses throughout Scotland with all the necessary information on prices and facilities. Completely revised every year.

SCOTLAND: WHERE TO STAY BED AND BREAKFAST £1.30

Nearly 2,000 places all over Scotland offering inexpensive accommodation with details of charges and facilities. Completely revised every year.

SELF-CATERING ACCOMMODATION IN SCOTLAND £1.40

Details of nearly 2,000 places for do-it-yourself accommodation—furnished cottages, chalets, holiday flats, caravans on site—all over Scotland. Completely revised every year.

CAMPING AND CARAVAN SITES IN SCOTLAND £1.10

Around 350 sites where touring caravans, and usually tents, are welcomed. Site finding is made easy with the reference maps provided and the information is completely revised every year.

ENJOY SCOTLAND PACK £3.90

A handy plastic wallet which contains the Scottish Tourist Board's Touring Map of Scotland (5 miles to the inch) showing beaches, historic sites, gardens, walks, museums; together with Scotland: 1001 Things to See, which describes and locates these places and tells you their hours of opening and admission charges. Both completely revised and updated for 1984 (available February)

TOURING MAP OF SCOTLAND £1.70

As above or available separately (available February)

SCOTLAND: 1001 THINGS TO SEE £2.30

As above or available separately (available February)

SCOTLAND FOR HILLWALKING £1.00

Over 60 or more difficult walks and scrambles on hills in different parts of Scotland, written by an expert.

WALKS AND TRAILS IN SCOTLAND £1.70

A selection of walks over a wide variety of terrain, most of which do not require specialist equipment and are suitable for children. Completely revised for 1984 (available February)

MUSEUMS AND GALLERIES IN SCOTLAND £1.80

An illustrated guide to over 300 museums and art galleries in Scotland, with details of their collections and facilities. Produced with the Council for Museums and Galleries in Scotland.

POSTERS

A series of attractive posters is available including Edinburgh, three on the Highlands (one on Skye, one on Glenfinnan and one on the Five Sisters of Kintail), the life and poems of Robert Burns, a piper, and a souvenir Wall Map of Scotland. Highland Cattle and the traditional sport of curling feature on two more, while an unusual montage of photographs of Scottish post-boxes is also available. Sizes and prices are detailed on the order form.

ALL PRICES INCLUDE POSTAGE & PACKAGE

ORDER FORM OVER PAGE

PUBLICATIONS ORDER FORM

Please mark the Scottish Tourist Board publications you would like, cut out the page and send it (with your money) to:—

**THE SCOTTISH TOURIST BOARD,
PO BOX 15, EDINBURGH EH1 1UY**

- ☐ **Scotland: Where to Stay Hotels and Guest Houses** ___ £1.90
- ☐ **Scotland: Where to Stay Bed and Breakfast** ________ £1.30
- ☐ **Self-Catering Accommodation in Scotland** _________ £1.40
- ☐ **Camping and Caravan Sites in Scotland** __________ £1.10
- ☐ **Enjoy Scotland Pack** _________________________ £3.90
- ☐ **Touring Map of Scotland** ______________________ £1.70
- ☐ **Scotland: 1001 Things to See** ___________________ £2.30
- ☐ **Scotland for Hillwalking** ______________________ £1.00
- ☐ **Museums and Galleries in Scotland** ______________ £1.80
- ☐ **Walks and Trails in Scotland** ___________________ £1.70

Posters

- ☐ **Piper** (24″ × 34″) ____________________________ £1.30
- ☐ **Edinburgh** (24″ × 34″) ________________________ £1.30
- ☐ **Land o' Burns** (27″ × 40″) _____________________ £1.30
- ☐ **Isle of Skye** (27″ × 40″) ______________________ £1.30
- ☐ **Souvenir Wall Map of Scotland** (24″ × 37″) ______ £1.30
- ☐ **Highland Cattle** (24″ × 34″) ___________________ £1.30
- ☐ **Curling** (24″ × 34″) __________________________ £1.30
- ☐ **Scottish Post Boxes** (24″ × 34″) _______________ £1.30
- ☐ **Five Sisters of Kintail** (27″ × 40″) ______________ £1.30
- ☐ **Glenfinnan** (19″ × 29″) _______________________ £1.10

YOUR NAME ____

ADDRESS ____

____

____

PLEASE MAKE ALL CHEQUES/POSTAL ORDERS PAYABLE TO THE SCOTTISH TOURIST BOARD.

TOTAL MONEY ENCLOSED   £

ALL PRICES INCLUDE POSTAGE AND PACKING

MAPS

Map 5
Map 3
Map 4
Map 1
Map 2
Inverness
Aberdeen
Dundee
Glasgow
Edinburgh
From London
MAJOR AIRPORTS
RAILWAY ROUTES

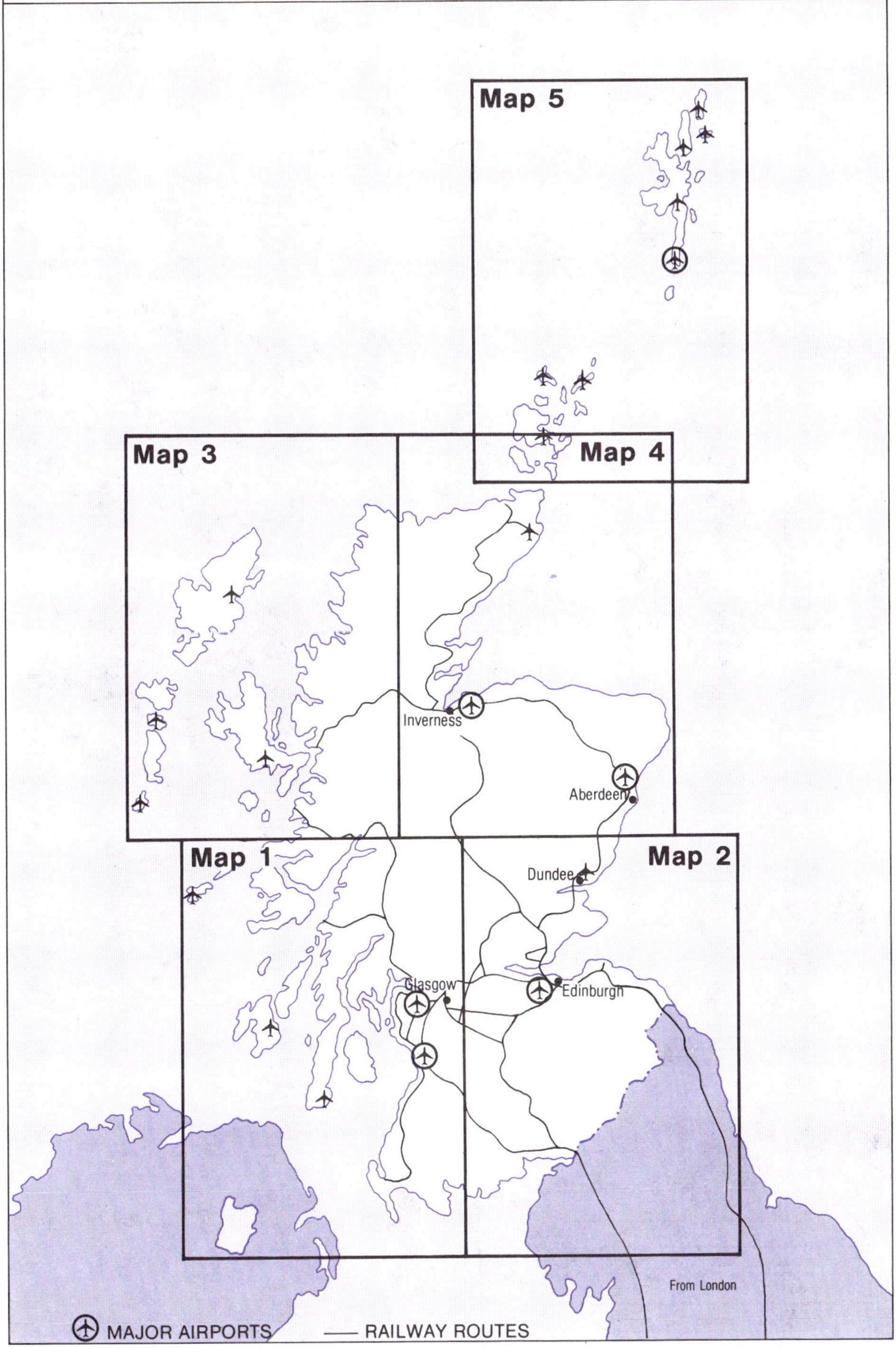

MAP 1

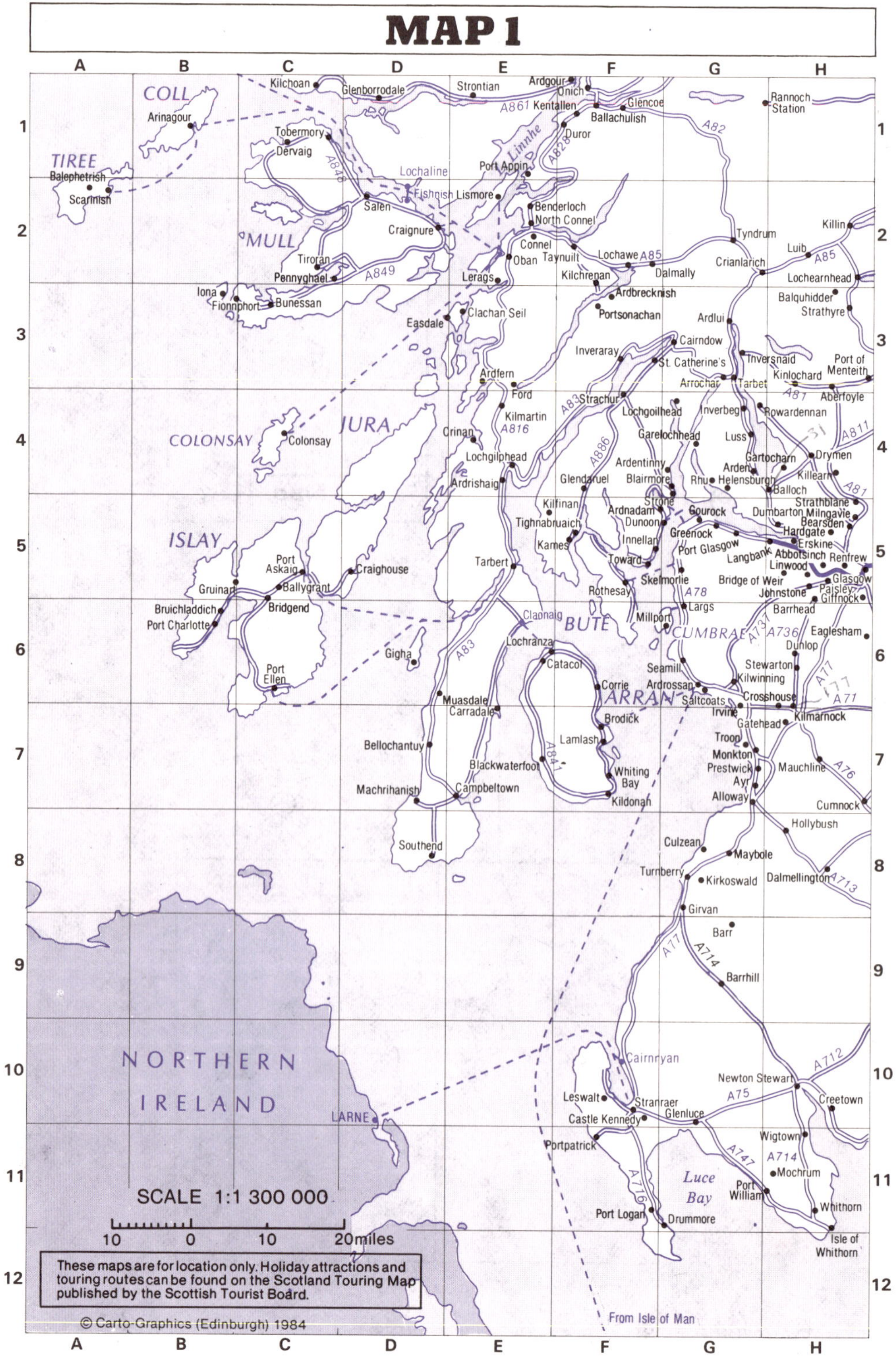

SCALE 1:1 300 000

10 0 10 20miles

These maps are for location only. Holiday attractions and touring routes can be found on the Scotland Touring Map published by the Scottish Tourist Board.

© Carto-Graphics (Edinburgh) 1984

MAP 2

Kinloch Rannoch
Strathtummel
Pitlochry
Kirkmichael
Glenisla
Kirriemuir
Montrose
Strathtay
Ballinluig
Bridge of Cally
Forfar
Inverkeilor
Fortingall
A827
Aberfeldy
Alyth
A926
Fearnan
A9
Blairgowrie
Meigle
Arbroath
Kenmore
A822
Dunkeld
A94
Coupar Angus
A929
A92
Lawers
Bankfoot
Kinclaven
Auchterhouse
Carnoustie
Amulree
Stanley
Dundee
Ardeonaig
Sma' Glen
St. Fillans
Perth
Scone
Newport on Tay
Comrie
A85
Crieff
Glencarse
Leuchars
Bridge of Earn
Muthill
Forgandenny
Abernethy
Cupar
St. Andrews
Kingsbarns
Auchterarder
Auchtermuchty
A91
Ladybank
Lathones
Crail
Callander
Greenloaning
Glenfarg
Strathmiglo
Freuchie
Largoward
Anstruther
Doune
A9
Blackford
Glendevon
Kinross
Leslie
Glenrothes
Pittenweem
Dunblane
Cleish
Kinnesswood
Leven
Upper Largo
Elie
Bridge of Allan
A91
Dollar
Thornton
Kippen
Blairlogie
Tillicoultry
M90
Cowdenbeath
Firth of Forth
Stirling
Alloa
Crossford
Dunfermline
Auchtertool
Kirkcaldy
Fintry
Airth
Culross
Aberdour
Kinghorn
North Berwick
Larbert
Bothkennar
Rosyth
Burntisland
Gullane
Dirleton
Dunbar
Bonnybridge
Grangemouth
Inverkeithing
Aberlady
East
Kilsyth
Falkirk
Polmont
South Queensferry
A1
Linton
Lennoxtown
Linlithgow
Winchburgh
Edinburgh
Musselburgh
Haddington
Stepps
Uphall
Riccarton
A6137
Gifford
Coldingham
Eyemouth
Chryston
Airdrie
Broxburn
Loanhead
Dalkeith
Pathhead
Humbie
Ayton
Bellshill
Chapelhall
M8
Currie
Roslin
Lasswade
Gorebridge
Longformacus
Chirnside
Duns
BERWICK upon TWEED
Uddingston
Whitburn
Newarthill
A71
A68
Carfraemill
A6105
Bothwell
Motherwell
Wishaw
Leadburn
A7
Oxton
Lauder
A697
Greenlaw
Hamilton
Carluke
A4703
West Linton
Stow
Earlston
Coldstream
East Kilbride
M74
A70
Camwath
A702
Peebles
Walkerburn
Galashiels
Melrose
Kelso
Strathaven
Lanark
Symington
Broughton
Innerleithen
A72
St. Boswells
Yetholm
Kirk Yetholm
A71
Biggar
Tweedsmuir
Yarrow
Selkirk
A698
A70
Abington
Crawford
A708
St. Mary's Loch
Ettrickbridge
Jedburgh
Elvanfoot
Ettrick Valley
Hawick
Camptown
New Cumnock
A68
Sanquhar
A702
Moffat
Thornhill
Beattock
Eskdalemuir
A7
A696
Johnstone Bridge
A74
Moniaive
A76
Lochmaben
Langholm
Newcastleton
Dalry
Hightae
Lockerbie
New Galloway
Dumfries
Collin
Canonbie
Crocketford
A75
A713
Carrutherstown
A69
Crossmichael
Kirkgunzeon
Glencaple
Annan
Gretna Green
NEWCASTLE
Castle Douglas
New Abbey
Powfoot
A75
Gatehouse of Fleet
Dalbeattie
Kirkbean
ENGLAND
Twynholm
Kippford
Colvend
Southerness
CARLISLE
Borgue
Rockcliffe
Kirkcudbright
A596
Solway Firth
M6
A1(M)

MAP 1
MAP 2

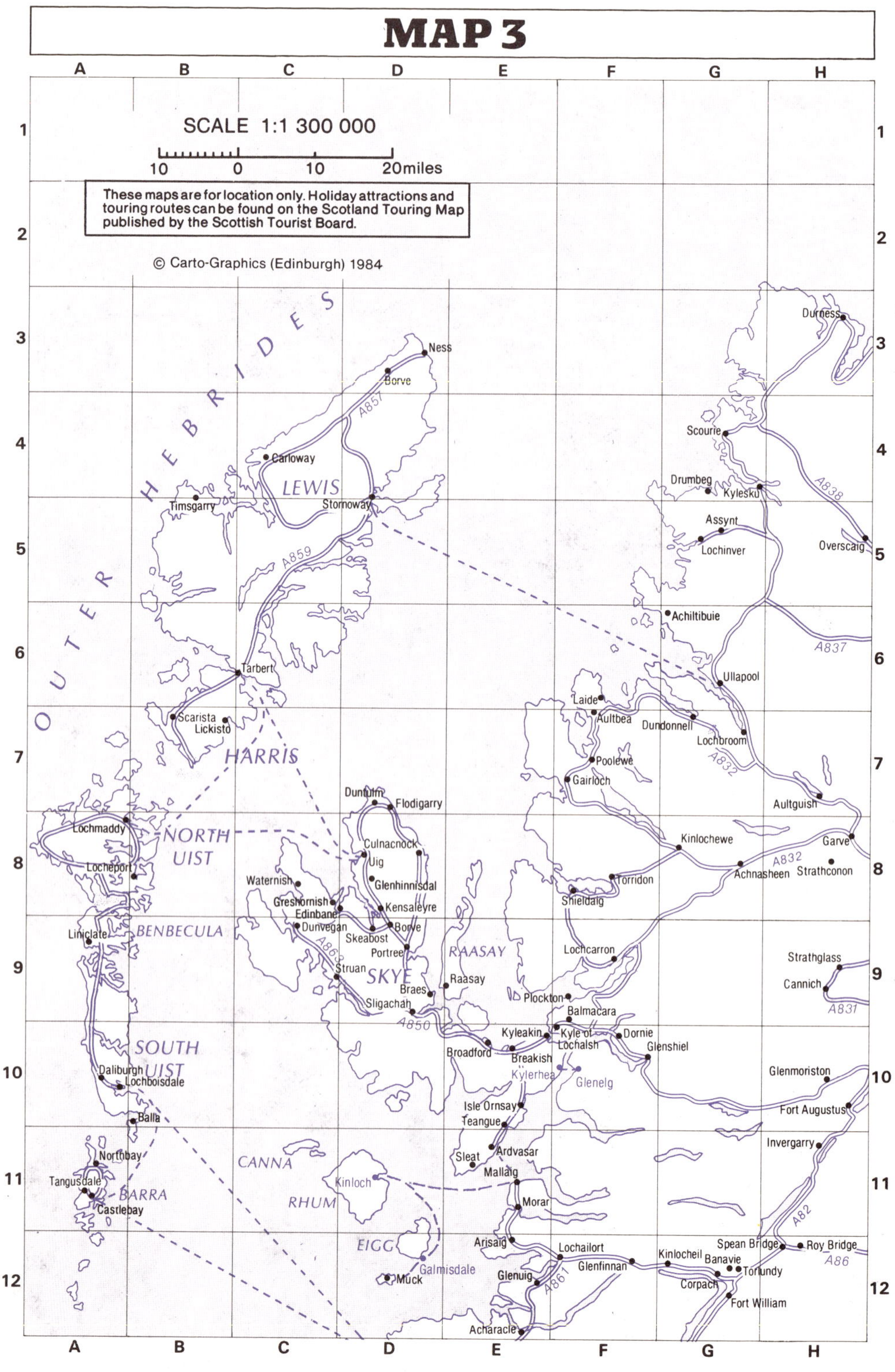

MAP 3
SCALE 1:1 300 000
10 0 10 20miles
These maps are for location only. Holiday attractions and touring routes can be found on the Scotland Touring Map published by the Scottish Tourist Board.
© Carto-Graphics (Edinburgh) 1984
OUTER HEBRIDES
Durness
Ness
Borve
A857
Scourie
Carloway
LEWIS
Drumbeg
Kylesku
A838
Timsgarry
Stornoway
Assynt
Lochinver
Overscaig
A859
Achiltibuie
A837
Tarbert
Ullapool
Laide
Scarista
Aultbea
Lickisto
Dundonnell
Lochbroom
HARRIS
Poolewe
A832
Gairloch
Aultguish
Duntulm
Flodigarry
Lochmaddy
Kinlochewe
Garve
NORTH
Culnacnock
UIST
Uig
A832
Locheport
Glenhinnisdal
Achnasheen
Strathconon
Waternish
Torridon
Greshornish
Kensaleyre
Shieldaig
Edinbane
Liniclate
Dunvegan
Borve
BENBECULA
Skeabost
A863
Portree
Lochcarron
Strathglass
Struan
RAASAY
SKYE
Cannich
Braes
Raasay
A831
Sligachah
Plockton
A850
Balmacara
Kyleakin
Kyle of
Dornie
SOUTH
Lochalsh
Glenshiel
Daliburgh
UIST
Broadford
Lochboisdale
Breakish
Glenmoriston
Kylerhea
Glenelg
Balla
Isle Ornsay
Fort Augustus
Teangue
Northbay
CANNA
Ardvasar
Invergarry
Tangusdale
Sleat
Mallaig
BARRA
Kinloch
A82
Castlebay
RHUM
Morar
EIGG
Arisaig
Spean Bridge
Roy Bridge
Galmisdale
Lochailort
Kinlocheil
A86
Muck
Glenuig
Glenfinnan
Banavie
Torlundy
A861
Corpach
Fort William
Acharacle

MAP 4

A
B
C
D
E
F
G
H
1
2
3
4
5
6
7
8
9
10
11
12
MAP 3
MAP 4
Stromness
Burray
Pentland Firth
Scrabster
Dunnet
Mey
John o' Groats
Thurso
Castletown
A836
Bettyhill
Tongue
Halkirk
Banniskirk
Watten
Wick
A895
Forsinard
Lybster
Latheron
A838
A836
A897
Helmsdale
A9
Lairg
Rogart
Golspie
Brora
Rosehall
Invershin
Dornoch Firth
Bonar Bridge
Dornoch
Ardgay
Edderton
Portmahomack
Tain
Kildary
A9
Balintore
Moray Firth
Alness
Invergordon
Evanton
Findhorn
Hopeman
Lossiemouth
Cullen
Rosehearty
Fraserburgh
Pennan
Buckie
Macduff
St Combs
Elgin
Garmouth
Portsoy
Banff
New Aberdour
A98
A98
Forres
Lhanbryde
Tynet
A97
Fochabers
A952
Strathpeffer
Dingwall
Rosemarkie
A941
A96
Old Deer
Contin
Fortrose
Nairn
Auldearn
Dallas
Peterhead
Conon Bridge
Rothes
Keith
Rothiemay
Muir of Ord
Croy
Aberlour
Craigellachie
A92
Beauly
Archiestown
Methlick
A981
Kiltarlity
Inverness
Glenlivet
Dufftown
Huntly
A831
Daviot
Ballindalloch
Struy
Old Meldrum
Ellon
A82
Farr
Grantown on Spey
Old Rayne
Moy
A9
Glenurquhart
Drumnadrochit
A59
Newburgh
Tomatin
Dulnain Bridge
Inverurie
Lewiston
Carrbridge
A947
Balmedie
Nethybridge
Tomintoul
Kintore
Foyers
Boat of Garten
Kildrummy
Kemnay
Invermoriston
A939
Strathdon
Glenkindie
A944
Aberdeen
Whitebridge
Aviemore
Tarland
Torphins
Banchory-Devenick
Kincraig
A980
Kingussie
Aboyne
Ballater
Banchory
A93
Newtonmore
Braemar
Laggan Bridge
A889
A9
Stonehaven
A86
A94
Dalwhinnie
Kinneff
Fettercairn
A92
Inverbervie
Bruar
Glen Clova
Gourdon
A93
Glenshee
Edzell
Laurencekirk
Blair Atholl
Cortachy
Calvine
Killiecrankie

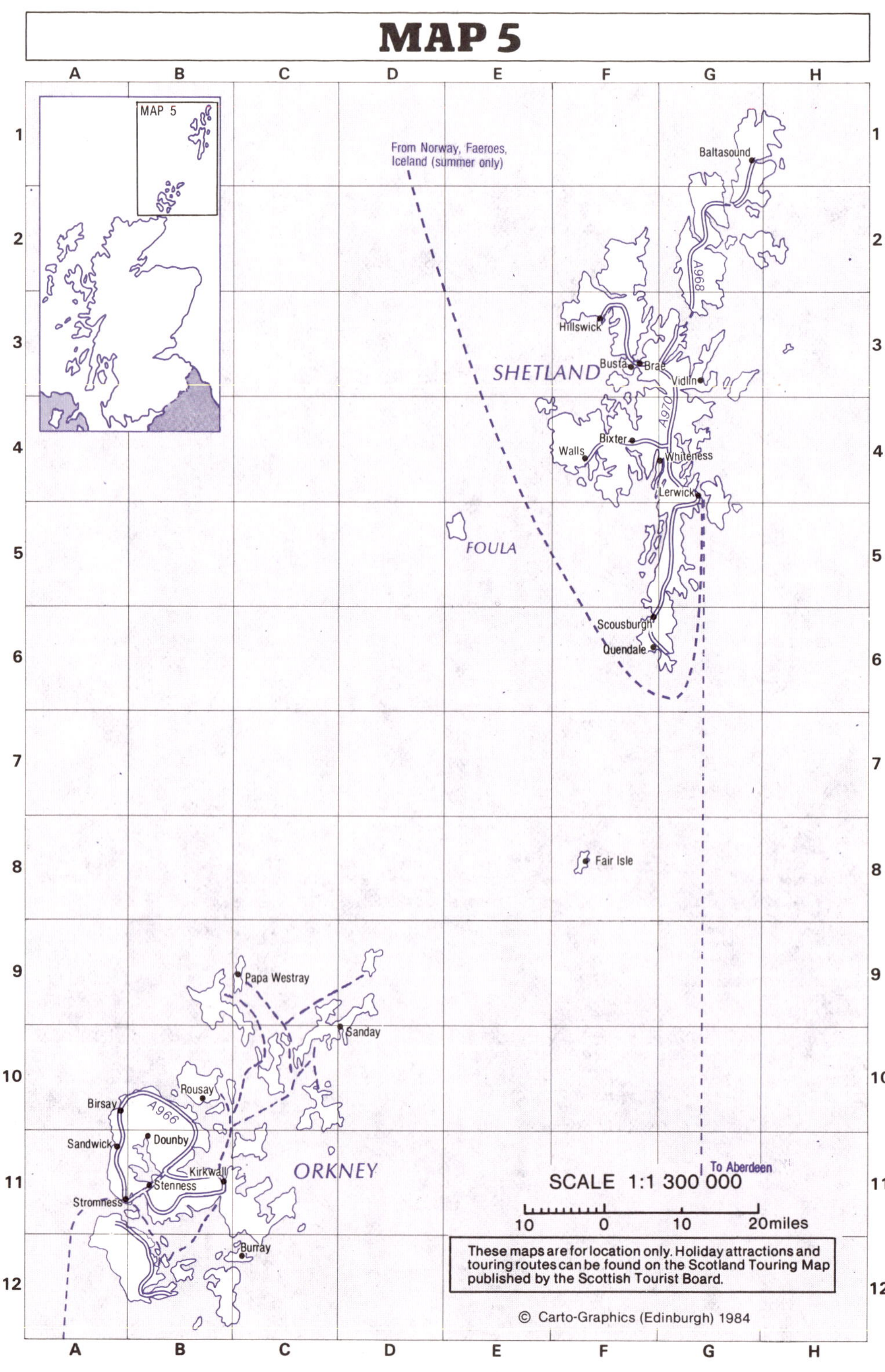

MAP 5
A B C D E F G H
From Norway, Faeroes, Iceland (summer only)
Baltasound
A968
Hillswick
SHETLAND
Busta Brae
Vidlin
A970
Bixter
Walls
Whiteness
Lerwick
FOULA
Scousburgh
Quendale
Fair Isle
Papa Westray
Sanday
Rousay
Birsay
A966
Sandwick
Dounby
Kirkwall
Stenness
ORKNEY
Stromness
To Aberdeen
SCALE 1:1 300 000
10 0 10 20miles
Burray
These maps are for location only. Holiday attractions and touring routes can be found on the Scotland Touring Map published by the Scottish Tourist Board.
© Carto-Graphics (Edinburgh) 1984

SCOTLAND
HOTELS AND
GUEST HOUSES 1984

Name and Address	Map Ref	Bedrooms	Services	Meals	Single room overnight £min/£max	Double/twin room overnight £min/£max	Per person daily £min/£max	Per person weekly £min/£max	Single	Double/twin	Family	Private	Public	Evening meals (Last order)	Parking (no. of cars)	Months open (1-12)	Symbols
ABBOTSINCH Renfrewshire	1 H5																
Excelsior Hotel, Glasgow Airport, PA3 2TR, Tel. 041 887 1212, Telex 777733		6	6	6	47.50 / -	63.50 / -	- / -	- / -	9	298	9	316	-	1830 / 2230	35	1-12	(symbols)
ABERDEEN	4 H10																
Aberdeen Airport Hotel, Skean Dhu, Argyll Road, AB2 0DU, Tel. Aberdeen 725252, Telex 739239		6	6	6	38.95 / -	43.95 / -	- / -	- / -	-	148	-	148	-	1700 / 2300	150	1-12	(symbols)
Albert & Victoria Private Hotel, 1-2 Albert Terrace, AB1 1XY, Tel. Aberdeen 641717		3	1	1	10.50 / 12.50	16.00 / 20.00	- / -	- / -	2	6	-	-	3	- / -	-	1-12	(symbols)
Amatola Hotel, 448 Great Western Road, Tel. Aberdeen 38724/5, Telex 739743		5	5	5	42.50 / 42.52	52.50 / 52.50	52.00 / 52.00	- / -	26	28	-	54	-	1830 / 2230	198	1-12	(symbols)
Atholl Hotel, 54 Kings Gate, AB9 2YN, Tel. Aberdeen 323505		5	6	4	30.00 / 35.00	34.00 / 40.00	38.00 / 43.00	- / -	13	26	-	39	-	1800 / 2130	96	1-12	(symbols)
Belvidere Hotel, 59 Queens Road, Tel. Aberdeen 323517		5	5	5	36.00 / 38.00	44.00 / 46.00	- / -	- / -	4	6	2	12	-	1800 / 2200	40	1-12	(symbols)
Broomfield Private Hotel, 15 Balmoral Place, AB1 6HR, Tel. Aberdeen 28758		2	3	2	11.00 / 11.00	20.00 / 20.00	14.50 / 14.50	- / -	2	6	1	-	3	1800 / 1900	20	1-12	(symbols)
Caledonian Thistle Hotel, Union Terrace, Tel. Aberdeen 640233, Telex 73758		5	5	6	43.50 / 49.50	51.00 / 59.00	- / -	- / -	33	43	3	56	10	1830 / 2145	35	1-12	(symbols)
Central Hotel, 93-95 Crown Street, AB1 2HH, Tel. Aberdeen 23685		3	3	4	16.00 / 25.00	26.50 / 28.00	- / -	- / -	6	9	6	9	6	1800 / 2000	10	-	(symbols)

VAT is shown at 15%: changes in this rate may affect prices.

Name and Address				Prices				Rooms						Facilities		
TOWN County — Establishment Address Telephone Telex	Map Ref — Bedrooms Services Meals			Bed and Breakfast — Single room overnight / Double/twin room overnight	Per person daily	B & B and evening meal — Per person weekly		No. of bedrooms — Single / Double/twin / Family / Private				No. of bath/shower rooms — Public	Evening meals	Parking (no. of cars)	Months open (1-12)	Symbols
ABERDEEN continued	4 H10			£min £max	£min £max	£min £max	£min £max						From Last order			Key on back fold-out

Dee Motel

Garthdee Road,
Aberdeen,
AB1 7AY.
Tel: (0224) 321474.

On the banks of the River Dee 1½ miles to south of city centre at start of ringroad system. All rooms with bath or shower, radio, telephone and colour TV. Twins/ double £29.50 singles £23.00 including continental breakfast and VAT. Special weekend rates available. World wide reservations service through any Comfort or World Motel Reservation Office.

Establishment	Bedrooms	Services	Meals	Single room overnight	Double/twin room overnight	Per person daily	Per person weekly	Single	Double/twin	Family	Private	Public	Evening meals (from/last order)	Parking	Months open	Symbols
Dee Motel, Garthdee Road, AB1 7AY, Tel. Aberdeen 321474, Telex 73212	5	3	5	24.50	32.50	-	-	28	47	-	75	-	1830 2145	300	1-12	T £ ⚓ Y 🐕 ✂ ▦ ⚒ ● ☎ ⊞ ▢ 🏷 C V ♘ ✎
Earls Court Hotel, 96 Queens Road, Tel. Aberdeen 321234, Telex 739743	5	5	5	40.00 40.00	48.50 48.50	50.00 50.00	350.00 350.00	13	7	-	21	-	1830 2230	60	-	£ Y ♨ ▦ 🏷 ● ☎ ▢ 🏷 C V ♘ ✈
Ferndale Hotel, 62 Bon-Accord Street, AB1 2EL, Tel. Aberdeen 24835	3	4	4	12.50 12.50	20.00 20.00	13.50 13.50	94.50 94.50	4	5	11	-	4	1730 1830	4	1-12	⚓ ♨ ▦ 🏷 ● ⊞ 🏷 C V

Glenwood Hotel

77-79 Bon Accord Street
Aberdeen.
Tel: 51612

Situated close to city centre and near bus and train stations. Swimming pool, putting and tennis courts nearby. Centrally heated, with radio in all rooms, the hotel caters for individual tastes with a daily change of menu. There is a 24 hour hot drinks and biscuit machine. Good reductions for children. Large private car park. Clay pigeon shooting can be arranged.

Establishment	Bedrooms	Services	Meals	Single room overnight	Double/twin room overnight	Per person daily	Per person weekly	Single	Double/twin	Family	Private	Public	Evening meals (from/last order)	Parking	Months open	Symbols
Glenwood Private Hotel, 77-79 Bon-Accord Street, AB1 2ED, Tel. Aberdeen 51612	3	3	2	11.50 11.50	21.00 21.00	15.50 16.50	105.00 112.00	2	6	6	-	4	1700 1800	12	1-12	T Y 🐕 ✂ ♨ ▦ 🏷 ⊞ 🏷 C V
Gloucester Hotel, 102 Union Street, AB9 1FT, Tel. Aberdeen 641095, Telex 76357	6	5	5	30.00	40.00	-	-	18	51	4	73	-	1800 2100	-	1-12	T £ ♨ Y 🐕 ♨ ▦ 🏷 ● ⚡ ☎ ⊞ ▢ 🏷 C V ♘
Gordon Hotel, Wellington Road, Nigg, Tel. Aberdeen 873012	3	3	4	21.50	33.00	-	-	11	15	-	17	3	1830 2130	80	1-12	T £ Y 🐕 ♨ ▦ 🏷 ● ☎ ⊞ ▢ 🏷 ❋ V
Guild Hotel, 22 Guild Street, AB1 2NF, Tel. Aberdeen 29411	2	3	3	16.00	31.50	-	-	4	9	2	12	3	1930 2230	-	1-12	T £ ♨ Y 🐕 ♨ ▦ 🏷 ● V

ABERDEEN

ABERDEEN continued — Map 4, H10

Name and Address	Map Ref	Bedrooms	Services	Meals	Single room overnight £min/£max	Double/twin room overnight £min/£max	Per person daily £min/£max	Per person weekly £min/£max	Single	Double/twin	Family	Private	Public	Evening meals From/Last order	Parking	Months open	Symbols
Holiday Inn Aberdeen Airport Riverview Dr., Farburn, Dyce Tel. Aberdeen 770011 Telex 739651		6	6	6	55.95 / -	68.50 / -	65.45 / -	- / -	86	68	-	154	-	1830 / 2300	-	1-12	
Holiday Inn Aberdeen Bucksburn Old Meldrum Road, Bucksburn Tel. Aberdeen 713911 Telex 73108		6	6	6	31.00 / 49.96	46.00 / 57.73	38.50 / 57.46	- / -	45	54	-	99	-	1800 / 2230	150	1-12	
Imperial Hotel Stirling Street AB9 2JY Tel. Aberdeen 29101 Telex 73365		5	5	5	25.00 / 33.50	30.00 / 43.00	31.00 / 39.50	217.00 / 276.50	44	62	4	100	7	1800 / 2200	-	1-12	
Inglewood Private Hotel 25 Kings Gate AB2 6BL Tel. Aberdeen 644358		3	3	2	10.00 / 12.00	18.00 / 20.00	15.00 / 17.00	- / -	1	1	1	-	2	1730 / 1800	2	1-12	
Kittybrewster Hotel 75 Powis Terrace AB2 3PY Tel. Aberdeen 46574		2	2	2	10.50 / 12.00	18.00 / 20.00	13.95 / 15.00	89.15 / 95.00	3	5	-	-	2	1800 / 1900	-	1-12	
Mannofield Hotel 447 Great Western Road AB9 6NL Tel. Aberdeen 35888		4	4	2	17.25 / 18.40	27.60 / 29.90	24.61 / 25.76	172.27 / 190.32	4	4	2	-	2	1830 / 1830	14	1-12	
New Marcliffe Hotel 53 Queens Road AB9 1QG Tel. Aberdeen 321371 Telex 73225		5	5	4	44.00 / 55.00	44.00 / 55.00	- / -	- / -	7	17	4	28	-	1900 / 2200	70	1-12	
Northern Hotel 1 Great Northern Road AB9 2UL Tel. Aberdeen 43342 Telex 53168		4	5	5	17.50 / 26.00	32.25 / 37.25	37.25 / 42.25	- / -	20	37	-	57	-	1700 / 2130	50	1-12	
Royal Hotel 1-3 Bath Street Tel. Aberdeen 25152/25694/25706		6	6	6	29.00 / -	37.00 / -	- / -	- / -	13	29	-	42	-	1830 / 2200	6	1-12	
Russell Private Hotel 50 St Swithin Street AB1 6XJ Tel. Aberdeen 323555/6		3	3	2	12.50 / 13.00	21.00 / 26.30	17.60 / 18.60	91.00 / 116.00	5	3	2	-	2	1800 / 1900	6	1-12	
Seton Lodge Hotel Station Road, Woodside AB2 2UL Tel. Aberdeen 42220/45250		4	3	5	20.00 / 25.00	30.00 / 32.00	22.00 / 35.00	154.00 / 245.00	-	7	-	7	-	1830 / 2145	-	1-12	

VAT is shown at 15%: changes in this rate may affect prices.

Name and Address	Map Ref	Bedrooms	Services	Meals	Bed and Breakfast – Single room overnight (£min / £max)	Bed and Breakfast – Double/twin room overnight (£min / £max)	B & B and evening meal – Per person daily (£min / £max)	B & B and evening meal – Per person weekly (£min / £max)	No. of bedrooms – Single	No. of bedrooms – Double/twin	No. of bedrooms – Family	No. of bedrooms – Private	No. of bath/shower rooms – Public	Evening meals (From / Last order)	Parking (no. of cars)	Months open (1-12)	Symbols (Key on back fold-out)
ABERDEEN continued	4 / H10																
Skean Dhu Hotel, Altens Souter Head Road, Altens AB1 4LF Tel. Aberdeen 877000 Telex 739631		6	6	6	38.95 / –	43.95 / –	–	–	–	221	–	221	–	1700 / 2300	400	1-12	
Skean Dhu Hotel, Dyce Farburn Terrace, Dyce AB2 0DW Tel. Aberdeen 723101 Telex 73473		6	6	6	35.95 / –	38.95 / –	–	–	–	221	–	221	–	1700 / 2300	300	1-12	
Struan Hotel 239 Great Western Road AB1 6DX Tel. Aberdeen 574484		5	5	4	16.50 / 29.00	24.00 / 37.00	20.00 / 36.50	139.50 / 215.00	2	12	3	13	1	1700 / 2100	14	1-12	
Tree Tops Crest Hotel 161 Springfield Road AB1 7SA Tel. Aberdeen 33377 Telex 73794		5	5	5	40.50 / –	51.00 / –	–	–	27	80	1	–	7	1900 / 2000	–	1-12	
Alelanro Guest House 272 Holburn Street AB1 6DD Tel. Aberdeen 575601		3	2	1	9.00 / 10.50	15.00 / 17.00	–	–	1	2	2	–	2	–	–	1-12	
Arkaig Guest House 43 Powis Terrace AB2 3PP Tel. Aberdeen 638872		3	2	1	9.00 / 10.00	16.00 / 18.00	–	–	2	3	2	–	2	–	–	1-12	
Ashgrove Guest House 34 Ashgrove Road AB2 5AD Tel. Aberdeen 44861		2	1	2	8.00 / 9.00	15.00 / 17.00	10.75 / 12.25	–	1	3	3	–	1	1745 / 1500	–	1-12	
Badenoch Guest House 359 Holburn Street AB1 6DQ Tel. Aberdeen 56833		2	2	1	8.00 / 10.00	14.00 / 16.00	–	–	3	2	2	–	2	–	–	1-12	
Belwade Guest House 139 Crown Street Tel. Aberdeen 50600		1	2	1	8.00 / –	15.00 / –	–	–	1	2	3	–	1	–	–	1-12	
Bracklinn Guest House 348 Great Western Road Tel. Aberdeen 37060		3	3	2	12.50 / 14.00	18.00 / 19.00	– / 20.00	–	3	2	1	1	2	1900 / 1900	2	1-12	
Cedars Guest House 339 Great Western Road AB1 6NW Tel. Aberdeen 23225		1	3	1	9.50 / 10.00	18.00 / 18.00	–	–	2	2	2	–	3	–	9	1-12	
Fourways Guest House 435 Great Western Road AB1 6NJ Tel. Aberdeen 30218		3	2	1	9.00 / 10.00	15.00 / 17.00	–	–	1	4	2	–	2	–	6	1-12	

ABERDEEN

Name and Address	Map Ref	Bedrooms	Services	Meals	Bed and Breakfast Single room overnight £min	£max	Double/twin room overnight £min	£max	B & B and evening meal Per person daily £min	£max	Per person weekly £min	£max	Single	Double/twin	Family	Private	Public	Evening meals From	Last order	Parking	Months open	Symbols
ABERDEEN continued	4 H10																					Key on back fold-out
Furain Guest House 92 N. Deeside Rd, Peterculter AB1 0QW Tel. Aberdeen 732189		3	2	1	10.00	-	14.00	-	-	-	-	-	-	4	1	-	2	-	-	6	1-12	
Glenmhor Guest House 318 Great Western Road AB1 6PL Tel. Aberdeen 27630		3	2	1	8.00	11.00	17.00	20.00	-	-	-	-	1	3	3	-	2	-	-	4	1-12	[T]
Granville Guest House 401 Great Western Road AB1 6NY Tel. Aberdeen 33043		3	3	1	9.00	11.00	15.00	17.00	-	-	-	-	-	2	2	-	2	-	-	-	1-12	[V]
Holburn Guest House 590 Holburn Street Tel. Aberdeen 25593		1	3	2	12.00	14.00	18.00	20.00	15.50	18.00	95.00	115.00	-	8	1	-	1	1730	1830	12	1-12	
Klibreck Guest House 410 Great Western Road AB1 6NR Tel. Aberdeen 36115		3	3	2	9.00	10.00	16.00	18.00	13.00	14.00	84.00	98.00	1	5	-	-	2	1800	1500	3	1-12	[V]
Morrison's Guest House 444 King Street AB2 3BS Tel. Aberdeen 637809		3	2	1	-	-	16.00	20.00	-	-	-	-	-	5	2	-	3	-	-	6	1-12	[T] [V]
Nutshell Guest House 301 Holburn Street AB1 6DP Tel. Aberdeen 51991		3	3	1	8.50	9.50	14.00	15.00	-	-	-	-	2	3	-	-	1	-	-	-	1-12	[C]
Open Hearth 349 Holburn Street AB1 6DQ Tel. Aberdeen 56888		3	2	1	8.50	9.50	14.00	15.00	-	-	-	-	5	5	2	-	3	-	-	6	1-12	[T] [C]
Ormesdale Guest House 302 Great Western Road AB1 6PL Tel. Aberdeen 25945/56741		3	3	1	9.00	12.00	18.00	18.00	-	-	-	-	1	3	3	-	2	-	-	-	1-12	[C]
Ravenscraig Guest House 69 Constitution Street AB2 1ET Tel. Aberdeen 646912		3	2	1	10.00	-	18.00	-	-	-	-	-	1	4	3	-	2	-	-	-	1-12	[M] [V]
Salisbury Guest House 12 Salisbury Terrace AB1 6QH Tel. Aberdeen 50447		3	1	2	8.00	9.00	15.00	16.00	11.00	12.00	-	-	1	2	2	-	2	1730	1830	-	1-12	
St Ola Guest House 421 Great Western Road AB1 6NJ Tel. Aberdeen 37186		1	3	1	8.50	-	15.00	-	-	-	-	-	1	3	3	-	1	-	-	5	1-12	[C] [V]
Stay-Mhor Guest House 62 Abergeldie Road AB1 6EH Tel. Aberdeen 585659		1	2	1	9.00	10.00	17.00	18.00	-	-	-	-	1	1	3	-	1	-	-	-	1-12	
Strathboyne Guest House 26 Abergeldie Terrace AB1 6EE Tel. Aberdeen 593400		3	3	2	8.00	8.50	15.00	16.00	11.25	11.75	77.00	80.00	2	3	2	-	2	1730	1800	1	1-12	[T] [C]

VAT is shown at 15%: changes in this rate may affect prices.

Name and Address	Map Ref	Bedrooms	Services	Meals	Single room overnight £min/£max	Double/twin room overnight £min/£max	Per person daily £min/£max	Per person weekly £min/£max	Single	Double/twin	Family	Private	Public	Evening meals From/Last order	Parking (no. of cars)	Months open (1-12)	Symbols
ABERDEEN continued	4 H10																Key on back fold-out
Terra Nova Guest House 114 Crown Street Tel. Aberdeen 573096		3	2	1	12.50 -	16.00 -	- -	- -	2	8	1	-	3	- -	-	1-12	
Western Guest House 193 Great Western Road AB1 6PS Tel. Aberdeen 56919		3	1	1	8.50 8.50	15.00 15.00	- -	- -	-	4	2	-	1	-	6	1-12	
University of Aberdeen Conference Office, Don Street AB9 2WW Tel. Aberdeen 40241 Ext 5171 Telex 73458		2	3	4	9.80 9.80	- -	- -	1175 -	-	-	-	221		1700 1830	250	3-4 7-10	
ABERDOUR Fife	2 C4																
The Fairways Hotel 17 Manse Street KY3 0TT Tel. Aberdour 860478		3	3	4	12.50 -	22.00 -	17.50 -	105.00 -	4	5	2	-	3	1900 2100	18	1-12	

Forth View Hotel

Aberdour, Fife.
Tel: (0383) 860402

Small, comfortable & secluded hotel on sea shore overlooking picturesque islands of the Forth. Many local amenities including: Silversands beach, golf, fishing, boating, cliff walks, climbing, canoeing etc.
Ideal family hotel. Modest rates. Personally managed by proprietors with fine reputation for home cooking. Easy reach of Edinburgh, Perth, St. Andrews.

Name and Address	Map Ref	Bedrooms	Services	Meals	Single room overnight £min/£max	Double/twin room overnight £min/£max	Per person daily £min/£max	Per person weekly £min/£max	Single	Double/twin	Family	Private	Public	Evening meals From/Last order	Parking (no. of cars)	Months open (1-12)	Symbols
Forth View Hotel Hawkcraig Point KY3 0TZ Tel. Aberdour 860402		3	3	3	11.00 12.00	19.00 22.00	16.00 -	- -	3	3	-	2		1900 -	-	4-10	
ABERFELDY Perthshire	2 B1																
Balnearn Private Hotel Crieff Road PH15 2BJ Tel. Aberfeldy 20431		3	3	2	9.20 10.35	18.40 20.70	13.80 16.10	96.60 96.60	4	7	2	-	3	1830 1900	17	1-12	
Breadalbane Arms Hotel Bridgend PH15 2DF Tel. Aberfeldy 20364		3	3	3	8.50 8.50	17.00 17.00	13.00 -	- -	8	17	1	1	6	1900 2000	20	4-10	
Coshieville Hotel Coshieville PH15 2NE Tel. Kenmore 319		4	4	4	10.00 15.00	20.00 30.00	18.00 22.00	115.00 126.00	-	6	1	7	-	1900 2130	40	1-12	
Crown Hotel Bank Street PH15 2BB Tel. Aberfeldy 20448		2	4	4	8.50 -	17.00 -	13.50 -	80.00 -	2	16	2	-	4	1700 2100	20	1-12	

Name and Address	Map Ref	Bedrooms	Services	Meals	Single room overnight (£min / £max)	Double/twin room overnight (£min / £max)	Per person daily (£min / £max)	Per person weekly (£min / £max)	Single	Double/twin	Family	Private	Public	Evening meals (From / Last order)	Parking (no. of cars)	Months open (1-12)	Symbols
ABERFELDY continued	2 B1																Key on back fold-out
Cruachan House Hotel, Kenmore Road, PH15 2BL, Tel. Aberfeldy 20545		3	3	5	12.60 / -	25.20 / -	17.50 / 22.00	- / -	2	7	-	2	2	1900 / 2100	25	1-12	(symbols)
Guinach House Hotel, Urlar Road, PH15 2ET, Tel. Aberfeldy 20251		3	3	4	11.00 / 12.00	22.00 / 24.00	17.50 / 18.50	100.00 / 120.00	2	4	2	-	3	1900 / -	8	3-10	(symbols)
Nessbank Private Hotel, Crieff Road, PH15 2BJ, Tel. Aberfeldy 20214		3	3	2	11.00 / -	22.00 / -	16.50 / -	100.00 / -	3	4	-	-	2	1900 / -	7	3-11	(symbols)
Palace Hotel, Breadalbane Terrace, PH15 2AG, Tel. Aberfeldy 20359		3	4	4	9.00 / 12.00	18.00 / 24.00	16.00 / 19.00	110.00 / 118.00	5	16	4	3	6	1900 / 2030	30	4-10	(symbols)
Weem Hotel, Weem, PH15 2LB, Tel. Aberfeldy 20381		3	4	4	8.00 / 12.00	16.00 / 24.00	16.00 / 19.00	110.00 / 130.00	3	8	1	3	4	1900 / 2030	25	1-12	(symbols)
Glenburn Guest House, Grandtully, PH15 2QX, Tel. Strathtay 330		-	-	-	8.00 / -	14.00 / -	12.00 / -	82.00 / -	1	7	1	-	5	1800 / 2000	12	1-12	(symbols)
ABERFOYLE Perthshire	1 H3																
Bailie Nicol Jarvie Hotel, FK8 3SZ, Tel. Aberfoyle 202		3	4	4	19.00 / -	35.00 / -	24.00 / -	145.00 / -	7	26	3	36	2	1900 / 2030	35	1-12	(symbols)
Covenanters Inn, FK8 3XB, Tel. Aberfoyle 347		4	5	4	19.00 / -	35.00 / -	24.00 / -	145.00 / -	5	38	4	47	-	1900 / 2030	50	1-12	(symbols)

VAT is shown at 15%: changes in this rate may affect prices.

Name and Address					Prices					Rooms				Facilities
TOWN County Establishment Address Telephone Telex	Map Ref Bedrooms / Services / Meals			Bed and Breakfast Single room overnight	Double/twin room overnight	Per person daily	B & B and evening meal Per person weekly	Single	Double/twin	Family	No. of bed-rooms Private	No. of bath/shower rooms Public	Evening meals (From Last order)	Parking (no. of cars) / Months open (1-12) / Symbols

| ABERFOYLE continued | 1 H3 | | | £min £max | £min £max | £min £max | £min £max | | | | From Last order | | Key on back fold-out |

FOREST HILLS HOTEL

Kinlochard, by Aberfoyle, Stirlingshire. Tel: 08777 277.

Serenely set on the beautiful north shore of Loch Ard and viewing onto the slopes of Ben Lomond. This elegant and friendly Hotel offers unrivalled facilities on an international scale.

The Hotel's leisure centre, opening April 1984, includes: An indoor swimming pool, jacuzzi, solarium, indoor curling rinks: badminton and squash courts. Other existing facilities include an outdoor heated swimming pool; tennis courts; sailing; windsurfing; rowing; fishing and pony trekking.

Fine à la carte dinner or informal bar meals are available with regular barbeques, entertainment and dinner-dances.

All hotel bedrooms have private bathrooms, colour T.V. with in-house video; tea/coffee making facilities and baby monitor.

Write or phone for full details of package breaks. Open all year. Conference facilities.

Establishment	Map Ref	Bedrooms	Services	Meals	Single room overnight	Double/twin room overnight	Per person daily	Per person weekly	Single	Double/twin	Family	Private	Public	Evening meals	Parking	Months open
Forest Hills Hotel Kinlochard FK8 3TL Tel. Kinlochard 277		5	5	5	- 28.00	- 46.00	- -	- -	3	14	-	10	3	1900 2100	40	1-12
Inverard Hotel Loch Ard Road FK8 3TD Tel. Aberfoyle 229		3	3	5	10.00 12.50	20.00 25.00	16.50 19.00	104.00 120.00	2	20	3	12	3	1900 2200	40	1-12
Dounans Outdoor Centre School Camp FK8 3UT Tel. Aberfoyle 291		-	-	3	5.70 5.70	11.40 11.40	6.70 8.20	39.35 48.65	24	Dormitories for Group Bookings			2	1700 -	50	4-10
ABERLADY East Lothian	2 E4															
Kilspindie House Hotel EH32 0RE Tel. Aberlady 319		3	3	5	10.00 13.00	20.00 26.00	16.50 19.50	119.00 135.00	4	9	-	5	2	1700 2130	42	1-12
ABERLOUR Banffshire	4 D8															
Aberlour Hotel High Street AB3 9QB Tel. Aberlour 287		4	4	5	13.90 14.95	23.90 25.20	18.90 22.30	130.20 137.55	8	11	-	15	4	1930 2030	21	1-12
Dowans Hotel AB3 9LS Tel. Aberlour 488		5	5	5	15.18 18.97	25.30 32.89	22.77 26.56	150.53 163.81	5	8	-	13	-	1900 2030	33	1-12

Name and Address	Map Ref	Bedrooms	Services	Meals	Single room overnight £min / £max	Double/twin room overnight £min / £max	Per person daily £min / £max	Per person weekly £min / £max	Single	Double/twin	Family	Private	Public	Evening meals (From / Last order)	Parking (no. of cars)	Months open (1-12)	Symbols
ABERNETHY Perthshire	2 C3																
Abernethy Hotel, Back Dykes, PH2 9JN, Tel. Abernethy 220		3	3	4	9.00 / -	15.00 / -	14.00 / -	60.00 / -	1	4	1	-	2	1630 / 2100	50	1-12	[symbols]
ABINGTON Lanarkshire	2 B7																
Abington Hotel, Carlisle Road, ML12 6SD, Tel. Crawford 467/8		3	3	5	14.00 / -	24.00 / 27.00	16.50 / 22.00	80.00 / 103.25	6	17	3	3	10	1800 / 2130	40	1-12	[symbols]
Glengonnar Outdoor Centre, Tel. Crawford 340		-	-	3	5.70 / 5.70	11.40 / 11.40	6.70 / 8.20	39.35 / 48.65	24	-	-	-	2	1700 / -	50	4-10	[symbols]
									Dormitories for Group Bookings								
ABOYNE Aberdeenshire	4 F11																
Birse Lodge Hotel, AB3 5EL, Tel. Aboyne 2253		4	4	4	16.00 / -	32.00 / -	21.00 / -	147.00 / -	3	13	-	16	1	1900 / 2030	30	3-10	[symbols]
Boat Inn, Charlestown Road, Tel. Aboyne 2137		4	3	5	12.00 / 12.00	24.00 / 24.00	17.00 / 17.00	99.00 / 99.00	-	5	-	3	1	1800 / 2200	20	1-12	[symbols]
Charleston Hotel, AB3 5HY, Tel. Aboyne 2475		3	3	5	9.25 / 10.25	16.50 / 18.50	15.50 / 16.50	85.00 / 95.00	1	4	2	-	2	1900 / 2030	30	1-12	[symbols]
Huntly Arms Hotel, AB3 5HS, Tel. Aboyne 2101		4	5	6	15.00 / 21.00	14.00 / 21.00	21.50 / 25.50	125.00 / 185.00	15	29	5	21	8	1830 / 2130	184	1-12	[symbols]
ACHARACLE, Ardnamurchan Argyll	3 E12																
Dalilea Farm Guest House, PH36 2JX, Tel. Salen 253		3	3	3	9.00 / -	17.00 / -	13.67 / -	88.50 / -	1	4	1	-	2	1900 / 1900	12	4-10	[symbols]
ACHILTIBUIE Ross-shire	3 G6																
Summer Isles Hotel, IV26 2YQ, Tel. Achiltibuie 282		4	3	3	15.50 / 17.50	31.00 / 50.00	30.50 / -	213.50 / -	3	12	-	7	4	1930 / 1930	15	4-10	[symbols]

Price sub-headings: £min / £max. Rooms: "From / Last order". Symbols key on back fold-out.

VAT is shown at 15%: changes in this rate may affect prices.

Name and Address		Prices					Rooms							Facilities	
TOWN County / Establishment Address Telephone Telex	Map Ref / Bedrooms / Services / Meals	Bed and Breakfast				B & B and evening meal	No. of bedrooms			No. of bath/shower rooms					Facilities	
		Single room overnight	Double/twin room overnight	Per person daily	Per person weekly		Single	Double/twin	Family	Private	Public	Evening meals From Last order	Parking (no. of cars)	Months open (1-12)	Symbols	
		£min £max	£min £max	£min £max	£min £max									Key on back fold-out	

the achnasheen hotel.

achnasheen · Ross-shire · scotland · 1022 2ef

Recent major improvements have enhanced a long established hostelry well-known for highland hospitality, comfort, excellent food and a well-stocked bar and cellar.

Favoured by railway enthusiasts because of its unique proximity to the famous scenic Kyle line favoured by the BBC Television Film, and ideally situated for touring and hill-walking, Achnasheen Hotel continues to fulfil its traditional role as a friendly hotel to which many return annually.

Highland Fling — Spring Special: 3-day Bargain Break, D, B & B (up to 23rd May 84). **£42.**

Mid-Summer Madness Offer: 3-day minimum stay, D, B & B (24th May-13th July 84) **£48.**

Above rates include daily Mini-Bus Tours to places of interest.

Name and Address	Bedrooms	Services	Meals	Single room overnight	Double/twin room overnight	Per person daily	Per person weekly	Single	Double/twin	Family	Private	Public	Evening meals (Last order)	Parking	Months open	Symbols
Achnasheen Hotel IV22 2EF Tel. Achnasheen 243	4	4	4	13.50 / 15.50	25.00 / 28.00	20.00 / 23.00	112.00 / 133.00	2	10	6	8	4	1900 / 2030	30	1-12	T £ ⚲ ♀ 🐕 🅟 ♿ ⚲ 🔌 C V ⚹ 🖃
Ledgowan Lodge Hotel Ledgowan IV22 2EJ Tel. Achnasheen 252 Telex 75605	4	4	5	18.00 / 21.00	28.00 / 37.00	27.00 / 30.00	140.00 / 210.00	2	12	4	10	3	1930 / 2130	25	4-10	T £ ⚲ ♀ 🐕 🅟 ▥ ♿ ⚲ 🔌 C ✳ 🏨 V ♘ ♪
AIRDRIE Lanarkshire — 2 A5																
Staging Post 8-10 Anderson Street Tel. Airdrie 67525	-	-	-	26.50 / -	37.00 / -	- / -	- / -	2	5	-	-	1	1800 / 2200	30	1-12	T £ ⚲ ♀ 🐕 🅟 ▥ ♿
Tudor Hotel 39 Alexander Street Tel. Airdrie 64144/63295	3	4	5	21.45 / 25.85	29.70 / 37.95	- / -	- / -	14	7	-	7	3	1800 / 2130	80	1-12	T £ ⚲ ♀ 🐕 ⚘ 🅟 ▥ ♿ ◑ ☏ 🖃 ☐ V

HOLIDAY SCOTLAND 1984

The most exciting collection of easy-to-book top value holidays in Scotland!

Get a free brochure now from your travel agent.

Name and Address	Map Ref	Bedrooms	Services	Meals	Prices — Bed and Breakfast				B & B and evening meal	Rooms — No. of bedrooms				No. of bath/shower rooms		Facilities		
TOWN County / Establishment Address Telephone Telex					Single room overnight £min £max	Double/twin room overnight £min £max	Per person daily £min £max	Per person weekly £min £max		Single	Double/twin	Family	Private	Public	Evening meals From Last order	Parking (no. of cars)	Months open (1-12)	Symbols Key on back fold-out
AIRTH, by Falkirk Stirlingshire	2 B4																	
Airth Castle Hotel FK2 8JF Tel. Airth 411 Telex 777975		5	5	5	27.00 39.00	33.00 48.00	- -	- -	3	19	1	23	-	1900 2145	55	1-12	
ALLOA Clackmannanshire	2 B4																	
Royal Oak Hotel Bedford Place FK10 1LJ Tel. Alloa 722423		6	3	5	15.95 -	22.50 -	- -	- -	2	8	3	11	1	1900 2200	40	1-12	
ALLOWAY Ayrshire	1 G7																	
Belleisle House Hotel Belleisle Park KA9 4DU Tel. Alloway 42331		5	5	4	23.00 26.00	30.00 40.00	30.00 33.00	210.00 231.00	2	14	2	14	2	1900 2045	40	1-12	
Burns Monument Hotel Tel. Alloway 42466		4	4	5	14.00 20.00	24.00 28.00	22.00 30.00	- -	-	7	2	8	-	1700 2100	-	1-12	
ALNESS Ross-shire	4 B7																	
Morven House Hotel Novar Road Tel. Alness 882323		3	3	3	9.20 -	20.70 -	12.65 -	- -	2	2	1	2	1	1800 2000	10	1-12	

Airth Castle Hotel

Airth, by Falkirk,
Stirlingshire, Scotland.
Telephone: Airth 411.

Airth Castle, dating from the 15th Century and set in its own country estate is an ideal location for a luxury stay in Central Scotland, whether on business or vacation.

Situated close to Stirling, Falkirk and Grangemouth, and conveniently positioned for motorway links (Junction 7, M9), half an hour's drive takes you to Edinburgh or Glasgow.

VAT is shown at 15%: changes in this rate may affect prices.

Name and Address	Map Ref	Bedrooms	Services	Meals	Single room overnight £min / £max	Double/twin room overnight £min / £max	Per person daily £min / £max	Per person weekly £min / £max	Single	Double/twin	Family	Private	Public	Evening meals From / Last order	Parking (no of cars)	Months open (1-12)	Symbols
ALYTH Perthshire	2 C1																
Alyth Hotel, Commercial Street, PH11 8AF, Tel. Alyth 2447		-	-	-	10.00 / -	20.00 / -	- / -	- / -	-	8	1	-	3	1700 / 2100	-	1-12	(symbols)
Lands of Loyal Hotel, PH11 8JQ, Tel. Alyth 2481		4	4	4	15.50 / 24.00	27.00 / 40.00	23.00 / 31.50	43.00 / 56.00	4	10	-	7	2	1900 / 2030	19	1-12	(symbols)
AMULREE Perthshire	2 B2																
Amulree Hotel, PH8 0EF, Tel. Amulree 218		3	4	5	11.00 / 12.50	22.00 / 25.00	18.50 / 20.00	120.00 / -	2	10	2	1	3	1900 / 2130	110	1-12	(symbols)
ANNAN Dumfriesshire	2 C10																
Central Hotel, St Johns Road, Tel. Annan 2257		3	4	4	12.00 / 14.00	22.00 / 24.00	- / -	- / -	5	7	6	6	4	1830 / 1915	27	1-12	(symbols)
Corner House Hotel, Tel. Annan 2754		3	3	4	11.50 / -	17.50 / -	15.20 / -	106.40 / -	2	26	3	1	6	1730 / 2000	50	1-12	(symbols)
Queensberry Arms Hotel, High Street, Tel. Annan 2024		3	4	5	21.00 / 21.00	36.00 / 36.00	19.50 / 19.50	117.00 / 117.00	4	21	2	5	-	1900 / 2100	35	1-12	(symbols)
Ravenswood Private Hotel, St Johns Road, DG12 6AW, Tel. Annan 2158		2	3	4	9.00 / 9.50	18.00 / 18.50	- / -	- / -	2	6	3	-	2	1750 / 1800	2	1-12	(symbols)
Warmanbie Hotel & Restaurant, DG12 5LL, Tel. Annan 2369		5	3	5	19.50 / 20.50	16.50 / 17.50	- / -	150.50 / 182.00	-	4	-	4	-	1845 / 2030	21	1-12	(symbols)
ANSTRUTHER Fife	2 E3																
Craws Nest Hotel, Bankwell Road, K10 3OA, Tel. Anstruther 310691		6	6	6	20.00 / 22.00	36.00 / 40.00	25.00 / 27.00	150.00 / 165.00	-	26	5	31	-	1900 / 2100	83	1-12	(symbols)
The Smugglers Inn, High Street, KY10 3DQ, Tel. Anstruther 310506		4	4	5	15.00 / 18.00	30.00 / 36.00	21.50 / 24.50	150.50 / 171.50	1	8	-	6	2	1900 / 2130	20	1-12	(symbols)

ARBROATH - ARDBRECKNISH, Dalmally

Name and Address	Map Ref	Bedrooms	Services	Meals	Single room overnight £min/£max	Double/twin room overnight £min/£max	Per person daily £min/£max	Per person weekly £min/£max	Single	Double/twin	Family	Private	Public	Evening meals From/Last order	Parking (no. of cars)	Months open (1-12)	Symbols
ARBROATH / Angus	2 E1																
Hotel Seaforth, Dundee Road, Tel. Arbroath 72232		1	3	4	15.00 / 20.00	27.00 / 40.00	20.75 / -	115.50 / -	7	11	2	10	4	1900 / 2130	150	1-12	[symbols]
The Kepties Hotel, 61 Keptie Street, DD11 3AN, Tel. Arbroath 72424		1	2	2	8.00 / -	16.00 / -	11.00 / -	75.00 / -	1	5	4	-	1	1800 / 1900	3	1-12	[symbols]
North Sea Hotel, Millgate Loan, Tel. Arbroath 73335		3	4	4	12.08 / -	23.00 / -	-	-	9	7	2	-	6	1700 / 2000	15	1-12	[symbols]
Towerbank Hotel, James Street, Tel. Arbroath 75987		3	4	5	12.00 / 14.00	18.00 / 20.00	14.50 / 20.00	91.00 / 135.00	2	2	3	-	2	1900 / 2100	12	1-12	[symbols]
Viewfield Hotel, Viewfield Road, Tel. Arbroath 72446		-	1	4	12.50 / 17.50	18.00 / 27.00	15.50 / 20.50	95.00 / 130.00	2	4	2	3	2	1700 / 1900	50	1-12	[symbols]
Waverley Hotel, 1 Catherine Street, Tel. Arbroath 73681		3	3	2	9.00 / -	16.00 / -	12.65 / -	70.00 / -	-	5	2	-	2	1730 / 1800	-	1-12	[symbols]
Windmill Hotel, Millgate Loan, Tel. Arbroath 72278		-	-	-	10.50 / 10.50	21.00 / 21.00	13.50 / 13.50	78.00 / 78.00	2	9	6	-	4	1700 / 2100	100	1-12	[symbols]
April Rise Guest House, 6 Rosemount Road, DD11 2AW, Tel. Arbroath 76827		3	3	2	6.00 / -	12.00 / -	8.50 / -	59.00 / -	-	-	3	-	1	1800 / 1200	-	1-12	[symbols]
Kingsley Guest House, 29-31 Marketgate, Tel. Arbroath 72417/73933		3	3	3	7.50 / -	15.00 / -	10.00 / -	59.00 / -	3	7	8	-	4	1730 / 1800	-	1-12	[symbols]
Sandhutton Guest House, 16 Addison Place, DD11 2AX, Tel. Arbroath 72007		3	3	1	-	14.00 / -	-	-	-	2	2	-	1	1730 / -	-	-	[symbols]
ARCHIESTOWN, Aberlour / Moray	4 D8																
Archiestown Hotel, IV34 7QX, Tel. Carron 218		3	3	3	12.00 / -	23.00 / -	17.50 / -	120.00 / -	5	5	-	-	4	1900 / -	38	1-12	[symbols]
ARDBRECKNISH, Dalmally / Argyll	1 F3																
Rockhill Farm Guest House, PA33 1BH, Tel. Kilchrenan 218		3	3	2	10.00 / -	16.00 / -	14.00 / -	88.50 / -	-	4	2	-	2	1900 / 1900	6	3-9	[symbols]

VAT is shown at 15%: changes in this rate may affect prices.

Name and Address	Map Ref	Bedrooms	Services	Meals	Single room overnight £min £max	Double/twin room overnight £min £max	Per person daily £min £max	Per person weekly £min £max	Single	Double/twin	Family	Private	Public	Evening meals From Last order	Parking (no. of cars)	Months open (1-12)	Symbols
ARDEN, by Alexandria Dunbartonshire	1 G4																
Lomond Castle Hotel & Log Cabin Complex Tel. Arden 681 Telex 776154		6	6	5	30.00 -	40.00 -	36.00 -	- -	6	15	-	21	-	1900 2200	400	1-12	
ARDENTINNY Argyll	1 G4																

ARDENTINNY HOTEL

AA**   RAC**

Explore the Cowal Peninsula—stay at Ardentinny Hotel in the Argyll Forest Park. An historic Inn, fully modernised with characterful "Harry Lauder Bar" and "Viking Lounge" overlooking Loch Long. Patio garden for alfresco lunches. In the evening choose from individually cooked Dinners including "Taste of Scotland" dishes or the informal Supper menu served in "The Buttery". Walking, sailing, golf and touring by car to Inveraray and other castles and some of Scotland's loveliest gardens. Inclusive Salmon/Trout Fishing and Stalking Holidays available. All rooms with Private Facilities. Special "Family Holiday" rates available.

Under the personal supervision of the owners
Sylvia and John Harris   **Telephone: 036 981 209/275**

INTER HOTEL * EGON RONAY

Name and Address	Map Ref	Bedrooms	Services	Meals	Single room overnight £min £max	Double/twin room overnight £min £max	Per person daily £min £max	Per person weekly £min £max	Single	Double/twin	Family	Private	Public	Evening meals From Last order	Parking (no. of cars)	Months open (1-12)	Symbols
Ardentinny Hotel PA23 8TR Tel. Ardentinny 209		4	4	6	16.50 17.50	30.00 32.00	20.00 24.50	135.00 155.00	2	7	2	11	-	1900 2130	25	3-11	
ARDEONAIG, by Killin Perthshire	2 A2																
Ardeonaig Hotel FK21 8SU Tel. Killin 400		3	3	3	16.00 18.00	32.00 36.00	26.00 28.50	170.00 185.00	-	14	-	14	1	2000 2100	40	1-10	

Name and Address	Map Ref	Single room overnight	Double/twin room overnight	Per person daily	Per person weekly	Single	Double/twin	Family	Private	Public	Evening meals	Parking (no. of cars)	Months open (1-12)	Symbols
		£min £max	£min £max	£min £max	£min £max						From Last order		Key on back fold-out

ARDFERN, by Lochgilphead — Argyll — Map Ref 1 / E3

THE GALLEY OF LORNE
Ardfern, by Lochgilphead, Argyll

Formerly a 16th-century Droving Inn, now a lively 10-bedroomed centrally-heated traditional pub by the sea. It is farmer-owned and has an informal restaurant serving home-produced mutton, vegetables, game, sea and loch food, with a range of wines and whiskies. Also self catering cottages.

Close to water sports and B.H.S. Riding School, Ceilidhs, Folk Music, Dancing. Other activities include Sailing, Fishing or relaxing with the locals.

AA approved. Open all year. Low season from £15 half board per day. Special rates on request. Wonderful base for touring and exploring: Oban 25 miles, Glasgow 100 miles, Lochgilphead 15 miles. **TELEPHONE: 085 25 284**

Establishment	Bedrooms / Services / Meals	Single room overnight	Double/twin room overnight	Per person daily	Per person weekly	Single	Double/twin	Family	Private	Public	Evening meals	Parking	Months open	Symbols
Galley of Lorne Hotel Tel. Barbreck 284	3 3 5	9.00 12.00	16.00 20.00	15.00 18.00	100.00 130.00	-	10	-	2	2	1800 2200	60	1-12	symbols
ARDGAY Sutherland — 4 / A6														
Inveroykel Lodge Hotel Strathoykel IV24 3DP Tel. Rosehall 200	3 4 5	9.50 11.00	19.00 22.00	14.50 16.00	90.00 105.00	1	4	-	-	2	1830 2130	20	1-12	symbols
Croit Mairi Guest House Kincardine Hill Tel. Ardgay 504	2 2 2	7.00 7.50	14.00 15.00	10.50 11.50	73.50 79.50	-	5	1	-	2	1900 1945	6	1-12	symbols
ARDGOUR, by Fort William Inverness-shire — 3 / G12														
Ardgour Hotel PH33 7AA Tel. Ardgour 225	3 3 4	10.50 -	19.00 -	16.00 -	104.00 -	3	5	2	1	4	1900 2130	-	1-12	symbols

VAT is shown at 15%: changes in this rate may affect prices.

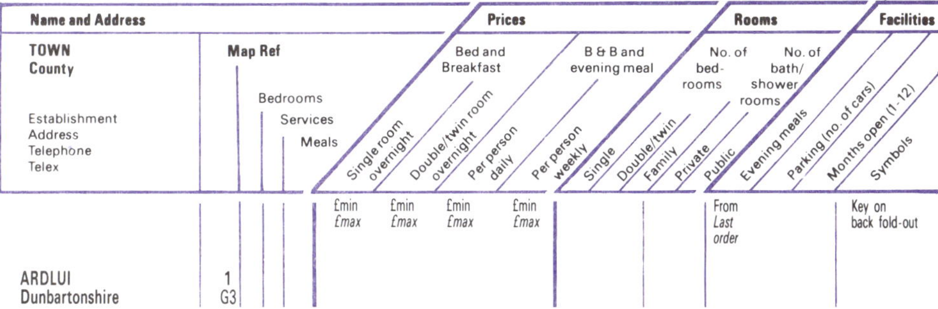

Name and Address	Map Ref	Bedrooms	Services	Meals	Single room overnight £min/£max	Double/twin room overnight £min/£max	Per person daily £min/£max	Per person weekly £min/£max	Single	Double/twin	Family	Private	Public	Evening meals From/Last order	Parking (no. of cars)	Months open (1-12)	Symbols
ARDLUI Dunbartonshire	1 G3																

ARDLUI HOTEL Loch Lomond Tel. Inveruglas (030 14) 243.

Nestled in the midst of the magnificent scenery on the shores at the head of Loch Lomond, the Ardlui Hotel commands a superb panoramic view of this most famous of Scottish Lochs.

The Hotel's landscaped front garden stretches in a gentle slope to the Loch itself. Beyond, the breathtaking grandeur of the Bonnie Banks unfolds along thickly wooded shores with their backcloth of Scottish mountains towering in splendour over all.

The Hotel is fully licensed with both bars open all day with an extensive bar snack menu available, which, as in our restaurant features our speciality! Fresh Loch Salmon, Sea Trout and Rainbow Trout.

If our guests' interest lie in boating or water ski-ing the hotel has its own slipway, moorings and berthing Pier. Boats are also available for hire for those wishing to fish for Salmon, Trout or Pike.

Proprietors: D. B. Squires, & C. P. Squires.

Name and Address	Map Ref	Bedrooms	Services	Meals	Single room overnight £min/£max	Double/twin room overnight £min/£max	Per person daily £min/£max	Per person weekly £min/£max	Single	Double/twin	Family	Private	Public	Evening meals From/Last order	Parking	Months open	Symbols
Ardlui Hotel Tel. Inveruglas 243		3	3	4	14.38 15.82	25.30 27.85	- -	- -	-	6	5	1	3	1900 2030	50	1-12	
ARDNADAM, by Dunoon Argyll	1 F5																
The Firpark Hotel & Restaurant Tel. Sandbank 210/506		-	-	-	17.75 -	27.50 -	- -	- -	2	3	1	2	2	1900 2100	30	1-12	
ARDRISHAIG, by Lochgilphead Argyll	1 E4																
Auchendarroch Hotel Tel. Ardrishaig 275		2	3	3	8.50 -	17.00 -	12.00 -	84.00 -	-	3	-	-	2	- 1900	6	4-10	
ARDROSSAN Ayrshire	1 G6																
The Beeches Guest House 56 Eglinton Road KA22 8NQ Tel. Ardrossan 64029		3	3	4	6.50 7.00	12.00 13.00	9.75 10.25	68.25 71.75	1	2	2	-	2	1700 2030	8	1-12	
Edenmore Guest House 47 Park House Road Tel. Ardrossan 62306		3	3	1	7.00 7.50	12.00 13.00	- -	- -	1	4	1	1	1	- -	10	1-12	
ARDVASAR, Sleat Isle of Skye, Inverness-shire	3 E11																
Ardvasar Hotel Tel. Ardvasar 223 Telex 75442		4	4	4	12.00 18.00	24.00 34.00	16.00 22.00	- -	1	10	1	4	4	1900 2030	30	4-10	

Name and Address	Map Ref	Bedrooms	Services	Meals	Bed and Breakfast — Single room overnight £min £max	Double/twin room overnight £min £max	Per person daily £min £max	B & B and evening meal — Per person weekly £min £max	Single	Double/twin	Family	Private	No. of bedrooms Public	No. of bath/shower rooms — From Last order	Evening meals	Parking (no. of cars)	Months open (1-12)	Symbols Key on back fold-out
ARINAGOUR Isle of Coll, Argyll	1 B1																	

Isle of Coll Hotel

AA ★ RAC
Arinagour,
Isle of Coll,
Argyll PA76 6SZ.
Tel. Coll 334 (STD 08793)

Fully Licensed,
Central Heating
Open all year round
May we send you
our brochure?

Name and Address	Bedrooms	Services	Meals	Single room overnight £min £max	Double/twin overnight £min £max	Per person daily £min £max	Per person weekly £min £max	Single	Double/twin	Family	Private	No. of bedrooms / Public	From Last order	Evening meals	Parking	Months open	Symbols
Isle of Coll Hotel PA78 6SZ Tel. Coll 334	3	4	5	13.60 17.00	24.80 31.00	24.00 25.00	168.00 175.00	2	5	2	-	2	1830 2130	35	1-12	T £ ♿ glass / horse / crossed / luggage / toilet / iron / electric / press / C / flower / building / V
Tigh-na-Mara Guest House Tel. Coll 354	3	3	5	8.00 -	16.00 -	15.00 -	105.00 -	1	4	3	-	3	1830 2230	9	4-10	♿ horse luggage radiator toilet iron electric C V
ARISAIG Inverness-shire	3 E12																
Arisaig Hotel Tel. Arisaig 210	3	3	5	14.00 -	28.00 -	23.00 -	- -	1	8	5	5	4	1930 2130	60	3-10	T luggage glass horse crossed radiator toilet electric hanger C flower building V hook flowers
Arisaig House Beasdale PH39 4NR Tel. Arisaig 622	5	5	3	18.50 48.00	48.00 86.00	33.00 62.50	184.80 350.00	1	11	2	14	2	1930 2030	15	4-10	T £ ♿ glass horse crossed luggage toilet phone iron hanger flower building hook K
Cnoc-na-Faire Hotel Back-of-Keppoch Tel. Arisaig 249	3	3	3	7.50 -	15.00 -	12.50 -	87.50 -	1	6	1	-	2	1800 2000	-	1-12	♿ glass horse radiator toilet V
ARROCHAR Dunbartonshire	1 G3																
Arrochar Hotel G83 7AU Tel. Arrochar 484	3	3	4	8.00 -	16.00 -	13.00 -	84.00 -	21	62	1	70	8	1830 2000	50	4-10	T ♿ glass horse radiator toilet iron flower V
Cobbler Hotel Tel. Arrochar 238	3	4	4	7.50 10.50	15.00 21.00	15.00 19.00	80.00 105.00	10	40	5	38	5	1900 2100	60	1-12	T £ ♿ glass horse radiator iron toilet electric flower building V hook
Loch Long Hotel G83 7AA Tel. Arrochar 434	3	4	4	9.00 11.00	18.00 22.00	14.00 17.00	80.00 100.00	13	43	3	7	9	1830 2000	60	4-11	T ♿ glass horse crossed radiator iron toilet electric C V hook
Greenbank Guest House Tel. Arrochar 305	4	2	4	7.50 8.50	13.00 15.00	- -	- -	1	2	1	-	1	1700 2100	6	1-12	horse radiator toilet flower V

VAT is shown at 15%: changes in this rate may affect prices.

Name and Address	Map Ref				Prices				Rooms							Facilities			
TOWN County / Establishment Address Telephone Telex		Bedrooms	Services	Meals	Bed and Breakfast			B & B and evening meal	No. of bedrooms					No. of bath shower rooms		Facilities			
					Single room overnight	Double/twin room overnight	Per person daily	Per person weekly	Single	Double/twin	Family	Private	Public			Evening meals	Parking (no. of cars)	Months open (1-12)	Symbols
ARROCHAR continued	1 G3				£min £max	£min £max	£min £max	£min £max						From Last order					Key on back fold-out
Lochside Guest House Tel. Arrochar 467		2	3	2	5.75 6.75	11.50 13.50	9.25 11.50	64.75 80.50	1	5	3	-	1	1800 1800		8	1-12		
Mansefield Guest House Tel. Arrochar 282		3	3	2	7.50 8.50	14.00 15.00	10.00 12.00	68.00 82.00	-	4	1	-	1	1900 2000		7	1-12		
ASSYNT Sutherland	3 G5																		
Inchnadamph Hotel IV27 4HL Tel. Assynt 202		3	3	4	13.00 -	26.00 -	18.50 -	127.50 -	13	12	5	7	7	1900 1945		34	3-11		
AUCHTERARDER Perthshire	2 B3																		
Cairn Lodge House Orchil Road Tel. Auchterarder 2634		4	3	5	20.00 25.00	30.00 35.00	29.00 37.00	- -	1	4	-	1	2	1900 2200		52	1-12		

Lochside ARROCHAR GUEST HOUSE

Telephone: ARROCHAR 467   J. A. & M. Sullivan

A small comfortable guest house with Garden directly on the shores of Loch Long, in magnificent Highland setting. 1½ miles from Loch Lomond. Ideal centre for touring, fishing, climbing. All bedrooms offer H/C, shaver points, heaters. Small boat hire, also chartered skippered sea fishing boats available, Anglers/clubs welcome. Good parking facilities open all year round. Under personal supervision of the proprietoress.

Collearn House Hotel

Auchterarder, Perthshire. Tel: 07646 3553

Situated only five minutes from the world famous golf courses of Gleneagles, and within easy reach of St. Andrews, Carnoustie and many other courses. Collearn is a Country House Hotel standing in its own grounds, and offers a high standard of accommodation, cuisine and personal service.

The bedrooms are spacious and well appointed: all have private bathrooms. The public rooms have retained the comfort, and character of former times.

Name and Address	Bedrooms	Services	Meals	Single room overnight	Double/twin room overnight	Per person daily	Per person weekly	Single	Double/twin	Family	Private	Public	From Last order	Evening meals	Months open	Symbols
Coll Earn House Hotel High Street PH3 1DF Tel. Auchterarder 3553/3554	5	4	5	18.00 25.00	35.00 50.00	23.00 23.00	161.00 161.00	1	6	1	8	-	1800 2200	60	1-12	
Gleneagles Hotel PH3 1NF Tel. Auchterarder 2231 Telex 76105	6	6	6	50.50 60.50	86.00 106.00	- -	- -	35	154	17	206	10	1900 2300	200	1-12	

Name and Address	Map Ref	Bedrooms	Services	Meals	Single room overnight £min/£max	Double/twin room overnight £min/£max	Per person daily £min/£max	Per person weekly £min/£max	Single	Double/twin	Family	Private	Public	Evening meals (From Last order)	No. of bath/shower rooms	Parking (no. of cars)	Months open (1-12)	Symbols
AUCHTERARDER continued	2 B3																	Key on back fold-out
Golf Inn 138 High Street PH3 1AD Tel. Auchterarder 2883		3	4	5	13.00 -	26.00 -	- -	- -	-	3	1	1	1	1900 2200	6		1-12	
Queens Hotel 20 High Street PH3 1DF Tel. Auchterarder 2493		2	2	3	10.00 -	19.00 -	14.00 -	- -	3	5	-	7	1	1630 2230	10		1-12	
Ruthven Tower Hotel Abbey Road PH3 1DN Tel. Auchterarder 2578		3	3	5	16.00 20.00	30.00 36.00	27.00 31.50	- -	2	20	1	10	3	1900 2100	40		1-12	
Star Hotel 113 High Street PH3 1AA Tel. Auchterarder 2407		1	3	4	8.00 10.00	14.00 18.00	12.00 15.00	60.00 75.00	1	3	1	-	-	1800 2200	-		1-12	
Deansland Guest House 17 High Street PH3 1DB Tel. Auchterarder 2528		3	3	1	8.00 -	14.00 -	- -	- -	1	2	-	-	1	- -	3		4-10	
AUCHTERHOUSE, by Dundee Angus	2 D2																	
The Old Mansion House Hotel Tel. Auchterhouse 366/367		5	4	5	32.00 35.00	40.00 44.00	- -	- -	1	4	2	6	-	1900 2130	50		1-12	
AUCHTERMUCHTY Fife	2 C3																	
The Boars Head Hotel The Square, High Street Tel. Auchtermuchty 318		3	2	4	10.00 12.00	18.00 20.00	14.00 18.00	80.00 105.00	-	3	-	-	2	1930 2100	2		1-12	
AUCHTERTOOL, by Kirkcaldy Fife	2 C4																	
Hotel Camilla Main Street Tel. Lochgelly 780590		-	-	-	10.00 16.60	19.00 25.00	- -	- -	1	10	2	13	-	1900 2030	10		1-12	
AULDEARN Nairn	4 C8																	
Lion Hotel Tel. Nairn 53204		3	3	3	8.50 -	17.00 -	11.00 -	72.00 -	7	10	4	3	3	1700 1930	12		1-12	

VAT is shown at 15%: changes in this rate may affect prices.

Name and Address		Map Ref	Bedrooms	Services	Meals	Prices							Rooms					Facilities	
						Bed and Breakfast				B & B and evening meal	No. of bedrooms			No. of bath/shower rooms					
TOWN County						Single room overnight	Double/twin room overnight	Per person daily	Per person weekly	Single	Double/twin	Family	Private	Public	Evening meals	Parking (no. of cars)	Months open (1-12)	Symbols	
						£min / £max	£min / £max	£min / £max	£min / £max						From / Last order			Key on back fold-out	

AULTBEA, by Achnasheen — Ross-shire — Map Ref 3 F7

AULTBEA HOTEL

AA   **AULTBEA, ROSS-SHIRE**   **RSAC**

On the shores of Loch Ewe—a small hotel with a very personal atmosphere, where good cooking combines with quiet comfort. Table d'hôte Dinner is offered, and à la carte Bar Meals. Inverewe Gardens are only 6 miles, and the sandy beaches of Gruinard Bay the same distance. Trout fishing is available on hill lochs and sea angling may be arranged. Mentioned in Arthur Epiron's "Travellers' Britain" and also a member of the "British Relais Routiers".

Telephone: STD 044 582 Aultbea 201

Establishment / Address / Telephone	Map Ref	Bedrooms	Services	Meals	Single room o/n	Double/twin o/n	Per person daily	Per person weekly	Single	Double/twin	Family	Private	Public	Evening meals	Parking	Months open
Aultbea Hotel, IV22 2HX, Tel. Aultbea 201		3	4	4	12.00 / 13.50	24.00 / 27.00	19.00 / 21.50	119.00 / 133.00	3	5	1	1	3	1730 / 2030	30	4-10
Drumchork Lodge Hotel, IV22 2HU, Tel. Aultbea 242		3	3	4	13.75 / 15.95	26.40 / 30.80	20.35 / 23.10	138.60 / 157.85	4	10	4	7	3	1900 / 2030	56	1-12
AULTGUISH, by Garve, Ross-shire	3 H7															
Aultguish Inn, Tel. Aultguish 254		3	4	4	10.75 / 11.85	21.50 / 23.70	16.95 / 18.75	107.00 / 118.00	6	19	3	-	7	1900 / 2100	50	1-12
AVIEMORE, Inverness-shire	4 C10															

For Family Favourites Families Favour it.

aviemore — THE AVIEMORE CENTRE · SCOTLAND

The all year all weather family resort offers unbeatable value in breathtaking unbeatable Highland scenery. From two to fourteen day holidays there is a package for all tastes. Ask about our Scot-Free Courtesy pass giving free access to many leisure facilities.
Write to Chalets Motel Manager, Aviemore Centre, Aviemore, Inverness-shire for a free leaflet. Tel: 0479 810624.

Establishment / Address / Telephone	Map Ref	Bedrooms	Services	Meals	Single room o/n	Double/twin o/n	Per person daily	Per person weekly	Single	Double/twin	Family	Private	Public	Evening meals	Parking	Months open
Aviemore Chalets Motel, Tel. Aviemore 810618		3	2	4	13.50 / 20.00	19.20 / 28.00	16.50 / 23.00	99.00 / 138.00	-	24	48	72	-	1800 / 2200	700	1-12
Badenoch Hotel, Tel. Aviemore 810261		5	5	5	14.70 / 27.30	27.30 / 37.80	18.10 / 30.10	84.00 / 112.00	2	75	-	61	9	1900 / 2130	50	1-12

Name and Address	Map Ref	Bedrooms	Services	Meals	Bed and Breakfast			B & B and evening meal	No. of bedrooms			No. of bath/shower rooms		Evening meals	Parking (no. of cars)	Months open (1-12)	Symbols
					Single room overnight	Double/twin room overnight	Per person daily	Per person weekly	Single	Double/twin	Family	Private	Public	From Last order			Key on back fold-out
					£min £max	£min £max	£min £max	£min £max									
AVIEMORE continued	4 C10																
Cairngorm Hotel Tel. Aviemore 810233		3	3	4	14.00 16.00	26.00 30.00	20.00 23.00	126.00 145.00	8	12	4	14	10	1900 2100	30	1-12	[symbols]
Corrour Hotel Inverdruie PH22 1QH Tel. Aviemore 810220		3	3	2	12.00 12.00	24.00 24.00	18.00 18.00	120.00 120.00	3	3	5	-	4	1830 -	12	12-11	[symbols]

HIGH RANGE MOTEL COMPLEX

Situated in its own silver birch woodland park and commanding a splendid view of the famous Lairig Ghru Pass and most prominent of all the peaks and ski runs of the Cairngorm mountains.

Motel Rooms: All with private bathroom, colour T.V., radio and baby listening service, tea making facilities. Bed and Continental Breakfast from £8.00 per person all inclusive.

Self Catering Chalets: Sleeping 2-6 persons from £50.00 per week.

Caravan Park: Designed to a very high standard of services including individual electricity hook up (240 volt — 5 amp) supply.

Tavern Bar & Bistro. Childrens Playpark.

For further information please phone or write.

Name and Address	Map Ref	Bedrooms	Services	Meals	Single room overnight	Double/twin room overnight	Per person daily	Per person weekly	Single	Double/twin	Family	Private	Public	Evening meals From Last order	Parking	Months open	Symbols
High Range Motel Complex PH22 1PS Tel. Aviemore 810636		5	-	-	- -	18.00 24.00	No Meals Provided		-	8	1	8	-	- -	50	1-12	[symbols]
The Ladbroke Freedom Inn Aviemore Centre PH33 1PF Tel. Aviemore 810781		6	4	5	- -	17.25 31.05	- -	- -	-	-	93	93	-	1900 2130	100	1-12	[symbols]
Lynwilg Hotel Loch Alvie PH22 1QB Tel. Aviemore 810207		3	4	5	10.00 12.00	19.00 22.00	13.00 16.50	98.00 108.00	3	7	1	2	2	1930 2100	40	1-12	[symbols]
Post House Hotel PH22 1PJ Tel. Aviemore 810771 Telex 75597		5	3	5	34.50 -	52.50 -	- -	- -	-	57	46	103	-	1900 2130	140	1-12	[symbols]
Stakis Coylumbridge Hotel PH22 1QN Tel. Aviemore 810661 Telex 75272		6	5	5	37.00 -	51.00 -	- -	- -	-	153	4	157	-	1800 2200	80	1-12	[symbols]

VAT is shown at 15%: changes in this rate may affect prices.

Name and Address (TOWN / County / Establishment / Address / Telephone / Telex)	Map Ref	Bedrooms	Services	Meals	Single room overnight £min £max	Double/twin room overnight £min £max	Per person daily £min £max	Per person weekly £min £max	Single	Double/twin	Family	Private	Public	Evening meals (Last order)	Parking (no of cars)	Months open (1-12)	Symbols
AVIEMORE continued — Map Ref 4 C10														From Last order			Key on back fold-out
Strathspey Thistle Hotel, Aviemore Centre, Tel. Aviemore 810681, Telex 75213	6	6	6		- / -	39.50 / 45.00	- / -	- / -	1	82	7	90	-	1900 2115	20	1-12	
Craiglea Guest House, PH22 1RH, Tel. Aviemore 810210	3	3	1		7.75 / -	15.50 / -	- / -	- / -	2	6	4	1	3	- / -	10	1-12	
Ravenscraig Guest House, PH22 1RP, Tel. Aviemore 810278	3	3	1		8.50 / 9.50	17.00 / 19.00	12.50 / 14.00	- / -	-	8	1	1	2	1830 / -	10	1-12	
AYR — Map Ref 1 G7																	
Aftongrange Hotel, 37 Carrick Road, Tel. Ayr 265679	4	3	4		13.00 / 15.00	22.00 / 24.00	- / -	- / -	1	5	2	5	1	1700 2000	30	1-12	
Ayrshire & Galloway Hotel, Killoch Place, Tel. Ayr 262626	4	4	4		12.00 / 20.00	22.00 / 30.00	18.00 / 26.00	- / -	10	12	3	8	5	1700 2030	15	1-12	

BEST VALUE IN TOWN, COMPETITIVELY PRICED

The Balgarth Hotel Welcomes You!

Accommodation. We offer modern, tastefully fitted bedrooms, with bath/shower. Warm relaxing decor, central heating, colour TV, telephone, teasmade, etc. superb a la carte/Table d'hote restaurant and modern cocktail bar. Beer garden. We will be pleased to arrange an Ayrshire golfing holiday for you.

8 Dunure Road, Doonfoot, Ayr. Tel: 0292 42441/2

Name and Address (TOWN / County / Establishment / Address / Telephone / Telex)	Map Ref	Bedrooms	Services	Meals	Single room overnight £min £max	Double/twin room overnight £min £max	Per person daily £min £max	Per person weekly £min £max	Single	Double/twin	Family	Private	Public	Evening meals (Last order)	Parking (no of cars)	Months open (1-12)	Symbols
The Balgarth Hotel, 8 Dunure Road, Doonfoot, Tel. Ayr 42441/2	5	4	5		14.00 / 18.00	26.00 / 32.00	20.00 / 24.00	- / -	6	7	2	11	2	1700 2200	100	1-12	
Beach Crest Hotel, 9 Queens Terrace, KA7 1DU, Tel. Ayr 264172	2	3	2		7.00 / 7.00	14.00 / 14.00	10.00 / 10.00	65.00 / 65.00	-	-	5	-	1	1750 / -	3	1-12	
Beechwood House Private Hotel, 39 Prestwick Road, Tel. Ayr 262093	3	3	2		7.00 / -	14.00 / -	- / -	- / -	-	6	2	-	1	1700 1800	3	1-12	
Caledonian Hotel, Dalblair Road, KA7 1UG, Tel. Ayr 69331, Telex 76357	6	5	6		15.00 / -	30.00 / -	- / -	- / -	56	62	3	121	-	1900 2115	60	1-12	
Chalmers Court Hotel, 36 Charlotte Street, KA7 1EA, Tel. Ayr 265458	2	2	2		7.00 / -	14.00 / -	9.50 / -	66.00 / -	1	3	3	-	1	1800 / -	6	1-12	

Name and Address	Map Ref	Bedrooms	Services	Meals	Single room overnight £min £max	Double/twin room overnight £min £max	Per person daily £min £max	Per person weekly £min £max	Single	Double/twin	Family	Private	Public	Evening meals From Last order	Parking	Months open	Symbols
AYR continued	1 G7																Key on back fold-out
The Chestnuts Hotel, 52 Racecourse Road, KA7 2UZ, Tel. Ayr 264393		3	4	5	12.50 –	25.00 –	17.00 –	110.00 –	3	7	4	7	3	1800 2145	45	1-12	(symbols)
Clifton Hotel, 19 Miller Road, KA7 2AX, Tel. Ayr 264521		4	4	4	9.50 10.00	17.00 22.00	15.50 16.00	85.00 90.00	2	7	2	5	2	1730 1800	16	1-12	(symbols)
Craiglea Hotel, 8 Cassillis Street, Tel. Ayr 69629		3	4	3	7.00 9.00	14.00 18.00	10.00 12.00	80.00 90.00	-	3	3	-	1	1800 -	-	1-12	(symbols)
Durward Hotel, 44 Prestwick Road, Tel. Ayr 262878		-	-	-	10.00 –	19.00 –	–	–	-	7	1	-	3	1800 2100	5	1-12	(symbols)
Elms Court Hotel, 21 Miller Road, Tel. Ayr 264191/82332		4	4	5	12.50 13.50	25.00 27.00	18.50 19.50	– –	4	8	7	11	3	1730 2030	50	1-12	(symbols)
Fort Lodge Hotel, 2 Citadel Place, Tel. Ayr 265232		3	4	4	14.00 17.00	26.00 34.00	18.00 21.00	115.00 136.00	1	3	2	-	2	1700 1900	7	1-12	(symbols)
Grosvenor House Hotel, 12 Charlotte Street, KA7 1DZ, Tel. Ayr 262153		3	2	2	6.00 7.00	12.00 14.00	9.00 10.00	60.00 67.00	1	1	5	-	1	1730 1730	4	1-12	(symbols)

Horizon Hotel
Fully Licensed.
Esplanade, Ayr.
Telephone: Ayr 264384.

The Hotel is on the seafront and five minutes from the bus station and town centre. Several Golf Courses nearby. Sandy Brach and Children's Play Area nearby. Sea fishing from harbour. Diningroom with the loveliest view in Ayr; overlooking the Heads of Ayr & the Isle of Arran. Most rooms with Private Shower & Toilets. All rooms have Tea/Coffee facilities. Central heating. Colour T.V. in all rooms. Dinner/Bed/Breakfast. Bar Lunches, High Teas with Home Baking. Under the constant personal supervision of the resident Proprietors Mr and Mrs James Meikle and their family.

Name and Address	Map Ref	Bedrooms	Services	Meals	Single room overnight £min £max	Double/twin room overnight £min £max	Per person daily £min £max	Per person weekly £min £max	Single	Double/twin	Family	Private	Public	Evening meals From Last order	Parking	Months open	Symbols
Horizon Hotel, The Esplanade, KA7 1DT, Tel. Ayr 264384		4	3	4	12.00 14.00	24.00 28.00	18.50 20.50	111.00 123.00	-	3	8	5	3	1800 2000	6	1-12	(symbols)

VAT is shown at 15%: changes in this rate may affect prices.

Name and Address	Map Ref	Bedrooms	Services	Meals	Single room overnight (£min / £max)	Double/twin room overnight (£min / £max)	Per person daily (£min / £max)	Per person weekly (£min / £max)	Single	Double/twin	Family	Private	Public	Evening meals (From / Last order)	Parking (no. of cars)	Months open (1-12)	Symbols
AYR continued	1 G7													From / Last order			Key on back fold-out
Lochinver Private Hotel 32 Park Circus KA7 2DL Tel. Ayr 265086		3	3	2	6.90 / -	13.80 / -	10.35 / -	72.45 / -	-	4	4	-	2	1700 / 1800	8	1-12	(facility symbols)
Marine Court Hotel Fairfield Road Tel. Ayr 267461		-	-	-	23.50 / 28.50	35.00 / 40.00	30.00 / 37.00	150.00 / 259.00	6	10	5	19	2	1900 / 2130	80	1-12	(facility symbols)
Monkwood Hotel 33-35 Carrick Road KA7 2RD Tel. Ayr 60952/263438		-	-	-	14.50 / -	22.00 / -	- / -	- / -	1	10	4	4	2	1700 / 2100	30	1-12	(facility symbols)
Old Race-Course Hotel Racecourse Road Tel. Ayr 262873		3	3	3	12.00 / 14.00	24.00 / 28.00	14.00 / 18.00	77.00 / 98.00	2	6	2	-	3	1700 / 2100	50	1-12	(facility symbols)
Rise Private Hotel 23 Eglinton Terrace KA7 1JJ Tel. Ayr 264623		2	1	2	5.50 / -	11.00 / -	7.50 / -	52.50 / -	-	4	2	-	1	1700 / -	-	1-12	(facility symbols)
The Roblin Hotel 9-11 Barns Street KA7 1XB Tel. Ayr 267595		2	2	2	9.20 / -	16.10 / -	11.50 / -	76.48 / -	1	11	6	-	5	1700 / 1815	20	1-12	(facility symbols)
Savoy Park Hotel Ltd 16 Racecourse Road Tel. Ayr 266112		5	5	4	20.00 / 25.00	37.00 / 45.00	30.00 / 35.00	178.00 / 200.00	3	13	3	19	5	1900 / 2030	90	1-12	(facility symbols)
Stakis Ayr Station Hotel Burns Statue Square KA7 3AT Tel. Ayr 263268		5	5	5	34.00 / -	46.00 / -	- / -	- / -	11	42	21	74	-	1800 / 2200	50	1-12	(facility symbols)
Windsor Hotel 6 Alloway Place Tel. Ayr 264689		3	3	2	10.50 / -	21.00 / -	14.50 / -	88.00 / -	2	5	3	-	3	1730 / -	-	1-12	(facility symbols)
Auchronie Guest House 8 Citadel Place KA7 1JN Tel. Ayr 265295		2	2	2	7.00 / 8.00	14.00 / 16.00	- / -	- / -	3	2	4	-	1	1700 / -	-	1-12	(facility symbols)
Cairnsmuir Guest House 35 Prestwick Road Tel. Ayr 265958		2	2	2	7.00 / 7.00	13.00 / 13.00	10.00 / 10.00	65.00 / 65.00	1	2	2	-	1	1700 / 1830	4	1-12	(facility symbols)
Cragallan Guest House 8 Queen's Terrace Tel. Ayr 264998		2	2	2	7.00 / 7.50	14.00 / 15.00	10.00 / 10.50	65.00 / 70.00	2	3	2	-	1	1730 / 1800	2	1-12	(facility symbols)
Daviot Guest House 12 Queen's Terrace Tel. Ayr 69678		2	2	2	7.00 / 7.50	14.00 / 15.00	10.00 / 11.00	65.00 / 70.00	-	3	1	-	2	- / -	-	-	(facility symbols)
Inverewe Board Residence 45 Bellevue Crescent KA7 2DP Tel. Ayr 265989		1	2	2	6.00 / -	12.00 / -	7.50 / -	50.00 / -	-	5	-	-	1	1730 / -	-	4-10	(facility symbols)

Name and Address (TOWN County / Establishment Address Telephone Telex)	Map Ref	Bedrooms	Services	Meals	Prices Bed and Breakfast: Single room overnight (£min £max)	Double/twin room overnight (£min £max)	Per person daily (£min £max)	B & B and evening meal: Per person weekly (£min £max)	Rooms: Single	Double/twin	Family	Private	Public	Evening meals (From Last order)	Parking (no. of cars)	Months open (1-12)	Symbols (Key on back fold-out)
AYR continued	1 G7																
Iona Boarding House 27 St Leonard's Road KA7 2PS Tel. Ayr 69541/83916		3	2	2	6.00 / 6.50	12.00 / 13.00	- / -	- / -	-	3	2	-	1	- / -	5	1-12	🛏🔥🚿⚓ C V
Queen's House 10 Queen's Terrace Tel. Ayr 265618		3	2	2	- / -	14.00 / -	10.00 / -	60.00 / -	-	2	3	-	1	1730 / 1730	2	1-12	🛏🔥🚿
Stanley Place Guest House 34 Dalblair Road KA7 1UL Tel. Ayr 263036		1	1	2	- / -	12.50 / 14.00	9.25 / 10.00	64.75 / 70.00	-	2	1	-	-	1830 / 1900	3	4-10	🛏🚿 C V
AYTON Berwickshire	2 G5																
Red Lion Hotel High Street Tel. Ayton 400		3	3	4	10.00 / 10.00	18.00 / 18.00	- / -	- / -	-	8	2	-	3	1900 / 2130	25	1-12	🛁🍷🐕🛏🔥 🚿 C ✳ V ♘
BALEPHETRISH Isle of Tiree, Argyll	1 A2																
Balephetrish House PA77 6UY Tel. Scarinish 549		1	3	3	8.05 / -	16.10 / -	13.80 / -	76.60 / -	1	3	1	-	1	1800 / -	10	1-12	💷🛁🐕🛏 C V
BALINTORE, Tain Ross-shire	4 C7																
Balintore Hotel Tel. Fearn 2219/2658		5	4	5	18.50 / -	32.00 / -	24.00 / -	- / -	1	4	1	6	-	1915 / 2030	50	1-12	💷🛁🍷🐕 🛏🔥🚿📞💷 🖵 C V ♘ ✎ 🧺
BALLA Isle of Eriskay, Western Isles	3 B10																

SILVERSANDS GUEST HOUSE
Eriskay—Outer Hebrides

Offering a majestic view. Own beach, and only a 10-minute car ferry sail from Ludag, South Uist. Central heating, wash basins, razor points. Tea facilities in all bedrooms. One free dinner with every three-night stay. Home baking, snacks, lunches, evening meals.

Non-Residents Welcome.

Write or telephone (087 86) 269 for details.

Name and Address	Map Ref	Bedrooms	Services	Meals	Single room overnight	Double/twin room overnight	Per person daily	Per person weekly	Single	Double/twin	Family	Private	Public	Evening meals	Parking	Months open	Symbols
Silver Sands Guest House Tel. Eriskay 269		-	-	-	9.50 / -	16.00 / -	15.50 / -	- / -	-	2	1	-	1	1800 / 1930	10	1-12	💷🛁🍴🛏 🔥🚿✂🧴 C ✳ V

VAT is shown at 15%: changes in this rate may affect prices.

Name and Address					Prices						Rooms						Facilities	
TOWN County Establishment Address Telephone Telex	Map Ref Bedrooms Services Meals				Bed and Breakfast			B & B and evening meal		No. of bed-rooms		No. of bath shower rooms						
					Single room overnight	Double/twin room overnight	Per person daily	Per person weekly	Single	Double/twin	Family	Private	Public	Evening meals	Parking (no. of cars)	Months open (1-12)	Symbols
					£min £max	£min £max	£min £max	£min £max						From Last order			Key on back fold-out
BALLACHULISH Argyll	1 F1																	

Ballachulish Hotel
BALLACHULISH   ARGYLL

Why not spend time relaxing in our beautiful Victorian coaching house overlooking Loch Leven and Loch Linnhe. Our hotel has recently been tastefully upgraded with Georgian Cocktail Bar, tea and coffee making facilities and radio and intercom in every bedroom. This year the hotel received an award for the high standard of its public rooms. We also have a games room and laundry facilities in the hotel. Most bedrooms have private facilities.

Our hotel has a fine reputation for good food and an extensive cellar.

The surrounding area is steeped in local folklore amidst the background of hills and glens. Local activities include Sailing, Fishing, Hill Walking, Water Skiing and Pony Trekking.

Why not let us help with your holiday plans?
Write or telephone 08552 239.

Name and Address	Map Ref	Bedrooms	Services	Meals	Single	Double/twin	Per person daily	Per person weekly	Single	Double/twin	Family	Private	Public	Evening meals	Parking	Months open	Symbols
Ballachulish Hotel PA39 4JY Tel. Ballachulish 239		4	5	4	10.25 13.50	21.00 27.00	19.00 22.00	- -	7	26	2	26	6	1900 2030	35	1-12	

Craigellachie Guest House
Ballachulish (by Glencoe), Argyll. Tel: 08552 531.

Close to the A82 road from Glasgow to the West Highlands near the shores of Loch Leven, this family run guest house features home cooking and a friendly atmosphere. All our rooms have hot and cold water, tea/coffee making facilities, heaters and electric blankets. There is a comfortable lounge with colour T.V. We also have a residents licence. Generous reductions for children. Ideal base for touring the West Highlands. Send S.A.E. for brochure. Resident proprietors, the Hill Family.

Name and Address	Map Ref	Bedrooms	Services	Meals	Single	Double/twin	Per person daily	Per person weekly	Single	Double/twin	Family	Private	Public	Evening meals	Parking	Months open	Symbols
Craigellachie Guest House PA39 4JB Tel. Ballachulish 531/264		3	3	2	5.95 6.95	11.90 13.90	9.70 10.70	64.75 67.90	1	7	2	-	3	1900 1900	4	1-10	
Craiglinnhe Guest House		1	2	2	- -	12.00 13.00	9.00 10.00	63.00 70.00	-	3	2	-	3	1900	5	4-10	
Lynleven Guest House Tel. Ballachulish 392		3	2	3	6.50	13.00	10.50 -	73.50 -	-	4	4	2	3	1830 2000	8	1-12	

Name and Address									Prices										Rooms							Facilities
TOWN County Establishment Address Telephone Telex	Map Ref	Bedrooms	Services	Meals				Bed and Breakfast Single room overnight	Double/twin room overnight	Per person daily	B & B and evening meal Per person weekly			Single	Double/twin	Family	No. of bedrooms Private	Public	No. of bath/shower rooms	Evening meals	Parking (no. of cars)	Months open (1-12)	Symbols
					£min £max	£min £max	£min £max	£min £max						From Last order		Key on back fold-out
BALLATER Aberdeenshire	4 E11																
Alexandra Hotel Bridge Square Tel. Ballater 55376		4	3	5	8.50 10.00	20.00 25.00	14.50 18.00	100.00 126.00	2	2	2	4	1	1700 2130	9	1-12	

ASPEN HOTEL

**Braemar Road, Ballater, Aberdeenshire.
Tel: 0338 55486.**

One of the traditional Hotels in this lovely area personally supervised by Resident Proprietors Mr and Mrs William Murdoch. Enjoy Royal Deeside and their hospitality. The Hotel is fully modernised with large private car park and is in an attractive and easily located situation. Convenient for golf, fishing, walking, pony trekking etc.
Open April-Mid October inclusive.

Name and Address	Bedrooms	Services	Meals	Single room overnight	Double/twin room overnight	Per person daily	Per person weekly	Single	Double/twin	Family	Private	Public	From Last order	Evening meals	Parking	Months open	Symbols
Aspen Hotel Braemar Road Tel. Ballater 55486	3	3	3	7.50 8.50	15.00 17.00	12.00 13.00	80.00 87.00	3	8	1	-	4	1845 -	16	4-10	
Coach House Hotel Netherley Place Tel. Ballater 55462	4	4	5	17.00 19.00	24.00 27.00	18.00 22.50	120.00 150.00	1	6	-	6	2	1700 2200	10	1-12	
Coyles Hotel Golf Road Tel. Ballater 55212	3	3	2	7.00 7.00	14.00 14.00	11.00 11.00	70.00 70.00	1	5	1	-	2	1900 1900	7	1-12	
Craigard Hotel AB3 5RR Tel. Ballater 55445	4	4	4	10.50 13.50	21.00 27.00	19.00 22.00	126.00 147.00	3	9	3	11	2	1900 2000	22	4-10	

Name and Address	Map Ref	Bedrooms	Services	Meals	Single room overnight	Double/twin room overnight	Per person daily	Per person weekly	Single	Double/twin	Family	Private	Public	Evening meals	Parking (no. of cars)	Months open (1-12)	Symbols
BALLATER continued	4 E11				£min £max	£min £max	£min £max	£min £max						From Last order			Key on back fold-out

DARROCH LEARG HOTEL
Ballater, Royal Deeside, Grampian.

Superbly situated, this beautiful hotel stands in 4 acres of garden and woodland overlooking the golf course and River Dee, with glorious views across the valley and Balmoral estate to the surrounding hills and most distant mountains, yet only 5 minutes walk from the centre of Ballater.

3 lounges, log fires, central heating, 23 bedrooms (19 with private bathroom), some with colour T.V., most with radio/intercom, and all with tea and coffee making facilities. If you want something special we suggest the Balmoral Room or perhaps the Alpine Room, (both have colour T.V. and south facing balcony).

There are also 2 self catering flats and the hotel is open for all meals. Residential and Restaurant Licence.

Illustrated brochure from Resident Proprietors Mr. and Mrs. C.D. Franks. Tel: 0338 55443
A.A., R.A.C., Michelin, Ashley Courtenay.

Name and Address	Bedrooms	Services	Meals	Single room overnight	Double/twin overnight	Per person daily	Per person weekly	Single	Double/twin	Family	Private	Public	Evening meals	Parking	Months open	Symbols
Darroch Learg Hotel AB3 5UX Tel. Ballater 55443	4	4	4	13.00 16.00	26.00 32.00	20.50 23.50	129.50 150.50	3	19	1	18	2	1900 2030	30	2-10	
Deeside Hotel Braemar Road AB3 5RQ Tel. Ballater 55420	3	3	4	12.00 13.00	20.00 23.00	15.00 18.00	95.00 115.00	-	5	1	1	2	1700 2100	32	1-12	
Gairnshiel Lodge Glengairn Tel. Ballater 55582	1	3	4	7.00 -	14.00 -	11.50 -	75.00 -	1	7	2	1	4	1800 2130	30	1-12	
Glen Lui Hotel AB3 5RP Tel. Ballater 55402	4	3	4	13.50 -	22.00 -	19.50 -	-	1	9	-	5	2	1900 2000	12	3-12	
The Green Inn Victoria Road Tel. Ballater 55701	1	2	4	7.50 -	15.00 -	-	-	-	3	-	1	1	1900 2100	-	1-11	

Scotland's Fishing Heritage

The sea has always played a vital part in the heritage of Scotland, this country with its wandering coastline and hundreds of islands. Today, for holidaymakers it means golden beaches, boat trips and birdwatching; for those who live on the coast it means a hard tradition of gaining a living from the sea.
You can learn about this tradition in the charming fishing villages on the coast, and in the fascinating museums which preserve it.
Write to the Scottish Tourist Board for a FREE pack telling you how to follow **SCOTLAND'S FISHING HERITAGE TRAIL.**

| Name and Address | | | | Prices | | | | | Rooms | | | | | Facilities | | |
TOWN County / Establishment Address Telephone Telex	Map Ref	Bedrooms	Services	Meals	Bed and Breakfast				B & B and evening meal	No. of bedrooms			No. of bath/shower rooms		Evening meals	Parking (no. of cars)	Months open (1-12)
					Single room overnight	Double/twin room overnight	Per person daily	Per person weekly	Per person weekly	Single	Double/twin	Family	Private	Public			
BALLATER continued	4 E11				£min £max	£min £max	£min £max	£min £max							From Last order		Key on back fold-out

Moorside House
Royal Deeside
Braemar Road,
Ballater,
Aberdeenshire

This A.A. award-winning establishment offers rooms with private bathrooms, and is attractively situated for touring the Highlands, hill walking and fishing. H&C, electric blankets, tea/coffee making facilities in all bedrooms. Full central heating. Residents' lounge with colour TV. Home grown produce. Ample car park. Fire certificate held. No service charge. Restricted Licence. Open all year. A.A., R.A.C. Listed.

Resident Proprietors: Mr and Mrs Ian Hewitt
Telephone Ballater 55492 (STD Code 0338).

Name and Address	Bedrooms	Services	Meals	Single room overnight	Double/twin overnight	Per person daily	Per person weekly	Single	Double/twin	Family	Private	Public	Last order	Parking	Months open
Moorside House Hotel, Braemar Road, AB3 5RL, Tel. Ballater 55492	4	3	2	11.00 / 12.00	18.00 / 20.00	15.50 / 17.00	100.00 / 110.00	-	6	2	4	2	1900 / 1900	10	3-11
Ravenswood Hotel, Braemar Road, Tel. Ballater 55539	3	3	4	11.00 / -	22.00 / -	16.50 / -	112.00 / -	1	3	3	2	2	1900 / 2130	30	1-12
Tullich Lodge Hotel, AB3 5SB, Tel. Ballater 55406	5	5	4	31.00 / 46.00	62.00 / 77.00	41.00 / 57.00	82.00 / 97.00	3	6	-	10	-	1930 / 2100	15	4-11
Westbank Hotel, Victoria Road, AB3 5QU, Tel. Ballater 55305	3	4	2	7.50 / 8.50	15.00 / 17.00	12.50 / 13.50	87.00 / 87.00	2	4	2	-	3	1830 / 1830	8	4-10
The Ballater Guest House, 34 Victoria Road, AB3 5QX, Tel. Ballater 55346	3	4	4	7.50 / -	14.00 / -	12.00 / -	75.00 / -	5	6	2	-	2	1900 / 2000	3	1-11
Dee Valley Guest House, 26 Viewfield Road, AB3 5RD, Tel. Ballater 55408	3	3	2	6.50 / 8.00	13.00 / 14.00	10.00 / 11.50	68.00 / 71.00	-	3	1	-	2	1800 / 1700	3	4-10

Royal Deeside

Glenbardie Guest House
Ballater, Aberdeenshire.

Glenbardie is a comfortable, family run, guest house. Ideally situated for: touring the Highlands, Hill Walking, Fishing, Golf, Bowls and Pony Trekking.

Ample car parking, large garden, home cooking, full central heating, H&C, electric blankets in all bedrooms, guest lounge with colour TV. Write for brochure. Resident Proprietors: Hugh and Isobel Craigie.

Telephone: Ballater 555 37

Name and Address	Bedrooms	Services	Meals	Single room overnight	Double/twin overnight	Per person daily	Per person weekly	Single	Double/twin	Family	Private	Public	Last order	Parking	Months open
Glenbardie Guest House, Braemar Road, AB3 5RQ, Tel. Ballater 55537	3	3	2	9.00 / -	16.00 / -	12.00 / -	78.00 / -	-	4	2	2	3	1830 / 1830	8	4-10
Killarney Guest House, AB3 5RS, Tel. Ballater 55465	2	2	2	6.50 / -	13.00 / -	10.00 / -	65.00 / -	1	3	1	-	1	1830 / 2000	6	4-10

VAT is shown at 15%: changes in this rate may affect prices.

Name and Address		Prices						Rooms						Facilities
TOWN County Establishment Address Telephone Telex	Map Ref Bedrooms / Services / Meals	Single room overnight	Double/twin room overnight	Per person daily	Per person weekly		Single	Double/twin	Family	Private	Public	Evening meals	Parking (no. of cars)	Months open (1-12)	Symbols

Name and Address	Map Ref	Bed	Ser	Meal	£min £max	£min £max	£min £max	£min £max	P/p wk	Single	D/twin	Family	Private	Public/From Last order	Evening meals	Parking	Months open	Symbols
BALLATER continued	4 E11																	Key on back fold-out
Morvada Guest House Braemar Road Tel. Ballater 55501		3	3	2	-	16.00	12.00	80.00	-	4	2	2	1	1900 -	6		4-10	

On Royal Deeside

Netherley Guest House

Ballater. Tel: Ballater (0338) 55792 or 55206

Comfortable family-run guest house. Quiet location near centre of village. Home cooking and baking with a choice of Lunch, High Tea or Dinner. Central Heating, Separate TV lounge, AA Listed.

Name and Address	Map Ref	Bed	Ser	Meal	Single	Double/twin	P/p daily	P/p wk	P/p wk2	Single	D/twin	Family	Private	Public/From Last order	Evening meals	Parking	Months open	Symbols
Netherley Guest House 2 Netherley Place AB3 5QE Tel. Ballater 55792		3	2	4	7.00 -	14.00 -	12.00 -	72.00 -	3	5	2	-	3	1900 -	-		2-12	
BALLINDALLOCH **Banffshire**	4 D9																	
Delnashaugh Hotel AB3 9AS Tel. Ballindalloch 210		4	3	4	10.50 12.50	21.00 25.00	16.50 19.50	125.00 135.00	2	4	-	4	1	1900 2100	-		1-12	
BALLINLUIG **Perthshire**	2 B1																	
Ballinluig Inn PH9 OLG Tel. Ballinluig 242		4	3	5	12.70 -	21.40 -	16.95 -	-	-	6	2	5	1	1800 2130	50		1-12	
Logierait Hotel Logierait PH9 OLJ Tel. Ballinluig 423		3	4	4	12.00 -	20.00 -	19.00 -	120.00 -	-	5	2	-	2	1700 2200	20		1-12	
BALLOCH **Dunbartonshire**	1 H4																	
Balloch Hotel G83 8LQ Tel. Alexandria 52579		4	3	5	15.67 19.53	25.30 31.35	-	-	2	8	3	6	2	1800 2000	20		1-12	
Balloch Myle Hotel Stirling Road Tel. Alexandria 52903		3	4	5	12.00 -	18.00 -	-	-	1	4	-	-	2	1800 2130	19		1-12	
Glenroy Hotel Balloch Road Tel. Alexandria 52494		-	-	-	10.00 -	20.00 -	-	-	1	5	1	3	1	1830 1945	30		1-12	
Tullichewan Hotel Tel. Alexandria 52052		3	3	6	15.08 17.08	23.15 27.15	20.96 22.96	149.56 -	2	12	1	6	2	1700 2200	50		1-12	

Name and Address				Prices						Rooms						Facilities	
TOWN / County / Establishment / Address / Telephone / Telex	Map Ref	Bedrooms	Services	Meals	Bed and Breakfast				B & B and evening meal		No. of bedrooms			No. of bath/ shower rooms		Evening meals	Parking (no. of cars)	Months open (1-12)	Symbols
					Single room overnight	Double/twin room overnight	Per person daily	Per person weekly	Single	Double/twin	Family	Private	Public				
BALLATER continued	4 E11				£min £max	£min £max	£min £max	£min £max					From Last order	Key on back fold-out			
Glen Alwyn Guest House Old Luss Road G83 8QW Tel. Alexandria 52860		3	2	1	7.00 8.00	14.00 14.00	- -	- -	-	3	-	-	1	- -	10	4-10	
BALLYGRANT Isle of Islay, Argyll	1 C5																
Ballygrant Inn Tel. Port Askaig 271/680		3	3	5	13.80 16.00	25.30 30.00	23.00 25.00	120.00 140.00	-	4	-	-	2	1900 2030	40	1-12	
BALMACARA, by Kyle of Lochalsh Ross-shire	3 F9																

Name and Address	Map Ref	Bedrooms	Services	Meals	B&B Single room overnight (£min / £max)	B&B Double/twin room overnight (£min / £max)	B&B + evening meal Per person daily (£min / £max)	B&B + evening meal Per person weekly (£min / £max)	No. of bedrooms Single	Double/twin	Family	No. of bath/shower rooms Private	Public	Evening meals (From / Last order)	Parking (no. of cars)	Months open (1-12)	Symbols
BALQUHIDDER continued Coshnachie Guest House FK19 8NZ Tel. Strathyre 258	1 H2	4	3	2	- / -	15.00 / -	12.25 / -	- / -	-	1	1	2	-	1900 / -	6	1-11	[symbols]
BALTASOUND, Unst **Shetland** Baltasound Hotel Tel. Baltasound 334	5 G1	3	3	3	12.00 / 17.00	16.00 / 24.00	17.00 / 22.00	116.00 / 130.00	-	10	-	2	2	1830 / 2030	-	1-12	[symbols]
Hagdale Lodge Tel. Baltasound 484		2	4	4	15.00 / 27.00	20.00 / 27.00	22.00 / 34.00	154.00 / 238.00	40	8	-	9	5	1900 / 2100	40	1-12	[symbols]
BANAVIE, by Fort William **Inverness-shire** Glen Loy Lodge PH33 7PD Tel. Gairlochy 200	3 G12	3	4	2	6.50 / 8.00	13.00 / 16.00	11.50 / 13.00	75.00 / 85.00	2	5	2	-	2	1900 / -	12	1-12	[symbols]
The Moorings Hotel PH33 7LY Tel. Corpach 550		4	4	4	9.00 / 20.00	18.00 / 32.00	17.75 / 24.75	- / -	2	15	1	6	4	1900 / 2030	25	1-12	[symbols]
BANCHORY **Kincardineshire** Banchory Lodge Hotel AB3 3HS Tel. Banchory 2625	4 F11	4	5	4	21.00 / 31.00	36.00 / 65.00	26.25 / 28.87	213.15 / 234.46	2	15	10	22	3	1900 / 2100	53	2-12	[symbols]
Tor-na-Coille Hotel Tel. Banchory 2242		6	4	5	18.50 / 24.00	36.00 / 40.00	27.50 / 33.00	175.00 / 225.00	2	22	1	25	-	1930 / 2130	60	1-12	[symbols]
BANCHORY-DEVENICK, by **Aberdeen** **Aberdeenshire** Ardoe House Hotel AB1 5YP Tel. Aberdeen 47355/6	4 H10	5	5	5	20.00 / 40.00	38.00 / 50.00	- / -	- / -	8	15	-	15	2	1900 / 2130	100	1-12	[symbols]
BANFF Banff Springs Hotel Tel. Banff 2881	4 F7	6	5	5	24.00 / 25.00	34.00 / 34.00	30.00 / 31.00	189.00 / 190.00	5	21	4	30	-	1830 / 2030	150	1-12	[symbols]
Carmelite House Private Hotel Low Street Tel. Banff 2152		3	3	2	8.95 / 11.75	17.90 / 23.50	12.90 / 16.25	- / -	2	3	4	-	2	1800 / 1900	6	1-12	[symbols]

Key on back fold-out

Name and Address	Map Ref	Bedrooms	Services	Meals	Bed and Breakfast — Single room overnight £min £max	Bed and Breakfast — Double/twin room overnight £min £max	Bed and Breakfast — Per person daily £min £max	B & B and evening meal — Per person weekly £min £max	Single	Double/twin	Family	Private	Public	No. of bath/shower rooms — Last order From / order	Evening meals	Parking (no. of cars)	Months open (1-12)	Symbols
BANFF continued	4 F7				£min £max	£min £max	£min £max	£min £max						From Last order				Key on back fold-out

THE COUNTY HOTEL BANFF *Telephone Banff (02612) 5353*

Elegant Georgian mansion with country-house atmosphere and fine views over Banff Bay.

The County offers every comfort of a prestigious small hotel and restaurant and is recognized by all the leading hotel and food guides. Friendly personal attention from the resident proprietors: **Michael MacKenzie** and **Frederic Symonds**.

Special facilities for golf and private fishing and ideal base for touring, walking, riding, sailing, shooting and **Grampian Heritage.**

Name and Address	Bedrooms	Services	Meals	Single room overnight	Double/twin room overnight	Per person daily	Per person weekly	Single	Double/twin	Family	Private	Public	Last order	Parking	Months open	Symbols
The County Hotel High Street AB4 1AE Tel. Banff 5353 Telex 73388	5	5	5	26.00 28.00	42.00 44.00	31.00 39.00	- -	2	4	-	6	-	1930 2130	16	1-12	[symbols]
Dounemount Hotel AB4 1PN Tel. Macduff 32262	4	4	4	11.95 -	21.00 -	19.00 -	92.00 -	2	4	2	2	3	1900 2100	50	4-10	[symbols]
Dunvegan House Hotel Low Street Tel. Banff 2374	3	3	5	9.50 9.50	19.00 19.00	- -	- -	-	2	2	-	2	1700 2200	-	1-12	[symbols]
Fife Lodge Hotel Sandyhill Road AB4 1BE Tel. Banff 2436	4	4	5	18.00 18.00	30.00 30.00	24.50 24.50	- -	-	5	1	6	-	1730 2000	200	1-12	[symbols]
Bridge Guest House 35a Bridge Street AB4 1HD Tel. Banff 5075	3	1	2	7.50 -	- -	10.00 -	- -	-	3	2	-	2	1830 1900	-	1-12	[symbols]
BANKFOOT **Perthshire** (Map Ref 2 B2)																
Bankfoot Hotel Main Street PH1 4AB Tel. Bankfoot 243	3	4	4	8.00 8.00	16.00 16.00	12.50 14.50	77.00 101.50	1	5	-	-	2	1900 2130	7	1-12	[symbols]
Hunters Lodge PH1 4DX Tel. Bankfoot 325	4	4	4	19.50 30.00	19.50 30.00	14.50 19.75	101.50 138.25	-	-	11	11	-	1700 2100	50	1-12	[symbols]

TOURIST INFORMATION CENTRES

All over Scotland there are Tourist Information Centres where friendly, well-informed staff will be pleased to give you information about:

PLACES TO STAY • PLACES TO VISIT • ROUTES TO TAKE • LOCAL EVENTS

There will be lots of helpful literature, some free and some saleable, and many Centres can help you book accommodation.

Look for the information symbol

    VAT is shown at 15%; changes in this rate may affect prices.

Name and Address		Map Ref	Bedrooms	Services	Meals	Single room overnight	Double/twin room overnight	Per person daily	Per person weekly	Single	Double/twin	Family	Private	Public	Evening meals From/Last order	Parking (no. of cars)	Months open (1-12)	Symbols
						£min £max	£min £max	£min £max	£min £max						From Last order			Key on back fold-out
BANNISKIRK Caithness		4 C3																

BANNISKIRK HOUSE GUEST HOUSE

Banniskirk (on A895) Caithness KW12 6XA   *Tel: 084 783 609*

This old Victorian mansion house delightfully set in 20 acres of wooded grounds is a haven of peace and quiet only 7 miles from Thurso and the Orkney Ferry. Wick and John 'o Groats easily reached. Guests enjoy fine food and personal attention. Comfortable rooms, with all modern amenities and convenient for golf. Sea, River and Loch fishing can be arranged. **OPEN MARCH TO OCT.**

BROCHURE ON REQUEST WITH S.A.E. FROM MR. & MRS. S. THOMSON

Name and Address	Map Ref	Bedrooms	Services	Meals	Single room overnight	Double/twin room overnight	Per person daily	Per person weekly	Single	Double/twin	Family	Private	Public	Evening meals From/Last order	Parking	Months open	Symbols
Banniskirk House Guest House KW12 6XA Tel. Halkirk 609		2	2	2	7.00 7.50	14.00 15.00	12.00 12.50	82.00 85.00	2	4	2	-	2	1830 1900	20	3-10	
BARR Ayrshire	1 G9																
The King's Arms Hotel Tel. Barr 230		3	3	4	10.35 -	18.70 -	15.35 -	94.50 -	-	3	-	-	1	1900 2200	8	1-12	
BARRHEAD Renfrewshire	1 H5																
Dalmeny Park Hotel Lochlibo Road Tel. 041 881 9211		4	4	5	27.50 32.50	34.50 38.50	37.00 42.00	-	-	18	1	10	4	1900 2200	120	1-12	
BARRHILL Ayrshire	1 G9																
Galloway Hotel 28 Main Street KA26 0PZ Tel. Barrhill 343		3	3	5	14.50 14.50	22.00 22.00	21.00 25.00	132.00 160.00	1	3	-	-	2	1800 2200	23	1-12	
BEARSDEN Dunbartonshire	1 H5																
Stakis Burnbrae Hotel Milngavie Road G61 3TA Tel. 041 942 5951		5	5	5	36.00 -	44.00 -	-	-	5	10	-	13	1	1830 2200	100	1-12	
Kilmardinny Riding Establishment Kilmardinny Farm, Milngavie Road Tel. 041 942 4404		3	2	1	7.00 -	14.00 -	-	-	4	4	-	-	4	-	10	1-12	
St Andrews College of Education G61 4QA Tel. 041 943 1424		2	2	3	10.12 -	-	-	-	210 Group Bookings Only	-	-	-	45	-	200	7-9	

Name and Address				Prices				Rooms									Facilities	
TOWN County Establishment Address Telephone Telex	Map Ref	Bedrooms	Services	Meals	Bed and Breakfast Single room overnight	Double/twin room overnight	Per person daily	Per person weekly	B & B and evening meal Single	Double/twin	Family	No. of bedrooms Private	Public	No. of bath/ shower rooms	Evening meals	Parking (no. of cars)	Months open (1-12)	Symbols
					£min £max	£min £max	£min £max	£min £max				From Last order			Key on back fold-out			
BEATTOCK Dumfriesshire	2 C8																	

AUCHEN CASTLE
HOTEL & RESTAURANT
Near Moffat, Dumfriesshire

A gracious, intimate country house with purpose built additional annexe in the lovely Scottish Borders. Spectacular views, 17 acres of grounds renowned for the shrubs and trees and a stocked trout loch. Private bath and shower rooms, very good cooking and owner managed.

BORDER BREAKS

Golf, Motoring, Fishing Holidays.
Telephone: Beattock (06833) 407.

Tour Scotland Member	A.A.
	Egon Ronay
	Good Hotel Guide

Name	Map Ref	Bedrooms	Services	Meals	Single room	Double/twin	Per person daily	Per person weekly	Single	Double/twin	Family	Private	Public	Last order	Evening meals	Parking	Months open	Symbols
Auchen Castle Hotel DG10 9SH Tel. Beattock 407	4	4	4		21.00 21.00	26.00 36.00	- -	- -	4	24	-	28	1	1900 2100	33	2-12		T £ ▣ 🍷 🐕 ▣ ▣ ▣ ▣ □ ▤ C ❋ ▦ V ♪ ⚓
Beattock House Hotel DG10 9QB Tel. Beattock 403	-	-	-		13.75 15.00	27.50 30.00	21.00 23.00	- -	1	4	2	2	2	1830 2130	30	1-12		🍷 🐕 ▣ ▣ C ❋ V ♪

Marchbankwood Country Hotel
BEATTOCK, DUMFRIESSHIRE

On A701 South of Beattock Village Telephone: 068 33 343

Friendly Country House set in 40 acres with magnificent views from every window. Stroll the grounds in the company of numerous wildlife. Relax in the cosy Bar Lounge with open fire. Facilities include Putting Green, Tennis Court, own 600-acre Rough Shoot. Horse-riding within 300 yards. Painting tuition. Good home cooking. Children and pets welcome. Open all year.

Name	Map Ref	Bedrooms	Services	Meals	Single room	Double/twin	Per person daily	Per person weekly	Single	Double/twin	Family	Private	Public	Last order	Evening meals	Parking	Months open	Symbols
Marchbankwood House Tel. Beattock 343	3	3	3		10.00 -	20.00 -	15.00 -	105.00 -	2	4	3	6	1	1900 2100	15	1-12		🍷 🐕 ▣ C ❋ V ⚲
Old Brig Inn & Posting House Tel. Beattock 401	3	3	4		12.50 12.50	21.00 23.50	19.00 19.00	99.00 108.00	3	3	2	2	2	1900 2030	24	1-12		£ 🍷 ▣ ▦ V

VAT is shown at 15%: changes in this rate may affect prices.

Name and Address / Town, County, Establishment, Address, Telephone, Telex	Map Ref	Bedrooms	Services	Meals	Single room overnight £min/£max	Double/twin room overnight £min/£max	Per person daily £min/£max	Per person weekly £min/£max	Single	Double/twin	Family	Private	Public	Evening meals From/Last order	Parking (no. of cars)	Months open (1-12)	Symbols
BEAULY — Inverness-shire	4 A8																
Priory Hotel, The Square, Tel. Beauly 782309		4	4	4	10.50 / 15.00	17.50 / 23.50	14.00 / 20.00	90.00 / 107.50	2	9	1	6	3	1730 / 2100	3	1-12	T £ ... C V
Arkton Guest House, West End, Tel. Beauly 782388		3	3	2	6.50 / -	13.00 / -	- / -	- / -	-	6	2	-	2	1800 / -	12	1-12	V
Chrialdon Guest House, Station Road, Tel. Beauly 782336		3	3	2	7.50 / 8.00	14.50 / 16.00	11.50 / 12.00	80.00 / 84.00	2	7	5	-	3	1900 / 1945	16	4-10	V
BELLOCHANTUY, by — Campbeltown, Argyll	1 D7																
Putechan Lodge Hotel, Tel. Glenbarr 266		5	5	5	16.00 / 18.00	22.00 / 30.00	- / -	- / -	-	12	1	8	2	1915 / 2130	30	2-12	T £ C V
BELLSHILL — Lanarkshire	2 A5																
Hattonrigg Hotel, Hattonrigg Road, Tel. Bellshill 748488		-	-	-	14.50 / -	29.00 / -	- / -	- / -	6	2	-	4	1	1830 / 2130	60	1-12	£
BENDERLOCH, by Connel — Argyll	1 E2																
Lynn of Lorne Hotel, Tel. Ledaig 278		3	3	4	10.50 / -	19.00 / -	16.50 / -	112.00 / -	1	20	-	2	6	1800 / 2100	40	1-12	T C V
Beach View Guest House, Tel. Ledaig 249		2	2	3	8.00 / 8.00	16.00 / 16.00	12.00 / 12.00	75.00 / 75.00	4	9	1	-	3	1800 / 1800	20	1-12	V
BETTYHILL — Sutherland	4 B3																
Bettyhill Hotel, KW14 7SP, Tel. Bettyhill 202		3	3	3	9.50 / -	19.00 / -	17.00 / -	- / -	5	17	-	5	3	1900 / 2000	33	1-12	V
Farr Bay Inn, Tel. Bettyhill 230		-	-	-	5.00 / 10.00	10.00 / 20.00	10.00 / 20.00	55.00 / 140.00	-	5	1	2	2	1800 / 2130	12	1-12	£ C V
BIGGAR — Lanarkshire	2 C6																
Hartree Country House Hotel, Tel. Biggar 20215		4	4	5	11.00 / 16.00	21.00 / 32.00	- / -	- / -	9	12	1	8	5	1900 / 2200	60	1-12	£ V
Shieldhill House Hotel, Quothquan, Tel. Biggar 20035		3	2	4	14.00 / 28.00	19.00 / -	19.00 / -	120.00 / -	5	14	1	8	3	1900 / 2145	150	1-12	T £ C V

Name and Address	Map Ref	Bedrooms	Services	Meals	Bed and Breakfast				B & B and evening meal					No. of bedrooms	No. of bath/shower rooms	Evening meals	Parking (no. of cars)	Months open (1-12)	Symbols
TOWN / County / Establishment / Address / Telephone / Telex					Single room overnight	Double/twin room overnight	Per person daily	Per person weekly	Single	Double/twin	Family	Private	Public						Symbols
BIGGAR continued	2 C6				£min £max	£min £max	£min £max	£min £max						From Last order					Key on back fold-out
Toftcombs Hotel Tel. Biggar 20142		3	2	4	12.00 12.00	24.00 24.00	18.00 18.00	119.00 119.00	3	4	1	-	2	1900 2030		-		1-12	
BIRSAY Orkney	5 A10																		
Orkney Field Centre, Links House KW17 2LX Tel. Birsay 221		-	2	3	- 6.00	- 12.00	- 12.50	- 87.50	1	2	4	-	2	1930 -		5		5-10	
BIXTER, West Mainland Shetland	5 F4																		
Bixter Guest House ZE2 9NA Tel. Bixter 200		3	2	2	6.50 -	- -	12.00 -	- -	1	2	-	-	1	1800 1900		3		4-9	
BLACKFORD Perthshire	2 B3																		
Blackford Hotel Moray Street PH4 1QF Tel. Blackford 246		4	4	3	11.00 14.00	18.50 22.00	14.00 -	- -	1	4	1	4	1	1800 2200		10		1-12	
BLACKWATERFOOT Isle of Arran	1 E7																		
Greannan Hotel Tel. Shiskine 200		3	3	5	11.50 -	23.00 -	15.00 -	105.00 -	5	6	1	-	2	1830 1900		50		1-12	

Name and Address	Bedrooms	Services	Meals	Single room overnight	Double/twin room overnight	Per person daily	Per person weekly	Single	Double/twin	Family	Private	Public	Evening meals	Parking	Months open	Symbols
Kinloch Hotel KA27 8ET Tel. Shiskine 286	4	4	4	12.00 14.50	24.00 29.00	19.50 23.00	136.50 157.50	10	36	-	46	8	1900 2000	50	1-12	

Name and Address	Map Ref	Bedrooms	Services	Meals	Single room overnight £min/£max	Double/twin room overnight £min/£max	Per person daily £min/£max	Per person weekly (B&B and evening meal) £min/£max	Rooms Single	Double/twin	Family	Private (bath/shower)	Public (bath/shower)	Evening meals From/Last order	Parking (no. of cars)	Months open	Symbols
BLACKWATERFOOT continued	1 E7																Key on back fold-out
Rock Hotel, Tel. Shiskine 225		3	3	3	12.00 / 13.00	24.00 / 26.00	17.00 / 18.50	112.00 / 125.00	1	4	4	-	2	1800 / 1900	1	1-12	T £ C V …
BLAIR ATHOLL Perthshire	4 C12																
Atholl Arms Hotel, PH18 5SG, Tel. Blair Atholl 205		3	4	4	10.50 / 12.00	21.00 / 24.00	16.00 / 18.00	100.00 / 106.00	7	19	2	9	9	1900 / 2030	26	1-12	T £ V …
Invergarry Guest House, The Terrace, Bridge of Tilt, PH18 5SZ, Tel. Blair Atholl 255		3	3	3	- / -	15.00 / -	12.50 / -	80.50 / -	-	3	4	-	1	1830 / 1700	12	4-10	…
BLAIRGOWRIE Perthshire	2 C1																

Altamount House Hotel

Telephone: (0250) 3512

A charming Georgian Mansion in 5 acres of secluded grounds and gardens yet only a 5-minute walk from the centre of town. The famous Rosemount Golf Course is close by. Lovely accommodation and superb cuisine are provided by the resident owners Ritchie and Sue Russell who will be pleased to send you full details on request.

Coupar Angus Road, Blairgowrie Perthshire PH10 6JN

Name and Address	Bedrooms	Services	Meals	Single room overnight £min/£max	Double/twin room overnight £min/£max	Per person daily £min/£max	Per person weekly (B&B and evening meal) £min/£max	Rooms Single	Double/twin	Family	Private (bath/shower)	Public (bath/shower)	Evening meals From/Last order	Parking (no. of cars)	Months open	Symbols
Altamount House Hotel, Coupar Angus Road, PH10 6JN, Tel. Blairgowrie 3512	-	-	-	15.00 / 15.00	30.00 / 30.00	25.00 / 25.00	175.00 / 175.00	2	3	2	2	2	1900 / 2100	40	1-12	£ C V …
Brig of Blair Hotel, Wellmeadow, PH10 6NQ, Tel. Blairgowrie 2589	-	-	-	7.50 / -	14.00 / -	9.50 / -	- / -	1	5	1	-	1	1830 / 2230	-	1-12	V …
Claymore House Hotel, 30 Wellmeadow, PH10 6AS, Tel. Blairgowrie 3570	2	1	3	7.50 / 8.00	13.00 / 14.00	12.00 / 13.00	80.00 / 86.00	1	2	2	-	1	1700 / 2100	10	1-12	T C V …
Golf View Hotel, Perth Road, Rosemount, PH10 6PY, Tel. Blairgowrie 2895	4	4	5	13.00 / 18.00	24.00 / 32.00	17.00 / 25.00	- / -	2	5	1	4	2	1800 / 2200	80	1-12	£ V …
Kinloch House Hotel, Kinloch, PH10 6SG, Tel. Essendy 237	4	4	4	22.50 / 22.50	29.00 / 34.00	23.75 / 31.75	166.25 / 222.25	2	7	1	7	2	1930 / 2100	50	1-12	T £ C V …
Kintrae House Hotel, Balmoral Road, Rattray, PH10 7AH, Tel. Blairgowrie 2106	3	5	5	9.50 / -	17.00 / -	14.00 / -	- / -	-	6	3	-	2	1830 / 1930	20	1-12	V …

Name and Address		Map Ref	Bedrooms	Services	Meals	Prices					Rooms							Facilities
TOWN County — Establishment Address Telephone Telex						Bed and Breakfast — Single room overnight	Double/twin room overnight	per person daily	B & B and evening meal — Per person weekly	Single	Double/twin	Family	Private	No. of bedrooms — Public	No. of bath/shower rooms	Evening meals — Last order	Parking (no. of cars)	Months open (1-12) — Symbols
BLAIRGOWRIE continued	2 C1					£min. £max	£min £max	£min £max	£min £max					From Last order		Key on back fold-out		

Muirton House Hotel

Essendy Road,
Blairgowrie,
Perthshire.
Tel: (0250) 2113.

Come and enjoy the home from home atmosphere, without the worry of washing up and bed making. The Hotel is set in three acres of secluded grounds outside Blairgowrie. An ideal centre for touring, fishing, golfing, shooting, ski-ing and pony trekking. All rooms have washbasins, some have ensuite facilities.
Special weekly terms and reductions for children.
Licensed. Dogs welcome.

Name and Address	Bedrooms	Services	Meals	Single room overnight	Double/twin room overnight	per person daily	Per person weekly	Single	Double/twin	Family	Private	Public	bath/shower	Last order	Parking	Months open
Muirton House Hotel Essendy Road PH10 6QU Tel. Blairgowrie 2113	4	3	4	12.50 16.00	25.00 32.00	19.00 22.50	110.00 135.00	1	5	2	-	2	1930 2130	50	1-12	
Queens Hotel 21 High Street PH10 6ET Tel. Blairgowrie 2217	3	4	4	13.80 -	21.50 -	20.15 -	- -	6	22	2	9	5	1900 2100	8	1-12	
The Rosemount Golf Hotel Golf Course Road, Rosemount PH10 6LG Tel. Blairgowrie 2604	4	3	5	11.00 12.50	22.00 22.00	- -	- -	-	10	2	12	-	1630 2200	75	1-12	

ROYAL HOTEL

Allan Street, Blairgowrie, Perthshire

47 bedrooms, five with private bathroom. A Georgian-fronted hotel privately owned and situated in the town centre. Licensed. Large comfortable cocktail lounge (serving bar lunches), sauna and solarium, television lounge. Games: table-tennis and bar billiards. All rooms have tea/coffee making facilities and central heating. Car and coach park. Children welcome.

Telephone: Blairgowrie (STD 0250) 2226

Name and Address	Bedrooms	Services	Meals	Single room overnight	Double/twin room overnight	per person daily	Per person weekly	Single	Double/twin	Family	Private	Public	bath/shower	Last order	Parking	Months open
Royal Hotel 53 Allan Street PH10 6AB Tel. Blairgowrie 2226	3	4	4	10.00 12.00	19.00 22.00	12.50 16.00	84.00 90.00	9	35	3	5	7	1700 1945	35	1-12	
Stormont Lodge Hotel Kirk Wynd PH10 6HN Tel. Blairgowrie 2853	4	4	4	10.00 12.50	20.00 25.00	16.00 18.50	105.00 120.00	1	7	-	3	2	- -	40	1-12	
Victoria Hotel Lower Mill Street PH10 6NF Tel. Blairgowrie 3100	-	-	-	8.50 -	15.00 -	12.50 -	- -	1	2	2	-	1	- -	24	1-12	

VAT is shown at 15%: changes in this rate may affect prices.

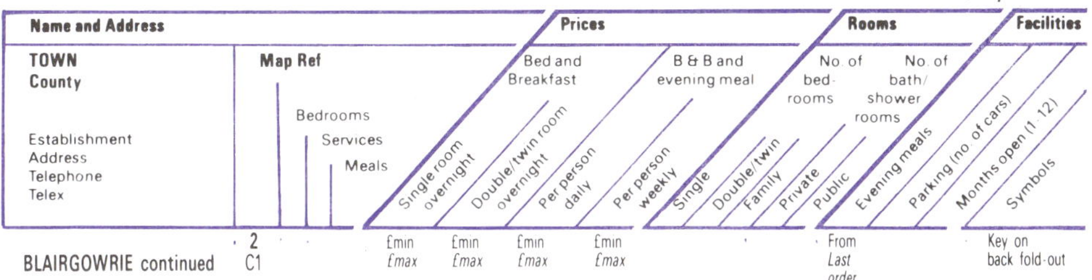

Name and Address	Map Ref	Bedrooms / Services / Meals	Prices — Bed and Breakfast				B & B and evening meal				Rooms			Facilities
TOWN / County / Establishment / Address / Telephone / Telex			Single room overnight	Double/twin room overnight	Per person daily	Per person weekly	Single	Double/twin	Family	Private	Public / Evening meals	No. of bedrooms	Months open (1-12)	Symbols
BLAIRGOWRIE continued	2 C1		£min £max	£min £max	£min £max	£min £max					From Last order	No. of bath/ shower rooms	Parking (no. of cars)	Key on back fold-out

BLAIRGOWRIE continued

Hatton Road, New Rattray, Blairgowrie.
A.A. & R.A.C. listed

Adjacent to the main Braemar Road yet secluded from traffic. A warm welcome awaits you at our early Victorian house, situated in extensive grounds. With views of the Sidlaw Hills and offering superior accommodation with six bedrooms (one ground floor), lounge with colour T.V. also a sun lounge.

Please write or telephone for brochure (0250 4605).

Name and Address	Bedrooms	Services	Meals	Single room overnight	Double/twin room overnight	Per person daily	Per person weekly	Single	Double/twin	Family	Private	Public	No. of bath/shower rooms	Parking	Months open	Symbols
Glenshieling Guest House, Hatton Road, Rattray, PH10 7HZ, Tel. Blairgowrie 4605	3	3	3	7.50 / 7.50	15.00 / 15.00	12.00 / 12.00	80.00 / 80.00	-	4	2	-	2	1900	18	1-12	
The Laurels Guest House, Golf Course Road, Rosemount, PH10 6LH, Tel. Blairgowrie 4920	3	3	4	7.50	15.00	12.00	81.00	1	3	1	-	1	1900 / 1830	8	1-12	

Name and Address	Bedrooms	Services	Meals	Single room overnight	Double/twin room overnight	Per person daily	Per person weekly	Single	Double/twin	Family	Private	Public	No. of bath/shower rooms	Parking	Months open	Symbols
Rosebank Guest House, Balmoral Road, PH10 7AF, Tel. Blairgowrie 2912	3	3	2	8.00 / 9.50	16.00 / 18.00	13.50 / 14.95	85.00 / 95.00	2	3	2	-	2	1900	12	1-12	
St Ninians Guest House, Perth Road, PH10 6EQ, Tel. Blairgowrie 2443	2	2	2	6.50	12.00	10.00	70.00	-	4	-	-	2	1830	4	1-12	
BLAIRLOGIE Stirlingshire (2 A4)																
Blairlogie House Hotel, FK9 5QE, Tel. Alva 61441	4	5	5	24.00	30.00	-	-	1	6	1	7	-	1830 / 2200	20	1-12	
BLAIRMORE, by Dunoon Argyll (1 G4)																
Stronchullin Farm Guest House, Tel. Ardentinny 246	1	-	2	7.00	14.00	12.00	84.00	1	2	1	-	2	1830	4	5-10	

Name and Address				Prices				Rooms									Facilities	
TOWN County / Establishment Address Telephone Telex	Map Ref	Bedrooms	Services	Meals / Bed and Breakfast / Single room overnight	Double/twin room overnight	Per person daily	Per person weekly	B & B and evening meal	Single	Double/twin	Family	Private	No. of bedrooms Public	No. of bath/ shower rooms	Evening meals	Parking (no. of cars)	Months open (1-12)	Symbols
				£min £max	£min £max	£min £max	£min £max						From Last order			Key on back fold-out	
BOAT OF GARTEN Inverness-shire	4 C10																
Boat Hotel PH24 3BH Tel. Boat of Garten 258	4	4	4	13.50 19.00	27.00 38.00	22.00 28.00	150.00 190.00	6	27	3	31	3	1900 2100	40	1-12			T 🛏 ♿ 🍷 🐕 ...

CRAIGARD HOTEL
Boat of Garten
Inverness-shire

OPEN ALL YEAR ROUND A.A. R.A.C. R.S.A.C.
Tel: BOAT OF GARTEN 206 STD 047-983 206
COLOUR BROCHURE AND TARIFF ON REQUEST
Prop: G.H. CAMERON, F.H.C.I.M.A., F.R.S.H., F.C.F.A.
ON STB PRESTEL DATA BASE PAGE 230.

A delightful country-house hotel with 22 bedrooms (8 with private bath). Every comfort. Cocktail Bar. Excellent Cuisine. Lock-ups. ACCESS TO 18 HOLE GOLF COURSE FROM HOTEL GROUNDS, FISHING (Permits for R. Spey from hotel), TENNIS, SKI-ING, PONY TREKKING, SAILING, CANOEING, OSPREY BIRD SANCTUARY NEARBY.

Name and Address	Map Ref	Bedrooms	Services	Meals	Single room overnight	Double/twin room overnight	Per person daily	Per person weekly	B&B and evening meal	Single	Double/twin	Family	Private	No. of bedrooms Public	From Last order	No. of bath/shower rooms	Evening meals	Parking	Months open	Symbols
Craigard Hotel Kinchurdy Road PH24 3BP Tel. Boat of Garten 206		4	4	4	11.50 14.50	23.00 29.00	19.00 22.00	112.00 126.00	5	13	4	8	4		1900 2000	35	1-12			
Moorfield House Hotel PH24 3BN Tel. Boat of Garten 646		2	3	2	8.00 -	16.00 -	13.50 -	89.00 -	1	3	2	-	1		1830 1800	12	1-10			
Heather Lea Guest House PH24 3BU Tel. Boat of Garten 674		3	3	2	6.50 -	13.00 -	10.50 -	72.00 -	1	5	1	-	2		1830 -	10	12-10			
Ryvoan Guest House Kinchurdy Road Tel. Boat of Garten 654		-	-	3	6.50 -	13.00 -	12.00 -	84.00 -	-	2	3	-	1		1830 -	6	1-12			

VAT is shown at 15%: changes in this rate may affect prices.

Name and Address	Map Ref	Bedrooms	Services	Meals	Bed and Breakfast — Single room overnight £min/£max	Double/twin room overnight £min/£max	Per person daily £min/£max	B & B and evening meal — Per person weekly £min/£max	No. of bedrooms — Single	Double/twin	Family	No. of bath/shower rooms — Private	Public	Evening meals From/Last order	Parking (no. of cars)	Months open (1-12)	Facilities (Symbols)

BONAR BRIDGE — Sutherland — Map Ref 4 A6

Guests at the Bridge Hotel are welcomed with a personal informality and professionalism that offer the best of both worlds. The Bridge is open to non-residents and is much used by ferry passengers to and from the Orkneys and Faroes, and by visitors staying to tour the Scottish Highlands. Every bedroom has tea and coffee-making facilities; independent heating, continental quilt, electric blanket, wash-hand basin; radio and intercom; telephone and colour T.V. Complimentary newspapers are usually available in time for breakfast, the first marvellous meal of the day. Lunchtime food is provided in the lounge bar, and an a la carte menu is served in the restaurant during the evening. *Aussi, ici on parle francais.*

BONAR BRIDGE, SUTHERLAND IV24 3EB
Telephone: Ardgay 204 (STD 086 32)
Guests: Ardgay 255   R.A.C.   AA****

Name and Address	Bedrooms	Services	Meals	Single room overnight	Double/twin room overnight	Per person daily	Per person weekly	Single	Double/twin	Family	Private	Public	Evening meals	Parking	Months open
Bridge Hotel, IV24 3EB, Tel. Ardgay 204	4	4	5	16.00 / 19.50	29.00 / 33.50	21.00 / -	120.00 / -	3	10	3	10	4	1800 / 2130	20	1-12
Dunroamin Hotel, IV24 3EA, Tel. Ardgay 236	3	3	4	9.00 / 9.00	18.00 / 18.00	15.00 / 15.00	90.00 / 90.00	2	2	-	-	2	- / 2030	24	1-12
Kyle Guest House, IV24 3EB, Tel. Ardgay 360	3	3	4	6.50 / -	13.00 / -	10.50 / -	70.00 / -	1	4	1	-	1	1900 / 2000	12	1-12

BONNYBRIDGE — Stirlingshire — Map Ref 2 B4

Name and Address	Bedrooms	Services	Meals	Single room overnight	Double/twin room overnight	Per person daily	Per person weekly	Single	Double/twin	Family	Private	Public	Evening meals	Parking	Months open
Norwood House Hotel, Larbert Road, FK4 1NX, Tel. Bonnybridge 812929	4	4	5	19.65 / -	27.85 / -	- / -	- / -	5	5	-	1	-	1900 / 2130	100	1-12
Royal Hotel, Falkirk Road, Tel. Bonnybridge 812429	1	2	3	11.50 / -	19.50 / -	- / -	- / -	-	4	-	-	2	1700 / 2100	-	1-12

BORGUE — Kirkcudbrightshire — Map Ref 2 A11

Name and Address	Bedrooms	Services	Meals	Single room overnight	Double/twin room overnight	Per person daily	Per person weekly	Single	Double/twin	Family	Private	Public	Evening meals	Parking	Months open
Borgue Hotel, Tel. Borgue 232	1	3	4	9.00 / -	18.00 / -	15.50 / -	90.00 / -	2	3	5	-	3	1830 / 1930	12	1-12
Senwick House Hotel, Tel. Borgue 236	3	3	4	13.50 / 15.00	27.00 / 30.00	21.50 / 24.50	130.00 / 150.00	2	7	1	4	2	1900 / 2130	50	1-12

Name and Address	Map Ref	Bedrooms	Services	Meals	Single room overnight £min £max	Double/twin room overnight £min £max	Per person daily £min £max	Per person weekly £min £max	Single	Double/twin	Family	Private	Public	Evening meals From / Last order	Parking (no. of cars)	Months open (1-12)	Symbols
BORVE Lewis, Western Isles — Borve House Hotel, Tel. Borve 223	3 D3	2	3	4	12.00 / 12.00	24.00 / 24.00	17.50 / -	- / -	-	3	1	-	2	1930 / 2200	10	1-12	(symbols)
BORVE, by Portree Isle of Skye, Inverness-shire — Grand View Guest House, 27 Borve, Tel. Skeabost Bridge 234	3 D9	1	1	2	6.00 / -	12.00 / -	9.00 / -	- / -	2	2	-	-	1	1830 / -	3	5-10	(symbols)
BOTHKENNAR, by Airth Stirlingshire — Powfoulis Manor Hotel, FK2 8PR, Tel. Airth 267	2 B4	5	4	5	22.00 / -	34.00 / -	- / -	- / -	2	19	-	16	2	1900 / 2300	200	1-12	(symbols)
BOTHWELL Lanarkshire — Bothwell Bridge Hotel, 89 Main Street, Tel. Bothwell 852246	2 A6	-	-	-	20.00 / -	27.00 / -	25.00 / -	- / -	3	7	2	-	2	1700 / 2000	160	1-12	(symbols)
BOTHWELL — Silvertrees Hotel, Silverwell Crescent, Tel. Bothwell 852311		-	-	-	25.50 / 26.50	31.00 / 32.00	32.10 / 33.10	224.70 / 231.70	5	18	1	24	-	1830 / 2100	104	1-12	(symbols)
BRAE, North Mainland Shetland — Brae Hotel, Tel. Brae 456, Telex 75183	5 F3	6	5	5	42.00 / 52.00	44.00 / 54.00	50.00 / 60.00	- / -	-	28	-	28	-	1830 / 2130	90	-	(symbols)
BRAEMAR Aberdeenshire — Braemar Lodge Hotel, Tel. Braemar 617	4 D11	3	3	4	9.00 / -	- / -	15.00 / -	- / -	1	4	3	-	3	1900 / -	21	5-10	(symbols)
BRAEMAR — Callater Lodge Hotel, AB3 5YQ, Tel. Braemar 275		3	3	2	10.00 / 10.00	20.00 / 20.00	16.80 / 16.80	106.00 / 106.00	1	7	1	-	3	1930 / 2000	42	12-10	(symbols)

VAT is shown at 15%: changes in this rate may affect prices.

| Name and Address | Map Ref | | | | Prices | | | | B & B and evening meal | | | | | Rooms | | | Facilities | |
TOWN County / Establishment Address Telephone Telex		Bedrooms	Services	Meals	Bed and Breakfast — Single room overnight	Double/twin room overnight	Per person daily	Per person weekly	Single	Double/twin	Family	Private	Public	No. of bedrooms / Evening meals	No. of bath/ shower rooms	Parking (no. of cars)	Months open (1-12)	Symbols
BRAEMAR continued	4 D11				£min £max	£min £max	£min £max	£min £max						From Last order			Key on back fold-out

Fife Arms Hotel

The Fife Arms Hotel—the pride of Royal Deeside, apart from a certain Balmoral Castle just down the road!

With ninety bedrooms, most with private bathroom, glorious views, three bars, entertainment every evening from April to October—there is plenty of "Life at the Fife".

You will be surprised how little it costs to savour our unrivalled facilities.

Mar Road, Braemar, Royal Deeside, Grampian, AB3 5YN.

Establishment	Map Ref	Bedrooms	Services	Meals	Single room overnight	Double/twin room overnight	Per person daily	Per person weekly	Single	Double/twin	Family	Private	Public	Bedrooms / Last order	Bath/shower	Parking	Months open	Symbols
Fife Arms Hotel, Mar Road, AB3 5YN, Tel. Braemar 644		5	5	5	15.25 -	25.50 -	19.75 -	-	17	60	13	42	16	1900 / 2015	107	1-12		
The Invercauld Arms Hotel, AB3 5YR, Tel. Braemar 605		5	4	5	20.00 -	40.00 -	-	-	8	47	5	39	4	1900 / 2030	100	1-10		
Moorfield Hotel, Chapel Brae, AB3 5YT, Tel. Braemar 244		4	4	4	15.00 -	23.00 -	24.00 -	150.00	2	6	2	4	1	1900 / 2000	20	1-12		
Cranford Guest House, 15 Glenshee Road, AB3 5YQ, Tel. Braemar 675		3	2	2	7.00 7.50	14.00 29.00	12.00 13.50	72.00 75.00	1	4	-	-	1	1830 / 2000	8	1-12		
Schiehallion Guest House, Glenshee Road, Tel. Braemar 679		3	2	2	6.50 6.50	13.00 14.00	10.50 11.00	68.00 72.00	1	8	2	2	2	1830 / 1800	10	12-10		
BRAES, by Portree Isle of Skye, Inverness-shire	3 D9																	
Cnoc Na H'Eaglaise Guest House, Conordan, Tel. Sligachan 229		3	4	2	6.00 -	12.00 -	-	-	-	3	-	-	1	1850 / -	6	4-10		
BREAKISH Isle of Skye, Inverness-shire	3 E10																	
Langdale Guest House, Waterloo, 1V42 8QE, Tel. Broadford 376		3	3	3	8.00 -	16.00 -	13.00 -	85.00 -	-	4	-	-	1	1800 / 1930	4	1-12		

Name and Address	Map Ref	Bedrooms	Services	Meals	Bed and Breakfast Single room overnight £min £max	Bed and Breakfast Double/twin room overnight £min £max	Bed and Breakfast Per person daily £min £max	B & B and evening meal Per person weekly £min £max	Single	Double/twin	Family	Private	No. of bedrooms Public	No. of bath/shower rooms From Last order	Evening meals	Parking (no. of cars)	Months open (1-12)	Symbols Key on back fold-out
BRIDGE OF ALLAN Stirlingshire	2 A4																	
Inverallan Lodge Hotel 116 Henderson Street FK9 4HF Tel. Bridge of Allan 832791		-	-	-	8.50 10.00	17.00 19.00	12.00 -	84.00 -	1	6	2	-	2	1700 2100	36	1-12	T ♨ ♿ ⚲ 🐕 ✂ 🛏 🛗 🚰 C V

ROYAL HOTEL
Henderson Street, Bridge of Allan.
Tel: 0786 832284.

This privately owned 3-star Hotel is set in the heart of Scotland and is the gateway to the Highlands. An ideal location for touring Scotland. Only 45 miles from Edinburgh and 35 miles from Glasgow. Loch Lomond and the Trossachs are easily accessible for day trips. Stirling Castle, Wallace Monument, Dunblane Cathedral, Blair Drummond Safari Park are to name but a few places of interest you must visit. The Hotel has thirty two bedrooms, many with private bathroom and TV. Ample lounge space. Pleasant lounge bar. Good food and friendly service. Attractive "Getaway Breaks" throughout the year with substantial reductions for children.
Telephone or write for further details and brochure.

Name and Address	Bedrooms	Services	Meals	Single room overnight £min £max	Double/twin room overnight £min £max	Per person daily £min £max	Per person weekly £min £max	Single	Double/twin	Family	Private	Public	From Last order	Evening meals	Parking	Months open	Symbols
Royal Hotel Henderson Street FK9 4HG Tel. Bridge of Allan 832284 Telex 778982	5	5	5	18.00 24.00	32.00 40.00	26.50 32.50	- -	7	23	2	14	7	1900 2045	50	1-12	T ♨ ♿ ⚲ 🐕 🛏 🛗 🚰 ● ⚑ ☎ ✉ 🖥 ♨ ⚽ C ✳ 🎪 V ♨ ∕
Walmer Hotel 90 Henderson Street FK9 4HA Tel. Bridge of Allan 832352	3	4	3	10.50 -	19.00 -	15.00 -	94.50 -	4	5	2	-	4	1800 1930	20	1-12	♿ ⚲ 🐕 🛏 🛗 ♿ ♨
BRIDGE OF CALLY, Blairgowrie Perthshire	2 C1																
Bridge of Cally Hotel PH10 7JJ Tel. Bridge of Cally 231	4	4	4	13.50 15.00	22.00 26.00	20.75 22.25	128.00 160.00	2	8	-	6	2	1930 2030	40	1-12	T ♨ ♿ ⚲ 🐕 🛏 🛗 🚰 ♨ ⚡ C ✳ 🎪 V ♨ ∕ 🎿 🎣
Corriefodly Hotel PH10 7JG Tel. Bridge of Cally 236	4	4	2	10.00 -	20.00 -	15.00 -	105.00 -	2	5	2	7	1	1700 1900	30	1-12	⚲ 🐕 🛏 🛗 🚰 ✳ ♨ ∕ 🎣
BRIDGE OF EARN Perthshire	2 C2																
Moncreiffe Arms Hotel Main Street PH2 9PJ Tel. Bridge of Earn 812931	3	3	4	18.00 -	25.00 -	- -	- -	2	8	3	4	3	1900 2100	90	1-12	♨ ♿ ⚲ 🐕 ✂ 🛏 🛗 🚰 🎪 V ♨

Name and Address (TOWN / County / Establishment / Address / Telephone / Telex)	Map Ref	Bedrooms	Services	Meals	Single room overnight £min/£max	Double/twin room overnight £min/£max	Per person daily £min/£max	Per person weekly £min/£max	Single	Double/twin	Family	Private	Public	Evening meals (From / Last order)	Parking (no. of cars)	Months open (1-12)	Symbols
BRIDGE OF WEIR — Renfrewshire; Gryffe Arms Hotel, Kilmalcolm Road, Tel. Bridge of Weir 613360	1 H5	5	3	3	16.50 / -	25.50 / -	- / -	- / -	-	14	3	13	3	1800 / 2300	150	1-12	Key on back fold-out
BRIDGEND — Isle of Islay, Argyll; Bridgend Hotel, Tel. Bowmore 212	1 C6	3	3	4	14.50 / -	29.00 / -	22.50 / -	- / -	2	9	-	-	-	1900 / 2130	60	1-12	
BROADFORD — Isle of Skye, Inverness-shire; Broadford Hotel, Tel. Broadford 204/5	3 E10	4	4	4	16.50 / 21.50	31.00 / 37.00	23.00 / 30.00	- / -	8	18	2	18	4	1930 / 2100	60	4-10	
Hebridean Hotel, Tel. Broadford 486		3	3	5	- / -	17.25 / 24.15	- / -	- / -	3	5	1	-	3	1800 / 2200	45	1-12	
Beul-na-Mara Guest House, Lower Harrapool, Tel. Broadford 487		2	2	1	- / -	13.00 / 15.00	- / -	- / -	1	4	1	-	2	- / -	-	4-9	
BRODICK — Isle of Arran; Altanna Hotel, Tel. Brodick 2232	1 F7	3	4	4	8.25 / 9.45	16.50 / 18.90	12.40 / 14.25	86.00 / 99.00	1	8	2	2	3	1830 / 1930	12	1-12	
Auchrannie Hotel, Tel. Brodick 2234		3	3	4	9.00 / 11.00	18.00 / 22.00	14.00 / 16.00	91.00 / 105.00	5	7	4	4	4	- / 1900	25	4-10	
Belvedere Private Hotel, Tel. Brodick 2397		3	3	2	8.00 / -	16.00 / -	11.50 / -	76.00 / -	1	5	-	1	1	1800 / -	5	1-12	
Douglas Hotel, Tel. Brodick 2155		4	6	6	17.50 / -	32.00 / -	26.00 / -	155.00 / -	6	17	4	6	9	1730 / 2100	100	1-12	

Name and Address	Map Ref	Bedrooms	Services	Meals	Prices — Bed and Breakfast — Single room overnight	Prices — Double/twin room overnight	Prices — Per person daily	B & B and evening meal — Per person weekly	Rooms — Single	Double/twin	Family	Private	Public	No. of bed-rooms	No. of bath/ shower rooms	Evening meals	Parking (no. of cars)	Months open (1-12)	Facilities / Symbols
BRODICK continued	1 F7				£min £max	£min £max	£min £max	£min £max						From Last order				Key on back fold-out

Ennismor Hotel Brodick 2265
Prop. Irene & Alistair McGill

Ideally situated on sea front only yards from ferry pier, a family hotel where children are most welcome. All rooms with H & C, electric blankets and heaters. Lounge bar and residents lounge with colour television. Dining room provides both table d'hote and a la carte meals. Package holidays can be arranged.

Establishment	Bedrooms	Serv	Meals	Single overnight	Double/twin overnight	Per person daily	Per person weekly	Single	Double/twin	Family	Private	Public	No. bedrooms	Bath/shower	Evening meals last order	Parking	Months	Symbols
Ennismor Hotel Tel. Brodick 2265	3	3	4	8.25 8.75	16.50 17.50	13.50 15.00	- -	1	11	4	4	2	1830 2000	16		1-10	T 🏨 👤 🐕 🍴 🛏 ⚡ C ❄ V U
Glenartney Hotel Tel. Brodick 2220	3	3	4	8.50 9.50	17.00 19.00	13.50 14.50	91.00 96.00	3	14	2	3	4	1830 1930	10		3-9	T 👤 🍷 🐕 🛏 🛋 ⚡ C V U 🪑
Gwyder Lodge Hotel Tel. Brodick 2377	-	-	-	8.50 -	17.50 -	13.50 -	- -	10	16	-	-	8	1830 1930	12		4-9	👤 🐕 🛏 ❄ V U
Heathfield Hotel Tel. Brodick 2204	3	4	2	7.75 -	15.50 -	12.00 -	83.00 -	2	4	2	-	3	1830 1900	20		4-11	🍷 🐕 🍴 🛏 ❄ U
Hotel Ormidale Tel. Brodick 2293	2	2	4	7.50 9.50	15.00 19.00	10.55 -	73.85 -	3	4	1	-	2	1700 2000	30		3-10	T 🍷 🐕 🛏 ❄ V U
Invercloy Hotel Tel. Brodick 2225	3	4	4	8.50 -	17.00 -	13.00 -	87.50 -	5	5	2	-	3	1830 1930	24		3-10	T 👤 🍷 🐕 🍴 🛏 ⚡ V U
Kingsley Hotel Tel. Brodick 2226	4	4	4	9.00 -	18.00 -	16.00 -	112.00 -	5	18	5	18	4	1830 1930	60		3-9	🍷 🐕 🛏 C ❄ V U
Tighnamara Private Hotel Tel. Brodick 2538/2340	3	2	2	7.50 -	15.00 -	12.00 -	84.00 -	-	3	3	-	2	1800 1630	3		4-10	🛏 ❄ V 🪑
Allandale Guest House KA27 8BJ Tel. Brodick 2278	4	3	2	8.00 8.80	16.00 17.60	12.65 14.00	88.55 98.00	1	3	2	6	1	- 1900	6		12-10	🐕 🛏 ⚡ ❄ V U
Dunvegan Guest House Tel. Brodick 2273	2	2	2	6.50 -	13.00 -	10.00 -	- -	-	3	-	-	1	-	3		6-9	🐕 🛏 V
Tuathair Guest House Tel. Brodick 2214	3	3	2	- -	- -	11.50 -	77.00 -	-	5	-	-	2	- 1800	5		4-10	🛏 U

Name and Address		Prices					B & B and evening meal				Rooms				Facilities

TOWN County / Establishment Address Telephone Telex	Map Ref	Bedrooms / Services / Meals	Single room overnight £min £max	Double/twin room overnight £min £max	Per person daily £min £max	Per person weekly £min £max	Single	Double/twin	Family	Private	Public No. of bedrooms From Last order	Evening meals No. of bath/shower rooms	Parking (no. of cars)	Months open (1-12)	Symbols Key on back fold-out

| **BRORA** Sutherland | 4 C6 | | | | | | | | | | | | | | |

The Links Hotel Brora Sutherland

Telephone Brora (04082) 225

Overlooking the Golf Course and Sea the Hotel has an unrivalled position on the East Coast. Golfers, Fishermen and visitors in general find a comfortable year round base for their stay. Excellent food and Highland Hospitality combine with the scenic beauty to provide a perfect short or long stay. Packages are available for Golfers and Fishermen, cheap rail and air travel are also built into special prices available only to Hotel guests. Prices vary from £12 B&B with Demi-pension and Full board terms at £140 per week, special rates for Children are offered. A'la Carte & Table D'Hote menus give the visitor a good choice at reasonable rates.

Proprietors: J.S. Howe, K. Howe

Establishment	Map Ref	Bedrms	Svc	Meals	Single overnight	Double overnight	Per person daily	Per person weekly	Single	Double/twin	Family	Private	Public	No. of bedrooms / Last order	Bath/shower	Parking	Months open	Symbols
Links Hotel KW9 6QS Tel. Brora 225		4	4	5	12.00 14.50	24.00 35.00	20.50 23.00	134.00 150.00	5	23	1	18	8	1900 2130	52	1-12	
Royal Marine Hotel KW9 6QS Tel. Brora 252		4	4	4	12.50 14.50	25.00 29.00	19.50 22.00	132.00 148.00	2	6	2	4	4	1900 2115	48	1-12	
Sutherland Arms Hotel KW9 6NX Tel. Brora 209/21209		2	3	4	11.00 -	19.00 -	13.50 17.50	100.00 -	4	5	1	-	3	1800 2000	-	1-12	

| **BROUGHTON** Peeblesshire | 2 C6 | | | | | | | | | | | | | | | | |
| Greenmantle Hotel ML12 6HQ Tel. Broughton 302 | | - | - | - | 18.50 - | 25.00 - | 27.00 - | 165.00 - | - | 6 | - | 2 | 1 | 1930 2100 | 60 | 1-12 | |

BROXBURN West Lothian	2 C5																
Buchan Arms Hotel Tel. Broxburn 856447		-	-	-	8.50 -	17.00 -	- -	- -	-	4	1	-	2	- 2100	15	1-12	
Strathbrock Hotel 56 East Main Street Tel. Broxburn 856469		2	2	2	7.00 8.00	14.00 14.00	9.00 11.00	50.00 70.00	2	1	1	-	1	1800 2100	4	1-12	

TOWN / County / Establishment / Address / Telephone / Telex	Map Ref	Bedrooms	Services	Meals	Single room overnight £min/£max	Double/twin room overnight £min/£max	Per person daily £min/£max	Per person weekly £min/£max	Single	Double/twin	Family	Private	Public	Evening meals From/Last order	Parking (no. of cars)	Months open (1-12)	Symbols
BRUAR, by Blair Atholl / **Perthshire**	**4** C12																Key on back fold-out
Bruar Falls Hotel / PH18 5TW / Tel. Calvine 243		3	3	4	8.35 / 10.35	16.70 / 20.70	14.95 / 16.95	97.50 / 118.00	1	6	-	-	2	1700 / 2100	30	1-12	
BRUICHLADDICH / **Isle of Islay, Argyll**	**1** B6																
Bruichladdich Hotel / PA49 7UN / Tel. Port Charlotte 305		3	4	3	13.50 / -	25.00 / -	18.50 / -	98.00 / -	-	5	1	-	2	1930 / 2030	8	1-12	
BUCKIE / **Banffshire**	**4** E7																
Cluny Hotel / 2 High Street / AB5 1AL / Tel. Buckie 32922		4	3	4	- / 15.75	- / 30.00	- / 23.25	- / 139.50	8	7	1	14	-	1700 / 2100	30	1-12	
Rathburn House Hotel / March Road / AB5 2BY / Tel. Buckie 31281/33925		-	-	-	9.50 / 10.50	19.50 / 21.00	13.50 / -	85.00 / 94.50	2	3	1	1	1	1700 / 1800	20	1-12	
St Andrews Hotel / St Andrew Square / AB5 1BT / Tel. Buckie 31227		3	4	4	12.50 / -	20.00 / -	15.00 / -	100.00 / -	1	15	1	3	6	1700 / 2000	40	1-12	
BUNESSAN / **Isle of Mull, Argyll**	**1** C3																
Ardfenaig House / PA67 6DX / Tel. Fionnphort 210		3	4	4	- / -	- / -	32.00 / 32.00	202.00 / 202.00	1	4	-	-	3	1930 / 1930	12	5-10	
BURNTISLAND / **Fife**	**2** C4																
Inchview Hotel / 69 Kinghorn Road / KY3 9EB / Tel. Burntisland 872239		4	4	5	15.00 / 15.00	26.00 / 26.00	- / -	- / -	2	6	3	10	1	1900 / 2145	20	1-12	
BURRAY / **Orkney**	**5** C12																
St Lawrence Motel / Tel. Burray 298		3	3	3	12.50 / -	20.40 / -	19.50 / -	136.50 / -	-	11	-	-	4	2230 / 2200	-	4-10	
BUSTA, North Mainland / **Shetland**	**5** F3																
Busta House / Tel. Brae 506		5	5	5	15.00 / 40.00	20.00 / 50.00	- / -	- / -	2	19	-	21	-	1900 / 2130	30	1-12	

VAT is shown at 15%: changes in this rate may affect prices.

Name and Address	Map Ref	Bedrooms	Services	Meals	Single room overnight	Double/twin room overnight	Per person daily	Per person weekly	Single	Double/twin	Family	Private	Public	Evening meals (From / Last order)	Parking (no. of cars)	Months open (1-12)	Symbols
					£min £max	£min £max	£min £max	£min £max						From Last order			Key on back fold-out
CAIRNDOW Argyll Cairndow Stagecoach Inn PA26 8BN Tel. Cairndow 286	1 G3	3	4	5	9.00 -	18.00 -	15.00 -	95.00 -	-	9	2	5	2	1900 2100	42	1-12	T ⌂£ 🛏 ♒ 🐕 ✂ ℞ ▦ ⚒ ☕ 🚪 ⚡ C ✳ ⌨ V ♨ ✎ ☒
CALLANDER Perthshire Ashlea House Hotel Bracklin Road FK17 8EN Tel. Callander 30325	2 A3	3	4	4	7.95 9.95	15.90 19.90	11.95 14.95	76.00 96.00	4	13	3	2	5	1900 1915	17	3-11	℞ ▦ ⚒ ☕ ⚡ C ✳ V ♨ ⚘
Bridgend House Hotel Bridge Street FK17 8AA Tel. Callander 30130		4	4	5	14.00 18.00	20.00 28.00	- -	- -	-	7	1	5	1	1700 2200	60	1-12	T ⌂£ ♒ 🐕 ✂ ℞ ▦ ⚒ ☎ ▢ ⚲ ✳ ⌨ V
Coppice Hotel Leny Road FK17 8AL Tel. Callander 30188		3	3	2	7.50 -	15.00 -	12.50 -	- -	1	4	1	-	1	1800 1930	20	2-12	⌂£ 🛏 ♒ 🐕 ℞ M ⚒ ☕ ✳
Dalgair House Hotel 113 Main Street FK17 8BQ Tel. Callander 30283		4	4	6	7.50 11.50	15.00 23.00	15.00 19.00	100.00 125.00	1	8	1	4	3	1700 2100	9	1-12	T ⌂£ 🛏 ♒ 🐕 ℞ ▦ ⚒ V ♨ ✎ ☒ ⚘ ✿
Dreadnought Hotel FK17 8AN Tel. Callander 30184 Telex 778215		3	3	4	8.00 -	16.00 -	13.00 -	84.00 -	27	65	-	20	-	1830 2000	-	4-10	T ♒ 🐕 ℞ ▣ ⌨ V

Dalgair House

113/115 Main Street
CALLANDER
Telephone: 0877 30283

Distinguished Town House on quiet main street, set in the beautiful Trossachs in the historic rural town of Callander. Family-run hotel and Taste of Scotland Member. Open all year. Invite enquiries for our Golf-inclusive holidays. 3-day Visitor Weekend Break; 4-day Special Xmas and New Year stays and our current summer holiday list. Conference facilities for small parties.

Name and Address	Map Ref	Bedrooms	Services	Meals	Prices										Rooms							Facilities

<table>
<tr><th rowspan="2">TOWN
County

Establishment
Address
Telephone
Telex</th><th rowspan="2">Map Ref

Bedrooms
Services
Meals</th><th colspan="4">Prices</th><th colspan="4"></th><th colspan="2">Rooms
No. of bed-rooms / No. of bath/shower rooms</th><th>Facilities</th></tr>
<tr><th>Bed and Breakfast
Single room overnight</th><th>Double/twin room overnight</th><th>Per person daily</th><th>B & B and evening meal
Per person weekly</th><th>Single</th><th>Double/twin</th><th>Family</th><th>Private / Public</th><th>Evening meals
From / Last order</th><th>Parking (no. of cars) / Months open (1-12)</th><th>Symbols
Key on back fold-out</th></tr>
</table>

CALLANDER continued — Map Ref 2 A3

Name and Address	Bedrooms	Services	Meals	£min £max	£min £max	£min £max	£min £max	Single	Double/twin	Family	Private	Public	Evening meals	Parking	Months open	Symbols
Glenorchy Hotel Leny Road FK17 8AL Tel. Callander 30329	3	4	4	9.50 11.50	19.00 23.00	16.00 18.00	105.00 115.00	2	11	1	6	3	1900 1915	12	1-12	
Highland House Hotel South Church Street FK17 8BN Tel. Callander 30269	4	4	2	8.50 9.50	16.50 18.50	15.75 17.25	104.75 110.25	3	6	1	3	2	1900 1930	10	2-10	
Lubnaig Hotel Leny Feus FK17 8AS Tel. Callander 30376	4	4	4	11.90 15.90	23.80 27.80	19.55 21.95	124.20 139.50	1	7	2	10	1	1900 2000	14	4-10	
Pinewood Hotel Leny Road FK17 8AP Tel. Callander 30111	3	3	4	9.00 10.00	18.00 20.00	15.00 16.00	105.00 112.00	3	10	3	2	3	1900 2030	30	4-10	

Glenorchy Hotel

Leny Road, Callander, Perthshire. Tel: Callander 30329

We have set out at Glenorchy to combine the best of traditional Scottish hospitality with the good things of modern life. The hotel is centrally heated and double glazed so that your comfort and warmth is assured in summer and winter. Each room has hot and cold water and a fitted electric shaver point. There is colour television in the spacious residents' lounge and ample car parking in the grounds. Fully licensed. Private bathrooms available. S.A.E. for terms.

Scotland's Guesthouse of the year 1981

Lubnaig Hotel
Callander

AA RAC BTA BHR Les Routiers

This small select internationally acclaimed hotel continues to offer outstanding value—all bedrooms with private facilities, superb food tastefully presented—personal attention in abundance. Large car park.
S.A.E. to Mrs Morna Dalziel,
Lubnaig Hotel, Leny Feus, Callander, Perthshire FK17 8AS.
Telephone: Callander (0877) 30376.

SCOTLAND'S COUNTRYSIDE IS UNIQUE!

So: stay on a farm or a croft — that's the best way to get to know the Scottish countryside! To help you find the ideal farmhouse, ask for the free brochure called *Scottish Farmhouse Holidays*. You'll be able to choose from a range of farms of all kinds.

Name and Address	Map Ref				Prices					Rooms							Facilities	
TOWN County / Establishment Address Telephone Telex		Bedrooms	Services	Meals	Single room overnight	Double/twin room overnight	Per person daily	Per person weekly		Single	Double/twin	Family	Private	Public	No. of bedrooms	No. of bath/shower rooms	Evening meals	Parking (no. of cars) / Months open (1-12) / Symbols
CALLANDER continued	2 A3				£min £max	£min £max	£min £max	£min £max						From Last order				Key on back fold-out

Riverview Hotel
Leny Rd.,
Callander.
Tel. Callander (0877) 30635

Detached stone built hotel peacefully situated opposite pleasant parkland and the River Teith. Riverview Hotel offers excellent home cooking, 7 comfortable rooms all with H&C and tea making facilities, lounge with colour TV, residents licence, free car park. Dinner, bed and breakfast from £12.50. B & B only £7. Mr & Mrs Little.

Name	Bedrooms	Services	Meals	Single room overnight	Double/twin room overnight	Per person daily	Per person weekly	Single	Double/twin	Family	Private	Public	Evening meals / last order	No. of bedrooms	Months open	Symbols
Riverview Hotel, Leny Road	3	3	3	7.00 / 7.00	14.00 / 14.00	12.00 / 12.00	84.00 / 84.00	2	3	1	1	-	1900 / 1915	6	3-10	
Roman Camp Hotel, FK17 8BG, Tel. Callander 30003	6	4	4	25.00 / 35.00	38.00 / 55.00	- / -	- / -	1	8	2	11	2	1900 / 2100	33	2-12	
Royal Hotel, Main Street, Tel. Callander 30651	-	-	-	- / -	16.00 / -	- / -	- / -	1	2	2	-	1	1700 / 2100	6	1-12	

Name	Bedrooms	Services	Meals	Single room overnight	Double/twin room overnight	Per person daily	Per person weekly	Single	Double/twin	Family	Private	Public	Evening meals / last order	No. of bedrooms	Months open	Symbols
Wolseley Park Hotel, Stirling Road, FK17 8DB, Tel. Callander 30261	3	3	3	9.20 / 9.20	17.80 / 17.80	14.65 / 14.65	90.00 / 90.00	1	13	4	-	3	1900 / 1830	22	4-10	

Name and Address				Prices									Rooms			Facilities	
TOWN County Establishment Address Telephone Telex	Map Ref	Bedrooms	Services	Meals	Bed and Breakfast				B & B and evening meal					No of bed rooms	No of bath/ shower rooms			
					Single room overnight	Double/twin room overnight	Per person daily	Per person weekly	Single	Double/twin	Family	Private	Public	Evening meals	Parking (no of cars)	Months open (1-12)	Symbols
CALLANDER continued	2 A3				£min £max	£min £max	£min £max	£min £max					From Last order				Key on back fold-out
Abbotsford Lodge Guest House Stirling Road FK17 8DA Tel. Callander 30066		3	4	3	8.00 -	16.00 -	14.00 -	89.50 -	1	11	7	-	7	1900 1900	20	1-12	

ARDEN HOUSE

Bracklinn Road
Callander
Perthshire

Mr and Mrs: J.S. McGregor

Tel: Callander 30235 (STD 0877)

AA and RAC Listed

Peacefully situated in its own attractive garden, with marvellous views of the hills and countryside. **Arden House** offers excellent home cooking, ten comfortable rooms with H and C, electric blankets, tea-makers and central heating, lounge with colour TV and a warm, friendly and relaxed atmosphere. Open all year with reduced off-season terms. Generous reductions for children. Ample car-parking space. *The TV home of "Dr Finlay's Casebook".*

Name and Address	Bedrooms	Services	Meals	Single room overnight	Double/twin room overnight	Per person daily	Per person weekly	Single	Double/twin	Family	Private	Public	From Last order	Evening meals	Months open	Symbols
Arden House Guest House Bracklinn Road FK17 8EQ Tel. Callander 30235	3	4	3	7.50 8.50	15.00 17.00	12.00 13.50	77.00 87.00	2	6	2	2	2	1900 -	15	1-12	
Ben Aan Guest House 158 Main Street FK17 8BG Tel. Callander 30317	2	2	2	6.50 6.50	13.00 13.00	11.00 11.50	77.00 80.00	1	3	2	-	1	1830 1900	5	1-12	
Edina Guest House 111 Main Street FK17 8BQ Tel. Callander 30004	3	3	2	6.61 7.20	13.22 14.40	10.64 11.22	69.00 73.60	1	8	2	3	2	1830 1930	8	1-12	
Greenbank Guest House 143 Main Street FK17 8BH Tel. Callander 30296	3	2	2	6.50 7.00	13.00 14.00	11.00 11.50	75.00 77.00	1	4	2	-	2	1900 1900	10	1-12	
Kinnell Guest House 24 Main Street FK17 8BB Tel. Callander 30181	3	2	3	6.00 7.50	12.00 15.00	10.00 11.50	65.00 75.00	2	3	3	-	2	1900 1915	7	1-12	
Linley Guest House 139 Main Street Tel. Callander 30087	3	3	2	7.00 -	14.00 -	- -	- -	-	4	1	-	2	1830 -	8	1-12	
Norwood House Guest House 12 South Church Street FK17 8BN Tel. Callander 30665	1	2	2	6.75 7.25	13.50 14.50	12.00 12.50	82.25 85.75	1	2	-	-	1	1830	-	2-11	
Rock Villa Guest House Bracklinn Road FK17 8EH Tel. Callander 30331	3	2	1	6.50 7.00	13.00 14.00	- -	- -	1	4	1	-	1	- -	6	4-10	
Tighnaldon Guest House 156 Main Street FK17 8BG Tel. Callander 30703	3	3	2	6.00 6.00	12.00 12.00	10.50 10.50	72.50 72.50	2	2	1	-	1	1900 1800	-	1-12	

VAT is shown at 15%: changes in this rate may affect prices.

Name and Address — TOWN / County / Establishment / Address / Telephone / Telex	Map Ref	Bedrooms	Services	Meals	Single room overnight £min / £max	Double/twin room overnight £min / £max	Per person daily £min / £max	Per person weekly £min / £max	Single	Double/twin	Family	Private	Public	Evening meals From / Last order	Parking (no. of cars)	Months open (1-12)	Symbols
CALLANDER continued	2 A3																Key on back fold-out
White Shutters Guest House, South Church Street, FK17 8BN, Tel. Callander 30442		3	2	1	6.50 / 7.00	13.00 / 14.00	- / -	- / -	1	3	-	-	1	- / -	-	3-10	
CALVINE Perthshire	4 B12																
The Struan Inn, PH18 5UB, Tel. Calvine 208		3	4	5	9.50 / -	17.00 / -	-	-	-	2	3	-	1	1930 / 2130	25	1-12	
CAMPBELTOWN Argyll	1 E7																
Ardshiel Hotel, Kilkerran Road, PA28 6JL, Tel. Campbeltown 52133		3	4	4	13.50 / -	25.50 / -	-	-	3	7	2	-	2	1730 / 2030	12	1-12	
Argyll Arms Hotel, Tel. Campbeltown 53431		3	3	4	10.50 / -	21.00 / -	-	-	3	25	2	5	7	1800 / 2000	10	1-12	
Dellwood Hotel, Drumore, Tel. Campbeltown 52465		2	2	2	7.00 / -	14.00 / -	11.00 / -	-	3	11	4	-	4	1800 / 1900	40	1-12	
Royal Hotel, Main Street, Tel. Campbeltown 52017		6	5	5	12.50 / 15.00	25.00 / 26.50	20.25 / 22.75	130.50 / 146.00	-	14	2	12	3	1700 / 2050	6	1-12	
White Hart Hotel, Main Street, Tel. Campbeltown 52440/53356		3	3	5	10.78 / -	18.25 / -	17.50 / -	97.50 / -	9	9	2	1	3	1730 / 2130	-	1-12	
Balegreggan Guest House, Balegreggan Road, PA28 6NN, Tel. Campbeltown 52062		3	2	2	7.50 / 8.00	15.00 / 16.00	10.00 / 11.50	65.00 / 75.00	-	3	1	-	1	1800 / 1800	6	2-11	
Seafield House, Kilkerran Road, Tel. Campbeltown 52741		3	4	3	7.50 / 9.50	15.00 / 19.00	11.00 / 13.00	77.00 / 91.00	-	5	1	-	2	1830 / 1900	5	1-12	

QUALITY ASSURED

The Thistle Commendation Scheme gives recognition to Holiday Static Caravan Sites in Scotland which provide first class caravans for hire, combined with very good facilities and an attractive environment. All sites have had a detailed inspection.

Look out for the Thistle Commendation plaques displayed by all the commended sites, or ask for the leaflet.

Name and Address	Map Ref	Bedrooms	Services	Meals	Single room overnight £min £max	Double/twin room overnight £min £max	Per person daily £min £max	Per person weekly £min £max	Single	Double/twin	Family	Private	Public	Evening meals From / Last order	Parking (no. of cars)	Months open (1-12)	Symbols
CAMPTOWN, by Jedburgh Roxburghshire	2 F7																
Jedforest Country House Hotel Tel. Camptown 274		4	4	4	15.00 -	25.00 -	21.00 -	135.00 -	-	8	3	4	3	1900 2030	50	1-12	
CANNICH Inverness-shire	3 H9																
Glen Affric Hotel Tel. Cannich 214		3	4	4	9.75 10.75	19.50 21.50	15.25 16.25	105.00 112.00	8	13	2	5	5	1900 2000	30	4-10	
Westward Guest House Tel. Cannich 225		4	3	2	6.75 6.75	13.50 13.50	10.50 10.50	75.00 75.00	-	3	-	1	1	- -	-	3-11	
CANONBIE Dumfriesshire	2 D9																
Cross Keys Hotel Tel. Canonbie 382		3	4	5	12.50 -	22.00 -	- -	- -	2	4	2	-	2	1700 2050	20	1-12	
Riverside Inn Tel. Canonbie 295		4	3	4	-	32.00 -	34.50 -	175.00 -	-	6	-	6	1	1930 2030	-	1-12	
CARFRAEMILL, by Lauder Berwickshire	2 E6																
Carfraemill Hotel Tel. Oxton 200		3	4	5	12.50 -	25.00 -	20.50 -	117.00 -	-	11	-	2	4	1900 2100	27	1-12	
CARLOWAY Lewis, Western Isles	3 C4																
Doune Braes Hotel PA86 9AA Tel. Carloway 252		2	3	4	12.00 -	24.00 -	19.00 -	130.00 -	3	6	3	-	4	1900 1930	100	1-12	
CARLUKE Lanarkshire	2 B6																
Wellbank Guest House 34 Kirkton Street Tel. Carluke 72050		3	3	2	7.00 7.00	14.00 14.00	12.00 -	- -	2	1	2	-	1	1700 1900	6	1-12	

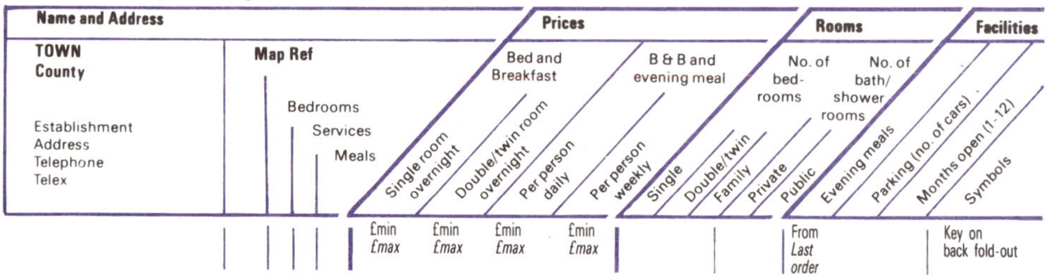

"First and Last" Hotel in Scotland on the A68

Jedforest Hotel
Near Jedburgh – Scotland
Telephone: Camptown 274

The Hotel stands in 50 acres, and has 1 mile of Trout Fishing. The kitchen is under the personal supervision of the Proprietor, Mr Dalgetty.
There are 4 bedrooms in a new Annex with private Shower Rooms, Toilet, TV, etc. 2 Star AA★★

VAT is shown at 15%: changes in this rate may affect prices.

Name and Address	Map Ref	Bedrooms	Services	Meals	Single room overnight £min/£max	Double/twin room overnight £min/£max	Per person daily £min/£max	Per person weekly £min/£max	Single	Double/twin	Family	Private	Public	Evening meals (From/Last order)	No. of bedrooms	No. of bath/shower rooms	Parking (no. of cars)	Months open (1-12)	Symbols (Key on back fold-out)
CARNOUSTIE Angus	2 E2																		
Almondbank Hotel, 29 Ireland Street, DD7 6AS, Tel. Carnoustie 59510		2	3	4	7.00 / -	14.00 / -	9.50 / -	66.50 / -	2	3	4	-	2	1800 / -	10	1-12	⟨symbols⟩		
Carlogie House Hotel, Carlogie Road, Tel. Carnoustie 53185		5	5	5	20.00 / 20.00	35.00 / 35.00	28.00 / -	168.00 / -	3	7	1	11	-	1900 / 2130	100	1-12	⟨symbols⟩		
Glencoe Hotel, 8 Links Parade, DD7 7JF, Tel. Carnoustie 53273		4	4	4	12.65 / -	28.00 / -	18.65 / -	130.55 / -	3	5	2	7	3	1930 / 2045	12	1-12	⟨symbols⟩		
Morven Hotel, 28 West Path, Tel. Carnoustie 52385		3	3	5	9.00 / 10.00	18.00 / 20.00	12.00 / 17.00	75.00 / 100.00	-	4	1	-	2	1700 / 2200	20	1-12	⟨symbols⟩		
Station Hotel, Station Road, Tel. Carnoustie 52447		4	4	5	9.00 / -	17.00 / -	12.50 / -	84.00 / -	2	6	2	3	2	1900 / 2130	14	1-12	⟨symbols⟩		
Braemore Guest House, 24 Dundee Street, DD7 7PF, Tel. Carnoustie 52076		3	2	2	6.00 / -	12.00 / -	9.50 / -	55.00 / -	-	4	-	-	1	- / 1800	1	4-10	⟨symbols⟩		
CARNWATH Lanarkshire	2 B6																		
Old Bush Hotel, 12 Main Street, Tel. Carnwath 333		3	4	5	8.00 / 10.00	13.00 / 15.00	9.50 / 15.00	55.00 / 75.00	1	3	-	-	1	1630 / 2130	20	1-12	⟨symbols⟩		
CARRADALE Argyll	1 E7																		
Ashbank Hotel, Tel. Carradale 650		3	3	4	- / -	16.00 / -	13.50 / 15.50	80.00 / 85.00	-	5	-	-	2	1900 / -	8	4-10	⟨symbols⟩		
Carradale Hotel, PA28 6RY, Tel. Carradale 223		4	4	4	12.00 / 14.00	24.00 / 28.00	20.00 / 21.00	105.00 / 119.00	6	14	2	7	4	1900 / 2200	22	1-12	⟨symbols⟩		
Dunncrannag Guest House, Tel. Carradale 224		1	2	2	6.50 / -	13.00 / -	10.00 / -	- / -	3	7	2	-	2	1800 / -	8	4-10	⟨symbols⟩		
Dunvalanree Guest House, Portrigh Bay, PA28 6SE, Tel. Carradale 226		3	3	2	7.00 / 7.50	14.00 / 15.00	9.00 / 10.00	63.00 / 70.00	1	8	3	-	3	1800 / -	9	4-10	⟨symbols⟩		

SCOTLAND'S FOR ME

64 pages of dazzling full colour packed with useful travel information, inclusive holidays, maps and details of how to enjoy the very best holiday in Scotland.

Ask your travel agent for your FREE copy.

Name and Address				Prices					Rooms						Facilities		
TOWN County / Establishment Address Telephone Telex	Map Ref	Bedrooms Services Meals		Bed and Breakfast			B & B and evening meal		No. of bedrooms				No. of bath/ shower rooms			Facilities		
				Single room overnight	Double/twin room overnight	Per person daily	Per person weekly	Single	Double/twin	Family	Private	Public	Evening meals	Parking (no. of cars)	Months open (1-12)	Symbols
				£min £max	£min £max	£min £max	£min £max					From Last order			Key on back fold-out

CARRBRIDGE
Inverness-shire — 4 C9

Name and Address	Bedrooms	Services	Meals	Single room	Double/twin room	Per person daily	Per person weekly	Single	Double/twin	Family	Private	Public	From / Last order	Parking	Months open	Symbols
Carrbridge Hotel Tel. Carrbridge 202 Telex 75160	3	5	5	14.00 -	28.00 -	- -	- -	11	40	4	13	7	1900 2130	30	1-12	
Dalrachney Lodge Private Hotel Tel. Carrbridge 252	3	4	4	9.50 -	18.00 -	14.00 -	84.00 -	3	5	2	-	5	1900 2100	20	1-12	
Old Manse Private Hotel Duthill PH23 3ND Tel. Carrbridge 278	3	3	2	8.00 8.00	16.00 16.00	12.50 12.50	77.00 77.00	2	4	2	-	3	1900 -	7	12-10	

STRUAN HOUSE HOTEL

Carrbridge, Inverness-shire PH23 3AU

Telephone: 047-984 242

Friendly family-run, fully licensed hotel, excellent centre for skiing, golf, riding, water sports, walking. Own hard tennis court. Austrian proprietor Karl Fuchs. Ski School with downhill and cross-country equipment for hire and instruction. Opposite Laendinvale Centre, 6 miles from Aviemore. Special accommodation rates for families and parties. For free brochure phone 047-984 242. **B. & B. £7. D. B. & B. £11 per day.**

Name and Address	Bedrooms	Services	Meals	Single room	Double/twin room	Per person daily	Per person weekly	Single	Double/twin	Family	Private	Public	From / Last order	Parking	Months open	Symbols
Struan House Hotel PH23 3AU Tel. Carrbridge 242	3	3	3	7.00 7.70	14.00 15.40	11.00 12.10	75.00 82.50	1	8	7	-	7	1900 -	30	1-12	
Ard-na-Coille Guest House Station Road Tel. Carrbridge 239	3	2	2	8.00 -	16.00 -	11.00 -	77.00 -	-	3	-	-	2	1830 -	7	1-12	
Carr Moor Guest House Carr Road PH23 3AD Tel. Carrbridge 244	3	3	2	6.50 7.00	13.00 14.00	10.00 11.00	66.00 74.00	-	3	1	-	1	1900 1900	4	1-12	
Keepers Cottage Guest House Tel. Carrbridge 621	3	3	3	7.00 -	14.00 -	11.00 -	75.00 -	-	2	1	-	1	1900 1900	4	1-10	

VAT is shown at 15%: changes in this rate may affect prices.

Name and Address	Map Ref	Bedrooms	Services	Meals	Single room overnight (£min / £max)	Double/twin room overnight (£min / £max)	Per person daily (£min / £max)	Per person weekly (£min / £max)	B & B and evening meal — Per person weekly	Single	Double/twin	Family	Private	Public	Evening meals (From / Last order)	Parking (no. of cars)	Months open (1-12)	Symbols
CARRBRIDGE continued	4 / C9																	Key on back fold-out
Kinchyle Guest House, PH23 3AA, Tel. Carrbridge 243		3	2	2	6.00 / 7.00	12.00 / 14.00	9.50 / 10.50	65.00 / 72.00		2	2	-	-	1	1830 / 1700	6	1-12	
CARRUTHERSTOWN, Dumfriesshire	2 / C10																	
Carrutherstown Hotel, Tel. Carrutherstown 268		2	2	3	8.05 / -	16.00 / -	12.00 / -	75.00 / -		-	6	1	-	3	1900 / 2100	20	1-12	
CASTLE DOUGLAS, Kirkcudbrightshire	2 / A10																	
Douglas Arms Hotel, Tel. Castle Douglas 2231		4	4	4	19.50 / -	33.00 / -	- / -	- / -		8	19	1	10	5	1900 / 2100	20	1-12	
Ernespie House Hotel, DG7 3JG, Tel. Castle Douglas 2188		3	3	4	12.00 / -	24.00 / -	18.00 / -	108.00 / -		3	6	6	5	3	1900 / 2000	130	1-12	
Imperial Hotel, Tel. Castle Douglas 2086		3	3	3	12.00 / 14.00	24.00 / 28.00	18.50 / 19.50	- / -		3	11	-	3	3	1730 / 1900	24	1-12	
Kings Arms Hotel, Tel. Castle Douglas 2097		3	4	4	12.00 / 14.00	24.00 / 28.00	21.00 / 24.00	119.00 / 140.00		6	9	1	6	4	1900 / 2000	17	1-12	
The Merrick Hotel, King Street, Tel. Castle Douglas 2173		3	3	4	8.00 / 8.50	15.00 / 16.50	11.50 / 12.50	73.00 / 80.00		1	4	2	-	1	1800 / 2000	6	1-12	
Cuil Park Guest House, Bridge of Dee, Tel. Bridge of Dee 213		3	3	3	6.50 / 6.50	13.00 / 13.00	10.00 / 10.00	65.00 / 65.00		-	8	2	-	3	1800 / 2000	10	1-12	
CASTLE KENNEDY, by Stranraer, Wigtownshire	1 / F10																	
Eynhallow Hotel, Tel. Dunragit 256		4	3	5	11.75 / -	23.50 / -	- / -	- / -		2	6	1	7	1	1830 / 2130	20	1-12	
CASTLEBAY, Isle of Barra, Western Isles	3 / A11																	
Castlebay Hotel, Tel. Castlebay 265		3	4	5	10.00 / 12.50	20.00 / -	15.50 / -	105.00 / -		1	6	2	-	4	1600 / 2030	10	1-12	
Craigard Hotel, Tel. Castlebay 200		3	3	3	11.00 / 12.00	20.00 / 22.00	18.00 / 19.00	105.00 / 110.00		-	6	1	-	2	1900 / 2000	30	1-12	
An Calla Guest House, Tel. Castlebay 270		-	-	-	7.00 / -	14.00 / -	10.00 / -	65.00 / -		1	4	-	-	2	1900 / 2000	7	4-10	
CASTLETOWN, Caithness	4 / D3																	
Seaforth Motel, Tel. Castletown 620		3	3	3	5.75 / 8.05	9.20 / 13.80	Rates for Room Only	-		-	5	-	5	-	1800 / 2045	40	1-12	

Prices shown are for guidance only. Please send SAE with each enquiry.

The prices and room columns are grouped as printed: **Prices** (Bed and Breakfast: Single room overnight, Double/twin room overnight, Per person daily; B & B and evening meal: Per person weekly), **Rooms** (No. of bedrooms: Single, Double/twin, Family; No. of bath/shower rooms: Private, Public; Evening meals From/Last order; Parking no. of cars) and **Facilities** (Months open 1‑12; Symbols — key on back fold‑out). Prices are given £min / £max.

Name and Address	Map Ref	Bedrooms	Services	Meals	Single room overnight	Double/twin room overnight	Per person daily	Per person weekly	Single	Double/twin	Family	Private	Public	Evening meals From / Last order	Parking (no. of cars)	Months open	Symbols
CATACOL — Isle of Arran	1 / E6																
Catacol Bay Hotel, Tel. Lochranza 231		3	4	4	8.50 / 9.00	17.00 / 18.00	13.00 / 13.50	91.00 / 94.50	2	2	2	-	2	1830 / 1900	40	1-12	[£]
Fairhaven, Tel. Lochranza 237		1	2	3	5.50 / -	11.00 / -	8.65 / -	61.00 / -	-	7	1	-	2	- / -	-	-	
CHAPELHALL, by Airdrie — Lanarkshire	2 / A5																
Laurel House Hotel, Main Street, Tel. Airdrie 63230		-	-	-	10.00	20.00	13.50	-	-	5	1	-	1	1800 / 1900	6	1-12	[V]
CHIRNSIDE, by Duns — Berwickshire	2 / F5																
Chirnside Country House Hotel, TD11 3LD, Tel. Chirnside 219		3	3	4	12.00 / 13.50	24.00 / 26.00	20.00 / 23.00	110.00 / 125.00	5	5	5	-	4	1900 / 2045	20	1-12	[£] [C] [V]
CHRYSTON — Lanarkshire	2 / A5																
Crow Wood House Hotel, Muirhead, Tel. 041 779 3861		-	-	-	21.00	31.50	-	-	8	10	-	10	-	1800 / 2130	100	1-12	[T] [£]
CLACHAN SEIL, by Oban — Argyll	1 / E3																
Willowburn Hotel, Tel. Balvicar 276		3	3	3	12.00 / 18.70	26.00 / 32.50	21.00 / 26.50	-	-	6	1	3	1	1900 / 2030	20	12-10	[T] [£]
CLEISH, Kinross — Kinross-shire	2 / C3																
Nivingston House Hotel, KY13 7LS, Tel. Cleish Hills 216		4	4	5	25.00	40.00	37.50	225.00	1	6	-	7	-	1900 / 2200	43	1-12	[T] [£] [C] [V]
COLDINGHAM — Berwickshire	2 / G5																
Shieling Hotel, Coldingham Bay, TD14 5PA, Tel. Coldingham 216		4	3	4	12.00	24.00	16.00	98.00	2	7	1	4	2	1830 / 1930	12	3-10	[C] [V]
COLDSTREAM — Berwickshire	2 / F6																
Hotel Majicado, 71 High Street, Tel. Coldstream 2112		3	3	4	10.00 / 10.00	20.00 / 20.00	12.00 / 18.00	84.00 / 140.00	2	4	1	-	2	1900 / 2030	-	1-12	[V]
Newcastle Arms Hotel, 50 High Street, TD12 4AS, Tel. Coldstream 2376		-	-	-	9.20	18.40	-	-	2	4	1	-	2	1800 / 2000	12	1-12	[V]
Lynnside Guest House, 1 Abbey Road, Tel. Coldstream 2682		2	3	5	7.00 / 7.00	13.00 / 13.00	9.50 / 9.50	66.50 / 66.50	-	3	1	-	2	1830 / 1630	5	1-12	[C] [V]

VAT is shown at 15%: changes in this rate may affect prices.

| Name and Address | Map Ref | | | | Prices | | | | B & B and evening meal | | | | | Rooms | | | Facilities |
TOWN / County / Establishment / Address / Telephone / Telex		Bedrooms	Services	Meals	Single room overnight	Double/twin room overnight	Per person daily	Per person weekly	Single	Double/twin	Family	Private	Public	No. of bedrooms	No. of bath/shower rooms	Evening meals	Parking (no. of cars) / Months open (1-12) / Symbols
					£min £max	£min £max	£min £max	£min £max						From Last order			Key on back fold-out
COLLIN, by Dumfries Dumfriesshire	2 C9																
Rockhall Hotel Tel. Collin 208		5	4	5	19.00 23.00	29.00 36.00	27.00 31.00	- -	3	6	-	5	1	1900 2100	80	1-12	
Stagecoach Hotel Tel. Collin 696		3	2	4	11.50 11.50	23.00 23.00	15.00 17.00	105.00 119.00	-	8	-	8	-	1830 2100	50	1-12	
COLONSAY, Isle of Argyll	1 C4																

Isles of Colonsay and Oronsay, Argyll

These favoured islands of the Inner Hebrides are tranquil, beautiful and unspoilt, the haunt of 170 species of birds, they are rich in antiquities, natural history and breathtaking scenery. There are magnificent sandy beaches, bays and strands, an 18-hole golf links, sailing dinghies, bicycles, fishing, yet no day-trippers, coach parties, etc.

Access is convenient, with three car ferries per week from Oban, which is also a main British Rail station.

Hotel accommodation is in the 18th century inn (open all year), which overlooks the harbour. Guests enjoy traditional comfort and hospitality, and table d'hote cuisine based on fresh local produce, they have the benefit of the hotel courtesy car and bicycles are supplied gratis.

Demi-pension from £17.50 including VAT and Service, family suite and family room available, for map and detailed information please contact THE HOTEL, Isle of Colonsay, Argyll, PA61 7YP. Telephone 09512 316.

Name and Address	Map Ref				Single room overnight	Double/twin room overnight	Per person daily	Per person weekly	Single	Double/twin	Family	Private	Public	No. of bedrooms	No. of bath/shower rooms	Evening meals	Months open
Isle of Colonsay Hotel PA61 7YP Tel. Colonsay 316		3	4	4	13.50 19.00	27.00 36.00	17.50 28.00	122.50 176.40	2	7	2	2	4	1930 1930	31	1-12	
COLVEND, by Dalbeattie Kirkcudbrightshire	2 B10																
Clonyard House Hotel Tel. Rockcliffe 372		3	3	4	11.50 12.00	22.00 24.00	16.50 19.00	112.00 130.00	1	1	3	1	1	1900 2045	35	1-12	
COMRIE Perthshire	2 A2																
Comrie Hotel Drummond Street PH6 2DY Tel. Comrie 70239		3	3	5	9.40 13.75	18.80 27.50	17.00 21.35	115.50 161.00	3	9	-	8	2	1730 2130	26	4-10	

Name and Address	Map Ref				Prices					Rooms							Facilities	
TOWN / County / Establishment / Address / Telephone / Telex		Bedrooms / Services / Meals			Bed and Breakfast				B & B and evening meal	No. of bedrooms				No. of bath/shower rooms			No. of / Parking (no. of cars) / Months open (1-12) / Symbols	
					Single room overnight	Double/twin room overnight	Per person daily	Per person weekly		Single	Double/twin	Family	Private	Public	Evening meals			
COMRIE continued	2 A2				£min £max	£min £max	£min £max	£min £max							From Last order		Key on back fold-out	

The Royal Hotel

Melville Square, Comrie, Perthshire, PH6 2DN.
Tel: (0764) 70200

Historic old coaching inn, Queen Victoria stayed, hence the 'Royal'. Since 1765 has been dispensing good food, fine wines, comfortable accommodation, courteous service and personal attention. All rooms have T.V., telephone, tea and coffee makers, electric blankets and self-selection heating control. B.T.A. commended, Egon Ronay, Ashley Courtenay, Michelin Guide, Relais Routier and A.A.** Ideal centre for golfers.

Name and Address	Bedrooms	Services	Meals	Single room overnight	Double/twin room overnight	Per person daily	Per person weekly	Single	Double/twin	Family	Private	Public	Evening meals last order	No. of bath/shower rooms	Parking	Months open	Symbols
Royal Hotel / Melville Square / PH6 2DN / Tel. Comrie 70200	5	4	5	14.00 15.50	28.00 31.00	22.25 23.75	44.50 47.50	4	9	3	10	3	1900 2130	34	1-12	
Mossgiel Guest House / Burrell Street / PH6 2JP / Tel. Comrie 70567	3	4	2	5.50 -	11.00 -	9.00 -	63.00 -	-	6	-	-	1	1930 1730	6	1-12	
CONNEL / Argyll / 1 E2																
Dunstaffnage Arms Hotel / Tel. Connel 209	4	3	5	9.00 15.00	16.00 24.00	15.00 21.00	95.00 135.00	-	15	2	17	1	1900 2200	50	1-12	

The Falls of Lora Hotel

AA★★ RAC★★ RSAC★★

Connel Ferry, by Oban, Argyll PA37 1PB
Tel: 0631-71 483

The Hotel, built in 1886, with its modern centrally heated wing, is set back from the A85 overlooking Loch Etive, only 5 miles from Oban–"The Gateway to the Highlands & Islands." An ideal centre for a touring, walking and sailing holiday or just relaxing in a friendly atmosphere. Fishing, Gliding, Water-skiing and Pony Trekking can be arranged. The resident owners guarantee you a warm welcome, personal attention, good food and service.

Accommodation to suit all tastes–
From Luxury room with a "four poster" bed and King size round bath–to inexpensive family rooms with bunk beds. FREE accommodation for children sharing parents' room.

Super Cocktail Bar with open log fire, over 50 brands of Whisky to tempt you, extensive Bar Menu.

2½-3 hours drive north-west of Glasgow or Edinburgh. Open all year, out of season mini-breaks.

A FINE OWNER-RUN SCOTTISH HOTEL

Name and Address	Bedrooms	Services	Meals	Single room overnight	Double/twin room overnight	Per person daily	Per person weekly	Single	Double/twin	Family	Private	Public	Evening meals last order	No. of bath/shower rooms	Parking	Months open	Symbols
Falls of Lora Hotel / PA37 1PB / Tel. Connel 483	4	5	5	9.50 26.50	15.00 53.00	13.50 32.50	- -	6	20	4	19	7	1900 2130	40	1-12	

Name and Address — TOWN / County / Establishment / Address / Telephone / Telex	Map Ref	Bedrooms	Services	Meals	Single room overnight (£min/£max)	Double/twin room overnight (£min/£max)	Per person daily (£min/£max)	Per person weekly (£min/£max)	Single	Double/twin	Family	Private	Public	Evening meals (From / Last order)	Parking (no. of cars)	Months open (1-12)	Symbols
CONON BRIDGE Ross-shire	4 A8																
Conon Hotel IV7 8HD Tel. Dingwall 61500		-	-	-	10.00 / -	20.00 / -	- / -	- / -	7	7	-	-	4	1830 / 2230	40	1-12	(symbols)
CONTIN, by Strathpeffer Ross-shire	4 A8																
Coul House Hotel IV14 9ED Tel. Strathpeffer 487		4	5	5	14.00 / 17.10	23.00 / 29.20	19.90 / 23.00	117.25 / 161.00	3	13	3	13	2	1915 / 2045	40	1-12	(symbols)
Craigdarroch Lodge Hotel Craigdarroch Drive Tel. Strathpeffer 265		4	5	5	13.50 / 15.50	27.00 / 31.00	23.00 / 25.00	161.00 / 175.00	2	15	2	11	2	1900 / 2130	20	1-12	(symbols)
CORPACH, by Fort William Inverness-shire	3 G12																
Corpach Hotel Tel. Corpach 223		2	3	2	7.80 / -	15.60 / -	12.80 / -	- / -	1	6	-	-	2	1830 / 1930	20	1-12	(symbols)
Loch Shiel Guest House Tel. Corpach 312		-	-	-	- / -	12.00 / 13.00	- / -	- / -	-	3	1	-	1	1830 / -	8	1-12	(symbols)
Mansfield Guest House Tel. Corpach 262		3	2	2	- / -	12.00 / -	10.00 / -	65.00 / -	-	1	3	-	2	1900 / -	10	1-12	(symbols)
CORRIE Isle of Arran	1 F6																
Corrie Hotel Tel. Corrie 273		3	3	4	9.00 / -	18.00 / -	14.00 / -	95.00 / -	8	9	2	-	7	1900 / 1930	15	4-10	(symbols)
Blackrock Guest House Tel. Corrie 282		1	3	2	8.00 / 8.00	16.00 / 16.00	11.75 / 11.75	80.00 / 80.00	3	5	1	-	2	1830 / 1900	8	1-11	(symbols)
CORTACHY, by Kirriemuir Angus	4 E12																
Royal Jubilee Arms Hotel Dykehead Tel. Cortachy 225/213		4	4	4	12.50 / -	25.00 / -	- / -	- / -	4	17	3	24	-	1800 / 2300	250	1-12	(symbols)

Secluded country house in 7 acres with beautiful views from the elegant dining room, unique octagonal lounge and most bedrooms. Perfect centre for 'explorers'; own salmon/trout fishing; log fires; many private bathrooms; known for good food and friendly atmosphere; weekly entertainment

Send for colour brochure and details of our fishing, golfing and pony-trekking holidays … also our 6 night 'Highland Passport' including dinner, bed, breakfast and 5 admissions to places of interest, eg. Cawdor Castle, Loch Ness Cruise, Inverewe Gardens … from £111.
Telephone Strathpeffer (09972) 478.

Name and Address (TOWN / County / Establishment / Address / Telephone / Telex)	Map Ref	Bedrooms	Services	Meals	Single room overnight £min/£max	Double/twin room overnight £min/£max	Per person daily £min/£max	Per person weekly £min/£max	Single	Double/twin	Family	Private	Public	Evening meals (From / Last order)	Parking (no. of cars)	Months open (1-12)	Symbols (Key on back fold-out)
COUPAR ANGUS Perthshire	2 C1																
The Moorfield House Hotel, Myreriggs, PH13 9HS, Tel. Coupar Angus 303		3	4	4	9.00 / -	18.00 / -	14.50 / -	95.00 / -	1	8	-	3	3	1800 / 2030	50	1-12	[symbols]
COWDENBEATH Fife	2 C4																
Struan Bank Private Hotel, 74 Perth Road, Tel. Cowdenbeath 511057		-	-	-	8.65 / 9.65	17.30 / 19.30	12.50 / -	-	3	5	-	-	2	1900 / 2100	6	1-12	[symbols]
Marchmont Guest House, 91 Broad Street, KY4 8JR, Tel. Cowdenbeath 510823		4	4	1	6.00 / 7.50	12.00 / -	-	-	3	1	2	1	2	- / -	-	4-10	[symbols]
CRAIGELLACHIE Banffshire	4 D8																
Craigellachie Hotel, Victoria Street, AB3 9SR, Tel. Craigellachie 204		4	4	4	17.50 / 19.50	33.00 / 37.00	25.00 / 27.00	150.00 / 162.00	13	16	3	23	-	1930 / 2100	70	3-9	[symbols]
Glenavon Hotel, Victoria Street, AB3 9SR, Tel. Craigellachie 354		3	3	4	8.00 / -	14.00 / -	12.00 / -	66.50 / -	-	1	3	-	1	1700 / 1830	10	1-12	[symbols]
CRAIGHOUSE Isle of Jura, Argyll	1 D5																
Jura Hotel, PA60 7UX, Tel. Jura 243		3	4	3	16.50 / 18.00	33.00 / 36.00	25.00 / 26.50	157.50 / 166.95	7	10	1	4	4	1900 / 2100	22	1-12	[symbols]
CRAIGNURE Isle of Mull, Argyll	1 D2																
Craignure Inn, Tel. Craignure 305		3	3	4	9.80 / -	- / -	15.30 / -	95.00 / -	1	2	1	-	1	1900 / 2000	30	1-12	[symbols]

Cairngorm Spey Valley, Glenshee, Glencoe, Lecht

Inclusive holidays and details of hotels, facilities and apres-ski in Scotland's major ski-ing centres.

FREE FROM

Scottish Tourist Board, PO Box 15, EDINBURGH EH1 1UY

VAT is shown at 15%: changes in this rate may affect prices.

Name and Address	Map Ref				Prices				Rooms								Facilities
TOWN County Establishment Address Telephone Telex		Bedrooms	Services	Meals	Bed and Breakfast Single room overnight	Double/twin room overnight	Per person daily	B & B and evening meal Per person weekly	Single	Double/twin	Family	Private	No. of bedrooms Public	No. of bath/shower rooms Evening meals	Parking (no. of cars)	Months open (1-12)	Symbols
CRAIGNURE continued	1 D2				£min £max	£min £max	£min £max	£min £max					From Last order			Key on back fold-out	

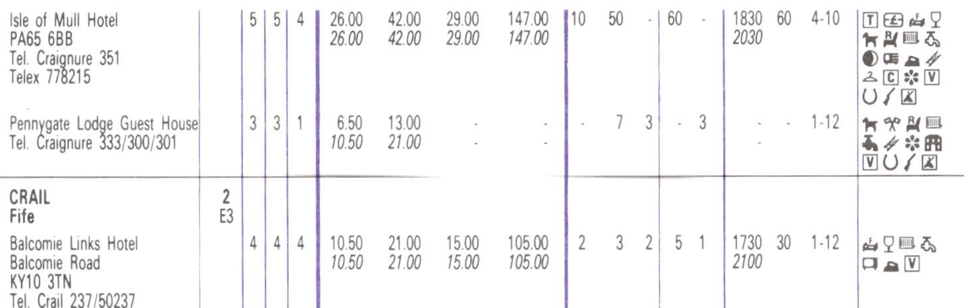

Isle of Mull Hotel, Craignure, Isle of Mull, Argyll. Tel. 068-02-351

The hotel overlooks Craignure Bay, the arrival point of the 45 minute ferry trip from Oban and is an ideal centre for touring Mull or visiting the Islands of Iona and Staffa. The new 9 hole golf course is only minutes from the hotel. 60 bedrooms with Private Bath and Tea and Coffee making facilities.

Name and Address	Bedrooms	Services	Meals	Single room overnight	Double/twin overnight	Per person daily	Per person weekly	Single	Double/twin	Family	Private	Public	Bedrooms/Last order	Bath/Evening meals	Parking	Months open	Symbols
Isle of Mull Hotel PA65 6BB Tel. Craignure 351 Telex 778215	5	5	4	26.00 26.00	42.00 42.00	29.00 29.00	147.00 147.00	10	50	-	60	-	1830 2030	60	4-10		
Pennygate Lodge Guest House Tel. Craignure 333/300/301	3	3	1	6.50 10.50	13.00 21.00	- -	- -	-	7	3	-	3	- -	-	1-12		
CRAIL Fife	2 E3																
Balcomie Links Hotel Balcomie Road KY10 3TN Tel. Crail 237/50237	4	4	4	10.50 10.50	21.00 21.00	15.00 15.00	105.00 105.00	2	3	2	5	1	1730 2100	30	1-12		

CROMA HOTEL
CRAIL, FIFE.   Tel. (03335) 239
AA ★ RAC ★

The Croma Hotel caters to families, golfers, etc. Daily or weekly terms available, discounts to groups. Bed and Breakfast available. Bar meals, afternoon teas, High teas, and Dinners served. Fully Licensed Lounge Bar.

The resident proprietors, Jack and Rosemarie Healy will welcome you most sincerely to the Croma Hotel.

Name and Address	Bedrooms	Services	Meals	Single room overnight	Double/twin overnight	Per person daily	Per person weekly	Single	Double/twin	Family	Private	Public	Bedrooms/Last order	Bath/Evening meals	Parking	Months open	Symbols
Croma Hotel 33-35 Nethergate KY10 3TU Tel. Crail 239/50239	4	5	5	8.00 10.00	16.00 20.00	14.00 15.50	85.00 95.00	-	9	-	4	3	1830 2230	10	4-10		
Golf Hotel 4 High Street Tel. Crail 500/50500	3	4	3	11.00 12.00	20.00 22.00	13.50 14.00	91.00 91.00	-	5	-	-	1	1700 2100	12	4-10		
Caiplie Guest House 51-53 High Street KY10 3RA Tel. Crail 564/50564	3	4	4	7.50 10.50	15.00 21.00	13.50 16.50	77.00 98.00	1	4	2	-	2	1900 2030	15	1-12		

Name and Address	Map Ref	Bedrooms	Services	Meals	Single room overnight £min/£max	Double/twin room overnight £min/£max	Per person daily £min/£max	Per person weekly £min/£max	Single	Double/twin	Family	Private	Public	Evening meals From/Last order	Parking (no. of cars)	Months open (1-12)	Symbols
CRAIL continued	1 / E3																Key on back fold-out
Gordons Hazelton Guest House, 29 Marketgate, KY15 4HF, Tel. Crail 250/50250		2	1	2	6.50 / 8.00	13.60 / 15.00	11.00 / 13.00	75.00 / 85.00	1	4	1	-	2	1800 / -	-	1-12	
CRAWFORD Lanarkshire	2 / B7																
Field End Guest House, ML12 6TN, Tel. Crawford 276		3	3	4	6.50 / 10.00	13.00 / 16.00	9.75 / 14.00	63.00 / 75.00	1	2	2	1	1	1830 / 2000	6	1-12	
CREETOWN, by Newton Stewart Wigtownshire	1 / H10																
Creetown Arms Hotel, Tel. Creetown 282		3	3	5	8.00 / -	15.00 / -	10.50 / 14.50	- / -	-	6	-	-	1	1900 / 2100	15	1-12	
The Boathouse Guest House, DG8 7DE, Tel. Creetown 335		3	3	2	8.00 / 9.00	14.00 / 16.00	12.00 / 13.00	80.00 / 85.00	-	2	1	-	1	1930 / 1800	6	1-12	
Hill of Burns, Tel. Creetown 487		1	2	3	12.50 / 14.50	25.00 / 29.00	20.50 / 22.50	135.00 / 145.00	1	3	-	2	3	2000 / 1800	10	1-12	
CRIANLARICH Perthshire	1 / G2																
Alltchaorain House Hotel, FK20 8RU, Tel. Crianlarich 283/212		4	4	4	9.00 / 11.00	18.00 / 22.00	14.00 / 16.00	95.00 / 105.00	1	7	1	3	2	1900 / -	12	1-12	
Crianlarich Hotel, FK20 8RW, Tel. Crianlarich 272		3	3	3	- / 9.00	- / 18.00	- / 11.50	- / -	-	25	6	-	6	1900 / 2000	30	4-10	
Craigbank Guest House, FK20 8QS, Tel. Crianlarich 279		3	3	2	7.50 / -	13.00 / -	10.50 / -	72.00 / -	-	3	1	-	1	1830 / -	6	1-12	
Glenardran Guest House, Tel. Crianlarich 236		3	3	4	9.00 / -	14.00 / -	11.00 / -	77.00 / -	1	3	2	-	1	1800 / 1915	4	1-12	
Mountgreenan Guest House, FK20 8RU, Tel. Crianlarich 286		3	3	3	7.00 / -	13.00 / -	10.50 / -	70.00 / -	-	4	1	-	2	1830 / -	6	1-12	
CRIEFF Perthshire	2 / B2																
Arduthie Hotel, Perth Road, PH7 3EQ, Tel. Crieff 3113		4	4	4	18.00 / 18.00	27.00 / 27.00	25.00 / 28.00	160.00 / 200.00	-	2	1	3	-	1700 / 2100	20	1-12	

VAT is shown at 15%: changes in this rate may affect prices.

Name and Address	Map Ref	Bedrooms	Services	Meals	Prices — Bed and Breakfast: Single room overnight £min/£max	Double/twin room overnight £min/£max	Per person daily £min/£max	B & B and evening meal: Per person weekly £min/£max	No. of bedrooms: Single	Double/twin	Family	No. of bath/shower rooms: Private	Public	Evening meals From/Last order	Parking (no. of cars)	Months open (1-12)	Symbols
CRIEFF continued	2 B2											From Last order				Key on back fold-out
Crieff Hydro, PH7 3LQ, Tel. Crieff 2401		4	4	4	13.65 / 17.75	27.30 / 35.50	14.00 / 24.00	98.00 / 168.00	65	67	68	105	25	1900 / 2000	90	1-12	
Crown Inn Hotel, 33 East High Street, PH7 3HY, Tel. Crieff 3283		3	3	5	9.00 / -	17.00 / -	- / -	- / -	1	5	-	-	1	1800 / 2130	12	1-12	
Cultoquhey Hotel, Gilmerton, PH7 3NE, Tel. Crieff 3253		-	-	-	7.50 / 8.50	15.00 / 17.00	11.00 / 15.00	77.00 / 105.00	1	16	3	-	4	1900 / 2000	50	4-10	
George Hotel, 57 King Street, PH7 3HB, Tel. Crieff 2089		3	3	4	9.00 / 12.50	18.00 / 25.00	15.00 / 19.00	95.00 / 110.00	6	19	2	4	4	1900 / 2100	35	1-12	
Gwydyr House Hotel, Comrie Road, PH7 4BP, Tel. Crieff 3277		3	3	4	10.00 / 10.00	20.00 / 20.00	16.25 / 16.25	105.00 / 105.00	2	4	4	-	3	1900 / 2000	15	4-10	
Keppoch House Hotel, Perth Road, Tel. Crieff 4341		3	3	6	11.00 / -	26.50 / -	15.50 / -	95.00 / -	1	5	-	-	2	1900 / 2130	12	1-12	
Kingarth Hotel, Perth Road, PH7 3EQ, Tel. Crieff 2060		3	4	4	9.75 / -	19.50 / -	15.75 / -	70.00 / -	4	7	3	1	7	1900 / 2000	15	3-11	
Leven House Hotel, Comrie Road, PH7 4BA, Tel. Crieff 2529		3	4	2	8.00 / -	16.00 / -	13.00 / -	88.00 / -	1	5	3	-	3	1830 / 1900	6	1-12	
Loch Monzievaird Chalets Hotel, Tel. Crieff 2586		3	3	1	- / -	25.00 / 29.00	- / -	- / -	-	13	-	13	-	- / -	25	1-12	
Lockes Acre Hotel, Comrie Road, PH7 4BP, Tel. Crieff 2526		3	3	3	- / -	17.00 / -	- / -	- / -	-	1	6	-	2	1800 / 1900	20	1-12	

Name and Address	Map Ref				Prices				B & B and evening meal				Rooms				Facilities
TOWN / County / Establishment / Address / Telephone / Telex		Bedrooms	Services	Meals	Single room overnight	Double/twin room overnight	Per person daily	Per person weekly	Single	Double/twin	Family	Private	Public	Evening meals	Parking (no. of cars)	Months open (1-12)	Symbols
					£min £max	£min £max	£min £max	£min £max						From Last order			Key on back fold-out
CRIEFF continued	2 B2																
Murraypark Hotel / Connaught Terrace / PH7 3DJ / Tel. Crieff 3731		5	4	5	14.00 17.00	28.00 34.00	24.50 28.50	154.00 189.00	2	11	2	10	2	1930 2130	50	1-12	Key on back fold-out
Rosebank Hotel / Millar Street / PH7 3AH / Tel. Crieff 2588		2	2	3	7.50 9.00	15.00 18.00	10.00 12.00	60.00 72.00	-	4	1	-	1	1800 2000	18	1-12	
Star Hotel / 45-47 East High Street / PH7 3HY / Tel. Crieff 2632		3	4	5	10.00 14.00	17.00 22.00	12.50 20.00	75.00 95.00	3	6	1	5	4	1700 2130	20	1-12	
Waverley Hotel / 7 James Square / PH7 3HX / Tel. Crieff 2652		2	1	1	7.50 -	14.00 -	11.50 -	80.50 -	1	3	2	-	1	1800 -	-	-	
Comely Bank Guest House / 32 Burrell Street / PH7 4DT / Tel. Crieff 3409/3834		3	3	2	6.50 6.50	13.00 13.00	9.50 9.50	59.50 59.50	2	2	3	-	3	1800 1900	-	1-11	
Dalchonzie House Guest House / 28 Burrell Street / PH7 4DT / Tel. Crieff 3423		3	3	2	- -	13.00 14.00	10.50 11.00	68.25 71.50	-	4	1	-	2	1830 -	-	4-10	
CRINAN, by Lochgilphead / Argyll	1 E4																
Crinan Hotel / Tel. Crinan 235 / Telex 778817		6	5	5	26.40 -	43.00 -	35.95 -	250.00 -	2	20	1	22	4	1900 2130	20	3-10	

Try a Taste of Scotland

Ask the Scottish Tourist Board for the colourful free booklet *A Taste of Scotland*. It lists around 200 places offering fine Scottish cooking, along with notes on regional specialities and recipes which you can try out at home.

While you're on holiday in Scotland, look for the Stockpot sign outside hotels and restaurants. It tells you that the menu offers not only traditional Scottish fare, but also examples of the creative skills of our chefs, using the best Scottish produce.

VAT is shown at 15%: changes in this rate may affect prices.

Name and Address: TOWN / County / Establishment / Address / Telephone / Telex	Map Ref / Bedrooms / Services / Meals	Prices — Bed and Breakfast: Single room overnight (£min £max)	Double twin room overnight (£min £max)	Per person daily (£min £max)	B & B and evening meal: Per person weekly (£min £max)	Rooms — No of bedrooms: Single	Double twin	Family	No of bath/shower rooms: Private	Public	Evening meals: From / Last order	Facilities: Parking (no of cars)	Months open (1-12)	Symbols
CROCKETFORD, by Dumfries Kirkcudbrightshire	2 B9													

Galloway Arms Hotel

FROM £165 per week, which includes Dinner, Bed & Breakfast, Picnic Tea, and half-day Mini Tour, or £96 for 4 days.

All rooms with Teamaking facilities and colour T.V. 60% rooms with Private Bath.

MINI TOUR HOLIDAY NO CAR!—NO PROBLEM:

A mini Tour Holiday is your answer at
THE GALLOWAY ARMS HOTEL, CROCKETFORD.

We offer you a series of half day tours in the Hotel's Mini Bus to places of scenic, historic and artistic interest off the beaten track in and around Romantic Galloway and Dumfries.

BOOKINGS AND INFORMATION
Tel. Crocketford (055669) 240. Mr and Mrs A. S. Hastings.

Name and Address	Map Ref / Services / Meals	Single room overnight	Double twin room overnight	Per person daily	Per person weekly	Single	Double twin	Family	Private	Public	Evening meals From / Last order	Parking	Months open	Symbols
Galloway Arms Hotel Tel. Crocketford 240	4 4 6	15.00 / 20.00	30.00 / 40.00	18.00 / 28.00	126.00 / 196.00	4	5	2	7	3	1700 / 2300	50	1-12	T £ …
Brae Guest House DG2 8QE Tel. Crocketford 253	4 2 2	10.00 / 12.00	16.00 / 18.00	15.00 / 19.00	100.00 / 130.00	-	3	1	1	2	1900 / 2000	6	4-9	…
CROSSFORD, by Dunfermline Fife	2 C4													

KEAVIL HOUSE HOTEL

Crossford, Dunfermline.
Telephone: Dunfermline 36258

Keavil House Hotel combines the delights of country house living with all the luxury of a first-class modern hotel. Visit us for our excellent cuisine: we serve lunch, bar lunch and dinner daily, high teas on Sundays only. We have 32 beautifully appointed bedrooms, all with private bath or shower and colour television. Disabled guests very welcome, rooms with special facilities available. Set in its own peaceful wooded grounds, Keavil House Hotel has a relaxing atmosphere ideal for both your friends, and your business associates. Special Weekend Breaks (two can stay for the price of one) from £11.00 per person bed and breakfast. Please write or telephone for our brochure.

SITUATED AT CROSSFORD BY DUNFERMLINE   AA***

Telephone (0383) 736258   Telex 728227

Name and Address	Services / Meals	Single room overnight	Double twin room overnight	Per person daily	Per person weekly	Single	Double twin	Family	Private	Public	Evening meals From / Last order	Parking	Months open	Symbols
Keavil House Hotel Tel. Dunfermline 736258	6 4 5	20.00 / 28.00	32.00 / 40.00	27.50 / -	- / -	4	26	2	32	-	1900 / 2130	70	1-12	T £ …

Establishment Address Telephone Telex	Map Ref	Bedrooms	Services	Meals	Single room overnight £min/£max	Double/twin room overnight £min/£max	Per person daily £min/£max	Per person weekly £min/£max	Single	Double/twin	Family	Private	Public	Evening meals From/Last order	Parking (no. of cars)	Months open (1-12)	Symbols
CROSSHOUSE, by Kilmarnock Ayrshire	1 H6																
Laurieland Hotel, 82 Irvine Road, Tel. Kilmarnock 35182		-	-	-	10.00 / -	20.00 / -	- / -	- / -	-	5	1	-	1	1700 / 2000	30	1-12	(symbols)
CROSSMICHAEL, by Castle Douglas Kirkcudbrightshire	2 A10																
Culgruff House Hotel, DG7 3AS, Tel. Crossmichael 230		3	5	4	12.65 / 12.65	23.00 / 23.00	19.55 / 21.85	115.00 / 123.05	2	13	2	1	4	1900 / 2000	58	1-12	(symbols)
CROY Inverness-shire	4 B8																
Kilravock Castle, IV1 2PJ, Tel. Croy 258		3	3	3	8.30 / 11.10	16.60 / 22.20	12.95 / 15.95	83.85 / 103.25	6	5	8	-	10	1900 / -	25	4-10	(symbols)
CULLEN, Buckie Banffshire	4 F7																
Bay View Hotel & Restaurant, 57 Seafield Street, AB5 2SU, Tel. Cullen 40260		4	4	5	14.50 / 14.50	25.00 / 25.00	17.50 / 17.50	114.00 / 114.00	1	4	3	2	2	1730 / 2130	11	12-10	(symbols)
Cullen Bay Hotel, AB5 2XA, Tel. Cullen 40432		3	3	4	13.00 / 14.00	26.00 / 28.00	18.00 / 20.00	112.00 / 126.00	2	14	1	4	4	1900 / 2130	164	1-12	(symbols)
Grant Arms Hotel, Grant Street, Tel. Cullen 40243		3	3	4	10.00 / -	16.00 / -	15.00 / -	100.00 / -	-	10	2	-	3	1800 / 1900	4	1-12	(symbols)
Royal Oak Hotel, 43-45 Seatown, AB5 2SD, Tel. Cullen 40252		3	3	4	9.25 / 9.75	18.00 / 20.00	14.20 / 18.00	95.00 / 105.00	1	5	2	-	2	1900 / 2200	20	1-12	(symbols)
The Seafield Arms Hotel, 19 Seafield Street, AB5 2SG, Tel. Cullen 40791		4	3	5	17.25 / 19.80	32.00 / 37.00	22.50 / 26.80	135.50 / 162.50	4	18	1	17	12	1900 / 2130	25	1-12	(symbols)
Three Kings Inn, 21 North Castle Street, AB5 2SA, Tel. Cullen 40538		3	3	3	8.50 / -	16.00 / -	14.00 / -	89.00 / -	-	5	-	-	2	1800 / 1830	10	1-12	(symbols)
Wakes Hotel, Seafield Place, AB5 2TE, Tel. Cullen 40251		3	3	4	8.00 / -	16.00 / -	11.00 / -	65.00 / -	1	17	5	-	4	1730 / 1900	20	1-12	(symbols)

VAT is shown at 15%: changes in this rate may affect prices.

Name and Address	Map Ref	Bedrooms	Services	Meals	Bed and Breakfast Single room overnight £min/£max	Double/twin room overnight £min/£max	Per person daily £min/£max	B & B and evening meal Per person weekly £min/£max	Single	Double/twin	Family	Private	Public	No. of bedrooms From/Last order	No. of bath/shower rooms	Evening meals	Parking (no. of cars)	Months open (1-12)	Symbols
CULNACNOCK, Portree **Isle of Skye, Inverness-shire** Blaracrian Guest House Tel. Staffin 208	3 D8	-	-	-	6.00 -	12.00 -	- -	- -	1	4	1	-	2	1830 -	10	3-9		*(Key on back fold-out)*
CULROSS **Fife** Red Lion Inn Main Street Tel. Newmills 880225	2 B4	-	-	-	10.00 -	20.00 -	13.00 -	91.00 -	1	4	-	-	1	1800 2000	30	1-12		*(Key on back fold-out)*
CULZEAN, by Maybole **Ayrshire** Ardlochan Guest House Maidens Tel. Kirkoswald 254	1 G8	3	2	4	10.00 -	18.00 -	13.00 -	91.00 -	-	4	1	-	2	1830 2000	10	1-12		*(Key on back fold-out)*
CUMNOCK **Ayrshire** Royal Hotel 1 Glaisnock Street KA18 1BP Tel. Cumnock 20822	1 H7	3	4	4	13.50 14.00	25.00 27.00	20.00 20.50	- -	1	9	2	-	3	1700 2100	10	1-12		*(Key on back fold-out)*
CUPAR **Fife** Cupar Arms Hotel Burnside Tel. Cupar 53240	2 D3	1	1	5	12.00 -	24.00 -	- -	- -	1	2	-	-	2	1900 2130	-	1-12		*(Key on back fold-out)*
CURRIE **Midlothian** Riccarton Arms Hotel 198 Lanark Road West EH14 5NX Tel. 031 449 2230	2 C5	2	1	1	11.00 13.00	17.00 19.00	- -	- -	-	4	1	-	1	- -	40	1-12		*(Key on back fold-out)*
DALBEATTIE **Kirkcudbrightshire** Galla Guest House Haugh-of-Urr Road DG5 4LP Tel. Dalbeattie 610425	2 B10	3	4	3	- 9.50	- 18.00	- 14.00	- 92.00	-	5	-	-	2	1800 1900	16	1-12		*(Key on back fold-out)*
DALIBURGH **S Uist, Western Isles** Borrodale Hotel Tel. Lochboisdale 444	3 A10	4	4	5	10.00 17.10	20.00 34.15	17.50 25.00	70.00 140.00	3	10	-	9	2	1900 2030	40	1-12		*(Key on back fold-out)*
DALKEITH **Midlothian** The County Hotel High Street Tel. 031 663 3495	2 D5	3	3	5	15.00 15.00	24.00 24.00	19.00 27.00	- -	-	15	4	17	3	1700 2200	6	1-12		*(Key on back fold-out)*
Birchlea Guest House 127 High Street Tel. 031 663 4280		3	1	1	7.50 9.00	14.00 16.00	- -	- -	-	6	2	-	1	- -	4	1-12		*(Key on back fold-out)*

Name and Address	Map Ref	Bedrooms	Services	Meals	Prices — Bed and Breakfast				B & B and evening meal					Rooms			Facilities		
TOWN / County / Establishment Address Telephone Telex					Single room overnight	Double/twin room overnight	Per person daily	Per person weekly	Single	Double/twin	Family	Private	Public	No. of bedrooms From / Last order	Evening meals	Parking (no. of cars)	Months open (1-12)	Symbols	
					£min £max	£min £max	£min £max	£min £max									Key on back fold-out		
DALLAS, Forres Moray	4 D8																		
Dallas Hotel Tel. Dallas 323		1	3	4	8.50 8.50	17.00 17.00	12.00 16.00	80.00 110.00	-	2	1	-	1	1800 2100	25	1-12			
DALMALLY Argyll	1 F2																		

Craig Lodge
Dalmally, Argyll

Highland Lodge, in beautiful garden, very comfortable for small numbers. Renowned for its good home cooking. All bedrooms have private bathrooms. Salmon fishing on own 4 miles secluded stretch of River Orchy (17 named pools)—July, Aug., Sept. Also good trout fishing on Loch Awe—April, May, June. Roe and Red Deer stalking. Billiard table and Games room. Outside badminton court. Also 3 self-catering houses (sleeping 6-10).
Colour brochure from:
Mr and Mrs Calum S. MacFarlane-Barrow. (Ref. STB).
Telephone Dalmally 216.

Name and Address	Map Ref	Bedrooms	Services	Meals	Single room overnight	Double/twin room overnight	Per person daily	Per person weekly	Single	Double/twin	Family	Private	Public	From / Last order	Evening meals	Parking	Months open	Symbols
Craig Lodge Guest House Tel. Dalmally 216		4	3	3	10.00 15.00	20.00 30.00	18.00 23.00	120.00 150.00	1	4	1	6	1	1900 2000	10	3-11		
Craig Villa Guest House Tel. Dalmally 255		3	4	3	- -	14.00 -	11.00 -	70.00 -	-	4	2	1	1	1800 1900	10	1-12		
Orchy Bank Guest House PA33 1AS Tel. Dalmally 370		3	3	3	7.50 9.50	14.00 17.00	11.50 14.50	75.00 105.00	2	4	2	-	2	1900 2100	8	1-12		
DALMELLINGTON Ayrshire	1 H8																	
Eglinton Hotel 50 Main Street KA6 7QL Tel. Dalmellington 550242		2	2	3	- -	18.00 -	- -	- -	-	4	-	-	1	1700 1900	6	1-12		

VAT is shown at 15%: changes in this rate may affect prices.

Name and Address	Map Ref	Bedrooms	Services	Meals	Single room overnight	Double/twin room overnight	Per person daily	Per person weekly	Single	Double/twin	Family	Private	Public	Evening meals	Parking	Months open	Symbols
DALRY Kirkcudbrightshire	2 A9																

THE LOCHINVAR HOTEL
DALRY, via CASTLE DOUGLAS DG7 3UP

Situated in the Glenkens Valley amidst some of the most beautiful scenery in Scotland. The hotel is centrally situated in South West Scotland in completely unspoiled countryside. An ideal place where one can unwind and relax, or find a different trail or route each day. Only one hour or 50 miles from Gretna, 18 bedrooms. Privately owned.

Telephone: Dalry (064 43) 210

A.A.   R.S.A.C.   R.A.C.**

Name and Address	Map Ref	Bedrooms	Services	Meals	Single room overnight	Double/twin room overnight	Per person daily	Per person weekly	Single	Double/twin	Family	Private	Public	Evening meals	Parking	Months open	Symbols
Lochinvar Hotel DG7 3UP Tel. Dalry 210		4	4	4	11.99 / 11.99	23.95 / 23.95	18.95 / 18.95	119.95 / 119.95	3	14	2	2	4	1900 / 1930	51	1-12	

MILTON PARK HOTEL

DALRY · CASTLE-DOUGLAS KIRKCUDBRIGHTSHIRE DG7 3SR
Telephone Dalry 286
Mr R. C. and Mrs Grayson
Good Hotel Guide
Ashley Courtenay Recommended
R.A.C. R.S.A.C.—Fully Licensed

Stands in its own grounds, beautiful landscape gardens. H. & C. all bedrooms. Electric blankets. Loch fishing. Brown Trout and Rainbow Trout. Ample parking. Brochure on application, S.A.E. please.

Name and Address	Map Ref	Bedrooms	Services	Meals	Single room overnight	Double/twin room overnight	Per person daily	Per person weekly	Single	Double/twin	Family	Private	Public	Evening meals	Parking	Months open	Symbols
Milton Park Hotel DG7 3SR Tel. Dalry 286		3	4	4	12.00 / 12.00	24.00 / 24.00	20.00 / 20.00	125.00 / 125.00	2	13	3	-	4	1930 / 1930	54	4-10	
DALWHINNIE Inverness-shire	4 B11																
Grampian Hotel PH19 1AB Tel. Dalwhinnie 210		-	-	-	12.00 / 12.00	24.00 / 28.00	15.00 / .	. / .	7	16	1	1	8	1900 / 2200	-	1-12	
Loch Ericht Hotel Tel. Dalwhinnie 257		3	3	4	12.50 / 15.00	22.50 / 25.00	17.50 / 20.00	90.00 / 110.00	-	23	4	27	-	1730 / 2100	50	1-12	

Name and Address				Prices				Rooms						Facilities	
TOWN County Establishment Address Telephone Telex	Map Ref	Bedrooms	Services	Meals	Single room overnight	Double/twin room overnight	Per person daily	Per person weekly	Single	Double/twin	Family	Private	Public	Evening meals	Parking (no. of cars)	Months open (1-12)	Symbols
					£min £max	£min £max	£min £max	£min £max						From Last order			Key on back fold-out
DAVIOT Inverness-shire	4 B9																
Meallmore Lodge Hotel Tel. Daviot 206		4	4	5	10.50 16.50	21.00 33.00	18.00 24.00	115.00 155.00	3	14	1	11	3	1900 2200	102	1-12	Key on back fold-out
DERVAIG, by Tobermory Isle of Mull, Argyll	1 C1																

BELLACHROY HOTEL

Dervaig, Isle of Mull, Scotland PA75 6QW
Telephone: Dervaig 225 or 314 (STD Code 068-84)

Peacefully situated midway between Tobermory and the beautiful sands of Calgary Bay this comfortable 17th Century Hotel offers a warm friendly atmosphere and excellent home cooking. River, loch and sea fishing are available nearby plus sea trips to Staffa and the bird sanctuaries of the Treshnish Isles during the summer. For visitors and Bed and Breakfast residents we provide Bar Suppers from mid-May to October. Bar Lunches served all year. Reduced rates for children sharing. Dogs welcome.

| Bellachroy Hotel Tel. Dervaig 225/314 (Res) | | 3 | 3 | 3 | 8.50 9.50 | 17.00 19.00 | 14.00 16.00 | 98.00 105.00 | - | 7 | 1 | - | 2 | 1900 2130 | 50 | 1-12 | |

Country House Hotel.

Donald and Wendy McLean invite you to enjoy the genuine Highland hospitality they offer, on the lovely Hebridean Island of Mull. The Island's Venison, Salmon, Lamb, Beef and our own garden produce are the basis of the menus. The comfort and elegance of what is our home and the uniquely personal attention we give our guests produces an atmosphere of indulgence. Special Holiday Packages available.

Telephone: (06884) 274 Dervaig, Isle of Mull.

| Druimnacroish Country House Hotel Tel. Dervaig 274/212 | | 6 | 4 | 4 | 28.00 28.00 | 56.00 56.00 | 38.00 38.00 | - - | 2 | 5 | - | 7 | - | 2000 - | 28 | 4-10 | |

Scotland's Fishing Heritage

The sea has always played a vital part in the heritage of Scotland, this country with its wandering coastline and hundreds of islands. Today, for holidaymakers it means golden beaches, boat trips and birdwatching; for those who live on the coast it means a hard tradition of gaining a living from the sea.

You can learn about this tradition in the charming fishing villages on the coast, and in the fascinating museums which preserve it.

Write to the Scottish Tourist Board for a FREE pack telling you how to follow **SCOTLAND'S FISHING HERITAGE TRAIL.**

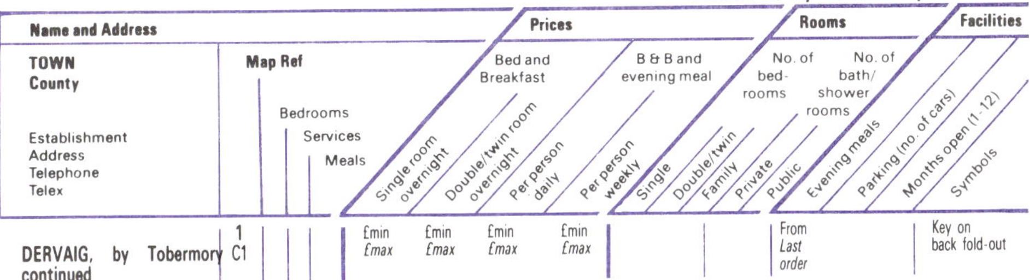

Name and Address	Map Ref	Bedrooms	Services	Meals	Bed and Breakfast Single room overnight	Double/twin room overnight	Per person daily	B & B and evening meal Per person weekly	Single	Double/twin	Family	Private	Public	Evening meals From / Last order	Parking (no. of cars)	Months open (1-12)	Symbols
TOWN County / Establishment Address Telephone Telex					£min £max	£min £max	£min £max	£min £max						From Last order			Key on back fold-out
DERVAIG, by Tobermory continued	1 C1																

Name and Address	Map Ref	Bedrooms	Services	Meals	Single room overnight	Double/twin room overnight	Per person daily	Per person weekly	Single	Double/twin	Family	Private	Public	Evening meals From / Last order	Parking	Months open	Symbols
Quinish House Guest House Quinish Estate Tel. Dervaig 223		4	3	2	11.00 -	21.00 -	18.00 -	- -	2	3	1	1	3	1930 1930	-	4-11	(symbols)
DINGWALL Ross-shire	4 A8																
National Hotel High Street Tel. Dingwall 62166		3	3	4	14.40 -	28.80 -	- -	- -	13	25	4	3	8	1900 2045	40	1-12	(symbols)
Royal Hotel High Street IV15 9HL Tel. Dingwall 62130		4	4	5	12.00 15.00	23.00 27.00	16.00 24.00	112.00 168.00	7	6	1	7	2	1730 2100	20	1-12	(symbols)
DIRLETON East Lothian	2 E4																
Castle Inn Tel. Dirleton 221		3	3	4	11.50 -	23.00 -	17.50 -	105.00 -	2	7	-	-	3	1900 2100	20	1-12	(symbols)
Open Arms Hotel EH39 5EG Tel. Dirleton 241		6	4	5	- 38.50	- 52.80	- -	- -	-	7	-	7	-	1900 2200	60	1-12	(symbols)
DOLLAR Clackmannanshire	2 B4																
Rumbling Bridge Hotel Rumbling Bridge Tel. Fossoway 325		3	3	5	10.00 10.00	20.00 20.00	15.00 20.00	105.00 140.00	8	17	1	-	6	1900 2130	50	1-12	(symbols)

Name and Address	Map Ref	Bedrooms	Services	Meals	Bed and Breakfast — Single room overnight £min £max	Bed and Breakfast — Double/twin room overnight £min £max	Per person daily £min £max	B & B and evening meal — Per person weekly £min £max	Single	Double/twin	Family	Private	Public	No. of bedrooms — From Last order	Evening meals	Parking (no. of cars)	Months open (1-12)	Symbols — Key on back fold-out
DORNIE, by Kyle of Lochalsh Ross-shire	**3** F10																	
Dornie Hotel 8-10 Francis Street Tel. Dornie 205		3	3	4	11.00 12.00	22.00 24.00	18.50 19.50	121.80 128.10	3	13	1	-	4	1900 2000	30	1-12	T £ 🛁 ♀ 🐕 🅟 ♿ ⚓ C V
Loch Duich Hotel Ardelve IV40 8DY Tel. Dornie 213		3	4	4	12.50 -	25.00 -	- -	- -	6	11	1	-	6	1900 2100	26	3-12	T £ ♀ 🐕 ✂ 🅟 ♿ 🛁 ⚡ ❄ 🎡 V ↺ ✎ ⓧ
Camuslongart Guest House Ardelve Tel. Dornie 357		2	2	2	7.00 8.00	14.00 16.00	- -	- -	-	3	1	-	2	1830 1730	6	4-11	🐕 ✂ 🅟 ▦ ♿ 🛁 ⚡ 🎡 V
DORNOCH Sutherland	**4** B6																	
Burghfield House Hotel IV25 3HN Tel. Dornoch 810212		-	-	-	- -	- -	24.00 -	- -	11	29	7	7	12	1930 2000	100	4-10	T £ 🛁 ♀ 🐕 🅟 ▦ ♿ 🛁 ⚡ C ❄ V ↺ 🐟

CARLINGBANK HOTEL

Church Street, Dornoch, Sutherland IV25 3LP
Tel. No: STD 0862 810335   J. G. Ward

★ Comfortable, modern, warm, hotel.
★ Close to the golf courses and beach.
★ Wide range of fresh local food served.
★ Inclusive golf breaks at Dornoch and other courses.
★ Private bathrooms and family suite available.

A WARM WELCOME ALL THE YEAR ROUND

| Carlingbank Hotel Church Street IV25 3LP Tel. Dornoch 335/810335 | | 4 | 4 | 5 | 10.00 15.00 | 18.00 26.00 | 14.00 19.00 | 84.00 122.50 | 1 | 8 | 1 | 4 | 2 | 1930 2300 | 20 | 1-12 | T 🛁 ♀ 🐕 ✂ 🅟 ♿ ⚓ C V ↺ ✎ |

TOURIST INFORMATION CENTRES

All over Scotland there are Tourist Information Centres where friendly, well-informed staff will be pleased to give you information about:

PLACES TO STAY ∙ PLACES TO VISIT ∙ ROUTES TO TAKE ∙ LOCAL EVENTS

There will be lots of helpful literature, some free and some saleable, and many Centres can help you book accommodation.

Look for the information symbol

Name and Address	Map Ref			Prices				B & B and evening meal				Rooms				Facilities	
TOWN County / Establishment Address Telephone Telex		Bedrooms / Services / Meals		Single room overnight £min £max	Double/twin room overnight £min £max	Per person daily £min £max	Per person weekly £min £max	Single	Double/twin	Family	Private	No. of bedrooms / Public	No. of bath/ shower rooms	Evening meals From Last order	Parking (no. of cars)	Months open (1–12)	Symbols / Key on back fold-out
DORNOCH continued	4 B6																
Dornoch Castle Hotel IV25 3SD Tel. Dornoch 216/810216	4	4	4	13.00 15.00	23.00 27.00	21.75 23.75	140.00 154.00	2	16	2	11	2	1930 2030	17	4-10	T ♿ 🛁 ♟ / 🐕 ✗ ♙ 🏠 / ♿ ✦ ❄ ♨ / V ♾ ✎ ❀
Dornoch Hotel Tel. Dornoch 351/810351 Telex 75160	3	4	4	13.00 -	26.00 -	- -	- -	21	84	3	20	20	1900 2100	50	3-11	T ♿ 🛁 ♟ / 🐕 ♙ ♿ ◐ / ✦ ♨ ✎ C / ❄ V ♾
Royal Golf Hotel Tel. Dornoch 283/810283 Telex 75160	5	5	5	21.00 -	42.00 -	- -	- -	8	26	2	30	1	1900 2130	20	1-12	T ♿ 🛁 ♟ / 🐕 ♙ 🏠 ♿ / ◐ ☎ ▭ ⬛ / ✎ ♿ C ✦ / V ♾ ✎
Trentham Hotel IV25 3HZ Tel. Dornoch 391/810391	3	3	5	9.00 9.50	16.00 18.00	15.00 18.00	85.00 90.00	1	4	1	-	2	1900 2100	20	1-12	🛁 ♟ 🐕 ♙ 🏠 / ♿ ♾
DOUNBY Orkney	5 B11																
Smithfield Hotel Tel. Harray 215	3	-	2	10.00 10.50	20.00 21.00	17.00 17.50	107.10 110.60	2	2	-	1	1	1900 -	-	5-10	🛁 ♟ 🐕 ♙ 🏠 / ♿ ⬛ ✎

Dornoch Castle
Dornoch, Sutherland

Open from April to October.
AA** RAC** 'Ashley Courtenay', 'Interplan' & 'Taste of Scotland' recommended.
Privately owned by the Ketchin family since 1979, the hotel has now one of the best restaurants in the region with a wine-list to match. All well-furnished 20 bedrooms are heated and most have private bathrooms. Elegant lounges, character bar and sunny terrace overlooking the well-kept formal gardens and putting lawn. Golf courses and lovely beaches within walking distance. Regular performances of the Dornoch Pipe Band in summer. Gymnasium and sunbed. Golf-packages (in early summer and autumn) from about £50.00 per person includes dinner, bed and breakfast and two days golf.
Resident Proprietors: Mr and Mrs Michael Ketchin. Brochure sent on request. Telephone (0862) 810216.

Name and Address	Map Ref	Bedrooms	Services	Meals	Single room overnight £min/£max	Double/twin room overnight £min/£max	Per person daily £min/£max	Per person weekly £min/£max	Single	Double/twin	Family	Private	Public	Evening meals From/Last order	Parking (no. of cars)	Months open (1-12)	Symbols
DOUNE Perthshire	2 A3																
Creity Hall Hotel, FK16 6AE, Tel. Doune 215		-	-	-	9.77	19.54	-	-	1	1	1	-	2	1900 2100	40	-	(symbols)
Highland Hotel, Main Street, Tel. Doune 536		3	3	4	8.00 / 15.00	13.00 / 24.00	12.00 / 30.00	48.00 / 105.00	1	4	1	-	2	1700 2130	2	1-12	(symbols)
DRUMBEG, by Lairg Sutherland	3 G4																
Drumbeg Hotel, IV27 4NW, Tel. Drumbeg 236		4	4	4	10.50 / 12.50	8.50 / 10.50	15.00 / 17.00	100.00 / 120.00	-	6	-	-	3	1900 2000	12	1-12	(symbols)
DRUMMORE, by Stranraer Wigtownshire	1 G11																
Queens Hotel, Tel. Drummore 300		3	3	3	9.20 / 10.35	-	14.95 / 16.20	95.00 / 105.00	-	4	3	-	3	1800 2100	-	1-12	(symbols)
DRUMNADROCHIT Inverness-shire	4 A9																
Benleva Hotel, IV3 6UH, Tel. Drumnadrochit 288		-	-	-	8.50 / 11.00	19.00 / 24.00	11.00 / 17.50	-	1	4	1	4	1	1900 2130	30	1-12	(symbols)

Loch Ness Lodge Hotel
Drumnadrochit, Inverness-shire

A Luxury hotel (yet our prices are reasonable) surrounded by the majestic peaks of the Western Highlands overlooking Drumnadrochit and the mysterious Loch Ness. All rooms with bath, radio. 3 Lounges, Coffee House, Clan Cakes, Whisky Cakes, Stable Bar. Regular Ceilidhs, Folk-Singing, Dancing. Ideal base for touring, hill-walking, pony-trekking, monster hunting.

D.B.B. from £17 per day.   **TELEPHONE: 04562 342**

Name and Address	Map Ref	Bedrooms	Services	Meals	Single room overnight	Double/twin room overnight	Per person daily	Per person weekly	Single	Double/twin	Family	Private	Public	Evening meals From/Last order	Parking (no. of cars)	Months open (1-12)	Symbols
Loch Ness Lodge Hotel, Tel. Drumnadrochit 342/383		1	-	4	15.00	24.00	19.00	112.00	12	43	4	53	2	1900 2100	50	3-10	(symbols)
Polmaily House, Tel. Drumnadrochit 343		4	4	4	18.50 / 18.50	37.00 / 40.00	-	-	4	4	3	5	2	1930 2130	25	4-11	(symbols)

VAT is shown at 15%: changes in this rate may affect prices.

Name and Address	Map Ref	Bedrooms	Services	Meals	Single room overnight	Double/twin room overnight	Per person daily	Per person weekly	Single	Double/twin	Family	Private	Public	Evening meals	Parking (no. of cars)	Months open (1-12)	Symbols
					£min £max	£min £max	£min £max	£min £max					From Last order			Key on back fold-out
DRYMEN Stirlingshire	1 H4																

Buchanan Arms Hotel, Drymen, Stirlingshire. Tel. 0360-60588

This historic and welcoming hotel is well known for its excellent restaurant and is superbly located within minutes of Loch Lomond and the Trossachs. 35 bedrooms with Private Bath, Tea and Coffee making facilities, colour T.V., Telephone and Radio/Intercom.

Name and Address	Bedrooms	Services	Meals	Single room overnight	Double/twin room overnight	Per person daily	Per person weekly	Single	Double/twin	Family	Private	Public	Last order	Evening meals	Parking	Months open	Symbols
Buchanan Arms Hotel G63 0BQ Tel. Drymen 60588 Telex 778215	4	5	5	34.00 34.00	48.00 48.00	32.00 32.00	168.00 168.00	2	30	3	35	3	1900 2130	60		1-12	
Hollybush Hotel Tel. Drymen 60205	3	2	5	10.00 12.00	24.00 30.00	14.50 16.50	98.00 112.00	-	5	-	-	2	2130 -	4		1-12	

WINNOCK HOTEL

Drymen
Your Gateway to the Highlands

The Winnock Hotel, in the charming village of Drymen, is ideal for the visitor who seeks the peacefulness of village life and yet it is only half an hour's drive from the city of Glasgow and three miles from Loch Lomond.

There is a range of accommodation to suit all pockets. Facilities available nearby include; golf, tennis, bowling, horse riding, water skiing, fishing and shooting.

Booking and information: Tel. Drymen (0360) 60245. *High Season:* June, July, August.

Name and Address	Bedrooms	Services	Meals	Single room overnight	Double/twin room overnight	Per person daily	Per person weekly	Single	Double/twin	Family	Private	Public	Last order	Evening meals	Parking	Months open	Symbols
Winnock Hotel The Square G63 0BL Tel. Drymen 60245	3	3	5	12.50 -	20.00 -	20.00 -	99.50 -	5	25	-	21	2	1700 2200	200		1-12	
DUFFTOWN, Keith Banffshire																4 E9	
Fife Arms Hotel 2 The Square AB5 4AD Tel. Dufftown 20220	1	2	4	10.00 10.00	18.00 18.00	- -	- -	1	1	-	-	1	1700 2000	6		1-12	

DUFFTOWN, Keith - DUMFRIES

Establishment / Address	Map Ref	Bedrooms	Services	Meals	Single room overnight £min/£max	Double/twin room overnight £min/£max	Per person daily £min/£max	Per person weekly £min/£max	Single	Double/twin	Family	Private	Public	Evening meals (From/Last order)	Parking (no. of cars)	Months open	Symbols
DUFFTOWN, Keith continued	4 / E9																Key on back fold-out
Tannochbrae Guest House, 22 Fife Street, AB5 3EH, Tel. Dufftown 20541		3	3	3	7.50 / 8.50	15.00 / 17.00	11.50 / 13.00	70.00 / 80.50	1	3	2	-	3	1800 / 1900	4	1-12	
DULNAIN BRIDGE, by ~~Grantown-on-Spey~~ **Moray**	4 / C9																
Muckrach Lodge Hotel, PH26 3LY, Tel. Dulnain Bridge 257		4	4	4	15.00 / -	28.00 / -	26.00 / -	-	2	6	1	4	4	1930 / 2015	53	1-12	V, K
Skye of Curr Hotel, PH26 3PA, Tel. Dulnain Bridge 345		4	4	4	13.50 / -	27.00 / -	22.00 / -	-	-	6	2	1	3	1830 / 2000	20	1-12	T, V
Balnacrive Guest House, Tel. Dulnain Bridge 228		3	3	3	6.00 / -	12.00 / -	10.00 / -	65.00 / -	1	2	2	-	2	1830 / 1800	10	1-12	C, V
Rosegrove Guest House, Skye of Curr, Tel. Dulnain Bridge 335		-	-	-	8.50 / -	-	12.00 / -	80.00 / -	1	4	1	-	3	-	12	1-12	T, C, V
DUMBARTON **Dunbartonshire**	1 / H5																
Dumbuck Hotel, Tel. Dumbarton 62148/63818		4	4	5	16.50 / 22.00	24.00 / 29.00	22.05 / 27.90	154.35 / 195.30	13	10	2	10	3	1900 / 2130	200	1-12	T, V
DUMFRIES	2 / B9																
Aberdour Hotel, Newall Terrace, Tel. Dumfries 54825		3	3	2	6.50 / 7.00	13.00 / 14.00	10.00 / 11.00	70.00 / 77.00	2	1	6	-	2	1800 / 1800	10	1-12	V
Birkhill Hotel, St Marys Street, Tel. Dumfries 53418		3	3	4	9.75 / -	17.00 / -	-	-	1	5	-	-	2	1800 / 2130	25	1-12	V
Cargenholm Hotel, New Abbey Road, Tel. Dumfries 54988		3	4	5	- / 12.50	- / 18.50	- / 17.50	- / 112.00	-	9	3	2	4	- / 2100	100	1-12	V
Dalston Hotel, Laurieknowe, Tel. Dumfries 54422		3	2	2	9.50 / -	19.00 / -	15.00 / -	100.00 / -	2	5	1	-	1	1800 / 1900	17	1-12	C, V
Eden Hotel, 17-21 English Street, Tel. Dumfries 54393		3	3	5	9.50 / -	17.00 / -	-	-	4	3	-	-	1	1700 / 2200	-	1-12	C
Edenbank Hotel, Laurie Knowe, Tel. Dumfries 52759		3	3	5	10.00 / -	16.00 / -	13.00 / 15.00	-	1	4	3	-	2	1830 / 2100	16	1-12	C, V
Fulwood Private Hotel, Lovers Walk, Tel. Dumfries 52262		3	3	1	7.00 / 7.50	13.00 / 13.00	-	-	-	3	2	-	1	-	-	1-12	

VAT is shown at 15%: changes in this rate may affect prices.

Name and Address (Town / County / Establishment, Address, Telephone, Telex)	Map Ref	Bedrooms	Services	Meals	Single room overnight (£min / £max)	Double/twin room overnight (£min / £max)	Per person daily (£min / £max)	Per person weekly (£min / £max)	Single	Double/twin	Family	Private	Public	Evening meals (From / Last order)	Parking (no. of cars)	Months open (1-12)	Symbols (Key on back fold-out)
DUMFRIES continued	2 B9																
Huntingdon Hotel, 32 Lovers Walk, Tel. Dumfries 54001		3	2	1	6.50 / 7.50	13.00 / 14.00	- / -	- / -	1	2	2	-	2	- / -	6	1-12	(symbols)
Moreig Hotel, 67 Annan Road, Tel. Dumfries 55524		3	3	4	9.50 / 11.50	19.00 / 23.00	11.75 / 17.50	82.25 / 122.50	4	5	-	1	2	1715 / 1930	50	1-12	(symbols)
Newall House Hotel, 22 Newall Terrace, Tel. Dumfries 52676		3	3	2	7.50 / 7.50	14.00 / 14.00	11.00 / 11.00	72.00 / 72.00	1	2	4	-	2	1800 / 1700	7	1-12	(symbols)
Nithsdale Hotel, 9 St Mary's Street, DG1 1HA, Tel. Dumfries 53452		3	3	4	9.50 / 10.50	18.00 / 20.00	- / -	- / -	5	7	1	-	3	1700 / 1830	-	1-12	(symbols)
Queensberry Hotel, 16 English Street, Tel. Dumfries 53526		4	3	5	12.65 / -	18.40 / -	16.15 / -	102.00 / -	4	12	2	7	4	1630 / 2200	-	1-12	(symbols)
Skyline Hotel, Irish Street, DG1 2NP, Tel. Dumfries 62416		4	4	4	13.50 / 15.50	25.00 / 28.00	20.00 / 22.00	108.00 / 118.00	1	3	2	2	2	1800 / 2000	18	1-12	(symbols)
Station Hotel, 49 Lovers Walk, DG1 1LT, Tel. Dumfries 4316		6	5	5	15.00 / 24.00	25.00 / 30.00	- / -	- / -	7	23		30	6	1900 / 2130	60	1-12	(symbols)
Waverley Hotel, St Marys Street, Tel. Dumfries 4588/4080/4848		3	3	4	11.00 / 16.00	20.00 / 28.00	14.00 / 16.00	- / -	7	22	6	2	9	1600 / 2100	20	1-12	(symbols)
Winston Hotel, Rae Street, DG1 1JD, Tel. Dumfries 54433		3	3	4	9.20 / -	18.40 / -	12.65 / -	85.00 / -	6	4	4	-	3	1800 / 1930	6	1-12	(symbols)
Glenlossie Guest House, 75 Annan Road, Tel. Dumfries 54305		3	2	1	7.00 / -	14.00 / -	- / -	- / -	1	4	-	-	1	- / -	6	1-12	(symbols)
Redlands Guest House, 54 Rae Street, Tel. Dumfries 52612		3	2	2	6.00 / 6.50	12.00 / 13.00	8.50 / 9.00	58.00 / 58.00	1	2	1	-	-	1800 / 1800	-	1-12	(symbols)
Saughtree Guest House, 79 Annan Road, DG1 3EG, Tel. Dumfries 52358		3	2	2	6.50 / -	13.00 / -	10.50 / -	73.50 / -	1	2	5	-	3	1800 / 1900	8	1-12	(symbols)
DUNBAR **East Lothian**	2 E4																
Battleblent Hotel, West Barns, Tel. Dunbar 62234		3	3	5	13.95 / 17.50	27.90 / 35.00	19.50 / -	132.50 / -	1	2	3	-	2	1900 / 1930	30	1-12	(symbols)
Bayswell Hotel, Bayswell Park, EH42 1AE, Tel. Dunbar 62225		5	5	5	16.80 / 25.00	26.00 / 35.00	21.00 / 28.00	125.00 / 170.00	1	12	1	10	1	1900 / 2030	16	1-12	(symbols)
Bellevue Hotel, Queens Road, Tel. Dunbar 62322		2	2	1	7.50 / 11.00	15.00 / 18.00	- / -	- / -	10	25	13	-	8	- / -	50	1-12	(symbols)

Name and Address	Map Ref	Bedrooms	Services	Meals	Bed and Breakfast				B & B and evening meal					No of bed rooms		No of bath/shower rooms	Facilities
TOWN County / Establishment Address Telephone Telex					Single room overnight	Double/twin room overnight	Per person daily	Per person weekly	Single	Double/twin	Family	Private	Public	Evening meals	Parking (no of cars)	Months open (1-12)	Symbols
DUNBAR continued	2 E4				£min £max	£min £max	£min £max	£min £max						From Last order			Key on back fold-out
Hillside Hotel Queens Road EH42 1LA Tel. Dunbar 62071/62797		3	5	5	7.50 -	15.00 -	14.04 -	98.28 -	3	6	5	3	2	1900 2200	20	1-12	
Bayview Guest House & Restaurant Bayswell Road EH42 1AB Tel. Dunbar 62778		3	3	2	8.00 -	16.00 -	13.50 -	94.50 -	-	3	4	-	1	1830 1930	-	1-12	
Kiloran Guest House 9 Marine Road EH42 1AR Tel. Dunbar 62286		3	2	2	7.00 8.00	14.00 16.00	8.50 10.00	- -	1	4	1	-	2	1800 2000	6	1-12	
Marine Guest House Marine Road EH42 1AR Tel. Dunbar 63315		3	2	2	7.00 7.00	14.00 14.00	10.00 10.00	60.00 60.00	2	4	3	-	2	1800 1800	-	1-12	
Springfield Guest House Belhaven Road EH42 1NH Tel. Dunbar 62502		3	3	2	10.50 -	19.00 -	16.00 -	100.00 -	1	4	2	-	1	1800 1800	8	1-12	
St Beys Guest House Bayswell Road Tel. Dunbar 63571		3	3	2	8.00 9.00	16.00 18.00	13.00 15.00	91.00 -	1	3	2	-	1	1830 1830	-	1-12	
DUNBLANE Perthshire	2 A3																

Altair Neuk Hotel

Doune Road,
Dunblane, FK15 9HR,
Perthshire.
Tel. (0786) 822562.
Visitors 822187.

Small family run hotel, offering eight attractive bedrooms, some with private facilities, and colour T.V. Our Restaurant serves lunches, high teas, à la carte dinner and suppers. Enjoy a warm welcome and personal service. An ideal base to relax after enjoying the scenic beauty of the central highlands. S.A.E. for colour brochure and tariff. "Taste of Scotland." British Relais Routier. Automobile Association. Travellers Britain.

Name and Address		Bedrooms	Services	Meals	Single room overnight	Double/twin room overnight	Per person daily	Per person weekly	Single	Double/twin	Family	Private	Public	Last order	Evening meals	Months open	Symbols
Altair Neuk Hotel Doune Road FK15 9HR Tel. Dunblane 822562/822187		3	4	5	12.00 14.50	- 24.00	- -	- -	2	4	2	2	2	1700 2100	10	1-12	
Cromlix House FK15 9JT Tel. Dunblane 822125		6	4	4	45.00 50.50	79.00 90.00	65.00 70.50	450.00 500.00	-	10	-	10	-	1930 2130	30	1-12	
Stakis Dunblane Hydro Hotel FK15 0HG Tel. Dunblane 822551 Telex 776284		5	5	5	37.00 -	51.00 -	- -	- -	25	88	13	126	-	1900 2200	200	1-12	

VAT is shown at 15%: changes in this rate may affect prices.

Name and Address	Map Ref	Bedrooms	Services	Meals	Single room overnight £min/£max	Double/twin room overnight £min/£max	Per person daily £min/£max	Per person weekly £min/£max	Single	Double/twin	Family	Private	Public	Evening meals From/Last order	Parking	Months open	Symbols
DUNBLANE continued	2 A3																Key on back fold-out
Westlands Hotel, Doune Road, FK15 9HT, Tel. Dunblane 822118		4	4	4	10.30 / 10.30	20.60 / 22.00	17.30 / 17.30	105.00 / 110.00	1	3	1	-	2	- / -	50	1-12	(symbols)
DUNDEE Angus	2 D2																
The Angus Thistle Hotel, Marketgait, Tel. Dundee 26874, Telex 76456		5	5	6	36.50 / 44.50	47.00 / 53.00	- / -	- / -	10	43	5	43	10	1900 / 2200	11	1-12	(symbols)
Ballinard Hotel, 26 Claypotts Road, Broughty Ferry, Tel. Dundee 739555		-	-	-	22.00 / -	30.00 / -	- / -	- / -	24	12	-	36	-	1900 / 2145	200	1-12	(symbols)
Cambustay Hotel, 8 Dalhousie Road, Broughty Ferry, Tel. Dundee 79290		3	3	4	14.50 / -	25.00 / -	- / -	- / -	3	3	1	-	3	1830 / 2100	123	1-12	(symbols)
Craigtay Hotel, 101 Broughty Ferry Road, Tel. Dundee 451142		4	4	2	14.95 / 14.95	23.00 / 23.00	- / -	- / -	3	12	3	18	-	1800 / 1900	30	1-12	(symbols)
Dunella Hotel, 76 Strathern Road, West Ferry, Tel. Dundee 74156		3	4	4	12.00 / 14.00	20.00 / 24.00	17.00 / 19.00	110.00 / 124.00	4	21	1	9	3	- / 2100	26	1-12	(symbols)
Dunlaw House Hotel, 10 Union Terrace, Tel. Dundee 21703		-	-	-	- / 10.00	- / 18.50	- / 14.50	- / 72.50	2	6	1	-	2	1700 / 1900	7	1-12	(symbols)
Invercarse Hotel, Perth Road, Tel. Dundee 69231, Telex 76608		6	5	5	17.00 / 33.75	25.00 / 45.50	24.70 / 41.45	- / -	21	6	-	27	-	1915 / 2145	200	1-12	(symbols)
Jerome Hotel, 2 Union Terrace, Tel. Dundee 23521		3	3	4	12.50 / -	20.50 / -	15.00 / -	90.00 / -	10	4	1	-	3	1800 / 1930	15	1-12	(symbols)
Magdalen Hotel, 5 Magdalen Place, Tel. Dundee 23541		3	3	2	8.75 / -	17.50 / -	12.00 / -	- / -	3	4	2	-	2	1730 / -	9	1-12	(symbols)
Park Hotel, 40 Coupar Angus Road, Tel. Dundee 610691		3	3	4	15.00 / -	23.00 / -	- / -	- / -	5	7	-	-	4	1830 / 2030	70	1-12	(symbols)
Royal Hotel, 5 Union Street, Tel. Dundee 24074, Telex 57515		3	5	4	17.75 / 25.65	26.65 / 37.40	- / -	- / -	21	37	-	7	9	1830 / 2030	-	1-12	(symbols)
Shaftesbury Hotel, 41 Shaftesbury Road, Tel. Dundee 67339		2	2	1	7.50 / 8.00	15.00 / 15.00	- / -	- / -	3	8	3	-	3	1800 / 1830	-	1-12	(symbols)
Swallow Hotel, Kingsway West, Invergowrie, DD2 5GT, Tel. Dundee 641122, Telex 53168		5	5	5	20.00 / 36.50	31.50 / 50.50	28.50 / 45.00	- / -	-	69	-	69	-	1900 / 2145	150	1-12	(symbols)

DUNDEE - DUNFERMLINE

Name and Address	Map Ref	Bedrooms	Services	Meals	Single room overnight £min/£max	Double/twin room overnight £min/£max	Per person daily £min/£max	Per person weekly £min/£max	Single	Double/twin	Family	Private	Public	Evening meals From/Last order	Parking	Months open	Symbols
DUNDEE continued	2 D2																Key on back fold-out
Tay Hotel, Whitehall Crescent, DD1 4AY, Tel. Dundee 21641, Telex 57515		4	5	5	19.60 / 27.95	30.10 / 41.15	- / -	- / -	48	36	3	30	12	1830 / 2130	-	1-12	
Taychreggan Hotel, 4 Ellieslea Road, Broughty Ferry, Tel. Dundee 78626		3	3	4	13.80 / 16.10	20.70 / 25.30	17.05 / 19.35	119.35 / 135.45	4	5	1	3	3	1730 / 1930	44	1-12	
Woodlands Hotel, 13 Panmure Terrace, Barnhill, Tel. Dundee 79548		3	4	4	14.00 / 17.00	22.00 / 27.00	17.50 / 21.00	- / -	5	13	1	9	3	1750 / 2200	100	1-12	
Raewood Guest House, 105 Magdalen Yard Road, Tel. Dundee 646576		-	-	-	6.00 / -	12.00 / -	8.00 / -	- / -	1	2	1	-	2	- / -	-	1-12	
Halls of Residence, The University of Dundee, DD1 4HN, Tel. Dundee 23181 Ext 240, Telex 76293		2	4	4	8.00 / -	16.00 / -	11.00 / -	77.00 / -	600	50	-	-	103	1800 / -	650	3-4 6-9	
DUNDONNELL Ross-shire	3 G7																
Dundonnell Hotel, IV23 2QS, Tel. Dundonnell 204		4	4	4	15.00 / 20.00	28.00 / 35.00	23.00 / 29.00	122.50 / 175.00	2	18	4	24	-	1900 / 2030	60	4-10	
(See ad. p. 85)																	
DUNFERMLINE Fife	2 C4																
Brucefield Hotel, Woodmill Road, KY11 4AD, Tel. Dunfermline 722199		3	4	3	- / 21.00	23.00 / 30.00	- / -	- / -	3	4	2	6	2	1830 / 2000	60	1-12	
The City Hotel, 18 Bridge Street, Tel. Dunfermline 722538		4	5	4	15.00 / 18.50	23.50 / 26.00	21.50 / 25.00	36.50 / 39.00	9	7	2	10	3	1900 / 2100	30	1-12	
Davaar House, 126 Grieve Street, Tel. Dunfermline 736463		4	4	4	13.00 / 13.00	20.50 / 20.50	17.75 / 17.75	99.75 / 115.25	1	5	-	6	-	1730 / 2000	8	-	
Halfway House Hotel, Main Street, Kingsleat, KY12 OTS, Tel. Dunfermline 731661		6	4	5	22.00 / 25.00	32.00 / 35.00	- / -	- / -	-	12	-	12	-	1900 / 2130	100	1-12	
King Malcolm Thistle Hotel, Wester Pitcorthie, KY11 JDS, Tel. Dunfermline 722611, Telex 727721		5	5	5	35.50 / 42.50	47.00 / 52.00	- / -	- / -	-	48	-	48	-	1830 / 2130	60	1-12	
Pitbauchlie House Hotel, Aberdour Road, Tel. Dunfermline 722282		5	5	4	18.00 / 22.00	25.00 / 30.00	- / -	- / -	-	29	2	27	2	1900 / 2030	90	1-12	

VAT is shown at 15%: changes in this rate may affect prices.

Name and Address	Map Ref	Bedrooms	Services	Meals	Prices								No. of bed-rooms	No. of bath/shower rooms	Facilities	
TOWN County / Establishment Address Telephone Telex					Single room overnight	Double/twin room overnight	Per person daily	Per person weekly	Single	Double/twin	Family	Private	Public / Evening meals	Parking (no. of cars)	Months open (1-12)	Symbols
DUNFERMLINE continued	2 C4				£min £max	£min £max	£min £max	£min £max					From Last order			Key on back fold-out
Garvock Guest House 82 Halbeath Road KY12 7RS Tel. Dunfermline 734689		3	3	2	7.50 -	15.00 -	11.50 -	60.00 -	1	3	1	- 2	1800 1930	7	1-12	
Pitreavie Guest House 3 Aberdour Road KY11 4PB Tel. Dunfermline 724244		3	2	1	8.00 -	15.00 -	- -	- -	1	3	1	- 2	- -	4	1-12	
DUNKELD Perthshire	2 B1															

Atholl Arms Hotel
Bridgehead, Dunkeld, Perthshire PH8 0AH.

Our family run hotel could be perfect for your holiday or short break. We offer friendly personal service in warm comfortable surroundings. Situated in central Perthshire, near the A9, it is ideal for touring, fishing, golfing or simply breaking your journey.

For further details write or ring:− (03502) 219.

AA/RAC** Relais Routiers, Good Hotel Guide, Minotels.

Name and Address	Map Ref	Bedrooms	Services	Meals	Single room overnight	Double/twin room overnight	Per person daily	Per person weekly	Single	Double/twin	Family	Private	Public / Evening meals	Parking	Months open	Symbols
Atholl Arms Hotel Tayside Terrace PH8 0AH Tel. Dunkeld 219		3	4	4	11.00 30.00	22.00 32.00	18.50 37.50	112.75 234.50	5	15	-	4 5	1900 2100	20	1-12	
Perth Arms Hotel High Street PH8 0AJ Tel. Dunkeld 270		-	-	-	8.50 11.00	17.00 22.00	- -	- -	-	6	-	- 1	1700 -	20	1-12	
Waterbury Guest House Murthly Terrace, Birnam PH8 0BG Tel. Dunkeld 324		3	2	2	6.00 7.50	12.00 15.00	10.00 11.50	70.00 80.00	1	4	1	- 2	1800 1800	4	1-12	
DUNLOP Ayrshire	1 H6															
Struther Farm Guest House 17 Newmill Road KA3 4DT Tel. Dunlop 346		3	3	2	7.50 -	15.00 -	14.50 -	96.50 -	-	4	2	- 3	1830 2030	20	1-12	

VAT is shown at 15%: changes in this rate may affect prices.

Name and Address	Map Ref	Bedrooms	Services	Meals	Single room overnight	Double/twin room overnight	Per person daily	Per person weekly	Single	Double/twin	Family	Private	Public	Evening meals	Parking (no. of cars)	Months open (1-12)	Symbols
					£min £max	£min £max	£min £max	£min £max					From Last order			Key on back fold-out
DUNNET Caithness	4 D2																
Northern Sands Hotel Tel. Barrock 270		3	2	5	12.00 12.00	24.00 24.00	18.00 19.00	106.00 109.00	5	8	-	2	3	2000 2200	40	1-12	
DUNOON Argyll	1 G5																
Abbeyhill Hotel Dhailling Road, Kirn PA23 8EA Tel. Dunoon 2204		4	4	5	20.00 22.00	32.00 35.00	26.50 28.50	150.00 160.00	4	6	2	12	-	1900 2100	40	1-12	

ABBOT'S BRAE HOTEL

**Bullwood, West Bay, Dunoon PA23 7QJ.
Tel Dunoon (0369) 5021.**

A country house family run hotel with magnificent sea views. Excellent amenities include teamakers, radio, colour T.V. in all rooms. Some with en-suite private bathrooms. 3 nights incl. dinner and VAT from £42. Special package deals include: Honeymoons, Golf, Forest Walks, 3-Centre.

Name and Address	Bedrooms	Services	Meals	Single room overnight	Double/twin room overnight	Per person daily	Per person weekly	Single	Double/twin	Family	Private	Public	Evening meals	Parking	Months open	Symbols
Abbot's Brae Hotel West Bay Tel. Dunoon 5021/2192	4	4	4	9.00 17.00	18.00 21.00	14.00 15.75	88.00 105.00	1	3	3	3	1	1830 1930	5	2-11	
Albany Hotel John Street Tel. Dunoon 3044	2	3	2	8.63 -	17.25 -	13.23 -	- -	1	6	2	-	2	1800 1700	-	1-12	
Ardenslate Hotel James Street, Hunter's Quay Tel. Dunoon 2068	3	3	4	10.00 -	20.00 -	14.50 -	94.50 -	3	3	3	-	3	1815 2030	7	4-10	
Argyll Hotel Argyll Street Tel. Dunoon 2059	3	3	4	10.25 -	20.50 -	13.00 -	- -	7	19	4	6	7	1830 2000	-	1-12	
Cedars Hotel Alexandra Parade, East Bay PA23 8AF Tel. Dunoon 2425	3	4	4	9.20 -	17.25 -	14.95 -	85.67 -	4	8	2	2	2	1900 1930	-	2-11	
Enmore Hotel Marine Parade PA23 8HH Tel. Dunoon 2230	4	5	5	20.00 -	- 58.00	30.00 -	182.00 -	3	10	3	9	2	1730 2030	20	1-12	
Esplanade Hotel West Bay PA23 7HU Tel. Dunoon 4070	3	4	4	9.50 12.50	19.00 25.00	14.00 17.00	80.00 100.00	4	36	13	16	13	1830 2030	12	4-10	
Lyall Cliff Hotel Alexandra Parade, East Bay PA23 8AW Tel. Dunoon 2041	4	4	4	9.00 12.00	18.00 25.00	14.00 17.00	91.50 110.00	2	7	3	5	2	1830 -	15	4-10	

Name and Address	Map Ref	Bedrooms	Services	Meals	Single room overnight £min/£max	Double/twin room overnight £min/£max	Per person daily £min/£max	Per person weekly £min/£max	Single	Double/twin	Family	Private	Public	No. of bedrooms From/Last order	No. of bath/shower rooms	Evening meals	Parking (no. of cars)	Months open (1-12)	Symbols
DUNOON continued	1 G5														From Last order				Key on back fold-out
Marlborough Hotel, Hunter's Quay, Tel. Dunoon 2439		4	4	4	7.50 / -	17.00 / -	11.50 / 12.50	75.00 / 80.00	2	-	4	-	2	1730 / 2130	6			1-12	
Rosscairn Private Hotel, Hunter Street, Kirn, Tel. Dunoon 4344		3	4	2	9.25 / 10.00	18.50 / 20.00	12.00 / 13.25	80.00 / 89.00	-	8	2	10	1	1900 / 1900	7			1-12	
Slatefield Hotel, Marine Parade, Kirn, Tel. Dunoon 4348		3	4	3	10.00 / 11.00	18.00 / 20.00	13.00 / 15.00	75.00 / 80.00	1	5	2	-	4	1830 / 1930	12			1-12	
St Ives Hotel, West Bay, Tel. Dunoon 2400/4825		3	3	4	9.50 / -	- / -	- / -	- / -	3	7	1	-	3	1900 / 1930	5			3-10	
Ann Mar Guest House, West Bay, Tel. Dunoon 5147		-	-	-	7.50 / -	15.00 / -	12.00 / -	84.00 / -	-	6	2	-	3	1800 / 1930	-			1-12	
Sebright Guest House, 41 Alexandra Parade, Tel. Dunoon 2099		3	2	2	7.50 / -	15.00 / -	10.00 / -	70.00 / -	-	3	2	-	1	1800 / 2000	5			1-12	
DUNS Berwickshire	2 F5																		
Barniken House Hotel, 18 Murray Street, Tel. Duns 82466		3	3	4	10.00 / -	18.00 / -	14.50 / -	95.00 / -	1	3	-	-	2	1800 / 1800	12			1-12	
Black Bull Hotel, Black Bull Street, Tel. Duns 83379		3	4	5	10.50 / -	19.00 / -	14.00 / 17.00	91.00 / 112.00	3	5	2	-	4	1830 / 2130	10			1-12	
White Swan Hotel, 32-34 Market Square, Tel. Duns 83338		-	-	-	8.50 / -	15.75 / -	- / -	- / -	-	4	2	-	2	1800 / 2100	8			1-12	
DUNTULM Isle of Skye, Inverness-shire	3 D7																		
Duntulm Castle Hotel, Tel. Duntulm 213		4	4	4	12.00 / -	22.00 / -	19.00 / -	- / -	5	20	2	7	8	1900 / 2030	-			1-12	
DUNVEGAN Isle of Skye, Inverness-shire	3 C9																		
Atholl House Hotel, Tel. Dunvegan 219		2	3	1	7.00 / 10.00	15.00 / 20.00	13.00 / 16.00	80.00 / 112.00	5	4	3	-	3	- / -	12			4-10	

VAT is shown at 15%: changes in this rate may affect prices.

Name and Address	Map Ref	Bedrooms / Services / Meals	Prices — Bed and Breakfast: Single room overnight	Double/twin room overnight	Per person daily	B & B and evening meal: Per person weekly	Rooms: Single	Double/twin	Family	Private	Public	No. of bath/shower rooms	Evening meals (Last order)	Parking (no. of cars)	Months open (1-12)	Facilities / Symbols
TOWN County — Establishment Address Telephone Telex			£min £max	£min £max	£min £max	£min £max					From		Last order			Key on back fold-out
DUNVEGAN continued	3 C9															

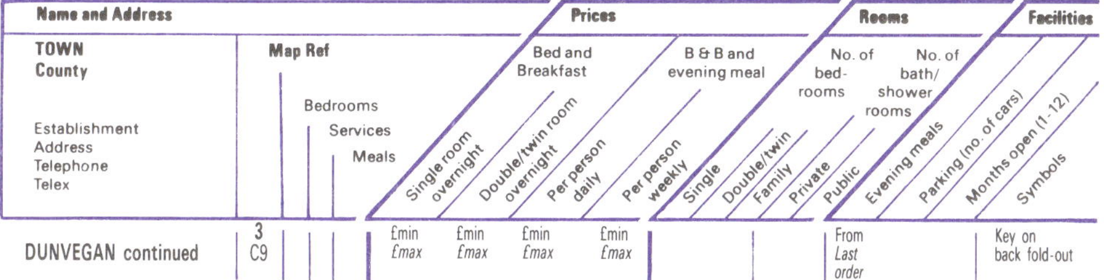

DUNVEGAN, with its historic castle standing proudly in lovely woods and its magnificent cliff scenery, is one of the most attractive areas of Skye. DUNVEGAN HOTEL is on the shore at the sheltered head of a sea loch. It was originally a way-side Inn and has been extended and modernised to offer a high standard of comfort. All areas are centrally heated, and the Bedrooms have private shower facilities. The Hotel is fully licensed (three bars) and there is a very extensive selection of fine Malt Whisky including the islands' own Talisker Malt. Local foods are prepared in the traditional way and there is also an a la carte service; chidrens' portions are available on some dishes.

EXTRA FACILITIES:
Nightly traditional entertainment. Sea angling and pleasure trips. Greenhill Guest House accommodation. Credit card facilities.

Name and Address	Map Ref	Bedrooms	Services	Meals	Single room overnight	Double/twin room overnight	Per person daily	Per person weekly	Single	Double/twin	Family	Private	Public	No. of bath/shower rooms	Evening meals (Last order)	Parking	Months open	Facilities
Dunvegan Hotel Tel. Dunvegan 202		4	4	4	12.00	22.00	18.00	115.00	-	4	2	-	2		1830 2130	40	4-10	
Argyll Guest House Kensalroag Tel. Dunvegan 230	1	2	2		5.25 5.75	10.50 11.50	8.75 9.00	-	1	4	1	-	2		1900 -	6	4-10	
Roskhill Guest House Roskhill Tel. Dunvegan 317	3	3	2		- -	14.50 15.00	12.00 12.75	84.00 86.00	-	3	2	-	1		1915 1800	6	3-12	
DURNESS Sutherland	3 H3																	
Parkhill Hotel IV27 4PN Tel. Durness 209		3	3	4	8.00 9.00	16.00 18.00	12.00 13.00	80.00 -	2	8	-	-	2		1900 2030	-	4-10	
West End Guest House Durine IV27 4PN Tel. Durness 246		2	3	2	- -	- -	12.75 -	- -	-	3	5	-	4		1900 2000	12	4-10	

TOURING AROUND?

It's easy to make your accommodation arrangements when you use the wide network of Tourist Information Centres in Scotland.
If you plan to stay in a certain area, call in at the Tourist Information Centre, where a **LOCAL BOOKING** will be made for you. Look for centres showing the **BLUE** bed symbols.

If you prefer to keep on the move, many Centres also operate the Book-a-Bed-Ahead scheme, through which you can make a booking anywhere in Scotland for the same night and subsequent nights—and at some Centres, for the next night and subsequent nights. Look for the **RED** bed symbol.

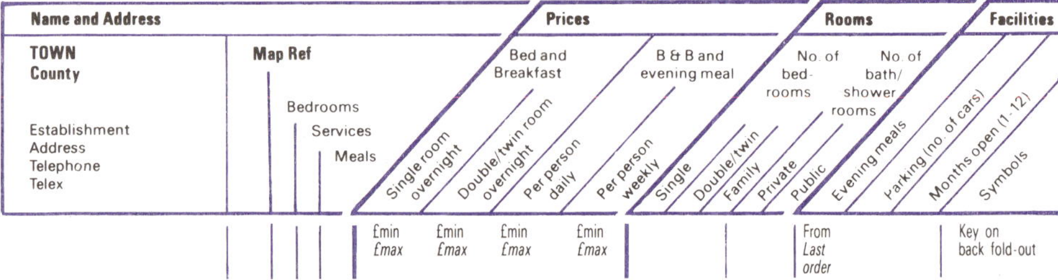

Name and Address	Map Ref	Bedrooms	Services	Meals	Single room overnight £min/£max	Double/twin room overnight £min/£max	Per person daily £min/£max	Per person weekly £min/£max	Single	Double/twin	Family	Private	Public	Evening meals From/Last order	Parking (no. of cars)	Months open (1-12)	Symbols

DUROR, by Appin
Argyll — Map Ref 1 F1

Have a really economical holiday in the Highlands.
Our menu is a blend of good home cooking with dishes that will appeal to the sophisiticate.
Half a mile from the Beach. Fishing, boating and riding—all available.

You will be staying at the Inn in which Allan Breck drank—
you will be drinking in our bar 'Kidnapped' scene of R. L. Stevenson's world famous book.

Send for colour brochure to:

DUROR HOTEL
Duror, Appin, Argyll.
Telephone: Duror (063 174) 219

Name and Address	Map Ref	Bedrooms	Services	Meals	Single room overnight £min/£max	Double/twin room overnight £min/£max	Per person daily £min/£max	Per person weekly £min/£max	Single	Double/twin	Family	Private	Public	Evening meals From/Last order	Parking	Months open	Symbols
Duror Hotel Tel. Duror 219		3	3	4	7.35 / 9.30	14.70 / 18.60	15.40 / 16.25	95.39 / 114.45	2	9	1	4	2	1900 / 2100	60	1-12	

Highland Lodge set in 5 acres of superb gardens overlooking Loch Linnhe. Excellent centre for hill walking, touring, island trips or just relaxation. Nearby Oban, Fort William and Glencoe. 5 miles from Ballachulish Bridge. Attentive staff under the personal supervision of the owners.

26 Modern Rooms—Bath en suite
Reasonably Priced—Relaxed Atmosphere
Children free accommodation in parents room
Interesting Food—Bar Buttery. Colour T.V. in all Bedrooms.
Good Hotel Guide ★ Egon Ronay
Ashley Courtenay ★
A.A. ★ ★ R.A.C.

Glen Duror, Appin, Argyll
Tel Duror (063 174) 268

'Special Breaks' available. A 'Tour Scotland' member see page 307

Name and Address	Map Ref	Bedrooms	Services	Meals	Single room overnight £min/£max	Double/twin room overnight £min/£max	Per person daily £min/£max	Per person weekly £min/£max	Single	Double/twin	Family	Private	Public	Evening meals From/Last order	Parking	Months open	Symbols
The Stewart Hotel PA38 4BW Tel. Duror 268		4	5	5	18.00 / 24.50	27.00 / 43.00	24.00 / 34.00	147.00 / 175.00	-	22	7	29	-	1900 / 2230	40	4-10	
EAGLESHAM **Renfrewshire**	1 H6																
Eglinton Arms Hotel Tel. Eaglesham 2631		5	4	5	26.00 / -	33.50 / -	- / -	- / -	7	5	-	12	-	1900 / 2200	50	1-12	

VAT is shown at 15%: changes in this rate may affect prices.

Name and Address / TOWN, County, Establishment, Address, Telephone, Telex	Map Ref	Bedrooms	Services	Meals	Single room overnight £min £max	Double/twin room overnight £min £max	Per person daily £min £max	Per person weekly £min £max	Single	Double/twin	Family	Private	Public	No. of bedrooms From / Last order	No. of bath/shower rooms	Evening meals	Parking (no. of cars)	Months open (1-12)
EARLSTON Berwickshire	2 E6																	
White Swan Hotel, The Square, Tel. Earlston 283		3	2	4	8.50 -	16.00 -	11.00 -	57.00 -	1	2	2	-	1	1800 2200	10		1-12
EASDALE, by Oban Argyll	1 D3																	
Easdale Inn, PA34 4RF, Tel. Balvicar 256		3	3	4	9.50 11.50	17.00 19.00	15.00 17.50	90.00 110.00	-	6	1	-	2	1930 2030	10		1-12
EAST KILBRIDE Lanarkshire	2 A6																	
Crutherland Hotel, Tel. East Kilbride 24611		6	5	5	22.00 25.00	30.00 30.00	- -	- -	16	6	2	16	4	1830 2230	250		1-12
The Queensway Motel, Eaglesham Road, Tel. East Kilbride 22747		-	-	-	17.00 -	28.50 -	- -	- -	-	10	-	10	-	1830 2300	100		1-12
The Stuart Thistle Hotel, Cornwall Way, Tel. East Kilbride 21161, Telex 778504		3	5	5	34.50 39.50	49.00 54.00	- -	- -	15	14	1	29	-	1900 2130	-		1-12
Torrance Hotel, Main Street, Tel. East Kilbride 25241		4	4	4	19.00 -	28.50 -	- -	- -	17	9	-	8	5	1700 2100	100		1-12
EAST LINTON East Lothian	2 E4																	
The Crown Hotel, Tel. East Linton 860335		1	2	2	10.00 -	20.00 -	14.00 -	84.00 -	-	3	2	-	2	1900 -	-		1-12
Harvesters Hotel, EH40 3DP, Tel. East Linton 860395/860429		4	4	4	15.00 25.00	30.00 40.00	22.50 32.50	161.00 189.00	2	5	3	7	2	1900 2030	46		1-12
EDDERTON, by Tain Ross-shire	4 B7																	
Aultnamain Inn, IV19 1LH, Tel. Edderton 238		3	3	5	12.00 15.00	22.00 25.00	18.00 23.00	112.00 115.00	-	3	-	-	1	1800 2200	30		1-12
EDINBANE Isle of Skye, Inverness-shire	3 C8																	
Edinbane Hotel, Tel. Edinbane 263		-	-	-	8.00 9.00	16.00 18.00	14.50 16.00	87.00 96.00	2	4	2	-	2	1900 2050	30		1-12

Name and Address		Prices					Rooms					Facilities			
TOWN / County / Establishment Address Telephone Telex	Map Ref / Bedrooms / Services / Meals	Bed and Breakfast — Single room overnight £min £max	Double/twin room overnight £min £max	Per person daily £min £max	B & B and evening meal — Per person weekly £min £max	No. of bedrooms — Single	Double/twin	Family	No. of bath/shower rooms — Private	Public	Evening meals — From / Last order	Parking (no. of cars)	Months open (1-12)	Symbols

Name and Address	Map Ref	Bedrooms	Services	Meals	Single room overnight £min £max	Double/twin room overnight £min £max	Per person daily £min £max	Per person weekly £min £max	Single	Double/twin	Family	Private	Public	Evening meals From/Last order	Parking	Months open	Symbols
EDINBURGH	2 D5																
Adria Hotel 11-12 Royal Terrace EH7 5AB Tel. 031 556 7875		4	4	2	13.80 / 18.40	23.00 / 29.90	- / -	- / -	2	18	5	6	7	- / -	-	1-12	
Afton Hotel 6 Grosvenor Crescent EH12 5EP Tel. 031 225 7033		3	2	1	12.50 / 15.00	21.00 / 24.00	- / -	- / -	-	7	2	1	2	- / -	-	1-12	
Ailsa Craig Hotel 24 Royal Terrace EH7 5AH Tel. 031 556 1022		4	4	4	9.77 / 10.92	19.55 / 21.85	14.37 / 15.52	86.25 / 93.15	3	7	3	3	3	- / -	-	1-12	
Albany Hotel 39 Albany Street EH1 3QY Tel. 031 556 0397/8 Telex 727079		3	6	6	28.50 / 35.50	31.00 / 46.50	- / -	- / -	5	15	1	21	-	1830 / 2200	-	1-12	
Alexander Hotel 21 Spring Gardens EH8 8HU Tel. 031 661 1157		2	3	1	7.00 / 8.00	15.00 / 15.00	- / -	- / -	1	4	2	-	1	- / -	6	1-12	
Allison Hotel 17 Mayfield Gardens EH9 2AX Tel. 031 667 8049		3	3	1	7.50 / 10.50	14.00 / 18.00	11.00 / 14.00	70.00 / 74.00	1	4	6	3	3	- / -	6	1-12	

Adria Hotel
11/12 Royal Terrace, Edinburgh EH7 5AB

Very central – Family supervised – Central heating – TV
Lounge – Hot and cold – Some private baths or showers –
Special terms for coach parties – A.A. Listed.
Office Tel: 031-556 7875 Guests: 031-556 2654

DON'T KNOW SCOTLAND TOO WELL?

You probably know whether you want to stay in the north-east, the south-west, or
some other part of the country—but you may not know all the little towns and
villages in that area.

That's where the MAPS in this book can help you.

Simply look at the page showing the area you have chosen, then check the names
marked on that part of the map. Each name has a corresponding entry in the text,
with a list of accommodation which you can contact.

It's easy!

VAT is shown at 15%: changes in this rate may affect prices.

Name and Address	Map Ref	Bedrooms	Services	Meals	Single room overnight	Double/twin room overnight	Per person daily	Per person weekly	Single	Double/twin	Family	Private	Public	Evening meals (From/Last order)	Parking (no. of cars)	Months open (1-12)	Symbols
EDINBURGH continued	2 D5				£min £max	£min £max	£min £max	£min £max						From Last order		Key on back fold-out	

This family run hotel has been expanded and improved over the last 25 years to now provide 45 bedrooms, 31 with private bathrooms and most served by a lift. It is fully licenced and with ample lounge and dining rooms.

ARDEN HOTEL

17-20 Royal Terrace, Edinburgh EH7 5AQ. Telephones 031-556 8688, 031-556 5879, 031-556 6904.

It is situated in a magnificent listed Georgian Terrace with wooded gardens to the front and rear. Yet this peaceful location is only a short walk from Princes Street and within easy reach of the bus and railway station.

Terms and brochure on request. Coach parties catered for – Special terms on application.

Name and Address	Bedrooms	Services	Meals	Single room overnight £min / £max	Double/twin room overnight £min / £max	Per person daily £min / £max	Per person weekly £min / £max	Single	Double/twin	Family	Private	Public	Evening meals From / Last order	Parking	Months open	Symbols
Arden Hotel 17-20 Royal Terrace EH7 5AQ Tel. 031 556 8688/5879/6904	4	4	2	13.80 / 27.60	23.00 / 40.25	- / -	- / -	5	22	18	31	4	1800 / 1900	-	1-12	(symbols)
Argus Hotel 14 Coates Gardens EH12 5LB Tel. 031 337 6159	2	3	2	9.00 / -	16.00 / -	- / -	- / -	3	5	2	3	2	- / -	-	1-12	(symbols)
Ashlyn Private Hotel 42 Inverleith Row EH3 5PY Tel. 031 552 2954	2	3	2	9.00 / -	16.50 / -	13.00 / -	91.00 / -	2	3	3	-	2	1830 / 1200	1	1-12	(symbols)
Avon Hotel 1-2 Spence Street EH16 5AG Tel. 031 667 8681	3	3	1	8.05 / 10.25	14.95 / 18.40	- / -	- / -	2	7	2	-	3	- / -	9	1-12	(symbols)
Balfour House Hotel 92 Pilrig Street EH6 5AY Tel. 031 554 2106	3	3	4	7.50 / 10.00	15.00 / 17.00	11.00 / 12.50	75.00 / 90.00	1	13	9	-	5	1800 / 1900	7	1-12	(symbols)
The Barnton Thistle Hotel Queensferry Road EH4 6AS Tel. 031 339 1144 Telex 727928	6	6	6	38.50 / 42.50	49.00 / 54.00	- / -	- / -	3	42	3	48	-	1900 / 2200	100	1-12	(symbols)
Belmont Hotel 10-11 Carlton Terrace EH7 5DD Tel. 031 556 6146	3	3	1	12.50 / 14.50	23.00 / 30.00	- / -	- / -	3	8	2	-	2	- / -	-	4-10	(symbols)
Beverley Hotel 40 Murrayfield Avenue EH12 6AY Tel. 031 337 1128	3	3	2	9.50 / 10.50	17.00 / 18.00	13.00 / -	- / -	3	4	2	-	2	1800 / -	-	1-12	(symbols)

Name and Address	Map Ref	Bedrooms	Services	Meals	Bed and Breakfast			B & B and evening meal	No. of bedrooms				No. of bath/shower rooms	Evening meals	Parking (no. of cars)	Months open (1-12)	Symbols
TOWN / County / Establishment / Address / Telephone / Telex					Single room overnight	Double/twin room overnight	Per person daily	Per person weekly	Single	Double/twin	Family	Private	Public				Key on back fold-out
EDINBURGH continued	2 D5				£min £max	£min £max	£min £max	£min £max						From Last order			
Boisdale Hotel, 9 Coates Gardens, EH12 5LG, Tel: 031 337 1134		4	3	2	12.00 14.00	24.00 28.00	15.50 17.50	- -	2	7	2	11	2	1830 2030	-	1-12	
Braid Hills Hotel, 134 Braid Road, EH10 6JD, Tel: 031 447 8888		4	5	5	21.00 28.50	30.00 46.00	27.50 31.50	- -	21	32	7	29	8	1900 2145	35	1-12	

"HAPPY TO ACCOMMODATE YOU"

**Bruntsfield Place, Edinburgh EH10 4HH.
Telephone 031-229 1393. Telex 727897 DOOCOT-G.**

A privately owned three-star hotel offering a friendly, personal service. The hotel, overlooking the Park a few minutes from Princes Street is modern and comfortable. Most rooms have private bathroom, colour T.V., radio and direct dial telephone. Fine food in the Park Restaurant. Relaxing Princes Cocktail Bar or our lively Kings Bar.

AA***

Name and Address	Bedrooms	Services	Meals	Single room overnight	Double/twin room overnight	Per person daily	Per person weekly	Single	Double/twin	Family	Private	Public	Evening meals (From Last order)	Parking	Months open	Symbols
Bruntsfield Hotel, 69-74 Bruntsfield Place, EH10 4HH, Tel: 031 229 1393, Telex 727897	4	5	5	20.00 26.00	28.00 42.00	28.00 32.00	- -	12	35	7	38	6	1830 2145	27	1-12	
Cairn Hotel, 10-18 Windsor Street, EH7 5JR, Tel: 031 556 2807	4	3	4	14.80 17.80	22.80 25.80	19.80 22.80	124.74 175.56	6	35	9	15	12	1800 2100	-	1-12	
Caledonian Hotel, Princes Street, EH1 2AB, Tel: 031 225 2433, Telex 72179	6	6	6	40.50 54.50	61.00 91.00	- -	- -	75	178	9	253	10	1900 2300	150	1-12	
Carlton Hotel, North Bridge, EH1 1SB, Tel: 031 556 7277, Telex 778215	5	5	5	37.00 37.00	54.00 54.00	35.00 35.00	189.00 189.00	49	45	4	97	-	1800 2100	-	1-12	
Christopher North House Hotel, 6 Gloucester Place, EH3 6EF, Tel: 031 225 2720	3	4	4	24.00 -	29.00 -	- -	- -		8	3	3	2	1830 2030	-	1-12	

(See ad. p. 95)

VAT is shown at 15%: changes in this rate may affect prices.

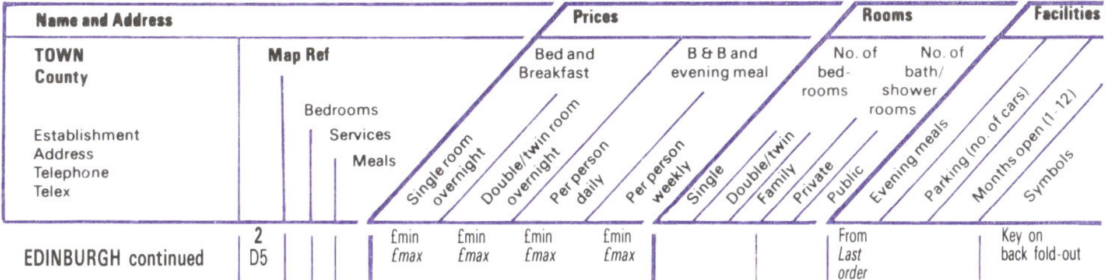

Clarendon Hotel,
Grosvenor Street, Edinburgh.
Tel. 031-337 7033
This quiet hotel lies conveniently in the attractive west-end of Edinburgh within easy walking distance of Princes Street. 50 bedrooms with Private Bath, Tea and Coffee making facilities and colour T.V.

Carlton Hotel,
North Bridge, Edinburgh.
Tel: 031-556 7277
One of the leading Edinburgh hotels, with an excellent Carvery Restaurant, situated close to Waverley Station overlooking Princes Street. 100 bedrooms with Private Bath, Tea and Coffee making facilities, colour T.V., Telephone and Radio/Intercom.

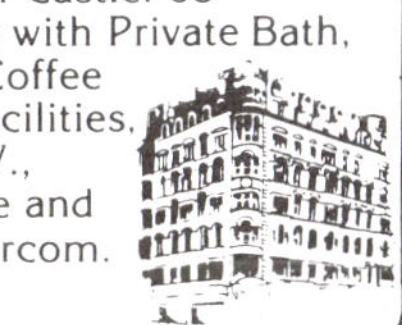

Old Waverley Hotel,
Princes Street, Edinburgh.
Tel. 031-556 4648
The hotel occupies one of the finest positions on Princes Street, opposite the Scott Monument, looking across the Gardens to Edinburgh Castle. 68 bedrooms with Private Bath, Tea and Coffee making facilities, colour T.V., Telephone and Radio/Intercom.

Name and Address	Bedrooms	Services	Meals	Single room overnight £min/£max	Double/twin room overnight £min/£max	Per person daily £min/£max	Per person weekly £min/£max	Single	Double/twin	Family	Private	Public	Evening meals From/Last order	Parking	Months open	Symbols
Clarendon Hotel, 22 Grosvenor Street, EH12 5EG, Tel. 031 337 7033, Telex 778215	3	4	4	33.00 / 33.00	46.00 / 46.00	31.00 / 31.00	161.00 / 161.00	9	36	5	50	4	1830 / 2030	-	4-10	T, symbols, V, C, U
Claymore Hotel, 6 Royal Terrace, EH7 5AG, Tel. 031 556 2693	3	4	3	10.00 / 10.00	20.00 / 20.00	- / -	- / -	2	7	2	-	4	- / -	-	1-12	symbols, C
Clifton Hotel, 18 Hopetoun Crescent, EH7 4AY, Tel. 031 556 1180	2	2	2	8.50 / -	17.00 / -	13.50 / -	80.00 / -	2	5	3	-	1	1800 / 1900	-	1-12	T, M, V
Clifton Private Hotel, 1 Clifton Terrace, Haymarket, EH12 5DR, Tel. 031 337 1002	2	3	2	9.20 / 10.35	18.40 / 20.70	12.65 / 13.80	- / -	2	3	5	-	2	1730 / 1730	-	1-12	M, V
The Counan Hotel, 6 Minto Street, EH9 1RG, Tel. 031 667 4454	2	1	2	10.00 / -	20.00 / 24.00	15.00 / 18.00	- / -	-	3	1	-	1	-	6	1-12	symbols
County Hotel, 8-10 Abercromby Place, EH3 6LF, Tel. 031 556 2333, Telex 727127	5	5	5	17.00 / 22.00	30.00 / 42.00	20.00 / 27.00	87.50 / 110.00	17	35	5	19	8	1830 / 2045	12	1-12	T, V, C, U, symbols
Craigelachie Private Hotel, 21 Murrayfield Avenue, EH12 6AU, Tel. 031 337 4076/2619	3	3	2	10.00 / 11.00	17.50 / 19.00	- / -	- / -	1	3	3	-	2	1830 / 1830	-	1-12	C, V, U
Cramond Brig Hotel, Queensferry Road, Cramond Brig, Tel. 031 339 4350	-	-	-	10.50 / -	21.00 / -	- / -	- / -	1	2	-	-	1	1830 / 2130	50	1-12	T, V

Name and Address	Map Ref	Bedrooms	Services	Meals	Prices: Bed and Breakfast — Single room overnight (£min/£max)	Double/twin room overnight	B & B and evening meal — Per person daily	Per person weekly	Rooms: No. of bedrooms — Single	Double/twin	Family	No. of bath/shower rooms — Private	Public	Evening meals (last order)	Parking (no. of cars)	Months open (1-12)	Symbols
EDINBURGH continued	2 D5				£min / £max	£min / £max	£min / £max	£min / £max				From		Last order			Key on back fold-out
Crest Hotel Edinburgh, Queensferry Road, EH4 EHL, Tel. 031 332 2442, Telex 72541		6	5	5	40.50 / -	55.00 / -	- / -	- / -	-	100	20	120	-	1830 2145	120	1-12	(see key)
Dean Hotel, 10 Clarendon Crescent, EH4 1PT, Tel. 031 332 0308		4	4	2	12.50 / 14.00	26.00 / 32.00	- / -	- / -	2	8	2	5	1	- / -	-	1-12	(see key)
Donmaree Hotel, 21 Mayfield Gardens, EH9 2BX, Tel. 031 667 3641/2		3	5	5	32.20 / -	46.00 / -	- / -	- / -	4	14	2	11	4	1830 2100	8	1-12	(see key)
Dorstan Private Hotel, 7 Priestfield Road, EH16 5HJ, Tel. 031 667 6721		4	3	2	8.75 / 9.50	17.50 / 22.00	15.00 / 15.75	- / -	2	10	2	4	3	- / -	9	1-12	(see key)
Drummond Hotel, 34 Drummond Place, EH3 6PW, Tel. 031 556 3261/3059		4	4	4	15.00 / 16.00	30.00 / 35.00	- / -	- / -	5	4	-	1	-	1830 2100	-	1-12	(see key)
Eglinton Hotel, 29-30 Eglinton Crescent, EH12 5BY, Tel. 031 337 2641		4	4	4	10.00 / 16.00	20.00 / 32.00	15.00 / 21.00	- / -	2	8	2	8	3	1830 2030	3	1-12	(see key)

Name and Address	Map Ref	Bedrooms	Services	Meals	Single room overnight £min/£max	Double/twin room overnight £min/£max	Per person daily £min/£max	Per person weekly £min/£max	Single	Double/twin	Family	Private	Public	Evening meals (Last order)	Parking (no. of cars)	Months open (1-12)	Symbols
EDINBURGH continued	2 D5													From Last order			Key on back fold-out
Ellersly House Hotel, Ellersly Road, EH12 6HZ, Tel. 031 337 6888, Telex 76357		5	5	5	17.50 / -	35.00 / -	- / -	- / -	15	41	1	57	-	1900 2100	30	1-12	

ELLWYN HOTEL

37-39 Moira Terrace, Edinburgh EH7 6TD
Tel: 031-669 1033

Privately owned, comfortable hotel on main bus route between beach and city. 11 bedrooms, all with H & C, some with shower, central heating and tea/coffee making facilities. Fully licensed. Elegant Lounge Bar and TV lounge. Excellent cuisine.

Proprietors, Mr and Mrs R. Patterson.

Name and Address	Bedrooms	Services	Meals	Single room overnight £min/£max	Double/twin room overnight £min/£max	Per person daily £min/£max	Per person weekly £min/£max	Single	Double/twin	Family	Private	Public	Evening meals (Last order)	Parking	Months open	Symbols
Ellwyn Hotel, 37-39 Moira Terrace, EH7 6TD, Tel. 031 669 1033	3	3	4	12.00 / 14.00	20.00 / 24.00	- / -	- / -	1	9	1	-	2	1830 / -	4	1-12	
Elmington House Private Hotel, 45 Leamington Terrace, EH10 4JS, Tel. 031 229 1164	3	2	2	8.50 / 9.50	17.00 / 19.00	12.50 / 17.00	80.00 / 112.00	2	4	-	-	2	1800 2000	-	1-12	
George Hotel, George Street, EH2 2PB, Tel. 031 225 1251, Telex 72570	6	6	6	31.50 / 43.00	42.00 / 58.00	43.20 / 54.70	302.40 / 382.90	56	139	1	196	-	1830 2030	25	1-12	
Georgian Hotel, 5-6 Dean Terrace, EH4 1ND, Tel. 031 332 4520	3	3	-	12.00 / 18.00	18.00 / 30.00	- / -	- / -	4	9	2	13	-	- / -	-	1-12	
Gillsland Hotel, 7 Gillsland Road, EH10 5BW, Tel. 031 337 1058/5735	3	3	3	12.00 / 12.00	21.85 / 21.85	18.40 / 18.40	- / -	2	6	1	-	3	1800 / -	20	1-12	
Glencairn Hotel, 19-21 Royal Circus, EH3 6TL, Tel. 031 225 5218	-	-	-	16.00 / -	30.00 / -	- / -	- / -	-	15	5	-	6	- / -	-	1-12	
Glendale House Hotel, 5 Lady Road, EH16 5PA, Tel. 031 667 6588	3	3	2	7.50 / 9.50	15.00 / 18.00	13.00 / 15.00	80.00 / 95.00	1	6	1	-	3	1800 / -	8	1-12	
Glenelg Hotel, 12-14 Leamington Terrace, EH10 4JN, Tel. 031 229 6481	3	2	4	8.50 / 15.00	17.00 / 30.00	13.00 / 20.00	60.00 / 140.00	2	3	3	-	2	1800 2100	5	1-12	
Glenisla Hotel, 12 Lygon Road, EH16 5QB, Tel. 031 667 4098	3	3	2	10.00 / 11.00	18.00 / 19.00	13.50 / 14.50	- / -	2	6	1	-	2	1830 / -	5	1-12	

Name and Address	Map Ref	Bedrooms	Services	Meals	Prices				Rooms						Facilities		
TOWN / County / Establishment / Address / Telephone / Telex					Bed and Breakfast		B & B and evening meal		No. of bedrooms			No. of bath/shower rooms					
					Single room overnight	Double/twin room overnight	Per person daily	Per person weekly	Single	Double/twin	Family	Private	Public	Evening meals	Parking (no. of cars)	Months open (1-12)	Symbols
EDINBURGH continued	2 D5				£min £max	£min £max	£min £max	£min £max					From Last order		Key on back fold-out
Glenora Hotel 14 Rosebery Crescent EH12 5JY Tel. 031 337 1186	2	3	2		9.00 -	17.50 -	- -	- -	2	4	3	- 3	1730 -	-	1-12	T ♀ ★ ℞ Ⓜ ⚘ ◪ Ⓒ Ⓥ

Glenorchy Hotel

Proprietors Audrey and Ken Russell

22 GLENORCHY TERRACE
EDINBURGH EH9 2DH
Telephone 031-667 5708

· Fire Certificate · Children welcome · Ten minutes City Centre
· Meals on request · Separate TV Lounge and Dining Room

Name and Address	Bedrooms	Services	Meals	Single room overnight	Double/twin room overnight	Per person daily	Per person weekly	Single	Double/twin	Family	Private	Public	Evening meals	Parking	Months open	Symbols
Glenorchy Hotel 22 Glenorchy Terrace EH9 2DH Tel. 031 667 5708	3	3	2	7.50 8.00	13.80 15.00	11.50 12.00	77.00 80.50	2	10	2	1 3		- -	1-12	T ★ ⚵ ℞ ▦ ⚘ ◪ Ⓒ ❋ Ⓥ ☺
Gloucester Hotel 10 Gloucester Place EH3 6EF Tel. 031 225 2378	4	5	1	14.00 22.00	20.00 36.00	- -	- -	3	7	2	7 1		- -	1-12	£ ♀ ★ ℞ ▦ ⚘ ⟞ Ⓒ ⌂

Golf View
Hotel

2 Marchhall Road
(off Dalkeith Road.)
Edinburgh,
EH16 5HR

● Residents' Licence. ● Adjacent to the Royal Commonwealth Swimming Pool and Tennis Courts ● A short putt from the first tee at Prestonfield Golf Course ● Large Private Car Park ● All rooms H & C and Shaver Points ● Full Central Heating ● Rooms with Private Bathrooms and Showers.
Under the personal supervision of the Proprietors, Mr and Mrs D'Ambrosio. Tel: 031-667 4812.
A.A., R.A.C. Listed.

Name and Address	Bedrooms	Services	Meals	Single room overnight	Double/twin room overnight	Per person daily	Per person weekly	Single	Double/twin	Family	Private	Public	Evening meals	Parking	Months open	Symbols
Golf View Hotel 2 Marchhall Road EH16 5HR Tel. 031 667 4812	4	3	1	11.93 -	17.25 25.30	- -	- -	2	6	3	6 4		- 12	3-10	♀ ★ ℞ ▦ ⚘ ◪ Ⓥ

COMPLAINTS

Any complaints or criticisms about individual establishments should where possible be taken up immediately with the management. In many cases the problems can be dealt with satisfactorily, thus avoiding any prolonged unhappiness during your stay.

If this procedure fails to remedy the grievance to your satisfaction, and particularly where serious complaints are concerned, please write to the local Tourist Organisation.

VAT is shown at 15%: changes in this rate may affect prices.

Name and Address	Map Ref	Bedrooms	Services	Meals	Single room overnight £min £max	Double/twin room overnight £min £max	Per person daily £min £max	Per person weekly £min £max	Single	Double/twin	Family	Private	Public	No. of bedrooms From Last order	No. of bath/shower rooms	Evening meals	Parking (no. of cars) / Months open (1-12)	Symbols Key on back fold-out
EDINBURGH continued	2 D5																	

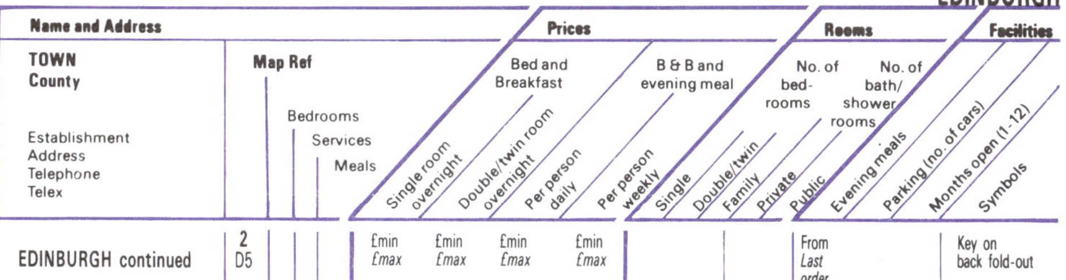

Gordon Bruce Hotel

Quiet situation overlooking private gardens.
Within easy reach of Princes Street. Private bath or shower.
T.V., Tea-making facilities.
RESTAURANT AND BAR.

12-16 South Learmonth Gardens, Edinburgh EH4 1EZ Telephone: 031-332 3232

Name and Address	Bedrooms	Services	Meals	Single room overnight	Double/twin room overnight	Per person daily	Per person weekly	Single	Double/twin	Family	Private	Public	No. of bedrooms / Last order	No. of bath/shower rooms	Evening meals	Parking	Months open	Symbols
Gordon Bruce Hotel/Kingswood Hotel–£ 14-16 South Learmonth Gardens EH4 1EZ Tel. 031 332 8248	4	4	4	18.50 –	21.50 –	25.50 –	164.50 –	7	28	5	40	-	1800 2045	-		1-12	
The Grange Hotel 8 White House Terrace, Grange Loan West EH9 2EU Tel. 031 667 5681	4	4	4	15.00 16.50	20.00 25.00	17.00 20.75	100.00 125.00	2	5	2	3	1	1900 2130	20		1-12	
Gray's Hotel 1 Hartington Gardens EH10 4LD Tel. 031 229 1019	2	3	1	8.00 8.50	15.00 16.00	9.50 10.00	66.00 68.00	2	4	2	-	2	1800 -	-		1-12	
Grosvenor Crest Hotel 7-21 Grosvenor Street EH12 5EF Tel. 031 226 6001 Telex 72445	5	5	5	36.50 –	49.00 –	- –	- –	31	80	17	128	-	1830 2130	-		5-12	
Hailes Hotel Wester Hailes Centre, Murrayburn Road EH14 2SW Tel. 031 442 3382	-	-	-	14.75 –	27.50 –	- –	- –	3	17	-	20	-	1830 2130	700		1-12	
Halcyon Hotel 8 Royal Terrace EH7 5AB Tel. 031 556 1032/3	3	3	1	9.20 11.50	17.25 18.40	- –	- –	4	6	6	-	4	- -	-		2-11	
Hamilton Lodge Hotel –£The Promenade, Portobello EH15 2DW Tel. 031 669 4366	3	2	2	10.00 12.00	19.00 21.00	13.00 15.00	75.00 80.00	-	7	-	-	2	- -	-		1-12	
Hampton Hotel 14 Corstorphine Road EH12 4QN Tel. 031 337 1130	3	4	1	11.50 –	21.85 –	-	-	1	8	1	-	1	- -	10		1-12	
Hanover House Hotel 26 Windsor Street EH7 5JR Tel. 031 556 1325	2	2	1	12.50 15.00	25.00 30.00	18.00 21.50	126.00 143.50	1	3	-	-	3	- -	1		1-12	

Name and Address / TOWN County — Establishment, Address, Telephone, Telex	Map Ref	Bedrooms	Services	Meals	Single room overnight £min/£max	Double/twin room overnight £min/£max	Per person daily £min/£max	Per person weekly £min/£max	Single	Double/twin	Family	Private	Public	Evening meals From/Last order	Parking (no. of cars)	Months open (1-12)	Symbols
EDINBURGH continued	2 D5													From Last order			Key on back fold-out
Harp Hotel, St Johns Road, EH12 8AX, Tel. 031 334 4750		4	4	5	19.50 / 22.50	33.00 / 40.00	26.00 / 29.00	126.00 / 140.00	6	14	-	8	6	1900 / 2130	35	1-12	
Heatherlea Hotel, Mayfield Gardens		2	2	2	9.75 / 10.90	18.40 / 20.70	14.65 / 15.80	95.00 / 103.00	2	3	4	-	2	1800 / 1800	6	1-12	
Howard Hotel, 32-36 Great King Street, EH3 6QH, Tel. 031 556 1393/4		5	5	5	26.00 / 34.50	40.00 / 53.00	30.00 / 39.00	- / -	8	14	3	25	-	1900 / 2130	14	1-12	

The Iona Hotel

17 Strathearn Place, Edinburgh, EH9 2AL

The Hotel you recommend to your friends for its Service, Comfort and Hospitable Welcome.

Central Heating

Cocktail Lounge   Fully Licensed   Parking

Bed and Breakfast from £17

A.A.   Telephone: 447 6264   R.A.C.

Name and Address	Map Ref	Bedrooms	Services	Meals	Single room overnight	Double/twin room overnight	Per person daily	Per person weekly	Single	Double/twin	Family	Private	Public	Evening meals From/Last order	Parking	Months open	Symbols
Iona Hotel, 17 Strathearn Place, EH9 2AL, Tel. 031 447 6264		3	4	4	17.00 / -	31.00 / -	24.00 / -	- / -	3	16	2	4	7	1900 / 2030	20	1-12	

AA & RAC Listed

KILDONAN LODGE HOTEL

27 Craigmillar Park, Edinburgh EH16 5PE

Think of us for your extra special holiday in Scotland

Independently owned and managed we offer you comfort, good food and friendly service

Licensed restaurant: Cocktail bar: Ample car parking: Full central heating.

Ask for our special bargain break brochure for holidays in April, May and June.

For reservations: Phone (031) 667 2793

Name and Address	Map Ref	Bedrooms	Services	Meals	Single room overnight	Double/twin room overnight	Per person daily	Per person weekly	Single	Double/twin	Family	Private	Public	Evening meals From/Last order	Parking	Months open	Symbols
Kildonan Lodge Hotel, 27 Craigmillar Park, EH16 5PE, Tel. 031 667 2793		3	3	5	9.50 / -	17.00 / -	13.75 / -	96.00 / -	1	2	6	-	3	1800 / 2130	20	1-12	
King James Thistle Hotel, 107 St James Centre, Leith St, EH1 3SW, Tel. 031 556 0111, Telex 727200		6	5	5	39.50 / 44.50	54.00 / 69.00	- / -	- / -	32	128	-	160	-	1830 / 2200	15	1-12	

VAT is shown at 15%: changes in this rate may affect prices.

Name and Address	Map Ref	Bedrooms	Services	Meals	Single room overnight £min/£max	Double/twin room overnight £min/£max	Per person daily £min/£max	Per person weekly £min/£max	Single	Double/twin	Family	Private	Public	Evening meals (From/Last order)	Parking (no of cars)	Months open	Symbols
EDINBURGH continued	2 D5													From Last order			Key on back fold-out
Kings Manor Hotel, 100 Milton Road East, EH15 2NP, Tel. 031 669 0444, Telex 727237		5	5	5	18.00 / 30.00	27.00 / 40.00	21.50 / 38.00	- / -	8	61	1	65	3	1900 / 2100	106	1-12	[symbols]
Ladbroke Dragonara Hotel, 69 Belford Road, EH4 3DG, Tel. 031 332 2545, Telex 727979 **(See ad. p. 102)**		6	6	5	50.50 / -	73.00 / -	- / -	- / -	27	115	-	142	-	1900 / 2230	90	1-12	[symbols]
Lady Nairne Hotel, 228 Willowbrae Road, EH8 7NG, Tel. 031 661 3396		3	3	4	18.00 / 20.00	26.00 / 30.00	- / -	- / -	7	18	-	25	-	1800 / 2230	50	1-12	[symbols]
Laggan House Private Hotel, 11 Spence Street, EH16 5AG, Tel. 031 667 5588		3	4	2	8.50 / 10.00	15.00 / 18.00	13.50 / 14.50	- / -		4	2	-	2	1830 / 1900	5	1-12	[symbols]
Lairg Private Hotel, 11 Coates Gardens, EH12 6LG, Tel. 031 337 1050/8493		-	-	-	9.00 / 12.00	18.00 / 24.00	13.00 / 15.00	90.00 / 100.00	2	6	4	10	2	1800 / 1900	-	1-12	[symbols]

Lauriston Private Hotel

9 Lauriston Park, Edinburgh EH3 9JA. Tel: 031-229 9530/1826.

Within easy walking distance of principal Theatres, the University, The Royal Infirmary. 10 minutes walk from the West End of Princes Street. Excellent public transport facilities, local car parks and free over-night street parking. Central heating. Private bathrooms and showers available. Large Dining Room, separate Cafeteria and Cocktail Lounge. Reduction of 10% on Bed and Breakfast for a week. Large reductions for children under 16 years.

Brochure on request.

Telex No: CHACOM G. 72465 J.F.

Name and Address	Map Ref	Bedrooms	Services	Meals	Single room overnight £min/£max	Double/twin room overnight £min/£max	Per person daily £min/£max	Per person weekly £min/£max	Single	Double/twin	Family	Private	Public	Evening meals (From/Last order)	Parking (no of cars)	Months open	Symbols
Lauriston Private Hotel, 9 Lauriston Park, EH3 9JA, Tel. 031 229 9530/1826, Telex 72465		3	3	4	9.50 / 10.50	17.00 / 20.00	13.50 / 15.00	88.55 / 98.00	10	10	7	2	5	1800 / 1945	-	1-12	[symbols]
Learmonth Hotel, 18-20 Learmonth Terrace, EH4 1PW, Tel. 031 343 2671, Telex 57515		4	5	5	18.80 / 26.75	28.75 / 39.65	- / -	- / -	11	44	7	24	7	1830 / 2130	-	1-12	[symbols]
Linden Hotel, 9-13 Nelson Street, EH3 6LF, Tel. 031 556 4344		4	5	4	15.00 / -	27.00 / -	- / -	- / -	1	14	5	2	4	- / -	1	1-12	[symbols]
Lochewe Hotel, 21 Royal Terrace, EH7 5AH, Tel. 031 556 6749		4	4	4	10.92 / 12.07	21.85 / 24.15	15.52 / 16.67	93.15 / 100.05	2	27	3	1	3	1800 / 2030	10	1-12	[symbols]

For the Finest Hotel Experience... a Few Minutes from Princes Street

The Ladbroke Dragonara Hotel

Now there's a new attraction to Edinburgh. The excitingly different 4 star Ladbroke Dragonara, where you'll find everything you need to complete your enjoyment of this historic city.

From the moment you arrive you'll find luxury and a warm welcome waiting for you. When you want a quiet drink just wander down to the Lounge Bar or experience the intimate Granary Bar — authentically renovated from an original 19th century mill. If you enjoy good food, you'll enjoy choosing from the superb a la carte menu in our magnificent Water of Leith Restaurant with a beautiful view of the water itself.

And you can look forward to a restful night in a luxurious bedroom with a private bathroom, colour T.V., radio, direct dial telephone and tea & coffee tray.

The Ladbroke Dragonara Hotel — it's what Edinburgh's been waiting for.

**Ladbroke Dragonara Hotel,
Belford Road, Edinburgh.
Tel: 031 332 2545**

Edinburgh

Name and Address	Map Ref	Bedrooms	Services	Meals	Bed and Breakfast Single room overnight £min £max	Bed and Breakfast Double/twin room overnight £min £max	B & B Per person daily £min £max	Per person weekly £min £max	B & B and evening meal Single	Double/twin	Family	No. of bedrooms Private	Public	No. of bath/shower rooms	Evening meals	Parking (no. of cars)	Months open (1-12)	Facilities Symbols
EDINBURGH continued	2 D5													From Last order			Key on back fold-out
Lovat Hotel 5 Inverleith Terrace EH3 5NS Tel. 031 556 2745		3	1	1	10.00 -	18.50 -	- -	- -	2	3	2	-	1	- -	-	1-12	ⵣ ♿ Ⓥ
Lygon Hotel 4 Lygon Road EH16 5QE Tel. 031 667 1374		3	3	2	9.00 9.50	16.00 17.00	13.00 13.50	- -	1	3	2	-	2	1800 1800	-	1-12	✂ 🛏 ▦ ♿ 🍳 Ⓥ

Once owned by the Earl of Maitland, the hotel stands in Georgian Edinburgh near to castle, Princes Street gardens, Museums, Royal Mile, bus and rail stations. Most theatres, cinemas and shopping areas are nearby.

Licensed restaurant and lounge bar. High teas. Colour TV lounge. Portable B/W TV sets available. Room tea making facilities. Full central heating. Intercom. Downies on all beds. 3/4 nights for price of 2/3. Special group rates for 2/3 day breaks.

Write or phone Alastair and Anne Milne 031-229 1467.

Name and Address	Bedrooms	Services	Meals	Single room overnight £min £max	Double/twin room overnight £min £max	Per person daily £min £max	Per person weekly £min £max	Single	Double/twin	Family	Private	Public	Evening meals	Parking	Months open	Symbols
Maitland Hotel 33 Shandwick Place, West Princes St EH2 4RG Tel. 031 229 1467	4	4	4	10.50 13.75	18.00 27.00	12.70 18.10	- -	12	11	4	8	3	1700 1945	-	1-12	T 💷 ♿ ⵣ 🛏 ▦ 🍳 🧴 🧥 🏨 Ⓥ
Malcolm Hotel 2 West Coates EH12 5JQ Tel. 031 337 2173	3	3	2	12.00 -	20.00 -	- -	- -	2	7	1	1	2	- -	6	1-12	T ⵣ 🐎 ✂ 🛏 ▦ 🍳 🧴 ⚡ 🏨
Mansion House Hotel & Motel Milton Road West EH15 3QF Tel. 031 661 4558	4	4	2	15.00 22.00	25.00 37.00	20.00 25.00	120.00 150.00	2	18	5	25	-	1930 2030	150	1-12	T ⵣ 🛏 ▦ 🍳 📺 🧴 ❇ 🏨 Ⓥ
Marchhall Hotel 14-16 Marchhall Crescent EH16 5HL Tel. 031 667 2743	3	3	2	9.50 12.00	18.50 22.00	13.50 16.00	80.00 84.00	2	6	4	-	3	1800 1830	-	1-12	♿ ⵣ 🛏 ▦ 🍳 ⬛ ↻

Name and Address				Prices								Rooms					Facilities			
TOWN / County / Establishment / Address / Telephone / Telex	Map Ref	Bedrooms	Services	Meals	Bed and Breakfast						B & B and evening meal		No. of bedrooms			No. of bath/shower rooms		Evening meals	Parking (no. of cars)	Months open (1-12)	Symbols
					Single room overnight	Double/twin room overnight	Per person daily		Per person weekly			Single	Double/twin	Family	Private	Public				
					£min £max	£min £max	£min £max		£min £max								From Last order		Key on back fold-out	
EDINBURGH continued	2 D5																			

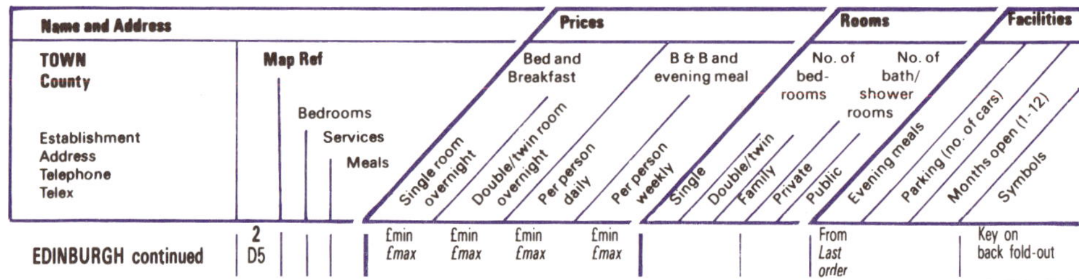

Name and Address	Bedrooms	Services	Meals	Single room o/n £min £max	Double/twin o/n £min £max	Per person daily £min £max	Per person weekly £min £max	Single	Double/twin	Family	Private	Public	Evening meals From/Last	Parking	Months open
McNair Hotel / 6 Links Gardens / Tel. 031 553 1111/2	3	4	4	9.20 / 13.80	18.40 / 30.00	12.80 / 17.40	80.00 / 120.00	2	4	2	6	2	1800 / 2000	-	1-12
Mount Royal Hotel / 53 Princes Street / EH2 2DQ / Tel. 031 225 7161 / Telex 727641	6	5	5	30.00 / -	46.00 / -	- / -	- / -	44	103	6	144	3	1800 / 2045	-	1-12
Murrayfield Hotel / 18 Corstorphine Road / EH12 6HN / Tel. 031 337 2207/1844 / Telex 53168	3	5	4	23.50 / -	33.50 / -	- / -	- / -	14	19	3	7	11	1800 / 2130	50	1-12
Myrim Hotel / 1 Royal Circus / EH3 6TL / Tel. 031 225 5332	4	4	3	14.00 / 22.00	22.00 / 26.00	- / -	- / -	1	4	2	7	-	- / -	-	1-12
Navaar House Hotel / 12 Mayfield Gardens / EH9 2BZ / Tel. 031 667 2828	3	3	1	8.00 / 12.00	16.00 / 24.00	- / -	- / -	1	2	3	-	1	-	5	-
New Town Hotel / 4 Darnaway Street / EH3 6BG / Tel. 031 226 6104	2	3	1	13.00 / 20.00	18.00 / 30.00	- / -	- / -	3	5	1	-	2	- / -	-	1-12
North British Hotel / Princes Street / EH2 2EQ / Tel. 031 556 2414 / Telex 72332	5	6	6	34.00 / 37.50	51.50 / 59.00	- / -	- / -	47	146	-	171	10	1900 / 2200	-	1-12
Northumberland Hotel / 31-33 Craigmillar Park / EH16 5PE / Tel. 031 667 6971	-	-	-	17.00 / 19.00	28.00 / 32.00	- / -	- / -	2	8	10	20	-	1900 / 2030	23	1-12
Old Waverley Hotel / 43 Princes Street / EH2 2BY / Tel. 031 556 4648 / Telex 778215	3	3	4	35.00 / 35.00	50.00 / 50.00	33.00 / 33.00	175.00 / 175.00	11	52	3	66	12	1830 / 2045	-	1-12

(See ad. p. 95)

VAT is shown at 15%: changes in this rate may affect prices.

Name and Address	Map Ref	Bedrooms	Services	Meals	Single room overnight £min/£max	Double/twin room overnight £min/£max	Per person daily £min/£max	Per person weekly £min/£max	Single	Double/twin	Family	Private	Public	Evening meals From/Last order	Parking	Months open	Symbols
EDINBURGH continued	2 D5													From Last order			Key on back fold-out

The Osbourne Hotel
(Incorporating Shelbourne Lounge Bar)

This comfortable city-centre Hotel is conveniently situated for Coach and Rail Stations. All Bedrooms have TV, Radio, Room-call and central heating. Restaurant. Coffee Shop. Lift and night porter.
53-59 York Place, Edinburgh. Tel: 031-556 2345.

Name and Address	Bed	Ser	Mls	Single room o/n	Double/twin o/n	Per person daily	Per person weekly	Single	Double/twin	Family	Private	Public	Evening meals	Parking	Months open
Osbourne Hotel 53-59 York Place EH1 3JD Tel. 031 556 5746/2345	4	5	4	12.00 / -	24.00 / -	18.00 / -	120.00 / -	8	14	6	10	10	1830 / 2000	6	1-12
Park Hotel 32-33 Royal Terrace EH7 5AH Tcl. 031 556 1156	4	4	4	10.92 / 14.37	21.85 / 28.75	15.52 / 18.97	93.15 / 113.85	1	19	8	15	3	1800 / 1930	-	1-12
Park View Hotel 68 Peffermill Road EH16 5LP Tel. 031 667 2032	-	-	-	11.50 / -	18.40 / -	-	-	-	10	4	-	2	- / 2030	30	1-12
Piries Hotel 4-8 Coates Gardens EH12 5LB Tel. 031 337 1108	-	-	-	9.77 / 11.00	19.55 / 22.00	-	-	4	9	7	-	4	-	-	1-12
Post House Hotel Corstorphine Road EH12 6UA Tel. 031 334 8221 Telex 727103	5	3	5	42.50	56.50	-	-	54	58	96	208	-	1900 / 2215	158	1-12
Prestonfield House Hotel Priestfield Road Tel. 031 667 8000 Telex 727396	1	3	5	40.00	52.00	-	-	-	5	-	-	3	1900 / 2200	200	1-12
Queensway Hotel 1 Queensferry Road EH4 3DJ Tel. 031 332 6492	5	5	5	15.00 / 15.00	22.00 / 25.00	-	-	1	4	1	6	1	1900 / 2230	30	1-12
Raeburn House Hotel 112 Raeburn Place EH4 1HG Tel. 031 332 2348	3	3	2	10.00 / 15.00	20.00 / 25.00	-	-	-	4	1	-	2	-	8	1-12
Redholme House Hotel 20 Colinton Road EH10 5QE Tel. 031 447 2286	3	5	5	12.50 / 16.00	23.00 / 30.00	19.50 / 23.00	130.00 / 150.00	4	11	3	1	3	1900 / 2030	18	1-12
Ritz Hotel 14-16 Grosvenor Street EH12 5EG Tel. 031 337 4315	5	5	4	13.80 / 25.30	25.30 / 39.10	-	-	6	28	6	28	2	1800 / 2030	-	1-12

(See ad. p. 106) *(Redholme House Hotel)*

Redholme House Hotel R.A.C.

Telephone: 031-447 2286 Reservations
447 7873 Guests

Here you can enjoy the complete comfort and quiet of a country mansion yet we are only a short distance from the city centre, with free parking space in the grounds.

18 comfortably furnished bedrooms (H&C).
A 50% reduction is made on the accommodation in small double bedrooms at certain quiet periods.
Single rooms for conferences.
Delightful olde style dining-room.
Special family rates.
Log fires and central heating or unmetered heaters.
We are accessible from the South, West and North without encountering city traffic.

Terms for Bed & Breakfast £10 daily + VAT
Weekly £63 + VAT

Reduced terms for families, party bookings and small conferences offered on request.

Guests from abroad especially welcomed for Christmas and New Year by the proprietors: Mr and Mrs J. F. G. Harris

Particulars from The Manager

20 Colinton Road, Edinburgh, EH10 5EQ

Name and Address	Map Ref				Prices					Rooms								Facilities
TOWN County Establishment Address Telephone Telex		Bedrooms	Services	Meals	Bed and Breakfast		B & B and evening meal			No. of bed-rooms				No. of bath/shower rooms				
					Single room overnight	Double/twin room overnight	Per person daily	Per person weekly	Single	Double/twin	Family	Private	Public	Evening meals	Parking (no. of cars)	Months open (1-12)	Symbols
EDINBURGH continued	2 D5				£min £max	£min £max	£min £max	£min £max					From Last order				Key on back fold-out
Rosehall Hotel 101 Dalkeith Road EH16 5AJ Tel. 031 667 9372	-	-	-		9.00 10.00	18.00 20.00	- -	- -	2	4	2	-	2	- -	-	1-12		
Roxburghe Hotel 38 Charlotte Square EH2 4HG Tel. 031 225 3921 Telex 727054	5	5	6		34.00 45.00	45.00 70.00	- -	- -	23	51	2	62	10	1800 2230	-	1-12		
Royal British Hotel 20 Princes Street EH2 2AW Tel. 031 556 4901 Telex 57515	4	5	5		19.60 27.95	30.10 41.15	- -	- -	22	44	6	39	8	1900 2130	-	1-12		
Royal Scot Hotel 111 Glasgow Road EH12 8NF Tel. 031 334 9191 Telex 727197	6	6	6		38.00 42.00	50.00 55.00	59.00 64.00	- -	17	177	56	250	-	1830 2230	250	1-12		
Rutland Hotel 3 Rutland Street EH1 2AE Tel. 031 229 3402	-	-	-		21.00 -	33.75 -	- -	- -	6	12	-	-	4	1830 2000	-	1-12		
Salisbury Hotel 45 Salisbury Road EH16 5AA Tel. 031 667 1264	3	3	2		7.50 9.00	15.00 18.00	- -	- -	3	8	4	2	4	- -	12	1-12		
Sgian-Dhu Hotel 8-9 Carlton Terrace EH7 5DD Tel. 031 556 1761	3	4	4		10.50 12.50	23.00 25.00	15.00 17.50	103.50 103.50	3	9	7	1	5	1800 1845	-	1-12		
Sighthill Hotel Calder Road Tel. 031 443 5151	-	-	-		15.25 -	31.25 -	- -	- -	8	2	-	10	-	1830 2130	100	1-12		
St Andrew Hotel 8-10 South St Andrew Street EH2 2AZ Tel. 031 556 8774	3	5	4		18.00 24.10	32.00 44.00	- -	- -	8	30	4	9	10	1800 2045	-	1-12		
Stakis Commodore Hotel West Marine Drive, Cramond Foreshore EH4 5EP Tel. 031 336 1700	5	5	5		37.00 -	49.00 -	- -	- -	-	49	-	49	-	1730 2200	75	1-12		

A YEAR-LONG FESTIVAL OF SCOTTISH HERITAGE

Tours and Trails, Exhibitions and Displays, Courses and Seminars, Concerts, Folk Concerts, Highland Games, and Sports are only some of the activities taking place throughout Scotland.

Ask your local Tourist Information Centre for details.

Name and Address		Prices					Rooms						Facilities		

TOWN / County / Establishment / Address / Telephone / Telex — **Map Ref** (Bedrooms, Services, Meals) — **Prices**: Bed and Breakfast (Single room overnight, Double/twin room overnight), B & B and evening meal (Per person daily, Per person weekly) — **Rooms**: No. of bedrooms (Single, Double/twin, Family), No. of bath/shower rooms (Private, Public) — **Facilities**: Evening meals, Parking (no. of cars), Months open (1-12), Symbols

	2 D5			£min £max	£min £max	£min £max	£min £max					From Last order			Key on back fold-out
EDINBURGH continued															

Stewart House Hotel

17 Merchiston Avenue, Edinburgh EH10 4PJ
031-229 5289 Guests 031-229 8869

R.A.C. R.S.A.C. Listed & Minotels   Fully Licensed

Comfortable and homely hotel with attractive cocktail lounge and colour TV lounge. Showers in all double and twin bedrooms, some with private bahroom. Central heating. Parking. Electric blankets on request. Sauna and Sunbed. 8 minutes city centre, good bus service 9, 10, 11, 16, 23 and 27. Colour TV, radios, baby sitting equipment installed in all bedrooms.
Under personal supervision of the proprietors: **Bruce and Rona Adam**

Name and Address	Bedrooms	Services	Meals	Single room overnight	Double/twin room overnight	Per person daily	Per person weekly	Single	Double/twin	Family	Private	Public	Evening meals (Last order)	Parking	Months open	Symbols
Stewart House Hotel, 17 Merchiston Avenue, EH10 4PJ, Tel. 031 229 5289	4	4	1	14.00 / 25.00	26.00 / 36.00	-	-	1	5	2	3	1	-	-	1-12	(symbols)
Suffolk Hall Hotel, 10 Craigmillar Park, EH16 5PG, Tel. 031 667 4810	4	4	5	18.00 / -	25.00 / 33.00	-	-	4	8	5	5	4	1830 / 2130	18	1-12	(symbols)
Terrace Hotel, 37 Royal Terrace, EH7 5AH, Tel. 031 556 3423	3	4	1	9.20 / -	17.48 / -	-	-	2	4	9	-	4	-	14	4-10	(symbols)
Thistle Court Hotel, 5 Hampton Terrace, EH12 5JD, Tel. 031 337 1314	4	3	3	15.50 / 17.25	20.70 / 23.00	-	-	-	6	4	6	2	1800 / 1900	12	1-12	(symbols)
Thrums Private Hotel, 14 Minto Street, Newington, EH9 1RQ, Tel. 031 667 5545	3	3	3	8.00 / 9.50	15.00 / 17.00	13.00 / 15.50	91.00 / 108.50	2	3	2	2	2	1900 / -	5	1-12	(symbols)
Victoria Hotel, 3-5 Forth Street, EH1 3JX, Tel. 031 556 1616	2	3	1	7.00 / 10.75	14.00 / 19.00	- / -	- / -	6	10	5	1	2	-	-	1-12	(symbols)
Walton Hotel, 79 Dundas Street, EH3 6SD, Tel. 031 556 1137	2	3	1	8.50 / 9.50	17.00 / 19.00	-	-	1	4	2	-	2	-	6	1-12	(symbols)

PAY A VISIT TO ROBERT BURNS' COUNTRY

Travel through some of Scotland's most attractive countryside, in the south west, and follow The Burns Heritage Trail. Easy to get to, it has something to interest everyone.

Send today for your free leaflet with map.

VAT is shown at 15%: changes in this rate may affect prices.

Name and Address TOWN County Establishment Address Telephone Telex	Map Ref	Bedrooms	Services	Meals	Prices: Bed and Breakfast: Single room overnight	Prices: Bed and Breakfast: Double/twin room overnight	Prices: B & B and evening meal: Per person daily	Prices: B & B and evening meal: Per person weekly	Rooms: No. of bedrooms: Single	Rooms: No. of bedrooms: Double/twin	Rooms: No. of bedrooms: Family	Rooms: No. of bath/shower rooms: Private	Rooms: No. of bath/shower rooms: Public	Facilities: Evening meals	Facilities: Parking (no. of cars)	Facilities: Months open (1-12)	Facilities: Symbols
EDINBURGH continued	2 D5				£min *£max*	£min *£max*	£min *£max*	£min *£max*						From *Last order*			Key on back fold-out

west end hotel

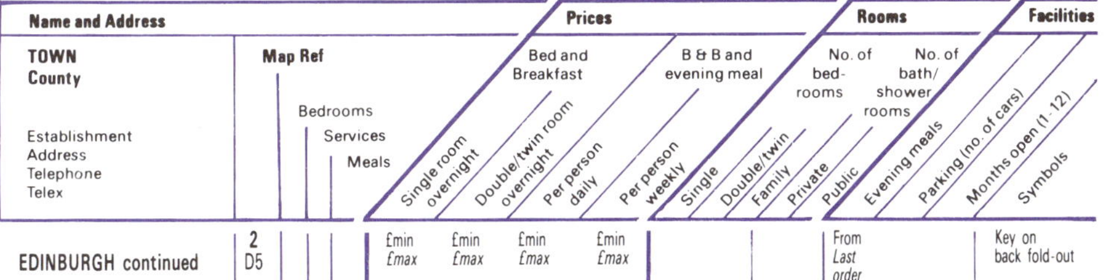

35 Palmerston Place, Edinburgh EH12 5AH
Tel: 031-225 3656, 225 4393

The West End Hotel famed for its Highland hospitality offers spacious accommodation at reasonable prices. The hotel is lively with regular ceilidh evenings and entertainment. It is also the home of the famed Eagle Pipers and Edinburgh Shetland fiddlers who give recitals every Wednesday and Thursday evenings.

The bedrooms have heating, H & C, Coloured T.V., electric blankets and radio and tea and coffee facilities. The hotel is fully licensed and a full meals service is available. Drop us a line and we will be pleased to quote to meet your requirements. Reduced prices for weekly stays and for children sharing. Ideally situated for easy access to all of Edinburgh's amenities and within walking distance of bus/rail terminals, cinemas/theatres and Princes Street. Personally supervised by proprietors Hugh & Sandra Maclean.

Establishment	Map Ref	Bedrooms	Services	Meals	Single room overnight	Double/twin room overnight	Per person daily	Per person weekly	Single	Double/twin	Family	Private	Public	Evening meals	Parking	Months open	Symbols
West End Hotel 35 Palmerston Place EH12 5AU Tel. 031 225 3656		3	4	4	11.00 *13.00*	22.00 *24.00*	- -	- -	3	4	2	-	2	1830 *2000*	-	1-12	T C V
Adelphi-Leonarde Guest House 14 Hartington Gardens EH10 4LD Tel. 031 229 6324		3	1	1	8.00 *9.50*	16.00 *19.00*	- -	- -	2	2	3	-	1	- -	-	1-12	V
Airlie Guest House 29 Minto Street EH9 1SB Tel. 031 667 3562		2	3	1	6.90 *9.20*	11.50 *18.40*	- -	- -	1	4	4	-	3	- -	10	1-12	T M C V
Allan Lodge Guest House 37 Queens Crescent EH9 2BA Tel. 031 668 2947		3	2	1	7.00 *9.00*	14.00 *18.00*	- -	- -	-	5	1	-	3	- -	5	1-12	V
Allanbank Guest House 3 Leamington Terrace EH10 4JW Tel. 031 229 2772		3	2	1	7.00 *8.00*	14.00 *16.00*	- -	- -	1	1	1	-	1	- -	-	1-12	C V
Allermuir Guest House 27 Downie Terrace EH12 7AU Tel. 031 334 1251		3	2	1	7.00 *8.00*	14.00 *16.00*	- -	- -	-	2	2	-	2	- -	4	1-12	
Alness Guest House 27 Pilrig Street EH6 5AN Tel. 031 554 1187		3	3	1	7.50 *8.50*	15.00 *17.00*	- -	- -	1	3	3	-	3	- -	2	1-12	T V
Amaragua Guest House 10 Kilmaurs Terrace EH16 5DR Tel. 031 667 6775		3	2	2	7.00 *10.00*	14.00 *19.00*	- -	- -	2	2	2	-	2	- -	-	1-12	T V

Name and Address	Map Ref	Bedrooms	Services	Meals	Single room overnight £min/£max	Double/twin room overnight £min/£max	Per person daily £min/£max	Per person weekly £min/£max	Single	Double/twin	Family	Private	Public	Evening meals From/Last order	Parking	Months open	Symbols
EDINBURGH continued	2 D5																
The Ard Thor Guest House 10 Mentone Terrace EH9 2DG Tel. 031 667 1647		3	2	1	7.50 / 11.50	14.00 / 18.00	- / -	- / -	2	2	2	-	2	- / -	-	1-12	[M] [C] [V]
Ardblair Guest House 1 Duddingston Crescent Tel. Edinburgh 669 2384		3	1	2	7.00 / -	14.00 / -	9.50 / -	60.00 / -	-	2	2	-	2	1700 / 1900	3	1-12	[V]
Ardenlee Guest House 9 Eyre Place EH3 5ES Tel. 031 556 2838		2	3	1	7.00 / 8.00	14.00 / 16.00	- / -	- / -	1	5	2	-	2	- / -	-	1-12	[M] [V]
Ardleigh Guest House 260 Ferry Road EH5 3AN Tel. 031 552 1833		3	2	1	9.00 / 11.00	14.00 / 16.00	- / -	- / -	-	2	4	-	3	- / -	-	1-12	[R] [C] [V]
Ardmor Guest House 74 Pilrig Street EH6 5AS Tel. 031 554 4944		3	2	1	7.50 / 8.00	15.00 / 16.00	- / -	- / -	-	2	1	-	1	- / -	-	1-12	[M] [C] [V]
Argyle Guest House 5 Hartington Place EH10 4LF Tel. 031 229 6645		2	3	1	8.00 / 8.50	16.00 / 16.00	- / -	- / -	2	4	1	-	1	- / -	-	1-12	[M] [V]
Arlington Guest House 11 Eyre Place EH3 5ES Tel. 031 556 6178		2	1	1	7.50 / 8.00	14.00 / 15.00	- / -	- / -	2	7	1	-	3	- / -	-	1-12	[T]
Ascot Guest House 98 Dalkeith Road EH16 5AF Tel. 031 667 1500		3	2	1	7.00 / 10.00	13.00 / 16.00	- / -	- / -	-	5	2	-	2	- / -	-	4-10	[V]

Ashdene House

**23 Fountainhall Road,
Edinburgh, EH9 2LN**
Tel: 031-667 6026
Telex: 72254
SCOTDEC 'G' (Ashdene)

Located in a pleasant street in a select area, 1½ miles from city centre, ASHDENE HOUSE offers its residents a quiet nights rest away from main road traffic.

A substantial Scottish Breakfast is served and dinner can be arranged. Free tea making facilities are standard in all rooms. Some rooms with private facilities.

Generous discounts arranged for family parties all year, and for the elderly in off season times.

Contact MRS DAULBY for brochure, and for help planning your itinerary.

Name and Address	Map Ref	Bedrooms	Services	Meals	Single room overnight £min/£max	Double/twin room overnight £min/£max	Per person daily £min/£max	Per person weekly £min/£max	Single	Double/twin	Family	Private	Public	Evening meals From/Last order	Parking	Months open	Symbols
Ashdene Guest House 23 Fountainhall Road EH9 2LN Tel. 031 667 6026 Telex 72254		3	2	2	8.00 / -	15.00 / -	12.00 / -	80.00 / -	-	3	2	1	2	1800 / -	2	1-12	[T] [R] [C] [V]
Ashling Guest House 47 Castle Street EH2 3BG Tel. 031 225 7796		3	2	1	7.50 / 10.00	15.00 / 18.00	- / -	- / -	2	5	-	-	2	- / -	-	1-12	

VAT is shown at 15%: changes in this rate may affect prices.

Name and Address	Map Ref	Bedrooms	Services	Meals	Single room overnight £min/£max	Double/twin room overnight £min/£max	Per person daily £min/£max	Per person weekly £min/£max	Single	Double/twin	Family	Private	Public	Evening meals From / Last order	Parking (no. of cars)	Months open (1–12)	Symbols
EDINBURGH continued	2 D5																Key on back fold-out
Ashwood Guest House, 20 Minto Street, EH9 1RQ, Tel. 031 667 8024		3	3	1	8.00 / 9.00	14.00 / 17.00	– / –	– / –	–	2	2	–	1	– / –	5	1-12	
Averon Guest House, 44 Gilmore Place, EH3 9NQ, Tel. 031 229 9932		1	2	1	6.50 / 9.00	13.00 / 16.00	– / –	– / –	1	3	1	–	2	1830 / –	3	1-12	C, V
Avondale Guest House, 10 South Gray Street, EH9 1TE, Tel. 031 667 6779		3	2	1	8.50 / –	15.00 / –	– / –	– / –	–	2	3	–	2	– / –	3	1-12	C, V
Balmoral Guest House, 32 Pilrig Street, EH6 5AL, Tel. 031 554 1857		3	3	1	7.50 / 8.50	15.00 / 17.00	– / –	– / –	–	4	3	–	2	– / –	2	1-12	T, C, V
Balquhidder Guest House, 94 Pilrig Street, EH6 5AY, Tel. 031 554 3377		1	1	1	7.50 / 8.50	14.00 / 16.00	9.00 / –	– / –	1	3	4	–	1	– / –	2	1-12	M, C, V
Barrosa Guest House, 21 Pilrig Street, EH6 5AN, Tel. 031 554 3700		2	2	1	8.50 / 12.00	16.00 / 20.00	– / –	– / –	1	3	3	1	2	– / –	2	1-12	M, V
Bayview, 48 Joppa Road, EH15 2ET, Tel. 031 669 4815		3	4	3	7.50 / 8.50	15.00 / 20.00	11.00 / 13.00	74.00 / 91.00	1	4	1	1	2	1800 / 1900	–	1-12	C, V
Beaumont, 113 Willowbrae Road, EH8 7HN, Tel. 031 661 3823		1	1	1	– / –	14.00 / 16.00	– / –	– / –	–	1	1	–	1	– / –	–	1-12	M
Bellrock Guest House, 105 Ferry Road, EH6 4ET, Tel. 031 554 2604		3	2	2	8.00 / 10.00	14.00 / 20.00	10.00 / 15.00	70.00 / –	1	3	3	–	2	1800 / 1900	1	1-12	V
Ben Doran Guest House, 11 Mayfield Gardens, EH9 2AX, Tel. 031 667 8488		2	3	2	9.50 / 10.00	17.00 / 20.00	– / –	– / –	–	4	5	–	2	– / –	6	1-12	T, C, V
Benlarig Guest House, 9 Mayfield Road, EH9 2NG, Tel. 031 667 4853		3	2	1	7.50 / 9.00	15.00 / 17.00	– / –	– / –	–	3	2	–	2	– / –	1	1-12	
Blairhaven Guest House, 5 Eyre Place, EH3 5ES, Tel. 031 556 3025		2	2	3	7.00 / 7.50	14.00 / 15.00	– / –	– / –	2	4	2	–	1	– / –	–	1-12	M, V
Bonnington Guest House, 202 Ferry Road, EH6 4NW, Tel. 031 554 7610		3	2	1	8.00 / 9.00	16.00 / 18.00	– / –	– / –	1	2	2	–	2	1800 / 1800	10	1-12	V
Brig O'Doon Guest House, 262 Ferry Road, EH5 3AN, Tel. 031 552 3953		3	2	1	8.50 / 9.00	14.00 / 16.00	– / –	– / –	–	4	2	–	2	– / –	–	1-12	

| Name and Address | Map Ref | Bedrooms | Services | Meals | Prices | | | | B & B and evening meal | | | | Rooms | | | | Facilities |
TOWN County / Establishment Address Telephone Telex					Bed and Breakfast: Single room overnight / Double/twin room overnight		Per person daily	Per person weekly	Single	Double/twin	Family	Private	No. of bedrooms: Public	No. of bath/shower rooms	Evening meals	Parking (no. of cars)	Months open (1-12) / Symbols
EDINBURGH continued	2 D5				£min £max	£min £max	£min £max	£min £max					From Last order				Key on back fold-out
Brucefield Guest House 8 Park Road EH6 4LF Tel. 031 552 3846	2	2	2		8.50 -	15.00 -	15.50 -	108.50 -	1	4	1	- 1	1900 1900	-		1-12	T ☂ M ☎ / ⊟ C V
Buchan Guest House 3 Coates Gardens EH12 5LG Tel. 031 337 1045	3	3	2		8.00 11.00	15.00 19.00	12.00 15.50	75.00 95.00	2	1	6	- 2	1730 1800	-		1-12	symbols / C ⊞ V
Buxstone Guest House 2 Hartington Gardens EH10 4LD Tel. 031 229 8664	3	2	1		7.50 8.50	15.00 17.00	10.00 12.00	- -	2	2	3	- 2	1730 1830	-		1-12	T symbols / V
Carrington 38 Pilrig Street EH6 5AN Tel. 031 554 4769	3	-	-		8.50 14.00	16.00 24.00	- -	- -	1	5	2	- 3	- -	6		1-12	symbols / V

Castle Guest House

38 Castle St Edinburgh EH2 3BN

Centrally situated, off Princes Street, within easy reach of bus, airport and rail terminals.
· Reasonable
· Own door key
· Access to rooms all day
· Good choice at breakfast
· Electric kettles available
· Highly recommended
Mr and Mrs J. C. Ovens, Tel. 225 1975

Name and Address	Bedrooms	Services	Meals	Single room overnight	Double/twin room overnight	Per person daily	Per person weekly	Single	Double/twin	Family	Private	Public	Bath/shower	Evening meals	Parking	Months open / Symbols
Castle Guest House 38 Castle Street EH2 3BN Tel. 031 225 1975	1	1	1	7.00 8.50	14.00 17.00	- -	- -	1	6	-	- 1	- -			1-12	symbols / V
Chalumna Guest House 5 Granville Terrace EH10 4PQ Tel. 031 229 2086	-	-	-	9.00 10.00	17.00 18.00	- -	- -	1	5	1	- 2	-		-		symbols M ⊠ V
Clarin Guest House 4 East Mayfield Street EH9 1SD Tel. 031 667 2433/9690	3	2	2	9.00 -	14.00 19.00	- -	- -	-	4	3	- 2	-	8		1-12	symbols / ⊞ V
Clashaidy Guest House 21 Kilmaurs Road EH16 5DA Tel. 031 667 2626	2	2	2	6.50 7.50	12.00 15.00	9.50 11.50	55.00 58.00	1	3	2	- 2	1830 -	-		1-12	symbols / C V
Claymore Guest House 68 Pilrig Street EH6 5AS Tel. 031 554 2500	2	3	1	- -	14.50 15.50	- -	- -	-	3	1	- 2	-	-		4-10	symbols / V
Craigholme Guest House 14 Downie Terrace EH12 7AU Tel. 031 334 6294	3	2	1	9.00 9.00	16.00 16.00	Bed and Breakfast -	- -	-	2	3	- 2	-	4		1-12	symbols / ⊠ V

VAT is shown at 15%: changes in this rate may affect prices.

Name and Address — TOWN / County / Establishment / Address / Telephone / Telex	Map Ref	Bedrooms	Services	Meals	Single room overnight £min/£max	Double/twin room overnight £min/£max	Per person daily £min/£max	Per person weekly £min/£max	Single	Double/twin	Family	Private	Public	Evening meals (From Last order)	No. of bath/shower rooms	Parking (no. of cars)	Months open (1-12)	Symbols (Key on back fold-out)
EDINBURGH continued	2 D5				£min £max	£min £max	£min £max	£min £max						From Last order				
Cree Guest House, 77 Mayfield Road, EH9 3AA, Tel. 031 667 3177	1	2	1		7.00 9.00	14.00 18.00	- -	- -	2	3	1	-	1	- -	-		1-12	[T] [M] [V]
Crion Guest House, 33 Minto Street, EH9 2BT, Tel. 031 667 2708	3	2	2		7.50 8.50	13.00 17.00	11.00 12.00	77.00 84.00	1	4	1	-	2	1800 -	1		1-12	[V]
Dargil Guest House, 16 Mayfield Gardens, EH9 2BZ, Tel. 031 667 6177	3	2	1		- -	14.00 -	- -	- -	-	1	3	-	1	- -	2		1-12	
Dickie Guest House, 22 East Claremont Street, EH7 4JP, Tel. 031 556 0903	3	4	1		8.00 -	16.00 -	- -	- -	1	2	1	-	2	- -	-		1-12	[V]
Drumorne Guest House, 82 Willowbrae Road, EH8 7HA, Tel. 031 661 4349	3	1	1		8.50 14.00	14.00 17.00	- -	- -	-	2	2	-	1	-	6		1-12	[V]
Fountainhall Guest House, 40 Fountainhall Road, EH9 2LW, Tel. 031 667 2544	2	2	1		9.00 11.00	15.00 18.00	- -	- -	1	3	3	-	2	-	2		1-12	[C] [V]
Galloway Guest House, 22 Dean Park Crescent, EH4 1PH, Tel. 031 332 3672, Telex 72165	3	3	2		8.00 12.00	16.00 24.00	12.00 16.00	76.00 100.00	1	6	3	1	3	1800 1830	-		1-12	[T] [V]
Garfield Guest House, 264 Ferry Road, EH5 3AN, Tel. 031 552 2369	3	2	1		8.50 9.00	14.00 16.00	- -	- -	1	4	2	-	2	-	-		1-12	[£] [V]
Gifford Guest House, 103 Dalkeith Road, EH16 5AJ, Tel. 031 667 4688	3	2	1		8.00 10.00	15.00 16.00	- -	- -	-	4	2	-	2	-	-		1-12	[C] [V]
Gil Dun Guest House, 9 Spence Street, EH16 5AG, Tel. 031 667 1368	3	2	-		9.00 10.00	16.00 18.00	14.00 15.00	- -	-	3	3	-	2	-	4		1-12	[C] [V]
Gilmore Guest House, 51 Gilmore Place, EH3 9NX, Tel. 031 229 5008	3	2	1		8.00 10.00	13.00 17.00	- -	- -	1	3	2	-	1	-	-		1-12	[T] [C]
Glen Park Guest House, 17 Glengyle Terrace, EH3 9LW, Tel. 031 229 9559	1	2	1		6.50 8.50	13.00 17.00	- -	- -	1	3	2	2	1	-	30		1-12	[£] [M] [C] [V]
Glenallan Guest House, 19 Mayfield Road, EH9 2NG, Tel. 031 667 1667	2	2	2		- -	14.00 18.00	10.00 13.00	63.00 84.00	-	4	2	-	2	1700 1800	8		1-12	[M]

EDINBURGH

EDINBURGH continued — Map Ref **2 D5**

VAT is shown at 15%: changes in this rate may affect prices.
Key on back fold-out.

Prices

Name and Address	Bedrooms	Services	Meals	Single room overnight £min / £max	Double/twin room overnight £min / £max	Per person daily £min / £max	Per person weekly £min / £max
Glenesk Guest House 39 Liberton Brae EH16 6AG Tel. 031 664 1529	3	1	1	5.50 / 7.50	11.00 / 15.00	- / -	- / -
Gorvic Guest House 14 Granville Terrace EH10 4PQ Tel. 031 229 6565	-	-	-	- / -	15.00 / 16.00	- / -	- / -
The Grange Guest House 8 Osborne Terrace EH12 5HG Tel. 031 337 4178	3	2	1	7.00 / 8.50	13.00 / 16.00	- / -	- / -
Grant's Guest House 2 Sciennes Road EH9 1LE Tel. 031 667 2847	2	2	1	6.00 / -	14.00 / -	- / -	- / -
Green Lady Guest House 10 Bruntsfield Crescent EH10 4EZ Tel. 031 447 2913	3	3	2	7.50 / 8.00	14.00 / 15.00	- / -	- / -
Grosvenor Guest House 1 Grosvenor Gardens EH12 5JU Tel. 031 337 4143	3	2	1	8.50 / 10.00	16.00 / 18.00	- / -	- / -
Haven Guest House 180 Ferry Road EH6 4NS Tel. 031 554 6559	3	3	1	8.00 / 10.00	16.00 / 18.00	- / -	- / -
Highland Park Guest House 16 Kilmaurs Terrace EH16 5DR Tel. 031 667 9204	3	2	1	7.00 / 8.00	14.00 / 16.00	- / -	- / -
Hillview Guest House 92 Dalkeith Road EH16 5AF Tel. 031 667 1523	3	3	2	8.00 / 18.00	16.00 / 36.00	- / -	- / -
Hollies Guest House 2 East Hermitage Place EH6 8AA Tel. 031 554 3763	1	2	1	8.00 / 11.00	14.00 / 18.00	11.00 / 15.00	- / -
International Guest House 37 Mayfield Gardens EH9 2BX Tel. 031 667 2511/9833	4	4	1	8.00 / 9.50	16.00 / 19.00	- / -	- / -
Ivy House Guest House 7 Mayfield Gardens, Newington EH9 2AX Tel. 031 667 3411	2	2	1	- / -	14.00 / 16.00	- / -	- / -
Kaimes Guest House 12 Granville Terrace EH10 4PQ Tel. 031 229 3401	3	2	1	- / -	15.00 / 17.00	- / -	- / -

Rooms and Facilities

Name	No. of bedrooms — Single	Double/twin	Family	No. of bath/shower rooms — Private	Public	Evening meals From / Last order	Parking (no. of cars)	Months open (1-12)	Symbols
Glenesk Guest House	2	2	-	2	-	- / -	5	1-12	
Gorvic Guest House	-	5	-	-	2	- / -	-	1-12	
The Grange Guest House	1	2	1	-	1	- / -	4	1-12	
Grant's Guest House	1	3	-	-	1	- / -	-	1-12	[M]
Green Lady Guest House	3	4	1	-	3	- / -	-	1-12	[M]
Grosvenor Guest House	-	4	3	2	2	- / -	-	1-12	
Haven Guest House	-	4	2	-	2	1700 / -	-	1-12	[V]
Highland Park Guest House	1	3	2	-	3	- / -	2	1-12	[V]
Hillview Guest House	3	3	1	1	2	1830 / 1900	3	1-12	
Hollies Guest House	-	3	3	-	2	- / -	-	1-12	[T] [M]
International Guest House	1	4	2	3	2	- / -	3	1-12	[V]
Ivy House Guest House	2	6	-	-	3	- / -	9	4-11	[M]
Kaimes Guest House	-	6	2	-	2	- / -	2	1-12	[T] [V]

Prices shown are for guidance only. The price columns show £min (upper figure) and £max (lower figure). "Evening meals" shows From / Last order. Facility symbols — Key on back fold-out.

Name and Address	Map Ref	Bedrooms	Services	Meals	Single room overnight (£min / £max)	Double/twin room overnight (£min / £max)	Per person daily (£min / £max)	Per person weekly (£min / £max)	Single	Double/twin	Family	Private	Public	Evening meals (From / Last order)	Parking (no. of cars)	Months open (1-12)	Symbols
EDINBURGH continued	2 / D5																Key on back fold-out
Kariba Guest House, 10 Granville Terrace, EH10 4PQ, Tel. 031 229 3773/1513		3	4	2	10.00 / -	16.00 / -	14.00 / -	- / -	1	4	2	-	2	1800 / 1900	3	1-12	(symbols)
Kenvie Guest House, 16 Kilmaurs Road, EH16 5DA, Tel. 031 668 1964		3	2	1	7.00 / -	14.00 / -	- / -	- / -	-	3	2	-	2	- / -	2	1-12	(symbols)
Kilmaurs Guest House, 9 Kilmaurs Road, EH16 5DA, Tel. 031 667 8315		3	2	1	7.50 / 8.00	15.00 / 16.00	- / -	- / -	1	3	2	-	2	- / -	1	1-12	(symbols)
Kingsley Guest House, 30 Craigmillar Park, EH16 5PS, Tel. 031 667 8439		3	3	1	6.00 / 8.00	12.00 / 16.00	- / -	- / -	1	3	4	-	2	- / -	7	1-12	(symbols)
Kingsview Guest House, 28 Gilmore Place, EH3 9NQ, Tel. 031 229 8004		2	2	2	8.50 / -	16.00 / -	13.00 / -	- / -	1	4	2	-	1	1900 / -	3	1-12	(symbols)
Kingsway Guest House, 5 East Mayfield, EH9 1SD, Tel. 031 667 5029		2	3	1	7.50 / 10.00	15.00 / 18.00	- / -	- / -	-	5	2	-	2	- / -	9	1-12	(symbols)
Kinnaird Guest House, 252 Morrison Street, EH5 8DT, Tel. 031 229 0992		3	1	1	8.50 / 9.50	17.00 / 19.00	- / -	- / -	-	6	2	1	2	- / -	-	-	(symbols)
Kinneil Guest House, 1 Bonnington Terrace, EH6 4BP, Tel. 031 554 4107		3	2	1	8.00 / -	15.00 / -	- / -	- / -	-	5	2	-	2	- / -	4	1-12	(symbols)
Kirkridge Guest House, 8 Kilmaurs Terrace, EH16 5PR, Tel. 031 667 6704		3	1	1	6.50 / 9.50	13.00 / 17.00	- / -	- / -	2	4	2	-	2	- / -	-	1-12	(symbols)
Kirtle Guest House, 8 Minto Street, EH9 1RG, Tel. 031 667 2813		2	2	1	- / -	14.00 / 18.00	- / -	- / -	-	4	4	-	2	- / -	5	1-12	(symbols)
Kriegie Guest House, 50 Mayfield Road, EH9 2NH, Tel. 031 667 5847		1	2	1	7.00 / 8.00	14.00 / 16.00	10.00 / 11.00	65.00 / 70.00	3	3	1	-	2	1800 / 1800	-	1-12	(symbols)
Lauderville Guest House, 52 Mayfield Road, EH9 2NH, Tel. 031 667 7788		3	2	2	7.50 / 8.50	14.00 / 16.00	11.00 / 12.00	75.00 / 80.00	1	3	1	-	1	1730 / -	-	1-12	(symbols)
Lindsay Guest House, 108 Polwarth Terrace, EH11 1NN, Tel. 031 337 1580		2	2	1	8.00 / 9.00	15.00 / 16.00	- / -	- / -	2	3	2	-	2	- / -	6	1-12	(symbols)
Lomond Guest House, 9 Zetland Place, EH5 3HU, Tel. 031 552 3901		3	3	2	8.00 / 8.50	16.00 / 17.00	12.00 / 12.50	84.00 / 87.50	-	4	3	2	3	1800 / 1800	3	1-12	(symbols)

Prices shown are for guidance only. Please send SAE with each enquiry.

Name and Address	Map Ref	Bedrooms	Services	Meals	Single room overnight £min/£max	Double/twin room overnight £min/£max	Per person daily £min/£max	Per person weekly £min/£max	Single	Double/twin	Family	Private	Public	Evening meals From/Last order	Parking (no. of cars)	Months open (1-12)	Symbols (Key on back fold-out)
EDINBURGH continued	2 D5																
Lorne Villa Guest House, 9 East Mayfield, EH9 1SD, Tel. 031 667 7159	2	2	2	1	9.00 / 11.00	15.00 / 18.00	- / -	- / -	1	3	2	-	1	-	6	1-12	T C V (+ symbols)
Manderley Guest House, 19 Milton Road East, EH15 2ND, Tel. 031 669 7978		1	1	1	- / -	18.00 / 18.00	- / -	- / -	-	3	-	-	1	-	-	-	V (+ symbols)
Marakech Guest House, 30 London Street, EH3 6NA, Tel. 031 556 4444		4	5	5	7.50 / 9.00	14.00 / 17.00	9.50 / 13.00	63.00 / 90.00	1	4	2	2	2	1900 / 2100	7	1-12	C V (+ symbols)
Maranatha Guest House, 90 Pilrig Street, EH6 5AY, Tel. 031 554 2106		3	3	4	7.50 / 10.00	15.00 / 17.00	11.00 / 12.50	75.00 / 90.00	-	4	4	-	2	1800 / 1900	2	1-12	T C V (+ symbols)
Marvin Guest House, 46 Pilrig Street, EH6 5AL, Tel. 031 554 6605		3	2	2	7.50 / 9.00	15.00 / 20.00	- / -	- / -	-	5	2	1	3	-	6	1-12	(symbols)
The Mayfield Guest House, 15 Mayfield Gardens, EH9 2AX, Tel. 031 667 8049		2	3	1	7.00 / 10.50	13.00 / 18.00	10.50 / 14.00	67.00 / 74.00	2	4	5	2	3	-	6	1-12	T M C (+ symbols)
Menzies Guest House, 33 Leamington Terrace, EH10 4JS, Tel. 031 229 4629		2	2	1	- / -	15.00 / 16.00	- / -	- / -	-	2	1	-	1	-	3	1-12	M C V (+ symbols)
Meriden Guest House, 1 Hermitage Terrace, EH10 4RP, Tel. 031 447 5476		1	1	1	10.00 / 11.00	16.00 / 17.00	- / -	- / -	-	4	1	2	2	-	-	1-12	(symbols)
Merlin Guest House, 14 Hartington Place, EH10 4LE, Tel. 031 229 3864/225 3510		1	1	1	7.00 / -	- / -	- / -	- / -	-	5	1	-	1	-	-	1-12	M (+ symbols)
The Mill, 46 East Claremont Street, EH7 4JR, Tel. 031 556 3605		3	1	1	6.50 / 7.50	13.00 / 15.00	9.00 / 10.00	- / -	-	3	1	-	1	-	-	1-12	(symbols)
Millfield Guest House, 12 Marchhall Road, EH16 5HR, Tel. 031 667 4428		2	2	2	7.50 / 8.50	14.00 / 16.00	- / -	- / -	-	4	2	-	2	-	2	-	M C V (+ symbols)
Morris Guest House, 42 Mayfield Road, EH9 2NH, Tel. 031 667 3117		3	2	1	8.00 / 10.00	16.00 / 20.00	- / -	- / -	1	2	2	-	1	-	6	1-12	(symbols)
Park View Villa Guest House, 254 Ferry Road, EH5 3AN, Tel. 031 552 3456		3	3	1	14.00 / 16.00	16.00 / 18.00	- / -	- / -	-	2	3	-	2	-	-	1-12	C V (+ symbols)
Parklands Guest House, 20 Mayfield Gardens, EH9 2BZ, Tel. 031 667 7184		3	2	1	- / -	14.00 / 16.50	- / -	- / -	-	5	1	-	2	-	-	1-12	(symbols)

VAT is shown at 15%: changes in this rate may affect prices.

Name and Address	Map Ref	Bedrooms	Services	Meals	Single room overnight £min £max	Double/twin room overnight £min £max	Per person daily £min £max	Per person weekly £min £max	Single	Double/twin	Family	Private	Public	Evening meals From Last order	No. of bath/shower rooms	Parking (no. of cars)	Months open (1-12)	Symbols
EDINBURGH continued (2 D5)																		Key on back fold-out
Parkview Guest House, 17 Downie Terrace, Corstorphine Road, EH12 7AU, Tel. 031 334 3455	2	1	1		8.00 / 9.00	15.00 / 16.00	- / -	- / -	-	2	2	-	1	- / -	4	1-12	
Quendale Guest House, 32 Craigmillar Park, EH16 5PS, Tel. 031 667 3171	-	-	-		6.00 / 7.50	12.00 / 14.00	7.00 / 8.50	45.00 / 50.00	2	4	2	-	2	- / -	6	1-12	
Quinton Lodge Guest House, 24 Polwarth Terrace, EH11 1NA, Tel. 031 229 4100	3	3	2		8.75 / -	15.50 / -	12.75 / -	- / -	1	4	1	-	2	1800 / 1800	8	1-12	
Ravensdown Guest House, 248 Ferry Road, EH5 3AN, Tel. 031 552 5438	3	4	1		10.00 / 12.50	15.00 / 17.00	- / -	- / -	-	5	3	-	2	- / -	3	1-12	
Ravensneuk Guest House, 11 Blacket Avenue, EH9 1RR, Tel. 031 667 5347	3	2	1		9.00 / 12.00	15.00 / 17.00	- / -	- / -	-	4	3	-	2	- / -	3	1-12	
Richmond Guest House, 20 Leopold Place, London Road, EH7 5LB, Tel. 031 556 3556	2	-	1		- / -	16.00 / 18.00	- / -	- / -	-	5	1	-	2	- / -	-	1-12	
Rigville Guest House, 1 Pilrig Street, EH6 5AH, Tel. 031 554 1116	1	2	1		8.00 / 8.50	16.00 / 17.00	- / -	- / -	2	5	1	-	2	- / -	-	1-12	
Rimswell Guest House, 33-35 Mayfield Gardens, EH9 2BX, Tel. 031 667 5851	3	3	1		7.00 / 9.50	14.00 / 17.00	- / -	- / -	3	4	2	-	5	- / -	6	1-12	
Robertson Guest House, 5 Hartington Gardens, EH10 4LD, Tel. 031 229 2652/3862	3	2	1		8.00 / 9.00	16.00 / 18.00	- / -	- / -	1	2	4	1	2	- / -	-	1-12	
Rosebank Guest House, 5 Upper Gilmore Place, EH3 9NW, Tel. 031 229 4669	3	2	1		7.00 / 8.50	13.00 / 15.00	10.00 / 11.50	70.00 / 72.00	-	5	-	-	2	- / -	-	1-12	
Rosedene Guest House, 4 Queens Crescent, EH9 2AZ, Tel. 031 667 5806	2	2	1		7.50 / 8.50	13.00 / 16.00	- / -	- / -	1	5	3	-	3	- / -	6	-	
Roselea Guest House, 11 Mayfield Road, EH9 2NG, Tel. 031 667 6115	3	2	3		8.00 / 10.00	16.00 / 20.00	11.50 / 14.00	77.00 / 98.00	-	2	4	-	2	1800 / 1830	3	1-12	
Roselea Guest House, 4 Kew Terrace, EH12 5JE, Tel. 031 337 8396	3	2	1		9.00 / 10.00	16.00 / 18.00	- / -	- / -	1	2	2	-	2	- / -	-	1-12	

Name and Address	Map Ref	Bedrooms	Services	Meals	Single room overnight £min/£max	Double/twin room overnight £min/£max	Per person daily £min/£max	Per person weekly £min/£max	Single	Double/twin	Family	Private	Public	Evening meals (Last order)	Parking (no. of cars)	Months open (1-12)	Symbols
EDINBURGH continued	2 D5													From Last order			Key on back fold-out
Rowan Guest House, 13 Glenorchy Terrace, EH9 2DQ, Tel. 031 667 2463		3	2	2	7.50 / 9.00	14.00 / 18.00	12.00 / 14.00	75.00 / 95.00	2	4	3	-	2	1800 / 1800	-	1-12	T, dog, R/, disabled, iron, //, V
Rowand Guest House, 7 Hermitage Terrace, EH10 4RP, Tel. 031 447 4089		3	2	2	9.00 / 9.00	15.00 / 16.00	- / -	- / -	1	2	3	-	2	- / -	-	1-12	T, dog, radiator, disabled
Salisbury View Guest House, 64 Dalkeith Road, EH16 5AE, Tel. 031 667 1133		2	2	2	7.00 / -	14.00 / -	- / -	- / -	1	5	2	-	2	- / -	-	1-12	dog, R/, M, disabled, C, V
Scott Guest House, 37 Leamington Terrace, EH10 4JS, Tel. 031 229 5391		3	2	1	8.00 / 10.00	15.00 / 18.00	- / -	- / -	-	2	1	-	1	-	2	1-12	£, R/, radiator, disabled
Shalimar Guest House, 20 Newington Road, EH9 1QS, Tel. 031 667 2827/0789		3	2	2	9.00 / 10.00	16.00 / 18.00	- / -	- / -	1	5	3	4	3	-	-	1-12	T, R/, radiator, disabled, iron, //
Sharon Guest House, 1 Kilmaurs Terrace, EH16 5BZ, Tel. 031 667 2002/2727		3	2	2	8.00 / 10.00	16.00 / 20.00	- / -	- / -	2	4	2	-	3	-	5	1-12	R/, radiator, disabled, iron
Sonas Guest House, 3 East Mayfield, EH9 1SD, Tel. 031 667 2781		2	2	2	8.00 / 11.00	14.00 / 18.00	- / -	- / -	-	5	2	-	2	-	6	1-12	dog, R/, radiator, house, V
Southdown Guest House, 20 Craigmillar Park, EH16 5PS, Tel. 031 667 2410		3	3	1	- / -	13.00 / 17.00	10.50 / 12.50	73.50 / 87.50	-	4	4	-	3	1800 / -	8	-	T, R/, radiator, box, C, V
Southside Guest House, 8 Newington Road, EH9 1QS, Tel. 031 667 5650		3	2	2	8.00 / -	15.00 / -	- / -	- / -	1	4	3	-	2	1830 / -	-	1-12	T, crossed tools, R/, radiator, disabled, iron, C, V

St Conan Guest House

Family Run Establishment

30 Minto Street, Edinburgh EH9 1SB. Tel: 031-667 8393

- High degree comfort & Hospitality
- Central Heating
- H&C. Shaver Points
- Tea making facilities
- Some rooms with showers
- TV Lounge

- Own key, access all day
- Private Car Park
- Fire Certificate
- Children Welcome

FULL SCOTTISH BREAKFAST

Name and Address	Map Ref	Bedrooms	Services	Meals	Single room overnight	Double/twin room overnight	Per person daily	Per person weekly	Single	Double/twin	Family	Private	Public	Evening meals (Last order)	Parking	Months open	Symbols
St Conans Guest House, 30 Minto Street, EH9 1SB, Tel. 031 667 8393		3	2	2	7.50 / 10.00	15.00 / 18.00	- / -	- / -	-	4	3	-	2	1750 / -	11	1-12	T, dog, R/, radiator, disabled, box, iron, V

VAT is shown at 15%: changes in this rate may affect prices.

Name and Address	Map Ref	Bedrooms	Services	Meals	Single room overnight £min / £max	Double/twin room overnight £min / £max	Per person daily £min / £max	Per person weekly £min / £max	Single	Double/twin	Family	Private	Public	Evening meals (From / Last order)	Parking (no. of cars)	Months open (1-12)	Symbols
EDINBURGH continued	2 D5																Key on back fold-out
St Margaret's Guest House, 18 Craigmillar Park, EH16 5PS, Tel. 031 667 2202		2	3	2	7.50 / 10.00	13.00 / 17.00	- / -	- / -	1	3	5	-	2	1730	8	1-12	T £ ... M ... C V
Straven Guest House, 3 Brunstane Road, EH15 2DL, Tel. 031 669 5580		2	2	1	7.00 / 8.00	13.00 / 14.00	- / -	- / -	-	4	2	-	2	- / -	-	1-12	... M ... V
Sylvern Guest House, 22 West Mayfield, EH9 1TQ, Tel. 031 667 1241		2	2	2	- / -	15.00 / 16.00	11.50 / 12.00	80.50 / 84.00	1	5	2	-	2	1800	8	-	...
Tania Guest House, 19 Minto Street, EH9 1RQ, Tel. 031 667 4144		3	2	2	9.00 / 10.00	15.00 / 18.00	- / -	- / -	-	4	2	-	2	1800 / 1900	2	1-12	T ... C V

Value for money – real Scottish home cooking and baking at

Teviotdale Guest House

Under personal supervision of Mrs. E.G. Riley. Small Exclusive Guest House offering superb Bed & Breakfast or a "Forget the Clock" self-catering holiday. Central heating and colour TV in all rooms. Vegetarians welcome, reductions for families and for senior citizens in off season. Central yet quiet, parking and frequent bus services. Princes Street 10 minutes by bus. S.A.E. for terms.
Proud winner of 1981 Farm Holiday Guides Diploma.
53 Grange Loan, Edinburgh EH9 2ER. 031-667 4376.
Founder Member of Edinburgh WHS Guest Houses Association.

Name and Address	Map Ref	Bedrooms	Services	Meals	Single room overnight £min / £max	Double/twin room overnight £min / £max	Per person daily £min / £max	Per person weekly £min / £max	Single	Double/twin	Family	Private	Public	Evening meals (From / Last order)	Parking (no. of cars)	Months open (1-12)	Symbols
Teviotdale Guest House, 53 Grange Loan, EH9 2ER, Tel. 031 667 4376		3	2	1	- / -	17.00 / -	14.00 / -	- / -	-	4	2	-	3	- / -	-	1-12	T ... V
The Thirty-Nine Steps Guest House, 62 South Trinity Road, EH5 3NX, Tel. 031 552 1349		3	2	2	8.00 / 9.00	15.00 / 17.00	10.50 / 12.50	60.00 / 75.00	1	3	2	-	1	1800 / 1830	-	1-12	... C V
Tiree Guest House, 26 Craigmillar Park, EH16 5PE, Tel. 031 667 7477		-	-	-	6.00 / 8.00	12.00 / 18.00	9.00 / 12.00	- / -	1	3	3	-	2	-	8	1-12	T £ ...
Villa Nina Guest House, 39 Leamington Terrace, EH10 4JS, Tel. 031 229 2644		3	2	2	7.50 / 8.00	13.00 / 14.00	- / -	- / -	-	4	2	-	2	1800 / 2000	-	1-12	T ... V
Villa San Monique Guest House, 4 Wilton Road, EH16 5NY, Tel. 031 667 1403		3	2	1	- / -	13.50 / 16.50	- / -	- / -	-	4	2	-	3	- / -	8	4-9	£ ...
Windsor Guest House, 11 Windsor Street, EH7 5LA, Tel. 031 556 4853		2	2	1	8.00 / 9.00	16.00 / 18.00	- / -	- / -	2	2	4	-	2	- / -	-	1-12	... M V

Name and Address	Map Ref	Bedrooms	Services	Meals	Single room overnight £min/£max	Double/twin room overnight £min/£max	Per person daily £min/£max	Per person weekly £min/£max	Single	Double/twin	Family	Private	Public	Evening meals From/Last order	Parking (no. of cars)	Months open (1-12)	Symbols
EDINBURGH continued	2 D5																Key on back fold-out
Winfield Guest House 12 Moston Terrace EH9 2DE Tel. 031 667 2540		3	2	1	8.00 / 9.00	15.00 / 17.00	12.00 / 14.00	84.00 / 90.00	1	4	3	-	2	- / -	-	-	[symbols]
Zetland House Guest House 186 St Johns Road EH12 8SG Tel. 031 334 3898		3	2	2	8.00 / 8.00	16.00 / 16.00	11.00 / 11.00	77.00 / 77.00	2	4	3	-	2	1830 / 1730	6	1-12	[symbols]
(Principal Warden) Carlyle Hall East Suffolk Road EH16 5PH Tel. 031 667 2262		1	3	3	8.50 / 9.00	15.00 / 16.00	11.50 / 12.00	21.00 / 22.00	265	53	-	-	50	1800 / -	300	3-4 7-9	[symbols]
Dunfermline College Cramond Road North Tel. 031 336 6001		2	2	3	9.20 / -	- / -	12.88 / -	90.00 / -	198	-	-	-	40	1730 / 1815	60	3-4 7-9	[symbols]
Patrick Geddes Hall Mound Place EH1 2LU Tel. 031 225 8400		2	4	1	10.75 / -	21.50 / -	14.09 / -	28.18 / -	17	30	-	-	14	- / -	-	7-9	[symbols]
Pollock Halls of Residence 18 Holyrood Park Road EH16 5AY Tel. 031 667 1971 Telex 72165		2	4	4	10.75 / -	21.50 / -	14.09 / -	28.18 / -	1500	8	-	-	250	1800 / 1900	140	3-4 7-9	[symbols]
Y W C A of Scotland Francis Kinnaird House, 13-14 Coates Cres EH3 7AG		-	-	-	6.50 / 7.50	11.00 / 13.00	7.50 / 9.50	52.50 / 66.50	4	4	4	-	3	1730 / 1800	-	1-12	Ladies Only [symbols]
EDZELL Angus	4 F12																
Central Hotel 18-20 Church Street Tel. Edzell 218		4	4	5	10.00 / 18.00	20.00 / 30.00	13.00 / 25.00	115.00 / 150.00	2	14	3	11	3	1700 / 2100	100	1-12	[symbols]
Glenesk Hotel Tel. Edzell 319		4	4	5	19.00 / 21.00	38.00 / 42.00	27.50 / -	168.00 / -	7	15	2	13	4	1900 / 2200	108	-	[symbols]
Panmure Arms Hotel 52 High Street Tel. Edzell 420		5	4	4	21.00 / -	36.00 / -	28.50 / -	- / -	-	12	4	16	-	1900 / 2100	-	1-12	[symbols]
ELGIN Moray	4 D7																
Braelossie Hotel Sheriffmill Road IV30 1AL Tel. Elgin 7181		3	3	5	16.00 / 19.50	27.50 / 29.50	19.50 / 25.00	120.00 / 155.00	1	2	2	-	1	1700 / 2100	55	1-12	[symbols]
City Hotel 191 High Street Tel. Elgin 7055		-	-	-	10.50 / -	19.50 / -	- / -	- / -	11	12	-	-	8	1700 / 2000	20	1-12	[symbols]

VAT is shown at 15%: changes in this rate may affect prices.

Eight Acres Hotel
Morriston Road, Sheriffmill, ELGIN

Telephone: 0343 3077

Set in extensive grounds on the main Elgin Inverness Road, this 58-bedroomed modern 3-Star Hotel (with full facilities) provides an ideal base from which to participate in the numerous local tourist activities.

The Hotel offers a large measure of comfort in its generous public areas. Our Cuisine, to High International Standard, offers both Table D'Hote and A La Carte — Bar lunches are also served.

Snooker, Pool and Darts are available in our Morriston Lounge Bar. Heated Indoor Pool.

Hotel Guests have the free use of the Elgin Sports Club offering Squash, Saunas, Solarium and Mini Gym.

Special Holiday Rates — Weekend or Full Week — Reductions for Children. Please write for brochure and our leaflet "Elgin as a Centre for Your Holiday".

Name and Address	Map Ref	Bedrooms	Services	Meals	Single room overnight £min/£max	Double/twin room overnight £min/£max	Per person daily £min/£max	Per person weekly £min/£max	Single	Double/twin	Family	Private	Public	Evening meals From/Last order	Parking (no. of cars)	Months open (1-12)
ELGIN continued	4 / D7															
Eight Acres Hotel, Sheriffmill, IV30 3UL, Tel. Elgin 3077/8		6	5	5	17.80 / 27.85	38.00 / 42.00	24.50 / -	170.00 / -	19	20	1	40	-	1800 / 2100	80	1-12
Hotel St Leonards, Duff Avenue, IV30 1QS, Tel. Elgin 7350		4	3	4	14.00 / 16.00	24.00 / 28.00	17.00 / -	- / -	3	12	2	8	3	2100 / 2000	40	1-12
Laichmoray Hotel, Maisondieu Road, Tel. Elgin 7832		2	4	4	17.00 / -	28.00 / -	- / -	- / -	6	16	1	-	7	1730 / 2130	54	1-12
Sunninghill Hotel, Hay Street, Tel. Elgin 7799		3	3	4	14.30 / -	24.20 / -	- / -	- / -	-	5	1	-	2	1800 / 2030	20	1-12
Torr House Hotel, 8 Moss Street, IV30 1LU, Tel. Elgin 2661		3	3	3	- / -	19.00 / -	- / -	96.50 / -	-	5	1	-	2	1630 / 1930	32	1-12
Southbank Guest House, 36 Academy Street, IV30 1LP, Tel. Elgin 7132		1	3	2	6.50 / -	13.00 / -	10.50 / -	70.00 / -	2	1	7	-	3	1800 / 1800	6	1-12
ELIE Fife	2 / E3															
Golf Hotel, Bank Street, KY9 1EF, Tel. Elie 330209		3	4	5	13.45 / 16.45	26.90 / 35.90	20.30 / 26.30	142.10 / 165.76	2	15	4	10	3	1930 / 2130	50	2-10

Name and Address	Map Ref	Bedrooms	Services	Meals	Single room overnight £min/£max	Double/twin room overnight £min/£max	Per person daily £min/£max	Per person weekly £min/£max	Single	Double/twin	Family	Private	Public	Evening meals From/Last order	Parking (no. of cars)	Months open (1-12)	Symbols
ELIE continued	2 E3																Key on back fold-out
Queens Hotel High Street Tel. Elie 330205		4	5	5	12.00 15.00	24.00 30.00	18.00 20.00	119.00 126.00	1	12	8	2	6	1900 2200	-	1-12	
The Elms Guest House 12 Park Place KY19 1DH Tel. Elie 330404		3	2	2	7.50 7.50	15.00 15.00	12.00 12.00	80.00 80.00	1	3	2	-	2	1800 1800	-	1-12	
ELLON Aberdeenshire	4 H9																

LADBROKE HOTEL ELLON (ABERDEEN)

From check-in to check-out you will enjoy the warm hospitality of our Ellon (Aberdeen) Hotel.

A drink, a meal and a good nights rest in a room with private bath and colour T.V. It's well worth stopping for.

Ladbroke Hotels

Ladbroke Hotel, Ellon, Aberdeenshire, AB4 9NP.
Tel: (0358) 20666 Telex: 739200.

Name and Address	Map Ref	Bedrooms	Services	Meals	Single room overnight £min/£max	Double/twin room overnight £min/£max	Per person daily £min/£max	Per person weekly £min/£max	Single	Double/twin	Family	Private	Public	Evening meals From/Last order	Parking (no. of cars)	Months open (1-12)	Symbols
Ladbroke Hotel AB4 9NP Tel. Ellon 20666		6	6	5	37.00 -	50.00 -	- -	- -	14	15	11	40	-	1900 2130	150	1-12	
New Inn Market Street AB4 9TD Tel. Ellon 20425		3	3	3	10.00 12.50	20.00 25.00	23.00 25.00	160.00 170.00	-	10	2	6	1	1700 -	20	1-12	
ELVANFOOT Lanarkshire	2 B7																
Glenelvan Hotel 79 Dumfries Road ML12 6TF Tel. Elvanfoot 254		-	-	-	7.50 -	15.00 -	9.40 -	59.50 -	1	2	2	-	2	1830 2100	6	1-12	
ERSKINE Renfrewshire	1 H5																
Crest Hotel Erskine Bridge PA8 6AN Tel. 041 812 0123 Telex 777713		6	5	5	42.00 -	54.00 -	- -	- -	25	175	-	200	-	1900 2200	350	1-12	
ESKDALEMUIR, by **Langholm** **Dumfriesshire**	2 D8																
Hart Manor Hotel Tel. Eskdalemuir 217		4	4	4	12.50 13.50	22.00 25.00	21.00 -	125.00 135.00	1	4	2	5	1	1830 2030	35	1-12	

VAT is shown at 15%: changes in this rate may affect prices.

Name and Address	Map Ref	Bedrooms	Services	Meals	Bed and Breakfast — Single room overnight £min / £max	Bed and Breakfast — Double/twin room overnight £min / £max	Bed and Breakfast — Per person daily £min / £max	B & B and evening meal — Per person weekly £min / £max	B & B and evening meal — Per person weekly	Single	Double/twin	Family	Private	Public	No. of bedrooms — From / Last order	Evening meals	Parking (no. of cars)	Months open (1-12)	Symbols
ETTRICK BRIDGE, by Selkirk Selkirkshire	2 D7																		Key on back fold-out
Ettrickshaws Country Hotel TD7 5HW Tel. Ettrick Bridge 229		5	4	5	13.00 / 18.00	22.00 / 30.00	20.00 / 24.00	133.00 / 161.00	-	5	1	5	1	1900 / 2130	15	2-12	
ETTRICK VALLEY Selkirkshire	2 D7																		
Tushielaw Inn Tel. Ettrick Valley 62205		3	3	4	9.00 / 9.50	18.00 / 19.00	12.50 / 15.00	80.50 / 108.50	-	2	1	-	1	1900 / 2130	10	1-12	
EVANTON Ross-shire	4 A7																		
Novar Arms Hotel Tel. Evanton 830210		3	3	4	10.00 / 10.00	20.00 / 20.00	12.50 / 17.50	62.50 / 87.50	5	6	1	-	2	1730 / 1930	52	1-12	
Wheel Inn Motel & Restaurant Novar Toll Tel. Evanton 830763		2	2	4	10.50 / -	20.00 / -	- / -	- / -		4	2	2	2	1730 / 2100	-	1-12	
EYEMOUTH Berwickshire	2 G5																		
Glenerne Hotel Albert Road Tel. Eyemouth 50401		2	2	3	7.50 / 7.50	15.00 / 15.00	11.00 / 13.00	77.00 / 85.00	-	8	-	-	1	1830 / -	-	4-10	
Home Arms Hotel TD14 5EY Tel. Eyemouth 50201		-	-	-	10.50 / 10.50	18.50 / 18.50	13.50 / 15.00	60.00 / 75.00	-	6	2	-	2	1630 / 1900	20	1-12	
FAIR ISLE Shetland	5 F8																		
Fair Isle Bird Observatory ZE2 9JU Tel. Fair Isle 258		-	-	3	- / -	- / -	12.65 / 20.70	64.40 / 103.50	4	6	2	-	3	1800 / 1800	-	4-10	
FALKIRK Stirlingshire	2 B4																		
Graeme Hotel 40 Grahams Road FK1 1HR Tel. Falkirk 28576		-	-	-	10.50 / -	19.00 / -	- / -	- / -	4	6	-	-	2	1700 / 1830	20	1-12	
Hotel Cladhan Kemper Avenue FK1 1UF Tel. Falkirk 27421		6	3	5	26.57 / -	34.16 / -	- / -	- / -	11	21	1	33	-	1700 / 2200	80	1-12	
Stakis Park Hotel Camelon Road, Arnothill FK1 5R7 Tel. Falkirk 28331		5	5	5	36.00 / -	46.00 / -	- / -	- / -	25	30	-	55	-	1900 / 2145	250	1-12	

Name and Address TOWN / County Establishment / Address / Telephone / Telex	Map Ref	Bedrooms	Services	Meals	Single room overnight £min / £max	Double/twin room overnight £min / £max	Per person daily £min / £max	Per person weekly £min / £max	Single	Double/twin	Family	Private	Public	Evening meals (Last order)	Parking (no. of cars)	Months open (1-12)	Symbols
FALKIRK continued	2 B4																Key on back fold-out
Ivanhoe Guest House 60 Stirling Road, Camelon FK1 4ER Tel. Falkirk 23034		2	2	1	7.50	15.00	-	-	1	4	2	-	1	-	12	1-11	(symbols)
FARR, by Inverness Inverness-shire	4 B9																

Dunlichity Lodge

Farr, by Inverness, IV1 2AN. Tel: Farr (08083) 282.

Situated 9 miles south of Inverness in a beautiful garden amid picturesque scenery, Dunlichity Lodge is a private house with tastefully furnished rooms and friendly atmosphere enjoying a reputation for comfort and good cooking–the ideal spot for your holiday in the Highlands.

Residents' licence; private bathrooms; electric blankets; inclusive terms and special rates for 3 days or more.

Brochure, personal welcome and attention from Commander and Mrs Ian Wedderburn.

Name and Address	Map Ref	Bedrooms	Services	Meals	Single room overnight	Double/twin room overnight	Per person daily	Per person weekly	Single	Double/twin	Family	Private	Public	Evening meals (Last order)	Parking	Months open	Symbols
Dunlichity Lodge Tel. Farr 282		4	3	3	9.50 / 9.50	19.00 / 25.00	16.00 / 19.00	94.00 / 115.00	1	2	-	2	1	1900 / 2100	4	4-10	(symbols)
FEARNAN, Aberfeldy Perthshire	2 A1																
Boreland Farm Hotel PH15 2PG Tel. Kenmore 212		3	2	3	6.50 / 8.30	- / -	11.50 / 13.30	42.00 / 54.60	1	4	2	-	2	1900 / 2100	20	4-10	(symbols)
Tigh-an-Loan Hotel PH15 2PF Tel. Kenmore 249		3	4	4	- / 10.50	- / 21.00	- / 15.50	- / 100.00	3	5	2	-	2	1900 / 1930	20	4-10	(symbols)
FETTERCAIRN Kincardineshire	4 F12																
Ramsay Arms Hotel AB3 1XX Tel. Fettercairn 334		4	4	4	18.00 / 18.00	28.00 / 28.00	19.00 / 25.00	105.00 / 175.00	3	6	2	11	-	1800 / 2100	15	1-12	(symbols)
FINDHORN, Forres Moray	4 C7																
Crown & Anchor Inn Tel. Findhorn 2243		3	2	3	10.00 / 12.50	20.00 / 25.00	- / -	- / -	1	5	-	-	1	1600 / 2200	15	1-12	(symbols)
FINTRY Stirlingshire	2 A4																
Clachan Hotel Tel. Fintry 237		3	3	4	11.00 / -	16.00 / -	- / -	- / -	-	2	2	-	1	1900 / 2145	-	1-12	(symbols)
Fintry Inn Tel. Fintry 224		3	4	5	8.50 / -	15.00 / -	13.50 / -	80.00 / -	-	3	1	-	1	1700 / 2100	45	1-12	(symbols)

VAT is shown at 15%: changes in this rate may affect prices.

Town / County / Establishment / Address / Telephone / Telex	Map Ref	Bedrooms	Services	Meals	Single room overnight £min £max	Double/twin room overnight £min £max	Per person daily £min £max	Per person weekly £min £max	Single	Double/twin	Family	Private	Public	No. of bath/shower rooms From Last order	Evening meals	Parking (no. of cars) / Months open (1-12)	Symbols

FIONNPHORT — Isle of Mull, Argyll — Map Ref **1 B3**

ACHABAN HOUSE
Fionnphort, Isle of Mull   Tel. No: STD 06817 205
Mr & Mrs T. P. Anderson

Small Georgian guest-house overlooking fresh-water loch (boat available) and only ½ mile from Iona ferry. Close to beautiful beaches. Ideal base for sight-seeing, boat-trips, pony-trekking, fishing, etc. We offer comfortable accommodation and excellent food using home-grown produce. C.H. in all rooms. Residents' lounge with log-fire. Open all year. Special Autumn Breaks. Details on request.

Establishment	Map Ref	Bd	Sv	Ml	Single overnight	Double/twin overnight	Per person daily	Per person weekly	Single	Double/twin	Family	Private	Public	Rooms From/Last order	Evening meals	Months open	Symbols
Achaban Guest House, PA66 6BL, Tel. Fionnphort 205		3	3	2	7.50 / 8.80	14.50 / 17.00	13.50 / 14.80	94.50 / 103.60	1	2	-	-	2	1830 / -	6	1-12	
FLODIGARRY Isle of Skye, Inverness-shire	3 D7																
Flodigarry Hotel, Tel. Duntulm 203		1	3	4	12.00 / 12.00	24.00 / 24.00	15.00 / 19.00	100.00 / 125.00	8	30	2	1	6	1900 / 2100	30	5-10	
FOCHABERS Moray	4 E8																
Gordon Arms Hotel, High Street, IV32 7DH, Tel. Fochabers 820508/9		4	3	5	18.00 / 24.00	32.00 / 38.00	22.00 / 26.00	130.00 / 160.00	-	17	-	8	3	1930 / 2130	50	1-12	
Grant Arms Hotel, High Street, IV32 7DH, Tel. Fochabers 820202		3	3	3	10.00 / -	17.00 / -	- / -	- / -	1	6	1	-	3	1700 / 1815	8	1-12	
Mains of Orton Lodge, Orton, IV32 7QE, Tel. Orton 240		3	4	5	16.00 / 22.00	- / -	- / -	- / -	2	3	-	-	2	1930 / -	20	1-12	
Spey Bay Hotel, Spey Bay, IV32 7PY, Tel. Fochabers 820424		4	3	4	- / 15.75	- / 30.00	- / 23.25	- / 139.50	2	8	-	8	2	- / 1900	100	1-12	
St Marys Lodge, Orton, IV32 7QH, Tel. Orton 240		3	4	5	16.00 / 22.00	- / -	- / -	- / -	1	3	-	-	2	1900 / -	10	1-12	
FORD, by Lochgilphead Argyll	1 E3																
Ford Hotel, PA31 8RH, Tel. Ford 273		2	3	4	12.50 / 13.50	25.00 / 27.00	20.50 / 21.50	125.00 / 135.00	2	8	1	5	2	1900 / 2000	20	1-12	

Name and Address	Map Ref	Bedrooms	Services	Meals	Single room overnight £min	£max	Double/twin room overnight £min	£max	Per person daily £min	£max	Per person weekly £min	£max	Single	Double/twin	Family	Private	Public	Evening meals From	Last order	Parking (no. of cars)	Months open (1-12)	Symbols
FORD, by Lochgilphead continued	1 E3																					Key on back fold-out
Tigh-an-Lodan Guest House Tel. Ford 287		3	3	2	7.50	7.50	15.00	15.00	11.00	11.00	77.00	-	-	3	-	-	3	1900	1900	5	4-10	(symbols)
FORFAR Angus	2 D1																					
Queens Hotel The Cross Tel. Forfar 62533		3	1	3	8.00	-	15.00	-	-	-	-	-	2	3	1	-	1	1700	1900	-	1-12	(symbols)
Royal Hotel Castle Street Tel. Forfar 62691		3	4	5	19.00	23.00	28.00	32.00	23.00	27.00	136.00	164.00	5	11	-	8	3	1700	2050	25	1-12	(symbols)
FORGANDENNY Perthshire	2 B3																					
Ardargie Lodge Hotel Path of Condie Road PH2 9DG Tel. Bridge of Earn 2234		3	3	4	9.50	9.50	19.00	19.00	22.00	27.00	-	-	4	7	-	-	4	1800	2100	50	1-12	(symbols)
FORRES Moray	4 C8																					
Carisbrooke Hotel Drumduan Road IV36 0BS Tel. Forres 72585		-	-	-	15.00	15.00	30.00	36.00	20.00	30.00	100.00	156.00	2	6	2	4	1	1700	2200	30	1-12	(symbols)
Heather Hotel Tytler Street IV36 0EL Tel. Forres 72377		4	4	4	11.50	11.50	23.00	23.00	15.00	15.00	-	-	2	3	1	3	1	1700	1845	12	1-12	(symbols)
Park Hotel Victoria Road IV36 0BN Tel. Forres 72328		-	-	3	12.00	-	24.00	-	17.50	-	121.50	-	3	6	3	2	3	1830	1900	30	1-12	(symbols)
Parkmount House Hotel St Leonard's Road IV36 0DW Tel. Forres 73312		3	3	4	9.75	9.75	19.50	19.50	15.75	15.75	60.00	60.00	1	5	2	-	3	1830	1930	15	1-12	(symbols)
Ramnee Hotel Victoria Road IV36 0BN Tel. Forres 72410		4	4	4	14.95	17.25	26.45	29.90	25.30	27.60	176.60	-	2	15	5	12	3	1900	2100	31	2-12	(symbols)
Royal Hotel Tytler Street IV36 0EL Tel. Forres 72617		3	4	5	13.50	-	23.00	29.90	15.70	-	-	-	1	15	4	6	5	1715	2030	50	1-12	(symbols)
Victoria Hotel 1 Tytler Street IV36 0EL Tel. Forres 72744		3	2	3	8.50	8.50	16.00	16.00	11.00	12.50	-	-	2	3	2	-	2	1700	1845	20	1-12	(symbols)
Moray Park Guest House Findhorn Road IV36 0TP Tel. Forres 72793		2	2	2	6.00	6.50	12.00	13.00	-	-	-	-	1	3	2	-	1	1730	1700	10	2-11	(symbols)

VAT is shown at 15%: changes in this rate may affect prices.

Name and Address				Prices					Rooms							Facilities
TOWN County Establishment Address Telephone Telex	Map Ref	Bedrooms	Services	Meals	Single room overnight	Double/twin room overnight	Per person daily	Per person weekly	Single	Double/twin	Family	Private	Public	No. of bedrooms / No. of bath/shower rooms	Evening meals	Parking (no. of cars)	Months open (1-12) / Symbols
					£min £max	£min £max	£min £max	£min £max						From Last order		Key on back fold-out
FORSINARD Sutherland	4 B4															
Forsinard Hotel KW13 6YT Tel. Halladale 221		4	3	4	14.00 14.00	24.50 24.50	19.75 21.50	125.00 140.00	6	8	-	8	2	1900 2100	30	1-12
FORT AUGUSTUS Inverness-shire	3 H10															

THE BRAE HOTEL

Fort-Augustus, Inverness-shire.
Tel: Fort-Augustus 6289 (STD Code 0320.)

Country House Hotel stands in its own spacious grounds. The 'Brae' is an intimate and friendly hotel; centrally heated throughout. Bedrooms with Private Bathrooms/Showers. Home cooking. Personally supervised.

Name and Address	Bedrooms	Services	Meals	Single room overnight	Double/twin room overnight	Per person daily	Per person weekly	Single	Double/twin	Family	Private	Public	Last order	Evening meals	Parking	Months open / Symbols
The Brae Hotel Tel. Fort Augustus 6289	4	4	4	9.00 10.50	18.00 21.00	15.00 16.50	100.00 120.00	-	5	3	4	1	1900 2000	10	4-10
Caledonian Hotel Tel. Fort Augustus 6256/6244	3	3	4	8.50 10.00	- -	14.00 16.00	90.00 100.00	2	9	1	1	4	1900 2100	20	4-9

INCHNACARDOCH LODGE HOTEL

LOCH NESS

Situated North of Fort Augustus, offering magnificent views of Loch Ness, this former Shooting Lodge specialises in traditional Scottish dishes and highland hospitality. Salmon and Trout fishing on Loch Ness, Boating, Hill Walking, Pony Trekking, Wind Surfing and Golfing are among the many activities offered from this touring centre, and in the evening relax over cocktails in Nessie's Nook Bar, to the music of our accordionist.

Marie and Donald MacFadyen   Telephone 0320 6258

Name and Address	Bedrooms	Services	Meals	Single room overnight	Double/twin room overnight	Per person daily	Per person weekly	Single	Double/twin	Family	Private	Public	Last order	Evening meals	Parking	Months open / Symbols
Inchnacardoch Lodge Hotel Loch Ness Tel. Fort Augustus 6258	4	3	5	14.00 15.50	28.00 31.00	19.50 21.00	- -	1	11	5	17	-	1900 2030	50	1-12
Lovat Arms Hotel Tel. Fort Augustus 6206	3	4	4	12.00 13.50	24.00 27.00	20.00 21.50	120.00 189.00	6	19	3	3	6	1900 2000	50	12-10
Richmond Guest House Tel. Fort Augustus 6221	3	3	4	8.50 -	17.00 -	14.00 -	90.00 -	2	4	2	1	3	1830 2100	-	1-12

Name and Address	Map Ref	Bedrooms	Services	Meals	Bed and Breakfast				B & B and evening meal				No. of bedrooms	No. of bath/shower rooms		Facilities		
TOWN County — Establishment Address Telephone Telex					Single room overnight	Double/twin room overnight	Per person daily	Per person weekly	Single	Double/twin	Family	Private	Public	Evening meals	Parking (no. of cars)	Months open (1-12)	Symbols	
					£min £max	£min £max	£min £max	£min £max					From Last order		Key on back fold-out		

FORT WILLIAM
Inverness-shire — 3 G12

ALEXANDRA HOTEL
The Parade, Fort William
Telephone: 0397 2241

The Alexandra Hotel is one of 4 Milton Hotels located throughout the Highlands. It is centrally situated adjacent to the shopping centre and has 92 rooms with tea and coffee-making facilities, telephone and colour T.V.s. Special weekend breaks and 7 or more night stays are available or you can take one of our tour holidays including hotels in Oban and Inverness.

Contact hotel direct or write to: Mhairi Cameron, Milton Hotels, Fort William, Inverness-shire, Tel. 0397 3139, for our colour "Highland Holiday" brochure.

Establishment	Bedrooms	Services	Meals	Single room overnight	Double/twin room overnight	Per person daily	Per person weekly	Single	Double/twin	Family	Private	Public	Evening meals (Last order)	Parking	Months open	Symbols
Alexandra Hotel PH33 6AZ Tel. Fort William 2241	5	5	4	16.50 -	33.00 -	-	99.00 -	11	75	6	68	5	1830 2100	40	1-12	T ⊞ ♨ ♟ ⛨ ⋈ ▥ ⚲ ● ⬓ ☎ ▭ ▢ ⚶ C ✳ V ◡

Clan Macduff Motel

27 Achintore Road
Fort William
Inverness-shire
PH33 6RW

Tel: 0397 2341

When in Fort William, stay at the Clan Macduff Motel. The comfort and freedom of a hotel at guest house prices. Dinner, bed and full breakfast from £13.50 per person.

Establishment	Bedrooms	Services	Meals	Single room overnight	Double/twin room overnight	Per person daily	Per person weekly	Single	Double/twin	Family	Private	Public	Evening meals (Last order)	Parking	Months open	Symbols
Clan MacDuff Motel PH33 6RW Tel. Fort William 2341	3	3	3	9.00 12.00	14.00 18.00	12.20 14.20	85.40 99.40	3	37	5	10	6	1830 2000	45	4-10	♟ ⛨ ⋈ ⚶ V ♫

VAT is shown at 15%: changes in this rate may affect prices.

Name and Address				Prices						Rooms					Facilities
TOWN County — Establishment Address Telephone Telex	Map Ref — Bedrooms / Services / Meals			Bed and Breakfast — Single room overnight	Double/twin room overnight	Per person daily	B & B and evening meal — Per person weekly	Single	Double/twin	Family	No. of bedrooms — Private	No. of bath/shower rooms — Public	Evening meals	Parking (no. of cars)	Months open (1-12) — Symbols
FORT WILLIAM continued	3 G12			£min £max	£min £max	£min £max	£min £max				From		Last order		Key on back fold-out

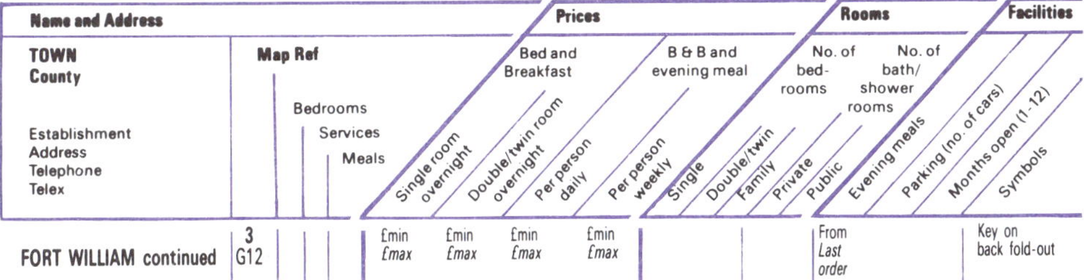

Croit Anna Hotel

Fort William, Inverness-shire
Scotland PH33 6RR.
Telephone 0397-2268/9.

This Hotel is situated 2½ miles south of Fort William on the A82 Inverness/Glasgow Road.

With its Lochside situation it commands views across Loch Linnhe to the Ardgour Hills.

The Accommodation consists of many rooms with Bath/Shower/Toilet, several having Colour T.V.

Morning Tea is available in the rooms.

The Service area comprises Dining Room, Lounge Bar, Residents Lounge, TV Lounge, Gift Shop, Glen Coe Suite Panoramic Lounge, and on premises Guest Launderette. The Hotel is owned and personally managed by the same family who designed and built it on a croft which has been held by the family for over 250 years.

Establishment	Bed	Serv	Meals	Single o/n	Double o/n	Per person daily	Per person weekly	Single	Double/twin	Family	Private	Public	Evening meals (Last order)	Parking	Months open
Croit Anna Hotel PH33 6RR Tel. Fort William 2268	4	3	4	16.30 -	30.50 -	24.05 -	168.35 -	22	78	-	62	15	1830 2030	60	4-10
Grand Hotel PH33 6DX Tel. Fort William 2928	4	5	4	11.50 -	22.00 -	17.50 -	-	2	29	2	25	6	1845 2030	25	1-12

IMPERIAL HOTEL

Fort William. Tel: 0397 2040.

Situated in the heart of Fort William, close to the shopping centre and with panoramic views of Loch Linnhe and the surrounding countryside. The Hotel offers the ideal base to explore and discover the beauty of the West Highlands by car or coach. It is one of the old established hotels in Fort William and has developed over the years a reputation for Highland hospitality and good food. The hotel has: 46 letting bedrooms with full central heating: Intercom and baby alarm in all rooms: TV room: Two lounges with panoramic views of Loch Linnhe: Tea and coffee facilities in all bedrooms: Rooms with Private Facilities.

Establishment	Bed	Serv	Meals	Single o/n	Double o/n	Per person daily	Per person weekly	Single	Double/twin	Family	Private	Public	Evening meals (Last order)	Parking	Months open
Imperial Hotel Tel. Fort William 2040	3	4	5	12.30 13.50	22.60 24.60	16.30 18.00	- -	9	25	4	2	7	1845 2015	24	1-12

Name and Address					Prices					Rooms					Facilities	
TOWN County / Establishment Address Telephone Telex	Map Ref	Bedrooms	Services	Meals	Single room overnight	Double/twin room overnight	Per person daily	Per person weekly	Single	Double/twin	Family	Private	Public	No. of bed-rooms	No. of bath/shower rooms	Evening meals	Parking (no. of cars)	Months open (1-12)	Symbols
FORT WILLIAM continued	3 G12				£min £max	£min £max	£min £max	£min £max					From Last order				Key on back fold-out

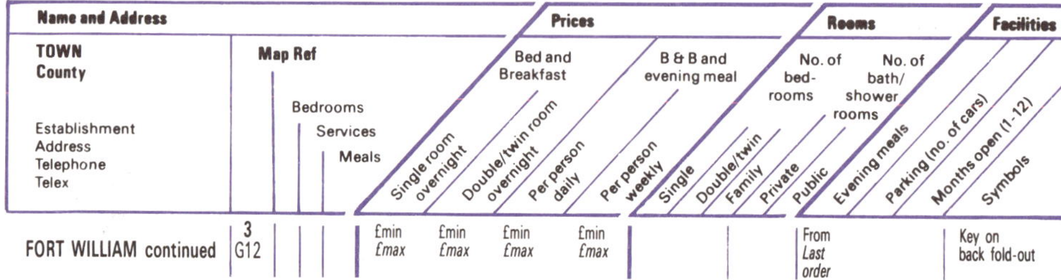

Establishment	Map Ref	Bedrooms	Services	Meals	Single room overnight	Double/twin room overnight	Per person daily	Per person weekly	Single	Double/twin	Family	Private	Public	No. of bed-rooms	No. of bath/shower rooms	Evening meals	Parking	Months open	Symbols
Ladbroke Hotel Achintore Road Tel. Fort William 3117		6	3	5	28.00 -	46.00 -	- -	- -	12	32	17	61	-	1830 2200	80		1-12	

MILTON HOTEL

North Road, Fort William, Inverness. Tel. STD 0397 2331

The Milton Hotel is one of 4 Milton Hotels located throughout the Highlands. It has 62 rooms and offers entertainment on same evenings of the week. Special Weekend Breaks and 7 or more night stays are available.

Contact hotel or write to Mhairi Cameron, Milton Hotels, Fort William, Inverness-shire (0397 3139) for our colour 'Highland Holiday' brochure.

Establishment	Map Ref	Bedrooms	Services	Meals	Single room overnight	Double/twin room overnight	Per person daily	Per person weekly	Single	Double/twin	Family	Private	Public	No. of bed-rooms	No. of bath/shower rooms	Evening meals	Parking	Months open	Symbols
Milton Hotel PH33 6TG Tel. Fort William 2331		3	5	4	14.50 -	29.00 -	- -	92.00 -	18	41	2	9	10	1830 2100	200		5-9	

VAT is shown at 15%: changes in this rate may affect prices.

Name and Address	Map Ref	Bedrooms	Services	Meals	Prices — Bed and Breakfast: Single room overnight (£min / £max)	Double/twin room overnight (£min / £max)	Per person daily (£min / £max)	B & B and evening meal: Per person weekly (£min / £max)	No. of bedrooms: Single	Double/twin	Family	No. of bath/shower rooms: Private	Public	Evening meals (Last order)	Parking (no. of cars)	Months open (1-12)	Symbols
TOWN / County / Establishment / Address / Telephone / Telex																	
FORT WILLIAM continued	3 G12				£min £max	£min £max	£min £max	£min £max						From Last order			Key on back fold-out
Milton Motor In / PH33 6TG / Tel. Fort William 2334	3	2	1		6.49 / -	9.00 / -	- / -	- / -	8	100	3	-	21	-	200	5-9	T R (symbols)
Nevis Bank Hotel / Tel. Fort William 2595	-	-	-		12.50 / 16.50	20.00 / 24.00	17.50 / -	- / -	5	17	1	6	4	1900 / 2030	20	1-12	R C V (symbols)
Stag's Head Hotel / High Street / Tel. Fort William 4144	3	4	4		14.50 / -	22.40 / -	17.20 / -	- / -	15	26	7	8	16	1830 / 2030	-	4-10	T £ R C V (symbols)
West End Hotel / PH33 6ED / Tel. Fort William 2614	-	-	-		14.50 / 21.00	25.00 / 32.00	- / -	- / -	2	43	4	25	6	1830 / 2030	45	1-12	T £ C V (symbols)
Achintee Farm Guest House / Achintee / Tel. Fort William 2240/3667	1	2	2		6.50 / 7.00	13.00 / 14.00	11.00 / 11.50	77.00 / 80.50	-	4	1	-	1	1800 / 1530	10	1-12	T R C V (symbols)
Ben View Guest House / Belford Road / Tel. Fort William 2966	3	3	2		6.90 / 9.20	13.80 / 18.40	11.50 / 14.95	81.50 / 104.65	2	11	2	-	6	1845 / 1930	20	3-11	R C (symbols)
Craig Nevis West Guest House / Belford Road / PH33 6BU / Tel. Fort William 2023	3	3	3		6.50 / 7.00	12.50 / 14.50	10.50 / 11.00	70.00 / 75.00	1	2	2	-	1	1830 / 1930	5	1-12	R C V (symbols)
Dariach Guest House / Cameron Road / Tel. Fort William 2644	2	2	1		6.00 / -	12.00 / -	- / -	- / -	1	-	3	-	1	- / -	4	4-10	R M V (symbols)
Glen Shiel Guest House / Achintore Road / PH33 6RW / Tel. Fort William 2271	3	3	1		7.00 / -	13.00 / -	- / -	- / -	1	4	1	-	3	-	6	4-10	R V (symbols)

Milton Motor In
North Road, Fort William
Telephone: 0397 2334

The Milton Motor In in FORT WILLIAM is located about 1 mile from the centre and is overlooked by Ben Nevis — Britain's highest mountain. It is adjacent to the Milton Hotel and offers inexpensive accommodation at rates from £4.99 for bed only. Special 2 or more night special packages are available. Cooked breakfast and three course dinners are available to all residents at the adjacent Milton Hotel which also has evening entertainment some evenings of the week. Contact **Motor In** direct or write to **Mhairi Cameron, Milton Hotels, Fort William, Inverness-shire (0397 3139)**, for our colour "Highland Holiday" Brochure.

Column key — **No. of bedrooms:** Single, Double/twin, Family · **No. of bath/shower rooms:** Private, Public · **Evening meals:** From / Last order

Establishment / Address	Map Ref	Bedrooms	Services	Meals	Single room overnight £min/£max	Double/twin room overnight	Per person daily	Per person weekly	Single	Double/twin	Family	Private	Public	Evening meals	Parking (no. of cars)	Months open (1-12)	Symbols
FORT WILLIAM continued	3 G12													From Last order			Key on back fold-out
Guisachan Guest House, Alma Road, Tel. Fort William 3797/4447		3	4	2	7.00 / 8.50	14.00 / 16.50	11.00 / 13.00	77.00 / 91.00	3	8	4	-	4	1830	15	1-12	(symbols)
Hillview Guest House, Achintore Road, Tel. Fort William 4349		3	3	2	6.00 / 7.00	12.00 / 14.00	10.00 / 11.00	70.00 / 77.00	1	6	2	-	2	1830	10	1-12	(symbols)
Innseagan Guest House, Achintore Road, PH33 6RW, Tel. Fort William 2452		4	4	2	-	-	12.00 / 15.00	81.00 / 103.00	3	21	2	12	3	1800 / 1900	26	4-10	(symbols)
Lochview Guest House, Heathercroft, off Argyll Terrace, PH33 6RE, Tel. Fort William 3149		3	3	2	-	13.00 / 15.00	10.50 / 11.75	69.50 / 77.00	-	5	2	1	2	1830 / 1830	8	4-10	(symbols)
Rhu Mhor Guest House, Alma Road, PH33 6BP, Tel. Fort William 2213		2	3	2	6.50	13.00	10.30	-	-	5	2	-	2	1900	7	3-10	(symbols)
Stronchreggan View Guest House, Achintore Road, PH33 6RW, Tel. Fort William 4644		3	3	2	-	14.00	11.50	80.50	-	3	4	-	3	1900 / 1900	7	4-10	(symbols)
Viewfield Guest House, Alma Road, Tel. Fort William 4763		-	-	-	6.00	12.00	9.50	-	2	4	-	-	1	1800 / 1900	12	1-12	(symbols)
FORTINGALL Perthshire	2 A1																
Fortingall Hotel, PH15 2NQ, Tel. Kenmore 367		3	4	4	12.50 / 16.00	20.00 / 26.00	19.95 / 26.00	125.00 / 165.00	2	15	-	1	4	1800 / 2100	36	4-10	(symbols)
FORTROSE Ross-shire	4 B8																
Platcock Guest House, 18 Church Street, IV10 8SQ, Tel. Fortrose 20569		3	5	5	8.00	15.00	11.50	72.50	1	2	3	-	2	1830	10	4-10	(symbols)

VAT is shown at 15%: changes in this rate may affect prices.

Name and Address	Map Ref	Bedrooms	Services	Meals	Bed and Breakfast				B & B and evening meal					No. of bedrooms	No. of bath/shower rooms	Evening meals	Parking (no. of cars)	Months open (1-12)	Facilities / Symbols
TOWN / County / Establishment / Address / Telephone / Telex					Single room overnight	Double/twin room overnight	Per person daily	Per person weekly	Single	Double/twin	Family	Private	Public					
					£min £max	£min £max	£min £max	£min £max						From Last order				Key on back fold-out
FORTROSE continued	4 B8																	
Saint Katherines Guest House / Union Street / Tel. Fortrose 20949		3	3	2	7.50 / 7.50	15.00 / 15.00	12.50 / 12.50	- / -	-	3	-	-	1	1830 / 1815	6	4-10	[symbols]
FOYERS / Inverness-shire	4 A10																	
Foyers Hotel / Tel. Gorthleck 216		3	4	4	9.00 / 9.00	18.00 / 18.00	13.50 / 13.50	94.50 / 94.50	2	6	1	-	3	1915 / 1900	30	1-12	[symbols]
FRASERBURGH / Aberdeenshire	4 H7																	
Station Hotel / Tel. Fraserburgh 3343		-	-	-	12.00 / -	22.00 / -	- / -	- / -	5	8	1	3	3	1700 / 2100	30	1-12	[symbols]
FREUCHIE, by Falkland / Fife	2 D3																	
Lomond Hotel / Parliament Square / KY7 7EY / Tel. Falkland 329		3	4	5	13.75 / 18.00	23.75 / 28.00	18.75 / 26.00	108.00 / 164.00	1	14	2	10	3	1830 / 2130	60	1-12	[symbols]
GAIRLOCH / Ross-shire	3 F7																	

Creag Mor Hotel.

Charleston, Gairloch, Ross-shire IV21 2AH. Telephone Gairloch 2068.

Overlooking the old harbour and quay, the Creag Mor Hotel is a family run establishment newly completed in 1976. Downstairs the dining room/lounge and the fully licensed bar are furnished in a comfortable old world style. The menu is traditional and locally caught fish makes frequent appearance in season. Upstairs there are nine bedrooms, four with self-contained bathrooms. All bedrooms have hot and cold water and there are downies on all the beds.

The Creag Mor Hotel is picturesquely situated in Gairloch, a uniquely beautiful region in the heart of Wester Ross.

Trout fishing, sea angling, golf and hill walking are among the many outdoor pursuits available to the visitor. The area abounds with beautiful beaches and famous tropical Inverewe gardens are only 5 miles from the hotel.

Brochure and tariff on request.

| Creag Mor Hotel / IV21 2AH / Tel. Gairloch 2068 | | 3 | 3 | 4 | 12.00 / 13.50 | 21.00 / 25.00 | 16.80 / 19.20 | 115.00 / 130.00 | - | 8 | 1 | 4 | 2 | 1900 / 2000 | 20 | 1-12 | [symbols] |

Name and Address	Map Ref	Bedrooms	Services	Meals	Prices				B & B and evening meal				Rooms					Facilities			
TOWN County — Establishment Address Telephone Telex					Bed and Breakfast								No of bed rooms	No of bath/shower rooms							
					Single room overnight	Double/twin room overnight	Per person daily	Per person weekly	Single	Double/twin	Family	Private	Public	Evening meals	Parking (no of cars)	Months open (1-12)	Symbols			
GAIRLOCH continued	3 F7				£min £max	£min £max	£min £max	£min £max					From Last order			Key on back fold-out				

Gairloch Hotel, Gairloch, Ross-shire. Tel. 0445-2001

This beautiful west Highland hotel overlooking the sea and long stretches of sand, offers the family holidaymaker superb facilities for safe sea bathing, excellent loch and sea angling, golf and tennis. 50 bedrooms most with Private Bath and all with Tea and Coffee making facilities.

Name and Address	Bedrooms	Services	Meals	Single room overnight	Double/twin room overnight	Per person daily	Per person weekly	Single	Double/twin	Family	Private	Public	From / Last order	Evening meals	Parking	Months open
Gairloch Hotel Tel. Gairloch 2001 Telex 778215	3	4	4	26.00 26.00	42.00 42.00	29.00 29.00	147.00 147.00	8	38	4	46	10	1900 2100	60		4-10
Glendale House Hotel South Erradale IV21 2AU Tel. Badachro 256	4	4	4	11.50 13.50	- -	17.50 21.50	- -	2	4	2	8	1	1915 2100	15		3-11
Millcroft Hotel Strath IV21 2BT Tel. Gairloch 2376 Telex 75605	4	4	5	10.00 14.50	20.00 29.00	- -	- -	1	11	-	4	2	1830 2100	23		1-12
Myrtle Bank Hotel IV21 2BS Tel. Gairloch 2004	3	3	4	9.50 10.00	18.00 20.00	16.00 16.50	112.00 116.00	1	11	-	1	5	1830 2000	24		4-10
The Old Inn IV21 2DB Tel. Gairloch 2006	4	4	4	14.00 -	28.00 -	20.50 -	- -	1	4	4	7	1	1900 2100	50		1-12
Shieldaig Lodge Hotel IV21 2AW Tel. Badachro 250	3	3	4	13.50 18.00	27.00 36.00	19.00 24.00	- -	2	10	3	3	4	1915 2015	20		4-10
Charleston Guest House IV21 2AH Tel. Gairloch 2497	3	1	2	6.00 6.00	12.00 12.00	10.00 10.00	70.00 70.00	2	5	2	-	2	1900 1900	9		3-10

THE GLENDALE

Tel: 0445 83 256

The Family Hotel that cares—top class comfort, traditional food and fine wines. Run by resident owners who invite you to come and enjoy yourself in a stress-free holiday environment—*Children sharing parents room accommodated free.*

Special Spring, Summer and Autumn Packages. For full details, brochure and tariff please write or phone:

The Glendale, South Erradale Gairloch, Wester Ross IV21 2AU Telephone Badachro 256 (STD 0445 83)

Member Wester Ross Hoteliers Association

VAT is shown at 15%: changes in this rate may affect prices.

Name and Address	Map Ref	Bedrooms	Services	Meals	Single room overnight	Double/twin room overnight	Per person daily	Per person weekly	Single	Double/twin	Family	Private	Public	Evening meals From / Last order	Parking (no. of cars)	Months open	Symbols
GAIRLOCH continued	3 F7				£min £max	£min £max	£min £max	£min £max						From Last order			Key on back fold-out

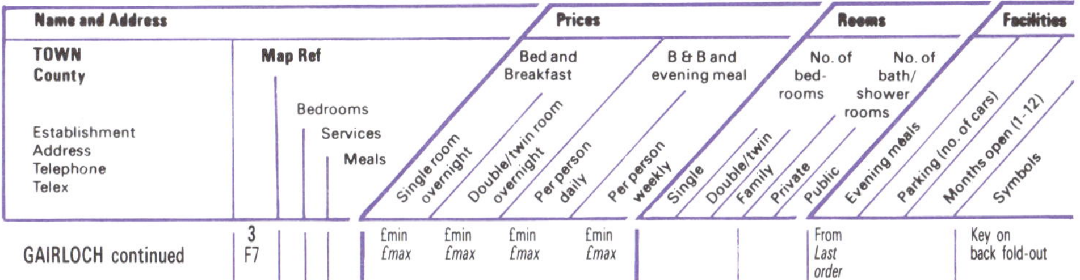

HORISDALE HOUSE

Strath, Gairloch
Wester Ross
Tel: Gairloch
(0445) 2151
AA Listed
Fire Certificate

"Purpose built Guest House with panoramic views of sea and mountains. We offer: comfortably furnished bedrooms equipped with teamakers; spacious lounge with open fire and separate dining room; traditional Scottish breakfasts and imaginative evening meals in friendly, relaxed atmosphere. Early bookings advised. SAE, please for details."

Name and Address	Map Ref	Bedrooms	Services	Meals	Single room overnight	Double/twin room overnight	Per person daily	Per person weekly	Single	Double/twin	Family	Private	Public	Evening meals From / Last order	Parking	Months open	Symbols
Horisdale House, Strath, IV21 2DA, Tel. Gairloch 2151	3	3	2	- / 9.00	- / 17.00	- / 14.00	- / -	1	7	1	-	3	1900 / 1700	22	4-10	
GALASHIELS Selkirkshire	2 E6																
Abbotsford Arms Hotel, Stirling Street, Tel. Galashiels 2517	-	-	-	10.00 / 14.00	18.00 / 22.00	16.25 / 20.25	105.00 / 140.00	-	10	-	5	1	1800 / 2100	-	1-12	
Douglas Hotel, Channel Street, Tel. Galashiels 2189	4	4	5	14.50 / -	24.00 / -	- / -	- / -	15	20	3	11	6	1700 / 2200	28	1-12	
Kings Hotel, Tel. Galashiels 2783	3	3	5	10.00 / 12.50	18.00 / 24.50	13.00 / 16.50	75.00 / 90.00	-	7	-	-	2	1630 / 2200	-	1-12	
Kingsknowes Hotel, Selkirk Road, TD1 3HY, Tel. Galashiels 3478	4	4	5	22.00 / 25.00	34.00 / 38.00	29.00 / 32.00	- / -	-	9	1	7	1	1900 / 2130	50	1-12	
Maxwell Hotel, Bridge Street, Tel. Galashiels 2176	3	3	4	8.50 / -	16.00 / -	14.50 / -	84.00 / -	3	12	1	-	4	1800 / 2000	-	1-12	
Royal Hotel, Channel Street, Tel. Galashiels 2918	-	-	-	13.25 / -	26.50 / -	- / -	- / -	5	14	3	1	4	1800 / 2100	-	1-12	
Woodlands House Hotel, Windyknowe Road, TD1 1RG, Tel. Galashiels 2829	6	5	5	19.50 / 23.00	29.50 / 34.00	29.50 / 44.00	- / -	3	6	-	9	-	1900 / 2200	28	1-12	
Buckholmburn Guest House, Edinburgh Road, Tel. Galashiels 2697	3	4	5	10.00 / 10.00	20.00 / 20.00	14.00 / -	- / -	1	4	3	-	2	1800 / 2130	15	1-12	
GARELOCHHEAD Dunbartonshire	1 G4																
Garelochhead Hotel, Tel. Garelochhead 810263	-	-	-	10.00 / -	19.00 / -	- / -	- / -	1	4	1	-	1	1700 / 2100	50	1-12	

Name and Address	Map Ref				Prices				B & B and evening meal				Rooms			Facilities
TOWN County / Establishment Address Telephone Telex		Bedrooms	Services	Meals	Bed and Breakfast								No. of bed-rooms	No. of bath/ shower rooms		Symbols
					Single room overnight	Double/twin room overnight	Per person daily	Per person weekly	Single	Double/twin	Family	Private	Public	Evening meals	Parking (no. of cars)	Months open (1-12)
					£min £max	£min £max	£min £max	£min £max					From Last order		Key on back fold-out
GARMOUTH, Fochabers Moray	4 E7															
Garmouth Hotel South Road IV32 7LU Tel. Spey Bay 226		-	-	-	15.00 -	20.00 -	22.00 -	- -	1	1	-	- -	- 2200	50	-	
GARTOCHARN, by Alexandria Dunbartonshire	1 H4															
Gartocharn Hotel G83 8RX Tel. Gartocharn 204		-	-	-	10.00 -	18.00 -	13.00 -	91.00 -	-	4	1	- 1	1630 2030	50	1-12	
GARVE Ross-shire	3 H8															
Garve Hotel IV23 2PR Tel. Garve 205		3	4	4	11.00 14.50	22.00 29.00	18.50 22.00	110.50 132.25	6	25	3	15 4	1900 2100	56	4-10	

Inchbae Lodge

Inchbae, by Garve, Ross-shire. Tel: 099 75 269.

Nestled amidst spectacular scenery on the banks of the River Blackwater, half way between Inverness and the West coast, Inchbae is the perfect centre for touring the Highlands.

Spend your days birdwatching, fishing, pony trekking, stalking, walking or simply unwinding. Spend your evenings enjoying the finest of fresh food including local salmon and venison.

Egon Ronay Recommended. RAC**AA.

Name and Address		Bedrooms	Services	Meals	Single room overnight	Double/twin room overnight	Per person daily	Per person weekly	Single	Double/twin	Family	Private	Public	From Last order	Evening meals	Months open	Symbols
Inchbae Lodge Aultguish IV23 9PG Tel. Aultguish 269		4	4	4	9.80 15.80	19.60 28.00	18.30 24.30	100.00 150.00	-	8	4	9 2	1930 2030	25	1-12	
Strathgarve Lodge IV23 2PO Tel. Garve 204		5	4	5	18.50 -	35.00 -	- -	- -	2	13	-	11 4	1900 2230	34	1-12	
GATEHEAD, by Kilmarnock Ayrshire	1 H7															
Old Rome Farmhouse Guest House Tel. Drybridge 850265	2	3	2		7.00 9.00	13.00 15.00	10.50 13.50	66.50 87.50	-	5	1	- 1	1900 2100	24	3-10	

VAT is shown at 15%: changes in this rate may affect prices.

Name and Address	Map Ref	Bedrooms	Services	Meals	Single room overnight £min/£max	Double/twin room overnight £min/£max	Per person daily £min/£max	Per person weekly £min/£max	Single	Double/twin	Family	Private	Public	Evening meals From/Last order	Parking (no. of cars)	Months open (1-12)	Symbols
GATEHOUSE-OF-FLEET Kirkcudbrightshire	2 A10																

ANGEL HOTEL

Gatehouse of Fleet, Kirkcudbrightshire DG7 2HP. Telephone: (055 74) 204. Proprietors: Norie and Irene Moir.

A small family hotel providing comfort, good food, and personal service in one of the most beautiful areas of Scotland. Golfing, fishing, shooting and sailing available locally. Fully licensed.

Name and Address	Bedrooms	Services	Meals	Single room overnight £min/£max	Double/twin room overnight £min/£max	Per person daily £min/£max	Per person weekly £min/£max	Single	Double/twin	Family	Private	Public	Evening meals From/Last order	Parking	Months open	Symbols
Angel Hotel, DG7 2HP, Tel. Gatehouse 204	3	3	4	9.50 / 9.50	19.00 / 19.00	- / -	- / -	1	4	2	-	2	1845 / 2045	15	1-12	
Anwoth Hotel, DG7 2JT, Tel. Gatehouse 217	-	-	-	13.00 / -	18.00 / -	18.00 / -	110.00 / -	2	11	2	2	5	1900 / 2100	14	1-12	
Bank O'Fleet Hotel, 47 High Street, Tel. Gatehouse 302	3	3	4	8.50 / 9.00	16.50 / 17.00	11.50 / 12.50	80.00 / 80.00	-	5	1	-	2	1830 / 2130	-	1-12	
Cally Palace Hotel, DG7 2DL, Tel. Gatehouse 341	5	5	5	22.50 / 22.50	44.00 / 51.50	27.50 / 32.50	173.95 / 204.75	6	37	17	60	1	1900 / 2130	100	2-12	
Murray Arms Hotel, DG7 2HY, Tel. Gatehouse 207	4	5	5	19.00 / 21.00	38.00 / 42.00	27.50 / 30.00	165.00 / 180.00	6	8	2	12	3	1930 / 2100	20	1-12	
Bobbin Guest House, 36 High Street, Tel. Gatehouse-of-Fleet 229	2	3	2	7.00 / -	14.00 / -	10.50 / -	70.00 / -	1	2	3	1	2	1800 / 2000	5	1-12	
GIFFNOCK Renfrewshire — Map Ref 1 H5																
Macdonald Thistle Hotel, Eastwood Toll, Tel. 041 638 2225, Telex 779138	6	5	6	37.50 / 42.50	44.00 / 49.00	- / -	- / -	27	30	1	58	2	1900 / 2200	200	1-12	
Orchard Park Hotel, 2 Park Road, Tel. 041 638 1044	-	-	-	- / -	27.00 / -	- / -	- / -	2	4	2	-	2	1730 / 2100	30	1-12	
Stakis Redhurst Hotel, Eastwoodmains Road, G46 6QE, Tel. 041 638 6465	5	5	5	37.00 / -	44.00 / -	- / -	- / -	10	6	-	10	6	1830 / 2200	60	1-12	

Name and Address	Map Ref	Bedrooms	Services	Meals	Single room overnight	Double/twin room overnight	Per person daily	Per person weekly	Single	Double/twin	Family	Private	Public	Evening meals From / Last order	Parking (no. of cars)	Months open	Symbols
GIFFORD East Lothian	2 E5																
Tweeddale Arms Hotel EH41 4QU Tel. Gifford 240		4	3	4	11.50 / 13.50	20.00 / 25.00	19.50 / 22.50	129.50 / 147.00	2	5	1	5	1	1900 / 2030	-	1-12	T £ ...
GIGHA, Isle of Argyll	1 D6																

GIGHA HOTEL Isle of Gigha, Argyll. Tel: 05835 254.

The lovely Isle of Gigha (pronounced 'Gee-a') is the innermost of the Hebrides, just 3 miles from mainland Argyll, only 2½ hours drive from Glasgow with a regular daily ferry service from Tayinloan.

The old inn has been tastefully restored and extended to form the Gigha Hotel — centrally heated with 9 twin-bedded rooms and renowned for its superb traditional Scottish cooking and baking, using local produce from the island's dairy farms and locally caught seafood.

Splendid views, sandy beaches, birds and wild flowers plus the world famous gardens of Achamore House with its collection of rhododendrons and exotic shrubs from many countries — the makings of a tranquil holiday.

Please write or telephone for colour brochure and further information.

Name and Address	Map Ref	Bedrooms	Services	Meals	Single room overnight	Double/twin room overnight	Per person daily	Per person weekly	Single	Double/twin	Family	Private	Public	Evening meals From / Last order	Parking (no. of cars)	Months open	Symbols
Gigha Hotel PA41 7AD Tel. Gigha 254		4	4	4	14.00 / -	28.00 / -	23.00 / -	46.00 / -	-	9	-	3	4	1900 / 2000	20	1-12	£ ... V
Post Office Guest House PA41 7AA Tel. Gigha 251		1	1	2	7.00 / -	14.00 / -	10.00 / -	65.00 / -	1	3	2	-	1	1830 / 1930	4	4-10	C ✱ V
GIRVAN Ayrshire	1 G8																
Auchendolly Hotel 30 Louisa Drive Tel. Girvan 4289		3	3	2	7.50 / 7.50	15.00 / 15.00	10.50 / 10.50	73.50 / 73.50	-	3	2	-	2	1800 / 1830	8	4-10	...
Hotel Westcliffe 15 Louisa Drive KA26 9AH Tel. Girvan 2128		4	4	4	10.00 / -	18.00 / -	26.00 / -	73.00 / -	1	11	8	6	4	1800 / 1800	-	1-12	T £ ...
Mansfield Private Hotel 22 The Avenue Tel. Girvan 4268/2492		3	4	2	8.00 / -	15.00 / -	10.75 / -	73.50 / -	2	5	3	-	2	- / -	10	1-12	C ✱ V
Queens Hotel Montgomerie Street Tel. Girvan 3670		2	2	4	7.50 / 7.50	14.00 / 14.00	10.50 / 10.50	63.00 / 63.00	1	7	1	-	2	1700 / 1930	15	1-12	T M V ...

VAT is shown at 15%: changes in this rate may affect prices.

Name and Address	Map Ref	Bedrooms	Services	Meals	Single room overnight £min/£max	Double/twin room overnight £min/£max	Per person daily £min/£max	Per person weekly £min/£max	Single	Double/twin	Family	Private	Public	Evening meals From/Last order	Parking (no. of cars)	Months open (1-12)	Symbols
GIRVAN continued	1 G8																Key on back fold-out
Gowanbrae Guest House, 45 Henrietta Street, KA26 9AL, Tel. Girvan 2316	1	1	2		7.00 / -	14.00 / -	9.20 / -	65.00 / -	1	3	2	-	1	1730 / 1800	6	4-10	[symbols]
Thistleneuk Guest House, 19 Louisa Drive, Tel. Girvan 2137	3	3	2		6.00 / -	12.00 / -	9.50 / -	56.00 / -	1	4	2	-	2	1800 / 1930	2	1-12	[symbols]
Trochrague Guest House, KA26 9QA, Tel. Girvan 2074	3	3	3		8.00 / -	16.00 / -	14.50 / -	101.50 / -	9	9	5	1	7	1800 / 1900	30	12-10	[symbols]
GLASGOW	1 H5																
Adamson Hotel, 4 Crookston Drive, Tel. 041 882 3047	3	3	2		9.00 / 9.00	16.00 / 16.00	- / -	- / -	4	4	-	-	2	1800 / -	10	1-12	[symbols]
Albany Hotel, Bothwell Street, G2 7EN, Tel. 041 248 2656, Telex 77440	6	6	6		49.50 / -	67.50 / -	- / -	- / -	174	77	-	251	-	1730 / 2245	25	1-12	[symbols]
Apsley Hotel, 903 Sauchiehall Street, Tel. 041 339 4999/334 3510	3	3	4		12.65 / -	19.55 / -	15.65 / -	91.00 / -	3	8	6	5	2	1750 / 2000	-	1-12	[symbols]
Arfon Hotel, 969 Sauchiehall Street, G3 7TQ, Tel. 041 334 7802	3	4	3		9.00 / 12.00	16.00 / 24.00	12.50 / 18.00	87.50 / 126.00	6	19	3	-	6	1800 / 2100	-	1-12	[symbols]
Beacons Hotel, 7 Park Terrace, Tel. 041 332 9438	6	6	6		18.50 / 32.95	27.50 / 38.95	24.50 / 38.95	171.50 / 272.65	10	26	-	36	-	1900 / 2300	-	1-12	[symbols]
Bellahouston Hotel, 517 Paisley Road West, Tel. 041 427 3146, Telex 778795	6	5	5		27.50 / 37.50	33.50 / 43.00	35.00 / 50.00	200.00 / 330.00	24	97	1	122	-	1900 / 2130	150	1-12	[symbols]
Blythswood Hotel, 320 Argyle Street, Tel. 041 221 4133	3	4	4		16.50 / -	27.50 / -	22.00 / -	154.00 / -	31	34	-	4	12	1815 / 2045	-	1-12	[symbols]
Boswell Hotel, 27 Mansionhouse Road, Tel. 041 632 9812	4	3	3		12.65 / 14.80	23.00 / 25.00	14.95 / 16.25	- / -	2	10	-	5	2	1800 / 1930	80	1-12	[symbols]
Burnbank Hotel, 67-85 West Princes Street, Tel. 041 332 4400	4	4	2		15.00 / 18.00	26.00 / 29.00	21.00 / 24.00	125.00 / 145.00	14	20	4	14	8	1800 / 1900	2	1-12	[symbols]

Prices shown are for guidance only. Please send SAE with each enquiry.

GLASGOW

Name and Address	Map Ref	Bedrooms	Services	Meals	Single room overnight £min/£max	Double twin room overnight £min/£max	Per person daily £min/£max	Per person weekly £min/£max	Single	Double twin	Family	Private	Public	Evening meals (Last order)	Parking (no of cars)	Months open (1-12)	Symbols
GLASGOW continued	1 H5													From Last order			Key on back fold-out
Cambridge Hotel, 41 Buccleuch Street, Tel. 041 333 9006	3	4	2	9.00 / 10.00	17.00 / 20.00	12.00 / 13.50	77.00 / 80.50	2	6	1	-	2	1800 / 1500	-	1-12	
Cavendish Hotel, 1 Devonshire Gardens, Great Western Rd, Tel. 041 339 2001	-	-	-	16.00 / 16.00	28.00 / 28.00	22.00 / 22.00	- / -	5	7	1	1	2	1800 / 2100	10	1-12	
Central Hotel, Gordon Street, G1 3SF, Tel. 041 221 9680, Telex 777771	5	5	6	18.50 / 37.50	25.00 / 44.00	- / -	- / -	129	80	4	170	20	1730 / 2200	-	1-12	
Crest Hotel Glasgow-City, 377-383 Argyle Street, G2 8LL, Tel. 041 248 2355, Telex 779652	6	5	5	37.00 / -	49.00 / -	- / -	- / -	43	79	-	120	-	1900 / 2145	-	1-12	
Crookston Hotel, 90 Crookston Road, Tel. 041 882 6142	4	5	4	14.00 / 19.50	19.95 / 25.50	19.95 / 25.45	- / -	12	9	2	10	5	1800 / 1950	50	1-12	
Duncans Hotel, 59 Union Street, Tel. 041 221 4580	3	5	2	13.80 / 16.10	23.00 / 27.60	15.30 / 18.50	107.10 / 129.50	24	29	2	6	8	1800 / 2000	-	1-12	
Dunvegan Hotel, 72 Queens Drive, Tel. 041 423 2706/2693	3	3	2	11.50 / 15.00	16.00 / 20.00	15.50 / 16.50	83.00 / -	6	16	3	3	7	1800 / 2000	30	1-12	
Ewington Hotel, 132 Queens Drive, Tel. 041 423 1152	4	5	4	15.00 / 18.00	29.00 / 32.00	19.00 / 25.00	124.00 / 160.00	25	22	1	18	10	1730 / 2200	12	1-12	
Hazelcourt Hotel, 232 Renfrew Street, Tel. 041 332 7737	3	3	1	9.50 / 10.50	17.00 / 19.00	- / -	- / -	2	3	4	-	2	1800 / 1900	-	1-12	
Holiday Inn Glasgow, Argyle Street, Anderston, Tel. 041 226 5577	6	6	6	55.50 / -	73.75 / -	65.00 / -	- / -	187	109	-	296	-	1830 / 2300	250	1-12	
Kelvingrove Hotel, 944 Sauchiehall Street, Tel. 041 339 0859	-	-	-	10.35 / 11.90	20.70 / 21.80	- / -	- / -	3	11	-	2	4	- / -	-	1-12	
Kirklee Hotel, 11 Kensington Gate, Tel. 041 334 5555/041 339 3828	4	4	1	18.00 / -	27.00 / -	- / -	- / -	-	8	3	11	-	- / -	-	1-12	

VAT is shown at 15%: changes in this rate may affect prices.

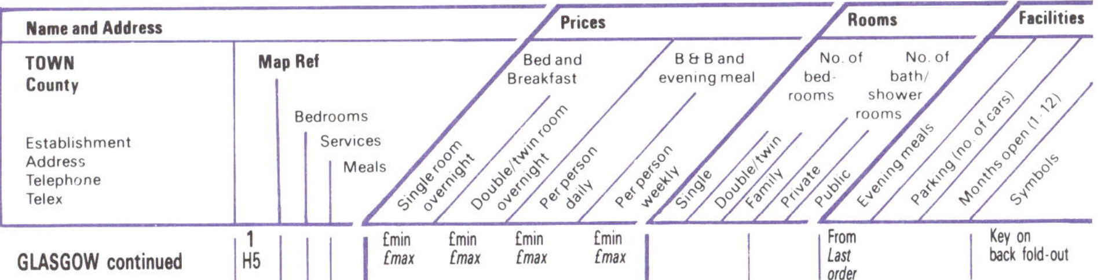

The column structure of the directory is:

Name and Address	Map Ref			Prices				Rooms							Facilities		
TOWN / County / Establishment / Address / Telephone / Telex	Bedrooms	Services	Meals	Bed and Breakfast — Single room overnight (£min / £max)	Double/twin room overnight (£min / £max)	Per person daily (£min / £max)	B & B and evening meal — Per person weekly (£min / £max)	Single	Double/twin	Family	Private	Public	No. of bath/shower rooms / Evening meals (From / Last order)	Parking (no. of cars)	Months open (1–12)	Symbols (Key on back fold-out)

GLASGOW continued — Map Ref 1 H5

Linwood Hotel

356 Albert Drive, Pollokshields, Glasgow, G41 5PJ.
Tel: 041–427 3646/1642
AA/RAC

Residential. 7 minutes City Centre. 14 minutes Glasgow Airport. 59 bus route from Renfield St or Union St to last stop in Albert Drive. Free car park. Map and brochure on request. Hot drinks available day or night.

Name and Address	Bedrooms	Services	Meals	Single room overnight	Double/twin room overnight	Per person daily	Per person weekly	Single	Double/twin	Family	Private	Public	Evening meals	Parking	Months open
Linwood Hotel, 356 Albert Drive, G41 5PJ, Tel. 041 427 1642/3646	3	4	1	10.00 / 11.00	20.00 / 22.00	-	-	10	4	2	-	3	-	7	1-12
Lorne Hotel, 923 Sauchiehall Street, Tel. 041 334 4891	4	5	5	18.50 / 29.95	27.50 / 36.95	24.50 / 35.95	121.50 / 251.65	34	45	4	47	20	1830 / 2145	30	1-12
Marie Stuart Hotel, 46-48 Queen Mary Avenue, Tel. 041 423 6363	3	5	4	12.75 / 21.90	23.50 / 29.90	16.75	-	13	16	2	9	5	1730 / 1900	50	1-12
Newlands Hotel, 288 Kilmarnock Road, Tel. 041 632 9171	-	-	-	17.00	29.50	-	-	11	5	1	17	-	1800 / 2130	20	1-12
North British Hotel, George Square, G2 1DS, Tel. 041 332 6711, Telex 778147	5	5	5	16.00 / 34.00	22.00 / 40.00	23.50 / 41.50	164.50 / 290.50	21	104	-	90	8	1800 / 2200	-	1-12
Park Court Hotel, 28 Balshagray Drive, Tel. 041 339 2143	2	3	1	7.00 / 9.00	14.00 / 16.00	-	-	9	4	1	-	3	-	6	1-12
Park Hotel, 960 Sauchiehall Street, G3 7TH, Tel. 041 334 1336	3	2	1	7.50 / 7.50	13.80 / 13.80	-	-	3	3	2	-	2	-	-	1-12
Queens Park Hotel, 10 Balvicar Drive, G42 8QT, Tel. 041 423 1123	3	5	4	10.95 / 11.50	21.00 / 30.25	15.65 / 16.20	-	8	25	4	3	7	1800 / 2000	10	1-12
Sherbrooke Hotel, 11 Sherbrooke Avenue, Tel. 041 427 4227	-	-	-	22.00 / 26.00	32.00 / 38.00	30.00	120.00	3	5	1	7	1	1800 / 2230	60	1-12
Smiths Hotel, 963 Sauchiehall Street, Tel. 041 339 6363	3	4	1	8.65 / 11.50	17.25 / 17.25	-	-	5	15	8	-	6	-	-	1-12
Stakis Burnside Hotel, East Kilbride Road, Burnside, G73 5EA, Tel. 041 634 1276, Telex 778704	5	5	5	34.00	43.00	-	-	4	12	-	13	3	1800 / 2100	100	1-12

GLASGOW

Name and Address	Map Ref	Bedrooms	Services	Meals	Single room overnight (£min/£max)	Double/twin room overnight (£min/£max)	Per person daily (£min/£max)	Per person weekly (£min/£max)	No. of bedrooms — Single	Double/twin	Family	Bath/shower — Private	Public	Evening meals (From/Last order)	Parking (no. of cars)	Months open	Symbols
GLASGOW continued	1 / H5																Key on back fold-out
Stakis Grosvenor Hotel Grosvenor Terrace, Gt Western Rd G12 0TA Tel. 041 339 8811 Telex 776247		6	5	6	48.00 / –	58.00 / –	– / –	– / –	–	81	12	93	–	1700 / 2230	112	1-12	(facility symbols)
Stakis Ingram Hotel 201 Ingram Street G1 1DQ Tel. 041 248 4401		5	5	5	40.00 / –	48.00 / –	– / –	– / –	45	45	–	90	–	1830 / 2145	25	1-12	(facility symbols)
Stakis Pond Hotel Great Western Road G12 0XP Tel. 041 334 8161 Telex 776573		5	5	5	38.00 / –	46.00 / –	– / –	– / –	–	134	3	137	–	1700 / 2300	150	1-12	(facility symbols)
Tinto Firs Thistle Hotel Kilmarnock Road Tel. 041 637 2353 Telex 778329		5	4	5	39.50 / 42.50	49.00 / –	– / –	– / –	25	5	–	24	3	1830 / 2200	45	1-12	(facility symbols)
White House Luxury Hotel Flats 12 Cleveden Crescent Tel. 041 339 9375		6	4	5	52.30 / 52.30	65.50 / 82.75	61.30 / 61.30	– / –	12	16	7	35	–	– / 2200	30	1-12	(facility symbols)
Wickets Hotel 52 Fortrose Street Tel. 041 334 9334		4	4	5	25.30 / 28.50	34.50 / 38.50	28.50 / 36.90	169.60 / 220.00	–	6	1	5	1	1800 / 2145	24	1-12	(facility symbols)
Woodside Hotel 405-407 North Woodside Rd Tel. 041 339 8620		2	3	2	8.00 / 12.00	15.00 / 18.50	10.75 / 14.75	70.00 / 90.00	2	6	–	–	4	1800 / 2100	–	1-12	(facility symbols)
The Alamo Guest House 46 Gray Street G3 7SE Tel. 041 339 2395		–	–	–	7.00 / –	12.00 / –	– / –	– / –	2	2	4	–	4	– / –	6	1-12	(facility symbols)
Aldara Guest House 5 Bentinck Street Tel. 041 339 0852/0928		3	2	1	– / –	12.00 / 14.00	– / –	– / –	–	2	3	–	2	– / –	–	1-12	(facility symbols)
Belle Vue Guest House 163 Hamilton Road, Mount Vernon Tel. 041 778 1077		2	3	2	10.50 / 10.50	17.00 / 17.00	11.50 / 13.50	70.50 / 94.50	3	6	2	1	2	1730 / 1830	10	1-12	(facility symbols)
Chez Nous Guest House 33 Hillhead Street Tel. 041 334 2977		3	4	1	8.50 / 9.00	15.00 / 16.00	– / –	– / –	7	7	3	–	3	– / –	9	1-12	(facility symbols)
Glades Guest House 142 Albert Road G42 8UF Tel. 041 423 4911		1	3	1	7.00 / 7.00	14.00 / 14.00	– / –	– / –	1	5	2	–	2	– / –	–	1-12	(facility symbols)
Reidholme Guest House 36 Regent Park Square G41 2AG Tel. 041 423 1855		2	3	2	7.00 / 7.50	14.00 / 15.00	11.00 / 11.50	– / –	1	4	1	–	2	1800 / –	–	1-12	(facility symbols)
Rosemundy Guest House 50 Bentinck Street Tel. 041 339 8220		3	2	1	8.00 / –	13.00 / –	– / –	– / –	2	4	3	–	3	– / –	3	1-12	(facility symbols)

VAT is shown at 15%: changes in this rate may affect prices.

Name and Address	Map Ref	Bedrooms	Services	Meals	Single room overnight £min/£max	Double/twin room overnight £min/£max	Per person daily £min/£max	Per person weekly £min/£max	No. of bedrooms Single	No. of bedrooms Double/twin	No. of bedrooms Family	Bath/shower Private	Bath/shower Public	Evening meals From/Last order	Parking (no. of cars)	Months open (1-12)	Symbols
GLASGOW continued	1 H5				£min/£max	£min/£max	£min/£max	£min/£max						From/Last order			Key on back fold-out
Wilkies Guest House 16 Hillhead Street G12 8PY Tel. 041 339 6898		3	2	1	7.50 / 8.00	15.00 / 16.00	- / -	- / -	2	10	3	1	4	-	8	1-12	
Dalrymple Hall, University of Glasgow 22 Belhaven Terrace West Tel. 041 339 5271		2	2	4	7.70 / 9.85	15.40 / 19.70	- / -	- / -	77	52	4	-	50	1730 / 1830	10	3-4 6-9	
Hostel Accommodation Jordanhill College, 76 South-brae Drive G13 1PP Tel. 041 959 1232 Ext 292		2	2	3	10.35 / -	19.00 / -	16.45 / -	90.00 / -	170	-	-	-	-	1700 / 1800	500	3-4 6-9	
Queen Margaret Hall 55 Bellshaugh Road Tel. 041 334 2192		2	2	4	7.70 / 10.00	15.40 / 20.00	11.00 / 13.30	68.10 / 91.35	330	10	-	-	50	1800 / 1900	50	3-4 6-9	
Residence Services Univ. of Strathclyde 73 Rottenrow East G4 0NG Tel. 041 552 4400 Ext 3560		3	3	3	12.00 / 12.00	20.00 / 20.00	14.50 / 16.50	87.00 / 99.00	65	120	5	-	25	1730 / 1830	-	1-12	
University of Glasgow, Wolfson Hall Garscube Estate, Maryhill Road Tel. 041 946 5252		-	-	-	7.70 / 9.85	15.40 / 19.70	- / -	- / -	213	18	-	4	39	1800 / 1900	100	3-4 7-10	
GLEN CLOVA, by Kirriemuir **Angus**	4 E12																
Ogilvy Arms Hotel Tel. Clova 222		3	3	3	10.00 / 14.50	20.00 / 29.00	14.00 / 23.00	98.00 / 161.00	-	7	-	4	2	1800 / 2100	30	1-12	

Excellent low cost accommodation in

Glasgow University Residences

Single and Twin Bedded Rooms
Bed and Breakfast from £7.70
Self-catering   from £5.00
PRICES INCLUDE V.A.T. @ 15%

Brochure and further details from:
Conference & Vacation Office
52 Hillhead Street
Glasgow G12 8PZ
Tel· 041-339 8855 Ext. 7385/7459

or contact direct:
Dalrymple Hall—041-339 5271
Queen Margaret Hall—
                041-334 2192
Maclay Hall—041-332 5056
(self-catering)

Name and Address				Prices				Rooms						Facilities	
TOWN County / Establishment Address Telephone Telex	Map Ref / Bedrooms / Services / Meals			Bed and Breakfast — Single room overnight	Double/twin room overnight	Per person daily	B & B and evening meal — Per person weekly	No. of bedrooms — Single	Double/twin	Family	Private	Public	No. of bath/shower rooms	Evening meals / Parking (no. of cars) / Months open (1-12)	Symbols
GLEN CLOVA, by Kirriemuir continued	4 E12			£min £max	£min £max	£min £max	£min £max							From Last order	Key on back fold-out

Rottal Lodge

Glen Clova, Angus DD8 4QT. Tel: 057 55 224.

Built by the Earl of Airlie around 1830 as a Shooting Lodge and recently converted to a small comfortable Hotel, offering good food, based mainly on local produce and prepared in our own kitchen. All 12 bedrooms individually decorated with private bath or shower. Ideal base for walking, fishing, golfing and visiting many places of historical interest in the area.

Name and Address	Map Ref	Bed	Serv	Meal	Single overnight	Double/twin overnight	Per person daily	Per person weekly	Single	Double/twin	Family	Private	Public	Last order	Parking	Months open	Symbols
Rottal Lodge DD8 4QT Tel. Clova 224		3	4	4	24.73 -	49.45 -	35.65 -	249.55 -	3	9	-	7	3	1930 2015	12	5-11	
GLENBORRODALE, by Ardnamurchan Argyll	1 D1																
Glenborrodale Castle Hotel PH36 4JP Tel. Glenborrodale 266		3	4	4	- -	- -	34.00 -	238.00 -	5	13	5	2	7	1900 2130	40	4-10	
GLENCAPLE Dumfriesshire	2 C10																
Nith Hotel Tel. Glencaple 213		3	4	4	13.20 -	26.40 -	- -	- -	2	6	2	4	3	1900 2030	20	1-12	

The Scottish Tourist Guides Association offers the services of trained guides at reasonable prices. Many are fluent in foreign languages.
UK bookings (during office hours) **031-229 3032.**
Details and charges from:
Mrs Jean Duncan, STGA Publicity Officer, 133 Hillhouse Road, Edinburgh EH4 7AF, or from the Scottish Tourist Board, 23 Ravelston Terrace, Edinburgh EH4 3EU.

DON'T KNOW SCOTLAND TOO WELL?

You probably know whether you want to stay in the north-east, the south-west, or some other part of the country—but you may not know all the little towns and villages in that area.

That's where the MAPS in this book can help you.

Simply look at the page showing the area you have chosen, then check the names marked on that part of the map. Each name has a corresponding entry in the text, with a list of accommodation which you can contact.

It's easy!

Name and Address	Map Ref				Prices					Rooms				Facilities	
TOWN County / Establishment Address Telephone Telex		Bedrooms	Services	Meals	Bed and Breakfast: Single room overnight	Double/twin room overnight	Per person daily	B & B and evening meal: Per person weekly	Single	Double/twin	Family	Private	Public	No. of bedrooms / No. of bath/shower rooms: Evening meals From Last order	Parking (no. of cars) / Months open (1-12) / Symbols
					£min £max	£min £max	£min £max	£min £max						From Last order	Key on back fold-out
GLENCARSE Perthshire	2 C2														
Newton House Hotel PH2 7LX Tel. Glencarse 250		3	3	5	21.00 30.00	24.00 36.00	38.00 46.00	180.00 210.00	2	4	-	-	2	1700 2130	40	1-12
GLENCOE Argyll	1 F1														
Clachaig Inn Tel. Ballachulish 252		3	4	3	11.00 12.00	20.00 24.00	- -	- -	2	6	2	4	2	1900 1945	40	1-12
Glencoe Hotel Tel. Ballachulish 245		4	4	5	9.50 12.50	19.00 25.00	- -	95.50 117.00	3	8	2	2	5	1800 2130	30	1-12

Newton House Hotel

Glencarse, Perthshire. (073) 886 250

Dear Visitor

Scotland is larger than it looks on the map.

You will tire of constant travel and never sleeping in the same bed twice.

Why not let us be your touring base?

I will meet you on arrival, show you to a room of character with a relaxing outlook. If you wish you can work up an appetite in the 1½ acres of grounds or you may wish a cat's nap, in which case I will wake you at the appointed time with a pot of tea.

Give you time to relax over an aperitif, take your dinner order from a choice of two menus, serve you excellent food, and offer an excellent choice of wines and liquers, not forgetting the vintage port.

Car parking is no problem, neither are children or dogs!

Come and see us.

Yours sincerely

Dennis H. Smith

Not the best known but known by the best.

Name and Address	Map Ref	Bedrooms / Services / Meals	Prices — Bed and Breakfast				B & B and evening meal		Rooms							Facilities		
TOWN County — Establishment Address Telephone Telex			Single room overnight £min £max	Double/twin room overnight £min £max	Per person daily £min £max	Per person weekly £min £max	Single	Double/twin	Family	Private	Public	From Last order	Evening meals	Parking (no. of cars)	Months open (1-12)	Symbols — Key on back fold-out		

| GLENCOE continued | 1 F1 | | | | | | | | | | | | | | | | | |

Kings House Hotel
Glencoe, Argyll

AA**   **RAC

This recently modernised 22 bed-roomed hotel stands amid breath-taking scenery at the head of one of Scotland's most famous glens. An ideal centre for either an activity holiday– skiing, walking, climbing and fishing are all readily available– or just a relaxing, 'away from it all' break.

Tel. Kings House (08556) 259

Name and Address	B	S	M	Single room o/n	Double/twin o/n	Per person daily	Per person weekly	Single	Double/twin	Family	Private	Public	Last order	Evening meals	Parking	Months open	Symbols
Kings House Hotel Tel. Kingshouse 259	4	4	4	15.00 / 19.00	28.00 / 34.00	22.00 / 27.00	- / -	4	17	1	10	4	1900 / 2015	100	3-10	
Dunire Guest House Tel. Ballachulish 318	3	2	2	7.00 / 8.50	14.00 / 17.00	10.50 / 12.50	70.00 / 86.00	1	2	3	-	3	1800 / -	10	1-12	
Scorry Breac Guest House Tel. Ballachulish 354	3	3	2	9.50 / -	14.00 / -	11.00 / -	75.00 / -	-	4	2	-	2	1800 / 1800	8	1-10	
GLENDARUEL Argyll	1 F4																
Glendaruel Hotel Tel. Glendaruel 274	3	4	4	11.00 / 11.00	16.00 / 18.00	- / -	- / -	1	4	-	-	1	1900 / 2030	10	1-12	
GLENDEVON, Dollar Clackmannanshire	2 B3																
Tormaukin Hotel FK14 7JY Tel. Glendevon 252	4	3	5	20.00 / 22.00	32.00 / 34.00	- / -	- / -	-	6	-	6	-	1830 / 2145	70	3-12	
GLENFARG Perthshire	2 C3																
The Bein Inn PH2 9PY Tel. Glenfarg 216/517	5	4	5	17.50 / -	24.50 / -	27.50 / -	138.00 / -	-	13	4	11	2	1900 / 2145	100	1-12	

VAT is shown at 15%: changes in this rate may affect prices.

Name and Address (TOWN / County / Establishment / Address / Telephone / Telex)	Map Ref	Bedrooms	Services	Meals	Single room overnight £min £max	Double/twin room overnight £min £max	Per person daily £min £max	Per person weekly £min £max	Single	Double/twin	Family	Private	Public	Evening meals (From / Last order)	Parking	Months open	Symbols
GLENFINNAN Inverness-shire	3 F12																
Glenfinnan House Hotel Tel. Kinlocheil 235		3	4	4	12.00 16.50	24.00 33.00	20.50 26.00	130.00 157.50	4	12	3	3	6	1930 2030	20	4-10	Key on back fold-out
Stage House Inn Tel. Kinlocheil 246		4	3	4	12.50 -	25.00 -	20.00 -	130.00 -	-	7	2	9	-	1900 2000	20	1-12	
GLENHINNISDAL, Snizort Isle of Skye, Inverness-shire	3 D8																
Garybuie Guest House Garybuie 4 Balmeanach Tel. Uig 310		2	2	3	6.50 -	13.00 -	9.50 -	63.00 -	1	1	2	-	2	1830 1600	5	1-12	
GLENISLA Perthshire	2 C1																

Kirkside House Hotel
Kirkton of Glenisla
by Blairgowrie Perthshire PH11 8PH
(on B951 between Kirriemuir & Glenshee)

Away from it all, natural and unspoiled beauty for the more discerning. Enjoy the informal, friendly and relaxed atmosphere, good food, comfort and personal attention of this small family run hotel.

Something for everyone. Peace and quiet, or the many outdoor activities (hillwalking, pony trekking, fishing, hang gliding etc.) Fully licensed. Centrally heated. Games room. Dog kennels. Seasonal rates and discounts. Open all year,

Telephone: Glenisla (057 582) 278

Name and Address	Map Ref	Bedrooms	Services	Meals	Single room overnight	Double/twin room overnight	Per person daily	Per person weekly	Single	Double/twin	Family	Private	Public	Evening meals	Parking	Months open	Symbols
Kirkside House Hotel Kirkton of Glenisla PH11 8PH Tel. Glenisla 278		3	4	4	10.00 11.75	20.00 23.50	16.00 18.50	103.50 117.00	1	4	1	1	1	1800 2100	20	1-12	
GLENKINDIE Aberdeenshire	4 H4																
Glenkindie Arms Hotel Tel. Glenkindie 288		3	3	3	9.50 -	18.00 -	- -	- -	1	-	2	-	2	1700 2100	-	1-12	
GLENLIVET, Ballindalloch Banffshire	4 D9																
Blairfindy Lodge Hotel AB3 9DJ Tel. Glenlivet 376		4	4	5	18.50 18.50	37.00 37.00	29.50 29.50	189.00 200.50	1	10	1	8	3	1930 2130	24	2-12	

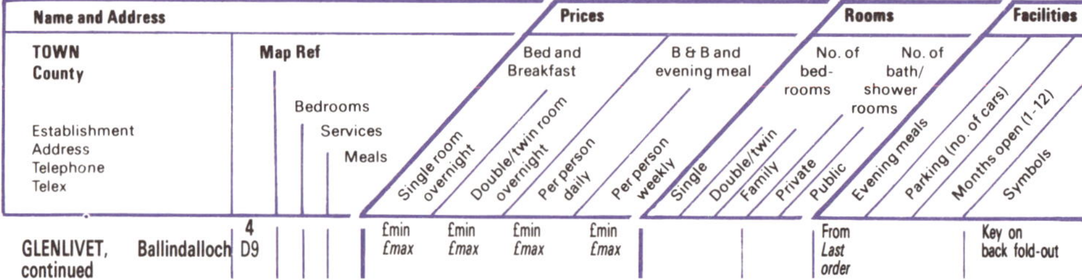

Name and Address		Prices						Rooms					Facilities			
TOWN County / Establishment Address Telephone Telex	**Map Ref** / Bedrooms / Services / Meals	Bed and Breakfast		B & B and evening meal				No. of bedrooms		No. of bath/shower rooms						
		Single room overnight	Double/twin room overnight	Per person daily	Per person weekly	Single	Double/twin	Family	Private	Public	Evening meals	Parking (no. of cars)	Months open (1-12)	Symbols
GLENLIVET, continued	4 D9	£min £max	£min £max	£min £max	£min £max				From Last order		Key on back fold-out

MINMORE HOUSE HOTEL
Glenlivet

Beautiful country house hotel set amidst 4 acres of landscaped gardens. This fine hotel with historical connections to the famous "The Glenlivet" distillery is in the heart of the Grampians on the whisky trail. All the rooms are furnished to a very high standard with many antiques, including oak panelled bar and elegant drawing room.

The service, meals and wines are of the same high quality. Personal attention is given to every detail. Swimming pool and tennis court.

Ideal centre for:– Bird Watching, Walking, Pony Trekking, Golf, Touring, Trout Fishing, Skiing etc. Arrangements made for:– **salmon** and sea trout fishing, rough and game shooting, deer stalking. Bargain Breaks Oct–mid May. Ski packages at the Lecht.

AA** Send for Brochure:– Minmore House Hotel, Glenlivet, Ballindalloch, Banffshire AB3 9DB. Tel: 08073 378.

Name and Address	Map Ref	Bedrooms	Services	Meals	Single room overnight	Double/twin room overnight	Per person daily	Per person weekly	Single	Double/twin	Family	Private	Public	Last order	Evening meals	Parking	Months open	Symbols
Minmore House Hotel AB3 9DB Tel. Glenlivet 378		4	4	5	13.50 15.50	27.00 37.00	19.00 27.00	130.00 180.00	2	8	-	10	1	1900 2200	29		1-12	
GLENLUCE Wigtownshire	1 G10																	
Auld Kings Arms 69 Main Street DG8 0PP Tel. Glenluce 280		3	4	5	7.00 8.00	14.00 16.00	10.00 12.00	58.00 80.00	4	13	5	2	6	1800 2330	60		1-12	
Judges Keep Hotel Tel. Glenluce 203		3	4	4	8.50 9.50	17.00 19.00	13.50 15.00	90.00 105.00	1	3	2	-	2	1700 2000	30		1-12	
Kings Arms Hotel Tel. Glenluce 219		3	4	4	9.20 -	18.40 -	14.70 -	90.00 -	2	5	1	2	2	1900 2000	16		1-12	
Torwood House, Hotel Tel. Glenluce 469		3	3	4	8.50 10.50	17.00 21.00	15.00 18.50	100.00 120.00	1	4	1	-	2	1900 2100	40		1-12	
Lochnagar Guest House 41 Main Street Tel. Glenluce 374		-	-	-	6.50 -	12.00 -	8.50 -	58.00 -	1	-	2	-	1	1830 1900	-		1-12	
Rowantree Guest House 38 Main Street Tel. Glenluce 244		2	2	2	6.00 7.50	12.00 15.00	10.00 12.00	60.00 70.00	1	4	2	1	1	1830 1830	8		1-12	

VAT is shown at 15%: changes in this rate may affect prices.

Name and Address	Map Ref	Bedrooms	Services	Meals	Single room overnight (£min £max)	Double/twin room overnight (£min £max)	Per person daily (£min £max)	Per person weekly (£min £max)	Single	Double/twin	Family	Private	Public	Evening meals (From Last order)	Parking (no. of cars)	Months open (1-12)	Symbols (Key on back fold-out)
GLENMORISTON Inverness-shire	3 H10																
Cluanie Inn Tel. Dalchreichart 40238		-	-	-	9.00 -	23.00 -	- -	- -	3	6	-	-	3	1900 2015	60	1-12	
Glenmoriston Arms Hotel Tel. Glenmoriston 206		3	3	4	12.50 -	25.00 -	17.00 -	-	2	7	1	2	2	1900 2100	24	4-11	
GLENROTHES Fife	2 D3																
Balgeddie House Hotel Leslie Road Tel. Glenrothes 742511		-	-	-	17.60 20.00	33.00 41.60	- -	- -	5	13	-	16	-	1900 2100	50	1-12	
The Forum Hotel 3 North Street Tel. Glenrothes 755340		-	-	-	14.75 -	25.50 -	- -	- -	4	7	-	11	-	1900 2200	-	1-12	
Rothes Arms Hotel South Parks Road KY6 1JD Tel. Glenrothes 753701		4	4	4	12.00 -	20.00 -	- -	- -	12	4	-	6	4	1900 2100	-	1-12	
GLENSHEE Perthshire	4 D12																
Dalmunzie House Hotel PH10 7QG Tel. Glenshee 224/225		4	4	4	15.00 17.00	28.00 44.00	23.50 26.50	139.00 190.00	5	14	-	9	4	2000 2030	42	1-10	
Spittal of Glenshee Hotel PH10 7QF Tel. Glenshee 215/229		-	-	-	15.80 15.80	27.84 31.60	20.88 22.77	146.16 159.39	2	19	8	5	6	1900 2015	80	1-12	

Name and Address				Prices								Rooms			Facilities	
TOWN County / Establishment Address Telephone Telex	Map Ref / Bedrooms / Services / Meals			Bed and Breakfast: Single room overnight	Double/twin room overnight	Per person daily	B & B and evening meal: Per person weekly	Single	Double/twin	Family	Private	No. of bedrooms Public / From Last order	No. of bath/shower rooms	Evening meals / Parking (no. of cars)	Months open (1-12)	Symbols
				£min £max	£min £max	£min £max	£min £max					From Last order			Key on back fold-out	
GLENSHIEL, by Kyle of Lochalsh Ross-shire	3 F10															

KINTAIL LODGE
Glenshiel, Ross-shire

Proprietor: CHRISTOPHER MAIN

This former shooting lodge on the road to Skye stands at the foot of the Five Sisters looking down Loch Duich. We are open all year (except November, Christmas and New Year). In summer we have boating, fishing, available on two rivers and sea angling in the hotel launch. In winter a warm house, open fires, lots of books, lovely walks with abounding wildlife — reduced rates and private bathrooms.

Always excellent fresh food and home baking.

It is an ideal centre for tourists who wish to hill-climb or walk and provides a central point for a day's motor run to Kyle of Lochalsh, Glenelg, the Isle of Skye, the Applecross peninsula, Loch Ness and Inverness.

★ *Ashley Courtenay recommended* ★

**Telephones:
Reception 059-981 275
Guests 059-981 262**

Establishment	Map Ref	Bedrooms	Services	Meals	Single room overnight	Double/twin room overnight	Per person daily	Per person weekly	Single	Double/twin	Family	Private	Public	From Last order	Bath/shower rooms	Months open	Symbols
Kintail Lodge Hotel IV40 8HL Tel. Glenshiel 275		3	4	5	13.00 18.00	26.00 36.00	20.00 25.00	140.00 160.00	4	10	2	-	6	1900 2100	20	1-12	
GLENUIG, Lochailort Inverness-shire	3 E12																
The Glenuig Inn PH38 4NG Tel. Lochailort 219		3	2	4	9.00 12.00	18.00 24.00	14.00 17.00	76.00 98.00	1	8	-	-	4	1900	30	1-12	
GLENURQUHART Inverness-shire	4 A9																
Kilmartin Hall Tel. Glenurquhart 269		5	5	5	35.00 45.00	45.00 65.00	47.00 56.00	280.00 320.00	-	-	6	6	-	1830 2100	22	1-12	
GOLSPIE Sutherland	4 B6																
Golf Links Hotel KW10 6TT Tel. Golspie 3408		4	4	3	15.00 18.00	28.00 34.00	21.00 25.00	126.00 165.00	2	8	-	5	2	1915 2000	18	1-12	
Park House Hotel & Restaurant Main Street KW10 6TG Tel. Golspie 3667		4	5	5	12.00 12.00	24.00 24.00	19.00 19.00	- -	-	4	1	-	3	2130	5	3-11	

VAT is shown at 15%: changes in this rate may affect prices.

Name and Address (Town / County / Establishment / Address / Telephone / Telex)	Map Ref	Bedrooms	Services	Meals	Single room overnight £min/£max	Double/twin room overnight £min/£max	Per person daily £min/£max	Per person weekly £min/£max	Single	Double/twin	Family	Private	Public	Evening meals (From / Last order)	Parking (no. of cars)	Months open (1-12)	Symbols
GOREBRIDGE / Midlothian	2 D5																
Middleton Hall Conference Centre / EH23 4RD / Tel. Gorebridge 20661		3	3	3	12.00 / 12.00	24.00 / 24.00	17.00 / 17.00	- / -	44	14	2	-	10	1900 / 1730	100	1-12	
Middleton Outdoor Centre / School Camp / EH23 4RD / Tel. Gorebridge 20314		-	-	3	5.70 / 5.70	11.40 / 11.40	6.70 / 8.20	39.35 / 48.65	24	-	-	-	2	1700 / -	-	4-10	
Dormitories for Group Bookings																	
GOURDON / Kincardineshire	4 G12																
Commercial Hotel / Tel. Inverbervie 282		3	3	3	10.00 / 12.00	16.00 / 18.00	15.00 / 17.00	95.00 / -	-	2	2	-	1	1800 / -	-	1-12	
GOUROCK / Renfrewshire	1 G5																
Queens Hotel / Ashburn Gate / Tel. Gourock 34586/7		3	3	3	11.00 / -	18.00 / -	- / -	- / -	10	6	2	1	4	1900 / 2100	-	1-12	
Spinnaker Hotel / Albert Road / Tel. Gourock 33107		3	3	3	10.00 / 12.50	20.00 / 24.00	- / -	- / -	2	2	-	-	1	- / -	-	1-12	
Stakis Gantock Hotel / Cloch Road / PA15 1AR / Tel. Gourock 34671		5	5	5	36.00 / -	46.00 / -	- / -	- / -	-	63	-	63	-	1900 / 2145	80	1-12	
GRANGEMOUTH / Stirlingshire	2 B4																
Avongrange Hotel / Kersiebank Avenue / FK3 0EN / Tel. Grangemouth 5711		-	-	-	16.00 / -	26.50 / -	- / -	- / -	6	8	-	14	-	1700 / 2045	10	1-12	
GRANTOWN-ON-SPEY / Moray	4 C9																
Ben Mhor Hotel / PH26 3EG / Tel. Grantown-on-Spey 2056		4	3	4	13.25 / 14.50	23.50 / 25.50	20.75 / 22.50	130.00 / 150.00	4	18	2	24	-	1900 / 2030	20	1-12	
Craiglynne Hotel / PH26 25X / Tel. Grantown-on-Spey 2597		3	3	4	8.00 / -	16.00 / -	13.00 / -	84.00 / -	18	59	4	69	6	1900 / 2030	75	4-10	
Dunvegan Hotel / PH26 3HX / Tel. Grantown-on-Spey 2301		3	3	3	8.75 / 10.95	17.50 / 21.90	14.55 / 16.75	83.70 / 100.50	-	4	5	-	2	1900 / 1930	9	1-12	
Garth Hotel / Castle Road / Tel. Grantown-on-Spey 2836		-	-	-	12.00 / 13.00	24.00 / 26.00	18.50 / 19.50	122.00 / 132.00	1	16	-	9	4	1900 / 2015	12	1-12	

Prices shown are for guidance only. Please send SAE with each enquiry.

Name and Address	Map Ref	Bedrooms	Services	Meals	Single room overnight	Double/twin room overnight	Per person daily	Per person weekly	Single	Double/twin	Family	Private	Public	Evening meals	Parking (no. of cars)	Months open (1-12)	Symbols
TOWN County — Establishment, Address, Telephone, Telex					£min £max	£min £max	£min £max	£min £max						From Last order			Key on back fold-out
GRANTOWN-ON-SPEY continued	4 C9																
Grant Arms Hotel Tel. Grantown-on-Spey 2526 Telex 75160	4	5	5		16.00	32.00	-	-	7	48	5	60	3	1900 2100	36	3-11	
Pines Hotel Woodside Avenue PH26 3JR Tel. Grantown-on-Spey 2092	2	3	2		7.50	15.00	11.75	75.25	2	6	2	-	2	1900 1900	4	4-9	
Seafield Lodge Hotel Woodside Avenue PH26 3JN Tel. Grantown-on-Spey 2152	4	3	4		12.65 16.10	25.30 28.75	20.13 20.70	128.80 155.90	3	11	-	9	2	1915 2015	50	4-10	
Spey Valley Hotel Seafield Avenue PH26 3EJ Tel. Grantown-on-Spey 2942	3	4	4		10.00 10.00	20.00 20.00	17.00 17.00	108.50 108.50	3	13	3	-	5	1900 2200	30	1-12	
Crann Tara Guest House High Street Tel. Grantown-on-Spey 2197	1	2	2		6.50 7.00	13.00 14.00	10.50 11.00	73.00 77.00	1	4	1	-	2	1830 1900	7	1-12	
Dar-il-Hena Guest House Grant Road PH26 3LA Tel. Grantown-on-Spey 2929	3	2	2		6.90	13.80	11.25	-	1	3	3	-	2	1900 -	10	4-10	

THE PINES HOTEL
Woodside Avenue, Grantown-On-Spey PH26 3JR

FIRST RATE : HOME COOKING : FRIENDLY ATMOSPHERE
QUIET SURROUNDINGS : EVERY COMFORT : CHILDREN WELCOME
CENTRAL TOURING POINT

**Under personal supervision of
Mrs M. A. Cooke**

Write for Brochure/Tariff
Tel: No. 0479-2092

Name and Address	Map Ref	Bedrooms	Services	Meals	Single room overnight	Double/twin room overnight	Per person daily	Per person weekly	Single	Double/twin	Family	Private	Public	Evening meals (From / Last order)	Parking (no. of cars)	Months open (1-12)	Symbols
GRANTOWN-ON-SPEY continued	4 C9				£min £max	£min £max	£min £max	£min £max						From / Last order			Key on back fold-out
Dunachton Guest House Grant Road PH26 31D Tel. Grantown-on-Spey 2098		3	3	2	6.90 -	13.80 -	11.25 -	75.00 -	2	3	2	-	2	1900 1900	9	1-12	(symbols)
Firhall Guest House PH26 3LD Tel. Grantown-on-Spey 3097		3	3	2	7.50 -	15.00 -	12.00 -	80.00 -	1	2	4	-	2	1900 -	10	1-12	(symbols)
Kinross Guest House Woodside Avenue PH26 3JR Tel. Grantown-on-Spey 2042		3	3	2	6.50 -	13.00 -	10.50 -	71.00 -	1	3	2	-	3	1900 -	6	1-12	(symbols)
Ravenscourt Guest House Seafield Avenue Tel. Grantown-on-Spey 2286		3	4	2	7.50 -	14.00 -	11.50 -	77.00 -	-	6	3	-	2	1900 1930	15	1-10	(symbols)
Riversdale Guest House Grant Road PH26 31D Tel. Grantown-on-Spey 2648		3	3	2	7.00 7.50	21.00 22.00	10.50 11.00	70.00 73.50	1	4	2	-	2	1900 -	10	1-12	(symbols)

UMARIA GUEST HOUSE

Woodlands Terrace, Grantown-on-Spey
Tel: (0479) 2104

Situated at the entrance to this charming Highland country town, this comfortable Victorian residence is an ideal centre for touring. Mountains, lochs, rivers, castles and coast, all within easy reach, and log fires, colour T.V. and good food when you return.

Tea Makers, Electric Blankets and ample car parking. Fishing, bird watching, walking, golf, winter sports, riding all available locally.

Name and Address	Map Ref	Bedrooms	Services	Meals	Single room overnight	Double/twin room overnight	Per person daily	Per person weekly	Single	Double/twin	Family	Private	Public	Evening meals (From / Last order)	Parking (no. of cars)	Months open (1-12)	Symbols
Umaria Guest House Woodlands Terrace PH26 3JU Tel. Grantown-on-Spey 2104		3	3	2	7.00 -	14.00 -	11.00 -	70.00 -	1	3	3	-	3	1830 1700	8	1-12	(symbols)
GREENLAW, Duns **Berwickshire**	2 F6																
Castle Hotel Tel. Greenlaw 217		4	4	5	9.00 9.00	15.00 17.50	10.00 12.75	70.00 89.25	1	3	1	-	2	1800 2200	20	1-12	(symbols)
Purves Hall Hotel TD10 6UJ Tel. Leitholm 558		4	5	4	19.00 23.00	34.00 38.00	29.50 33.50	185.85 211.05	2	6	-	8	-	1930 2045	30	3-1	(symbols)
Bridgend Guest House West High Street TD10 6XA Tel. Greenlaw 270		3	3	3	6.00 7.50	12.00 15.00	9.00 12.00	63.00 84.00	-	3	2	-	1	1900 -	5	1-12	(symbols)
GREENLOANING **Perthshire**	2 B3																
Allanbank Hotel FK15 0LX Tel. Braco 205		4	4	5	10.00 12.00	20.00 44.00	15.00 22.00	84.00 105.00	-	2	2	3	1	1800 2130	100	1-12	(symbols)

GREENOCK - GULLANE

<table>
<tr><th rowspan="2">Name and Address
TOWN / County
Establishment / Address / Telephone / Telex</th><th rowspan="2">Map Ref</th><th>Bed-
rooms</th><th>Ser-
vices</th><th>Meals</th><th colspan="6">Prices — Bed and Breakfast</th><th colspan="2">B & B and evening meal</th><th colspan="5">Rooms — No. of bedrooms / bath-shower</th><th>Evening meals (From / Last order)</th><th>Parking (no. of cars)</th><th>Months open (1-12)</th></tr>
<tr><th></th><th></th><th></th><th>Single room overnight £min</th><th>£max</th><th>Double/twin room overnight £min</th><th>£max</th><th>Per person daily £min</th><th>£max</th><th>Per person weekly £min</th><th>£max</th><th>Single</th><th>Double/twin</th><th>Family</th><th>Private</th><th>Public</th><th></th><th></th><th></th></tr>

<tr><td>GREENOCK
Renfrewshire</td><td>1
G5</td><td></td><td></td><td></td><td></td><td></td><td></td><td></td><td></td><td></td><td></td><td></td><td></td><td></td><td></td><td></td><td></td><td></td><td></td><td></td></tr>
<tr><td>Pamrosa Hotel
8 Brougham Street
Tel. Greenock 20238</td><td></td><td>6</td><td>3</td><td>3</td><td>15.50</td><td>15.50</td><td>19.50</td><td>19.50</td><td>19.00</td><td>24.00</td><td>133.00</td><td>168.00</td><td>-</td><td>7</td><td>-</td><td>-</td><td>2</td><td>1730
2130</td><td>14</td><td>1-12</td></tr>

<tr><td>GRESHORNISH
Isle of Skye, Inverness-shire</td><td>3
C8</td><td></td><td></td><td></td><td></td><td></td><td></td><td></td><td></td><td></td><td></td><td></td><td></td><td></td><td></td><td></td><td></td><td></td><td></td><td></td></tr>
<tr><td>Greshornish House Hotel
Tel. Edinbane 266/255</td><td></td><td>4</td><td>4</td><td>5</td><td>14.00</td><td>16.00</td><td>26.00</td><td>34.00</td><td>21.00</td><td>24.00</td><td>140.00</td><td>150.00</td><td>-</td><td>4</td><td>2</td><td>4</td><td>3</td><td>1900
-</td><td>25</td><td>1-12</td></tr>

<tr><td>GRETNA GREEN
Dumfriesshire</td><td>2
D10</td><td></td><td></td><td></td><td></td><td></td><td></td><td></td><td></td><td></td><td></td><td></td><td></td><td></td><td></td><td></td><td></td><td></td><td></td><td></td></tr>
<tr><td>Crossways Inn
Tel. Gretna 284</td><td></td><td>6</td><td>6</td><td>5</td><td>11.50</td><td>12.50</td><td>23.00</td><td>25.00</td><td>18.00</td><td>19.50</td><td>90.00</td><td>100.00</td><td>2</td><td>2</td><td>2</td><td>6</td><td>-</td><td>1800
2230</td><td>40</td><td>1-12</td></tr>
<tr><td>Gretna Chase Hotel
CA6 5JB
Tel. Gretna 517</td><td></td><td>3</td><td>4</td><td>5</td><td>18.00</td><td>21.00</td><td>30.00</td><td>36.00</td><td>-</td><td>-</td><td>-</td><td>-</td><td>2</td><td>7</td><td>1</td><td>3</td><td>2</td><td>1900
2130</td><td>50</td><td>1-12</td></tr>
<tr><td>Solway Lodge Hotel
Annan Road
Tel. Gretna 266</td><td></td><td>4</td><td>4</td><td>4</td><td>12.50</td><td>13.50</td><td>23.00</td><td>24.00</td><td>-</td><td>-</td><td>-</td><td>-</td><td>-</td><td>9</td><td>1</td><td>7</td><td>1</td><td>2100
2100</td><td>30</td><td>1-12</td></tr>
<tr><td>Greenlaw Guest House
Tel. Gretna 361</td><td></td><td>-</td><td>-</td><td>-</td><td>7.25</td><td>7.50</td><td>13.50</td><td>14.00</td><td>-</td><td>-</td><td>-</td><td>-</td><td>2</td><td>5</td><td>1</td><td>-</td><td>3</td><td>-
-</td><td>8</td><td>4-11</td></tr>
<tr><td>Surrone House Guest House
Annan Road
Tel. Gretna 341</td><td></td><td>4</td><td>4</td><td>2</td><td>13.80</td><td>-</td><td>20.70</td><td>-</td><td>15.35</td><td>-</td><td>100.00</td><td>-</td><td>-</td><td>5</td><td>1</td><td>6</td><td>-</td><td>1900
2030</td><td>-</td><td>1-12</td></tr>

<tr><td>GRUINART, Bridgend
Isle of Islay, Argyll</td><td>1
B5</td><td></td><td></td><td></td><td></td><td></td><td></td><td></td><td></td><td></td><td></td><td></td><td></td><td></td><td></td><td></td><td></td><td></td><td></td><td></td></tr>
<tr><td>Loch Gruinart Guest House
Tel. Port Charlotte 212</td><td></td><td>1</td><td>2</td><td>2</td><td>6.50</td><td>7.00</td><td>13.00</td><td>14.00</td><td>11.00</td><td>12.00</td><td>70.00</td><td>77.00</td><td>1</td><td>4</td><td>-</td><td>-</td><td>2</td><td>1800
1900</td><td>6</td><td>1-12</td></tr>

<tr><td>GULLANE
East Lothian</td><td>2
E4</td><td></td><td></td><td></td><td></td><td></td><td></td><td></td><td></td><td></td><td></td><td></td><td></td><td></td><td></td><td></td><td></td><td></td><td></td><td></td></tr>
<tr><td>Bisset's Hotel
Tel. Gullane 842230</td><td></td><td>-</td><td>-</td><td>-</td><td>14.00</td><td>16.00</td><td>25.00</td><td>30.00</td><td>23.00</td><td>25.00</td><td>144.00</td><td>-</td><td>6</td><td>17</td><td>3</td><td>-</td><td>7</td><td>1900
2030</td><td>37</td><td>1-12</td></tr>
<tr><td>Greywalls Hotel
Muirfield
Tel. Gullane 842144
Telex 727396</td><td></td><td>5</td><td>5</td><td>5</td><td>20.00</td><td>40.00</td><td>40.00</td><td>80.00</td><td>35.95</td><td>55.95</td><td>-</td><td>-</td><td>7</td><td>16</td><td>-</td><td>23</td><td>1</td><td>1930
2130</td><td>60</td><td>1-12</td></tr>
<tr><td>Mallard Hotel
Tel. Gullane 843288</td><td></td><td>3</td><td>3</td><td>4</td><td>11.00</td><td>13.50</td><td>23.00</td><td>28.60</td><td>18.00</td><td>21.00</td><td>126.00</td><td>147.00</td><td>4</td><td>17</td><td>2</td><td>5</td><td>5</td><td>1900
2100</td><td>20</td><td>1-12</td></tr>
</table>

VAT is shown at 15%: changes in this rate may affect prices.

Name and Address	Map Ref	Bedrooms	Services	Meals	Single room overnight £min/£max	Double/twin room overnight £min/£max	Per person daily £min/£max	Per person weekly £min/£max	Single	Double/twin	Family	Private	Public	Evening meals (Last order)	Parking (no. of cars)	Months open (1-12)	Symbols
HADDINGTON East Lothian	2 E5																
Browns' Hotel 1 West Road Tel. Haddington 2254		4	4	2	18.00 / -	34.00 / -	30.50 / -	213.50 / -	1	5	-	4	1	1930 / 2100	8	1-12	
Maitlandfield Hotel Tel. Haddington 2287		3	2	2	10.00 / -	20.00 / -	13.00 / -	70.00 / -	4	2	5	2	2	1900 / 1900	50	1-12	
HALKIRK Caithness	4 C3																
Ulbster Arms Hotel KW12 6XY Tel. Halkirk 206		3	3	5	11.00	22.00	17.00	-	13	17	-	22	1	- / -	37	1-12	
HAMILTON Lanarkshire	2 A6																
Avonbridge Hotel Carlisle Road Tel. Hamilton 285001		6	1	5	20.00	27.00	25.00	-	5	40	1	37	6	1700 / 2250	120	1-12	
HARDGATE Dunbartonshire	1 H5																
Cameron House Hotel Glasgow Road G81 5PJ Tel. Duntocher 73535		3	3	5	19.80	33.00	26.12	182.84	12	5	-	17	-	1900 / 2130	-	1-12	
HAWICK Roxburghshire	2 E7																
The Buccleuch Hotel 1 Trinity Street Tel. Hawick 72368		3	4	4	10.00 / 10.00	18.00 / 25.00	12.80 / -	- / -	9	7	2	3	5	1700 / 2200	12	1-12	
Elm House Hotel 17 North Bridge Street TD9 9BD Tel. Hawick 72866		4	4	5	10.00 / 15.00	18.00 / 24.00	- / -	- / -	1	10	4	7	2	1830 / 2100	14	1-12	
Kirklands Hotel West Stewart Place Tel. Hawick 72263		5	4	5	17.50 / 22.50	30.00 / 33.00	22.00 / 24.00	140.00 / 145.00	-	6	-	3	1	1900 / 2130	20	1-12	

Kirklands Hotel AA★★ RAC★★

Hawick, Scottish Borders

Egon Ronay; Ashley Courtenay; Michelin; Routiers, Recommended. B.T.A. Commended Hotel/Restaurant. Charming Small Hotel pleasantly situated in the beautiful Scottish Borders. Conveniently placed for visiting the Abbeys, Stately Homes and magnificent surrounding countryside. Riding, Fishing, Golf, Swimming all near by. Personally supervised by the proprietors, we specialise in superb cuisine, with first class, friendly service. Radio, colour TV, Tea making facilities all rooms. Private Bathrooms available. Ample Parking. Tel: Hawick (0450) 72263.

Name and Address TOWN County Establishment Address Telephone Telex	Map Ref	Bedrooms	Services	Meals	Prices — Bed and Breakfast — Single room overnight £min £max	Double/twin room overnight £min £max	Per person daily £min £max	Per person weekly £min £max	B & B and evening meal — Single	Double/twin	Family	Private	Rooms — No. of bedrooms Public	Evening meals From Last order	No. of bath/ shower rooms	Parking (no. of cars)	Months open (1-12)	Facilities — Symbols — Key on back fold-out
HAWICK continued	2 E7																	
Teviotdale Lodge Country Hotel Commonside Tel. Teviotdale 232		-	4	5	15.00 -	23.00 -	17.45 -	118.00 -	1	6	1	2 1	1900 2100	30	1-12		(symbols)
Bridge House Guest House Sandbed TD9 0HD Tel. Hawick 73351		2	1	4	8.00 -	16.00 -	10.00 -	63.00 -	-	9	1	- 2	- -	-	1-12		(symbols)
West Buccleuch Guest House Roberton Tel. Selkirk 62230		1	3	4	9.75 -	19.50 -	17.25 -	- -	1	6	1	- 2	1800 2100	18	1-12		(symbols)
HELENSBURGH Dunbartonshire	1 G4																	
Commodore Hotel West Clyde Street Tel. Helensburgh 6924		6	5	6	23.00 27.00	35.00 40.00	31.50 35.50	199.50 227.50	-	45	-	45 -	1900 2130	80	1-12		(symbols)
HELMSDALE Sutherland	4 C5																	
Belgrave Arms Hotel KW8 6JX Tel. Helmsdale 242		3	3	4	9.00 9.00	18.00 18.00	13.75 13.75	95.00 95.00	5	6	-	- 3	1830 1930	17	1-12		(symbols)
Bridge Hotel KW8 6JA Tel. Helmsdale 219		3	5	4	8.50 -	17.00 -	14.50 -	- -	8	16	2	- 7	1900 2030	30	1-12		(symbols)

Navidale House Hotel

Helmsdale, Sutherland. Tel: 043 12 258.

A traditional Highland Country House Hotel with all modern comforts. Set in 5 acres overlooking the Moray Firth. The ideal base for touring Sutherland and Caithness. A la carte menu, all home cooking. Inclusive holidays combining fishing, golf, gold panning etc. Weekly terms, substantial reductions for children. Stay for a day or a week, you will receive a warm welcome.

Name and Address	Map Ref	Bedrooms	Services	Meals	Single room overnight	Double/twin room overnight	Per person daily	Per person weekly	Single	Double/twin	Family	Private	From Last order	Evening meals	Parking	Months open
Navidale House Hotel KW8 6JS Tel. Helmsdale 258		3	4	4	9.50 11.45	19.00 22.90	13.00 17.95	91.00 113.10	4	17	-	1 9	1930 2015	26	1-12	(symbols)
HIGHTAE, by Lockerbie Dumfriesshire	2 C9															
Royal Four Towns Hotel Tel. Lochmaben 402		3	2	2	8.50 -	17.00 -	13.00 -	85.00 -	1	- 3	-	1	1830 1930	20	1-12	(symbols)

Name and Address	Map Ref	Bedrooms	Services	Meals	Prices				B & B and evening meal					Rooms				Facilities	
TOWN County / Establishment Address Telephone Telex					Bed and Breakfast / Single room overnight	Double/twin room overnight	Per person daily	Per person weekly	Single	Double/twin	Family	Private	Public	No. of bedrooms / Evening meals	No. of bath/shower rooms	Parking (no. of cars)	Months open (1-12)	Symbols	
					£min £max	£min £max	£min £max	£min £max						From Last order			Key on back fold-out	
HILLSWICK, North Mainland Shetland	5 F3																		
St Magnus Bay Hotel Tel. Hillswick 209		4	4	5	12.50 19.50	25.00 -	18.50 25.50	122.50 143.50	6	20	2	9	5	1930 2100	60	1-12	T⌂⚓♀ 🐕✕🛏▥ ♿🛥⚡ 🖥©🅿Ⓥ	
HOLLYBUSH Ayrshire	1 H8																		

Hollybush House Hotel

Hollybush, by Ayr, Ayrshire   Telephone 0292-56 214

Beautiful old Country House in some 40 acres of garden, woodland and river. All fresh food cooked to order. Egon Ronay Crown and RAC and AA 3-star. Ideally situated for golf, fishing or shooting holidays and only 15 minutes from Prestwick Airport. Under the personal supervision of Bob and Margaret White. **American representative: Mark Barnes (phone 415-931 5225).**

Name and Address	Map Ref	Bedrooms	Services	Meals	Single room overnight	Double/twin room overnight	Per person daily	Per person weekly	Single	Double/twin	Family	Private	Public	No. of bedrooms / Last order	Evening meals	Parking	Months open	Symbols
Hollybush House Hotel KA6 7EA Tel. Dalrymple 214		4	5	5	15.00 20.00	20.00 30.00	22.50 25.50	- -	2	9	1	7	2	1900 2130	54	1-12		T⌂⚓♀ 🐕🛏▥♿ 🖥▬⚡© ✿🅿Ⓥ◡ ♪✎⊠
HOPEMAN, Elgin Moray	4 D7																	
Station Hotel 36 Harbour Street IV30 2RU Tel. Hopeman 830258		-	-	-	9.50 -	- -	14.00 -	- -	-	2	3	-	2	1800 -	10	1-12		⚓♀🐕🛏♿ Ⓥ
HUMBIE East Lothian	2 E5																	
Johnstounburn House Tel. Humbie 696 Telex 727897		5	5	5	40.00 -	64.00 -	- -	- -	-	11	-	11	-	1900 2100	100	1-12		T⌂⚓♀ 🐕✕🛏▥ ♿◑◡🖥▢ 🛥⚡⚘© ✿🅿Ⓥ✎ 🏆
HUNTLY Aberdeenshire	4 F9																	
Castle Hotel AB5 4SH Tel. Huntly 2696		4	4	5	14.50 16.50	26.00 28.00	23.00 28.00	119.00 136.00	3	19	2	4	4	1700 2200	20	1-12		T⌂⚓♀ 🐕🛏▥♿ 🖥▬⚡© ✿🅿Ⓥ◡ ♪
Hill Hotel AB5 5HX Tel. Huntly 2734		3	4	5	10.93 -	19.55 -	13.80 -	96.60 -	-	5	-	-	2	1700 2130	20	1-12		T⚓♀🐕🛏 ▥♿🛥✿ Ⓥ

Name and Address	Map Ref	Bedrooms	Services	Meals	Single room overnight £min £max	Double/twin room overnight £min £max	Per person daily £min £max	Per person weekly £min £max	Single	Double/twin	Family	Private	Public From Last order	Evening meals	Parking (no. of cars) / Months open (1-12)	Symbols Key on back fold-out
INNELLAN, by Dunoon **Argyll**	1 F5															
Springfield Hotel Sandy Beach PA23 7SP Tel. Innellan 261		3	4	5	10.20 13.00	20.40 20.40	14.80 18.60	85.00 100.00	2	6	2	-	2	1845 2130	15	1-12	🅃 ♟ ♘ 🐕 ♞ ♜ ▦ ♿ ☎ ⚡ ⚓ 🄲 ✿ 🆅 ∪ ✎ 🄺
INNERLEITHEN **Peeblesshire**	2 D6															
St Ronans Hotel Tel. Innerleithen 830380		3	2	2	8.00 10.00	16.00 20.00	12.00 -	84.00 -	1	3	1	-	1	1800 2000	12	1-12	♟ 🐕 ♿ 🆅 ∪

Tighnuilt House Hotel

Situated in the Tweed Valley overlooking the River Tweed, surrounded by gardens and forest area amongst one of the finest scenic settings in Scotland. The hotel is unique in its architectural design and quality. Centrally heated throughout also log fires in lounge. Ample parking space. All rooms recently tastefully decorated; special feature three large family rooms. Tea, Coffee and Refreshments served on request. Golf, Shooting, Fishing, Forest Walks, Nature Trails, Picnic Areas, Hill Climbing, Pony-Treks arranged. The hotel has three private beats for Salmon and Sea Trout. There is 9 miles of Brown Trout Fishing on Association Water. Shooting Parties arranged from nearby Estates. Home cooking. Very highly recommended. **For further details write or phone 0896-830491 and ask for George or Sybil Buchan**

PEEBLES ROAD, INNERLEITHEN, PEEBLESSHIRE

Name and Address	Map Ref	Bedrooms	Services	Meals	Single room overnight £min £max	Double/twin room overnight £min £max	Per person daily £min £max	Per person weekly £min £max	Single	Double/twin	Family	Private	Public From Last order	Evening meals	Parking / Months open	Symbols
Tighnuilt House Hotel Peebles Road Tel. Innerleithen 830491		4	3	4	9.50 12.50	19.00 24.50	15.00 18.50	105.00 -	1	2	3	-	3	1900 2030	14	1-12	♟ 🐕 ♞ ♜ ▦ ♿ ☎ ⚡ ✿ ∪ ♪ ✎ 🄺
Traquair Arms Hotel Traquair Road Tel. Innerleithen 830229		3	4	5	12.75 20.75	23.00 31.00	19.00 27.00	114.00 162.00	2	6	1	1	2	1700 2200	18	1-12	🅃 🄵 ♟ ♘ 🐕 ♞ ▦ ♿ ☎ ⚡ 🄲 🆅 ∪
INVERARAY **Argyll**	1 F3															
Argyll Arms Hotel Tel. Inveraray 2466		3	3	4	8.00 13.00	16.00 26.00	12.50 21.00	80.00 126.00	8	20	2	6	6	1900 2030	30	1-12	🅃 🄵 ♟ ♘ 🐕 ♞ ♜ ▦ ♿ ☎ ⚡ 🄲 ♻ 🆅 ∪ ✎ 🄺
Fern Point Hotel Tel. Inveraray 2170		4	4	5	8.00 16.00	16.00 32.00	- -	- -	1	1	4	5	1	1800 2200	20	1-12	🅃 ♟ ♘ 🐕 ♞ ♜ ▦ ♿ ☎ ⚡ ⚓ 🄲 ✿ ♻ 🆅 ∪ ✎ 🄺
George Hotel Tel. Inveraray 2111		3	3	3	8.50 10.00	17.50 20.00	14.00 16.00	95.00 100.00	2	12	-	2	6	1900 2000	-	1-12	🅃 🄵 ♟ ♘ 🐕 ♞ ♿ ⚡ ∪ ♻ 🆅 ∪

VAT is shown at 15%: changes in this rate may affect prices.

Prices — Bed and Breakfast / B & B and evening meal

Name and Address (Town / County / Establishment / Address / Telephone)	Map Ref	Bedrooms	Services	Meals	Single room overnight £min / £max	Double/twin room overnight £min / £max	Per person daily £min / £max	Per person weekly £min / £max
INVERARAY continued	1 F3							
Loch Fyne Hotel — Tel. Inveraray 2148		3	3	3	8.50 / –	17.00 / –	– / –	– / –
The Mckinlay Arms Hotel, Dalchenna — Tel. Inveraray 2160		3	3	5	10.50 / –	17.00 / –	16.00 / –	– / –
INVERBEG, by Luss — Dunbartonshire	1 G4							
The Inverbeg Inn, G83 8PD — Tel. Luss 678		4	5	6	18.00 / 26.50	24.00 / 40.00	26.00 / 42.50	– / –
INVERBERVIE — Kincardineshire	4 G12							
The Star Hotel, 78 King Street — Tel. Inverbervie 278		3	3	4	10.00 / –	18.00 / –	– / –	– / –
Anchorage Guest House — Tel. Inverbervie 393		1	2	2	5.00 / –	10.00 / –	– / –	– / –
INVERGARRY — Inverness-shire	3 H11							
Glengarry Castle Hotel, PH35 4HW — Tel. Invergarry 254		4	4	4	14.00 / 19.50	24.00 / 32.00	18.50 / 25.50	122.50 / 171.50
Inn On The Garry — Tel. Invergarry 206/7		5	4	5	18.50 / –	37.00 / –	29.00 / –	– / –

Rooms — Facilities

Establishment	No. of bedrooms: Single	Double/twin	Family	No. of bath/shower rooms: Private	Public	Evening meals From / Last order	Parking (no. of cars)	Months open (1-12)
Loch Fyne Hotel	6	18	1	–	5	– / –	40	1-12
The Mckinlay Arms Hotel	–	3	1	–	1	1900 / 2200	20	1-12
The Inverbeg Inn	2	11	1	7	2	1900 / 2300	84	1-12
The Star Hotel	2	3	1	–	1	1800 / 2000	20	1-12
Anchorage Guest House	2	2	1	–	1	1800 / 1900	–	1-12
Glengarry Castle Hotel	6	20	4	17	5	1900 / 2015	36	4-10
Inn On The Garry	1	9	–	10	–	1900 / 2230	50	3-11

(Facilities columns carry key symbols — Key on back fold-out.)

Name and Address	Map Ref	Bedrooms	Services	Meals	Single room overnight £min/£max	Double/twin room overnight £min/£max	Per person daily £min/£max	Per person weekly £min/£max	Single	Double/twin	Family	Private	Public	Evening meals (From / Last order)	Parking (no. of cars)	Months open (1-12)	Symbols
INVERGARRY continued	3 H11				£min £max	£min £max	£min £max	£min £max						From / Last order			Key on back fold-out
Tomdoun Hotel, Tel. Tomdoun 218		3	4	4	11.00 / -	21.00 / -	16.00 / -	105.00 / -	2	6	2	1	3	1900 / 2200	25	3-10	
Craigard Guest House, PH35 4HG, Tel. Invergarry 258		3	3	2	7.50 / 8.65	15.00 / 17.30	11.50 / 13.25	73.50 / 84.50	2	3	2	-	2	1930 / 1930	6	4-10	
Faichem Lodge Guest House, Faichem, Tel. Invergarry 314		3	3	2	6.00 / -	12.00 / -	10.00 / -	-	-	1	1	-	1	1900 / 1900	5	1-12	
Lundie View Guest House, PH35 4HN, Tel. Invergarry 291		3	3	2	6.50 / -	13.00 / -	10.50 / -	72.00 / -	1	2	3	-	2	1930 / 2000	8	1-12	
INVERGORDON Ross-shire	4 B7																
Viewfirth Hotel, Saltburn Road, IV18 0HH, Tel. Invergordon 852527		3	4	5	12.65 / -	22.00 / -	-	-	5	3	-	-	3	1800 / 2130	6	1-12	
INVERKEILOR, by Arbroath Angus	2 E1																
Lunan Bay Hotel, Tel. Inverkeilor 265		6	3	5	15.00 / 25.00	25.00 / 34.00	-	-	2	6	2	10	-	1900 / 2100	104	1-12	
INVERKEITHING Fife	2 C4																
Forth Craig Private Hotel, 90 Hope Street, Tel. Inverkeithing 418440		5	3	3	13.50 / 13.50	22.00 / 22.00	19.50 / 19.50	122.50 / 136.50	2	3	-	5	-	1830 / 2000	8	1-12	
The Royal Hotel, 34-36 High Street, KY11 1NN, Tel. Inverkeithing 412427		3	4	4	11.00 / -	18.50 / -	14.00 / -	-	4	7	-	-	3	1830 / 1930	-	1-12	
INVERMORISTON Inverness-shire	4 A10																

Tigh-na-Bruach
Invermoriston
On the shores of Loch Ness
R.A.C. and A.A. listed
Ideal centre for touring. Comfort assured. Dinner Bed and Breakfast terms, nightly and weekly. Brochure on request.
Proprietrix: **Miss Sheena Paterson**
Telephone: **Glenmoriston (0320) 51208**

Name and Address	Bedrooms	Services	Meals	Single room overnight	Double/twin room overnight	Per person daily	Per person weekly	Single	Double/twin	Family	Private	Public	Evening meals	Parking	Months open	Symbols
Tigh-na-Bruach Hotel, Tel. Glenmoriston 51208	3	3	2	9.20 / -	18.40 / -	13.80 / -	80.50 / -	1	4	2	-	2	1930 / 1930	12	4-10	

VAT is shown at 15%: changes in this rate may affect prices.

Name and Address	Map Ref	Bedrooms	Services	Meals	Single room overnight £min/£max	Double/twin room overnight £min/£max	Per person daily £min/£max	Per person weekly £min/£max	No. of bedrooms Single	No. of bedrooms Double/twin	No. of bedrooms Family	No. of bath/shower rooms Private	No. of bath/shower rooms Public	Evening meals From/Last order	Parking (no. of cars)	Months open (1-12)	Symbols
INVERNESS	4 B9																
Beaufort Hotel, 11 Culduthel Road, Tel. Inverness 222897		5	5	5	19.00 / 22.00	34.00 / 36.00	25.00 / 32.00	- / -	5	12	4	21	-	1900 / 2200	53	1-12	symbols
Brae Ness Hotel, 16-17 Ness Bank, Tel. Inverness 231732		4	4	4	10.50 / 11.75	18.00 / 19.50	14.25 / 15.50	85.00 / 97.50	1	10	3	7	3	1830 / 1930	10	4-11	symbols
Caledonian Hotel, Church Street, IV1 1DX, Tel. Inverness 235181, Telex 76357		6	5	5	15.00 / -	30.00 / -	- / -	- / -	60	60	-	120	-	1830 / 2130	50	1-12	symbols
Corriegarth Hotel, Heathmount Road, off Kingsmills Road, Tel. Inverness 231893		-	-	-	8.05 / -	16.10 / -	- / -	- / -	2	7	-	-	4	1830 / 1930	7	1-12	symbols
Craigmonie Hotel, Annfield Road, Tel. Inverness 231649		5	5	5	18.25 / 22.50	15.50 / 18.25	20.25 / 23.75	131.00 / 154.00	4	22	3	29	-	1830 / 2200	60	1-12	symbols
Cuchullin Lodge Hotel, 43 Culduthel Road, Tel. Inverness 231945/231613		4	4	5	12.00 / 18.00	22.00 / 31.00	17.50 / -	99.75 / -	3	10	2	8	3	1900 / 2145	24	1-12	symbols
Culloden House, Tel. Inverness 790461, Telex 75402		6	4	5	49.00 / -	75.00 / 99.00	- / -	- / -	-	20	-	20	-	1900 / 2130	40	1-12	symbols
Cummings Hotel, Church Street, Tel. Inverness 232531		3	5	4	15.00 / 17.00	28.00 / 32.00	20.00 / 22.00	120.00 / 140.00	5	31	2	5	10	1800 / 2000	25	1-12	symbols

BRAE NESS HOTEL
Ness Bank, Inverness IV2 4SF
Tel: 0463 231732
AA   RAC

A small private hotel situated beside the River Ness, 5 minutes walk from the town centre. We offer excellent home cooking and baking including traditional Scottish fare and local produce.

Brochure and travel inclusive holiday details on request.

Name and Address		Map Ref	Bedrooms	Services	Meals	Prices — Bed and Breakfast			B & B and evening meal	Rooms — No. of bedrooms			No. of bath/shower rooms		Evening meals		Parking (no. of cars)	Months open (1-12)	Facilities — Symbols
TOWN / County / Establishment / Address / Telephone / Telex						Single room overnight	Double/twin room overnight	Per person daily	Per person weekly	Single	Double/twin	Family	Private	Public	From	Last order			Key on back fold-out
INVERNESS continued		4 B9				£min £max	£min £max	£min £max	£min £max						From Last order				
Drumossie Hotel / Perth Road / Tel. Inverness 236451 / Telex 777967			3	5	4	17.00 23.00	30.00 36.00	21.50 27.00	120.00 150.00	25	53	3	52	6	1830	2030	80	1-12	
Dunain Park / Tel. Inverness 230512			4	4	4	- -	35.00 60.00	- -	- -	-	5	1	4	1	1930	2100	31	3-10	

DRUMOSSIE HOTEL
Perth Road, Inverness. Tel: 0463 236451

Overlooking Inverness and the Moray Firth the Drumossie is an ideal centre for touring the Highland region.

Loch Ness, Glen Affric and Aviemore are all within easy reach with Cawdor Castle, Culloden Battlefield and Fort George only a short drive away. Our reception staff are fully briefed on suggested day trips and local facilities.

Good food, an excellent wine cellar and a regular programme of entertainment which includes: Ceilidhs, Dances and Folk Singing, all combine to give the Drumossie the reputation it enjoys.

All rooms have radio, telephone and tea making facilities. Rooms with bath or shower also have colour TV.

Attractive weekend and midweek breaks from £17 per day.

Write or phone for further details and colour brochures.

Try a Taste of Scotland

Ask the Scottish Tourist Board for the colourful free booklet *A Taste of Scotland*. It lists around 200 places offering fine Scottish cooking, along with notes on regional specialities and recipes which you can try out at home.

While you're on holiday in Scotland, look for the Stockpot sign outside hotels and restaurants. It tells you that the menu offers not only traditional Scottish fare, but also examples of the creative skills of our chefs, using the best Scottish produce.

VAT is shown at 15%: changes in this rate may affect prices.

Name and Address		Map Ref	Bedrooms / Services / Meals	Prices				Rooms						Facilities		
TOWN County	Establishment Address Telephone Telex			Bed and Breakfast — Single room overnight / Double/twin room overnight		B & B and evening meal — Per person daily / Per person weekly		No. of bedrooms — Single / Double/twin / Family			No. of bath/shower rooms — Private / Public		Evening meals	Parking (no. of cars)	Months open (1-12)	Symbols
INVERNESS continued		4 B9		£min £max	£min £max	£min £max	£min £max				From	Last order			Key on back fold-out	

GLENMHOR HOTEL

Ness Bank, Inverness.
Telephone: 0463-234308.

Beautifully and quietly situated on the banks of the Ness near town centre. Ample car parking.

All bedrooms have radio, colour TV, baby listening and tea/coffee makers.

Free accommodation in some rooms for children accompanying two adults.

Excellent restaurant specialising in seafood and local produce.

Bistro offering informal, inexpensive food.

Reduced weekend rates most of the year from as little as £9.95 per person.

Establishment	Bedrooms	Services	Meals	Single room overnight	Double/twin room overnight	Per person daily	Per person weekly	Single	Double/twin	Family	Private	Public	Last order	Evening meals	Months open	Symbols
Glen Mhor Hotel 10 Ness Bank IV2 4SG Tel. Inverness 234308/9	4	5	5	10.50 17.50	21.00 35.00	15.00 -	105.00 -	7	18	1	15	6	1800 2130	16	1-12	
Glenmoriston Hotel 20 Ness Bank Tel. Inverness 223777 Telex .	-	-	-	16.00 21.00	25.00 36.00	- -	- -	7	12	2	10	4	1900 2100	30	1-12	
Haughdale Hotel Ness Bank Tel. Inverness 233065	3	3	3	14.50 -	27.00 -	22.50 -	155.00 -	14	23	3	-	6	1800 2030	20	1-12	

QUALITY ASSURED

The Thistle Commendation Scheme gives recognition to Holiday Static Caravan Sites in Scotland which provide first class caravans for hire, combined with very good facilities and an attractive environment. All sites have had a detailed inspection.

Look out for the Thistle Commendation plaques displayed by all the commended sites, or ask for the leaflet.

Name and Address					Prices						Rooms					Facilities
TOWN County Establishment Address Telephone Telex	**Map Ref**	Bedrooms	Services	Meals	Bed and Breakfast Single room overnight	Double/twin room overnight	Per person daily	B & B and evening meal Per person weekly	Single	Double/twin	No. of bedrooms Family	Private	No. of bath/shower rooms Public	Evening meals	Parking (no. of cars)	Months open (1-12) Symbols
INVERNESS continued	4 B9				£min £max	£min £max	£min £max	£min £max					From Last order			Key on back fold-out

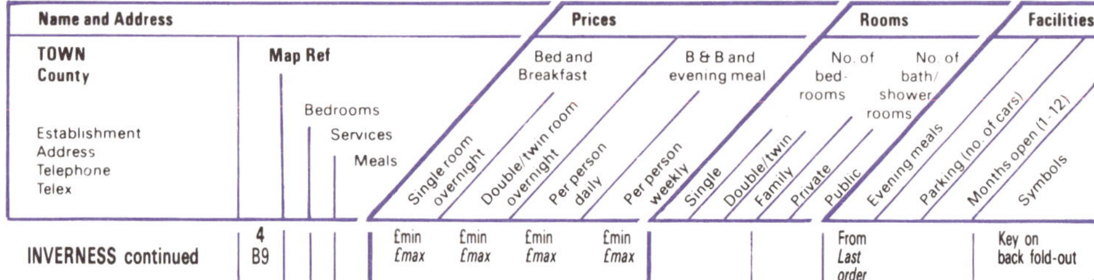

Set in three acres of gardens one mile south of the centre of town, this lovely 18th century mansion combines truly high standards of cuisine and modern comforts with friendly, personal service. Our 54 bedrooms have private bathrooms, colour television, telephones and radio, and offer the choice of bed sittingrooms, family rooms, superb 'doubles' and very well appointed twin and single bedded rooms. Excellent Restaurant, and private Dining Rooms. Private squash courts and adjacent to the fine 18 hole Inverness Golf Course. Parking for 100 cars. Kingsmills Hotel is personally supervised by the proprietors Angus and Lilian Macleod who look forward with their staff to the pleasure of welcoming you. Please write for our brochure and tariff, **Kingsmills Hotel, Culcabock Road, Inverness. Tel. (0463) 237166. Telex 75566.** *** AA plus HBL Awards, Egon Ronay, RAC & RSAC ***

Name and Address	Bedrooms	Services	Meals	Single room overnight	Double/twin room overnight	Per person daily	Per person weekly	Single	Double/twin	Family	Private	Public	Evening meals	Parking	Months open	Symbols
Kingsmills Hotel Culcabock Road Tel. Inverness 237166 Telex 75566	6	6	5	33.50 42.00	46.00 58.00	- -	- -	-	42	12	-	-	1800 2130	100	1-12	

From check-in to check-out you will enjoy the warm hospitality of our Inverness Hotel.

A drink, a meal and a good nights rest in a room with private bath and colour T.V. It's well worth stopping for.

Ladbroke Hotels
Ladbroke Hotel, Nairn Road, Inverness IV2 3TR. Tel: (0463) 239666 Telex: 75377.

Name and Address	Bedrooms	Services	Meals	Single room overnight	Double/twin room overnight	Per person daily	Per person weekly	Single	Double/twin	Family	Private	Public	Evening meals	Parking	Months open	Symbols
Ladbroke Hotel Nairn Road Tel. Inverness 239666 Telex 75377	6	5	5	41.00 -	53.00 -	- -	- -	26	70	12	108	-	1830 2200	150	1-12	

Name and Address	Map Ref	Bedrooms	Services	Meals	Prices				Rooms							Facilities		
TOWN / County / Establishment / Address / Telephone / Telex					Bed and Breakfast			B & B and evening meal		No. of bedrooms		No. of bath/shower rooms						
					Single room overnight	Double/twin room overnight	Per person daily	Per person weekly		Single	Double/twin	Family	Private	Public	Evening meals	Parking (no. of cars)	Months open (1-12)	Symbols
INVERNESS continued	4 B9				£min £max	£min £max	£min £max	£min £max						From Last order			Key on back fold-out

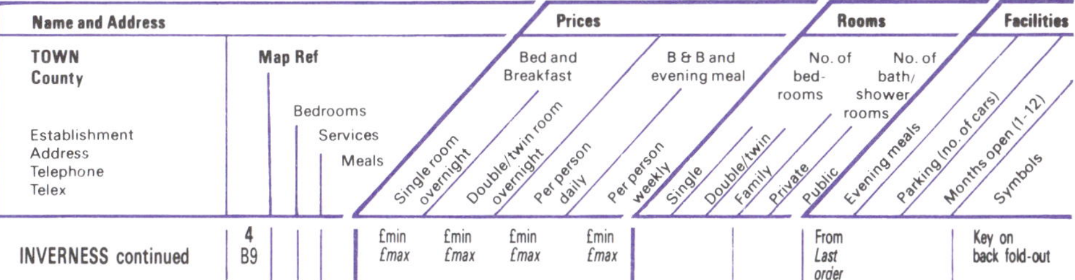

Larchfield Hotel
INVERNESS

Larchfield Hotel is an 18th Century listed building of architectural historic interest, situated on the banks of the River Ness, which runs through Inverness, Capital of the Highlands.

Facing the hotel, across the river, is the modern Eden Court Theatre and Inverness Cathedral. The hotel is an ideal centre for touring the North of Scotland, with its majestic scenery and many places of historic interest.

Our Struan Dining Room specialises in fresh local produce, and is open to non-residents. The hotel is under the personal supervision of the owner, Mrs C. Houston.

15 Ness Bank, Inverness IV2 4SF.
Telephones: Visitors (0463) 237315.
Reception: (0463) 233874.

Name and Address	Bedrooms	Services	Meals	Single room overnight	Double/twin room overnight	Per person daily	Per person weekly	Single	Double/twin	Family	Private	Public	Last order	Parking	Months open	Symbols
Larchfield Hotel / 15 Ness Bank / Tel. Inverness 233874	4	4	4	11.50 -	18.40 -	16.10 -	- -	5	10	4	2	8	1800 2030	6	1-12	
Lochardil Hotel / Stratherrick Road / Tel. Inverness 235995	4	4	4	17.25 19.55	- -	- -	- -	-	6	1	5	2	1900 2100	100	1-12	
Macdougall Clansman Hotel / Church Street / Tel. Inverness 231683	4	4	2	12.50 -	24.00 -	18.00 -	118.00 -	3	13	2	7	3	1800 1900	-	1-12	
Moray Park Hotel / Island Bank Road / Tel. Inverness 233528	4	4	4	8.50 10.00	17.00 20.00	15.00 16.50	99.75 110.25	1	4	2	3	2	1900 1730	10	1-12	
Moyness Private Hotel / Bruce Gardens / Tel. Inverness 233836	3	3	2	7.00 -	14.00 -	11.00 -	77.00 -	3	3	3	-	2	1900 2000	14	1-12	
Muirtown Motel / 11 Clachnaharry Road / IV3 6LT / Tel. Inverness 234860	5	4	4	18.00 -	24.00 -	23.00 -	- -	-	25	11	36	-	1730 2100	120	1-12	

TOWN County Establishment Address Telephone Telex	Map Ref Bedrooms Services Meals			Prices					Rooms						Facilities	
				Bed and Breakfast			B & B and evening meal		No. of bedrooms			No. of bath/shower rooms					
				Single room overnight	Double/twin room overnight	Per person daily	Per person weekly	Single	Double/twin	Family	Private	Public	Evening meals	Parking (no. of cars)	Months open (1-12)	Symbols
INVERNESS continued	4 B9			£min £max	£min £max	£min £max	£min £max					From Last order			Key on back fold-out

PALACE HOTEL
Ness Walk Inverness
Telephone: 0463 223243

The PALACE HOTEL is one of 4 Milton Hotels located throughout the Highlands. It has 82 rooms with tea and coffee-making facilities and TV in every room. Special weekend breaks and 7-night or more stays are available or you can take one of our touring holidays including hotels in Oban and Fort William.

Contact hotel direct or write to Mhairi Cameron, Milton Hotels, Fort William, Inverness-shire (0397 3139) for our full-colour 'Highland Holiday' brochure.

Name and Address																	
Palace Hotel Ness Walk Tel. Inverness 223243	4	5	4	16.50 -	33.00 -	- -	99.00 -	8	62	12	50	9	1800 2100	30	1-12		T ♨ ⚓ ♉ ♞ ♝ ♿ ◐ ♒ ☎ ▱ ⚓ C V ♻
Queensgate Hotel Queensgate Tel. Inverness 237211 Telex 75235	5	5	5	15.00 20.00	25.00 32.50	22.00 27.00	140.00 200.00	20	37	3	60	-	1830 2130	-	1-12		T ♨ ⚓ ♉ ⚔ ♝ ▦ ♿ ◐ ♒ ☎ ▱ ⚓ ♻ V ♻ ♪ ⚒ ⚔
Rannoch Lodge Hotel 25 Southside Road Tel. Inverness 234816/233114	4	4	4	14.95 17.25	26.00 30.00	20.00 25.00	120.00 150.00	5	9	-	4	3	1900 2130	26	1-12		⚓ ♉ ⚔ ♝ ▦ M ♿ ▱ ⚓ ⚡ ⚓ C ✽ V ♻

Redcliffe Hotel
Gordon Terrace Inverness (0463) 232767

* Quiet secluded location within 3 minutes walk of town centre
* Excellent A la Carte Menu including traditional Scottish Dishes and Extensive Wine List
* Ample Car Parking
* Under Personal Supervision of Proprietors
Brochure on Request

Name and Address																	
Redcliffe Hotel 1 Gordon Terrace Tel. Inverness 232767	4	3	3	11.90 13.90	23.80 27.80	17.90 19.90	112.00 125.00	2	3	2	2	2	1830 2030	13	1-12		T ♉ ♞ ⚔ ♝ ▦ ♿ ⚓ ⚡ ⚓ C V ♻
Riverside House Ness Bank Tel. Inverness 231052	3	3	2	8.50 9.50	17.00 19.00	13.50 14.50	91.00 98.00	3	3	4	-	2	1800 1900	-	1-12		T ♝ ▦ ♿ V

VAT is shown at 15%: changes in this rate may affect prices.

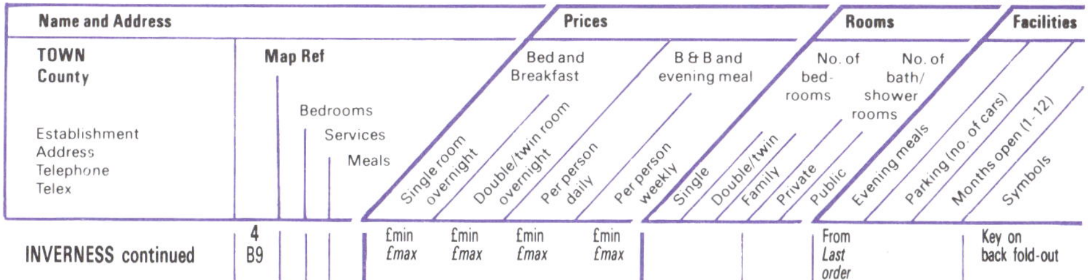

| INVERNESS continued | 4 B9 | | | £min £max | £min £max | £min £max | £min £max | | | | | From Last order | | Key on back fold-out |

Station Hotel

Academy Street, Inverness.
Tel: 0463 231926.

Whenever you step through the elegant pillared entrance, you are made welcome in finest Highland fashion in this famous and friendly 3-star hotel. Centrally located adjacent to all the town's amenities. Most bedrooms have private bathrooms and all have colour television. Our award-winning restaurant is truly an experience in dining. Bargain breaks available in low seasons. Brochure on request.

Establishment / Address / Telephone	Bedrooms	Services	Meals	Single room overnight	Double/twin room overnight	Per person daily	Per person weekly	Single	Double/twin	Family	Private	Public	Last order	Parking	Months open
Station Hotel, Academy Street, Tel. Inverness 231926	6	5	5	21.50 / 33.50	36.00 / 52.00	29.00 / 42.00	180.00 / 220.00	29	34	2	52	2	1900 / 2100	10	1-12
Whin Park Hotel & Restaurant, 17 Ardross Street, Tel. Inverness 232549	4	4	4	10.00 / 14.00	18.00 / 24.00	16.50 / 21.00	115.50 / 147.00	-	4	4	4	1	1830 / 2130	6	1-12
Abermar Guest House, 25 Fairfield Road, Tel. Inverness 239019	4	2	1	7.00 / 7.50	14.00 / 15.00	- / -	- / -	2	6	1	3	2	- / -	8	1-12
Advie Lodge Guest House, 31 Crown Drive, Tel. Inverness 235119	2	3	2	7.00 / 7.00	14.00 / 14.00	12.00 / 12.00	84.00 / 84.00	1	3	1	-	1	1800 / 1830	3	1-12
Ardnacoille Guest House, 1a Annfield Road, Tel. Inverness 233451	3	2	2	7.00 / 8.00	14.00 / 16.00	11.00 / 12.00	75.00 / 81.00	-	4	1	-	2	1900 / 1900	6	4-10
Arran Guest House, 42 Union Street, Tel. Inverness 232115	3	2	1	- / -	14.00 / -	- / -	- / -	-	5	2	-	2	- / -	-	1-12
Blair Ord Guest House, 10 Ballifeary Road, 1V3 5PJ, Tel. Inverness 235572	2	3	1	6.00 / 8.00	12.00 / 16.00	- / -	- / -	2	6	3	-	2	-	8	4-10
Clachnaharry Guest House, 41 Clachnaharry Road, Tel. Inverness 231432	3	3	2	8.00 / 9.50	14.00 / 16.00	12.50 / 14.00	80.50 / 91.00	-	5	3	-	3	1830 / 1900	10	1-12
Craigside Guest House, 4 Gordon Terrace, Tel. Inverness 231576	4	3	2	- / -	16.00 / 18.50	12.00 / 15.00	80.00 / 100.00	-	5	1	4	1	1900 / -	4	3-12
Crownleigh Guest House, 6 Midmills Road, Tel. Inverness 220316	3	2	2	5.50 / 7.50	11.00 / 14.00	9.50 / 11.50	66.50 / 80.50	2	3	1	-	2	- / 1800	-	1-12
Four Winds Guest House, 42 Old Edinburgh Road, Tel. Inverness 230397	3	4	1	7.50 / 8.00	15.00 / 16.00	- / -	50.00 / -	2	3	2	-	2	- / -	15	1-12
Glencairn Guest House, 19 Ardross Street, Tel. Inverness 232965	3	2	1	7.50 / 7.50	14.00 / 15.00	- / -	- / -	1	8	2	-	5	- / -	6	1-12
Glencairn Guest House, 30 Argyle Street, Tel. Inverness 231857	-	-	-	7.00 / -	14.00 / -	- / -	- / -	1	1	3	-	1	- / -	4	1-12

Prices shown are for guidance only. Please send SAE with each enquiry.

Name and Address	Map Ref	Bedrooms	Services	Meals	Single room overnight (£min / £max)	Double/twin room overnight (£min / £max)	Per person daily (£min / £max)	Per person weekly (£min / £max)	Single	Double/twin	Family	Private	Public	Evening meals (From / Last order)	Parking	Months open	Symbols
INVERNESS continued	4 B9																Key on back fold-out
Gowanlea Guest House 11 Ballifeary Road Tel. Inverness 234906		3	2	1	6.50 / 7.00	13.00 / 14.00	- / -	- / -	1	2	-	-	1	- / -	-	1-12	
Inverglen Guest House 7 Abertarff Road Tel. Inverness 237610		3	3	4	7.50 / 9.00	14.00 / 17.00	11.00 / 12.50	65.00 / 75.00	1	2	3	-	2	1800 / 1800	5	1-12	
Ivybank 28 Old Edinburgh Road Tel. Inverness 232796		3	2	1	6.50 / -	13.00 / -	- / -	- / -	-	3	-	-	1	- / -	-	4-10	
Leinster Lodge Guest House 27 Southside Road 1V2 4XA Tel. Inverness 233311		3	3	1	7.50 / 7.50	15.00 / 15.00	- / -	- / -	1	3	2	-	2	- / -	7	1-12	
Redwood Guest House 19 Culduthel Road Tel. Inverness 232427		-	-	-	- / 6.50	- / 13.00	- / -	- / -	3	4	3	-	2	- / -	12	1-12	
Silverwells 28 Ness Bank Tel. Inverness 234658		3	3	-	- / -	14.00 / -	- / -	- / -	-	4	1	-	2	- / -	-	1-12	
St Ann's Guest House 37 Harrowden Road Tel. Inverness 236157		3	3	2	7.50 / 8.75	15.00 / 20.50	12.00 / 14.75	74.00 / 95.50	2	4	1	4	2	1815 / 1915	3	4-10	
Taymount Guest House 27 Crown Drive Tel. Inverness 232741		4	3	2	6.00 / 6.50	12.00 / 13.00	10.00 / 10.00	65.00 / 65.00	-	2	1	-	3	1800 / -	3	1-12	
Tigh-a'-Mhuilinr Guest House 2 Kingsmills Gardens Tel. Inverness 238257		1	2	2	9.00 / -	16.00 / -	13.00 / -	- / -	2	2	-	-	2	1900 / -	5	1-12	
INVERSHIN, by Lairg **Sutherland**	4 A6																
Invershin Hotel IV27 4ET Tel. Invershin 202		4	4	6	9.00 / 12.00	18.00 / 24.00	16.00 / 18.00	70.00 / 78.00	6	16	2	13	5	1900 / 2150	50	1-12	
INVERSNAID **Stirlingshire**	1 G3																
Inversnaid Hotel FK8 3TU Tel. Inversnaid 223		3	3	4	10.35 / 13.23	20.70 / 24.15	16.30 / 19.75	80.00 / 103.00	4	27	11	-	8	1900 / 2000	106	1-12	
INVERURIE **Aberdeenshire**	4 G9																
Gordon Arms Hotel Market Place AB5 9SA Tel. Inverurie 20314		3	3	4	12.75 / -	19.50 / -	- / -	- / -	7	4	-	-	2	1700 / 1945	-	1-12	
Kintore Arms Hotel 83 High Street Tel. Inverurie 21367		3	4	4	17.00 / 20.00	22.00 / 27.00	20.00 / 27.00	120.00 / 170.00	4	7	2	-	5	1700 / 1945	70	1-12	

VAT is shown at 15%: changes in this rate may affect prices.

Name and Address	Map Ref	Bedrooms	Services	Meals	Single room overnight £min £max	Double/twin room overnight £min £max	Per person daily £min £max	Per person weekly £min £max	Single	Double/twin	Family	Private	Public	Evening meals From / Last order	Parking (no. of cars)	Months open (1-12)	Symbols
IONA, Isle of Argyll	1 B3																

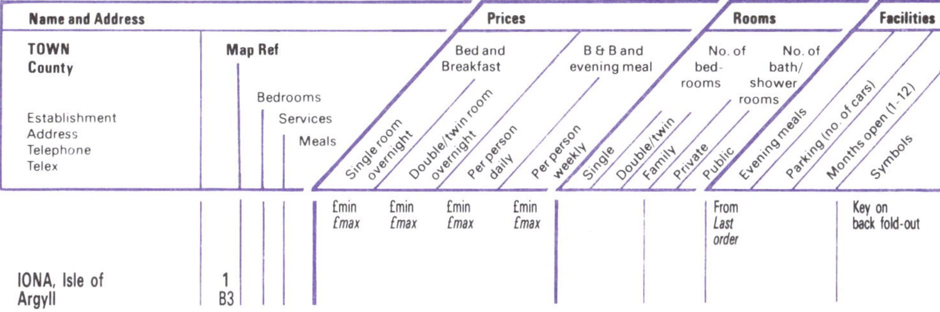

argyll hotel isle of iona

Argyll. Tel: 06817-334

A delightful friendly hotel, situated in the village overlooking the Sound of Iona. We serve excellent home cooking, home-grown vegetables and our own baking. Residents license with a good selection of wines.

Come and stay with us for a refreshing holiday on this beautiful island. Ring or write to Mrs Fiona Menzies for brochure.

Name and Address	Map Ref	Bedrooms	Services	Meals	Single room overnight	Double/twin room overnight	Per person daily	Per person weekly	Single	Double/twin	Family	Private	Public	Evening meals	Parking	Months open	Symbols
Argyll Hotel PA76 6SJ Tel. Iona 334	1	3	3		13.00 / 15.00	22.00 / 34.00	18.00 / 24.00	105.00 / 143.00	10	11	-	2	4	1900 / 1900	-	4-10	
St Columba Hotel Tel. Iona 304		3	3	3	13.20 / 14.60	24.00 / 26.60	18.00 / 19.80	99.00 / 110.00	10	19	-	2	7	1900 / -	-	4-10	
IRVINE Ayrshire	1 G6																
Annfield House 6 Castle Street Tel. Irvine 78903/4	-	-	-		22.00 / -	32.00 / -	- / -	- / -	2	8	-	10	-	1850 / 2150	-	1-12	
Claremont Hotel 68-76 Byres Road Tel. Kilwinning 53938	3	5	4		14.00 / 16.50	27.00 / 29.00	- / -	- / -	9	9	2	12	2	1700 / 2130	60	1-12	
ISLE ORNSAY Isle of Skye, Inverness-shire	3 E10																
Duisdale Hotel Tel. Isle Ornsay 202	3	3	4		14.00 / -	28.00 / -	23.75 / -	155.75 / -	8	12	2	5	5	1900 / 2030	30	4-10	
Kinloch Lodge Hotel Kinloch Tel. Isle Ornsay 214 Telex 75442	4	4	4		20.00 / 28.00	40.00 / 56.00	32.80 / 40.80	- / -	2	5	-	5	3	2000 / 2030	30	1-12	
Post Office Guest House Tel. Isle Ornsay 201	2	3	1		6.00 / -	12.00 / -	- / -	- / -	-	6	-	-	2	- / -	10	3-10	

Name and Address				Prices				Rooms						Facilities
TOWN / County / Establishment / Address / Telephone / Telex	Map Ref / Bedrooms / Services / Meals			Bed and Breakfast — Single room overnight (£min £max)	Double/twin room overnight (£min £max)	Per person daily (£min £max)	B & B and evening meal — Per person weekly (£min £max)	No. of bedrooms — Single	Double/twin	Family	Private	No. of bath/shower rooms — Public	Evening meals — From Last order / Parking (no. of cars) / Months open (1-12)	Symbols — Key on back fold-out

Name and Address	Map Ref	Bed	Serv	Meal	Single o/n	Double o/n	Per person daily	Per person weekly	Single	Double	Family	Private	Public	Last order / Parking / Months	Symbols
ISLE OF WHITHORN Wigtownshire	1 H11														

The Queen's Arms Telephone: Whithorn 369
Isle of Whithorn, Wigtownshire

A comfortable old inn, modernised to give guests all facilities without destroying its character. Food emphasis is on Scots cooking and local specialities – fish, lobster, Galloway beef and Sorbie cheese. Winners of AA rosette for food for 3 years running. We can arrange sail and power boats for sea angling, local cruises and sailing. There are 5 golf courses within easy reach of the hotel

Proprietors: George and Kay Barr.

Name and Address	Map Ref	Bed	Serv	Meal	Single o/n	Double o/n	Per person daily	Per person weekly	Single	Double	Family	Private	Public	Last order / Parking / Months	Symbols
Queens Arms Hotel Tel. Whithorn 369		3	4	5	10.95 / -	21.90 / -	17.95 / -	120.00 / -	3	7	-	4	2	1930 2145 10 3-10	
JEDBURGH Roxburghshire	2 E7														
Ferniehirst Mill Lodge TD8 6PQ Tel. Jedburgh 63279		3	3	2	11.50 / 12.65	23.00 / 25.30	19.55 / 22.65	129.95 / 150.65	2	9	-	9	2	1830 2000 16 12-10	
Glenbank Hotel Castlegate Tel. Jedburgh 62258		-	-	-	11.50 / 14.50	23.00 / 29.00	17.50 / 20.50	110.00 / 120.00	2	4	2	2	2	1900 2030 30 1-12	
Kenmore Bank Guest House Oxnam Road Tel. Jedburgh 62369		3	3	3	8.00 / 8.00	16.00 / 16.00	10.00 / 10.00	70.00 / 70.00	-	4	2	-	2	1800 2100 7 1-12	
JOHN O'GROATS Caithness	4 E2														
John O'Groats House Hotel KW1 4YR Tel. John O'Groats 203		3	4	4	11.50 / -	20.75 / -	- / -	- / -	2	14	1	7	5	1900 2100 53 4-10	
Seaview Hotel Tel. John O'Groats 220		3	4	4	8.00 / -	16.00 / -	14.00 / -	98.00 / -	1	7	1	2	2	- 2000 21 1-12	
Caber-feidh Guest House KW1 4YR Tel. John O'Groats 219		2	2	2	6.00 / -	10.00 / -	- / -	- / -	2	5	3	-	3	1800 1900 14 3-11	
JOHNSTONE Renfrewshire	1 H5														
Lynnhurst Hotel Park Road Tel. Johnstone 24331/24600		5	4	5	13.80 / 20.25	28.55 / 33.15	22.05 / 28.50	154.35 / 199.50	16	13	2	21	2	1830 2100 70 1-12	

VAT is shown at 15%: changes in this rate may affect prices.

Name and Address — TOWN / County / Establishment / Address / Telephone / Telex	Map Ref	Bedrooms	Services	Meals	Bed and Breakfast — Single room overnight £min £max	Double/twin room overnight £min £max	Per person daily £min £max	B & B and evening meal — Per person weekly £min £max	Single	Double/twin	Family	Private	Public	No. of bath/shower rooms — From Last order	Evening meals	Parking (no. of cars)	Months open (1-12)	Symbols — Key on back fold-out
JOHNSTONE BRIDGE Dumfriesshire	2 C9																	
Dinwoodie Lodge Country House Hotel DG11 2SL Tel. Johnstone Bridge 289		3	4	5	15.00 17.50	25.00 28.00	- -	- -	1	5	3	2	2	1700 2130	100	1-12	[symbols]
KAMES, by Tighnabruaich Argyll	1 F5																	
Kames Hotel PA21 2AF Tel. Tighnabruaich 489		3	3	4	8.50 12.00	17.00 24.00	16.00 -	112.00 -	1	6	3	-	2	1900 2000	12	1-12	[symbols]
KEITH Banffshire	4 E8																	
Ashley Lodge Hotel Church Road AB5 3BQ Tel. Keith 2335		3	5	5	9.50 -	16.95 -	14.50 -	85.00 -	6	3	3	-	2	1830 2130	25	1-12	[symbols]
Royal Hotel Church Road AB5 3BR Tel. Keith 2528/2313		-	-	-	11.00 17.00	19.00 27.00	17.50 23.50	105.00 120.00	4	10	1	3	4	1700 2100	24	1-12	[symbols]
KELSO Roxburghshire	2 F6																	

Cross Keys Hotel
Kelso TD5 7HL Tel: 0573 23303

***AA ***RAC

Most Rooms with Bath/Shower. All with own Colour Television, In House Films. Tea/Coffee Making Facilities. Direct Dial Telephone. Night Service.

THE TRYST 'N' TREE RESTAURANT
"The Best Food in Town". Early Travellers Supper — 6.00 pm-9.00 pm. Price from £2.95 inclusive. Dinner-7.00 pm-9.00 pm. Price £8.50 inclusive. À la carte Menu with Scottish and Continental Specialities. Friday Night is "Italian Night Menu" by popular request.

WHIPMANS BAR LUNCHES
From 12.00-2.00pm. The wide selection of freshly cooked food and its central position, make the Whipmans Bar the natural choice for a good Bar Lunch in Kelso.

Name and Address		Bedrooms	Services	Meals	Single room overnight £min £max	Double/twin room overnight £min £max	Per person daily £min £max	Per person weekly £min £max	Single	Double/twin	Family	Private	Public	From Last order	Evening meals	Parking	Months open	Symbols
Cross Keys Hotel 36-37 The Square Tel. Kelso 23303		5	5	5	16.00 21.00	28.00 34.00	21.00 28.00	- -	7	13	3	13	4	1900 2100	10	1-12	[symbols]

Name and Address	Map Ref			Prices					Rooms						Facilities	
TOWN County Establishment Address Telephone Telex		Bedrooms	Services / Meals	Bed and Breakfast Single room overnight	Double/twin room overnight	Per person daily	B & B and evening meal Per person weekly	Single	Double/twin	Family	Private	No. of bedrooms Public	No. of bath/shower rooms Evening meals	Parking (no. of cars)	Months open (1-12)	Symbols
KELSO continued	2 F6			£min £max	£min £max	£min £max	£min £max					From Last order		Key on back fold-out		

Queens Head Hotel

Bridge Street, Kelso, Borders. Tel: Kelso (0573) 24636

A modernised 18th century Inn full of character, and set in one of the most beautiful of the Border towns. A perfect centre for exploring the Borders and Lothians.

Basic cost £42 — any 3 nights (£48 in July and August). Extra days £14.
Private bathrooms available at small extra cost.
Free morning papers at breakfast.

Name and Address	Bedrooms	Services	Meals	Single room overnight	Double/twin room overnight	Per person daily	Per person weekly	Single	Double/twin	Family	Private	Public	Evening meals (From/Last order)	Bath/shower rooms	Months open	Symbols
Queens Head Hotel 20 Bridge Street TD5 7JD Tel. Kelso 24636	3	4	4	10.20 13.00	18.90 20.90	16.40 17.50	98.00 112.00	-	5	4	1	2	1700 2000	-	1-12	(symbols)
Sunlaws House Hotel TD5 8JZ Tel. Roxburgh 331	6	5	5	30.00 36.00	48.00 56.00	42.50 48.50	- -	4	9	1	14	-	1930 2130	44	1-12	(symbols)
Bellevue Guest House Bowmont Street Tel. Kelso 24588	3	3	2	7.50 -	14.00 -	10.50 -	- -	3	3	2	-	2	1830 1830	7	1-12	(symbols)
Maxmill Park Guest House Maxmill Park Tel. Kelso 24468	3	2	2	7.75 8.75	15.50 17.50	11.25 12.25	78.00 88.00	-	5	1	3	2	1800 -	10	1-12	(symbols)
KEMNAY **Aberdeenshire** — Map Ref 4 G10																
Park Hill Lodge Hotel Tel. Kemnay 2789	3	2	4	10.00 12.00	20.00 24.00	16.00 19.00	104.00 118.00	1	2	2	-	2	1900 2130	30	1-12	(symbols)

SCOTLAND'S COUNTRYSIDE IS UNIQUE!

So: stay on a farm or a croft — that's the best way to get to know the Scottish countryside! To help you find the ideal farmhouse, ask for the free brochure called *Scottish Farmhouse Holidays*. You'll be able to choose from a range of farms of all kinds.

Town / County / Establishment / Address / Telephone / Telex	Map Ref	Bedrooms	Services	Meals	Single room overnight £min/£max	Double/twin room overnight £min/£max	Per person daily £min/£max	Per person weekly £min/£max	Single	Double/twin	Family	Private	Public	Evening meals From / Last order	Parking (no. of cars)	Months open (1-12)	Symbols
KENMORE Perthshire	2 A1																Key on back fold-out
Kenmore Hotel, The Square, PH15 2NU, Tel. Kenmore 205 (See ad. p. 174)		4	4	4	17.00 / 23.00	34.00 / 46.00	24.50 / 30.50	164.50 / 210.00	3	31	4	38	-	1915 / 2100	100	1-12	
Loch Tay Guest House, Croft-Na-Caber, Sth Loch Rd, PH15 2HW, Tel. Kenmore 236		3	3	2	- / -	20.00 / -	18.00 / -	119.00 / -	-	2	1	-	1	1715 / 2030	20	1-12	
KENSALEYRE, by Portree Isle of Skye, Inverness-shire	3 D8																
Macdonald Hotel, Tel. Skeabost Bridge 339		4	3	4	12.00 / 17.00	24.00 / 34.00	16.50 / 25.50	115.50 / 164.50	4	7	-	7	1	1830 / 1930	20	4-10	
Corran Guest House, Eyre, Tel. Skeabost Bridge 311		-	-	-	7.00 / 7.00	14.00 / 14.00	10.00 / 10.00	70.00 / 70.00	1	2	3	-	2	1900 / 1830	10	1-12	
KENTALLEN, by Appin Argyll	1 F1																
Ardsheal House, PA38 4BX, Tel. Duror 227		3	3	3	28.00 / 42.00	40.00 / 64.00	42.00 / 56.00	238.00 / 322.00	-	12	-	8	2	2000 / 2030	20	4-10	
KILCHOAN, Ardnamurchan Argyll	1 C1																
Sonachan Hotel, Tel. Kilchoan 211		3	4	5	9.78 / -	- / -	17.25 / -	- / -	-	5	2	-	2	1900 / 1930	8	3-10	
KILCHRENAN, by Taynuilt Argyll	1 F2																
Ardanaiseig Hotel, Tel. Kilchrenan 333		6	4	5	- / -	- / -	42.50 / -	- / -	-	14	-	14	-	1930 / 2200	40	4-10	
Taychreggan Hotel, PA35 1HQ, Tel. Kilchrenan 211		4	4	4	15.00 / 25.00	30.00 / 50.00	26.00 / 36.00	52.00 / 72.00	1	16	-	14	1	1930 / 2100	30	4-10	
KILDARY Ross-shire	4 B7																
Jackdaw Hotel, Barbaraville, Tel. Kildary 2312		4	3	5	15.00 / 17.50	25.00 / 30.00	- / -	160.00 / -	12	8	-	20	-	1700 / 2200	24	1-12	

THE KENMORE HOTEL

Scotland's oldest Inn
Established in 1572

B.T.A. Commended Country House Hotel

A.A. *** R.A.C.   EGON RONAY

Beautifully situated in Kenmore, one of Scotland's loveliest villages, now a conservation area and surrounded by countryside listed for its outstanding natural beauty THE KENMORE HOTEL offers a unique combination of old world charm, elegance and comfort matched only by its excellent cuisine, cellar and personal service.

**Reduced rates on our own Taymouth Castle Golf Course
(Par 69)**

Salmon and Trout Fishing on our own private beats on the Tay.

*For Hotel brochure and reservations apply to:
Mr Ian Mackenzie, Manager
Telephone: Kenmore (08873) 205*

KENMORE, PERTHSHIRE

Name and Address (Town / County / Establishment)	Map Ref	Bedrooms	Services	Meals	Single room overnight £min/£max	Double/twin room overnight £min/£max	Per person daily £min/£max	Per person weekly £min/£max	Single	Double/twin	Family	Private	Public	Evening meals From/Last order	Parking (no. of cars)	Months open (1-12)	Symbols
KILDONAN / Isle of Arran / Kildonan Hotel, Tel. Kildonan 207	1 F7	3	4	4	8.50 / 12.50	17.00 / 25.00	15.00 / 19.00	83.00 / 113.00	7	18	4	2	6	1915 / 2030	70	1-12	(symbols)
KILDRUMMY, by Alford / Aberdeenshire / Kildrummy Castle Hotel, AB3 8RA, Tel. Kildrummy 288	4 E10	5	4	5	20.50 / 25.50	33.00 / 45.00	23.00 / 33.00	154.00 / 196.00	2	9	2	10	1	1900 / 2130	40	3-12	(symbols)
Mossat Guest House, Mossat, AB3 8PL, Tel. Kildrummy 355		3	2	4	- / -	17.00 / -	- / -	- / -	-	1	2	-	1	1700 / 2000	5	1-12	(symbols)
KILFINAN, by Tighnabruaich / Argyll / Kilfinan Hotel, PA21 2EP, Tel. Kilfinan 223/208	1 E5	5	3	4	16.50 / 20.00	20.00 / 25.00	26.50 / 30.00	- / -	-	11	-	11	-	1900 / 2130	20	1-12	(symbols)
KILLEARN / Stirlingshire / Black Bull Hotel, G63 9NG, Tel. Killearn 50215	1 H4	4	3	5	15.68 / 19.53	25.30 / 31.35	- / -	- / -	2	9	1	5	3	1700 / 2030	60	1-12	(symbols)
KILLIECRANKIE / Perthshire	4 C12																

Killiecrankie Hotel By Pitlochry, Perthshire.

AA ** RAC, Egon Ronay, Ashley Courtenay, Relais Routiers, Taste of Scotland and Good Hotel guides.

· Fully licensed country Hotel overlooking Pass of Killiecrankie
· Renowned for good food and well balanced wine list
· Bar meals a speciality, with suppers to 10 pm
· Non-residents, children and dogs very welcome
Resident Proprietors:
Duncan and Jennifer Hattersley Smith and Emma.

Name and Address	Map Ref	Bedrooms	Services	Meals	Single room overnight £min/£max	Double/twin room overnight £min/£max	Per person daily £min/£max	Per person weekly £min/£max	Single	Double/twin	Family	Private	Public	Evening meals From/Last order	Parking (no. of cars)	Months open (1-12)	Symbols
Killiecrankie Hotel, PH16 5LG, Tel. Pitlochry 3220		4	3	5	12.00 / 15.00	24.00 / 30.00	19.35 / 24.20	129.00 / 161.00	1	9	2	8	2	2200 / 2200	32	4-10	(symbols)
Garry Guest House, PH16 5LW, Tel. Pitlochry 3219		2	3	2	7.50 / -	13.50 / -	- / -	- / -	1	3	1	-	1	- / -	10	4-10	(symbols)

Name and Address	Map Ref	Bedrooms	Services	Meals	Single room overnight £min £max	Double/twin room overnight £min £max	Per person daily £min £max	Per person weekly £min £max	Single	Double/twin	Family	Private	Public	Evening meals Last order	Parking (no. of cars)	Months open (1-12)	Symbols
KILLIN Perthshire	1 H2																

BRIDGE OF LOCHAY HOTEL

Half-mile Killin, on banks of River Lochay. Eighteen bedrooms, all with H. & C. some private Bathrooms. Part central heating. Log fires. Two lounges, Bar lounges. Mountaineering. Trout fishing. Golf.

Tel. Office 272; Guests 230
Proprietor: A.G. Symon

Name and Address	Bedrooms	Services	Meals	Single room overnight	Double/twin room overnight	Per person daily	Per person weekly	Single	Double/twin	Family	Private	Public	Evening meals Last order	Parking	Months open	Symbols
Bridge of Lochay Hotel FK21 8TS Tel. Killin 272	3	3	4	11.00 -	22.00 -	18.00 -	- -	4	13	1	7	4	1900 2030	43	4-10	⌖
Craigard Hotel FK21 8UT Tel. Killin 285	3	3	4	8.50 -	15.00 -	- -	- -	1	6	2	-	2	1700 2015	12	1-12	⌖

Dall Lodge Hotel *Killin. Perthshire*

A small family-run licensed hotel on the outskirts of the village of Killin, overlooking the River Lochay.

Emphasis is placed on Scottish dishes, the hotel being a member of the Taste of Scotland scheme. All bedrooms have tea/coffee making facilities and electric blankets. Residents lounge with colour T.V. and log fires. Boats available for trout fishing; salmon fishing by arrangement. Private bathrooms available.

Write or telephone for brochure:
Mr and Mrs W. Bourne, Killin (05672) 217.

Name and Address	Bedrooms	Services	Meals	Single room overnight	Double/twin room overnight	Per person daily	Per person weekly	Single	Double/twin	Family	Private	Public	Evening meals Last order	Parking	Months open	Symbols
Dall Lodge Hotel FK21 8TN Tel. Killin 217	3	3	4	10.60 -	19.20 -	15.85 16.85	95.50 101.50	3	5	2	2	2	1900 2000	10	4-10	⌖
Falls of Dochart Hotel FK21 8UW Tel. Killin 237	3	3	4	8.50 10.50	17.00 21.00	14.00 16.00	93.50 102.00	-	6	2	1	2	1600 2030	25	4-10	⌖

VAT is shown at 15%: changes in this rate may affect prices.

Name and Address	Map Ref	Bedrooms	Services	Meals	Prices: Single room overnight	Double/twin room overnight	Per person daily	Per person weekly	B & B and evening meal: Single	Double/twin	Family	Private	Rooms: Public	No. of bedrooms / Last order	No. of bath/shower rooms	Evening meals / Parking (no. of cars)	Months open (1-12)	Facilities / Symbols
TOWN County / Establishment, Address, Telephone, Telex					£min £max	£min £max	£min £max	£min £max						From Last order				Key on back fold-out
KILLIN continued	1 H2																	

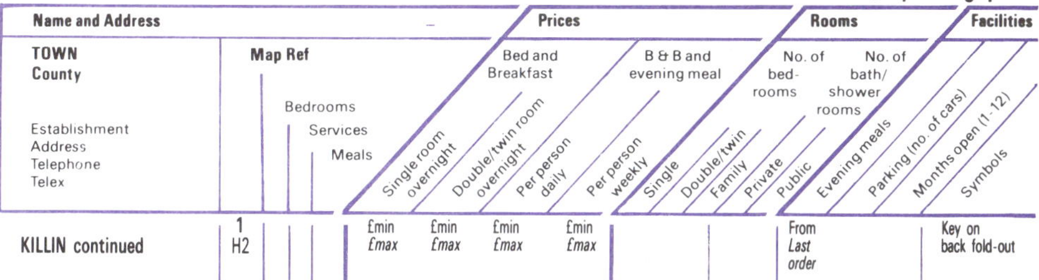

KILLIN HOTEL

Telephone: Killin 296./573.

KILLIN PERTHSIRE **AA   RAC   RSAC

Ideal touring centre situated in beautiful countryside with 8 miles salmon and trout fishing on Loch Tay. Boats and outboards available. Golf course nearby. 30 Bedrooms (all with hot and cold) including 17 private suites. Central heating throughout. Lift. Extensive parking and lock-ups. Fully licensed. Good food and comfort. Open 21/3 to 15/10

Resident Proprietors: **Mr. & Mrs. D. Proctor**

The friendly world of Best Western

Fine independent hotels throughout Britain and the world
CENTRAL RESERVATIONS: 01-940 9766

Name and Address	Bedrooms	Services	Meals	Single room overnight	Double/twin room overnight	Per person daily	Per person weekly	Single	Double/twin	Family	Private	Public	Bedrooms / Last order	Bath/shower	Evening meals / Parking	Months open	Symbols
Killin Hotel, FK21 8TP, Tel. Killin 296	4	4	5	14.75 / 19.25	26.25 / 29.50	22.10 / 26.60	139.00 / 167.00	7	23	-	13	4	1900 / 2015	59	3-10		
Morenish Lodge Hotel, Morenish, FK21 8TX, Tel. Killin 258	3	3	4	13.00 / -	22.00 / -	18.00 / -	105.00 / -	-	12	-	3	3	1900 / 2000	24	3-10		
Queens Court Hotel, FK21 8TN, Tel. Killin 349	3	3	4	10.35 / 10.35	16.10 / 18.40	- / -	- / -	1	3	4	-	3	1830 / 2100	35	1-12		
Craigbuie Guest House, Main Street, FK21 8UH, Tel. Killin 439	3	2	2	- / -	12.00 / -	10.00 / -	65.00 / -	-	5	2	-	2	1830 / 1830	6	4-10		
KILMARNOCK Ayrshire																	
Broomhill Hotel, 57 London Road, Tel. Kilmarnock 23711	2	3	4	9.00 / 10.00	18.00 / 20.00	14.00 / 16.00	- / -	1	4	1	-	2	1800 / 1900	30	1-12		
Burnside Hotel, 18 London Road, Tel. Kilmarnock 22952	1	1	1	7.50 / 8.00	14.00 / 15.00	10.50 / 11.00	70.00 / 77.00	2	9	-	-	2	1730 / 1900	10	1-12		
Howard Park Hotel, 136 Glasgow Road, KA3 1UT, Tel. Kilmarnock 31211, Telex 53168	5	5	5	29.50 / 29.50	39.00 / 39.00	36.65 / 36.65	- / -	-	46	-	46	-	1900 / 2130	300	1-12		
Rowallan Castle, Tel. Kilmaurs 38254	4	4	2	27.50 / -	48.00 / -	48.00 / -	- / -	3	11	-	7	7	2030 / 2300	105	1-12		
KILMARTIN, by Lochgilphead Argyll (Map Ref 1 E4)																	
Kilmartin Hotel, Tel. Kilmartin 244/250	3	3	4	9.90 / 9.90	19.80 / 19.80	14.30 / 18.70	100.10 / 130.90	-	4	1	-	2	1900 / 2030	-	1-12		

(See ad. p. 178)

MORENISH LODGE HOTEL
Loch Tayside, Killin

"The hotel with a view"

Enjoy traditional Highland hospitality in this delightfully situated former shooting lodge with panoramic views over Loch Tay.

The resident proprietors look forward to welcoming you with friendly service amidst attractive and congenial surroundings. All bedrooms (some with private bathrooms), have H. & C., electric fires and blankets and tea-making facilities. Public areas including T.V. lounge, reading room and cocktail bar are centrally heated.

Situated 2¾ miles from Killin in the shadow of Ben Lawers, renowned for its alpine flora. Morenish Lodge is in an ideal position to enjoy a variety of outdoor pursuits including fishing, sailing and hill walking. For touring the Highlands or simply finding total relaxation our location cannot be bettered.

We think we offer the ideal hotel for those who appreciate the countryside and the tranquil pleasures it offers, at very reasonable terms.

REDUCED TERMS FOR STAYS OF 3 DAYS OR MORE.
SPECIAL WEEKLY TARIFF.

Please write or telephone for brochure.
Telephone: 05672 258.
Proprietors: MAUREEN and GRAEME NAYLOR.

Name and Address (Town / County / Establishment)	Map Ref	Bedrooms	Services	Meals	Single room overnight £min/£max	Double/twin room overnight £min/£max	Per person daily £min/£max	Per person weekly £min/£max	Single	Double/twin	Family	Private	Public	Evening meals From / Last order	Parking (no. of cars)	Months open (1-12)	Symbols
KILSYTH Stirlingshire — Coachman Hotel, Parkfoot Street, Tel. Kilsyth 821649	2 A5	5	3	4	17.25 -	27.60 -	- -	- -	-	9	1	10	-	1830 2045	100	1-12	(symbols)
KILTARLITY Inverness-shire — Brockie's Lodge Hotel, Tel. Kiltarlity 257	4 A9	3	4	4	9.00 -	18.00 -	15.50 -	- -	1	7	-	-	2	1830 2200	60	1-12	(symbols)
KILWINNING Ayrshire — Montgreenan Mansion House Hotel, Tel. Kilwinning 57733	1 G6	6	6	6	30.00 40.00	45.00 70.00	45.50 52.00	- 250.00	-	11	-	11	-	1900 2230	85	1-12	(symbols)
KINCLAVEN, by Stanley Perthshire — Ballathie House Hotel, PH1 4QN, Tel. Meikleour 268	2 C2	5	4	5	15.00 27.00	30.00 50.00	- -	- -	13	15	2	30	-	1900 2145	50	1-11	(symbols)
KINCRAIG Inverness-shire — Invereshie House, PH21 1NA, Tel. Kincraig 332	4 B10	4	4	5	14.00 -	28.00 -	24.00 -	150.00 -	1	4	1	1	3	2000 2200	24	1-11	(symbols)
Ossian Hotel, Tel. Kincraig 242		3	4	5	14.00 14.00	27.00 27.00	22.00 26.00	- -	-	5	1	-	3	1930 2200	20	2-12	(symbols)
March House Guest House, Tel. Kincraig 388		3	2	2	6.50 -	13.00 -	10.50 -	70.00 -	-	5	1	-	1	1830 1930	8	1-10	(symbols)

March House
Lagganlia Kincraig Inverness-shire

Relax in the pine-scented air of Glenfeshie set between the Cairngorms and the old forest of Inshriach. March House is purpose built with your comfort in mind. Most rooms have a private shower and there is a log fire in the lounge. Our reputation for good food is growing. We can arrange gliding, skiing, riding, sailing and canoeing holidays tailored to your needs. The terrain is excellent for bird-watching, walking, photography etc.
AA Listed. Brochure Tel. 054 04 388.
Proprietors Mr and Mrs Ron Convery.

Prices shown are for guidance only. Please send SAE with each enquiry.

Name and Address	Map Ref	Bedrooms	Services	Meals	Bed and Breakfast			B & B and evening meal	No. of bedrooms			No. of bath/shower rooms		Evening meals	Parking (no. of cars)	Months open (1-12)	Facilities
Establishment / Address / Telephone / Telex					Single room overnight £min £max	Double/twin room overnight £min £max	Per person daily £min £max	Per person weekly £min £max	Single	Double/twin	Family	Private	Public	From Last order			Symbols (Key on back fold-out)
KINGHORN Fife	2 D4																
Rossland Motel & Leisure Centre, Pettycur Road, Tel. Kinghorn 890577		-	-	-	9.25	18.50	-	-	-	5	-	5	-	-	65	1-12	T ⌂ ♨ ⚑ ▦ ♿ 🖵 ☐ C ♪
KINGSBARNS, by St Andrews Fife	2 E3																
Cambo Arms Hotel, Main Street, KY16 8TA, Tel. Boarhills 226		3	3	2	7.50 7.50	14.00 14.00	- -	- -	1	2	-	1	2	-	36	1-12	♨ 🐕 ⚑ ♿ ⌂ ⚡ ✿ 🏠 V ♘
KINGUSSIE Inverness-shire	4 B11																

Columba House Hotel

Manse Road, Kingussie
(054 02 402)

A small, privately-owned country house hotel with extensive views of surrounding mountains. Recently modernised. The secluded walled garden supplies in season much of the fruit and vegetables for the hotel. Inclusive terms cover full Scottish breakfast and splendid dinner. Carefully selected wines at reasonable prices complete the day's enjoyment. Open all year for walking and climbing, fishing, golf, bird watching, touring, pony trekking and ski-ing, according to season.

Name and Address	Bedrooms	Services	Meals	Single room overnight	Double/twin room overnight	Per person daily	Per person weekly	Single	Double/twin	Family	Private	Public	Evening meals	Parking	Months open	Facilities
Columba House Hotel, Manse Road, PH21 1JF, Tel. Kingussie 402	4	4	4	10.00 12.00	20.00 22.00	20.00 22.00	112.00 116.00	2	4	1	3	1	1900 2000	10	1-12	♨ 🐕 ✂ ⚑ ▦ ♿ 🛏 ⚡ ✿ V ♘ ✦ ⛷ ⚒
The Osprey Hotel, PH21 1EN, Tel. Kingussie 510	3	4	4	9.00 13.00	18.00 26.00	17.00 21.00	105.00 147.00	1	8	1	-	3	1930 -	10	1-10	T ⌂ ♨ 🐕 ✂ ⚑ ▦ ♿ 🛏 ⚡ ⌿ V ♘ ⚒ ❀

Situated in the centre of the village, nearly 1,000 ft. above sea level just off A9 highway.

Comfortable, homely, centrally heated and noted for its excellent food and service. Ground floor bedrooms also rooms with private bath available.

Fully Licensed

Telephone: 05402 236

Brochure on request

Name and Address	Bedrooms	Services	Meals	Single room overnight	Double/twin room overnight	Per person daily	Per person weekly	Single	Double/twin	Family	Private	Public	Evening meals	Parking	Months open	Facilities
Royal Hotel, PH21 1HX, Tel. Kingussie 236	2	3	4	7.50 12.50	15.00 21.00	14.00 19.00	85.00 115 00	7	25	3	4	8	1900 2030	18	1-12	T ⌂ ♨ 🐕 ✂ ⚑ ▦ ♿ ⚡ V ♘ ⛷

VAT is shown at 15%: changes in this rate may affect prices.

Name and Address	Map Ref			Prices				B & B and evening meal					Rooms			Facilities	
TOWN / County / Establishment / Address / Telephone / Telex		Bedrooms / Services / Meals		Single room overnight £min £max	Double/twin room overnight £min £max	Per person daily £min £max	Per person weekly £min £max	Single	Double/twin	Family	Private	Public	No. of bath/shower rooms (Evening meals From Last order)	Evening meals	Parking (no. of cars)	Months open (1-12)	Symbols (Key on back fold-out)
KINGUSSIE continued — 4 B11																	
Scotts Hotel / PH21 HE / Tel. Kingussie 351		4	4	4 — 6.50 / 7.50	13.00 / 15.00	11.50 / 14.00	77.00 / 97.00	-	5	7	12	-	1900 / 2100	28	1-12	(symbols)
Silverfjord Hotel / PH21 1ES / Tel. Kingussie 292		3	4	4 — 10.50 / -	19.00 / -	15.50 / -	- / -	-	6	1	1	3	1900 / 2000	6	1-12	(symbols)
Star Hotel / Tel. Kingussie 431		3	4	4 — 7.00 / 9.00	14.00 / 16.00	12.00 / 14.00	65.00 / 75.00	2	15	6	-	9	1900 / 2200	12	1-12	(symbols)
Sonnhalde Guest House / East Terrace / Tel. Kingussie 266		4	3	2 — 7.00 / 7.50	14.00 / 15.00	11.00 / 11.50	75.00 / 78.00	1	3	2	-	3	1900 / 2000	8	1-11	(symbols)
Tirveyne Guest House / West Terrace / Tel. Kingussie 667		3	1	2 — 6.00 / 7.00	12.00 / 14.00	10.00 / 11.00	70.00 / 77.00	2	3	2	-	1	1800 / 2000	10	1-12	(symbols)
KINLOCH RANNOCH / Perthshire — 2 A1																	
Dunalastair Hotel / PH16 5PW / Tel. Kinloch Rannoch 323		4	5	4 — 10.95 / 13.95	21.90 / 27.90	18.90 / 21.90	124.64 / 143.54	2	18	3	10	10	1930 / 2030	36	1-12	(symbols)
Loch Rannoch Hotel / PH16 5PS / Tel. Kinloch Rannoch 201		5	5	6 — - / 28.00	- / 46.00	- / -	- / -	-	13	-	13	-	1900 / 2045	50	1-12	(symbols)

A small and friendly hotel with leisure and sports facilities on an international scale.

Set in 250 acres of the most spectacular countryside in Scotland, overlooking Loch Rannoch.

For the exclusive use of our guests we offer: an indoor swimming pool: spa bath; sauna; solarium; squash courts; bicycles; trim-trail and tuition on our dry ski slope; sailing; windsurfing; canoeing and hillwalking with resident instructors.

Two restaurants offer either informal grillroom or fine à la carte dining whilst our lounge bar features regular ceilidhs and traditional entertainment.

All hotel bedrooms have private bathrooms, colour T.V. with in-house video, tea/coffee making facilities and baby monitor.

Write or phone for full details of packaged breaks. Open all year.

LOCH RANNOCH HOTEL Kinloch Rannoch,
by Pitlochry, Perthshire. Tel: (08822) 201.

Name and Address / TOWN County / Establishment Address Telephone Telex	Map Ref	Bedrooms	Services	Meals	Bed and Breakfast — Single room overnight £min £max	Double/twin room overnight £min £max	Per person daily £min £max	B & B and evening meal — Per person weekly £min £max	Single	Double/twin	Family	Private	Rooms — No. of bedrooms / Public From Last order	No. of bath/shower rooms	Evening meals	Parking (no. of cars)	Months open (1-12)	Facilities Symbols
KINLOCHARD, by Aberfoyle Perthshire — Altskeith Hotel FK8 3FL Tel. Kinlochard 266	1 H3	3	4	4	9.50 9.50	19.00 19.00	- -	- -	-	6	1	-	1	1800 2100	25	1-12		Key on back fold-out
KINLOCHEIL, Fort William Inverness-shire — Dailanna Guest House PH33 7NP Tel. Kinlocheil 253	3 G12	3	2	2	7.00 8.00	14.00 15.00	11.00 12.00	70.00 77.00	-	1	1	-	1	1900 -	6	4-10		
KINLOCHEWE, by Achnasheen Ross-shire — Kinlochewe Hotel IV22 2PA Tel. Kinlochewe 253	3 G8	3	3	4	16.00 -	26.00 -	21.95 24.95	153.65 174.65	2	8	-	1	3	1900 2000	22	3-11		
KINNEFF Kincardineshire — Corbieknowe Guest House DD10 0TB Tel. Catterline 341	4 G12	3	3	4	8.50 8.50	15.00 15.00	11.00 12.00	75.00 80.00	1	2	3	-	2	1800 1900	9	1-12		
KINNESSWOOD, Kinross Kinross-shire — Lomond Country Inn Main Street KY13 7HN Tel. Scotlandwell 253	2 C3	-	-	-	- -	25.00 -	- -	- -	3	10	-	10	1	1900 2200	43	1-12		
KINROSS — Croftbank Hotel 30 Station Road KY13 7TG Tel. Kinross 63819	2 C3	5	3	5	12.00 18.00	20.00 30.00	18.00 30.00	112.00 205.00	1	2	2	2	1	1930 2130	20	1-12		

VAT is shown at 15%: changes in this rate may affect prices.

Name and Address	Map Ref	Bedrooms	Services	Meals	Bed and Breakfast Single room overnight	Bed and Breakfast Double/twin room overnight	Bed and Breakfast Per person daily	B & B and evening meal Per person weekly	Single	Double/twin	Family	Private	Public	Evening meals	Parking	Months open	Symbols
KINROSS continued	2 C3				£min £max	£min £max	£min £max	£min £max					From Last order			Key on back fold-out

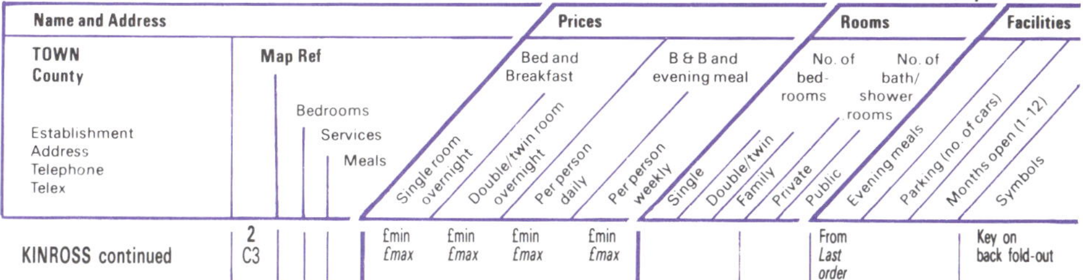

The grass is always greener at the GREEN HOTEL . . .

Hardly surprising, when you consider there's and 18-hole golf course, croquet lawn, putting green, and surrounding gardens all belonging to this first-class hotel.

And if you're keen on the ice there's our 4-sheet CURLING RINK (Season Mid-September to Mid-April), inquire about our specially priced curling holiday breaks.

Why not bring the family? They'll love the indoor pool, games room, saunas, solarium, and squash courts, There's candlelight dinner dances every Friday and Saturday. It's all part of the Green Hotel Service.

Write or phone for a brochure to:
Wolfgang F. J. Geissler, Manager,
or make your booking now.

Name and Address	Map Ref	Bedrooms	Services	Meals	Single room overnight	Double/twin room overnight	Per person daily	Per person weekly	Single	Double/twin	Family	Private	Public	Evening meals	Parking	Months open	Symbols
Green Hotel 2 The Muirs KY13 7AS Tel. Kinross 63467		6	6	6	27.50 30.00	40.00 44.00	23.50 28.00	167.65 182.00	14	24	5	48	-	1900 2230	60	1-12	
KINTORE Aberdeenshire	4 G10																
Crown Hotel Northern Road Tel. Kintore 32204/32358		3	4	4	12.00 16.00	20.00 26.00	- -	- -	1	5	1	-	1	1700 1930	60	1-12	
Torryburn Hotel Tel. Kintore 32269		3	4	4	12.65 15.00	23.00 26.00	18.00 -	95.00 -	2	4	1	-	2	- -	100	1-12	
KIPPEN Stirlingshire	2 A4																
Cross Keys Inn Tel. Kippen 293		1	2	4	12.00 -	17.50 -	- -	- -	-	3	-	-	1	1915 2100	8	5-9	
KIPPFORD Kirkcudbrightshire	2 B10																
Anchor Hotel Tel. Kippford 205		3	3	4	11.00 11.00	22.00 22.00	17.00 19.00	119.00 133.00	5	6	-	-	3	1900 2030	30	4-10	
KIRK YETHOLM Roxburghshire	2 F6																
Border Hotel Tel. Yetholm 237		3	3	4	9.50 -	19.00 -	14.00 -	87.50 -	1	3	-	-	2	1900 2130	8	1-12	
KIRKBEAN, by Dumfries Kirkcudbrightshire	2 B10																
Cavens Guest House Tel. Kirkbean 234		4	3	2	12.00	24.00	20.00	140.00	-	5	1	6	-	1845 -	6	1-12	

Name and Address	Map Ref			Prices					Rooms						Facilities	
TOWN County / Establishment Address Telephone Telex		Bedrooms Services Meals		Bed and Breakfast Single room overnight / Double/twin room overnight / Per person daily			B & B and evening meal Per person weekly		No. of bedrooms Single / Double/twin / Family / Private				No. of bath/shower rooms Public	Evening meals	Parking (no. of cars)	Months open (1-12) Symbols
				£min £max	£min £max	£min £max	£min £max						From Last order			Key on back fold-out

KIRKCALDY Fife — Map Ref 2 D4

Name and Address	Bed	Serv	Meal	Single room	Double/twin	Per person daily	Per person weekly	S	D	F	Priv	Pub	Last order	Eve meals	Parking	Months	Symbols
Dunnikier House Hotel, Dunikier Way, KY1 3LP, Tel. Kirkcaldy 266630/268393	4	5	5	18.00 23.00	33.00 38.00	26.00 -	- -	9	8	-	6	3	1900 2130	150	1-12	
The Forth Motel, Boreland Road, Tel. Kirkcaldy 253324	4	3	5	14.55 16.00	22.14 25.00	20.00 21.00	140.00 -	-	10	1	11	-	1730 2030	40	1-12	
Royal Oak Hotel, Rosslyn Street, KY1 3HT, Tel. Kirkcaldy 52242/52689	3	4	1	8.00 -	16.00 -	- -	- -	4	1	-	-	1	- -	40	1-12	
Station Hotel, 4 Bennochy Road, Tel. Kirkcaldy 262461	3	4	5	16.00 23.00	28.00 36.00	22.00 30.00	140.00 190.00	6	26	3	9	8	1800 2230	25	1-12	
Strathearn Hotel, 2 Wishart Place, Tel. Kirkcaldy 52210	-	-	-	13.00 -	20.00 -	- -	- -	-	5	2	7	-	1700 2100	61	1-12	

KIRKCUDBRIGHT — Map Ref 2 A11

Name and Address	Bed	Serv	Meal	Single room	Double/twin	Per person daily	Per person weekly	S	D	F	Priv	Pub	Last order	Eve meals	Parking	Months	Symbols
Commercial Hotel, Tel. Kirkcudbright 30407	2	2	3	8.50 8.50	19.00 19.00	11.50 11.50	80.00 80.00	3	1	1	-	2	1800 1900	4	1-12	
Gordon House Hotel, 116 High Street, Tel. Kirkcudbright 30670	3	3	4	9.70 9.70	19.40 19.40	14.00 14.00	95.00 95.00	4	8	1	-	3	1900 1930	-	1-12	
Mayfield Hotel, DG6 4ET, Tel. Kirkcudbright 30523	3	4	4	11.00 -	22.00 -	17.00 -	- -	6	13	3	-	6	1845 2000	35	1-12	

Dunnikier House Hotel

Dunnikier Park, Kirkcaldy, Fife KY1 3LP
Telephone: 268393 Residents: 266630
VAT Reg. No. 270 0136 07

Dunnikier House Hotel, originally the ancestral home of the Oswald family, was built over 200 years ago as a wedding present for one of the Oswald sons. Whilst the original characteristics have been retained, our hotel can now offer every modern facility.

Dine in our Oswald room and see why the A.A. granted us the coveted three forks and spoons award. See for yourself our excellent choice of wines and delight in our friendly atmosphere.

Visit our impressive Dysart room with its magnificent oak panelling and its carved oak fireplace, log fire and romantic paintings of old Dysart. Wherever you are in the vicinity, come and visit us. We guarantee you won't be disappointed.

VAT is shown at 15%: changes in this rate may affect prices.

Name and Address	Map Ref	Bedrooms	Services	Meals	Bed and Breakfast — Single room overnight	Bed and Breakfast — Double/twin room overnight	Bed and Breakfast — Per person daily	B & B and evening meal — Per person weekly	Single	Double/twin	Family	Private	Public	Evening meals	Parking (no of cars)	Months open (1-12)	Symbols
					£min / £max	£min / £max	£min / £max	£min / £max					From / Last order				Key on back fold-out
KIRKCUDBRIGHT continued	2 A11																
Royal Hotel Tel. Kirkcudbright 30551		4	3	4	10.00 / 12.50	20.00 / 25.00	- / -	- / -	4	14	2	7	4	1700 / 2100	10	1-12	T ⊞ ⌸ ♈ / 🐕 ♙ ▥ ♿ / ▦ ⬙ ⚡ C / V ♘ /
Selkirk Arms Hotel Old High Street DG6 4JG Tel. Kirkcudbright 30402		3	3	4	12.40 / 13.65	24.80 / 27.30	19.65 / 21.65	118.00 / 130.00	7	15	4	4	7	1845 / 1930	18	1-12	T ⊞ ⌸ ♈ / 🐕 ♙ ♿ ⬙ / ⚡ ✽ ⛺ V / ♘
Anchorlee Guest House 95 St Mary's Street Tel. Kirkcudbright 30793		3	3	2	- / -	13.00 / 16.00	12.50 / 15.00	- / -	-	2	1	-	2	1800 / -	4	1-12	♙ ♿ ✽
Castle Guest House 16 Castle Street Tel. Kirkcudbright 30204		3	3	3	8.00 / -	16.00 / -	12.00 / -	- / -	1	3	1	-	2	1800 / -	-	1-12	⊞ ⌸ 🐕 ♙ / ▥ ♿ ⬙ C / V ♘
Mansfield Guest House St Mary's Street Tel. Kirkcudbright 30657		3	3	2	6.50 / -	13.00 / -	11.00 / -	70.00 / -	2	4	2	-	2	1800 / 1800	6	1-12	🐕 ♙ ▥ ♿ / V
KIRKGUNZEON, by Dumfries Kirkcudbrightshire	2 B10																
Cowans Farm Guest House Tel. Kirkgunzeon 284		3	4	3	- / -	16.00 / -	11.50 / -	80.00 / -	-	6	-	-	2	1800 / -	12	1 12	♈ 🐕 ♙ ▥ ♿ / ✽ /
KIRKMICHAEL Perthshire	2 C1																

The Log Cabin Hotel

Special Ski Package   Special Golf Package
Special Walkers Package

is located in the delightful highlands of Scotland. 900 feet above sea-level amidst the forest pine, breathtaking scenery and wildlife, in the village of Kirkmichael equidistant between Pitlochry and Blairgowrie on the A924. The 13 twin-roomed hotel offers an atmosphere in keeping with its strong Norwegian whole log structure, heartwarming log fires with an unsurpassed view across Strathardle from the Restaurant where the Scottish food is perfectly prepared and pleasantly presented. A Tyrolean bar, ceilidh, folk groups and rousing après-ski evenings. Nearby there is ski-ing at Glenshee, the Festival Theatre at Pitlochry, numerous championship golf courses, pony-trekking, canoeing and climbing, salmon and trout fishing on the River Ardle, together with boats in various trout lochs.

Send for our brochure to: **BRIAN SANDELL**
LOG CABIN HOTEL
Kirkmichael, Perthshire Tel. Strathardle (025 081) 288

Name and Address	Map Ref	Bedrooms	Services	Meals	Single room overnight	Double/twin room overnight	Per person daily	Per person weekly	Single	Double/twin	Family	Private	Public / Last order	Evening meals	Parking	Months open	Symbols
The Log Cabin Hotel Glen Derby, Balnald PH10 7NB Tel. Strathardle 288		4	5	6	- / -	26.00 / 32.00	- / -	- / -	-	9	4	13	-	1930 / 2100	60	1-12	T ⊞ ⌸ ♈ / 🐕 ✕ ♙ ▥ / ♿ ▦ ⬙ ⚡ / C ✽ ⛺ V / ♘ / ▣

Name and Address	Map Ref	Bedrooms	Services	Meals	Bed and Breakfast Single room overnight £min/£max	Double/twin room overnight £min/£max	B & B and evening meal Per person daily £min/£max	Per person weekly £min/£max	Single	Double/twin	Family	Private	Public	Evening meals From/Last order	Parking (no of cars)	Months open (1-12)	Symbols
KIRKMICHAEL continued	2 C1																Key on back fold-out
Strathlene Hotel PH10 7NT Tel. Strathardle 347		3	4	4	10.50 11.50	18.00 20.00	15.50 16.50	93.00 99.00	-	5	2	1	2	1830 2100	3	1-12	
KIRKOSWALD Ayrshire	1 G8																
Kirkton Jean's Hotel KA19 8HY Tel. Kirkoswald 220		4	3	4	16.00 -	28.00 -	19.00 -	117.00 -	-	9	-	9	1	1900 2100	30	1-12	
Shanter Hotel 47 Main Road Tel. Kirkoswald 653		3	3	4	9.50 12.50	17.00 21.00	- -	- -	-	4	-	-	3	1800 2000	-	1-12	
KIRKWALL Orkney	5 B11																
Albert Hotel Tel. Kirkwall 2021		-	-	-	9.20 9.20	18.40 18.40	11.50 11.50	80.50 80.50	2	10	1	1	2	1700 1830	4	1-12	

Name and Address	Bedrooms	Services	Meals	Single room overnight £min/£max	Double/twin room overnight £min/£max	Per person daily £min/£max	Per person weekly £min/£max	Single	Double/twin	Family	Private	Public	Evening meals From/Last order	Parking	Months open	Symbols
Ayre Hotel Ayre Road KW15 1QX Tel. Kirkwall 2197	4	4	5	12.50 17.50	22.00 28.50	- -	- -	11	19	1	4	6	1830 2030	24	1-12	
Foveran Hotel St Ola Tel. Kirkwall 2389	4	4	5	16.00 17.50	25.00 28.50	23.50 25.00	135.50 173.00	3	5	-	3	2	1900 2130	12	1-12	
Kirkwall Hotel Harbour Street KW15 1LF Tel. Kirkwall 2232	4	4	4	14.00 -	28.00 -	- -	- -	15	23	2	12	11	1800 2000	-	1-12	
Royal Hotel Victoria Street Tel. Kirkwall 3477	3	5	4	13.90 -	25.80 -	20.00 -	- -	13	19	1	10	8	1830 2000	-	1-12	

VAT is shown at 15%: changes in this rate may affect prices.

Name and Address	Map Ref	Bedrooms	Services	Meals	Single room overnight	Double/twin room overnight	Per person daily	Per person weekly	Single	Double/twin	Family	Private	Public	Evening meals (From/Last order)	Parking (no. of cars)	Months open	Symbols
					£min £max	£min £max	£min £max	£min £max						From Last order			Key on back fold-out
KIRKWALL continued	5 B11																
St Ola Hotel Harbour Street		-	-	-	9.20 9.20	18.40 18.40	11.50 11.50	80.50 80.50	3	4	-	-	1	1830 2000	-	1-12	
West End Hotel Main Street Tel. Kirkwall 2368		2	3	2	7.50 7.50	13.80 13.80	10.00 10.00	70.00 70.00	2	7	4	-	5	1830 1900	2	1-12	
Bellavista Guest House Carness Road Tel. Kirkwall 2306		3	3	2	8.00 8.00	16.00 16.00	13.00 13.00	91.00 91.00	1	7	-	-	2	1830	8	1-12	
KIRRIEMUIR Angus	2 D1																
Newton Hotel 51 Glamis Road Tel. Kirriemuir 2755		3	2	2	8.50 -	15.00 -	- -	- -	3	3	-	-	2	1830 1930	-	4-10	
Thrums Hotel Tel. Kirriemuir 2758		-	-	-	8.00 9.00	15.00 20.00	10.00 12.00	60.00 70.00	4	8	1	-	3	1800 2100	2	1-12	
Carriden Guest House Shielhill Road DD8 4PN Tel. Kirriemuir 2449/72449		3	2	2	6.50 -	13.00 -	10.50 -	70.00 -	2	4	-	-	1	1800 1930	6	4-10	
KYLE OF LOCHALSH Ross-shire	3 F10																
North West Hotel IV40 8AB Tel. Kyle 4204		3	3	4	10.00 12.00	20.00 25.00	16.00 17.00	100.00 120.00	3	5	1	-	1	1900 2100	40	1-12	
Tingle Creek Hotel Erbusaig Tel. Kyle of Lochalsh 4430		3	5	4	- -	24.15 28.75	10.00 12.00	- -	-	7	3	-	5	1900 1500	40	1-12	
Island View Guest House Badicaul Tel. Kyle 4453		3	3	3	8.00 -	15.00 -	13.00 -	- -	1	5	-	-	1	1900 -	-	3-11	
KYLEAKIN Isle of Skye, Inverness-shire	3 E10																
Dunringell Hotel 1V41 8PR Tel. Kyle 4180		3	4	2	10.25 12.25	20.50 24.50	16.00 18.00	91.00 105.00	3	3	4	1	2	1900 2000	25	3-10	
Marine Hotel Tel. Kyle 4585		3	3	4	11.50 12.50	23.00 25.00	18.00 20.00	111.25 121.25	11	14	-	-	6	1900 1945	10	4-10	
Triton Hotel Tel. Kyle 4585		3	3	4	11.50 12.50	23.00 25.00	18.00 20.00	111.25 121.25	8	21	1	-	8	1900 1945	10	4-10	
White Heather Hotel 1V41 8PL Tel. Kyle 4577		3	4	4	10.95 -	19.50 -	18.00 -	- -	5	16	-	-	4	1900 2000	12	4-10	
KYLESKU Sutherland	3 G4																
Kylesku Hotel IV27 4HW Tel. Kylestrome 231		3	2	4	9.00 10.00	18.00 20.00	15.50 16.00	90.00 92.00	2	5	-	-	1	1900 2000	8	3-10	

Name and Address	Map Ref	Bedrooms	Services	Meals	Bed and Breakfast Single room overnight £min £max	Double/twin room overnight £min £max	Per person daily £min £max	B & B and evening meal Per person weekly £min £max	Single	Double/twin	Family	Private	Public	Evening meals From Last order	Parking (no. of cars)	Months open (1-12)	Symbols Key on back fold-out
LADYBANK Fife	2 D3																
Fernie Castle Hotel Letham Tel. Letham 209		6	4	5	20.00 20.00	34.00 40.00	30.00 35.00	- -	2	7	2	11	-	1930 2045	80	1-12	
LAGGAN BRIDGE, by Newtonmore Inverness-shire	4 B11																

Set in the most beautiful part of **SPEY VALLEY,** the hotel owned and operated by Bill and Rachel Haighton, is an ideal base for walking, fishing, photography or visiting places of interest. Food and comfort are the main considerations of the owners. Licensed bar, central heating. **Midweek Special Packages.**

MONADHLIATH HOTEL
Laggan Bridge, by Newtonmore, Inverness-shire
Telephone: 052 84 273/276

Name and Address	Map Ref	Bedrooms	Services	Meals	Single room overnight £min £max	Double/twin room overnight £min £max	Per person daily £min £max	Per person weekly £min £max	Single	Double/twin	Family	Private	Public	From Last order	Parking	Months open	Symbols
Monadhliath Hotel Tel. Laggan Bridge 276 or 273		3	3	5	10.00 11.00	18.00 19.00	16.00 17.00	105.00 115.00	-	5	3	-	3	1900 2130	40	1-12	
LAIDE Ross-shire	3 F6																
Ocean View Hotel Sand IV22 2ND Tel. Aultbea 385		3	3	4	7.50 9.50	15.00 19.00	13.00 15.00	91.00 105.00	2	5	1	1	2	1900 2100	30	1-12	

A YEAR-LONG FESTIVAL OF SCOTTISH HERITAGE

Tours and Trails, Exhibitions and Displays, Courses and Seminars, Concerts, Folk Concerts, Highland Games, and Sports are only some of the activities taking place throughout Scotland.

Ask your local Tourist Information Centre for details.

Name and Address		Map Ref				Prices							Rooms								Facilities		
TOWN County						Bed and Breakfast				B & B and evening meal			No. of bed-rooms				No. of bath/shower rooms						
Establishment Address Telephone Telex			Bedrooms Services Meals			Single room overnight	Double/twin room overnight	Per person daily	Per person weekly	Single	Double/twin	Family	Private	Public	Evening meals	Parking (no. of cars)	Months open (1-12)	Symbols						
						£min £max	£min £max	£min £max	£min £max						From Last order			Key on back fold-out					
LAIRG Sutherland		4 A6																					

Name and Address	Bedrooms	Services	Meals	Single room overnight	Double/twin room overnight	Per person daily	Per person weekly	Single	Double/twin	Family	Private	Public	From / Last order	Evening meals	Parking	Months open	Symbols
Achany House IV27 4ED Tel. Lairg 2433	4	4	3	13.00 16.00	26.00 33.00	21.50 26.00	135.50 164.00	2	4	-	6	-	1930 2030	10	1-12		
Aultnagar Lodge Hotel IV27 4EX Tel. Invershin 245	4	4	4	9.00 10.00	18.00 24.00	15.75 18.75	101.50 122.50	8	14	3	12	5	1900 2030	55	1-12		

Sutherland Arms Hotel, Lairg, Sutherland. Tel: 0549-2291

An attractive country house hotel of great character overlooking Loch Shin and only half an hour from the seaside and golfing resorts of Golspie and Dornoch. Excellent loch and river fishing. 24 bedrooms most with private bath, and all with tea and coffee making facilities.

Name and Address	Bedrooms	Services	Meals	Single room overnight	Double/twin room overnight	Per person daily	Per person weekly	Single	Double/twin	Family	Private	Public	From / Last order	Evening meals	Parking	Months open	Symbols
Sutherland Arms Hotel IV27 4AT Tel. Lairg 2291 Telex 778215	3	4	4	26.00 26.00	42.00 42.00	29.00 29.00	147.00 147.00	2	22	-	18	-	1930 2030	25	4-10		
LAMLASH Isle of Arran	1 F7																
Bay Hotel Tel. Lamlash 224	3	4	2	8.00 -	15.00 -	12.00 -	84.00 -	6	11	3	-	3	1800 1800	12	5-9		

LAMLASH - LARGOWARD

Name and Address	Map Ref	Bedrooms	Services	Meals	Single room overnight	Double/twin room overnight	Per person daily	Per person weekly	Single	Double/twin	Family	Private	Public	Evening meals	Parking (no. of cars)	Months open (1-12)	Symbols
					£min £max	£min £max	£min £max	£min £max					From Last order				Key on back fold-out
LAMLASH continued	1 F7																
Glenisle Hotel Tel. Lamlash 258		3	4	2	6.95 11.00	13.90 22.00	10.35 14.25	72.45 99.75	2	10	4	3	3	1800 -	18	3-10	
Marine House Hotel Tel. Lamlash 298		3	3	3	8.65 -	17.30 -	11.50 -	80.50 -	1	12	6	6	4	1800 -	16	4-10	
Myrtle Bank Guest House Tel. Lamlash 354		1	3	2	6.50 -	13.00 -	10.00 -	70.00 -	2	2	-	-	1	- -	3	1-12	
Westfield Guest House Tel. Lamlash 428		2	2	2	6.50 8.00	13.00 16.00	10.00 12.00	60.00 70.00	1	3	2	-	2	1800 2000	4	1-12	
HF Holidays Ltd Altachorvie KA27 8LG Tel. Lamlash 286 Telex 922296		2	3	4	7.40 9.90	14.80 19.70	12.40 16.90	70.00 107.00	14	17	3	12	14	1900 1930	40	3-12	
LANARK	2 B6																
Clydesdale Hotel 15 Bloomgate Tel. Lanark 3565		3	3	4	13.80 19.00	22.36 25.30	- -	- -	2	6	2	1	4	1800 2200	6	1-12	
LANGBANK Renfrewshire	1 H5																
Gleddoch House Hotel PA14 6YE Tel. Langbank 711 Telex 779801		6	5	5	44.00 51.00	62.00 75.00	- -	- -	8	10	-	18	1	1930 2130	75	1-12	
LANGHOLM Dumfriesshire	2 D9																
Eskdale Hotel DG13 0JH Tel. Langholm 80357		3	4	5	11.00 12.50	19.50 22.50	14.00 15.50	90.00 98.50	5	7	2	3	3	1900 2200	14	1-12	
Holmwood House Hotel Holmwood Drive Tel. Langholm 80211		3	3	5	11.00 13.00	20.00 24.00	16.00 -	110.00 -	1	5	1	2	1	1830 2130	25	1-12	
Langholm Restaurant & Guest House 81 High Street Tel. Langholm 80378		3	3	3	7.00 -	14.00 -	9.00 -	18.00 -	-	2	2	-	1	1630 1900	-	1-12	
LARBERT Stirlingshire	2 B4																
Red Lion Hotel The Cross Tel. Larbert 562304		-	-	-	18.97	25.00	- -	- -	1	4	-	-	1	1800 2230	17	1-12	
LARGOWARD Fife	2 E3																
Staghead Hotel KY9 1HX Tel. Peat Inn 205		3	3	4	9.00 -	18.00 -	- -	- -	-	3	-	-	1	1900 2100	60	1-12	

VAT is shown at 15%: changes in this rate may affect prices.

Name and Address	Map Ref	Bedrooms	Services	Meals	Single room overnight £min £max	Double/twin room overnight £min £max	Per person daily £min £max	Per person weekly £min £max	Single	Double/twin	Family	Private	Public	From Last order	Evening meals	Parking (no. of cars)	Months open (1-12)	Symbols
LARGS Ayrshire	1 G6																	
Burnlea Hotel Burnlea Road KA30 8BX Tel. Largs 672372/674201		3	3	2	7.50 8.00	15.00 16.00	11.00 12.00	77.00 84.00	2	6	2	1	4	1845		15	4-10	
Charleston Hotel Charles Street KA30 8HL Tel. Largs 672543		3	4	5	12.50 -	21.00 -	- -	- -	1	6	3	2	2	1830 2145		18	1-12	
Corbiere Hotel 110 Irvine Road Tel. Largs 673707		3	4	5	9.00 9.25	18.00 18.50	14.75 15.00	- -	1	7	1	-	3	1800 2130		16	1-12	
Elderslie Hotel John Street Tel. Largs 686460		4	4	4	14.50 16.50	29.00 33.00	21.00 23.00	136.85 149.45	7	16	2	13	4	1900 2030		40	1-12	
Glen-Eldon Hotel 2 Barr Crescent KA30 8PX Tel. Largs 673381		4	4	4	12.00 -	24.00 -	18.50 -	- -	1	6	2	9	-	1830 1945		18	3-1	
Haylie Hotel Irvine Road Tel. Largs 673207		4	4	4	9.50 12.00	19.00 24.00	14.50 19.00	- -	2	7	1	3	2	1800 2000		12	4-10	
Hutton Park Hotel Esplanade KA30 8PD Tel. Largs 673184		2	3	4	7.00 10.00	12.50 17.50	10.00 12.50	- -	2	14	5	-	4	1800 1915		21	1-12	
Mackerston Hotel Mackerston Place KA30 8BY Tel. Largs 673264		-	-	-	10.25 -	18.50 -	13.75 -	96.25 -	20	30	6	3	21	1800 2000		-	4-10	

LARGS

LARGS continued — Map Ref: 1 G6

Prices columns — **Bed and Breakfast:** Single room overnight, Double/twin room overnight, Per person daily (each £min / £max). **B & B and evening meal:** Per person weekly (£min / £max). **Rooms** — No. of bedrooms: Single, Double/twin, Family; No. of bath/shower rooms: Private, Public. **Evening meals:** From / Last order.

Name and Address	Bedrooms	Services	Meals	Single room overnight £min/£max	Double/twin room overnight £min/£max	Per person daily £min/£max	Per person weekly £min/£max	Single	Double/twin	Family	Private	Public	Evening meals (From/Last order)	Parking (no. of cars)	Months open (1-12)	Symbols
Springfield Hotel, North Bay, KA30 8NE, Tel. Largs 673119	4	4	5	14.00 / 16.25	24.00 / 28.50	20.00 / 22.25	120.00 / 133.50	6	30	5	15	9	1630 / 2100	80	1-12	[symbols]
St Helens Hotel, Esplanade, KA30 8NE, Tel. Largs 672328	3	4	4	15.40 / -	29.43 / -	- / -	- / -	4	22	2	4	7	2000 / 2200	36	1-12	[symbols]
Willow Bank Hotel, 96 Greenock Road, KA30 8PG, Tel. Largs 672311	3	4	4	11.50 / 15.00	20.00 / 22.00	13.50 / 17.50	87.50 / 115.50	4	21	3	6	8	1830 / 2030	30	1-12	[symbols]
Aubery Guest House, 22 Aubery Crescent, Tel. Largs 672330	-	-	-	7.00 / -	14.00 / -	8.25 / -	57.75 / -	-	4	2	-	1	1730 / -	6	4-10	[symbols]
Avondale Guest House, 8 Aubery Crescent, KA30 8PR	-	-	-	- / -	13.00 / -	9.50 / -	65.00 / -	-	4	2	-	3	1730 / -	6	5-9	[symbols]
Braemore Guest House, 15 Charles Street, Tel. Largs 673308	3	4	2	7.50 / -	13.00 / -	11.00 / -	70.00 / 77.00	-	5	1	-	2	1800 / 1800	10	1-12	[symbols]
Carlton Guest House, 10 Aubery Crescent, Tel. Largs 672313	-	-	-	6.50 / 6.50	12.00 / 12.00	9.50 / 9.50	66.50 / 66.50	-	4	2	-	1	1800 / -	6	4-10	[symbols]
Crawfordlea Guest House, 12 Charles Street, KA30 8HJ, Tel. Largs 675825	1	2	2	6.50 / 6.50	13.00 / 13.00	10.00 / 10.00	70.00 / 70.00	1	3	-	-	1	1800 / -	-	-	[symbols]
Elmore Guest House, 14 Glenburn Crescent, KA30 8PB, Tel. Largs 672835	1	3	2	7.00 / 7.00	14.00 / 14.00	8.50 / 8.50	59.50 / 59.50	-	3	1	-	1	1730 / -	3	1-12	[symbols]
Holmesdale Guest House, 74 Moorburn Road, KA30 9DE, Tel. Largs 674793	3	3	2	7.00 / -	14.00 / -	10.00 / -	66.50 / -	2	4	2	-	2	1800 / 2100	4	11-9	[symbols]
Lea-Mar Guest House, 20 Douglas Street, KA30 8PS, Tel. Largs 672447	2	2	2	8.00 / -	13.00 / -	11.00 / -	- / -	-	5	1	-	1	1800 / -	5	1-12	[symbols]
Red Gables Guest House, 17 Stanlane Place, Tel. Largs 673250	3	3	2	- / -	12.00 / -	- / -	- / -	-	3	1	-	1	1830 / -	-	1-12	[symbols]
St Annes Guest House, Mackerston Place, Tel. Largs 674026	-	-	-	7.50 / -	15.00 / -	12.50 / -	- / -	1	3	-	-	2	1900 / 2000	-	1-12	[symbols]
Sunbury Guest House, 12 Aubery Crescent, KA30 8PR, Tel. Largs 673086	2	3	2	7.00 / 8.00	14.00 / 14.00	11.00 / 11.00	70.00 / 70.00	-	3	3	-	2	1800 / 1830	8	4-10	[symbols]
Tigh-na-Ligh Guest House, 104 Brisbane Road, KA30 8NN, Tel. Largs 673975	3	3	2	8.00 / 8.50	14.00 / 15.00	11.50 / 12.00	- / -	-	4	2	-	1	1730 / 1900	4	1-12	[symbols]

Key on back fold-out

VAT is shown at 15%: changes in this rate may affect prices.

Name and Address	Map Ref				Prices				Rooms						Facilities		
TOWN County Establishment Address Telephone Telex		Bedrooms / Services / Meals			Bed and Breakfast		Per person daily	B & B and evening meal Per person weekly	Single	Double/twin	Family	Private	No. of bedrooms / Public	No. of bath/shower rooms / Evening meals	Parking (no. of cars)	Months open (1-12)	Symbols	
					Single room overnight	Double/twin room overnight												
LARGS continued	1 G6				£min £max	£min £max	£min £max	£min £max					From Last order	Key on back fold-out				

Whin Park
16 Douglas Street, Largs, Ayrshire KA30 8PS *(STD Code 0475)* : *Largs 673437*

Attractive guest house near sea front where a pleasant walk reveals the scenic beauty of the Firth of Clyde.

A friendly welcome and good food awaits you at "Whin Park" which is personally managed by Mrs Henderson.

Facilities include: 3-course dinner with coffee, H & C, teamakers and heaters in all rooms. Parking. Comfortable Lounge. Phone or write for brochure.

Establishment	Map Ref	Bed	Serv	Meal	Single overnight	Double/twin overnight	Per person daily	B&B+EM weekly	Single	Double/twin	Family	Private	Beds / Public	Bath / EM	Parking	Months	Symbols
Whin-Park Guest House 16 Douglas Street Tel. Largs 673437		3	3	2	7.50 8.00	13.00 14.00	10.50 11.30	68.00 75.00	-	4	1	- 1	1800 -	6	4-10		
LASSWADE Midlothian Melville Castle Hotel Tel. 031 663 6633/4 Telex 727289	2 D5	3	4	5	16.00 18.00	25.00 35.00	25.00 -	112.00 -	2	20	1	4 6	1800 2200	200	1-12		
LATHERON Caithness Forse House Hotel Tel. Latheron 213	4 D4	3	6	5	12.80 -	24.00 -	16.80 -	110.00 -	6	20	3	2 10	1900 2100	20	1-12		
Latheronwheel Hotel Tel. Latheron 209		3	3	4	9.50 10.00	19.00 20.00	12.50 17.00	78.50 100.00	1	1	2	- 1	1700 2100	10	1-12		
LATHONES Fife Lathones Hotel KY9 1JE Tel. Peat Inn 219	2 E3	2	2	2	8.50 8.50	17.00 17.00	13.00 13.00	- -	-	6	-	6 -	1930 2230	40	1-12		
LAUDER Berwickshire Black Bull Hotel Tel. Lauder 208	2 E6	4	4	5	13.80 14.40	27.40 28.75	20.80 23.00	- -	2	9	2	3 2	1930 2130	16	1-12		
Eagle Hotel Tel. Lauder 426		3	3	6	8.00 12.00	16.00 24.00	10.50 14.50	- -	2	2	2	- 1	1800 2200	6	1-12		
Lauderdale Hotel 1 Edinburgh Road TD2 6TW Tel. Lauder 231		-	-	-	10.00 -	20.00 -	- -	- -	1	9	-	9 -	1900 2300	52	1-12		

Prices shown are for guidance only. Please send SAE with each enquiry.

Name and Address	Map Ref	Bedrooms	Services	Meals	Single room overnight £min £max	Double/twin room overnight £min £max	Per person daily £min £max	Per person weekly £min £max	Single	Double/twin	Family	Private	Public	Evening meals (Last order)	Parking	Months open	Symbols
LAURENCEKIRK Kincardineshire Boars Head Hotel High Street Tel. Laurencekirk 346	4 G12	3	3	4	8.50 -	15.00 -	- -	- -	1	6	1	1	1	1900 2100	20	1-12	
LAWERS, by Aberfeldy Perthshire Ben Lawers Hotel PH15 2PA Tel. Killin 436	2 A2	3	3	3	8.50 10.00	17.00 20.00	14.00 15.50	93.00 104.00	2	3	1	-	2	1930 2245	20	1-12	
LEADBURN Midlothian Leadburn Inn Tel. Penicuik 73052	2 C5	-	-	-	8.50 8.50	16.00 16.00	14.50 -	- -	1	2	2	-	1	1830 2100	100	1-12	
LENNOXTOWN Stirlingshire Glazert Bank Hotel Tel. Lennoxtown 310790	2 A5	4	4	5	13.50 -	20.00 -	16.45 20.00	115.15 140.00	-	5	-	5	-	1700 2200	60	1-12	
LERAGS, Oban Argyll	1 E2																

Name and Address	Map Ref	Bedrooms	Services	Meals	Single room overnight £min £max	Double/twin room overnight £min £max	Per person daily £min £max	Per person weekly £min £max	Single	Double/twin	Family	Private	Public	Evening meals (Last order)	Parking	Months open	Symbols
Foxholes Hotel Cologin Tel. Oban 64982		3	3	3	17.00 22.00	20.00 24.00	15.00 19.00	98.00 133.00	-	5	1	1	2	1830 2200	6	1-10	

VAT is shown at 15%: changes in this rate may affect prices.

Name and Address	Map Ref	Bedrooms	Services	Meals	Prices				B & B and evening meal					Rooms			Facilities
TOWN / County / Establishment / Address / Telephone / Telex					Bed and Breakfast				Single	Double/twin	Family	Private	Public	No. of bedrooms (From/Last order)	Evening meals	Parking (no. of cars) / Months open (1-12)	Symbols
					Single room overnight	Double/twin room overnight	Per person daily	Per person weekly									
					£min £max	£min £max	£min £max	£min £max						From Last order			Key on back fold-out
LERWICK Shetland	5 G4																
Craiglea Private Hotel, St Olaf Street, Tel. Lerwick 2826		3	3	2	12.00 -	18.00 22.00	16.00 20.00	115.00 125.00	5	5	1	6	-	1830 1930	-	1-12	
Grand Hotel, Commercial Street, Tel. Lerwick 2018		3	3	4	21.85 -	32.20 -	29.85 -	-	12	8	2	1	4	1830 2115	3	1-12	
Kveldsro Hotel, Tel. Lerwick 2195		4	4	5	24.73 24.73	45.43 45.43	-	-	5	9	-	9	2	1830 2030	24	1-11	
The Lerwick Thistle Hotel, South Road, Tel. Lerwick 2166, Telex 75128		3	5	5	39.50 46.50	44.00 51.00	-	-	12	48	-	60	-	1830 2100	60	1-12	
Queen's Hotel, Commercial Street, Tel. Lerwick 2826		4	4	4	20.00 25.00	25.00 30.00	25.00 30.00	120.00 140.00	14	30	-	22	7	1830 2030	-	1-12	
Shetland Hotel, Tel. Lerwick 5515		6	5	5	43.00 48.00	48.00 52.00	48.00 53.00	336.00 371.00	-	60	4	64	-	1700 2200	100	1-12	
Glen Orchy Guest House, 20 Knab Road, Tel. Lerwick 2031		3	3	1	- -	16.00 20.00	- -	-	-	5	1	-	2	- -	-	1-12	
Solheim Guest House, King Harald Street, ZE1 0EQ, Tel. Lerwick 3613		2	3	1	9.00 10.00	16.00 18.00	-	-	1	2	-	-	1	- -	-	1-12	
LESLIE Fife	2 D3																
Rescobie Hotel, Valley Drive, Tel. Glenrothes 742143		4	4	3	13.75 18.70	27.50 31.90	20.75 25.70	145.25 179.90	2	6	-	3	2	1930 1930	15	1-12	
LESWALT, by Stranraer Wigtownshire	1 F10																
Lochnaw Castle, DG9 0RW, Tel. Leswalt 227		4	4	4	14.00 17.00	28.00 34.00	19.80 22.80	110.00 135.00	2	3	-	3	1	1800 2100	7	1-12	
LEUCHARS Fife	2 D2																
St Michaels Inn, Tel. Leuchars 220		3	3	5	15.00 20.00	20.00 25.00	14.00 16.50	98.00 115.50	-	6	-	-	2	1700 2130	100	1-12	
LEVEN Fife	2 D3																
Hunting Lodge, Durie Street, Tel. Leven 24562		3	3	4	8.00 -	14.00 -	10.00 -	60.00 -	2	3	-	-	1	1800 1900	-	1-12	

Name and Address	Map Ref	Bedrooms	Services	Meals	Single room overnight £min £max	Double/twin room overnight £min £max	Per person daily £min £max	Per person weekly £min £max	Single	Double/twin	Family	Private	Public	From Last order	Evening meals	Parking (no. of cars)	Months open (1-12)	Symbols
LEWISTON, Drumnadrochit **Inverness-shire**	4 A9																	
Lewiston Arms Hotel Tel. Drumnadrochit 225		3	3	4	9.00 10.00	18.00 20.00	14.00 16.00	- -	1	7	-	- 2	1900 2000	20	1-12		
LHANBRYDE, Elgin **Moray**	4 D8																	
St Andrews Hotel Garmouth Road IV30 3PD Tel. Lhanbryde 2698		4	3	4	10.00 -	20.00 -	- -	- -	-	- 5	5	-	1800 2100	20	1-12		
LICKISTO **Harris, Western Isles**	3 B7																	
Two Waters Guest House 4 Lickisto		3	3	3	7.00 7.50	14.00 15.00	11.50 12.50	- -	-	4	- 1	1	1900 -	10	4-10		
LINICLATE **Isle of Benbecula, Western Isles**	3 A9																	
Inchyra Guest House 27 Liniclate PA88 5PY Tel. Benbecula 2176		4	4	4	9.50 -	19.00 -	14.40 -	91.00 -	-	3	- 1	1	1800 1930	6	1-12		
LINLITHGOW **West Lothian**	2 B5																	
St Michael's Hotel High Street Tel. Linlithgow 842217		3	3	4	12.50 15.00	23.00 25.00	- -	- -	2	4	-	- 2	1800 2000	1	1-12		
Star & Garter Hotel High Street Tel. Linlithgow 845485		3	3	4	12.50 -	20.00 -	20.00 -	100.00 -	-	6	-	- 1	1830 2230	12	1-12		
LINWOOD **Renfrewshire**	1 H5																	
Golden Pheasant Hotel 1 Moss Road Tel. Johnstone 21266		5	3	4	- 18.70	- 29.70	- -	- -	3	9	- 12	-	1830 2030	80	1-12		
LISMORE, Isle of **Argyll**	1 E2																	
Isle of Lismore Guest House Tel. Lismore 207		1	3	3	8.50 8.50	17.00 17.00	13.50 13.50	85.00 85.00	1	5	-	- 2	1900 2100	6	1-12		
LOANHEAD **Midlothian**	2 D5																	
Inveravon House Inveravon Road		3	4	3	9.50 9.50	17.00 19.50	12.50 18.00	86.00 125.00	3	4	3	- 2	1745 -	50	1-12		
LOCHAILORT **Inverness-shire**	3 F12																	
Glenshian Lodge Hotel PH38 4LZ Tel. Lochailort 235		2	2	2	9.20 -	18.40 -	16.10 -	80.50 -	2	5	-	- 1	1950 2000	20	4-10		

VAT is shown at 15%: changes in this rate may affect prices.

Name and Address	Map Ref	Bedrooms	Services	Meals	Bed and Breakfast Single room overnight £min £max	Bed and Breakfast Double/twin room overnight £min £max	Bed and Breakfast Per person daily £min £max	B & B and evening meal Per person weekly £min £max	Single	Double/twin	Family	Private	No. of bedrooms Public	No. of bath/shower rooms	Evening meals From Last order	Parking (no. of cars)	Months open (1-12)	Symbols
LOCHAILORT continued	3 F12																Key on back fold-out
Lochailort Inn Road To The Isles PH38 4LZ Tel. Lochailort 208		3	3	5	10.00 12.50	20.00 25.00	14.00 17.00	99.00 119.00	1	6	1	-	3	1700 2130	20	1-12	
LOCHAWE Argyll	1 F2																

Carraig Thura Hotel
Overlooking Kilchurn Castle

There is no finer place for your holiday than this family-run country house, overlooking romantic Kilchurn Castle and beautiful Lochawe. Built in the style of a Scottish baronial castle, with comfort and cuisine fit for a king.

Free fishing for Salmon and Trout.

Full central heating. 16 rooms with bath en suite.

Open—March to December.

Resident Proprietors:
Mr and Mrs R. G. Holbrook.
Telephone: Dalmally (08382) 210.

Name and Address	Bedrooms	Services	Meals	Single room overnight	Double/twin room overnight	Per person daily	Per person weekly	Single	Double/twin	Family	Private	Public	bath/shower rooms	Evening meals	Parking	Months open	Symbols
Carraig Thura Hotel Tel. Dalmally 210	4	3	4	14.00 -	22.00 -	22.00 -	139.00 -	2	15	3	16	3	1900 2030	50	4-11	
HF Holidays Ltd Loch Awe House PA33 1AQ Tel. Dalmally 261 Telex 922296	2	3	4	7.40 9.90	14.80 19.70	12.40 16.90	70.00 120.91	14	38	9	-	9	1900 1930	52	3-10	
LOCHBOISDALE S Uist, Western Isles	3 A10															
Lochboisdale Hotel Tel. Lochboisdale 332	-	-	-	12.00	22.00	15.00	-	6	14	-	8	3	1900 2030	30	1-12	
The Grianaig Guest House Garryhallie Tel. Lochboisdale 406	4	3	2	8.00 -	16.00 -	13.50 -	144.50 -	-	7	-	3	1	- -	7	1-12	
LOCHBROOM, by Garve Ross-shire	3 G7															
Tir Aluinn Hotel Leckmelm IV23 2RJ Tel. Ullapool 2074	3	3	2	12.65 14.00	25.30 28.00	18.40 19.75	128.80 138.25	2	12	-	3	4	1900 2000	20	6-9	

Name and Address	Map Ref	Bedrooms	Services	Meals	Single room overnight £min/£max	Double/twin room overnight £min/£max	Per person daily £min/£max	Per person weekly £min/£max	Single	Double/twin	Family	Private	Public	Evening meals From/Last order	Parking (no. of cars)	Months open (1-12)	Symbols
LOCHCARRON Ross-shire	3 F9																
Lochcarron Hotel, IV54 8YS, Tel. Lochcarron 226		3	3	4	13.00 / 14.00	26.00 / 28.00	20.50 / 22.00	- / -	3	4	-	4	3	1930 / 2030	30	1-12	(symbols)
LOCHEARNHEAD Perthshire	1 H2																
Craigroyston Hotel & Restaurant, FK19 8PU, Tel. Lochearnhead 229		4	4	5	12.00 / 17.00	19.00 / 25.00	16.00 / 22.00	99.00 / 155.00	2	13	-	4	3	- / 2130	22	4-10	(symbols)
Mansewood Country House, FK19 8NS, Tel. Lochearnhead 213		3	3	3	12.00 / 13.50	18.00 / 21.00	14.00 / 15.50	90.00 / 100.00	-	6	-	3	1	1900 / 1930	10	4-10	(symbols)
Tigh-na-Crich Guest House, FK19 8PR, Tel. Lochearnhead 235		3	3	2	- / -	13.00 / 15.00	- / -	- / -	-	4	1	-	1	- / -	6	4-10	(symbols)
LOCHEPORT N Uist, Western Isles	3 B8																
Langass Lodge Hotel, Tel. Locheport 285		3	3	5	12.50 / -	24.00 / -	20.50 / -	130.00 / -	-	4	-	-	2	1900 / 2130	25	1-12	(symbols)
LOCHGILPHEAD Argyll	1 E4																
Argyll Hotel, Tel. Lochgilphead 2221		3	4	4	10.29 / -	17.90 / -	- / -	- / -	5	5	-	1	3	1830 / 2030	16	1-12	(symbols)
Victoria Hotel, Tel. Lochgilphead 2176		3	3	4	10.00 / -	20.00 / -	15.75 / -	- / -	3	6	-	-	2	1730 / -	-	1-12	(symbols)
Kilmory Guest House, Paterson Street, Tel. Lochgilphead 2773		3	3	4	6.95 / -	13.00 / -	10.50 / -	70.00 / -	1	3	3	-	2	1700 / 1900	16	1-12	(symbols)
LOCHGOILHEAD Argyll	1 G4																
Carrick Castle Hotel, Tel. Lochgoilhead 251		6	3	5	15.00 / 19.00	10.00 / 14.00	21.50 / 25.50	106.50 / 120.50	-	21	-	21	-	1700 / 2100	50	1-12	(symbols)
Lochgoilhead Hotel, PA24 8AA, Tel. Lochgoilhead 208		3	3	5	8.00 / -	15.00 / 16.00	- / -	- / -	1	4	-	-	1	1800 / 2200	20	1-12	(symbols)

Scotland's Fishing Heritage

The sea has always played a vital part in the heritage of Scotland, this country with its wandering coastline and hundreds of islands. Today, for holidaymakers it means golden beaches, boat trips and birdwatching; for those who live on the coast it means a hard tradition of gaining a living from the sea.

You can learn about this tradition in the charming fishing villages on the coast, and in the fascinating museums which preserve it.

Write to the Scottish Tourist Board for a FREE pack telling you how to follow **SCOTLAND'S FISHING HERITAGE TRAIL.**

VAT is shown at 15%: changes in this rate may affect prices.

Name and Address	Map Ref	Bedrooms	Services	Meals	Single room overnight £min £max	Double/twin room overnight £min £max	Per person daily £min £max	Per person weekly £min £max	Single	Double/twin	Family	Private	Public	Evening meals From Last order	Parking	Months open	Symbols
LOCHINVER, by Lairg Sutherland	3 G5																

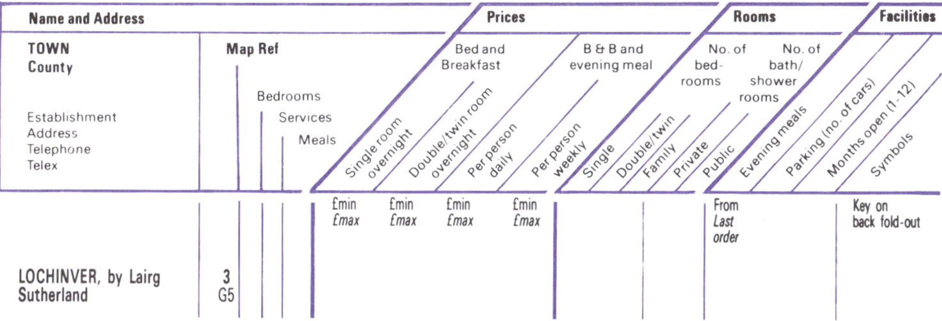

Name and Address	Map Ref	Bedrooms	Services	Meals	Single room overnight	Double/twin room overnight	Per person daily	Per person weekly	Single	Double/twin	Family	Private	Public	Evening meals	Parking	Months open	Symbols
Culag Hotel IV27 4LE Tel. Lochinver 209		4	5	5	- 18.50	- 37.00	- 27.50	154.00 192.50	14	30	1	19	9	1900 2100	50	4-10	
Park House Hotel IV27 4JY Tel. Lochinver 259/320		3	4	5	10.35 -	20.70 -	15.00 -	- -	1	3	-	-	2	1830 2130	15	1-12	
Ceol-na-Mara Guest House Badnaban IV27 4LR Tel. Lochinver 325		3	3	2	8.75 -	- -	14.00 -	- -	-	3	-	-	1	1900 -	4	4-10	
Hillcrest Guest House Tel. Lochinver 391		3	4	2	8.00 -	16.00 -	12.75 -	85.00 -	1	3	-	-	2	1830 1900	4	1-12	
LOCHMABEN Dumfriesshire	2 C9																
Balcastle Hotel Tel. Lochmaben 239		-	-	-	10.35 12.00	18.50 20.00	13.50 15.85	90.00 -	1	3	-	3	-	1900 2200	100	1-12	
Kings Arms Hotel Tel. Lochmaben 238		3	-	-	8.63 -	17.25 -	- -	- -	2	3	1	-	2	-	10	1-12	
Beaufort Guest House Tel. Lochmaben 295		2	3	2	5.50 6.00	10.75 11.75	9.50 9.50	65.50 67.50	1	3	1	-	1	1700 1800	7	2-11	
LOCHMADDY N Uist, Western Isles	3 A8																
Lochmaddy Hotel Tel. Lochmaddy 331		-	-	-	13.50 14.50	26.00 28.00	21.00 22.00	- -	6	9	-	2	4	1930 2100	50	1-12	

Name and Address	Map Ref	Bedrooms	Services	Meals	Single room overnight (£min/£max)	Double/twin room overnight (£min/£max)	Per person daily (£min/£max)	Per person weekly (£min/£max)	Single	Double/twin	Family	Private	Public	Evening meals (From/Last order)	Parking (no. of cars)	Months open (1-12)	Symbols
LOCHRANZA — Isle of Arran	1 E6																
Butt Lodge Hotel, Tel. Lochranza 240		3	3	3	9.00 / -	18.00 / -	12.60 / -	- / -	-	3	3	-	1	1900 / -	10	1-12	
Lochranza Hotel, Tel. Lochranza 223		2	3	3	9.00 / -	18.00 / -	12.50 / -	84.00 / -	1	9	-	-	2	1830 / 2100	12	1-12	
LOCKERBIE — Dumfriesshire	2 C9																
Bluebell Hotel, DG11 2ES, Tel. Lockerbie 2309		3	3	4	9.50 / 16.50	16.50 / 16.50	- / -	- / -	-	6	1	-	2	1700 / 2100	40	1-12	
Dryfesdale Hotel, Tel. Lockerbie 2427		4	4	4	16.00 / 20.00	24.00 / 34.00	- / -	- / -	4	6	2	6	3	1900 / 2030	100	1-12	
Kings Arms Hotel, High Street, Tel. Lockerbie 2410		3	3	4	9.00 / -	16.00 / -	- / -	- / -	5	8	2	-	4	1700 / 2200	8	1-12	
Lockerbie House Hotel, DG11 2RD, Tel. Lockerbie 2610		4	5	5	17.50 / 25.00	30.00 / 40.00	- / -	- / -	8	21	1	16	4	1800 / 2130	150	1-12	
Queens Hotel, Annan Road, Tel. Lockerbie 2415		4	4	5	12.75 / 17.50	25.00 / 30.00	20.50 / 25.50	125.00 / 154.00	4	10	2	6	3	1700 / 2100	126	1-12	
Ravenshill House Hotel, Dumfries Road, Tel. Lockerbie 2882		4	3	5	12.50 / -	20.00 / -	19.50 / 22.00	- / -	1	3	2	4	1	1900 / 2200	40	1-12	
Somerton House Hotel, Carlisle Road, Tel. Lockerbie 2583		4	3	3	13.00 / 15.00	24.00 / 27.00	19.50 / 21.50	- / -	-	5	1	3	2	1900 / 2150	91	1-12	
Rosehill Guest House, Carlisle Road, Tel. Lockerbie 2378		3	2	1	7.00 / 7.00	13.00 / 13.00	- / -	- / -	1	3	2	-	1	- / -	4	1-12	
LONGFORMACUS — Berwickshire	2 F5																
Rathburne Country House Hotel, Tel. Longformacus 232		3	3	6	14.00 / -	18.00 / -	- / -	- / -	3	6	2	3	2	1930 / 2230	41	1-12	
LOSSIEMOUTH — Moray	4 D7																
Huntly House Hotel, Stotfield Road, IV31 6QP, Tel. Lossiemouth 2085		3	4	5	14.30 / 17.60	23.10 / 26.40	- / -	- / -	-	9	3	2	4	1900 / 2145	30	1-12	

VAT is shown at 15%: changes in this rate may affect prices.

Name and Address	Map Ref	Bedrooms	Services	Meals	Bed and Breakfast — Single room overnight (£min/£max)	Double/twin room overnight (£min/£max)	Per person daily (£min/£max)	B & B and evening meal — Per person weekly (£min/£max)	Single	Double/twin	Family	Private	No. of bedrooms (Public)	No. of bath/shower rooms	Evening meals / Last order	Parking (no. of cars)	Months open (1-12)	Symbols
LOSSIEMOUTH continued	4 D7				£min / £max	£min / £max	£min / £max	£min / £max					From Last order			Key on back fold-out
Laverock Bank Hotel, St Gerardines Road, IV31 6RA, Tel. Lossiemouth 2350		3	4	4	9.00 / -	18.00 / -	13.50 / -	- / -	2	7	1	-	4	1800 2130	12	1-12	
Skerrybrae Hotel, Stotfield Road, IV31 6QT, Tel. Lossiemouth 2040		4	4	5	12.00 / 12.00	24.00 / 24.00	18.00 / -	- / -	2	3	2	2	2	1900 2100	24	1-12	
Beachview Guest House, Stotfield Road, IV31 6QS, Tel. Lossiemouth 3053		3	3	2	6.00 / 7.00	12.00 / 14.00	9.50 / 10.50	62.00 / 67.00	2	4	4	-	3	1830	12	4-10	
LUIB, by Crianlarich Perthshire	1 H2																
Suie Lodge Hotel, FK20 8QT, Tel. Killin 417		3	3	4	8.50 / 9.50	17.00 / 17.00	10.50 / 16.00	98.00 / 100.00	2	3	3	-	3	1900 2200	50	1-12	
LUSS, by Alexandria Dunbartonshire	1 G4																

Colquhoun Arms Hotel
LUSS : LOCH LOMOND
Alexandria : Dunbartonshire
Telephone: Luss (043 686) 282
Telex 727289

The COLQUHOUN ARMS HOTEL is on the A82, 25 miles north-west of Glasgow, commanding a view of Luss Village, one of the prettiest villages in Scotland, and Loch Lomond. The hotel is centrally heated, fully licensed and furnished in the Scottish tradition. The dining room has an "Olde Worlde" atmosphere and is complemented by excellent food. There are three well-stocked bars with log fires burning during the winter months. Now well established is Glendarroch Tearoom, named after the famous STV series "Take the High Road". Here, home baking is served all through the summer months.

*AA*** *Les Routiers Establishment*

Name and Address		Bedrooms	Services	Meals	Single room overnight	Double/twin room overnight	Per person daily	Per person weekly	Single	Double/twin	Family	Private	No. of bedrooms	No. of bath/shower rooms	Evening meals / Last order	Parking	Months open	Symbols
Colquhoun Arms Hotel, Tel. Luss 282		3	5	6	12.50 / 15.00	22.50 / 26.00	20.00 / 22.50	125.00 / 150.00	8	18	3	5	6	1800 2230	60	1-12	
LYBSTER Caithness	4 D4																
Bayview Hotel, Tel. Lybster 346		3	3	6	10.50 / -	18.00 / -	19.50 / -	120.00 / -	1	2	-	-	1	1930 2330	25	1-12	

Name and Address	Map Ref			Prices					Rooms								Facilities
TOWN County — Establishment Address Telephone Telex		Bedrooms / Services / Meals		Single room overnight £min £max	Double/twin room overnight £min £max	Per person daily £min £max	Per person weekly £min £max	Single	Double/twin	Family	Private	Public	No. of bedrooms From / Last order	No. of bath/shower rooms	Evening meals	Parking (no. of cars)	Months open (1-12)	Symbols (Key on back fold-out)

MACDUFF — Banffshire — 4 F7

DEVERON HOUSE HOTEL
UNION ROAD, MACDUFF, BANFF
Telephone: 0261 32309

The Hotel has been fully modernised and is centrally heated. We offer our guests a high standard of cuisine and accommodation. All bedrooms are tastefully furnished and decorated, each with comfortable beds, colour television, radio-baby listening service, tea and coffee tray. We have 18 bedrooms; 15 of these are beautifully appointed with private bathrooms, including either bath or shower en suite. Your comfort and service are carefully maintained by our well trained and efficient staff. Their friendly attitude ensures hospitality in the true Scottish tradition.

Establishment	Bedrooms	Services	Meals	Single room o/n	Double/twin o/n	Per person daily	Per person weekly	Single	Double/twin	Family	Private	Public	Bedrooms (last order)	Bath/shower	Evening meals	Parking	Months open
Deveron House Hotel, 25-27 Union Road, Tel. Macduff 32309	4	4	5	19.00 / 22.00	31.00 / 40.00	24.00 / 29.00	137.00 / 170.00	5	8	4	15	2	1700 / 2130	36			1-12

Fife Arms Hotel
Macduff
Telephone: 0261 32408

Overlooking Harbour — comfort, warmth, local atmosphere offered, with good food, local fish a speciality, served 11 a.m.-11 p.m. "Taste of Scotland" fare at weekends. Accommodation includes: Bath/shower, tea/coffee, central heating, radio, intercom, alarm. Hairdressing Salon, Motor Launch, Children's Play Area, Pool Room, Video Films, Dancing. Golf, Tennis, Bowling, Angling, Pony Trekking, Scenic Country/Cliff Walks, Yachting, sandy beaches. Package holidays offered.

Further particulars/enquiries:
Mr and Mrs W. Alcock, Proprietors.

Establishment	Bedrooms	Services	Meals	Single room o/n	Double/twin o/n	Per person daily	Per person weekly	Single	Double/twin	Family	Private	Public	Bedrooms (last order)	Bath/shower	Evening meals	Parking	Months open
Fife Arms Hotel, Shore Street, AB4 1UB, Tel. Macduff 32408	4	4	5	12.50 / -	24.00 / -	- / -	- / -	2	9	2	6	3	1700 / 2230	12			1-12
Shore Hotel, Shore Street, Tel. Macduff 32704	2	3	4	9.00 / -	15.00 / -	- / -	- / -	-	4	1	-	1	1830 / 2130	-			1-12

VAT is shown at 15%: changes in this rate may affect prices.

Name and Address	Map Ref	Bedrooms	Services	Meals	Bed and Breakfast — Single room overnight £min £max	Double/twin room overnight £min £max	Per person daily £min £max	Per person weekly £min £max	B & B and evening meal — Single	Double/twin	Family	Private	No. of bedrooms Public	No. of bath/shower rooms — From Last order	Evening meals	Parking (no. of cars)	Months open (1-12)	Symbols
MACHRIHANISH, by Campbeltown Argyll	1 D7																	
Ardell House		3	3	2	10.00 / 10.00	20.00 / 20.00	15.50 / 16.00	95.00 / 100.00	1	9	-	4	2	1900 / 2000	10	1-12	♀ 🐕 ♨ ▦ ♿ ⚡ C ✿ V ♘
MALLAIG Inverness-shire	3 E11																	

Marine Hotel
Mallaig
0687 2217
AA ** RAC **

Conveniently situated for Railway Station and the Isle of Skye Ferry, in the centre of a quiet idyllic fishing village.
Stay and enjoy fresh fish at its best.
Free hill loch fishing.
Many island boat trips available.
Special weekly (start any day) and weekend rates.
Write to S. Henderson for brochure and tariff.

Name and Address	Bedrooms	Services	Meals	Single room overnight £min £max	Double/twin room overnight £min £max	Per person daily £min £max	Per person weekly £min £max	B & B evening meal Single	Double/twin	Family	Private	Public	From Last order	Evening meals	Parking	Months open	Symbols
Marine Hotel Tel. Mallaig 2217	4	4	4	9.50 / 12.00	19.00 / 23.00	15.50 / 18.00	90.00 / 100.00	3	18	2	6	5	1830 / 2000	5	1-12	T 📺 ♨ ♀ 🐕 🍴 ▦ ▥ ♿ ⚡ C V
West Highland Hotel Tel. Mallaig 2210	4	4	4	14.00 / 18.50	24.00 / 34.00	22.00 / 26.00	138.60 / 163.80	5	16	5	10	6	1845 / 2030	30	4-10	T 📺 ♨ ♀ 🐕 ▦ ▥ ♿ 🪨 ⚡ C ✿ V ♪ ✎ 🎿
Hillside Guest House Tel. Mallaig 2253	2	1	1	6.50 / -	- / -	- / -	- / -	-	5	1	-	1	- / -	6	4-10	▦ ♿
MAUCHLINE Ayrshire 1 H7																
Loudoun Arms Hotel Tel. Mauchline 596	-	-	-	7.50 / 7.50	15.00 / 15.00	- / -	- / -	1	5	1	-	2	1800 / 1900	14	5-9	♀ ▦ ▥ ♿ 🏕 V
MAYBOLE Ayrshire 1 G8																
Cassillis Hotel Cassillis Road Tel. Maybole 82274	-	-	-	8.00 / -	16.00 / -	10.00 / -	- / -	-	3	1	-	1	1700 / 2000	-	1-12	♨ ♀ 🐕 ▦ ▥ ♿ 🪨 ⚡ C
MEIGLE Perthshire 2 C1																
Kings of Kinloch Hotel PH12 8QX Tel. Meigle 273	4	4	5	17.50 / 20.00	30.50 / 32.50	24.50 / 25.50	171.50 / 178.50	3	4	-	1	2	1930 / 2045	40	2-12	T 📺 ♀ 🐕 🍴 ▦ ♿ 🪨 ⚡ C ✿ 🏕 V ♘ ✎ 🎿
Scottish National Camps Association Belmont Outdoor Centre PH12 8TG Tel. Meigle 275	-	-	3	5.70 / 5.70	11.40 / 11.40	6.70 / 8.20	39.35 / 48.65	24	Dormitories for Group Bookings		-	2	1700 / -	50	4-10	T ♨ ▦ ▥ 🪨 ⚡ ✿ V 🔍 ♘

Name and Address	Map Ref	Bedrooms	Services	Meals	Prices Bed and Breakfast Single room overnight £min £max	Double/twin room overnight £min £max	Per person daily £min £max	B & B and evening meal Per person weekly £min £max	Single	Double/twin	Family	Private	Public	Rooms No. of bedrooms From Last order	No. of bath/shower rooms	Evening meals	Parking (no. of cars)	Months open (1-12)	Facilities Symbols
MELROSE Roxburghshire	2 E6																		
Bon Accord Hotel Market Square Tel. Melrose 2645		-	-	-	12.00	24.00	-	-	2	4	3	-	2	1700 2145	-	1-12			

Burt's Hotel, Melrose, Roxburghshire

RAC ** AA ** RSAC
Ashley Courtenay Recommended
Egon Ronay Pub Guide Recommended
Telephone Melrose (089 682) 2285

A delightful hotel, built in 1722 and now listed as a building of architectural interest. Centrally situated in Melrose Market Square, 24 centrally heated bedrooms, 10 with private bathroom, all with radio and room-call, family bedrooms also available. Television Lounge, Residents Lounge, Cocktail Bar with open fires. Dining room overlooking garden and offering both traditional and continental cuisine, with a fine selection of wines. Bar meals are served lunch time and evening. Private Car Park. An ideal centre for touring the beautiful Scottish Border Country.

For brochure write to: Graham and Anne Henderson, Proprietors.

Name and Address	Bedrooms	Services	Meals	Single room overnight £min £max	Double/twin room overnight £min £max	Per person daily £min £max	Per person weekly £min £max	Single	Double/twin	Family	Private	Public	From Last order	No. of bath/shower	Months open	Symbols
Burts Hotel Market Square Tel. Melrose 2285	4	4	5	14.00 16.00	26.00 30.00	21.00 25.00	140.00 160.00	4	17	2	11	5	1900 2130	32	1-12	
George & Abbotsford Hotel High Street Tel. Melrose 2308 Telex 53168	3	3	5	14.00 -	25.00 -	18.00 -	-	13	23	1	17	6	1900 2130	102	1-12	
Kings Arms Hotel High Street Tel. Melrose 2143	3	3	4	11.50 -	23.00 -	17.50 -	122.50 -	2	6	-	2	2	1900 2030	9	1-12	
Waverley Castle Hotel TD6 9AA Tel. Melrose 2244	4	5	4	19.00	35.00	24.00 -	145.00	25	70	5	100	-	1900 2030	200	1-12	
METHLICK Aberdeenshire (4 G9)																
Gight House Hotel Sunnybrae AB4 0BP Tel. Methlick 389	3	3	4	8.00 -	16.00 -	10.50 -	62.00 -	-	4	-	-	1	1700 2100	30	1-12	

Name and Address	Map Ref	Bedrooms	Services	Meals	Single room overnight £min	£max	Double/twin room overnight £min	£max	Per person daily £min	£max	Per person weekly £min	£max	Single	Double/twin	Family	Private	Public	Evening meals From / Last order	Parking (no. of cars)	Months open (1-12)	Symbols
MEY, by Thurso / Caithness	4 / D2																				
Berriedale Arms Hotel / Tel. Barrock 244		-	-	-	8.50	-	15.00	-	10.50	13.00	55.00	80.00	-	1	2	-	2	1900 / 2200	10	1-12	[symbols]
MILLPORT / Isle of Cumbrae, Bute	1 / G6																				
The Angus Hotel / Barend Street / KA28 0BL / Tel. Millport 397		1	3	3	10.00	-	20.00	-	12.00	-	84.00	-	-	3	4	-	1	1800 / 1830	-	1-11	[symbols]
Fairhaven Hotel / Balloch Bay / Tel. Millport 821		-	-	-	8.50	-	17.00	-	14.00	-	-	-	1	4	-	-	1	- / -	-	1-12	[symbols]
Mansewood Hotel / George Street / Tel. Millport 379		3	4	3	-	-	18.00	-	12.00	-	-	-	-	2	3	-	2	1750 / 1850	28	1-12	[symbols]
Millerston Hotel / West Bay Road / Tel. Millport 480		3	3	5	8.00	-	16.00	-	-	-	-	-	1	2	2	-	1	1900 / 2130	12	1-12	[symbols]
Royal George Hotel / Quayhead / Tel. Millport 301		3	3	4	8.00	8.00	15.00	15.00	-	-	-	-	1	4	-	-	1	1700 / 2030	-	1-12	[symbols]
Westbourne Hotel / Westbay Road / Tel. Millport 530423		4	4	4	11.50	11.50	23.00	23.00	-	-	-	-	1	2	2	3	1	1900 / 2200	20	1-12	[symbols]
MILNGAVIE / Dunbartonshire	1 / H5																				
Black Bull Thistle Hotel / Main Street / Tel. 041 956 2291 / Telex 778323		3	5	5	34.50	39.50	41.00	47.00	-	-	-	-	5	22	-	28	-	1830 / 2130	70	1-12	[symbols]
Barloch Guest House / 82 Strathblane Road / G62 8DH / Tel. 041 956 1432		1	1	1	9.00	-	17.00	-	-	-	-	-	-	5	-	-	2	- / -	-	1-12	[symbols]

PAY A VISIT TO ROBERT BURNS' COUNTRY

Travel through some of Scotland's most attractive countryside, in the south west, and follow The Burns Heritage Trail. Easy to get to, it has something to interest everyone.

Send today for your free leaflet with map.

Name and Address			Prices				Rooms							Facilities
TOWN County / Establishment Address Telephone Telex	Map Ref / Bedrooms Services Meals		Bed and Breakfast / Single room overnight / Double/twin room overnight / Per person daily			B & B and evening meal / Per person weekly	No. of bedrooms / Single Double/twin Family			No. of bath/shower rooms / Private Public		Evening meals / From Last order	Parking (no. of cars)	Months open (1-12)	Symbols / Key on back fold-out
			£min £max	£min £max	£min £max	£min £max								
MOCHRUM, by Port William Wigtownshire	1 H11													

GREENMANTLE HOTEL
MOCHRUM, NEWTON STEWART, WIGTOWNSHIRE DG8 9LY.
TEL: 098 87 357.

Set peacefully in one acre, here is the perfect centre for touring this beautiful south-west corner of Scotland. Originally 17th-century country manse, now offering comfortable, centrally heated, en-suite bedrooms, residents lounge, restaurant/dining-room, and lounge-bar.

Open year-round; excellent home cooking; reductions for children; special off-peak week-end breaks. Fishing, Golf, etc. nearby.

Brochure from resident proprietors Alan & Jess Cairns. A.A. and R.A.C. listed.

Establishment	Bedrooms	Services	Meals	Single room overnight	Double/twin room overnight	Per person daily	Per person weekly	Single	Double/twin	Family	Private	Public	Evening meals (last order)	Parking	Months open	Symbols
Greenmantle Hotel DG8 9LY Tel. Port William 357	4	4	5	9.50 13.50	19.00 27.00	16.00 20.00	98.00 119.00	2	3	2	6	1	1930 2100	30	1-12	
MOFFAT **Dumfriesshire**	2 C8															
Annandale Hotel DG10 9HF Tel. Moffat 20013	3	3	4	12.00 13.00	24.00 26.00	17.00 18.00	-	7	19	4	5	6	1800 2030	50	3-12	
Beechwood Country House Hotel DG10 9RS Tel. Moffat 20210	5	4	5	13.00 18.00	26.00 36.00	22.50 27.50	150.00 185.00	2	6	-	6	2	1930 2130	20	2-12	
Bonnington Hotel High Street DG10 9DL Tel. Moffat 20317	3	3	4	10.00 -	19.00 -	15.00 -	-	4	6	1	-	3	1530 1930	-	1-12	
Buccleuch Arms Hotel High Street Tel. Moffat 20003	3	3	4	10.00 10.10	20.00 20.00	15.00 15.00	-	2	11	1	-	3	1900 2100	6	1-12	

Establishment	Bedrooms	Services	Meals	Single room overnight	Double/twin room overnight	Per person daily	Per person weekly	Single	Double/twin	Family	Private	Public	Evening meals (last order)	Parking	Months open	Symbols
Ladbroke Hotel Tel. Moffat 20464	4	3	5	31.50 -	46.00 -	-	-	4	43	4	48	2	1830 2130	70	1-12	

VAT is shown at 15%: changes in this rate may affect prices.

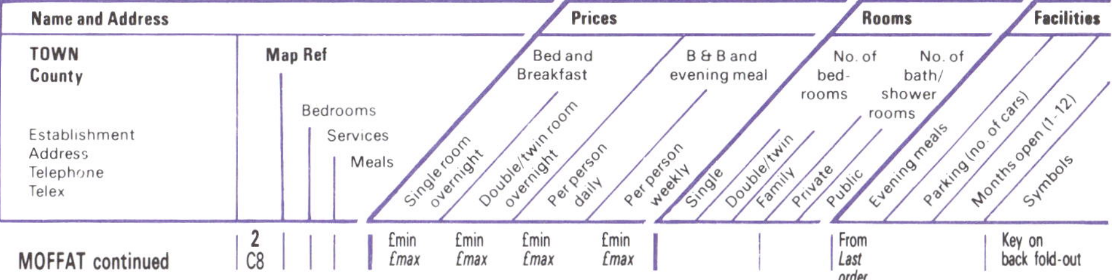

Name and Address	Map Ref	Bedrooms	Services	Meals	Bed and Breakfast: Single room overnight £min £max	Double/twin room overnight £min £max	Per person daily £min £max	Per person weekly £min £max	Single	Double/twin	Family	Private	Public	Evening meals From / Last order	Parking (no. of cars)	Months open (1-12)	Symbols
MOFFAT continued	2 C8															Key on back fold-out

Moffat House Hotel
Moffat, Dumfriesshire DG10 9HL

Moffat House Hotel is a fine example of an 18th Century Adam mansion house. Extensively refurbished, we offer a relaxing, comfortable atmosphere either to break your journey north/south (1 mile off the A74) or to base yourselves for a longer stay in the beautiful Galloway countryside. Most rooms with private bathrooms, all with heating, colour TV lounge, cocktail bar and sun lounge, you can be sure of a warm welcome and good food with the emphasis on fresh, local produce.

Contact the resident proprietors on Moffat 20039 (0683).

Name and Address	Map Ref	Bedrooms	Services	Meals	Single room overnight	Double/twin room overnight	Per person daily	Per person weekly	Single	Double/twin	Family	Private	Public	Evening meals From / Last order	Parking	Months open	Symbols
Moffat House Hotel, Tel. Moffat 20039		4	4	4	16.00 / 18.00	29.00 / 33.00	24.50 / 26.50	145.00 / 155.00	3	9	3	11	1	1900 / 2045	46	1-12	
Red House Hotel, Wamphray, DG10 9NF, Tel. Johnstone Bridge 214		3	3	3	12.45 / -	24.90 / -	18.70 / -	130.50 / -	4	4	-	-	2	1930 / 2030	20	4-10	
Star Hotel, High Street, Tel. Moffat 20156		2	2	4	10.00 / -	18.00 / -	- / -	- / -	-	7	1	-	2	1830 / 2030	-	1-12	
The Arden House Guest House, DG10 9HG, Tel. Moffat 20220		4	3	3	6.50 / 7.00	13.00 / 15.00	10.50 / 12.00	73.50 / 84.00	-	7	2	4	2	- / 1845	9	1-11	

Bridge Guest House

Well Road,
Moffat,
Dumfries-shire.
Tel: (0683) 20383.

A comfortable, family run Guest House set in a quiet residential area, ideal for touring with golf, fishing and riding available locally. All our rooms with H & C, tea-making facilities and electric blankets. TV lounge. Car parking in our own ground. Special rates for children. Pets welcome. AA listed.

Name and Address	Map Ref	Bedrooms	Services	Meals	Single room overnight	Double/twin room overnight	Per person daily	Per person weekly	Single	Double/twin	Family	Private	Public	Evening meals From / Last order	Parking	Months open	Symbols
Bridge Guest House, Well Road, DG10 9JT, Tel. Moffat 20383		2	3	2	8.00 / -	14.00 / -	11.00 / -	70.00 / -	-	3	3	-	2	1800 / -	10	2-11	
Buchan Guest House, Beechgrove, Tel. Moffat 20378		3	3	3	-	12.00 / -	10.00 / -	70.00 / -	1	6	2	-	1	1830 / 1900	6	1-12	
Cabana Guest House, Ballplay Road, DG10 9JX, Tel. Moffat 20400		3	4	2	7.00 / 7.00	12.00 / 12.00	9.50 / 10.00	65.00 / 70.00	2	2	-	-	2	1830 / 1900	5	3-10	

Name and Address	Map Ref	Bed-rooms	Services	Meals	Single room overnight £min £max	Double/twin room overnight £min £max	Per person daily £min £max	Per person weekly £min £max	Single	Double/twin	Family	Private	Public	Evening meals Last order	Parking (no. of cars)	Months open (1-12)	Symbols
MOFFAT continued	2 C8																Key on back fold-out
Greenbank Guest House, Well Road, DG10 9BT, Tel. Moffat 20074		4	3	4	-	15.00	12.50 -	83.50 -	-	3	2	-	2	1830 1900	5	4-10	

Name and Address	Bed-rooms	Services	Meals	Single room overnight £min £max	Double/twin room overnight £min £max	Per person daily £min £max	Per person weekly £min £max	Single	Double/twin	Family	Private	Public	Evening meals Last order	Parking	Months open	Symbols
Hartfell Guest House, Hartfell Crescent, DG10 9AL, Tel. Moffat 20153	3	3	4	8.60 8.60	17.20 17.20	14.60 14.60	95.00 95.00	2	4	3	-	4	1830 1900	10	2-12	
Ivy House Guest House, High Street, Tel. Moffat 20279	3	3	2	- -	13.00 13.00	10.00 10.00	- -	-	3	1	-	1	1800 1800	-	1-12	
Ram Lodge Guest House, High Street	3	3	4	6.50 7.50	13.00 15.00	9.75 10.75	63.00 70.00	1	2	3	-	1	1600 2100	-	1-12	
Rockhill Guest House, 14 Beech Grove, DG10 9RS, Tel. Moffat 20283	3	3	2	7.00 7.50	14.00 15.00	12.00 12.50	79.00 82.50	2	5	3	-	2	1830 1730	-	3-10	
St Olaf Guest House, Eastgate, Dickson Street, DG10 9AE, Tel. Moffat 20001	3	3	2	6.50 6.50	13.00 13.00	10.25 10.25	71.75 71.75	1	3	3	-	1	1845 1800	4	4-10	
Wellview Guest House, Ballplay Road, Tel. Moffat 20184	3	3	4	6.00 8.00	12.00 16.00	10.00 14.00	68.00 98.00	1	4	2	2	3	1800 1900	12	1-12	
MONIAIVE Dumfriesshire (Map Ref 2 A9)																
Craigdarroch Arms Hotel, Tel. Moniaive 205	3	4	5	9.00 10.00	18.00 20.00	14.00 15.00	98.00 105.00	1	7	-	-	2	1700 2100	8	1-12	

SCOTLAND'S COUNTRYSIDE IS UNIQUE!

So: stay on a farm or a croft — that's the best way to get to know the Scottish countryside! To help you find the ideal farmhouse, ask for the free brochure called *Scottish Farmhouse Holidays.* You'll be able to choose from a range of farms of all kinds.

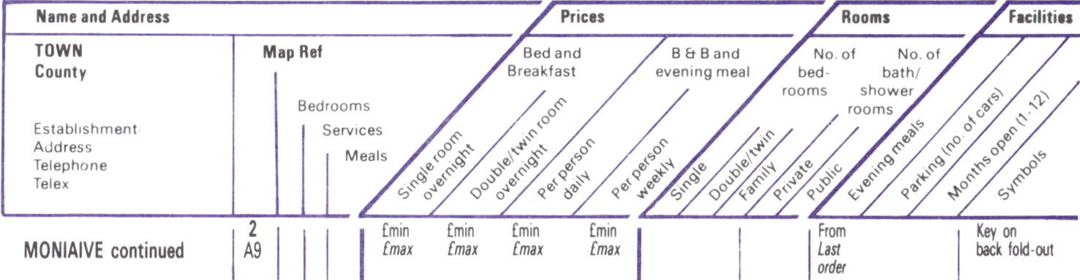

Name and Address	Map Ref				Prices					Rooms						Facilities		
TOWN / County / Establishment / Address / Telephone / Telex		Bedrooms	Services	Meals	Bed and Breakfast				B & B and evening meal	No. of bedrooms				No. of bath/ shower rooms		Facilities		
					Single room overnight	Double/twin room overnight	Per person daily	Per person weekly		Single	Double/twin	Family	Private	Public		Evening meals	Parking (no. of cars)	Months open (1-12)	Symbols
MONIAIVE continued	2 A9				£min £max	£min £max	£min £max	£min £max						From Last order		Key on back fold-out

WOODLEA HOTEL
Moniaive · Dumfriesshire · Scotland
Telephone Moniaive 209 STD 084 82

Robin and Sandi McIver invite you to stay at their friendly country hotel. Good food and wine (Recommended Gourmet Publication) and comfortable rooms. Ideal centre from which to explore unspoilt Galloway. Plenty for the family to do: Swimming, Tennis, Badminton, Kiddies' Play Area, Bike Hire, plus other attractions in our spacious garden. Also Games Room for wet weather and evenings. WARNING: If you want an impersonal, formal, always-talk-in-whispers hotel, then don't come here.

Name and Address	Bd	Sv	Ml	Single overnight	Double overnight	Per person daily	Per person weekly	B&B Single	Double/twin	Family	Private	Public	Last order	Evening meals	Parking	Months open	Symbols
Woodlea Hotel / Tel. Moniaive 209	3	4	5	9.80 / 13.50	23.60 / 25.60	16.00 / 20.00	80.00 / 110.00	3	8	4	3	4	1930 / 2030	40	12-10	
MONKTON, by Prestwick / Ayrshire — Map Ref 1 G7																
Adamton House Hotel / KA9 2SQ / Tel. Prestwick 70678	-	-	-	22.00 / 22.00	38.00 / 38.00	32.50 / 37.50	185.00 / 220.00	7	17	6	30	-	1930 / 2130	1	1-12	
MONTROSE / Angus — Map Ref 2 E1																
Central Hotel / 118 High Street / Tel. Montrose 2152	-	-	-	12.00 / -	24.50 / -	- / -	- / -	4	13	3	1	2	1700 / 2030	-	1-12	
Corner House Hotel / 131-133 High Street / DD10 8QW / Tel. Montrose 3126	3	4	5	16.00 / 25.00	26.00 / 32.00	- / -	- / -	4	8	1	2	3	1800 / 2100	-	1-12	
Links Hotel / Mid Links / Tel. Montrose 2288	-	-	-	23.00 / 25.00	33.00 / 35.00	- / -	- / -	3	16	3	18	2	1830 / 2245	50	1-12	
Park Hotel / John Street / Tel. Montrose 3415 / Telex 76367	5	5	5	20.00 / -	35.00 / -	25.00 / -	180.00 / -	12	43	4	52	2	1830 / 2130	106	1-12	
The Pipers Private Hotel / 11 Union Place / Tel. Montrose 2298	3	3	2	8.00 / -	15.00 / -	11.50 / -	77.50 / -	1	3	2	-	2	1800 / 2000	-	1-12	
The Limes Guest House / 15 King Street / Tel. Montrose 2399	3	4	2	8.00 / -	14.50 / -	11.00 / -	77.00 / -	1	8	2	-	3	1800 / 1900	8	1-12	
Linksgate Guest House / 11 Dorward Road / Tel. Montrose 72273	-	-	•	8.00 / -	16.00 / -	11.50 / -	70.00 / -	-	2	4	-	2	1800 / -	6	1-12	

Prices shown are for guidance only. Please send SAE with each enquiry.

Name and Address TOWN County / Establishment Address Telephone Telex	Map Ref	Bedrooms	Services	Meals	Bed and Breakfast — Single room overnight £min £max	Double/twin room overnight £min £max	Per person daily £min £max	Per person weekly £min £max	B & B and evening meal — Per person weekly	Single	Double/twin	Family	Private	Rooms — No. of bedrooms Public	No. of bath/shower rooms From Last order	Evening meals	Parking (no. of cars)	Months open (1-12)	Facilities — Symbols Key on back fold-out
MORAR, by Mallaig Inverness-shire	3 E11																		
Morar Hotel PH40 4PA Tel. Mallaig 2346		4	4	4	14.00 17.50	24.00 34.00	22.00 25.50	138.60 160.00	6	21	4	12	6	1845 2030	50	4-10		T 🏊 ♟ 🐕 🛏 ▥ 🚿 🍳 🚲 C V ↻ ⚓ ✗ 🅇
Glengorm Guest House PH40 4PA Tel. Mallaig 2165		1	1	2	-	12.00 -	9.50 -	66.50 -	-	2	1	-	1	1800 1800	3	4-9		🐕 🛏 V
MOTHERWELL Lanarkshire	2 A6																		
Garrion Hotel Merry Street Tel. Motherwell 64561		4	5	5	20.00 25.00	29.00 34.00	25.95 30.95	- -	35	17	-	35	6	1830 2130	50	1-12		T ﾃ 🏊 ♟ 🐕 🍳 🍽 ▥ 🚿 ◑ 🛗 📞 🚐 ⬚ 🛎 🚲 C ✳ V ↻
Strathclyde Guest House 90 Hamilton Road Tel. Motherwell 64076/63691		1	4	2	7.50 9.00	14.00 -	11.00 12.00	- -	2	4	2	-	2	1700 1900	14	1-12		🏊 🛏 ▥ V
MOY Inverness-shire	4 B9																		

Dennis and Valerie Simpson welcome you to their charming and comfortable Guest-House set amid pinewoods and moorland just off the A9 10 miles south of Inverness. Ideally situated for touring the Highlands.

· Open all seasons · Residents' licence · Good Home-cooking
· All bedrooms with H & C and tea-making facilities
· One bedroom with private facilities
· C. H. throughout
· Residents' lounge and car park

Name and Address	Map Ref	Bedrooms	Services	Meals	Single room overnight £min £max	Double/twin room overnight £min £max	Per person daily £min £max	Per person weekly £min £max	B & B evening meal weekly	Single	Double/twin	Family	Private	Public	Bath/shower From Last order	Evening meals	Parking	Months open	Symbols
Invermoy House IV13 7YE Tel. Tomatin 271		3	4	2	8.00 8.00	16.00 19.50	12.50 14.25	80.00 92.25	1	6	-	1	2	1930 2000	10	1-12		T ♟ 🐕 🛏 ▥ 🚿 🛎 🚲 C ✳ 📻 V ↻ ⚓
MUASDALE, by Tayinloan Argyll	1 D6																		
Tighnacladich Guest House PA29 6XD Tel. Glenbarr 237		1	2	2	6.00 6.50	12.00 13.00	9.00 9.50	63.00 66.50	-	2	1	-	2	1830 -	5	4-10		🐕 🛏 ✳
MUCK, Isle of Inverness-shire	3 D12																		
Port Mhor House Port Mhor Tel. Mallaig 2365		1	3	3	7.50 7.50	15.00 15.00	12.00 12.00	72.00 72.00	1	5	2	-	3	1930 2100	-	4-10		🏊 ♟ 🐕 🍽 🛏 🚿 ◑ 🛎 🚲 C ✳ V

VAT is shown at 15%: changes in this rate may affect prices.

Name and Address	Map Ref	Bedrooms	Services	Meals	Single room overnight £min £max	Double/twin room overnight £min £max	Per person daily £min £max	Per person weekly £min £max	Single	Double/twin	Family	Private	Public	Evening meals From Last order	Parking (no. of cars)	Months open (1-12)	Symbols Key on back fold-out
MUIR OF ORD Ross-shire	4 A8																
Ord House Hotel IV6 7UH Tel. Muir of Ord 870492		4	4	4	11.75 17.60	23.50 35.20	19.75 25.60	138.25 153.60	2	14	1	8	3	1900 2030	25	4-10	T 🏇 ...
MUSSELBURGH East Lothian	2 D5																
Drummore Motor Inn Hotel North Berwick Road Tel. 031 665 2302		5	5	5	16.50 -	30.00 -	20.50 -	125.00 -	-	-	47	47	-	1800 2130	200	1-12	T ...
Sweethope House Hotel Carberry Road, Inveresk Tel. 031 665 3005		-	-	4	12.50 -	- -	19.50 -	- -	1	2	3	-	1	- .	6	1-12	...
Woodside Hotel 30 Linkfield Road Tel. 031 665 2155		2	3	5	10.50 12.00	18.50 20.00	15.00 21.00	90.00 105.00	-	3	2	-	-	1900 2130	51	1-12	...
Craigesk Guest House 10 Albert Terrace EH21 7LJ Tel. 031 665 3344/3170		3	2	1	6.00 -	12.00 -	- -	- -	1	2	2	-	1	-	6	1-12	...
MUTHILL, by Crieff Perthshire	2 B3																
Drummond Arms Willoughby Street PH5 2AB Tel. Muthill 233		2	2	2	- -	15.00 15.00	20.00 -	- -	-	1	2	-	1	1830 1900	20	1-12	...
NAIRN	4 C8																
Alton Burn Hotel Tel. Nairn 53325		3	4	5	12.00 14.00	24.00 28.00	- -	- -	6	23	4	5	7	1900 2030	40	4-10	T ...
Ardgour Hotel Seafield Street Tel. Nairn 54230		3	3	3	- 7.50	- 15.00	- 11.00	- 74.00	-	8	2	-	2	1815 -	8	3-10	...
Braeval Hotel Crescent Road Tel. Nairn 52341		3	4	2	8.75 9.50	16.00 17.50	13.00 13.50	90.00 95.00	1	6	2	-	3	1830 1930	-	4-10	...
Carnach Country House Hotel Inverness Road IV12 5NT Tel. Nairn 52094		4	5	5	11.00 15.00	20.00 30.00	18.00 22.00	122.50 150.50	1	4	3	5	3	1830 2130	20	1-12	...

Name and Address	Map Ref	Bedrooms	Services	Meals	Bed and Breakfast Single room overnight £min £max	Double/twin room overnight £min £max	Per person daily £min £max	B & B and evening meal Per person weekly £min £max	Single	Double/twin	Family	Private	Public	Evening meals From / Last order	Parking (no. of cars)	Months open (1-12)	Symbols
NAIRN continued	4 C8																Key on back fold-out
The Clifton Hotel Tel. Nairn 53119		4	5	6	22.50 28.00	36.00 50.00	- -	170.00 245.00	3	11	2	9	1	1900 2200	20	3-11	(symbols)
Golf View Hotel Tel. Nairn 52301 Telex 777967		6	6	5	27.00 30.00	42.00 50.00	34.00 37.00	175.00 196.00	5	50	-	55	6	1900 2130	30	1-12	(symbols)
Hebron House Seabank Road Tel. Nairn 52459		3	3	2	7.00 -	14.00 -	13.00 -	82.00 -	2	5	2	-	5	1830 1830	8	-	(symbols)
Lothian House Hotel Crescent Road Tel. Nairn 53555		2	2	2	9.00 -	16.00 -	13.00 -	- -	2	4	2	-	2	1800 1900	10	1-12	(symbols)
Millford Hotel Mill Road Tel. Nairn 53941		3	4	5	11.00 -	20.00 -	15.50 -	90.00 -	1	6	1	-	3	1800 2100	20	1-12	(symbols)

GOLF VIEW HOTEL

Seabank Road, Nairn. Tel: 0667 52301

In Nairn famous for its beaches and Golf Courses, you have the ideal, 4 star Egon Ronay recommended, family hotel, complete with excellent sporting facilities. Free tennis, sauna, heated outdoor swimming pool, games room and the Nairn Championship Golf Course on the doorstep.

All rooms have bath or shower, radio, telephone, colour TV and trouser press.

Midweek and weekend bargain breaks from £21 per day.

Inclusive Golfing Holidays from £24 per day.

Golf Weeks – professional tuition, competitions, etc., March, May, October.

Family suites available with substantial discounts for children.

Write or phone for further details and colour brochures.

VAT is shown at 15%: changes in this rate may affect prices.

Name and Address	Map Ref				Prices				Rooms						Facilities		
TOWN County Establishment Address Telephone Telex		Bedrooms	Services	Meals	Bed and Breakfast			B & B and evening meal	No. of bedrooms			No. of bath/shower rooms					
					Single room overnight	Double/twin room overnight	Per person daily	Per person weekly	Single	Double/twin	Family	Private	Public	Evening meals	Parking (no. of cars)	Months open (1-12)	Symbols
NAIRN continued	4 C8				£min £max	£min £max	£min £max	£min £max						From Last order			Key on back fold-out

NEWTON HOTEL
Nairn. Tel: 0667 53144

Only 14 miles from Inverness, set in 27 acres of secluded grounds, with magnificent views of the Moray Firth this 4 star Egon Ronay recommended hotel provides an unspoiled haven for peace and relaxation. There is a 9 hole putting green and sheltered tennis court a few steps from the main entrance and the Nairn Championship Golf Course and 9 hole Newton Course are only a few hundred yards away.

Sauna, solarium and keep fit equipment are also available. Facilities of our sister hotel, the Golf View, only a short walk away, are available to all guests.

All rooms have bath or shower, radio, telephone, colour TV and trouser press.

Midweek and weekend breaks from £21 per day.

Inclusive Golfing Holidays from £24 per day.

Write or phone for further details and colour brochures.

Name and Address	Bedrooms	Services	Meals	Single room overnight	Double/twin room overnight	Per person daily	Per person weekly	Single	Double/twin	Family	Private	Public	Evening meals	Parking	Months open	Symbols
Newton Hotel Tel. Nairn 53144 Telex 777967	6	6	5	27.00 30.00	44.00 50.00	34.00 37.00	175.00 196.00	12	33	-	45	-	1900 2130	40	4-10	
Ramleh Hotel 2 Academy Street Tel. Nairn 53551	-	-	-	9.00 10.00	17.00 18.00	13.00 14.50	- -	3	6	3	-	2	1800 1730	14	1-12	
Ross House Hotel Seabank Road Tel. Nairn 53731	3	4	4	9.50 11.25	19.90 22.50	14.95 16.95	94.50 108.50	2	10	4	2	4	1900 2030	17	1-12	

QUALITY ASSURED

The Thistle Commendation Scheme gives recognition to Holiday Static Caravan Sites in Scotland which provide first class caravans for hire, combined with very good facilities and an attractive environment. All sites have had a detailed inspection.

Look out for the Thistle Commendation plaques displayed by all the commended sites, or ask for the leaflet.

Name and Address	Map Ref			Prices				Rooms								Facilities
TOWN / County / Establishment / Address / Telephone / Telex		Bedrooms / Services / Meals		Bed and Breakfast			B & B and evening meal	No. of bedrooms			No. of bath/shower rooms		Evening meals	Parking (no. of cars)	Months open (1-12)	Symbols
				Single room overnight	Double/twin room overnight	Per person daily	Per person weekly	Single	Double/twin	Family	Private	Public				
NAIRN continued	4 C8			£min £max	£min £max	£min £max	£min £max						From / Last order			Key on back fold-out

ROYAL MARINE HOTEL
NAIRN SCOTLAND
AA ★★★ RAC ★★★

The Royal Marine Hotel is under the management of the resident proprietors Mr & Mrs Scott & Family.

The hotel is situated on the sea front with its miles of golden sands and has unsurpassed views over the Moray Firth, 43 bedrooms most with private facilities, lift, attractive grounds.

Let Us Arrange Your Complete Holiday.

Golf on 2 Championship courses, Bowling, Squash, Pony Trekking, Hill Walking, Loch & River Fishing, Day-Out Route Maps, Evening Entertainment.

Brochures & Tariffs on request for your golf or touring holiday. **Tel. 0667-53381**

Open All Year.

Establishment	Bed	Serv	Meals	Single room overnight	Double/twin room overnight	Per person daily	Per person weekly	Single	Double/twin	Family	Private	Public	Evening meals	Parking	Months open
Royal Marine Hotel, IV12 4EA, Tel. Nairn 53381	4	4	4	17.50 / 21.00	28.00 / 34.00	22.00 / 29.50	140.00 / 185.00	8	26	9	34	4	1900 / 2100	34	1-12
Washington Hotel, Tel. Nairn 53351	3	3	4	10.00 / 11.50	20.00 / 23.00	15.00 / 16.50	90.00 / 103.00	2	9	8	6	4	1900 / -	21	1-12
Waverley Hotel, High Street, Tel. Nairn 53001	3	3	3	9.50 / 10.00	19.00 / 20.00	13.00 / 16.00	- / -	2	6	2	-	3	1700 / 2100	-	1-12
Windsor Hotel, Albert Street, Tel. Nairn 53108	6	6	6	16.50 / 19.50	30.00 / 35.00	24.95 / 27.50	151.60 / 169.20	30	26	4	41	7	1900 / 2130	50	1-12
Greenlawns Guest House, Seafield Street, Tel. Nairn 52738	2	3	3	- / -	18.00 / 22.00	13.50 / 13.50	85.00 / 144.00	-	6	3	2	2	1800 / -	7	4-10
Orcadia Guest House, 2 Castle Lane, Tel. Nairn 52350	3	3	2	7.25 / -	14.50 / -	10.75 / -	70.00 / -	2	-	4	-	2	1750 / 1750	-	1-12
Sunny Brae Guest House, Marine Road, IV12 4EA, Tel. Nairn 52309	3	3	2	9.50 / 10.50	19.00 / 21.00	15.00 / 16.00	92.00 / 101.00	3	4	2	-	4	1900 / 1700	14	4-10
NESS — Lewis, Western Isles (Map Ref 3 D3)															
Cross Inn, Cross, Tel. Port of Ness 378	1	3	4	9.00 / 10.00	18.00 / 20.00	14.00 / 14.50	90.00 / 95.00	1	1	2	-	1	1830 / 2000	30	1-12

VAT is shown at 15%: changes in this rate may affect prices.

Name and Address	Map Ref	Bedrooms	Services	Meals	Single room overnight £min/£max	Double/twin room overnight £min/£max	Per person daily £min/£max	Per person weekly £min/£max	Single	Double/twin	Family	Private	Public	Last order	Parking (no. of cars)	Months open (1-12)	Symbols
NETHYBRIDGE Inverness-shire	4 C10																
Nethybridge Hotel Tel. Nethybridge 203/267		4	4	4	17.00 19.00	37.00 38.00	24.00 27.00	133.00 165.00	13	48	1	61	5	1900 2100	30	1-12	[symbols]
NEW ABBEY, by Dumfries Kirkcudbrightshire	2 B10																
Criffel Inn 2 The Square Tel. New Abbey 244		4	3	4	10.00 11.00	20.00 22.00	16.00 18.00	98.00 108.00	1	3	-	-	1	1830 -	8	1-12	[symbols]
NEW ABERDOUR Aberdeenshire	4 G7																
The Beach House Hotel AB4 4HR Tel. New Aberdour 277		-	-	-	12.00 -	20.00 -	15.00 -	100.00 -	-	3	2	1	1	1700 2100	30	1-12	[symbols]
Commercial Hotel Tel. New Aberdour 226		3	3	3	6.50 -	13.00 -	9.50 -	57.00 -	-	4	5	-	2	1700 2400	10	1-12	[symbols]
NEW CUMNOCK Ayrshire	2 A8																
Lochside House Hotel KA18 4PN Tel. New Cumnock 629		3	4	5	12.50 18.00	22.00 30.00	15.50 28.00	98.00 150.00	-	7	1	1	2	1700 2200	26	1-12	[symbols]
NEW GALLOWAY Kirkcudbrightshire	2 A9																
Ken Bridge Hotel DG7 3PR Tel. New Galloway 211		3	3	4	9.00 10.00	- -	15.00 16.00	85.00 90.00	1	8	3	2	3	1830 2100	30	1-12	[symbols]
Leamington Private Hotel High Street DG7 3RN Tel. New Galloway 327		3	3	4	9.78 9.78	18.40 18.40	15.53 15.53	97.75 97.75	1	7	1	1	2	1900 -	-	3-10	[symbols]
NEWARTHILL Lanarkshire	2 A5																
Silverburn Hotel Loanhead Road Tel. Holytown 732503		-	-	-	17.50 -	29.00 -	- -	- -	9	3	-	5	1	1900 2030	80	1-12	[symbols]
NEWBURGH Aberdeenshire	4 H9																
Udny Arms Hotel Tel. Newburgh 444 Telex 739187		5	4	5	26.00 -	39.50 -	- -	- -	11	15	-	26	-	1830 2200	57	1-12	[symbols]

Name and Address	Map Ref	Bedrooms	Services	Meals	Bed and Breakfast — Single room overnight £min £max	Double/twin room overnight £min £max	Per person daily £min £max	B & B and evening meal — Per person weekly £min £max	Single	Double/twin	Family	Private	Public	Evening meals — Last order	Parking (no. of cars)	Months open (1-12)	Symbols (Key on back fold-out)
NEWCASTLETON Roxburghshire	2 E9																
Grapes Hotel Tel. Liddesdale 245		2	2	3	8.00 9.00	16.00 18.00	13.80 14.80	- -	1	2	1	-	1	1830 -	10	1-12	(symbols)
Liddesdale Hotel Tel. Liddesdale 255		3	3	4	9.50 10.00	19.00 20.00	15.00 18.00	105.00 105.00	1	3	-	-	1	1900 2100	-	1-12	(symbols)
NEWPORT ON TAY Fife	2 D2																

Sandford Hill Hotel *Ltd.*

Near Wormit, Newport-on-Tay, Fife DD6 8RG.
Telephone: Newport-on-Tay 541802 (STD 0382)

Set on a sheltered hill side close to the A914 road which links the Tay and Forth Road bridges this charming country house hotel is well situated for touring or holidays in the area. A few minutes car journey takes the visitor from the quiet of the country to the bustle of Dundee and the major cities of Central Scotland are all within easy reach. Also close by is the picturesque Fife coast or the mountain scenery of Perthshire and Angus. All the major golf courses — St Andrews, Carnoustie, Rosemount and Gleneagles — are ideally grouped around the area. A high standard of accommodation, a superb range of menus and friendly service combined with weekend and midweek breaks throughout the year make a visit well worth while.

Name and Address		Bedrooms	Services	Meals	Single room overnight £min £max	Double/twin room overnight £min £max	Per person daily £min £max	Per person weekly £min £max	Single	Double/twin	Family	Private	Public	Evening meals — Last order	Parking	Months open	Symbols
Sandford Hill Hotel Wormit DD6 8RG Tel. Newport On Tay 541802		5	4	5	21.00 24.70	33.00 39.00	22.50 34.00	150.00 185.00	2	11	2	13	1	1900 2130	50	1-12	(symbols)

VAT is shown at 15%: changes in this rate may affect prices.

Name and Address			Prices						Rooms				Facilities	
TOWN County Establishment Address Telephone Telex	Map Ref Bedrooms Services Meals		Bed and Breakfast Single room overnight / Double/twin room overnight / Per person daily			B & B and evening meal Per person weekly			No. of bedrooms Single / Double/twin / Family / Private		No. of bath/shower rooms Public	Evening meals	Parking (no. of cars)	Months open (1-12)	Symbols
			£min £max	£min £max	£min £max	£min £max				From Last order	Key on back fold-out			
NEWTON STEWART Wigtownshire	1 H10													

BRUCE HOTEL

Newton Stewart, Wigtownshire DG8 6JL, Scotland. (0671 2294)

AA*** RAC***, Egon Ronay, Ashley Courtenay

A small comfortable 3 star Hotel, run by the Wyllie family to give personal and friendly service, is recommended by Egon Ronay and Ashley Courtney.

All bedrooms have en suite bathroom, radio, colour television, G.P.O. telephone and tea making facilities. Many of the bedrooms have beautiful views of the Galloway Hills. We offer free golf on the local course.

Our two tiered Dining Room offers an open and bright breakfast room with panoramic views of the hills, and an intimate candle-lit restaurant for dinner when our chef and his team have the opportunity to create for you, excellent food, with friendly unassuming service.

We will gladly send you our current Brochure and Tariff including details of Bargain Breaks.

Establishment	Bedrooms	Services	Meals	Single room overnight £min £max	Double/twin overnight £min £max	Per person daily £min £max	Per person weekly £min £max	Single	Double/twin	Family	Private	Public	Evening meals (Last order)	Parking	Months open	Symbols
Bruce Hotel Tel. Newton Stewart 2294	6	4	4	15.00 21.00	30.00 36.00	24.00 31.00	161.00 210.00	1	14	2	16	1	1930 2100	20	1-12	
Creebridge House Hotel DG8 6NP Tel. Newton Stewart 2121	4	5	5	14.00 18.50	28.00 37.00	23.00 28.00	147.50 180.00	3	16	1	12	3	1930 2130	40	1-12	
Crown Hotel DG8 6EF Tel. Newton Stewart 2727	3	4	4	11.00 18.00	22.00 30.00	19.00 23.00	128.00 148.00	2	8	1	5	3	1730 2030	16	1-12	
Galloway Arms Hotel Tel. Newton Stewart 2282	4	5	6	16.00 18.00	30.00 35.00	23.00 25.00	161.00 175.00	3	18	2	17	-	1700 2300	22	1-12	
Grapes Hotel Victoria Street Tel. Newton Stewart 2266	3	4	5	10.92	21.84	-	-	1	6	2	-	2	1500 1730	30	-	

Name and Address				Prices					Rooms					Facilities			
TOWN County Establishment Address Telephone Telex	Map Ref Bedrooms | Services | Meals			Bed and Breakfast				B & B and evening meal				No. of bedrooms	No. of bath/shower rooms				Facilities
				Single room overnight	Double/twin room overnight	Per person daily	Per person weekly	Single	Double/twin	Family	Private	Public	Evening meals	Parking (no. of cars)	Months open (1-12)	Symbols	
NEWTON STEWART continued	1 H10			£min £max	£min £max	£min £max	£min £max					From Last order			Key on back fold-out	

Kirroughtree Hotel

Newton Stewart, Galloway, SW Scotland

Tel (0671) 2141   **AA ★ ★ ★ RAC ★ ★ ★**

DO YOU ENJOY REALLY GOOD FOOD?

If so you should definitely come to Kirroughtree Hotel, because our New Chef has received the highest rating of any Chef in Scotland for his cuisine from the various Good Food Guides. Luxurious Country House Hotel, built in 1719, full of traditional character, in 8 acres, with beautiful views.

* All bedrooms are luxuriously furnished and have coloured bathroom suites, colour TV/Radio, telephone etc, incl 7 groundfloor and family rooms, plus 4 honeymoon suites which are an absolute dream.
* Two exquisite dining rooms, one of which for non-smokers and public rooms which are the ultimate in taste and beauty.
* FREE GOLF for residents at 2 to 3 courses, Lawn Tennis, Putting & Bowling in hotel grounds.
* One of the mildest climates in Britain because of the Gulf Stream.
* **HIGHLY RECOMMENDED FOR ITS PLEASANT ATMOSPHERE, COMFORT, TASTY FOOD AND WINES. Please send for brochure, you will be delighted with the value for money.**

Establishment	Bedrooms	Services	Meals	Single room o/n	Double/twin o/n	Per person daily	Per person weekly	Single	Double/twin	Family	Private	Public	Last order	Evening meals	Parking	Months open
Kirroughtree Hotel Tel. Newton Stewart 2141	6	5	5	21.00 25.00	42.00 50.00	32.00 40.00	196.00 228.00	3	18	3	24	-	1900 2130	60	3-12	
Rowallan House Hotel DG8 6JB Tel. Newton Stewart 2520	5	3	5	15.00 15.00	24.00 24.00	- -	125.00 125.00	-	4	-	4	-	1900 2130	18	1-12	
Corsbie Villa Guest House Corsbie Road Tel. Newton Stewart 2124 or 2041	2	3	3	7.00 8.00	14.00 16.00	11.00 12.00	77.00 84.00	2	7	1	-	3	- 1800	20	1-12	
Duncree Guest House King Street Tel. Newton Stewart 2001	3	4	3	7.50 8.50	14.00 15.00	10.50 11.50	73.50 80.00	1	6	2	-	2	1800 1700	25	1-12	
Flower Bank Guest House Minnigaff Tel. Newton Stewart 2629	3	4	2	7.25 -	15.00 -	11.00 -	72.00 -	-	3	2	-	2	1900 1800	10	1-12	
Glen Cree Guest House 6 Albert Street Tel. Newton Stewart 3317	1	2	3	6.50 -	13.00 -	9.50 -	66.50 -	1	4	1	-	1	1800 1700	-	1-12	
Millburn Guest House King Street Tel. Newton Stewart 2039	2	4	2	7.50 7.50	15.00 15.00	11.00 11.00	77.00 77.00	-	4	3	-	2	1800 1800	7	1-12	
NEWTONMORE Inverness-shire 4 B11																
Ard-Na-Coille Hotel Tel. Newtonmore 214	4	4	4	9.00 13.00	16.00 24.00	16.00 20.00	105.00 130.00	2	6	2	4	2	1930 2015	20	1-10	

VAT is shown at 15%: changes in this rate may affect prices.

Name and Address	Map Ref	Bedrooms	Services	Meals	Single room overnight £min £max	Double/twin room overnight £min £max	Per person daily £min £max	Per person weekly £min £max	Single	Double/twin	Family	Private	Public	Evening meals From Last order	Parking (no. of cars)	Months open (1-12)	Symbols / Facilities
NEWTONMORE continued	4 B11																Key on back fold-out
Badenoch Hotel PH20 1AS Tel. Newtonmore 246		3	3	3	8.46 -	16.92 -	13.14 -	80.14 -	7	6	1	-	3	1900	10	4-10	T 🛏 🐎 ✂ ℞ 🐌 ❄ V ♘ ⚓
Craigerne Hotel Tel. Newtonmore 281		-	-	-	- -	- -	13.75 -	- -	4	9	-	-	5	1900 1935	22	4-10	🛏 🐎 ℞ 🐌 🪨 ⚡ C ❄ V ♘ ✎
Craigower Lodge Outdoor Centre Golf Course Road Tel. Newtonmore 319		3	2	3	6.00 7.00	12.00 14.00	9.35 9.35	56.10 56.10	-	3	7	1	4	1830 1830	14	1-12	T 🛏 🍷 🐎 ℞ ▦ 🐌 ☐ 🪨 ⚡ �̲ C ❄ V ♘ ✎ 🅇 ⚓ ⚓
Glen Hotel PH20 1DD Tel. Newtonmore 203		4	3	4	12.50 14.50	10.50 12.50	17.00 19.00	107.50 119.50	1	5	3	4	2	1900 2030	40	1-12	T £ 🛏 🍷 🐎 ℞ ▦ 🐌 🪨 ⚡ V ♘ ✎ 🅇
Pines Hotel Station Road Tel. Newtonmore 271		3	3	3	8.50 9.50	17.00 19.00	12.50 13.50	84.50 87.50	1	2	3	-	2	1900 2000	8	1-12	🛏 🍷 ✂ ℞ 🐌 ⚡ C ❄ V ♘ ⚓
Alvey House Guest House Tel. Newtonmore 260		3	3	3	9.00 10.00	18.00 20.00	13.00 14.00	84.00 91.00	2	3	2	1	2	1900 1900	12	12-10	T 🍷 ✂ ℞ 🐌 🪨 ⚡ ❄ V ♘ ⚓
Coig Na Shee Guest House Fort William Road PH20 1DG Tel. Newtonmore 216		3	3	2	9.00 10.00	18.00 20.00	14.50 16.50	91.00 108.00	1	4	1	-	2	1900 1830	8	2-11	T 🐎 ✂ ℞ ▦ 🐌 🪨 C ❄ V ♘ ✎ 🅇 ⚓ 🌱
Glen Quoich Guest House Glen Road Tel. Newtonmore 461		3	3	2	8.50 -	17.00 -	14.00 -	90.00 -	2	1	3	-	2	1900 1900	6	1-12	🐎 ℞ 🐌 C V ♘ ✎ ⚓ 🌱

Spey Valley Lodge

Station Road, Newtonmore, Inverness-shire, Scotland. Tel. (05403) 398

Open all year. Situated in its own half acre grounds. Magnificent views. Personally supervised by owners. Specialise in Swiss and home cooking. French, Italian and English spoken. There are six bedrooms, each H&C water, central heating, television and shaving points. Facilities include tea/coffee making. Two shower rooms.

Newtonmore, Spey Valley offer numerous variety of sports including winter skiing. Beautiful sight seeing. Tariff per person per night £8 BB. Double room per person per night £16 BB. Evening meal £4. Per person per week £80 BB. Supplement £3 festive season.

Name and Address	Map Ref	Bedrooms	Services	Meals	Single room overnight	Double/twin room overnight	Per person daily	Per person weekly	Single	Double/twin	Family	Private	Public	Evening meals From Last order	Parking	Months open	Symbols
Spey Valley Lodge Guest House Station Road PH20 1AR Tel. Newtonmore 398		3	4	5	8.00 9.20	16.00 18.40	12.00 13.80	84.00 96.00	2	2	2	-	2	1900 2200	8	1-12	🛏 🐎 ✂ ℞ ▦ 🐌 ☐ ⚡ C ❄ V ♘ ⚓ 🅅
NORTH BERWICK East Lothian	2 E4																
Blenheim House Hotel EH39 4AF Tel. North Berwick 2385		4	3	5	12.50 13.50	25.00 27.00	21.00 23.00	120.00 120.00	2	7	2	6	2	1900 2100	30	1-12	🛏 🍷 ℞ ▦ 🐌 ⚡ ❄ V
Brentwood Private Hotel Clifford Road EH39 4PP Tel. North Berwick 2783		3	3	3	7.00 -	14.00 -	11.00 -	- -	1	6	3	-	3	1800 -	6	1-12	🛏 ℞ ▦ 🐌 V

Name and Address	Map Ref	Bedrooms	Services	Meals	Single room overnight £min/£max	Double/twin room overnight £min/£max	Per person daily £min/£max	Per person weekly £min/£max	Single	Double/twin	Family	Private	Public	Evening meals From/Last order	Parking	Months open	Symbols
NORTH BERWICK continued	2 E4																
Forth Lodge Hotel Marine Parade Tel. North Berwick 2238		3	3	2	- -	22.00 -	17.00 -	- -	-	4	2	-	2	1830 1900	12	1-11	C
Marine Hotel Cromwell Road EH39 4LZ Tel. North Berwick 2406 Telex 727363		6	5	4	33.50 -	52.50 -	- -	- -	6	69	10	85	-	1900 2130	200	1-12	T £ C V
Nether Abbey Hotel Dirleton Avenue Tel. North Berwick 2802		4	4	4	12.65 12.65	25.30 25.30	18.40 19.50	88.00 88.00	2	15	6	7	3	1900 2000	60	3-10	C V

Point Garry Hotel

West Bay Road
North Berwick
A.A. ** R.A.C.

Commanding a superb view over the golf course and Firth of Forth. Opposite the 1st tee. Rooms with private bath/shower. Full central heating. Billiard Room. First-class cuisine. Personal supervision of resident proprietors. Fully Licensed.

Proprietors: Mr and Mrs E. W. Stewart
Telephone: North Berwick 2380

Name and Address	Map Ref	Bedrooms	Services	Meals	Single room overnight £min/£max	Double/twin room overnight £min/£max	Per person daily £min/£max	Per person weekly £min/£max	Single	Double/twin	Family	Private	Public	Evening meals From/Last order	Parking	Months open	Symbols
Point Garry Hotel EH39 4AW Tel. North Berwick 2380		4	3	5	13.75 15.40	25.00 28.00	19.25 20.90	120.00 130.00	2	9	4	8	2	1930 2030	15	4-10	C V
Royal Hotel Station Road EH39 4AT Tel. North Berwick 2401		3	3	5	10.50 12.50	21.00 25.00	17.00 19.00	110.00 124.00	15	29	5	20	9	1900 2130	10	3-10	T £ C V
Bayview Guest House 22 Melbourne Road Tel. North Berwick 2859		3	3	2	- -	14.00 15.00	10.50 11.50	70.00 77.00	-	2	2	-	1	1800 -	-	6-9	C V
Cragside Guest House Marine Parade Tel. North Berwick 2879		3	2	2	7.50 -	15.00 -	11.50 -	75.00 -	1	4	2	-	2	1830 1900	4	4-10	V
Craigview Guest House 5 Beach Road Tel. North Berwick 2257		3	2	2	- -	16.00 -	11.00 -	75.00 -	-	4	1	-	2	1800 1800	5	1-12	C
NORTH CONNEL Argyll	1 E2																
Lochnell Arms Hotel PA37 1RF Tel. Connel 408		4	3	5	10.00 13.00	20.00 26.00	15.00 19.00	105.00 133.00	1	8	2	9	1	1900 2200	100	1-12	T £ V
Ossians Hotel PA37 1RB Tel. Connel 322		3	3	4	13.00 14.00	26.10 28.00	18.00 18.00	126.00 126.00	2	12	-	4	6	1900 2030	50	4-10	C V
NORTHBAY Isle of Barra, Western Isles	3 A11																
Northbay Guest House Tel. Northbay 255		-	-	-	7.00 7.00	14.00 14.00	10.00 10.00	70.00 70.00	1	2	1	1	1	1800 2100	6	1-12	C V

VAT is shown at 15%: changes in this rate may affect prices.

Name and Address	Map Ref	Bedrooms	Services	Meals	Single room overnight £min £max	Double/twin room overnight £min £max	Per person daily £min £max	Per person weekly £min £max	Single	Double/twin	Family	Private	Public	Evening meals From Last order	Parking (no. of cars)	Months open (1-12)	Symbols
OBAN **Argyll**	1 E2																
Ach-Na-Mara Hotel Esplanade Tel. Oban 62683		2	3	2	8.00	14.95	7.47	80.00	2	8	2	-	3	1830	12	3-11	🐕 ♨ ♿

Alexandra Hotel,
Oban, Argyll.
Tel. 0631-62381

This peaceful hotel has an unsurpassed view over Oban's active harbour, and is within easy walking distance of the town's shopping centre with activities for all tastes.

59 bedrooms most with Private Bath and all with Tea and Coffee making facilities.

Great Western Hotel,
Oban, Argyll.
Tel. 0631-63101

Situated in the centre of Oban's seafront and only minutes from the shopping centre, this distinguished hotel commands a superb view across the Firth of Lorn and the departure points of the island ferries and fishing boats. 76 bedrooms most with Private Bath and all with Tea and Coffee making facilities.

Name and Address	Map Ref	Bedrooms	Services	Meals	Single room overnight £min £max	Double/twin room overnight £min £max	Per person daily £min £max	Per person weekly £min £max	Single	Double/twin	Family	Private	Public	Evening meals From Last order	Parking (no. of cars)	Months open (1-12)	Symbols
Alexandra Hotel Corran Esplanade PA34 5AA Tel. Oban 62381 Telex 778215		3	5	4	26.00 26.00	42.00 42.00	29.00 29.00	147.00 147.00	9	46	1	41	13	1830 2030	35	4-10	
Argyll Hotel Esplanade Tel. Oban 62353		4	5	5	8.50 13.00	16.00 28.00	11.00 19.50	77.00 125.00	4	23	3	8	9	1700 2100	40	1-12	
Atholl Hotel George Street PA34 5NT Tel. Oban 62426		2	2	1	7.00 7.00	14.00 14.00	- -	- -	2	9	-	-	1	- -	-	4-10	

Try a Taste of Scotland

Ask the Scottish Tourist Board for the colourful free booklet *A Taste of Scotland*. It lists around 200 places offering fine Scottish cooking, along with notes on regional specialities and recipes which you can try out at home.

While you're on holiday in Scotland, look for the Stockpot sign outside hotels and restaurants. It tells you that the menu offers not only traditional Scottish fare, but also examples of the creative skills of our chefs, using the best Scottish produce.

Name and Address	Map Ref	Bedrooms	Services	Meals	Prices				Rooms								Facilities
TOWN / County / Establishment / Address / Telephone / Telex					Bed and Breakfast: Single room overnight	Double/twin room overnight	Per person daily	B & B and evening meal: Per person weekly	Single	Double/twin	Family	Private	Public	Evening meals (Last order)	Parking (no. of cars)	Months open (1-12)	Symbols (Key on back fold-out)
OBAN continued	1 E2				£min £max	£min £max	£min £max	£min £max						From / Last order			

BALMORAL HOTEL
Craigard Road, Oban, Argyll

This very comfortable, town centre hotel is personally managed by the owners. We offer a relaxed, friendly atmosphere, old-fashioned service, and excellent food (with the accent on steaks and local seafoods).

Restaurant, Lounge and Cocktail Bars. Heating in all bedrooms, some with private shower/W.C.

For brochure and Tariff, contact Mr or Mrs D. Garland (0631) 62731 or 62274.

Name and Address	Bedrooms	Services	Meals	Single room overnight	Double/twin room overnight	Per person daily	Per person weekly	Single	Double/twin	Family	Private	Public	Evening meals	Parking	Months open	Symbols
Balmoral Hotel / Craigard Road / Tel. Oban 62731	3	4	5	9.00 -	18.00 -	14.00 -	93.00 -	4	10	-	2	3	1830 2145	-	4-10	(symbols)

CALEDONIAN HOTEL
Station Square, Oban, Argyll
Tel. STD 0631 63133

The Caledonian Hotel is one of 4 Milton Hotels located throughout the Highlands. It has 72 rooms with tea and coffee making facilities. Special weekend breaks and 7 nights or more stay rates are available or you can take one of our touring holidays including our hotels in Fort William and Inverness.

Contact hotel direct or **Mhairi Cameron, Milton Hotels, Fort William, Inverness-shire (0397) 3139** for our colour 'Highland Holiday' brochure.

Name and Address	Bedrooms	Services	Meals	Single room overnight	Double/twin room overnight	Per person daily	Per person weekly	Single	Double/twin	Family	Private	Public	Evening meals	Parking	Months open	Symbols
Caledonian Hotel / Station Square / PA34 5RT / Tel. Oban 63133	5	5	4	16.50 -	33.00 -	- -	99.00 -	15	49	8	33	13	1830 2100	4	4-10	(symbols)
Claredon Hotel / Shore Street / Tel. Oban 62522	2	3	2	8.50 -	17.00 -	- -	- -	8	15	1	-	4	1830 2000	-	4-10	(symbols)
Cologin Motel / Cologin, Lerags / Tel. Oban 64501	3	3	4	- -	11.50 16.50	8.25 10.75	56.00 72.00	-	26	-	15	15	1700 2400	50	1-12	(symbols)
Columba Hotel / North Pier / Tel. Oban 62183	3	5	4	12.00 13.50	24.00 27.00	17.00 18.00	- -	11	40	3	14	12	1900 2000	9	4-10	(symbols)

VAT is shown at 15%; changes in this rate may affect prices

Name and Address: TOWN, County, Establishment, Address, Telephone, Telex	Map Ref	Bedrooms	Services	Meals	Single room overnight £min £max	Double/twin room overnight £min £max	Per person daily £min £max	Per person weekly £min £max	Single	Double/twin	Family	Private	No. of bedrooms From Last order	Public	Evening meals	Parking (no. of cars)	Months open (1-12)	Symbols
OBAN continued	1 E2																	Key on back fold-out
Corran House Hotel, Esplanade, Tel. Oban 62343	3	3	2		- / -	16.10 / 17.26	11.50 / 12.65	- / -	-	14	4	4	7	1845 / 1845	-	4-10		🐕 symbols
Corrimar Hotel, Esplanade, PA34 5AQ, Tel. Oban 62476	4	5	2	9.00 / 13.00	18.00 / 26.00	16.00 / 20.00	100.00 / 120.00	4	9	3	8	3	1830 / 1830	10	3-10		symbols
Crathie Hotel, Duncraggan Road, PA34 5DT, Tel. Oban 62619	3	3	2	7.00 / 8.00	13.00 / 16.00	9.50 / 10.50	63.00 / 70.00	2	6	1	-	2	1830 / 1830	12	4-10		symbols
Crown Hotel, Shore Street, Tel. Oban 62468	-	-	-	7.50 / -	15.00 / -	12.50 / -	- / -	4	8	3	-	4	1830 / 2000	20	3-11		symbols
Glenburnie Private Hotel, Esplanade, Tel. Oban 62089	2	3	1	8.22 / 9.00	16.44 / 18.96	- / -	- / -	1	9	3	3	4	- / -	13	5-10		symbols
Glencairn Hotel, Esplanade, Tel. Oban 62187	-	-	-	6.50 / 8.00	13.00 / 16.00	- / -	- / -		6	4	2	2	- / -	10	4-10		symbols
Glenrigh Private Hotel, Esplanade, Tel. Oban 62991	3	3	2	6.90 / -	13.80 / -	11.50 / -	80.00 / -	3	5	3	-	3	1830 / 1900	12	4-10		symbols
Great Western Hotel, Esplanade, PA34 5PP, Tel. Oban 63101, Telex 778215	3	4	4	26.00 / 26.00	42.00 / 42.00	29.00 / 29.00	147.00 / 147.00	12	60	2	66	2	1900 / 2030	30	4-10		symbols

Heatherfield Private Hotel

Albert Road, Oban, Argyll. Tel: 0631 62681.

Situated in a quiet location close to Oban's main shopping centre. Heatherfield is a comfortable well appointed private hotel, enjoying the privacy of its own grounds, car parking. Close proximity to swimming pool, tennis court, steamer and rail terminal etc.

Good food in this family run hotel.

S.A.E. for brochure and tariff.

Prop. Bob and Anne Mossman.

Name and Address	Map Ref	Bedrooms	Services	Meals	Single room overnight £min £max	Double/twin room overnight £min £max	Per person daily £min £max	Per person weekly £min £max	Single	Double/twin	Family	Private	From Last order	Public	Evening meals	Parking	Months open	Symbols
Heatherfield Private Hotel, Albert Road, PA34 5EJ, Tel. Oban 62681	2	3	2	7.00 / 8.00	14.00 / 16.00	11.00 / 13.00	78.00 / 82.00	1	6	3	-	3	1900 / 1930	10	1-12		symbols
Kilchrenan Hotel, Esplanade, Tel. Oban 62663	2	2	1	9.00 / -	- / -	- / -	- / -	-	8	1	-	3	- / -	8	4-10		symbols
Kings Knoll Hotel, Dunollie Road, Tel. Oban 62536	3	4	4	7.50 / 9.50	15.00 / 19.00	12.50 / 14.50	87.50 / 101.50	2	12	4	-	5	/ 1930	9	4-10		symbols

| Name and Address | Map Ref | | | | Prices | | | | Rooms | | | | | | | Facilities |
TOWN County Establishment Address Telephone Telex		Bedrooms	Services	Meals	Bed and Breakfast — Single room overnight	Bed and Breakfast — Double/twin room overnight	Bed and Breakfast — Per person daily	B & B and evening meal — Per person weekly	Single	Double/twin	Family	Private	Public	Evening meals (Last order)	Parking (no. of cars)	Months open (1-12)	Symbols
OBAN continued	1 E2				£min £max	£min £max	£min £max	£min £max					From	Last order			Key on back fold-out

Knipoch hotel

By Oban, Argyll, Scotland.
Telephone 085 26 251.

- Excellent food with both table d'hôte and à la carte menus.
- Beautiful furnishings.
- A magnificent situation six miles south of Oban beside the main A816, on the shores of Loch Feochan.
- Each of the 23 bedrooms has a view of the sun setting over the loch. They are also exquisitely furnished, including private bathroom, radio, TV, telephone and central heating in all of them.
- Full licensed and open to non-residents.

AA*** Egon Ronay Recommended
At your service – The Craig Family, Proprietors.

For The Scottish Western Highlands

Name and Address	Map Ref / Bed / Serv / Meals	Single room overnight	Double/twin room overnight	Per person daily	Per person weekly	Single	Double/twin	Family	Private	Public	Evening meals (Last order)	Parking	Months open	Symbols
Knipoch Hotel Tel. Kilninver 251	5 5 6	25.00 32.50	50.00 65.00	41.50 49.00	290.50 343.00	-	23	-	23	-	1900 2230	30	1-12	T £ …

Name and Address	Map Ref / Bed / Serv / Meals	Single room overnight	Double/twin room overnight	Per person daily	Per person weekly	Single	Double/twin	Family	Private	Public	Evening meals (Last order)	Parking	Months open	Symbols
Lancaster Hotel Esplanade Tel. Oban 62587	3 3 4	12.00 -	24.00 -	17.75 -	-	5	23	-	5	5	1830 2000	20	1-12	
Palace Hotel George Street Tel. Oban 62294	3 3 5	9.50 11.00	18.00 20.00	- -	-	2	7	7	7	3	1730 2130	-	1-12	

Name and Address				Prices				Rooms					Facilities			
TOWN County	Map Ref			Bed and Breakfast			B & B and evening meal	No. of bedrooms			No. of bath/shower rooms					
Establishment Address Telephone Telex	Bedrooms	Services	Meals	Single room overnight	Double/twin room overnight	Per person daily	Per person weekly	Single	Double/twin	Family	Private	Public	Evening meals	Parking (no. of cars)	Months open (1-12)	Symbols
OBAN continued	1 E2			£min £max	£min £max	£min £max	£min £max						From Last order			Key on back fold-out

PARK HOTEL
The Esplanade, Oban. Tel: 0631 63621

Set on the Esplanade overlooking Oban bay and only a few hundred yards from the ferry to the islands of Mull, Iona and Staffa, the Park is an ideal base for a real Highland Holiday. By road you can visit Glencoe, Ben Nevis and Inveraray. Hotel lounges, bars and restaurant all overlook the bay and an excellent variety of meals is offered. Regular entertainment is provided in the Sheraton lounge bar including Ceilidhs, Folk Singing, and Dancing.

All rooms have radio, telephone and free tea making facilities.

Rooms with bath or shower also have colour TV.

Attractive weekend and midweek breaks from £17.00. per day with substantial discounts for children.

Write or phone for further details and colour brochures.

Name and Address	Bedrooms	Services	Meals	Single room overnight	Double/twin room overnight	Per person daily	Per person weekly	Single	Double/twin	Family	Private	Public	Evening meals	Parking	Months open	Symbols
Park Hotel Esplanade Tel. Oban 63621 Telex 777967	3	5	4	17.00 23.00	30.00 36.00	21.50 27.00	120.00 150.00	11	68	2	39	10	1830 2030	16	1-12	
Queens Hotel Esplanade PA34 5AG Tel. Oban 62505	3	3	4	10.00 -	20.00 -	15.00 -	95.00 -	11	31	3	45	-	1830 2000	20	4-10	
Regent Hotel Esplanade Tel. Oban 62341	4	4	4	12.00 -	24.00 -	18.00 -	100.00 -	20	45	11	36	13	1900 2030	11	1-12	
Rowan Tree Hotel George Street Tel. Oban 62954	4	4	4	19.00 -	32.00 -	24.00 -	- -	-	24	-	16	4	1900 2100	18	1-12	

ROYAL HIGHLAND HOTEL Breadalbane Street, Oban Tel: OBAN (0631) 64520

A pleasant friendly hotel situated in a quiet street close to the centre of the town and convenient for Coach, Rail and Sea Terminals and most entertainments.

* T.V.   * Laundry facilities   * H & C all rooms
* Single, Twin, Double & Family rooms   * Ground floor rooms
* Excellent food

Phone or write to the proprietor

G. MacLachlan

Enclosing SAE & Requirements

Name and Address	Bedrooms	Services	Meals	Single room overnight	Double/twin room overnight	Per person daily	Per person weekly	Single	Double/twin	Family	Private	Public	Evening meals	Parking	Months open	Symbols
The Royal Highland Hotel Breadalbane Street Tel. Oban 64520	3	2	2	6.00 13.00	12.00 16.00	8.50 11.50	58.00 80.50	4	17	3	-	7	1815 1815	5	4-11	

Name and Address — TOWN County, Establishment, Address, Telephone, Telex	Map Ref	Bedrooms	Services	Meals	Prices — Bed and Breakfast: Single room overnight £min £max	Double/twin room overnight £min £max	Per person daily £min £max	B & B and evening meal: Per person weekly £min £max	Single	Double/twin	Family	Private	Public	Rooms — No. of bedrooms From Last order	No. of bath/shower rooms	Evening meals	Parking (no. of cars)	Months open (1-12)	Facilities — Symbols Key on back fold-out
OBAN continued	1 E2																		
Royal Hotel, Argyll Square, PA34 4BE, Tel. Oban 63021, Telex 76357		4	4	4	17.50 -	35.00 -	- -	- -	49	68	1	26	20	1830 2000	-	4-10			Key on back fold-out
Soroba House Hotel, Soroba Road, Tel. Oban 62628		5	4	5	12.00 -	24.00 -	- -	- -	4	20	-	24	-	1800 2300	100	1-12			
Sutherland Hotel, Esplanade, Tel. Oban 62539		3	3	2	7.00 8.00	14.00 16.00	11.50 12.00	80.50 80.50	1	8	2	-	3	1830 1900	10	4-10			
Thistle Hotel, Breadalbane Place, Tel. Oban 63132		3	2	5	8.00 -	16.00 -	- -	- -	1	1	4	-	2	1800 2130	-	4-9			

WELLPARK HOTEL Esplanade Oban, Argyll PA34 5AQ

This sea front hotel commands magnificent views of the Bay and Islands of Kerrera, Mull and Lismore. It is quiet at night and has private parking. All bedrooms have H.&C., central heating and electric blankets, and many have private shower rooms. Special family room rates! Special dinner, bed and breakfast inclusive daily rates from £12.65 incl. VAT.
The high standard of food, comfort and service offered is excellent value.

For free colour brochure write to Mr and Mrs R. B. DICKISON.
S.A.E. please.   **Telephone: 0631 62948.**

Name and Address	Map Ref	Bedrooms	Services	Meals	Single room overnight £min £max	Double/twin room overnight £min £max	Per person daily £min £max	Per person weekly £min £max	Single	Double/twin	Family	Private	Public	From Last order	No. of bath/shower rooms	Evening meals	Parking	Months open	Facilities
Wellpark Hotel, Esplanade, Tel. Oban 62948		3	3	2	- -	17.24 18.40	12.65 13.80	- -	-	13	2	3	4	1900 1930	11	4-10			
Woodside Hotel, Tweedale Street, Tel. Oban 62184		-	-	-	7.00 -	14.00 -	- -	- -	-	3	2	-	2	- -	-	1-12			

TOURIST INFORMATION CENTRES

All over Scotland there are Tourist Information Centres where friendly, well-informed staff will be pleased to give you information about:

PLACES TO STAY • PLACES TO VISIT • ROUTES TO TAKE • LOCAL EVENTS

There will be lots of helpful literature, some free and some saleable, and many Centres can help you book accommodation.

Look for the information symbol

VAT is shown at 15%: changes in this rate may affect prices.

Name and Address	Map Ref	Bedrooms	Services	Meals	Bed and Breakfast — Single room overnight (£min/£max)	Double/twin room overnight (£min/£max)	Per person daily (£min/£max)	Per person weekly (£min/£max)	Single	Double/twin	Family	Private	Public	Evening meals (From/Last order)	Parking (no. of cars)	Months open (1-12)	Symbols
OBAN continued	1 E2				£min / £max	£min / £max	£min / £max	£min / £max						From / Last order		Key on back fold-out	
Ardblair Guest House, Dalriach Road, PA34 5JB, Tel. Oban 62668	3	4	2		5.50 / 7.00	11.00 / 14.00	9.50 / 11.00	- / -	3	15	4	-	8	1830 / -	11	5-9	
Arichonan Guest House, Longsdale Road, Tel. Oban 62553	3	-	-		7.50 / -	15.00 / -	- / -	- / -	-	2	2	1	-	- / -	4	-	
Armadale Guest House, Dunollie Road, PA34 5PH, Tel. Oban 62981	3	2	2		6.50 / 7.00	12.00 / 13.00	9.00 / 9.50	60.00 / 65.00	2	3	2	-	1	1830 / 1845	-	4-10	
Braehead Guest House, Albert Road, Tel. Oban 63341	3	3	2		- / -	13.00 / -	10.00 / -	70.00 / -	-	5	1	-	2	1830 / 1830	6	1-12	
Craigvarran Guest House, Ardconnel Road, Tel. Oban 62686	2	2	1		5.00 / 8.00	12.00 / 18.00	- / -	- / -	4	3	1	-	2	- / -	10	1-11	
Elmbank Guest House, Croft Road, Tel. Oban 62545	3	3	4		7.00 / 8.00	14.00 / 16.00	11.00 / 12.00	- / -	1	4	2	-	2	- / -	12	1-12	
Glenbervie Guest House, Dalriach Road, Tel. Oban 64770	-	-	-		7.00 / 7.50	14.00 / 15.00	11.00 / 12.00	77.00 / 84.00	2	4	2	-	1	1830 / -	7	1-12	
Glenroy Guest House, Rockfield Road	3	3	2		6.00 / -	12.00 / -	9.00 / -	50.00 / -	3	4	2	-	3	1800 / 1900	6	1-12	
Harbour View Guest House, Shore Street	-	-	-		- / -	11.00 / 13.00	- / -	- / -	-	2	2	-	2	- / -	-	1-12	

"Ardblair" OBAN'S LEADING GUEST HOUSE

We have a magnificent view overlooking Oban Bay across Kerrera to the mountains of Mull, and a beautiful Sun Lounge to sit and enjoy it from: there is also a separate TV Lounge. It's easy to find us if you are coming by the A85, just turn left half way down the hill as you enter Oban, and come up past the Tennis Courts, Swimming Pool and the Bowling Green, and there we are! Our Garden has a Car Park for up to 12 cars, and the Esplanade is only 3 minutes' walk. After a day of touring you can expect a hearty five course dinner, and you have the option of arranging your meals daily, also our "help yourself" snack corner gives you Teas, Coffees, Cake and Biscuits anytime you want them. For early holidays there are special terms and our bedrooms have unmetered heating. Anyway, send us a s.a.e. and we will be happy to send you fuller details, including photographs of "Ardblair".

BILL and DOROTHY REID
Phone: 0631 62668 A.A. and R.A.C. listed

Name and Address	Map Ref				Prices				Rooms								Facilities
TOWN / County / Establishment / Address / Telephone / Telex		Bedrooms	Services	Meals	Bed and Breakfast: Single room overnight	Double/twin room overnight	Per person daily	B & B and evening meal: Per person weekly	No. of bedrooms: Single	Double/twin	Family	Private	No. of bath/shower rooms: Public	Evening meals	Parking (no. of cars)	Months open (1-12)	Symbols
OBAN continued	1 E2				£min £max	£min £max	£min £max	£min £max					From Last order				Key on back fold-out

Kelvin Guest House & Restaurant

Shore Street, Oban.
Telephone 0631 62150.

Centrally situated close to station, pier and buses and convenient for shops.

Electric blankets and central heating in all rooms. A la carte meal service and a wide range of snacks available all day. Fully licensed with a good selection of wines and spirits. Quiet, spacious bar serving snacks during licensing hours.

Adequate parking space. Open for breakfast 8 am, last orders for dinner 8.30 pm.

Name and Address	Bedrooms	Services	Meals	Single room o/n	Double/twin room o/n	Per person daily	Per person weekly	Single	Double/twin	Family	Private	Public	Last order	Parking	Months open	Symbols
Kelvin Guest House / Cawdor Place, Shore Street / Tel. Oban 62150	3	4	4	8.00 / 8.00	16.00 / 16.00	- / -	- / -	3	14	2	-	7	1630 / 2030	10	4-10	
Rosebank Guest House / Dalriach Road / PA34 5EQ / Tel. Oban 62095	3	3	3	- / -	- / -	12.00 / 12.50	84.00 / 87.50	-	4	-	-	1	1900 / -	6	1-12	
Roseneath Guest House / Dalriach Road / Tel. Oban 64262	3	3	2	6.00 / 8.75	12.00 / 17.50	9.75 / 12.75	65.00 / 81.00	2	6	2	-	2	1815 / -	10	1-12	

Dinner, Bed & Breakfast at

Sand Villa Guest House

Breadalbane St., Oban.
Tel. Oban (0631) 62803

A large well appointed Guest House ideally situated on the level part of the town and convenient to most entertainments, coach, rail and sea terminals.
- H&C in rooms • Colour T.V.
- Laundry facilities • Full central heating
- Car parking • Excellent Food

(Special weekly terms available July and August). Phone or write to the Proprietor enclosing SAE and requirements.

Name and Address	Bedrooms	Services	Meals	Single room o/n	Double/twin room o/n	Per person daily	Per person weekly	Single	Double/twin	Family	Private	Public	Last order	Parking	Months open	Symbols
Sand Villa Guest House / Breadalbane Street / Tel. Oban 62803	-	2	2	6.00 / 9.00	12.00 / 16.00	8.50 / 11.00	- / -	-	11	6	-	2	1800 / 1800	8	1-12	
St Annes Guest House / Dunollie Road / Tel. Oban 62743	3	3	1	5.50 / -	11.00 / -	- / -	- / -	1	4	2	-	1	- / -	-	1-12	
Thornloe Guest House / Albert Road / Tel. Oban 62879	3	4	2	7.00 / -	14.00 / -	11.00 / -	- / -	1	6	1	-	2	1830 / -	7	4-10	

VAT is shown at 15%; changes in this rate may affect prices.

Name and Address	Map Ref	Bedrooms	Services	Meals	Single room overnight (£min / £max)	Double/twin room overnight (£min / £max)	Per person daily (£min / £max)	Per person weekly (£min / £max)	Single	Double/twin	Family	Private	Public	Evening meals (From / Last order)	Parking	Months open	Symbols
OBAN continued	1 E2																Key on back fold-out
Westmount Guest House, Dalriach Road, Tel. Oban 62884		3	3	1	6.50 / -	13.00 / -	- / -	- / -	-	3	5	-	1	-	12	4-10	
Willowdene Guest House, Glencruitten Road, Tel. Oban 64601		2	2	2	- / -	12.00 / -	9.50 / -	- / -	-	3	1	-	1	1830	8	3-10	
OLD DEER Aberdeenshire	4 H8																
Aden Arms Hotel, Tel. Mintlaw 2573/2922		-	-	-	8.00 / -	14.00 / -	12.00 / -	- / -	-	6	-	-	2	1730 / 2000	30	1-12	
OLD MELDRUM Aberdeenshire	4 G9																
Meldrum House, AB5 0AE, Tel. Old Meldrum 2294		5	4	5	37.95 / 46.81	49.33 / 58.19	49.95 / 58.81	- / -	1	8	-	9	1	1900 / 2200	50	3-12	
OLD RAYNE, by Insch Aberdeenshire	4 F9																
The Lodge Hotel, AB5 6RY, Tel. Old Rayne 205		4	3	4	11.50 / 11.50	18.50 / 18.50	17.50 / 17.50	107.50 / 107.50	2	4	-	4	1	1700 / 2000	10	1-12	
ONICH Inverness-shire	1 F1																
Allt-Nan-Ros Hotel, PH33 6RY, Tel. Onich 210		3	4	3	8.00 / -	16.00 / -	14.50 / -	100.00 / -	6	14	-	-	7	1930 / 2030	30	4-10	
Creag Dhu Hotel, PH33 6RY, Tel. Onich 238		4	5	5	14.50 / 16.50	29.00 / 33.00	23.00 / 25.00	150.50 / 164.50	5	14	1	8	4	1900 / 2030	25	4-10	
Creag Mhor Hotel, PH33 6RY		3	3	5	12.00 / 14.00	24.00 / 26.00	18.00 / -	112.00 / -	6	12	-	3	3	1900 / 2130	24	4-10	
Nether Lochaber Hotel, Corran, Tel. Onich 235		-	-	-	9.20 / -	18.40 / -	16.65 / -	- / -	1	3	1	-	1	1930 / 2030	8	1-12	
Onich Hotel, PH33 6RY, Tel. Onich 214		4	4	5	11.00 / -	22.00 / -	19.00 / -	- / -	5	13	4	7	4	1800 / 2230	50	1-12	
Tigh-an-Righ Private Hotel, Tel. Onich 255		3	4	3	6.00 / 6.00	12.00 / 12.00	10.00 / 10.00	- / -	-	2	3	-	1	1830 / 2030	20	1-12	
Cuilcheanna Guest House, PH33 6SD, Tel. Onich 226		3	3	2	7.00 / 8.00	14.00 / 16.00	12.50 / 14.00	79.00 / 87.00	1	6	2	-	3	1900 / -	9	4-10	

For the Creag Dhu Hotel: (See ad. p. 230)

Name and Address				Prices						Rooms					Facilities		
TOWN County Establishment Address Telephone Telex	**Map Ref** Bedrooms Services Meals			Bed and Breakfast Single room overnight	Double/twin room overnight	Per person daily	B & B and evening meal Per person weekly	Single	Double/twin	No. of bedrooms Family	Private	No. of bath/shower rooms Public		Evening meals	Parking (no. of cars)	Months open (1-12)	Symbols
ONICH continued	1 F1			£min £max	£min £max	£min £max	£min £max					From Last order				Key on back fold-out	

Glenmorven Guest House
Onich, Fort William, Inverness-shire PH33 6RY
Telephone: (085 53) 247

Glenmorven enjoys a panorama of mountain and loch ,views from Glencoe in the east to Ardgour and Morven in the west. There is a large garden where you may relax in peace and privacy. All the touring and sporting facilities of Lochaber are readily available. We offer every comfort with good food and personal supervision at all times by the resident proprietors, Andrew and Jean Coke. Residents' Licence.

Establishment	Map Ref	Bedrooms	Services	Meals	Single room overnight	Double/twin room overnight	Per person daily	Per person weekly	Single	Double/twin	Family	Private	Public	Evening meals	Parking	Months open	Symbols
Glen Morven Guest House PH33 6RY Tel. Onich 247		3	3	2	- -	- -	14.25 -	99.75 -	1	4	2	-	4	1900 1900	20	1-10	
Marine House		1	1	2	6.00 6.50	12.00 13.00	11.50 12.00	78.00 80.00	1	4	1	-	1	- 1930	8	4-9	
HF Holidays Ltd Alltshellach PH33 6SA Tel. Onich 357 Telex 922296		2	3	4	7.40 9.90	14.80 19.70	12.40 16.90	70.00 117.00	10	22	9	12	5	1900 1930	40	3-9	
OVERSCAIG, by Lairg Sutherland	3 H5																
Overscaig Hotel IV27 4NY Tel. Merkland 203		3	4	4	11.50 -	21.00 -	17.50 -	115.00 -	3	7	-	4	2	1900 2030	30	4-10	
OXTON Berwickshire	2 E6																
Tower Hotel Tel. Oxton 235		-	-	-	11.00 11.00	16.00 16.00	16.00 23.00	107.00 150.00	1	2	1	3	2	1700 2300	-	1-12	
PAISLEY Renfrewshire	1 H5																
Broadstones Private Hotel 17 High Calside PA2 6BY Tel. 041 889 4055		3	3	1	10.50 11.00	18.00 19.00	- -	- -	1	5	2	-	3	- -	12	1-12	
Rockfield Hotel 125 Renfrew Road Tel. 041 889 6182		5	3	5	- 25.85	- 32.45	- -	- -	9	11	-	20	2	1830 2030	50	1-12	
Stakis Watermill Hotel Lonend PA1 1SR Tel. 041 889 3201		5	5	5	36.00 -	46.00 -	- -	- -	21	27	3	51	-	1700 2215	50	1-12	

Prices shown are for guidance only. Please send SAE with each enquiry.

Name and Address	Map Ref	Bedrooms	Services	Meals	Single room overnight £min/£max	Double/twin room overnight £min/£max	Per person daily £min/£max	Per person weekly £min/£max	Single	Double/twin	Family	Private	Public	Evening meals From/Last order	Parking (no. of cars)	Months open (1-12)	Symbols
PAPA WESTRAY Orkney Papay Community Co-operative Ltd Beltane House Tel. Papa Westray 267/238	5 C9	2	2	3	12.50 / -	23.00 / -	15.00 / -	100.00 / -	-	4	-	4	-	1800 / 1800	30	1-12	(key on back fold-out)
PATHHEAD Midlothian Stair Arms Hotel Tel. Ford 320	2 D5	4	4	5	17.50 / -	28.00 / -	- / -	- / -	1	5	1	-	2	1900 / 2130	102	1-12	(key on back fold-out)
PEEBLES County Hotel 35 High Street Tel. Peebles 20595	2 D6	-	-	-	11.00 / 15.00	22.00 / 30.00	16.00 / 20.00	85.00 / 112.00	1	4	1	-	2	1800 / 2100	4	1-12	(key on back fold-out)

Cringletie House Hotel, Peebles

Privately owned – personally run – set in 28 acres – just 2 miles from Peebles, and only 20 miles from Edinburgh. All bedrooms have magnificent views.

Restaurant recommended by Egon Ronay and other guides.
Fully licensed. Open to non-residents.
B.T.A. commended.
Telephone: Eddleston 233.
Mr and Mrs Stanley Maguire.

Name and Address	Bedrooms	Services	Meals	Single room overnight £min/£max	Double/twin room overnight £min/£max	Per person daily £min/£max	Per person weekly £min/£max	Single	Double/twin	Family	Private	Public	Evening meals From/Last order	Parking (no. of cars)	Months open (1-12)	Symbols
Cringletie House Hotel Eddleston EH45 8PL Tel. Eddleston 233	4	3	4	17.50 / 19.50	35.00 / 41.00	29.50 / 31.50	- / -	4	12	-	11	1	1930 / 2030	40	3-12	(key on back fold-out)
Cross Keys Northgate Tel. Peebles 20748	3	2	3	8.00 / 10.50	16.00 / -	12.00 / 14.50	85.00 / 85.00	4	2	2	-	1	1900 / 2000	5	1-12	(key on back fold-out)
Dilkusha Hotel & Restaurant Chambers Terrace Tel. Peebles 20590	5	4	5	18.00 / 20.00	14.00 / 16.00	23.00 / 25.00	161.00 / 175.00	1	4	1	6	-	1900 / 2130	19	1-12	(key on back fold-out)

SCOTLAND'S FOR ME

64 pages of dazzling full colour packed with useful travel information, inclusive holidays, maps and details of how to enjoy the very best holiday in Scotland.

Ask your travel agent for your FREE copy.

VAT is shown at 15%; changes in this rate may affect prices.

Name and Address	Map Ref	Bedrooms	Services	Meals	Prices				Rooms							Facilities		
TOWN County / Establishment Address Telephone Telex					Bed and Breakfast: Single room overnight / Double/twin room overnight / Per person daily			B & B and evening meal: Per person weekly	No. of bedrooms: Single / Double/twin / Family			No. of bath/shower rooms: Private / Public		Evening meals	Parking (no. of cars)	Months open (1-12)	Symbols
PEEBLES continued	2 D6				£min £max	£min £max	£min £max	£min £max						From Last order		Key on back fold-out

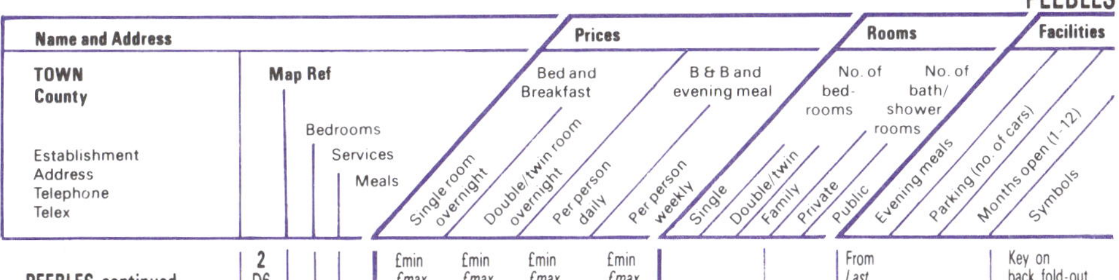

Green Tree Hotel, Peebles

Tel: Peebles 20582

Comfortable privately owned hotel, convenient for buses to Edinburgh and Galashiels. Specialising in Scottish High Teas. Personal supervision.

Name and Address	Map Ref	Bedrooms	Services	Meals	Single room overnight	Double/twin room overnight	Per person daily	Per person weekly	Single	Double/twin	Family	Private	Public	Evening meals	Parking	Months open	Symbols
Green Tree Hotel 41 Eastgate Tel. Peebles 20582		3	5	4	9.50 -	19.00 -	- -	- -	5	9	3	3	4	1600 1900	6	1-12	
Kingsmuir Hotel Springhill Road Tel. Peebles 20151		4	5	5	12.00 -	22.00 -	18.00 -	115.00 -	3	4	1	1	2	1800 2130	20	4-11	
The Park Hotel Innerleithen Road Tel. Peebles 20451 Telex 53168		4	5	5	20.90 27.00	25.70 40.80	29.15 35.25	204.05 246.75	12	20	-	21	5	1900 2100	60	1-12	

COMFORTABLE ACCOMMODATION ∗ IDEAL LOCATION FOR TOURING
ATTENTIVE STAFF ∗ PITCH 'N' PUTT ∗ TENNIS ∗ 30 ACRES OF GROUNDS
GYM ∗ SAUNA **A PEEBLES HYDROLIDAY. MUCH MORE THAN YOUR AVERAGE HOLIDAY.** MAGNIFICENT SCENERY.
GOOD FOOD AND WINE — RIDING ∗ GOLF
BADMINTON FISHING
SQUASH SNOOKER
FAST ACCESS TO EDINBURGH AND GLASGOW ∗ SUMMER EXTRAS AT
NO EXTRA COST ∗ SMALL PRICES *Scotland's for me!* **Peebles Hydro**
FOR SMALL CHILDREN ∗ GREAT
RATES FOR ADULTS ∗ BOOK NOW. Peebles EH45 8LX. Telephone. 0721 20602 Telex. 72568.

Name and Address	Map Ref	Bedrooms	Services	Meals	Single room overnight	Double/twin room overnight	Per person daily	Per person weekly	Single	Double/twin	Family	Private	Public	Evening meals	Parking	Months open	Symbols
Peebles Hotel Hydro Innerleithen Road Tel. Peebles 20602		6	5	5	26.00 33.00	30.00 65.00	22.00 40.00	- -	26	83	26	135	-	1930 2100	200	1-12	

Name and Address				Prices						Rooms					Facilities		
TOWN County Establishment Address Telephone Telex	Map Ref	Bedrooms	Services	Meals	Bed and Breakfast Single room overnight	Double/twin room overnight	Per person daily	B & B and evening meal Per person weekly	Single	Double/twin	Family	Private	Public	No. of bedrooms Evening meals	No. of bath/shower rooms Parking (no. of cars)	Months open (1-12)	Symbols
PEEBLES continued	2 D6				£min £max	£min £max	£min £max	£min £max						From Last order	Key on back fold-out		

AA★   # Riverside Hotel   *RAC★*
Peebles. Tel. (0721) 20776

A small family Hotel situated in its own grounds which overlook and have access to the banks of the River Tweed.

Situated in quiet surroundings within five minutes' walk from the town centre the Hotel is off the Peebles–Glasgow Road (A72). Ample car parking in the Hotel's car park.

The Hotel is fully licensed with Residents' Lounge overlooking the River, Television Lounge. All Bedrooms provided with Hot and Cold Water, Shaver Points, Electric Radiators and Electric Blankets.

Name and Address	Map Ref	Bedrooms	Services	Meals	Single room overnight	Double/twin room overnight	Per person daily	Per person weekly	Single	Double/twin	Family	Private	Public	Bedrooms / Last order	Evening meals	Parking	Months open	Symbols
Riverside Hotel Glasgow Road Tel. Peebles 20776		3	4	4	9.00 10.00	18.00 20.00	14.00 15.00	82.00 90.00	1	5	2	-	2	1900 2000	41	1-12		T 📠 ♈ ♔ ☠ ♨ ✽
Tontine Hotel High Street EH45 8AJ Tel. Peebles 20892		5	5	5	33.00 -	49.50 -	-	-	6	28	3	37	-	1900 2130	30	1-12		T £ ♈ ♔ ☠ ♨ 📞
Venlaw Castle Hotel Tel. Peebles 20384		4	3	4	13.50 14.50	25.00 27.00	19.50 20.50	120.00 125.00	-	8	4	5	4	1900 2000	22	4-10		T £ ♈ ♔ ☠ ✽

PENNAN, by Fraserburgh Aberdeenshire	4 G7																

The Pennan Inn
Tel: New Aberdour (034 66) 201

Whether Walking or Motoring Drop Down to **PENNAN**. Spectacular cliff views with village nestling by the sea beneath. Sit on the Front. Swim in the Harbour. Enjoy refreshments in the unique atmosphere of The Pennan Inn. Meet resident Proprietor Les Rose. Excellent accommodation. Food of the region served. Bar lunches daily. Open to non residents. Children welcome. Teamasters, showers and hair dryers in all rooms.

Name and Address	Map Ref	Bedrooms	Services	Meals	Single room overnight	Double/twin room overnight	Per person daily	Per person weekly	Single	Double/twin	Family	Private	Public	Bedrooms / Last order	Evening meals	Parking	Months open	Symbols
Pennan Inn AB4 4JB Tel. New Aberdour 201		4	4	4	14.00 -	- -	23.00 -	- -	-	8	-	-	1	1900 2200	10	1-12		T £ ♈ ♔ ☠ ♨

PENNYGHAEL Isle of Mull, Argyll	1 C2																
Kinloch Hotel Tel. Pennyghael 204/229		3	4	4	10.35 -	20.50 -	16.35 -	120.00 -	1	2	2	1	1	1900 2030	20	1-12		📠 ♈ ♔ ☠ ♨

Name and Address					Prices									Rooms				Facilities
TOWN County Establishment Address Telephone Telex	Map Ref	Bedrooms	Services	Meals	Single room overnight	Double/twin room overnight	Per person daily	Per person weekly	Single	Double/twin	Family	Private	Public	No. of bedrooms	Evening meals	Parking (no. of cars)	Months open (1-12)	Symbols
					£min £max	£min £max	£min £max	£min £max						From Last order				Key on back fold-out
PERTH	2 C2																	
Balcraig House By Scone Tel. Perth 51123/4/5		5	5	5	32.50 35.00	50.00 70.00	46.00 48.50	303.25 318.00	-	10	-	10	-	1900 2300	23	1-12	
County Hotel 26 County Place PH2 8EE Tel. Perth 23618/23355/6/7		-	-	-	11.50 -	22.00 -	- -	- -	2	14	3	16	3	1800 2100	9	1-12	

THE INCH PARK HOTEL

The Hotel is close to the railway and bus stations and the motor rail terminal, and within walking distance of the City and its excellent shopping centre facilities. The Hotel has a large car park and is fully licensed with a well apointed lounge bar. Central heating throughout.

St. Leonards Bank, Perth, Scotland
Telephone 0738 22451

Establishment	Map Ref	Bedrooms	Services	Meals	Single room overnight	Double/twin room overnight	Per person daily	Per person weekly	Single	Double/twin	Family	Private	Public	No. of bedrooms	Evening meals	Parking	Months open
Inch Park Hotel 2 St Leonards Bank PH2 8EB Tel. Perth 22451	3	3	4		9.00 -	16.00 -	12.65 -	80.00 -	3	7	3	-	3	1700 2100	50	1-12	
Isle of Skye Hotel 18 Dundee Road PH2 7AB Tel. Perth 24471	6	5	5		- 25.00	- 38.00	- 33.00	- 54.00	11	26	7	44	1	1830 2200	80	1-12	
Letham House Hotel Huntingtower Road, Crieff Road PH1 2SG Tel. Perth 27674	3	3	3		8.00 8.00	15.00 15.00	13.00 13.00	85.00 85.00	1	3	1	-	2	1800 1900	35	1-12	
Lovat Hotel 90-92 Glasgow Road PH2 0LT Tel. Perth 36555/6/7	3	6	5		14.00 22.00	20.00 30.00	- -	- -	2	18	5	14	3	1700 2230	60	1-12	
Market Hotel Caledonian Road PH1 5QU Tel. Perth 29347	3	2	3		11.00 -	20.00 -	- -	- -	1	6	1	-	3	1600 2000	-	1-12	
Royal George Hotel Tay Street PH1 5LD Tel. Perth 24455	5	5	5		33.00 -	52.50 -	- -	- -	15	26	2	43	-	1900 2200	32	1-12	

PERTH

Map Ref: **2 C2**

PERTH continued

Name and Address	Bedrooms	Services	Meals	Single room overnight £min/£max	Double/twin room overnight £min/£max	Per person daily £min/£max	Per person weekly £min/£max	Single	Double/twin	Family	Private	Public	Evening meals (last order)	Parking	Months open	Symbols
Salutation Hotel, 34 South Street, PH2 8PH, Tel. Perth 22166, Telex 76357	6	5	5	12.00 / -	24.00 / -	- / -	- / -	20	37	5	55	6	1800 / 2030	-	1-12	Key on back fold-out
Stakis City Mills Hotel, West Mill Street, PH1 5QP, Tel. Perth 28281	5	5	5	36.00 / -	46.00 / -	- / -	- / -	13	65	-	78	-	1700 / 2200	50	1-12	
Station Hotel, Leonard Street, PH2 8HE, Tel. Perth 24141, Telex 76481	5	5	5	18.00 / 29.00	32.00 / 42.00	24.00 / 35.00	105.00 / 126.00	18	35	2	42	7	1900 / 2100	59	1-12	
Tay Motel, 153 Dunkeld Road, PH1 5AU, Tel. Perth 22804	4	4	4	16.50 / -	26.00 / -	20.50 / -	- / -	-	12	8	20	-	1830 / 2130	120	1-12	
Victoria Hotel, 61 Princes Street, PH2 8LJ, Tel. Perth 24351	1	4	3	8.50 / 9.50	16.00 / 17.00	11.70 / 12.70	22.40 / 23.40	4	7	1	-	1	1700 / 1930	6	1-12	
Clark Kimberley Guest House, 57-59 Dunkeld Road, PH1 5RP, Tel. Perth 37406	3	2	1	7.50 / 7.50	13.00 / 13.00	- / -	- / -	2	4	2	-	2	- / -	10	1-12	
Clunie Guest House, 12 Pitcullen Crescent, PH2 7HT, Tel. Perth 23625	4	4	2	8.00 / -	16.00 / -	12.00 / -	84.00 / -	1	5	1	2	2	1800 / 1800	8	1-12	
The Darroch Guest House, 9 Pitcullen Crescent, PH2 7HT, Tel. Perth 36893	3	4	2	8.50 / -	16.00 / -	12.50 / -	80.00 / -	-	3	3	-	2	1800 / -	10	1-12	
The Gables Guest House, 24-26 Dunkeld Road, PH1 5RW, Tel. Perth 24717	2	4	1	8.00 / -	14.00 / -	- / -	- / -	-	4	4	-	2	- / -	8	1-12	
Hazeldene Guest House, Pitcullen Crescent, PH2 7HT, Tel. Perth 23550	3	3	2	7.50 / 9.00	13.00 / 15.00	10.00 / 12.00	68.00 / 77.00	-	4	1	-	1	1830 / 1830	10	1-12	
Iona Guest House, 2 Pitcullen Crescent, PH2 7HT, Tel. Perth 27261	3	4	2	7.50 / -	14.00 / -	- / -	- / -	2	3	1	-	2	1800 / 1800	5	1-12	
Kinnoull Guest House, 5 Pitcullen Crescent, PH2 7HT, Tel. Perth 34165	4	4	2	8.00 / -	13.50 / -	11.00 / -	70.00 / -	-	3	1	4	-	1800 / -	5	1-12	

VAT is shown at 15%; changes in this rate may affect prices.

Name and Address	Map Ref	Bedrooms	Services	Meals	Prices				Rooms							Facilities		
TOWN County / Establishment Address Telephone Telex					Single room overnight	Double/twin room overnight	Per person daily	Per person weekly	Single	Double/twin	Family	Private	Public	Evening meals	Parking (no. of cars)	Months open (1-12)	Symbols	
PERTH continued	2 G7				£min £max	£min £max	£min £max	£min £max						From Last order		Key on back fold-out		

Pitcullen Guest House
17 PITCULLEN CRESCENT PERTH PH2 7HT
Tel: (0738) 26506 and 28265
Family run friendly home situated in the heart of Scotland offering excellent value for money.
Write or phone Mrs J. Grainger for brochure.
★★★ AA and RAC LISTED ★★★

Name and Address	Bedrooms	Services	Meals	Single	Double/twin	Per person daily	Per person weekly	Single	Double/twin	Family	Private	Public	Evening	Months	Symbols
Pitcullen Guest House 17 Pitcullen Crescent PH2 7HT Tel. Perth 26506/28265	3	4	2	7.00 -	14.00 -	10.50 -	70.00 -	1	5	2	-	2	1800 -	8	1-12	T 🐕 ♨ 🖥 ⚅ ♿ 🛏 C V ⊍ ✓
Rowan Bank Guest House 3 Pitcullen Crescent PH2 7HT Tel. Perth 21421	3	3	2	7.00 -	14.00 -	10.50 -	70.00 -	-	2	3	-	2	1730 2000	6	1-12	🐕 ♨ 🖥 ♿ 🛏 C V ⊍

Struan
7 Strathview Terrace, A94/Scone Road, Perth. Tel. (0738) 37687/38478.

Situated about one mile from town centre, the house offers superior accommodation in comfortable homely atmosphere, well appointed rooms all centrally heated and with colour T.V. Residents' lounge, pleasant outlook over cricket park. Private parking. A high reputation is enjoyed for home cooked food served in the bright sunny restuarant–morning coffee, lunch, high tea, dinner, and supper–open till 10pm. Restricted hotel licence. Open all year. Send for brochure and prices to Mrs Isla Smart.

Name and Address	Bedrooms	Services	Meals	Single	Double/twin	Per person daily	Per person weekly	Single	Double/twin	Family	Private	Public	Evening	Months	Symbols
Struan House 7 Strathview Terrace PH2 7HY Tel. Perth 37687	4	4	5	- -	17.00 19.00	13.50 14.50	89.50 96.50	-	3	-	1	1	1700 2130	6	1-12	♿ 🍸 🐕 ♨ 🖥 ♿ 🗆 🛏 C ✳ V
Tatra Guest House 1 Pitcullen Crescent PH2 7HT Tel. Perth 25951	3	5	1	7.50 -	14.00 -	- -	- -	-	2	2	-	2	-	8	1-12	T 🐕 ✗ ♨ 🖥 ♿ 🛏 C V ⊍ ✓

Name and Address	Map Ref	Bedrooms	Services	Meals	Single	Double/twin	Per person daily	Per person weekly	Single	Double/twin	Family	Private	Public	Evening	Months	Symbols
PETERHEAD Aberdeenshire	4 H8															
Albert Hotel 75 Queen Street AB4 6TU Tel. Peterhead 2391		3	4	5	12.00 15.00	18.00 22.00	15.00 18.00	95.00 112.00	1	7	2	-	5	1800 2030	6	1-12	♿ 🍸 🐕 ♨ 🖥 ♿ ● 🗆 🛏 ⚓ C V ⊍
Bayview Hotel 3 St Peter Street Tel. Peterhead 2523		-	-	-	14.00 -	18.00 -	-	-	5	13	2	10	3	1700 2100	25	1-12	♿ 🍸 🐕 ✗ ♨ 🖥 ♿ 🗆 🛏 ⚓ ∥ ⚓ C 📶 V

Name and Address	Map Ref	Bedrooms	Services	Meals	Single room overnight £min/£max	Double/twin room overnight £min/£max	Per person daily £min/£max	Per person weekly £min/£max	Single	Double/twin	Family	Private	Public	Evening meals (From/Last order)	Parking (no. of cars)	Months open (1-12)	Symbols
PETERHEAD continued	4 H8																Key on back fold-out
Waterside Inn Tel. Peterhead 71121 Telex 739413		6	5	6	21.00 / 35.00	30.00 / 40.00	- / -	- / -	-	40	80	120	-	1700 / 2230	220	1-12	T £ V C …
Brae Guest House 9 Harbour Street		1	4	1	6.00 / -	12.00 / -	- / -	- / -	2	5	3	-	4	- / -	10	1-12	…
Carrick Guest House 16 Merchant Street AB4 6DU Tel. Peterhead 70610		1	2	2	6.00 / -	12.00 / -	- / -	- / -	2	5	-	-	2	1700 / 1830	4	1-12	V …
Glendale Guest House 29 Merchant Street Tel. Peterhead 3985		1	2	2	5.55 / -	11.50 / -	7.50 / -	42.00 / -	2	3	5	-	3	1630 / 1900	-	1-12	C V …
PITLOCHRY Perthshire	2 B1																
Acarsaid Hotel 8 Atholl Road PH16 5BX Tel. Pitlochry 2389		4	3	4	13.25 / -	26.50 / -	20.75 / -	41.50 / -	2	17	1	19	3	1830 / 1930	18	4-10	T C V …
Adderley Private Hotel 23 Toberargan Road PH16 5HG Tel. Pitlochry 2433		2	3	2	- / -	- / -	12.50 / 13.75	84.50 / 92.50	1	8	1	-	3	1830 / 1830	9	4-10	M …

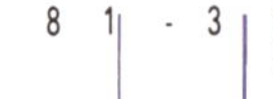

Adderley Private Hotel
Toberargan Road, Pitlochry, Scotland.
Telephone 0796 2433.

Small private hotel run personally by proprietors Atholl and Margaret Davidson.

Situated approx 3 minutes walk from town centre. Free car parking. A.A. Listed.

HOLIDAY SCOTLAND 1984
The most exciting collection of easy-to-book top value holidays in Scotland!
Get a free brochure now from your travel agent.

VAT is shown at 15%: changes in this rate may affect prices.

Name and Address	Map Ref			Prices					Rooms						Facilities		
TOWN County / Establishment Address Telephone Telex		Bedrooms / Services / Meals		Single room overnight	Double/twin room overnight	Per person daily	Per person weekly	Single	Double/twin	Family	Private	Public	Evening meals	Parking (no. of cars)	Months open (1-12)	Symbols	
PITLOCHRY continued	2 B1			£min £max	£min £max	£min £max	£min £max					From Last order			Key on back fold-out	

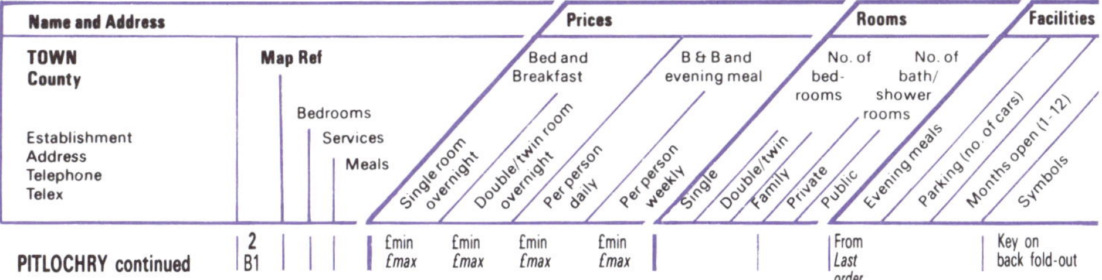

Airdaniar Hotel *Pitlochry, Perthshire PH16 5AR ★ AA & RAC ★*

Tel. (Office) Pitlochry 2266, (Guests) Pitlochry 2041, STD Code 0796. Resident Proprietors: Andrew & Sue Mathieson.

This charming Hotel is under the personal supervision of the owners and splendidly situated in one of the most beautiful areas of Scotland. The Hotel is a large Scottish stone-built house set in attractive gardens overlooking beautiful countryside and within easy reach of buses and station. It is a ten-bedroom family Hotel renowned for its good food and friendly atmosphere. There are two lounges, colour TV and a Cocktail Bar. All bedrooms have H & C, electric fires and blankets, radio/intercom, tea and coffee making facilities. Rooms with private facilities are available.

Fishing is available on some of the best hill lochs in Perthshire, and The New Theatre and Fish Ladder are within easy walking distance.

Write or telephone for our brochure and terms. Bed and Breakfast; Dinner, Bed and Breakfast; and Special Spring/Autumn Breaks are available.

Name and Address	Bedrooms	Services	Meals	Single room overnight	Double/twin room overnight	Per person daily	Per person weekly	Single	Double/twin	Family	Private	Public	From/Last order	Evening meals	Parking	Months open	Symbols
Airdaniar Hotel 160 Atholl Road PH16 5AR Tel. Pitlochry 2266	3	3	4	13.75 14.75	23.50 25.50	18.75 21.75	124.25 145.45	1	7	2	4	2	1830 2000	14	4-10		
Atholl Palace Hotel Atholl Road PH16 5LY Tel. Pitlochry 2400 Telex 76406	6	5	5	33.50 -	54.50 -	- -	- -	15	73	4	92	-	1830 2100	150	1-12		
Balrobin Hotel 14 Higher Oakfield PH16 5HT Tel. Pitlochry 2901	3	3	3	8.00 -	16.00 -	13.00 -	87.50 -	1	5	2	2	1	1830 1930	8	4-10		

Birchwood Hotel

**East Moulin Road
Pitlochry
Telephone (0796) 2477
A.A.★★ R.A.C.★★
–Ashley Courtenay
Recommended.**

Lovely Country House Hotel in 4 Acres of Gardens and Woodlands. Ideal Centre for Walking, Touring, Golfing and Fishing. Well known for its Excellent Cuisine. Tea/Coffee Facilities in all Bedrooms, most with Private Bathrooms. Operated by Proprietors Personally ensuring High Standard of Comfort and Service . . . Residential Licence.

Apply for Brochure and Tariff including details of Early and Late Season Special Terms. Bargain Breaks, and Package Holidays.

OPEN ALL YEAR.

Name and Address	Bedrooms	Services	Meals	Single room overnight	Double/twin room overnight	Per person daily	Per person weekly	Single	Double/twin	Family	Private	Public	From/Last order	Evening meals	Parking	Months open	Symbols
Birchwood Hotel 2 East Moulin Road PH16 5DW Tel. Pitlochry 2477	4	4	4	12.50 14.00	25.00 28.00	18.50 20.00	121.50 133.00	1	12	3	13	1	1830 1930	25	1-12		

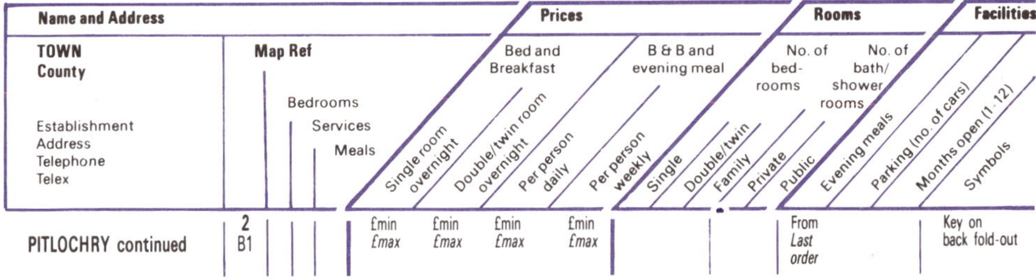

Name and Address	Map Ref				Prices					Rooms				Facilities		
TOWN County Establishment Address Telephone Telex		Bedrooms Services Meals			Bed and Breakfast			B & B and evening meal		No. of bedrooms		No. of bath/shower rooms				
					Single room overnight	Double/twin room overnight	Per person daily	Per person weekly	Single	Double/twin	Family	Private	Public	Evening meals	Parking (no. of cars)	Months open (1-12)	Symbols
PITLOCHRY continued	2 B1				£min £max	£min £max	£min £max	£min £max				From Last order			Key on back fold-out

Family owned and managed in quiet central location.

BEDROOMS (23) 18 P/B or Shr, all TV, Radio, Tea/Coffee tray, 1 Bedroom for Disabled guests.

LICENSED RESTAURANT noted for its tasty lunch, snacks, variety of Table D'Hote and a la Carte dinners with speciality dishes and desserts.

TARIFFS include **have a Break and Theatre Break** short stays, **Senior Citizens and Summer Special Holidays.**

SPECIAL INTEREST HOLIDAYS — Painting, golf and Holiday with Flowers.

Colour brochure and full details from Resident Proprietors, Mr & Mrs W. G. Falconer.

R.A.C. ★★ A.A. ★★ and H L Quality Awards.

Ashley Courtenay Recommended.

Name and Address				Single room overnight	Double/twin room overnight	Per person daily	Per person weekly	Single	Double/twin	Family	Private	Public	Evening meals	Parking	Months open	Symbols
Burnside Hotel 19 West Moulin Road PH16 5EA Tel. Pitlochry 2203	4	4	4	16.42 -	28.62 -	23.96 -	- -	3	12	8	19	2	1830 2030	30	3-11	T £ 🛏 🍷 🐕 ✕ 🍴 ▥ ♿ 🛎 □ 🗞 ⚡ C ✷ V ∪

Castlebeigh Hotel

****AA   Central Highlands   Pitlochry**
****RAC   Telephone: 0796 2925**

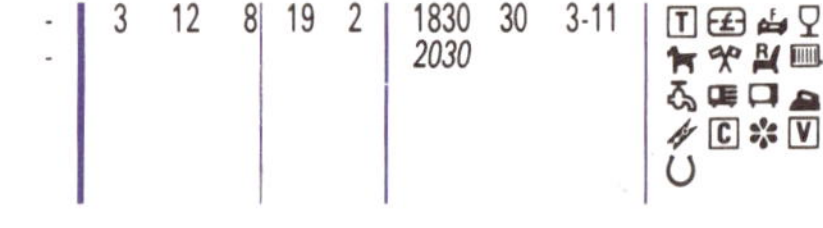

Castlebeigh a Country House Hotel in $2\frac{1}{2}$ acres, convenient to the town and Festival Theatre, commands superb views across Ben Y Vrackie mountain, and the Cocktail Lounge offers fine views down the Valley of the Tummel.

Twenty-one spacious and beautifully appointed bedrooms with private bathrooms en suite all with interior sprung divans, electric blankets, continental quilts and tea and coffee facilities.

Colour T.V.–Reading Lounge–Central Heating and Car Park.

April-20 May: 21 September-November 1984. From £18.50 per night. Dinner and Breakfast.

Alan and Betty Lawson offer highland hospitality, good food, comfort and service.

Name and Address				Single room overnight	Double/twin room overnight	Per person daily	Per person weekly	Single	Double/twin	Family	Private	Public	Evening meals	Parking	Months open	Symbols
Castlebeigh Hotel 10 Knockard Road PH16 5HJ Tel. Pitlochry 2925/2091	4	4	4	12.90 14.00	25.80 28.00	18.50 20.50	129.52 143.50	5	16	-	21	-	1845 1945	36	4-10	🍷 🐕 ▥ ♿ 🛏 ⚡ ✷ ∪

Name and Address	Map Ref	Bedrooms	Services	Meals	Single room overnight £min / £max	Double/twin room overnight £min / £max	Per person daily £min / £max	Per person weekly £min / £max	Single	Double/twin	Family	Private	Public	Evening meals (Last order)	Parking (no. of cars)	Months open (1-12)	Symbols
PITLOCHRY continued	2 B1													From / Last order			Key on back fold-out
Claymore Hotel, 162 Atholl Road, PH16 5AR, Tel. Pitlochry 2888		3	3	4	13.00 / -	26.00 / -	20.50 / -	128.50 / -	2	9	1	3	3	1830 / 2030	25	4-10	[symbols]
Craig Urrard Hotel, 10 Atholl Road, PH16 5BX, Tel. Pitlochry 2346		3	4	4	13.20 / 13.20	22.40 / 22.40	18.80 / 18.80	114.00 / -	1	6	5	4	4	1830 / 2000	12	1-12	[symbols]
Craigard Hotel, Strathview Terrace, Lettoch Road, PH16 5AZ, Tel. Pitlochry 2592		4	4	4	14.25 / -	25.50 / -	20.10 / -	133.00 / -	3	6	1	6	1	1830 / 1930	10	3-10	[symbols]
Craigvrack Hotel, West Moulin Road, PH6 5EQ, Tel. Pitlochry 2399		4	4	4	9.00 / -	18.00 / -	16.50 / -	105.00 / -	2	13	4	9	3	1830 / 2000	20	4-10	[symbols]
Fasganeoin Hotel, Perth Road, PH16 5DJ, Tel. Pitlochry 2387		3	3	4	10.50 / 11.50	21.00 / 23.00	15.50 / 17.00	103.50 / 114.00	2	3	4	-	2	1830 / 1930	20	4-10	[symbols]

Craig Urrard Hotel
Pitlochry A.A.*

A family hotel situated in its own grounds close to the Festival Theatre. The golf course and other amenities are nearby. The hotel is comfortable, friendly with a relaxing atmosphere. Licensed. Excellent food and wine. Brochure on request from the resident proprietors. Tea and coffee making facilities in all rooms.

Telephone: Pitlochry 2346 (STD 0796)

Craigard Hotel

Pitlochry
Strathview Terrace
Tel: (0796) 2592 AA★★

Enjoy a holiday of quality at Craigard with its superb appointments, excellent food and relaxed atmosphere.

Standing in beautiful grounds with lovely views of the Tummel Valley and surrounding hills this family run hotel offers 10 bedrooms, all with tea/coffee facilities, colour televisions and majority with private facilities. Please write/telephone for colour brochure/tariff, 4 day touring package, and golfing holiday details.

A 'Traveller's Britains' Hotel.

Prices shown are for guidance only. Please send SAE with each enquiry.

Name and Address	Map Ref			Prices						Rooms					No. of bedrooms		No. of bath/shower rooms	Facilities			
TOWN County / Establishment Address Telephone Telex		Bedrooms	Services	Meals	Bed and Breakfast				B & B and evening meal	Single	Double/twin	Family	Private	Public	From Last order			Evening meals	Parking (no. of cars)	Months open (1-12)	Symbols
					Single room overnight	Double/twin room overnight	Per person daily	Per person weekly	Per person weekly												
PITLOCHRY continued	2 B1				£min £max	£min £max	£min £max	£min £max							From Last order						Key on back fold-out
Fisher's Hotel 75-79 Atholl Road PH16 5BN Tel. Pitlochry 2000		4	5	4	17.75 23.00	33.50 43.00	21.50 31.00	140.00 210.00	24	44	9	51	14		1830 2030	66	1-12				
Green Park Hotel Clunie Bridge Road PH16 5JY Tel. Pitlochry 2537		4	4	4	16.50 -	33.00 -	24.75 -	173.00 -	9	29	-	27	6		1830 2000	44	3-10				

Moulin Inn

By Pitlochry, Perthshire
Telephone: 0796 2196

★ ★ AA

The Moulin Inn, which forms two sides of the Village Square of Moulin, has been developed around the original 17th Century Coaching Inn, and nestles at the foot of Ben-y-Vrackie.

This unspoilt Village in the heart of Scotland, and within walking distance of Pitlochry and all its amenities, is an ideal centre for Family holidays.

Under the personal supervision of Michael and Mary Davies, the Inn, with 23 bedrooms, 10 with private bathrooms en suite), offers modern comfort, traditional friendly service and good food.

All forms of leisure activities can easily be arranged, ie Theatre and Castle visits, Golf, Fishing, Pony-trekking etc. Brochure and Tariff forwarded on request.

Name	Bedrooms	Services	Meals	Single room overnight	Double/twin room overnight	Per person daily	Per person weekly	Single	Double/twin	Family	Private	Public	Last order	Evening meals	Months open
Moulin Inn 11-13 Kirkmichael Road, Moulin PH16 5EH Tel. Pitlochry 2196	4	3	4	15.00 16.50	28.00 31.00	20.00 21.50	126.00 135.45	3	19	1	10	6	1800 2100	40	1-12

VAT is shown at 15%: changes in this rate may affect prices.

Name and Address				Prices					Rooms								Facilities
TOWN County Establishment Address Telephone Telex	Map Ref	Bedrooms	Services	Meals	Single room overnight	Double/twin room overnight	Per person daily	Per person weekly	Single	Double/twin	Family	Private	Public	No. of bed-rooms	No. of bath/ shower rooms	Evening meals	Parking (no. of cars)	Months open (1-12) Symbols / Facilities
PITLOCHRY continued	2 B1				£min £max	£min £max	£min £max	£min £max					From Last order				Key on back fold-out

Pine Trees Hotel

Strathview Terrace, Pitlochry.
Telephone 0796 2121.
Ashley Courtenay recommended
*** Country House AA RAC RSAC

An exceptionally well appointed family run hotel with spacious comfortable public rooms, an atmosphere of friendliness, warmth and relaxation, and an enviable reputation for good food and wine.

It is situated in 14 acres of private grounds yet is less than 15 minutes walk to the town centre and to the golf course.

A nine hole putting green and a practice golf range are available in the hotel grounds and are of course free of charge to guests.

Salmon and trout fishing can normally be arranged.

Establishment	Bedrooms	Services	Meals	Single room overnight	Double/twin room overnight	Per person daily	Per person weekly	Single	Double/twin	Family	Private	Public	No. of bed-rooms	Evening meals (last order)	Parking	Months open
The Pine Trees Hotel Strathview Terrace PH16 5QR Tel. Pitlochry 2121	4	4	5	11.00 18.50	22.00 38.00	19.50 28.00	129.50 189.00	4	23	2	20	3		1830 2045	70	4-12

Pitlochry Hydro Hotel, Pitlochry, Perthshire. Tel. 0796-2666

An attractive hotel overlooking the town with its own 9 hole golf course and tennis court. Set in the centre of beautiful Perthshire countryside. Pitlochry is well known for its Festival Theatre and 18 hole golf course.
62 bedrooms with Private Bath, Tea and Coffee making facilities and colour T.V.

Establishment	Bedrooms	Services	Meals	Single room overnight	Double/twin room overnight	Per person daily	Per person weekly	Single	Double/twin	Family	Private	Public	No. of bed-rooms	Evening meals (last order)	Parking	Months open
Pitlochry Hydro Hotel Knockard Road PH16 5JH Tel. Pitlochry 2666 Telex 778215	3	5	4	28.00 28.00	46.00 46.00	31.00 31.00	161.00 161.00	14	44	4	58	4		1830 2030	85	4-10
Scotlands Hotel 32-46 Bonnethill Road PH16 5BT Tel. Pitlochry 2292	4	5	4	23.90 -	41.80 -	- -	- -	12	34	14	47	7		1830 2230	50	1-12
Tigh-Na-Cloich Hotel Larchwood Road PH16 5AS Tel. Pitlochry 2216	4	3	4	10.00 13.50	20.00 27.00	15.00 19.50	100.50 130.50	3	9	2	7	3		1830 2100	9	3-10

Name and Address	Map Ref	Bedrooms	Services	Meals	Single room overnight £min/£max	Double/twin room overnight £min/£max	Per person daily £min/£max	Per person weekly £min/£max	Single	Double/twin	Family	Private	Public	Evening meals (From/Last order)	Parking (no. of cars)	Months open (1-12)	Symbols
PITLOCHRY continued	2 B1																Key on back fold-out
Wellwood Hotel, 13 West Moulin Road, PH16 5EA, Tel. Pitlochry 2879		3	3	4	11.50 / -	23.00 / -	17.50 / -	115.00 / -	3	11	2	-	-	1930 / 2200	13	4-10	T, V
Carra Beag Guest House, 16 Toberargan Road, PH16 5HG, Tel. Pitlochry 2835		2	2	1	7.00 / 7.50	14.00 / 15.00	11.50 / 12.25	77.00 / 80.00	2	5	3	1	2	1800 / 1900	12	1-12	M
Craigmore Guest House, 27 West Moulin Road, PH16 5EF, Tel. Pitlochry 2123		3	3	2	8.25 / 10.00	16.50 / 20.00	13.75 / 15.50	91.50 / 103.00	2	11	3	3	4	- / 1830	14	3-10	C, V
Derrybeg Guest House, 18 Lower Oakfield, PH16 5DS, Tel. Pitlochry 2070		3	3	2	7.00 / 8.00	14.00 / 16.00	12.00 / 13.00	80.00 / 85.00	1	4	3	-	2	1830 / 2000	12	1-12	C, V
Duntrune Guest House, 22 East Moulin Road, PH16 5HY, Tel. Pitlochry 2172		3	3	2	8.50 / 9.50	17.00 / 19.00	12.50 / 13.50	81.25 / 87.75	2	4	1	-	1	1830 / -	8	4-10	V
Kinnaird Guest House, Kirkmichael Road, PH16 5JL, Tel. Pitlochry 2843		3	4	2	8.50 / -	17.00 / -	12.50 / -	83.00 / -	1	4	2	-	2	1830 / -	8	4-10	T
Mansewood Guest House, 11 Nursing Home Brae Rd, PH16 5HP, Tel. Pitlochry 2366		2	2	1	6.50 / -	13.00 / -	- / -	- / -	1	5	2	-	2	- / -	8	4-10	V
Tir Aluinn Guest House, 10 Higher Oakfield, PH16 5HT, Tel. Pitlochry 2418		3	3	1	- / -	13.00 / 14.00	- / -	- / -	-	3	1	-	2	- / -	4	5-10	
Viewmore Guest House, 27 Atholl Road, PH16 5BX, Tel. Pitlochry 2065		3	3	1	7.00 / 7.50	14.00 / 15.00	- / -	- / -	1	5	2	-	2	- / -	8	4-12	V
Atholl Baptist Centre, 20 Atholl Road, PH16 5BX, Tel. Pitlochry 3044		3	3	3	6.44 / -	12.88 / -	8.74 / 9.69	58.12 / 61.16	2	2	8	-	4	1830 / 1830	12	1-12	V

Bonskeid House

Pitlochry, Perthshire
Tel: Pitlochry
(0796) 3208

Bonskeid House is a Y.M.C.A. Holiday and Conference Centre set in the Scottish Highlands, 5 miles from Pitlochry. It is a large house taking up to 115 guests. All bedrooms have wash-hand basins and there are 3 lounges, a large dining room, and good games facilities – tennis court, billiard room, table tennis, putting, etc., – also easy access to the river for fishing and swimming. The house is open from mid-February to mid-November.

Name and Address	Map Ref	Bedrooms	Services	Meals	Single room overnight £min/£max	Double/twin room overnight £min/£max	Per person daily £min/£max	Per person weekly £min/£max	Single	Double/twin	Family	Private	Public	Evening meals (From/Last order)	Parking (no. of cars)	Months open (1-12)	Symbols
YMCA Bonskeid House, PH16 5NP, Tel. Pitlochry 3208		2	2	3	6.90 / 6.90	13.80 / 13.80	11.20 / 11.20	78.40 / 78.40	5	25	15		12	1830 / 1830	25	2-11	M, V

VAT is shown at 15%: changes in this rate may affect prices.

Name and Address				Prices				B & B and evening meal					Rooms				Facilities
TOWN County / Establishment Address Telephone Telex	Map Ref	Bedrooms	Services	Meals	Bed and Breakfast				Single	Double/twin	Family	Private	No. of bedrooms Public	No. of bath/shower rooms Evening meals	Parking (no. of cars)	Months open (1-12)	Symbols (Key on back fold-out)
					Single room overnight £min £max	Double/twin room overnight £min £max	Per person daily £min £max	Per person weekly £min £max					From Last order				
PITTENWEEM Fife	2 E3																
Eight Gable Hotel Viewforth Place Tel. Anstruther 311646		3	4	3	12.00 -	22.00 -	16.00 -	110.00 -	-	2	1	-	1	1800 2100	32	1-12	(symbols)
PLOCKTON Ross-shire	3 F9																
The Haven Hotel IV52 8TW Tel. Plockton 223		3	4	4	13.00 14.50	22.00 25.00	17.50 19.00	108.50 119.00	2	6	4	4	3	1900 1945	8	3-10	(symbols)
Plockton Hotel 41 Harbour Street IV52 8TN Tel. Plockton 274		3	3	4	- -	20.00 -	- -	- -	-	1	1	-	1	1830 2000	-	1-12	(symbols)
POLMONT Stirlingshire	2 B4																
Inchyra Grange Hotel Grange Road FK2 0YB Tel. Polmont 711911 Telex 777693		5	5	5	28.50 33.00	41.00 46.00	- -	- -	1	29	-	30	-	1900 2130	100	1-12	(symbols)
Polmont Bank Hotel Main Street Tel. Polmont 712433		-	-	-	9.50 -	18.00 -	- -	- -	3	4	1	-	2	1800 2100	150	1-12	(symbols)
Whyteside Hotel Gilston Crescent FK2 0XP Tel. Polmont 712394		3	3	5	18.00 -	25.00 -	- -	- -	1	4	-	-	1	1900 2030	100	1-12	(symbols)
POOLEWE Ross-shire	3 F7																
Pool House Hotel IV22 2LE Tel. Poolewe 272		4	3	4	12.00 14.50	24.00 29.00	19.00 21.50	119.00 133.00	4	10	-	3	4	1900 2030	40	4-10	(symbols)
Corriness Guest House IV22 2JU Tel. Poolewe 262		3	3	4	8.00	16.00	14.00	90.00	1	4	1	-	3	1900 -	20	1-12	(symbols)

(See ad. p. 246)

A YEAR-LONG FESTIVAL OF SCOTTISH HERITAGE

Tours and Trails, Exhibitions and Displays, Courses and Seminars, Concerts, Folk Concerts, Highland Games, and Sports are only some of the activities taking place throughout Scotland.

Ask your local Tourist Information Centre for details.

"CORRINESS" POOLEWE

"Corriness" is situated in the village of Poolewe, at the head of Loch Ewe.

"Corriness" stands in its own grounds of 2.5 acres and is central for walking and touring Wester Ross. There are 7 bedrooms, all with h & c and heating. Meals are substantial and varied.

Inverewe Gardens (National Trust) are half a mile and Gairloch Golf Course (9 hole) is 6 miles.

Sea-angling trips can be arranged and local boats for hire, brown trout fishing is obtainable and there are good sandy beaches in the area.

Terms for Dinner, Bed and Breakfast from £14 per day, per person
Packed lunch or lunch in Dining Room

Inquiries to:
Mrs S. E. Urquhart, "Corriness", Poolewe,
Wester Ross IV22 2JU
Tel. Poolewe 262 (STD 044 586)

The column legend for the listings table reads:

Name and Address — TOWN, County; Establishment, Address, Telephone, Telex · **Map Ref** · Bedrooms · Services · Meals · **Prices** (£min / £max): *Bed and Breakfast* — Single room overnight, Double/twin room overnight, Per person daily; *B & B and evening meal* — Per person weekly · **Rooms**: No. of bedrooms (Single, Double/twin, Family), No. of bath/shower rooms (Private, Public) · **Facilities**: Evening meals (From Last order), Parking (no. of cars), Months open (1-12), Symbols (Key on back fold-out)

The Airds Hotel
Port Appin, Argyll.

Under personal supervision of resident proprietors. Mr. and Mrs. E. Allen. Telephone Appin (063 173) 236.

The Airds Hotel is an old Ferry Inn, dating from around 1700. The Hotel is a haven of peace, overlooking Loch Linnhe, the island of Lismore and the majestic mountains of Morvern.

In 1983, the hotel was one of only 5 hotels in Scotland to be awarded Red Stars and a Rosette by the Automobile Association for accommodation, food and service considered to be outstanding within the classification. Also listed in Ashley Courtenay, Egon Ronay. BTA Commended.

Name and Address	Map Ref	Bedrooms	Services	Meals	Single room overnight (£min/£max)	Double/twin room overnight	Per person daily	Per person weekly	Single	Double/twin	Family	Private	Public	Evening meals (last order)	Parking	Months open	Symbols
PORT APPIN — Argyll	1 E1																
The Airds Hotel, PA38 4DF, Tel. Appin 236		4	4	4	18.00 / 18.00	36.00 / 40.00	30.00 / 32.00	200.00 / 214.00	2	10	1	9	3	1930	30	4-10	
Linnhe House, Tel. Appin 245		3	3	2	8.50 / 9.50	17.00 / 19.00	14.00 / 16.00	90.00 / 100.00	1	3	1	-	1	1930	6	4-10	
PORT ASKAIG — Isle of Islay, Argyll	1 C5																
Port Askaig Hotel, PA56 7RD, Tel. Port Askaig 245		4	4	5	17.75 / 19.00	29.00 / 31.00	24.00 / 26.00	145.00 / 160.00	1	8	-	4	3	-	26	1-12	
PORT CHARLOTTE — Isle of Islay, Argyll	1 B6																
Lochindaal Hotel, Tel. Port Charlotte 202		3	3	3	9.50 / -	- / -	15.50 / -	- / -	3	3	-	-	2	1800 / 2000	3	-	
Port Charlotte Hotel, Tel. Port Charlotte 321 or 379		4	3	4	12.50 / -	25.00 / -	- / -	- / -	4	6	1	4	2	1900 / 2100	10	1-12	
PORT ELLEN — Isle of Islay, Argyll	1 C6																
Dower House Hotel, Kildalton, Tel. Kildalton 225		3	3	4	12.00 / 16.00	22.00 / 28.00	19.50 / 23.50	132.30 / 145.90	2	3	1	6	-	1930 / 2100	12	1-12	
Islay Hotel, Tel. Port Ellen 2260		3	3	5	10.00 / 14.00	19.00 / 27.00	- / -	- / -	2	9	1	-	2	1830 / 2230	18	1-12	
White Hart Hotel, Tel. Port Ellen 2311		3	4	4	13.00 / -	25.00 / -	20.50 / -	130.00 / -	3	13	3	5	4	1900 / 2000	20	1-12	

Name and Address	Map Ref	Bedrooms	Services	Meals	Bed and Breakfast: Single room overnight (£min £max)	Double/twin room overnight (£min £max)	Per person daily (£min £max)	B & B and evening meal: Per person weekly (£min £max)	Single	Double/twin	Family	Private	Public	No. of bed-rooms From Last order	Evening meals	Parking (no. of cars)	Months open (1-12)	Symbols (Key on back fold-out)
PORT GLASGOW Renfrewshire	1 G5																	
Clune Brae Hotel Boglestone Tel. Port Glasgow 704226		-	-	-	14.00 -	23.00 -	- -	- -	1	9	-	10	-	1830 2000	20	1-12		
PORT LOGAN, by Stranraer Wigtownshire	1 F11																	
Logan Lodge Hotel DG9 9NG Tel. Ardwell 282		3	4	5	10.00 10.00	20.00 20.00	15.00 15.00	95.00 95.00	1	3	1	1	2	1830 2130	-	4-10		
PORT WILLIAM Wigtownshire	1 H11																	
Commercial Hotel Tel. Port William 243		3	2	3	7.50 -	13.00 -	11.00 -	70.00 -	-	3	-	-	1	1800 1800	-	1-12		
Eagle Hotel Tel. Port William 280		-	-	-	10.00 -	20.00 -	- -	- -	3	2	2	-	1	1900 2000	-	1-12		

Monreith Arms Hotel

AA. RAC, RSAC appointed　　　　**PORT WILLIAM**

13 bedrooms (2 single, 4 double, 5 twin, 2 family) 5 public bathrooms
Partial central heating, coal fires Morning coffees, lunches, afternoon teas, dinners
(last orders 8 pm) fully licensed

BATHING ● GOLF ● BOWLING ● SEA ANGLING

Proprietors: **Mr. & Mrs. A. R. Jardine**
Port William, Wigtownshire
Telephone: Port William (098 87) 232

Name and Address	Map Ref	Bedrooms	Services	Meals	Single room overnight (£min £max)	Double/twin room overnight (£min £max)	Per person daily (£min £max)	Per person weekly (£min £max)	Single	Double/twin	Family	Private	Public	No. of bed-rooms From Last order	Evening meals	Parking	Months open	Symbols
Monreith Arms Hotel DG8 9SE Tel. Port William 232		3	3	4	11.30 -	22.60 -	17.20 -	120.40 -	2	9	2	1	5	1900 2030	-	1-12		
PORT OF MENTEITH Perthshire	1 H3																	
Lake Hotel FK8 3RA Tel. Port of Menteith 258		3	3	4	12.00 -	23.00 -	18.00 -	106.75 -	2	12	-	2	3	1930 2030	-	4-10		
PORTMAHOMACK Ross-shire	4 C7																	
Castle Hotel IV20 1YE Tel. Portmahomack 263		3	3	3	9.00 11.00	17.00 20.00	15.00 19.00	100.00 130.00	1	4	-	-	1	1900 2000	5	1-12		
Oyster Catcher Hotel Main Street Tel. Portmahomack 279		3	4	4	9.00 11.00	18.00 22.00	- -	- -	4	2	1	-	2	1800 2100	5	1-12		

VAT is shown at 15%: changes in this rate may affect prices.

Name and Address					Prices					Rooms				Facilities
TOWN County / Establishment Address Telephone Telex	Map Ref	Bedrooms / Services / Meals	Single room overnight	Double/twin room overnight	Per person daily	Per person weekly	Single	Double/twin	Family	Private	Public	Evening meals	Parking (no. of cars)	Months open (1-12)
			£min £max	£min £max	£min £max	£min £max					From Last order			Key on back fold-out

PORTPATRICK   1
Wigtownshire   F11

FERNHILL HOTEL ***AA.   R.A.C.***
Portpatrick

This small well appointed hotel offers comfort and superb food to residents and non residents alike.

Delightfully situated, the hotel has 15 bedrooms, 13 having private bath or shower. Superb food from cordon bleu chef available both in restaurant and cocktail bar. Seafood a speciality.

Free golf at nearby Dunskey Golf Club (400 yards) is available to residents during the weekdays (Monday-Friday) of April, May, June/September and October of 1984.

Illustrated brochure on request from the owners Mr & Mrs Hugh Harvie.

Telephone PORTPATRICK (077 681 220) 220

Establishment	Bedrooms	Services	Meals	Single room overnight	Double/twin overnight	Per person daily	Per person weekly	Single	Double/twin	Family	Private	Public	From/Last order	Evening meals	Months open
Fernhill Hotel Tel. Portpatrick 220	4	4	5	15.50 -	31.00 -	24.00 -	168.00 -	2	9	4	12	1	1800 2200	40	3-11
Knockinaam Lodge Hotel Tel. Portpatrick 471	4	4	5	- -	- -	30.00 42.00	200.00 284.00	1	10	-	8	1	1915 2100	50	3-1
Mount Stewart Hotel DG9 8LE Tel. Portpatrick 291	3	4	5	12.50 14.00	25.00 28.00	- -	- -	1	2	5	-	2	1830 2130	25	1-12
Portpatrick Hotel Tel. Portpatrick 333	4	5	5	13.00 22.00	29.00 44.00	18.00 27.00	108.50 175.00	16	39	8	30	9	1900 2100	70	4-10
Rickwood Private Hotel Tel. Portpatrick 270	3	2	2	10.50 -	21.00 24.00	15.50 17.00	103.00 110.00	1	3	2	3	1	1900 1930	10	4-10

ROSLIN HOTEL PORTPATRICK

iDEAL SITUATION OVERLOOKING SEA
100 YARDS FROM GOLF COURSE

H. & C. in all rooms ★ **Excellent Cuisine** ★ **Residential Licence**

Electric Kettles   *Children Welcome*

Open all year   Fire Certificate Granted   Electric Blankets all rooms

3 Day Bargain Breaks

Proprietors: J. & H. LENNOX   **Tel: PORTPATRICK 241**

Establishment	Bedrooms	Services	Meals	Single room overnight	Double/twin overnight	Per person daily	Per person weekly	Single	Double/twin	Family	Private	Public	From/Last order	Evening meals	Months open
Roslin Hotel Heugh Road Tel. Portpatrick 241	3	3	5	8.50 -	17.00 -	14.00 -	- -	3	10	-	-	2	1830 2000	-	1-12
South Cliff House Hotel Tel. Portpatrick 411	3	2	3	9.00 10.00	18.00 20.00	13.00 15.00	80.00 95.00	1	4	1	-	1	1830 2100	20	1-11

Name and Address	Map Ref	Bedrooms	Services	Meals	Single room overnight (£min/£max)	Double/twin room overnight (£min/£max)	Per person daily (£min/£max)	Per person weekly (£min/£max)	Single	Double/twin	Family	Private	Public	Evening meals From/Last order	Parking (no. of cars)	Months open (1-12)	Symbols
PORTPATRICK continued	1 F11				£min £max	£min £max	£min £max	£min £max						From Last order			Key on back fold-out
Blinkbonnie Guest House DG9 8LG Tel. Portpatrick 282		3	3	2	8.00 / 9.00	14.00 / 15.00	11.50 / 12.25	80.50 / 85.25	-	5	1	-	2	1830 / 1830	6	2-11	(symbols)
Broomknowe Guest House School Brae Tel. Portpatrick 365		1	3	2	- / -	14.50 / -	12.00 / -	- / -	-	1	2	-	1	1830 / 1600	3	4-10	(symbols)
PORTREE Isle of Skye, Inverness-shire	3 D9																

Bosville Hotel & Restaurant

Office: Tel: 0478 2846 Visitors: Tel: 0478 2120
Personally Supervised by Murdo and Marie Macleod
Restaurant on ground floor, Hotel above. Overlooking Portree Bay on main road.
Parking in front. All bedrooms with hot and cold water and tea-making equipment.
Shaver points. Family rooms available. Access to rooms at all times – own key. Baths
and showers, private bathrooms available. Home baking – liberal and varied menus.
TV Lounge. Tours arranged. Terms on application. Fire certificate held.
All bookings by telephone must be confirmed by letter.

Name and Address	Bedrooms	Services	Meals	Single room overnight (£min/£max)	Double/twin room overnight	Per person daily	Per person weekly	Single	Double/twin	Family	Private	Public	Evening meals From/Last order	Parking	Months open	Symbols
Bosville Hotel & Restaurant Bosville Terrace Tel. Portree 2846	4	3	4	9.50 / -	17.00 / -	12.75 / -	- / -	-	9	2	2	2	1700 / 2000	8	4-10	(symbols)
Coolin Hills Hotel Tel. Portree 2003	4	5	4	15.00 / 18.00	27.00 / 36.00	22.00 / 25.00	41.00 / 50.00	7	16	5	15	5	1830 / 2000	100	1-12	(symbols)

Meg & John Isles Welcome you to—

* *A delightful small hotel, ideally situated in Portree's main square.*

* *Good food and Wine.*

* *Licensed Restaurant.*

* *Central heating and all amenities with a high standard of decor throughout.*

Telephone: PORTREE 2129

Name and Address	Bedrooms	Services	Meals	Single room overnight (£min/£max)	Double/twin room overnight	Per person daily	Per person weekly	Single	Double/twin	Family	Private	Public	Evening meals From/Last order	Parking	Months open	Symbols
The Isles Hotel Tel. Portree 2129	3	3	4	10.75 / -	21.50 / -	- / -	- / -	4	6	1	-	4	1830 / 2030	-	4-10	(symbols)
King's Haven Hotel 11 Bosville Terrace Tel. Portree 2290/2228	3	3	4	- / -	29.00 / -	23.50 / -	164.50 / -	1	5	1	5	1	1930 / 2100	-	3-10	(symbols)
Portree Hotel Tel. Portree 2511	3	3	4	10.12 / -	20.24 / -	- / -	- / -	9	15	2	-	6	1830 / 2000	-	1-12	(symbols)

VAT is shown at 15%: changes in this rate may affect prices.

Name and Address	Map Ref				Prices					Rooms					Facilities			
TOWN County Establishment Address Telephone Telex		Bedrooms	Services	Meals	Bed and Breakfast			B & B and evening meal		No. of bed-rooms			No. of bath/ shower rooms		Evening meals	Parking (no. of cars)	Months open (1-12)	Symbols
					Single room overnight	Double/twin room overnight	Per person daily	Per person weekly	Single	Double/twin	Family	Private	Public				
PORTREE continued	3 D9				£min £max	£min £max	£min £max	£min £max						From Last order		Key on back fold-out	

ROSEDALE HOTEL
Telephone: (0478) 2531
Portree Isle of Skye LV51 9DB
20-bedroom, family-owned hotel with unrivalled waterfront situation. Tastefully and carefully modernised. Fully licensed with two modern bars. Two residents' lounges. Restaurant overlooking harbour. Colour brochure free.

Name and Address	Bedrooms	Services	Meals	Single room overnight	Double/twin room overnight	Per person daily	Per person weekly	Single	Double/twin	Family	Private	Public	Evening meals	Parking	Months open	Symbols
Rosedale Hotel Beaumont Crescent Tel. Portree 2531	3	3	4	17.00 18.00	26.00 33.00	21.00 26.00	140.00 175.00	4	15	2	18	4	1900 2000	12	5-10	
Royal Hotel Tel. Portree 2525	-	-	-	15.00 17.00	33.00 36.00	20.00 27.00	- -	6	17	3	17	2	1900 2030	28	1-12	
Tongadale Hotel Wentworth Street Tel. Portree 2115	3	4	6	9.50 -	16.95 -	14.00 -	- -	8	17	4	-	5	- 2200	-	1-12	
Almondbank Guest House Viewfield Road Tel. Portree 2696	3	3	2	7.50 9.00	15.00 18.00	12.00 13.50	- -	-	3	2	-	3	- 1800	6	4-10	
Craiglockhart Guest House Beaumont Crescent Tel. Portree 2233	3	3	2	8.50 8.50	17.00 19.00	13.50 15.80	85.00 95.00	2	4	2	2	3	1900 1900	4	1-12	
Dunalasdair Guest House Sluggans Tel. Portree 2893	3	2	2	7.00 8.00	14.00 16.00	12.00 13.00	78.00 85.00	-	4	1	-	2	1900 2000	8	1-12	
Springfield Guest House Tel. Portree 2505	3	4	2	9.20 9.20	18.40 18.40	14.95 14.95	- -	2	6	1	-	3	- 1830	20	1-12	
Woodside Guest House 2 Blaven Park Tel. Portree 2598	3	2	1	7.25 9.00	14.50 18.00	- -	- -	-	4	3	-	2	- -	15	1-12	

Scotland's Fishing Heritage

The sea has always played a vital part in the heritage of Scotland, this country with its wandering coastline and hundreds of islands. Today, for holidaymakers it means golden beaches, boat trips and birdwatching; for those who live on the coast it means a hard tradition of gaining a living from the sea.

You can learn about this tradition in the charming fishing villages on the coast, and in the fascinating museums which preserve it.

Write to the Scottish Tourist Board for a FREE pack telling you how to follow **SCOTLAND'S FISHING HERITAGE TRAIL.**

Name and Address	Map Ref	Bedrooms	Services	Meals	Single room overnight £min £max	Double/twin room overnight £min £max	Per person daily £min £max	Per person weekly £min £max	Single	Double/twin	Family	Private	Public	Evening meals (Last order)	Parking (no. of cars)	Months open (1-12)	Symbols
PORTSONACHAN **Argyll**	1 F3																

Portsonachan Hotel

Lochaweside, by Dalmally, Argyll PA33 1BL
Telephone: Kilchrenan (086 63) 224
Telegrams: 'Hotel' Portsonachan

Deep in the Western Highlands, yet easily accessible, this cosy Hotel nestles on the south side of Loch Awe. Ideal for most outdoor pursuits, or for simply relaxing, we offer superb cooking in comfortable surroundings.

Whether your interest is fishing, walking, boating or shooting, Christopher and Caroline Trotter will make sure that all your needs are catered for.

Christopher prepares a different menu daily, using the best of local produce in traditional recipes with a personal touch. Write or telephone for brochure, or to reserve accommodation.

Name and Address	Bedrooms	Services	Meals	Single room o/n £min £max	Double/twin room o/n £min £max	Per person daily £min £max	Per person weekly £min £max	Single	Double/twin	Family	Private	Public	Evening meals (Last order)	Parking	Months open	Symbols
Portsonachan Hotel Tel. Kilchrennan 224	3	4	4	- -	- -	22.00 25.50	138.60 160.65	2	15	2	3	6	2000 2100	20	1-12	
PORTSOY **Banffshire** 4 F7																
Boyne Hotel 2 North High Street Tel. Portsoy 2242	3	4	5	7.00 9.00	14.00 18.00	9.00 10.00	59.00 63.00	2	10	2	-	3	1800 2100	-	1-12	
POWFOOT, by Annan **Dumfriesshire** 2 C10																
Powfoot Golf Hotel Links Avenue DG12 5PN Tel. Cummertrees 254	3	3	4	12.00 17.00	23.00 29.00	19.00 24.00	126.00 161.00	3	16	1	7	3	1900 2030	40	1-12	
PRESTWICK **Ayrshire** 1 G7																
Auchencoyle Hotel 13 Links Road Tel. Prestwick 78316	3	3	4	9.00 10.75	18.00 21.50	12.50 14.25	78.75 89.75	2	1	3	3	1	1700 2100	20	1-12	
Carlton Hotel 187 Ayr Road Tel. Prestwick 76811	5	5	5	21.50 -	37.00 -	19.00 28.75	133.00 147.00	-	35	2	37	4	1900 2130	150	1-12	
Golf View Hotel 17 Links Road KA9 1QG Tel. Prestwick 77764	3	3	3	9.00 10.00	18.00 20.00	12.00 13.00	84.00 91.00	1	4	2	-	1	1800 1900	10	1-12	

VAT is shown at 15%: changes in this rate may affect prices.

| Name and Address | | | | Prices | | | | | B & B and evening meal | | | | Rooms | | | Facilities |
TOWN County — Establishment Address Telephone Telex	Map Ref	Bedrooms	Services / Meals	Single room overnight £min £max	Double/twin room overnight £min £max	Per person daily £min £max	Per person weekly £min £max	Per person weekly	Single	Double/twin	Family	Private	No. of bedrooms — Public / From Last order	No. of bath/shower rooms — Evening meals	Parking (no. of cars) / Months open (1-12)	Symbols

PRESTWICK continued — Map Ref 1 / G7 — Key on back fold-out

Establishment	Bedrooms	Services	Meals	Single overnight	Double/twin overnight	Per person daily	Per person weekly	Single	Double/twin	Family	Private	Public	From / Last order	Evening meals	Parking / Months	Symbols
Kincraig Hotel, 39 Ayr Road, KA9 1SY, Tel. Prestwick 79480	3	3	2	7.50 / 8.00	14.00 / 14.50	11.50 / 11.50	75.00 / 75.00	2	5	1	-	3	1800 / -	8	1-12	(symbols)
North Beach Hotel, 5-7 Link's Road, KA9 1QC, Tel. Prestwick 79069	3	4	4	9.50 / 10.50	18.00 / 18.00	14.00 / 15.00	82.50 / 84.00	2	6	1	-	3	1730 / 2000	20	1-12	(symbols)
Parkstone Hotel, Esplanade, KA9 1QN, Tel. Prestwick 77286	4	4	4	16.25 / -	27.25 / -	- / -	- / -	7	20	2	12	6	1700 / 2030	60	1-12	(symbols)

QUEENS HOTEL

The Esplanade Prestwick

The Queens Hotel is situated on the Esplanade enjoying a delightful view of the Firth of Clyde and Isle of Arran.

Many sporting facilities such as golf, fishing and sailing, etc., are available. An ideal centre for touring Burns Country. Prestwick International Airport is 1 mile away.

Bar Snacks. Table d'Hote Dinner. Last orders 9.30 p.m. Fully Licensed. T.V. Room. H. & C. in all rooms.

Write or Telephone: **PRESTWICK 70501** *for further details.*

Establishment	Bedrooms	Services	Meals	Single overnight	Double/twin overnight	Per person daily	Per person weekly	Single	Double/twin	Family	Private	Public	From / Last order	Evening meals	Parking / Months	Symbols
Queens Hotel, Esplanade, 34 Ardayre Road, KA9 1RO, Tel. Prestwick 70501	3	5	5	13.50 / -	27.00 / -	20.00 / -	115.00 / -	8	16	3	12	6	1900 / 2130	44	1-12	(symbols)
St Nicholas Hotel, 41 Ayr Road, Tel. Prestwick 79568	4	4	5	13.00 / 14.00	26.00 / -	16.00 / 17.00	112.00 / 119.00	3	7	3	4	3	1700 / 2100	50	1-12	(symbols)
Towans Hotel & Motel, Powmill Road, KA9 2NY, Tel. Prestwick 77831	4	5	5	12.50 / 14.50	22.00 / 24.50	- / -	- / -	7	40	8	36	5	1800 / 2030	100	1-12	(symbols)
Villa Marina Hotel, 19 Links Road, KA9 1QC, Tel. Prestwick 70396	3	4	2	8.50 / -	17.00 / -	11.50 / -	80.50 / -	1	3	1	-	1	1800 / 1830	9	1-12	(symbols)
Medwyn Guest House, 3 Regent Park, Station Road, KA9 1AQ, Tel. Prestwick 77204	3	3	2	7.50 / -	14.00 / -	10.00 / -	- / -	1	1	1	-	2	1730 / -	-	1-12	(symbols)

Name and Address	Map Ref	Bedrooms	Services	Meals	Single room overnight £min/£max	Double/twin room overnight £min/£max	Per person daily £min/£max	Per person weekly £min/£max	Single	Double/twin	Family	Private	Public	No. of bedrooms From/Last order	Evening meals	Parking (no. of cars)	Months open (1-12)	Symbols
QUENDALE Shetland	5 F6																	Key on back fold-out
Silverlea Guest House		-	-	-	9.00 / 10.00	16.00 / 18.00	14.00 / 15.00	84.00 / 90.00	3	1	-	-	2	1800 / 1930	-	1-12	
RAASAY, by Kyle Ross-shire	3 E9																	

Isle of Raasay Hotel

Isle of Raasay Hotel, Isle of Raasay,
by Kyle of Lochalsh IV40 8PB. Tel: 047 862 222

This New hotel overlooks the Narrows of Raasay with splendid views of the mountains of Skye. Raasay offers sea-angling, trout-fishing, hill walking etc. Interesting for amatear naturalists and geologists. Come over the sea from Sconser, Skye – only 15 minutes on the Car Ferry. Brochure from Isle of Raasay Hotel, Raasay, Kyle IV40 8PB.

Name and Address		Bedrooms	Services	Meals	Single room overnight	Double/twin room overnight	Per person daily	Per person weekly	Single	Double/twin	Family	Private	Public	No. of bedrooms	Evening meals	Parking	Months open	Symbols
Isle of Raasay Hotel IV40 8PB Tel. Raasay 222/226		5	4	4	14.00 / -	28.00 / -	23.00 / -	145.00 / -	1	11	-	12	-	1900 / 1945	12	4-9		
RANNOCH STATION Perthshire	1 G1																	
Moor of Rannoch Hotel PH17 2QA Tel. Bridge of Gaur 238		3	3	5	12.50 / 12.50	25.00 / 25.00	19.75 / 19.75	138.25 / 138.25	2	4	-	-	2	1900 / 2100	10	1-12		
RENFREW	1 H5																	
Dean Park Hotel 91 Glasgow Road Tel. 041 886 3771 Telex 779032		5	5	5	28.00 / -	34.00 / -	25.00 / -	150.00 / -	45	69	6	120	1	1830 / 2145	250	1-12		

Glynhill Hotel AA★★★

Paisley Rd. Renfrew
(nr. Glas. Airport)
041-886 5555

One mile from Glasgow Airport, 8 minutes via M8 to Glasgow Centre. Comfortable, privately owned & ideally based for touring. 80 bedrooms, all with private bathrooms, colour TV, tea/coffee makers and fresh fruit, 2 fourposter bedrooms. Specially priced family rooms.

Reduced terms FRI/SAT/SUN. Dinner, B & B from £20 per person per night. Dinner Dances every FRI & SAT. Gourmet restaurant, first class food and service. Reductions for children.

Name and Address		Bedrooms	Services	Meals	Single room overnight	Double/twin room overnight	Per person daily	Per person weekly	Single	Double/twin	Family	Private	Public	No. of bedrooms	Evening meals	Parking	Months open	Symbols
Glynhill Hotel 169 Paisley Road Tel. 041 886 5555 Telex 779536		6	5	5	19.00 / 28.00	25.50 / 34.50	21.25 / 25.75	144.00 / 198.50	2	53	25	80	2	1800 / 2230	200	1-12		

VAT is shown at 15%: changes in this rate may affect prices.

Name and Address	Map Ref	Bedrooms	Services	Meals	Single room overnight £min/£max	Double/twin room overnight £min/£max	Per person daily £min/£max	Per person weekly £min/£max	Single	Double/twin	Family	Private	Public	Evening meals From/Last order	Parking (no. of cars)	Months open (1-12)	Symbols
RENFREW continued	1 H5																
Stakis Normandy Hotel, Inchinnan Road, PA4 9EJ, Tel. 041 886 4100, Telex 778897		5	5	5	42.00 / -	50.00 / -	- / -	- / -	95	45	2	142	-	1830 / 2215	150	1-12	[symbols]
RHU Dunbartonshire	1 G4																
Ardencaple Hotel, Shore Road, G83 8LA, Tel. Rhu 820200		4	3	5	16.78 / 20.63	26.40 / 32.45	- / -	- / -	1	7	2	4	2	1900 / 2100	70	1-12	[symbols]
Rosslea Hall Hotel, Tel. Rhu 684/685/707		6	4	5	27.00 / 27.00	40.00 / 40.00	25.00 / 25.00	160.00 / 160.00	3	19	1	23	-	1900 / 2130	31	1-12	[symbols]
RICCARTON Midlothian	2 C5																
Heriot-Watt University, Controller of Catering & Residences, EH14 4AS, Tel. 031 449 5111		-	-	-	10.29 / -	18.64 / -	- / -	- / -	220	84	-	-	57	1715 / 1830	600	3-4, 7-10	[symbols]
ROCKCLIFFE, by Dalbeattie Kirkcudbrightshire	2 B10																
Barons Craig Hotel, DG5 4QE, Tel. Rockcliffe 225		4	4	4	21.50 / 33.30	39.90 / 59.00	29.30 / 42.40	- / -	8	16	3	20	4	1900 / 2100	54	4-10	[symbols]
ROGART Sutherland	4 B6																
Rovie Farm Guest House, 1V28 3TZ, Tel. Rogart 209		3	3	3	6.50 / 7.00	13.00 / 14.00	11.00 / 11.50	77.00 / 77.00	-	6	-	-	2	1830 / -	4	3-10	[symbols]
ROSEHALL Sutherland	4 A6																
Achness House Hotel, IV27 4BD, Tel. Rosehall 239		-	-	-	15.50 / 20.50	31.00 / 32.00	23.00 / 28.00	154.00 / 189.00	2	10	-	7	2	1930 / -	-	3-10	[symbols]
ROSEHEARTY, by Fraserburgh Aberdeenshire	4 G7																
Bay Hotel, The Square, AB4 4JL, Tel. Rosehearty 393		3	5	5	9.00 / 16.00	- / -	- / -	- / -	-	8	2	-	2	1830 / 2100	40	1-12	[symbols]
Cliff View Hotel, 1 Cairnhill Road, AB4 4JU, Tel. Rosehearty 238		-	-	-	- / -	20.00 / -	- / -	- / -	1	4	-	-	1	1830 / 2030	-	1-12	[symbols]

Name and Address					Prices								Rooms			Facilities
TOWN County / Establishment Address Telephone Telex	Map Ref	Bedrooms	Services	Meals	Bed and Breakfast				B & C and evening meal				No. of bed-rooms	No. of bath/ shower rooms		**Facilities**
					Single room overnight	Double/twin room overnight	Per person daily	Per person weekly	Single	Double/twin	Family	Private	Public / Evening meals	Parking (no. of cars)	Months open (1-12)	Symbols
					£min £max	£min £max	£min £max	£min £max					From Last order			Key on back fold-out

ROSEMARKIE — Ross-shire — Map Ref 4 B8

Marine Hotel
Rosemarkie Ross-shire

This long established golfing and family Hotel, privately owned and personally run, is beautifully situated on the southern shores of the Black Isle. There are over 50 bedrooms, many with private bathroom and fine 18 hole golf course, tennis, sailing, sandy beaches and safe bathing all available nearby.

Special terms—April, May, June, Sept., and for children. Write for brochure or telephone Fortrose (0381) 20253.

Name and Address	Map Ref	Bedrooms	Services	Meals	Single overnight	Double/twin overnight	Per person daily	Per person weekly	Single	Double/twin	Family	Private	Public	No. bed-rooms	No. bath/shower	Months open
Marine Hotel IV10 8UL Tel. Fortrose 20253		3	4	4	9.50 -	19.00 -	16.50 -	98.50 -	12	38	4	13	8	1915 2030	50	4-9
ROSLIN Midlothian — 2 D5																
Royal Hotel		3	4	5	13.00 15.00	20.00 22.00	19.00 21.00	- -	2	5	1	1	1	1800 2230	8	1-12
ROSYTH Fife — 2 C4																
Wendonana Private Hotel Kings Road Tel. Inverkeithing 415298		3	2	3	11.50	-	-	-	-	6	-	-	2	1800 2000	5	1-12
ROTHES Moray — 4 D8																
Rothes Glen Hotel IV33 7AH Tel. Rothes 254		4	4	5	22.20 -	40.40 -	-	-	1	15	3	11	5	1900 2030	30	3-11
Station Hotel 51 New Street IV33 7BJ Tel. Rothes 240		3	3	4	10.00 11.00	19.00 20.00	16.00 18.00	105.00 110.00	4	6	-	-	3	1900 2100	8	1-12
ROTHESAY Isle of Bute — 1 F5																
Ardmory House Hotel Ardmory Road, Ardbeg Tel. Rothesay 2346		4	4	5	10.50 -	21.00 -	17.00 -	105.00 -	-	2	4	6	-	1900 2130	20	1-12
Ardyne Hotel 38 Mount Stuart Road Tel. Rothesay 2052		3	3	2	7.50 -	15.00 -	10.50 -	60.00 -	2	8	2	6	2	1800 -	2	5-9
Bayview Private Hotel 21-22 Mountstuart Road Tel. Rothesay 2339		3	3	2	8.50 9.00	17.00 18.00	11.50 12.50	77.00 84.00	3	17	-	-	5	1800 -	10	4-10

Name and Address	Map Ref	Bedrooms	Services	Meals	Single room overnight (£min/£max)	Double/twin room overnight (£min/£max)	Per person daily (£min/£max)	Per person weekly (£min/£max)	Single	Double/twin	Family	Private	Public	Evening meals (From/Last order)	Parking (no. of cars)	Months open (1-12)	Symbols
ROTHESAY continued	1 F5				£min £max	£min £max	£min £max	£min £max						From Last order			Key on back fold-out
Blair-Bank Private Hotel 3 Mountstuart Road Tel. Rothesay 2277		2	2	2	7.00 / 7.50	- / -	9.00 / 9.50	- / -	1	3	3	-	1	1730 / -	-	4-9	
Craigmore Hotel Crichton Road Tel. Rothesay 3533		2	3	3	6.50 / 8.50	12.00 / 15.00	8.00 / 10.50	45.00 / 69.00	5	15	6	-	4	1800 / 2130	6	4-10	
George Hotel 25 Argyle Street Tel. Rothesay 2198		-	-	-	9.50 / 10.50	17.00 / 19.00	12.00 / 14.00	73.00 / 78.00	4	12	2	-	4	- / 1800	-	4-10	
Glenburn Hotel Glenburn Road Tel. Rothesay 2500 Telex 75160		4	5	5	17.00 / -	34.00 / -	- / -	- / -	13	83	7	45	9	1900 / 2030	60	1-12	
Grand Marine Hotel Argyle Street Tel. Rothesay 3145		3	4	4	9.60 / 10.60	19.20 / 21.20	12.20 / 14.00	85.40 / 98.00	5	23	3	3	5	1800 / 1900	-	4-10	
Hillside Hotel Serpentine Road Tel. Rothesay 3675		3	3	2	8.50 / -	16.00 / -	10.50 / -	70.00 / -	-	6	2	-	1	1800 / -	20	1-12	
Invercraig Hotel 39 Mount Stuart Road Tel. Rothesay 2323		2	2	2	8.50 / 9.50	17.00 / 19.00	11.00 / 12.00	77.00 / 84.00	2	8	2	-	2	1800 / -	5	1-12	
Royal Hotel Albert Place Tel. Rothesay 3044		3	5	6	10.50 / -	21.00 / -	14.00 / -	- / -	2	14	5	-	8	1800 / 2130	-	1-12	
St Ebba Hotel 37 Mountstuart Road Tel. Rothesay 2683		3	4	4	12.50 / 14.50	23.00 / 28.00	18.50 / 20.50	91.00 / 115.00	6	7	3	8	2	1800 / 1900	6	4-10	
Victoria Hotel 55 Victoria Street Tel. Rothesay 3553		-	-	-	10.50 / -	21.00 / -	14.50 / -	- / -	4	17	2	1	5	1900 / 2100	-	1-12	
Kinnell House 1 Argyle Place Tel. Rothesay 2669		3	3	2	- / -	13.50 / 15.00	8.00 / 8.50	56.00 / 59.50	-	2	1	-	1	1800 / -	3	4-10	
Lyndhurst Guest House 29 Battery Place Tel. Rothesay 4799		3	3	3	7.50 / -	15.00 / -	10.00 / -	70.00 / -	1	5	1	-	2	1730 / 1800	4	1-12	

Glenburn Hotel
Rothesay, Isle of Bute

Overlooking the Kyles of Bute, this family hotel has many facilities such as tennis, table tennis, putting, billiard room, badminton, free golf and also free swimming at the pool 80 yards from the hotel. A holiday with something different, our island hotel will make your stay comfortable, complete with good service and good food. Full details and brochure from

The GLENBURN HOTEL, Rothesay.
Tel: (0700) 2500.

Name and Address	Map Ref	Bedrooms	Services	Meals	Single room overnight £min £max	Double/twin room overnight £min £max	Per person daily £min £max	Per person weekly £min £max	Single	Double/twin	Family	Private	Public	Evening meals From Last order	Parking (no. of cars)	Months open (1-12)	Symbols
ROTHESAY continued	1 F5																Key on back fold-out

Special Packaged Offer.

7 days dinner, B & B, 6 lite bite vouchers, 6 days entertainment and ferry travel to the island, all-in from £69 inclusive. **MORNINGSIDE** is entirely reserved yet only minutes from pier, town centre and golf course. Bedrooms are well appointed including tea makers, large comfortable lounge with adjoining TV room and central heating.

Mrs W. Shaw, Morningside, Mount Pleasant, Rothesay, Isle of Bute. Telephone Rothesay (0700) 3526 for brochures.

Name and Address	Map Ref	Bedrooms	Services	Meals	Single room overnight	Double/twin room overnight	Per person daily	Per person weekly	Single	Double/twin	Family	Private	Public	Evening meals From / Last order	Parking	Months open	Symbols
Morningside Guest House 1 Mountpleasant Road Tel. Rothesay 3526		3	3	3	7.00 7.00	12.00 14.00	10.00 10.00	63.00 65.00	1	6	2	-	3	1830 1900	-	4-10	T 🐕 🛏 ♿ 🪑 V ♻
Sunnyside Guest House 12 Argyle Place Tel. Rothesay 2351		2	3	2	6.50 7.00	13.00 14.00	9.00 9.50	60.00 65.00	1	3	2	-	1	1730 -	-	4-9	🐕 🛏 M ♿ V
ROTHIEMAY, Huntly **Aberdeenshire**	4 F8																
Forbes Arms Hotel AB5 5LT Tel. Rothiemay 248		2	3	3	12.65 12.65	25.20 25.20	20.70 20.70	141.68 141.68	2	2	-	-	1	1900 1900	10	3-10	T 🚿 🍷 🐕 🛏 M ♿ C V
ROUSAY **Orkney**	5 B10																
Taversoe Hotel KW17 2PT Tel. Rousay 325		3	4	3	8.50 -	17.00 -	14.00 -	98.00 -	-	2	-	-	1	1900 -	8	1-12	T 🚿 🍷 🐕 🛏 ♿ V ♻

PAY A VISIT TO ROBERT BURNS' COUNTRY

Travel through some of Scotland's most attractive countryside, in the south west, and follow The Burns Heritage Trail. Easy to get to, it has something to interest everyone.

Send today for your free leaflet with map.

VAT is shown at 15%: changes in this rate may affect prices.

Name and Address	Map Ref			Prices					Rooms								Facilities
TOWN County / Establishment Address Telephone Telex		Bedrooms / Services / Meals		Bed and Breakfast			B & B and evening meal		No. of bedrooms			No. of bath/shower rooms					Symbols
				Single room overnight	Double/twin room overnight	Per person daily	Per person weekly		Single	Double/twin	Family	Private	Public	Evening meals / Last order	Parking (no. of cars)	Months open (1-12)	
				£min £max	£min £max	£min £max	£min £max							From Last order			Key on back fold-out

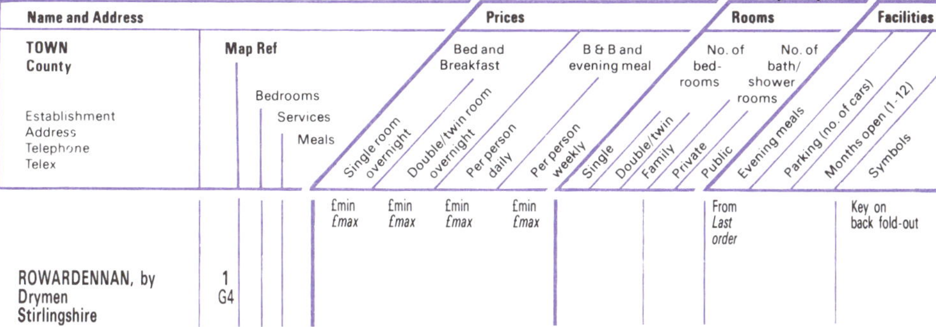

ROWARDENNAN HOTEL

COME UP TO SCOTLAND AND SEE LOCH LOMOND. Stay at the famous ROWARDENNAN HOTEL situated on the loch shore and in the lee of Ben Lomond.

This is a family hotel designed for people who love walking – hill climbing – boating – fishing – and the great outdoors.

All rooms have central heating. Public Rooms and Bars have log fires. Our Dining Room serves Home Baking and our extensive menu includes most Scottish Traditional Dishes.

A Warm Welcome awaits you at Rowardennan Hotel, Rowardennan by Drymen, Glasgow G63 0AR.

Send for our brochure – it may alter your holiday plans this summer. **Write or phone 036 087 273.**

Our weekly terms are unbeatable.

Town / Establishment	Map Ref	Bedrooms	Services	Meals	Single room overnight	Double/twin room overnight	Per person daily	Per person weekly	B&B eve (wk)	Single	Double/twin	Family	Private	Public	Evening meals (last order)	Parking	Months open	Symbols
ROWARDENNAN, by Drymen Stirlingshire	1 G4				£min £max	£min £max	£min £max	£min £max							From Last order			
Rowardennan Hotel Loch Lomond G63 0AR Tel. Balmaha 273		3	4	5	12.00 -	20.00 -	15.00 -	- -	-	7	2	1	3		1930 2150	50	3-10	T ♨ ♀ 🐕 ⚕ 🎱 ♿ ⚡ C 🏨 V ☕ ♪ ⚘
ROY BRIDGE Inverness-shire	3 H12																	
Kinchellie Croft Motel PH31 4AW Tel. Spean Bridge 265		2	3	3	8.00 9.00	15.00 16.00	12.50 13.00	79.00 82.00	2	6	2	-	2		1900 -	10	4-10	🐕 ⚕ M ♿ 🍳 C ❋ ☕
Roy Bridge Hotel Tel. Spean Bridge 236		3	3	3	7.95 7.95	15.90 15.90	13.45 13.45	90.00 90.00	-	5	2	-	2		1830 2030	20	1-12	T ♨ ♀ 🐕 ⚕ 🎱 ♿ ❋ 🏨 V ♪
Stronlossit Hotel Tel. Spean Bridge 253		-	-	-	9.50 9.50	17.00 17.00	14.00 14.00	98.00 98.00	-	11	2	-	2		1900 2100	40	1-12	T ♨ ♀ 🐕 ⚕ 🎱 ♿ ☐ 🍳 ⚡ ❋ V ☕
SALEN Isle of Mull, Argyll	1 D2																	
The Craig Hotel Tel. Aros 347		3	3	3	12.00 -	21.00 -	18.00 -	120.00 -	-	7	-	-	2		1915 -	8	1-12	♨ ♀ 🐕 ⚕ ♿ 🍳 ⚡ C V ☕ ✗ ✉

Name and Address	Map Ref	Bedrooms	Services	Meals	Prices					Rooms							Facilities			
TOWN / County / Establishment / Address / Telephone / Telex					Bed and Breakfast — Single room overnight	Double/twin room overnight	Per person daily	Per person weekly	B & B and evening meal — Single	Double/twin	Family	Private	No. of bedrooms — Public	No. of bath/shower rooms	Evening meals	Parking (no. of cars)	Months open (1-12)	Symbols		
SALEN continued	1 D2				£min £max	£min £max	£min £max	£min £max					From Last order				Key on back fold-out			
Glenforsa Hotel / PA72 6JN / Tel. Aros 377		3	3	4	15.00 17.50	27.00 32.00	21.00 23.50	135.00 150.00	-	14	-	7	2	1900 2030	29	4-10			
Salen Hotel / Tel. Aros 324		3	4	4	9.00 10.00	18.00 20.00	14.00 16.00	98.00 112.00	5	6	2	-	3	1900 2000	40	1-12			
SALTCOATS / Ayrshire	1 G6																		
Stanley Hotel / Ardrossan Road / Tel. Saltcoats 68866		4	3	4	10.50 12.50	16.50 18.50	- -	- -	1	5	-	2	1	1900 2000	20	1-12			
St Francis Guest House / 22 Montgomerie Crescent / Tel. Saltcoats 62785		-	-	-	6.00	12.00	- -	- -	3	2	2	-	-	- -	-	-			
SANDAY / Orkney	5 C10																		
Belsair Guest House / KW17 2BJ / Tel. Sanday 206		1	3	3	6.50 -	13.00 -	10.00 -	70.00 -	1	2	-	-	1	1800 -	3	1-12			
SANDWICK, by Stromness / Orkney	5 A11																		
Keldroseed Guest House / KW16 3HY / Tel. Sandwick (Orkney) 628		3	3	3	9.00 -	18.00 -	13.50 -	84.00 -	-	3	-	-	1	2000 2200	5	1-12			
SANQUHAR / Dumfriesshire	2 A8																		
Mennockfoot Lodge Hotel / Tel. Sanquhar 382		3	4	4	13.00 14.00	18.50 20.50	18.00 -	- -	-	8	1	3	3	1900 2045	25	1-12			

Delightfully situated in secluded grounds by Sound of Mull and Forsa River with own Sea Trout and Salmon fishing free to guests. Good Loch and Sea fishing also available. Splendid centre for touring, walking and climbing.

14 twin and double bedrooms, 7 with private bathrooms.

Magnificent views from all public rooms. Ample space for private parking. Very good food and varied menu with well stocked wine cellar. Fully licensed. Excellent airstrip ½ mile long, always available for private aircraft. Brochure and particulars of car ferry services from resident proprietors..

ATTRACTIVE NORWEGIAN LOG HOTEL

Ashley Courtenay, Egon Ronay and Taste of Scotland.

Mr. & Mrs. R. Scott-Howitt. Tel: AROS (06803) 377

Isle of Mull GLENFORSA HOTEL By Salen

VAT is shown at 15%: changes in this rate may affect prices.

Name and Address		Map Ref				Prices					Rooms						Facilities	
TOWN County Establishment Address Telephone Telex			Bedrooms	Services	Meals	Bed and Breakfast		B & B and evening meal			No. of bedrooms		No. of bath/shower rooms					
						Single room overnight	Double/twin room overnight	Per person daily	Per person weekly	Single	Double/twin	Family	Private	Public	Evening meals	Parking (no. of cars)	Months open (1-12)	Symbols
SANQUHAR continued		2 A8				£min £max	£min £max	£min £max	£min £max					From Last order				Key on back fold-out

NITHSDALE HOTEL
Sanquhar   Tel. 06592 506

Fully Licensed and Residential Hotel
AA ★ RAC ★ RSAC
Recommended by British Relais Routiers. Ideal small country hotel for walking, golfing and fishing in the River Nith for salmon and trout — Local Angling Association has 12 miles of water. Map of river on request; also brochure.

Resident Proprietors: Margaret and Robert Spiers

Name and Address	Bedrooms	Services	Meals	Single room overnight	Double/twin overnight	Per person daily	Per person weekly	Single	Double/twin	Family	Private	Public	From/Last order	Evening meals	Parking	Months open	Symbols
Nithsdale Hotel DG4 6DJ Tel. Sanquhar 506	3	3	4	9.75 10.75	19.50 21.50	15.25 16.25	118.00 125.00	1	3	2	-	1	1800 2030	-	1-12		T £
Drumbringan Guest House 53 Castle Street Tel. Sanquhar 409	-	-	-	7.00 7.50	14.00 15.00	10.50 12.00	72.00 82.00	-	2	2	-	1	1900 2000	5	1-12		
SCARINISH Isle of Tiree, Argyll	1 A2																

Tiree Lodge Hotel
ISLE OF TIREE, INNER HEBRIDES PA77

Come to Tiree for a holiday with a difference. Panoramic scenery, sandy beaches, and enjoy the comfort and cuisine offered at Tiree Lodge Hotel. Fully licensed, TV Room, all rooms centrally heated, H & C or Private Bathroom. Facilities include Golf, Bikes, Car Hire and Sea Angling and Diving Parties of 10 aboard the 26' Fishing Vessel "Frigg"

Further details write for Colour Brochure.

Telephone 08792 368.

Name and Address	Bedrooms	Services	Meals	Single room overnight	Double/twin overnight	Per person daily	Per person weekly	Single	Double/twin	Family	Private	Public	From/Last order	Evening meals	Parking	Months open	Symbols
Tiree Lodge Hotel Tel. Scarinish 353/368/317	3	3	3	10.00 11.00	20.00 22.00	16.00 -	96.00 -	1	8	1	1	2	1900 -	15	1-12		
SCARISTA Harris, Western Isles	3 B7																
Scarista House Tel. Scarista 238				20.00 20.00	40.00 40.00	32.00 32.00	196.00 196.00	-	7	-	7	-	2000 -	6	1-12		
SCONE Perthshire	2 C2																
Wheel Inn Motor Hotel Angus Road PH2 6RA Tel. Scone 51518	5	5	5	14.00 20.00	22.00 30.00	22.00 28.00	154.00 196.00	-	13	1	14	-	1900 2230	200	1-12		

Prices shown are for guidance only. Please send SAE with each enquiry.

Name and Address	Map Ref	Bedrooms	Services	Meals	Single room overnight	Double/twin room overnight	Per person daily	Per person weekly	Single	Double/twin	Family	Private	Public	Evening meals (From/Last order)	Parking (no. of cars)	Months open (1-12)	Symbols
SCOURIE Sutherland	3 G4				£min £max	£min £max	£min £max	£min £max						From Last order			Key on back fold-out

Name and Address	Map Ref	Bedrooms	Services	Meals	Single room overnight	Double/twin room overnight	Per person daily	Per person weekly	Single	Double/twin	Family	Private	Public	Evening meals	Parking	Months open	Symbols
Eddrachilles Hotel Badcall Bay IV27 4TH Tel. Scourie 2080		4	4	4	15.60 19.20	26.00 32.40	18.40 24.70	130.00 143.00	-	9	1	10	-	1830 2030	20	1-12	
Scourie Hotel IV27 4SX Tel. Scourie 2396		4	3	4	10.50 14.00	21.00 28.00	16.50 20.50	115.50 150.50	9	13	1	11	3	1950 2050	30	3-10	
SCOUSBURGH, South Mainland Shetland	5 F6																
Spiggie Lodge Hotel Tel. Sumburgh 60563		3	4	5	15.00 -	28.00 -	- -	- -	-	4	-	-	2	1930 2130	6	1-12	
SCRABSTER, by Thurso Caithness	4 C2																
Scrabster Hotel Tel. Thurso 2814		3	3	4	9.05 9.05	18.10 18.10	11.55 19.00	- -	1	5	-	-	2	1900 2100	10	1-12	
SEAMILL Ayrshire	1 G6																
Galleon Inn Tel. West Kilbride 822375		3	4	4	9.00 13.50	17.00 26.00	12.00 20.00	- -	4	3	-	-	1	1830 2030	25	1-12	
SELKIRK	2 E7																
County Hotel High Street Tel. Selkirk 21233		-	-	-	9.50 -	19.00 -	13.50 -	- -	1	5	1	-	1	1800 2100	6	1-12	
Glen Hotel Yarrow Terrace Tel. Selkirk 20259		3	3	5	10.00 -	20.00 -	13.75 -	- -	2	4	2	-	3	- -	12	-	

VAT is shown at 15%: changes in this rate may affect prices.

Name and Address	Map Ref	Bedrooms	Services	Meals	Bed and Breakfast Single room overnight £min £max	Double/twin room overnight £min £max	Per person daily £min £max	Per person weekly £min £max	B & B and evening meal Single	Double/twin	Family	Private	No. of bedrooms Public	No. of bath/shower rooms From Last order	Evening meals	Parking (no. of cars)	Months open (1-12)	Symbols
SELKIRK continued	2 E7				£min £max	£min £max	£min £max	£min £max					From Last order				Key on back fold-out
Heatherlie Hill Hotel Heatherlie Park Tel. Selkirk 21200		3	4	4	11.00 12.00	20.00 22.00	16.50 18.00	112.00 126.00	1	2	2	1 1	1900 2000	15	1-12		
Philipburn House Hotel Tel. Selkirk 20747/21690 **(See ad. p. 264)**		4	4	5	18.00 25.00	24.00 36.00	25.00 36.00	- -	-	4	12	12 1	1930 2100	15	2-12		
SHIELDAIG, Strathcarron Ross-shire	3 F8																

Tigh an Eilean
Shieldaig, Strathcarron, Ross-shire
Tel. Shieldaig (052 05) 251

A small family-run hotel situated on the shore of Loch Torridon amidst magnificent mountain scenery. All comforts, good home-cooking, licensed. Perfect centre for either hill-walking or exploring by car. Weekly terms available. Ring or write for brochure. A.A. Listed.

Name and Address	Map Ref	Bedrooms	Services	Meals	Single room overnight £min £max	Double/twin room overnight £min £max	Per person daily £min £max	Per person weekly £min £max	Single	Double/twin	Family	Private	Public	Bath/shower From Last order	Evening meals	Parking	Months open	Symbols
Tigh-an-Eilean Hotel IV54 8XN Tel. Shieldaig 251		3	3	3	13.00 14.00	24.00 26.00	19.50 20.50	122.85 129.15	3	9	1	- 6	1900 2000	20	5-10		
SKEABOST, by Portree Isle of Skye, Inverness-shire	3 D9																
Skeabost House Hotel Tel. Skeabost Bridge 202		3	5	4	15.00 20.00	28.00 40.00	24.00 29.00	164.50 199.50	7	16	3	16 4	1900 2000	64	4-10		
SKELMORLIE Ayrshire	1 G5																
Manor Park Hotel Tel. Wemyss Bay 520832		6	4	5	22.00 -	- 44.00	31.00 -	164.00 -	3	11	4	17 1	1900 2130	120	2-12		
SLEAT Isle of Skye, Inverness-shire	3 E11																
Hotel Eilean Iarmain Camus Chros Tel. Isle Ornsay 266 Telex 75252		3	3	4	11.00 -	22.00 -	20.00 -	- -	2	11	-	- 4	1930 2030	10	1-12		
SLIGACHAN Isle of Skye, Inverness-shire	3 D9																
Sligachan Hotel Tel. Sligachan 204		3	3	4	17.50 19.00	34.00 38.00	25.50 27.00	164.50 178.50	8	15	-	9 5	1900 2030	26	5-10		

Prices shown are for guidance only. Please send SAE with each enquiry.

PHILIPBURN HOUSE HOTEL
Selkirk

Resident Owners: Jim and Anne Hill

Recommended: Egon Ronay, Ashley Courtenay Gourmet Guides

PHILIPBURN is a lovely 18th century house standing in its own wooded grounds high above the historic vales of Ettrick and Yarrow and with holiday thoughts turning towards Scotland Jim and Anne Hill would love to extend a warm welcome to you to come and stay at Philipburn in the heart of romantic Scottish Borderland.

The charming old house, built in 1751, some years after Covenanters and Royalists fought it out at the Battle of Philiphaugh, the site of which lies in the fields below the estate, was recently carefully and sypathetically modified to become the distinguished Scottish family hotel now famous for the warm hospitality, comfort and perfect cooking.

We have loads to keep the children happy during the

day from tree house to trampoline but in the evening with junior snug in his pine bunk and after a last dip in the heated swimming pool, stroll down to the Souters Bar, always alive with talk and laughter, sit back around the log fires and examine the mouth watering menu and the famous wine list with the blissful realisation that a whole holiday at Philipburn lies before you.

We hope that you will come and stay with us in this most beautiful and unspoiled part of the country and when you are not exploring the ancient castles or abbeys or fishing in the nearby rivers, you'll find that we have:

* Gardens and Woodlands in which to roam
* A heated and filtered swimming pool
* Playground and adventure area with woodland houses, chutes, sandpit, trampoline
* Games room and table tennis
* Outdoor badminton in our sheltered garden
* Riding and fishing
* Baby listening in every bedroom or suite
* Laundry room with coin operated washing machines, spin drier, ironing
* Catering arranged for children and babies, high chairs, etc.
* Shop with all the 'necessaries' you are bound to forget
* The Cuisine ranging from perfectly cooked family fare at lunchtime with home-made soups, rich stews and fruit-filled pies to dinner service where freshly caught fish may be flamed in brandy and simmered in rich wine sauce or young grouse stuffed with wild raspberries and wrapped in bacon and whisky-soaked sprigs of heather – the sweet trolley is always a masterpiece of confection making a wonderfully elegant ending to your meal.

For colour brochure and further information
write to Jim and Anne Hill or telephone 0750 20747 · 21690

Name and Address	Map Ref	Bedrooms	Services	Meals	Single room overnight £min £max	Double/twin room overnight £min £max	Per person daily £min £max	Per person weekly £min £max	Single	Double/twin	Family	Private	Public	From Last order	Evening meals	Parking (no. of cars) / Months open (1-12)	Symbols
SMA'GLEN, Crieff **Perthshire**	2 B2																Key on back fold-out
Foulford Inn PH7 3LN Tel. Crieff 2407		3	3	5	9.50 -	19.00 25.00	12.50 16.50	78.00 106.00	4	7	-	1	3	1630 2200	50	1-12	🐾🍷🐕🎿 🛏🛁♿ⓒ ❄🎱Ⓥ☕ 🏓🎿🅺
SOUTH QUEENSFERRY **West Lothian**	2 C4																

Forth Bridges Moat House

South Queensferry, West Lothian. Tel: 031-331 1199.

The Sign of Courtesy

Offering a unique location overlooking the Forth Road and Rail Bridges.
The hotel is a modern 3 star. All 108 bedrooms have private bathroom, colour TV, radio and telephone.
Choice of 2 restaurants. The Pantile offering à la carte cuisine and the En Route for a quick snack. 2 bars and a snooker room.

Name and Address	Map Ref	Bedrooms	Services	Meals	Single room overnight	Double/twin room overnight	Per person daily	Per person weekly	Single	Double/twin	Family	Private	Public	From Last order	Evening meals	Months open	Symbols
Forth Bridges Moat House EH30 9SF Tel. 031 331 1199 Telex 727430		6	5	5	38.50 -	49.85 -	46.25 -	-	15	78	15	108	-	1845 2145	100	1-12	
Hawes Inn Tel. 031 331 1990		2	2	5	19.00 -	29.00 -	-	-	4	3	-	-	4	1830 2130	80	1-12	
SOUTHEND, by **Campbeltown** **Argyll**	1 D8																
Keil Hotel Tel. Southend 253		3	4	5	11.00 16.00	22.00 26.00	16.00 19.00	105.00 120.00	2	13	3	5	8	1930 2130	40	1-12	
SOUTHERNESS **Kirkcudbrightshire**	2 B10																
Paul Jones Hotel DG2 8AZ Tel. Kirkbean 205		4	1	4	10.00 -	20.00 -	-	-	-	7	-	7	-	1800 2130	30	1-12	
SPEAN BRIDGE **Inverness-shire**	3 H12																
Letterfinlay Lodge Hotel Tel. Invergloy 222		4	4	4	12.00	22.00	20.00	-	2	12	1	5	6	1900 2030	100	3-10	

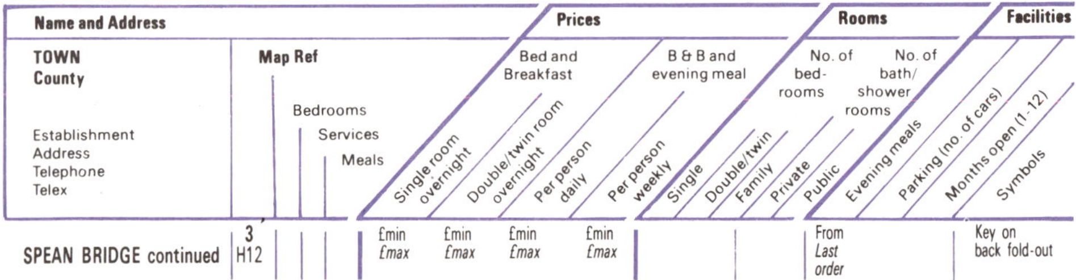

HOLIDAYS IN THE SPEAN BRIDGE HOTEL

Inverness-Shire. Tel: 039781 250.

Relax before the warmth of open log fires, enjoy good food and comfortable accommodation. Fishing on the River Spean; Golf on our 'local' 9 hole 'challenge'; Mountain climb or walk the Ben Nevis range — or just simply sightsee the breathtaking views all around. From here you are within two hours drive from the Isle of Skye, Inverness, Aviemore, Mallaig and Oban; with Ben Nevis, Fort William, Glencoe and Loch Ness so close what more can you ask?

Hotel Facilities Include: Lounge, T.V. Lounge, Table Tennis, Memberhip of Golf Course, Fishing 'rights', Two Bars, Ballroom and Dining Room, A Self Catering Flat and 24 bedrooms, 70% with Private Bathroom.

For further details write or telephone Bruce and Mairi Murray, Spean Bridge Hotel.

Name and Address	Map Ref	Bedrooms	Services	Meals	Single room overnight £min/£max	Double/twin room overnight £min/£max	Per person daily £min/£max	Per person weekly (B&B) £min/£max	B & B and evening meal per person weekly	Single	Double/twin	Family	Private	Public	Evening meals From/Last order	Parking	Months open	Symbols
SPEAN BRIDGE continued	3 / H12																	
Spean Bridge Hotel Tel. Spean Bridge 250		4	6	5	11.50/13.50	23.00/29.00	19.50/21.50	120.00/140.00		5	15	4	16	5	1730/2200	40	1-12	(facility symbols)
Spean Bridge Motor Inn		3	4	5	7.00/8.00	14.00/16.00	9.50/11.00	65.00/75.00	-	-	9	3	2	2	1600/2300	42	3-11	(facility symbols)
Barbagiani Guest House Tirindrish Tel. Spean Bridge 437		3	2	2	-/-	13.00/13.00	11.50/11.50	77.00/77.00	-	-	4	1	-	2	1930/1900	12	1-12	(facility symbols)
Coire Glas Guest House Tel. Spean Bridge 272		3	3	4	7.50/-	13.00/-	11.50/-	75.00/75.00	1	1	10	2	2	3	1830/1915	20	3-11	(facility symbols)
Druimandarroch Guest House PH34 4EU Tel. Spean Bridge 335		2	3	4	9.00/-	13.00/-	11.50/-	75.00/-	-	-	4	3	-	2	1930/1900	12	3-12	(facility symbols)
Forest Lodge Guest House South Laggan PH34 4EA Tel. Invergarry 219		3	3	2	9.00/9.00	22.00/22.00	11.00/11.00	73.50/73.50	-	-	5	2	-	2	1930/1930	9	2-11	(facility symbols)
Lesanne Guest House Tel. Spean Bridge 231		3	3	3	8.50/-	13.00/-	11.50/-	80.00/-	-	-	4	1	-	2	1900/1830	8	4-10	(facility symbols)
ST ANDREWS Fife	2 / E3																	
Ardgowan Hotel 2 Playfair Terrace, North Street Tel. St Andrews 72970		3	3	5	10.00/14.00	20.00/28.00	13.00/18.00	85.00/125.00		4	10	2	1	3	1700/2100	-	1-12	(facility symbols)
Argyle House Private Hotel 127 North Street Tel. St Andrews 73387/77007		3	4	2	8.00/11.00	16.00/22.00	13.00/16.00	85.00/105.00		2	12	4	-	6	1800/1800	-	4-10	(facility symbols)

VAT is shown at 15%: changes in this rate may affect prices.

Name and Address	Map Ref			Prices				B & B and evening meal					Rooms			Facilities
TOWN / County / Establishment / Address / Telephone / Telex		Bedrooms / Services / Meals		Bed and Breakfast — Single room overnight	Double/twin room overnight	Per person daily	Per person weekly	Single	Double/twin	Family	Private	Public	No. of bedrooms — Evening meals	No. of bath/shower rooms — Parking (no. of cars)	Months open (1-12)	Symbols
ST ANDREWS continued	2			£min / £max	£min / £max	£min / £max	£min / £max						From / Last order			Key on back fold-out
Arran House / 5 Murray Park / Tel. St Andrews 74724	3	2	1	7.50 / 9.00	14.00 / 18.00	- / -	- / -	-	3	3	-	2	- / -	-	1-12	�”🖼♿
Hazelbank Hotel / 28 The Scores / KY16 9AS / Tel. St Andrews 72466	3	4	3	7.00 / 10.00	15.00 / 20.00	12.00 / 15.00	70.00 / 95.00	2	5	3	-	4	1800 / 1830	-	1-12	T 🐕 🖼 ♿ ▭ C V
Kinburn Hotel / Double Dykes Road / KY16 9DS / Tel. St Andrews 73620	3	3	4	12.75 / 12.75	23.50 / 28.00	17.00 / 19.25	102.00 / 116.00	11	11	2	8	6	1900 / -	25	1-12	🖼♿ ✳ V
Links Hotel & Niblick Restaurant / Golf Place / Tel. St Andrews 72059	6	5	5	20.00 / 24.00	32.00 / 38.00	26.50 / -	- / -	2	4	-	6	-	1800 / 2100	-	1-12	T 🖼♿ ● ☎ ▭ V
Old Course Hotel / Tel. St Andrews 74371 / Telex 76280	6	6	6	- / 48.00	- / 85.00	- / 55.00	330.00 / -	5	120	-	125	-	1900 / 2200	150	1-12	T 🖼♿ ● ☎ ▭ C ✳ V
Rufflets Hotel / Strathkinness Low Road / KY16 9TX / Tel. St Andrews 72594	6	4	5	25.00 / 25.00	42.00 / 42.00	33.00 / 33.00	210.00 / 210.00	4	15	2	21	1	1900 / 2130	106	1-12	T 🖼♿ ☎ ▭ C ✳ V

RUSACKS MARINE HOTEL
St Andrews (0334-74321)

Rusacks opened in 1887 to look after the needs of golfers and their families. Almost 100 years later we continue to provide first class 4-star hotel facilities. Our 50 rooms and suites have private bathrooms, colour T.V.'s and radios. Out of season golf packages are available with play over all four St. Andrews courses. March, April and October including golf weeks with professional tuition, competitions and entertainment, from around £26.00 per person per day, including D.B.&B..

From July 1983 we have the added facility of the Links Rooms — full clubhouse facilities for ladies and gentlemen, where you can have a snack or a full meal. Grannie Clark's room is available for private parties of up to 50 golfers.

Telephone today for further information or write to ERIC H. BROWN, MANAGING DIRECTOR.

Name and Address	Map Ref			Prices				B & B and evening meal					Rooms			Facilities
Rusacks Marine Hotel / Pilmour Links / Tel. St Andrews 74321 / Telex 76357	6	6	5	28.00 / 36.00	50.00 / 66.00	34.00 / 39.00	217.00 / 252.00	8	32	10	50	4	1900 / 2130	30	1-12	T ♿ ● ☎ C V

Name and Address	Map Ref	Bedrooms	Services	Meals	Single room overnight £min	£max	Double/twin room overnight £min	£max	Per person daily £min	£max	Per person weekly £min	£max	Single	Double/twin	Family	Private	Public	Evening meals From	Last order	Parking (no. of cars)	Months open (1-12)	Symbols
ST ANDREWS continued	2 E3																					Key on back fold-out
The Russell Hotel, 26 The Scores, KY16 9AS, Tel. St Andrews 73447		3	4	4	14.00	-	28.00	-	-	-	-	-	1	4	3	-	2	1900	2130	-	1-12	(symbols)
The Scores Hotel, The Scores, KY16 9BB, Tel. St Andrews 72451		5	5	5	21.50	26.50	43.00	47.00	26.00	35.00	-	-	-	30	-	30	1	1900	2100	-	1-12	(symbols)
St Andrews Golf Hotel, 40 The Scores, Tel. St Andrews 72611		5	5	5	25.00	27.00	42.00	46.00	27.00	30.00	-	-	2	15	8	22	2	1900	2130	-	1-12	(symbols)
Yorkston Hotel, 68-70 Argyle Street, KY16 9BU, Tel. St Andrews 72019		3	3	2	9.50	-	17.00	-	13.80	-	85.00	-	3	8	1	-	3	1830	-	-	1-12	(symbols)
Beachway Guest House, 4-8 Murray Park, KY16 9AW, Tel. St Andrews 73319		3	4	2	8.00	11.00	14.00	19.00	12.00	14.25	82.00	93.00	2	12	4	-	5	1800	1800	-	1-11	(symbols)
Cleveden Guest House, 3 Murray Place, KY16 9AP, Tel. St Andrews 74212		3	3	1	8.00	8.50	16.00	17.00	-	-	-	-	2	2	2	-	2	-	-	10	1-12	(symbols)
Craigmore Guest House, 3 Murray Park, KY16 9AW, Tel. St Andrews 72142		3	3	2	7.50	11.50	15.00	23.00	-	-	-	-	1	-	4	1	2	1800	1815	-	4-11	(symbols)
Kerelaw Guest House, 5 Playfair Terrace, North St, Tel. St Andrews 75906		3	4	2	-	-	16.00	18.00	13.00	14.00	87.00	93.00	-	3	3	1	2	1830	1930	-	1-12	(symbols)
Lorimer Guest House, 19 Murray Park, KY16 9AW, Tel. St Andrews 76599		3	2	2	7.00	-	14.00	-	11.95	-	80.00	-	2	1	2	-	2	1830	-	-	1-12	(symbols)
Number Ten Guest House, 10 Hope Street, KY16 9HJ, Tel. St Andrews 74601		3	4	2	8.50	-	15.00	-	12.45	-	81.00	-	3	4	3	-	3	1800	1815	-	1-12	(symbols)
Peover Guest House, 22 Murray Park, KY16 9AW, Tel. St Andrews 75787		3	3	1	-	-	15.00	23.00	-	-	-	-	-	3	1	1	1	-	-	-	5-10	(symbols)
Waldon Guest House, 16 The Links, Tel. St Andrews 73036		4	4	3	12.00	-	24.00	-	-	-	-	-	2	7	-	9	-	1900	2200	-	1-12	(symbols)
ST BOSWELLS Roxburghshire	2 E7																					
Buccleuch Arms Hotel, Tel. St Boswells 22243		3	2	4	12.00	17.50	23.00	32.00	19.50	25.00	123.00	157.50	2	12	2	6	3	1900	2100	100	1-12	(symbols)

VAT is shown at 15%: changes in this rate may affect prices.

Name and Address				Prices				Rooms							Facilities			
TOWN County / Establishment Address Telephone Telex	Map Ref	Bedrooms	Services	Meals	Bed and Breakfast — Single room overnight	Double/twin room overnight	Per person daily	B & B and evening meal — Per person weekly	Single	Double/twin	Family	Private	No. of bedrooms — Public	No. of bath/shower rooms	Evening meals	Parking (no. of cars)	Months open (1-12)	Symbols
ST BOSWELLS continued	2 E7				£min £max	£min £max	£min £max	£min £max					From Last order					Key on back fold-out

Dryburgh Abbey Hotel,

St. Boswells, Roxburghshire.

"... A handsome house to lodge a friend; a river at my garden's end. A terrace walk and half a rood, of land to plant a wood".

The author may well have been thinking of Dryburgh Abbey Hotel when penning those lines.

Attractive and comfortable accommodation. Friendly, courteous service. Well prepared and tastefully presented traditional fare using produce from our well stocked garden. Well balanced wine list.

An 11th Century setting–secluded among wooded Border hills. With the murmuring waters of the 'Chiming Tweed' close by. All of this represents one of the finest hotels in Border country.

Come for a weekend, a week or a fortnight. Either way, you'll be well looked after–and very welcome. For accommodation rates and tariffs, call or write D.A. Hogg, F.H.C.I.M.A., Resident Manager, 0835 22261.

AA***RAC, Egon Ronay. A British Tourist Authority Commended Country Hotel.

Establishment	Map Ref	Bedrooms	Services	Meals	Single room overnight	Double/twin room overnight	Per person daily	Per person weekly	Single	Double/twin	Family	Private	Public	bath/shower	Evening meals / Last order	Parking	Months open	Symbols
Dryburgh Abbey Hotel Tel. St Boswells 22261		4	4	4	19.80 23.40	35.00 53.50	30.80 37.95	124.00 192.30	6	20	1	19	6		1900 2030	124	1-12	T ⊞ ♿ ♈ ⚞ ⚘ ♙ ▦ ⚒ ⊟ ⚙ ⚡ C ❋ ♨ V ∪ ✎
ST CATHERINE'S Argyll	1 F3																	
Thistle House St Catherine Tel. Inveraray 2209		3	2	2	9.50 -	19.00 -	16.50 -	112.00 -	-	5	1	-	2		1900 1900	12	5-9	⚞ ♙ ▦ ⚒ ❋
ST COMBS Aberdeenshire	4 H7																	
Tufted Duck Hotel Tel. Inverallochy 2481		5	4	5	19.95 -	31.95 -	26.00 -	- -	7	11	-	18	-		1900 2130	100	1-12	⊞ ♿ ♈ ⚞ ♙ ▦ ⚒ ⚡ ⊟ ▢ ⚏ ⚡ ⊟ ❋ V ∪ ✎
ST FILLANS Perthshire	2 A2																	
Achray House Hotel PH6 2NF Tel. St Fillins 231(off)320(guest)		3	4	5	- -	20.00 28.00	16.50 20.50	103.95 129.15	-	2	1	-	-		1900 2100	12	1-12	⊞ ♿ ♈ ♙ ▦ ⚒ ⚏ ⚡ V
Drummond Arms Hotel PH6 2NF Tel. St Fillans 212		3	4	5	15.50 18.50	29.00 31.00	25.00 26.00	175.00 182.00	10	22	4	14	7		1700 2130	68	4-10	T ⊞ ♿ ♈ ⚞ ⚘ ♙ ⚒ ♨ ⚡ C ❋ ♨ V ∪
Four Seasons Hotel PH6 2NF Tel. St Fillans 333		6	4	5	24.50 29.50	41.00 51.00	33.50 38.50	220.50 255.50	-	12	6	18	-		1900 2200	50	4-10	T ⊞ ♿ ♈ ⚞ ⚘ ⚘ ♙ ▦ ⚒ ⚘ ▢ ⚡ ⚎ C ❋ V ∪ ✎ ⊠ ⚲

ST MARY'S LOCH - STIRLING

Name and Address	Map Ref	Bedrooms	Services	Meals	Single room overnight £min/£max	Double/twin room overnight £min/£max	Per person daily £min/£max	Per person weekly £min/£max	Single	Double/twin	Family	Private	Public	Evening meals From/Last order	Parking (no. of cars)	Months open (1-12)	Symbols
ST MARY'S LOCH Selkirkshire	2 D7																
Rodono Country Hotel & Restaurant Tel. Cappercleuch 232		3	3	4	11.00 / –	22.00 / –	17.25 / –	117.00 / –	2	7	2	–	3	1600 / 2030	30	1-12	
Tibbie Shiels Inn Tel. Cappercleuch 231		3	4	5	8.50 / 10.00	17.00 / 20.00	11.00 / 18.00	84.00 / 105.00	–	4	1	–	1	1700 / 2130	50	1-12	
STANLEY, Perth Perthshire	2 C2																
Tayside Hotel 51-53 Mill Street PH2 4NL Tel. Stanley 249		3	3	5	8.50 / 10.50	17.00 / 21.00	17.00 / 19.00	–	3	10	4	9	3	1900 / 2130	46	1-12	
STENNESS Orkney	5 B11																
Standing Stones Hotel KW16 3JX Tel. Stromness 449		3	4	4	12.36 / –	21.85 / –	18.68 / –	120.75 / –	6	13	1	–	5	1800 / 2030	70	1-12	
STEPPS Lanarkshire	2 A5																
Garfield Hotel Cumbernauld Road Tel. 041 779 2111		5	5	5	18.50 / 29.95	27.50 / 36.95	24.50 / 35.95	171.50 / 251.65	10	10	2	22	–	1900 / 2200	80	1-12	
STEWARTON Ayrshire	1 H6																
Chapeltoun House Hotel Chapeltoun KA3 3ED Tel. Stewarton 82696		5	5	5	35.00 / –	60.00 / –	50.50 / –	–	–	6	–	6	–	1900 / 2130	50	1-12	
STIRLING	2 A4																
Golden Lion Hotel 8 King Street FK8 1BD Tel. Stirling 5351		4	6	5	24.00 / –	36.00 / –	–	–	12	63	–	43	7	1900 / 2200	45	1-12	
Heritage Hotel 16 Allan Park FK8 2QG Tel. Stirling 3660		4	5	5	18.50 / 18.50	26.60 / 26.60	22.00	–	–	4	–	4	–	1800 / 2200	12	1-12	
Hollybank Hotel & Restaurant Glasgow Road, St Ninians Tel. Bannockburn 812311		2	3	4	15.00 / –	22.00 / –	–	–	1	4	1	–	1	1700 / 2200	26	1-12	
Park Lodge Hotel 32 Park Terrace		5	3	5	20.00 / 25.00	30.00 / 36.00	32.00 / 35.00	–	1	8	–	9	–	1800 / 2200	17	1-12	

VAT is shown at 15%: changes in this rate may affect prices.

Name and Address	Map Ref	Bedrooms	Services	Meals	Single room overnight £min/£max	Double/twin room overnight £min/£max	Per person daily £min/£max	Per person weekly £min/£max	Single	Double/twin	Family	Private	Public	Evening meals From/Last order	Parking	Months open	Symbols
STIRLING continued	2 A4																Key on back fold-out
Stakis Station Hotel, Murray Place, FK8 2BX, Tel. Stirling 2017		5	5	5	30.00 / -	38.00 / -	- / -	- / -	5	18	2	25	1	1700 / 2230	17	1-12	
Terraces Hotel, 4 Melville Terrace, FK8 2ND, Tel. Stirling 2268		4	5	5	16.95 / -	26.50 / -	- / -	- / -	2	13	-	10	1	1900 / 2100	25	1-12	
Dalglennan Guest House, 4 Allan Park, FK8 2QF, Tel. Stirling 3432		2	2	1	7.00 / 8.00	13.00 / 14.00	- / -	- / -	-	8	2	-	4	- / -	6	1-12	
Firgrove Guest House, 13 Clifford Road, FK8 2AQ, Tel. Stirling 5805		3	3	1	7.00 / 8.00	14.00 / 15.00	- / -	- / -	-	2	3	1	2	- / -	6	1-12	
Mia-Roo Guest House, 37 Snowdon Place, FK8 2JP, Tel. Stirling 3979		2	2	1	7.00 / -	14.00 / -	- / -	- / -	2	4	2	-	2	- / -	2	1-12	
University of Stirling, FK9 4LA, Tel. Stirling 3171		3	5	4	8.50 / 10.50	- / -	11.50 / 14.00	69.00 / 84.00	1060	46	-	21	24	1800 / 1855	2200	1-2 6-9	
STONEHAVEN Kincardineshire	4 G11																
The Commodore Hotel, Cowie Park, Tel. Stonehaven 62936		5	5	5	18.00 / 25.00	18.00 / 35.00	25.95 / 32.95	- / -	-	40	-	40	-	1900 / 2200	200	1-12	
County Hotel, Arduthie Road, Tel. Stonehaven 64386		5	4	5	15.00 / 17.50	28.00 / 30.00	22.50 / 25.00	157.50 / 175.00	-	8	4	10	10	1900 / 2200	50	1-12	
Heugh Hotel, AB3 2EE, Tel. Stonehaven 62379		4	3	4	17.00 / -	26.50 / -	10.00 / -	102.00 / -	3	6	1	2	1	1900 / 2100	56	1-12	
St Leonards Hotel, Tel. Stonehaven 62044		-	-	-	25.00 / -	35.00 / -	32.50 / -	- / -	2	12	1	5	3	1900 / 2100	-	-	

Prices shown are for guidance only. Please send SAE with each enquiry.

Name and Address	Map Ref			Prices				Rooms					Facilities			
TOWN County	Bedrooms	Services	Meals	Single room overnight	Double/twin room overnight	Per person daily	Per person weekly	Single	Double/twin	Family	Private	Public	Evening meals (From / Last order)	Parking (no. of cars)	Months open (1-12)	Symbols
Establishment Address Telephone Telex				£min £max	£min £max	£min £max	£min £max						From Last order			Key on back fold-out
STORNOWAY Lewis, Western Isles	3 D4															

Caberfeidh Hotel,

Manor Park, Stornoway, Isle of Lewis. Telephone 0851 2604
A.A. rated ★★★ Licensed

Situated in its own five acre grounds on the outskirts of Stornoway the Caberfeidh is just a few hundred yards from the town's charming 18 hole golf course set in the lovely grounds of Stornoway Castle.

***A.A. Rated. ***Egon Ronay Recommended. ***Most rooms have colour TV. All have Radio, Telephone and Baby Listening.

***Our Viking Lounge Bar is the ideal place for a tasty Buffet Lunch or a friendly Evening Drink.

This Hotel is one of the most modern and highly rated on Lewis. All bedrooms with private bathroom. If any are unlet at 4.00 pm you may book in at a specially reduced rate. For further details please contact direct or Stornoway Tourist Office. Enjoy *** comfort and hospitality without blowing the holiday budget.

Name and Address	Bedrooms	Services	Meals	Single room overnight	Double/twin room overnight	Per person daily	Per person weekly	Single	Double/twin	Family	Private	Public	Evening meals	Parking	Months open	Symbols
Caberfeidh Hotel Manor Park Tel. Stornoway 2604	4	4	4	24.75 26.75	35.50 38.00	23.75 36.75	142.50 220.50	2	37	-	39	-	1930 2130	120	1-12	
County Hotel Francis Street Tel. Stornoway 3250	3	3	4	14.95 -	23.00 -	- -	- -	5	6	-	-	3	1900 2130	-	1-12	
Royal Hotel Cromwell Street Tel. Stornoway 2109	-	-	-	13.50 -	27.00 -	- -	- -	9	9	3	-	4	1830 2030	-	1-12	

VAT is shown at 15%: changes in this rate may affect prices.

Name and Address	Map Ref	Bedrooms	Services	Meals	Prices: Bed and Breakfast – Single room overnight £min £max	Double/twin room overnight £min £max	Per person daily £min £max	B & B and evening meal – Per person weekly £min £max	Rooms: No. of bedrooms – Single	Double/twin	Family	No. of bath/shower rooms – Private	Public	Evening meals From Last order	Parking (no. of cars)	Months open (1-12)	Facilities / Symbols
STORNOWAY continued	3 D4														Key on back fold-out

Name and Address	Bedrooms	Services	Meals	Single overnight	Double/twin overnight	Per person daily	Per person weekly	Single	Double/twin	Family	Private	Public	Evening meals	Parking	Months open	Symbols
Seaforth Hotel, James Street, PA87 2QN, Tel. Stornoway 2740	4	4	4	23.75 / 25.75	34.50 / 37.00	23.25 / 35.75	139.50 / 214.50	18	49	5	70	1	1930 / 2130	50	1-12	T £ 👜 🍷 🐕 ♨ 🖥 ♿ ● 🚻 📠 🚭 ⚓ C V ☎ 🍴 K
Hebridean Guest House, Bayhead, PA87 2DZ, Tel. Stornoway 2268	3	4	4	9.00 / -	18.00 / -	13.00 / -	- / -	7	3	-	-	2	1900 / 2200	-	1-12	👜 🍷 ♨ 🖥 ♿ 🚢 ⚓ V
Park Guest House, 30 James Street, PA87 2QN, Tel. Stornoway 2485	3	2	1	6.50 / 7.00	13.00 / 14.00	- / -	- / -	2	4	-	-	1	- / -	-	1-12	🐕 ♨ 🖥 ♿ 🚢 🚭 V
Tower Guest House, 32 James Street, Tel. Stornoway 3150	-	-	-	8.00 / 8.50	15.00 / 15.50	12.50 / 13.00	- / -	2	2	-	-	2	1800 / 1830	-	1-12	♨ 🖥 ♿ 🚭 ❄ 📻 V ☎
STOW, Selkirkshire (2 E6)																
Manor Head House Hotel, Tel. Stow 201	-	-	-	10.00 / -	20.00 / -	15.00 / -	- / -	-	6	2	-	2	1900 / 2230	53	1-12	👜 🍷 🐕 ♨ 🖥 ♿ C ❄ 📻 V ☎ 🎵
STRACHUR, Argyll (1 F4)																
Creggans Inn, Tel. Strachur 279, Telex 727396	5	5	5	23.50 / 27.00	37.00 / 51.00	35.50 / 39.00	- / -	5	17	1	21	1	1930 / 2130	70	1-12	T £ 👜 🍷 🐕 ♨ 🖥 ♿ ● 📞 📠 🚢 C ❄ V ☎ 🎵 🍴

Name and Address	Map Ref	Bedrooms	Services	Meals	Single room overnight £min/£max	Double/twin room overnight £min/£max	Per person daily £min/£max	Per person weekly £min/£max	Single	Double/twin	Family	Private	Public	Evening meals (From/Last order)	Parking	Months open	Symbols
STRANRAER Wigtownshire	1 F10																
Corsewall Arms Hotel, Kirkcolm, DG9 0NN, Tel. Kirkcolm 228		3	4	4	8.50/8.50	17.00/18.00	13.25/-	92.75/-	6	5	-	1	3	1730/1930	40	1-12	(symbols)
George Hotel, DG9 7RJ, Tel. Stranraer 2487/8		4	5	4	15.00/17.00	25.00/27.00	22.50/24.50	130.00/140.00	3	24	1	12	7	1900/2100	31	1-12	(symbols)
North West Castle Hotel, Tel. Stranraer 4413		6	5	5	18.00/20.00	30.00/37.50	23.00/25.50	141.75/166.25	14	52	17	83	4	1830/2130	100	1-12	(symbols)
Royal Hotel, Hanover Street, Tel. Stranraer 2426		4	5	3	8.50/-	16.50/-	12.00/-	88.00/-	2	4	1	-	1	1830/2000	6	1-12	(symbols)
Ruddicot Hotel, London Road, DG9 8AJ, Tel. Stranraer 2684		-	-	-	8.00/8.00	16.00/16.00	11.75/11.75	82.25/82.25	4	1	1	-	1	1800/1900	6	4-10	(symbols)
Dunhaven Guest House, 21 Agnew Crescent, Tel. Stranraer 3118		2	2	2	8.00/9.00	14.00/15.00	9.00/10.00	60.00/65.00	-	4	2	-	2	1700/1830	-	1-12	(symbols)
Harbour Guest House, Market Street, Tel. Stranraer 4626		3	4	2	-/-	13.00/-	8.50/-	59.50/-	-	3	2	-	2	1700/1800	5	1-12	(symbols)
Lochview Guest House, 52 Agnew Crescent		3	2	2	7.50/8.50	13.00/14.00	10.50/11.00	-/-	-	4	2	-	2	1730/1150	6	1-12	(symbols)
Marine Guest House, 23 Agnew Crescent, Tel. Stranraer 3370		2	2	2	6.50/6.50	13.00/13.00	8.50/8.50	59.50/59.50	4	2	1	-	2	1750/1850	2	1-12	(symbols)
STRATHAVEN Lanarkshire	2 A6																
Bucks Head, 16 Townhead Road, Tel. Strathaven 20184		3	3	5	10.00/10.00	18.00/18.00	13.50/15.50	94.50/108.50	1	7	-	-	2	1830/2130	10	1-12	(symbols)
Springvale Hotel, 18 Letham Street, Tel. Strathaven 21131		-	-	-	10.00	18.00	14.00	98.00	4	8	2	2	3	1630/1845	8	1-12	(symbols)
STRATHBLANE Stirlingshire	1 H5																
Country Club Hotel, G36 94H, Tel. Blanefield 70491		5	4	5	30.00/-	40.00/-	40.00/-	250.00/-	2	8	-	10	-	1900/2130	100	1-12	(symbols)

VAT is shown at 15%; changes in this rate may affect prices.

Name and Address	Map Ref	Bedrooms	Services	Meals	Prices: Bed and Breakfast — Single room overnight £min £max	Prices: Bed and Breakfast — Double/twin room overnight £min £max	Prices: Bed and Breakfast — Per person daily £min £max	Prices: B & B and evening meal — Per person weekly £min £max	Rooms: Single	Rooms: Double/twin	Rooms: Family	Rooms: Private	Rooms: Public	No. of bedrooms / bath/shower rooms: From Last order	Evening meals	Parking (no. of cars)	Months open (1-12)	Facilities / Symbols
STRATHBLANE continued Kirkhouse Inn G63 9AA Tel. Blanefield 70621	1 H5	6	5	6	21.00 23.00	27.00 31.00	29.75 31.75	119.00 130.00	6	13	-	14	5	1900 2130	360	1-12	Key on back fold-out
STRATHCONON, by Muir of Ord Ross-shire East Lodge Hotel IV6 7QQ Tel. Strathconon 222	3 H8	4	4	5	11.50 16.00	23.00 32.00	19.50 25.00	- -	-	10	-	10	-	1900 2030	25	1-12	
STRATHDON Aberdeenshire Colquhonnie Hotel AB3 8UN Tel. Strathdon 210	4 E10	3	3	4	9.00 -	16.00 -	17.00 -	112.00 -	2	5	3	-	3	1900 1930	20	1-12	
STRATHGLASS, by Beauly Inverness-shire Tomich Hotel Tomich IV4 7LY Tel. Cannich 212	3 H9	3	4	3	6.50 6.50	- -	11.00 11.00	77.00 77.00	-	5	-	-	1	1900 2000	10	4-10	
STRATHMIGLO Fife The Tavern 109 High Street Tel. Strathmiglo 229	2 C3	1	2	3	8.00 11.00	16.00 22.00	10.50 11.50	75.00 112.00	-	4	-	-	2	1800 1430	9	1-12	
STRATHPEFFER Ross-shire Ben Wyvis Hotel Tel. Strathpeffer 323 Telex 75160	4 A8	3	5	4	13.00 -	26.00 -	- -	- -	32	79	1	9	15	1900 2100	40	1-12	

QUALITY ASSURED

The Thistle Commendation Scheme gives recognition to Holiday Static Caravan Sites in Scotland which provide first class caravans for hire, combined with very good facilities and an attractive environment. All sites have had a detailed inspection.

Look out for the Thistle Commendation plaques displayed by all the commended sites, or ask for the leaflet.

Name and Address				Prices				Rooms						Facilities		
TOWN County / Establishment Address Telephone Telex	Map Ref / Bedrooms / Services / Meals			Bed and Breakfast — Single room overnight	Double/twin room overnight	Per person daily	B & B and evening meal — Per person weekly	No. of bedrooms — Single	Double/twin	Family	No. of bath/shower rooms — Private	Public	Evening meals	Parking (no. of cars)	Months open (1-12)	Symbols
STRATHPEFFER continued	4 A8			£min £max	£min £max	£min £max	£min £max						From Last order			Key on back fold-out

Brunstane Lodge
Strathpeffer Spa

Small, fully licensed family Hotel. Peaceful and secluded setting overlooking the village, only 100m from the picturesque Strathpeffer Spa Golf Course.

With comfortable bedrooms (two with PBs) and quality home cooking we endeavour to make your stay pleasant and friendly for a reasonable price. (Special rates for children).

Please write for brochure or telephone David & Sheila Green, Strathpeffer (099 72) 261. Also ask for details of our special golf package, "Golf without crowds".

View from the Brunstane Lodge paddock looking down the 'Strath' towards Dingwall.

Establishment	Bedrooms	Services	Meals	Single room overnight	Double/twin room overnight	Per person daily	Per person weekly	Single	Double/twin	Family	Private	Public	Evening meals	Parking	Months open	Symbols
Brunstane Lodge Hotel IV14 9AT Tel. Strathpeffer 261	3	4	3	9.50 10.00	19.00 20.00	16.00 17.00	110.00 114.00	2	3	2	2	1	1930 2000	10	5-10	
Dunraven Lodge Hotel IV14 9DE Tel. Strathpeffer 210	4	4	4	11.00 13.50	18.00 23.00	18.50 21.00	92.00 107.00	-	12	2	-	5	1900 2030	14	1-12	
HF Holidays Ltd Balmoral Lodge IV14 9AT Tel. Strathpeffer 670 Telex 922296	2	3	4	7.40 9.90	14.80 19.70	12.40 16.90	70.00 115.56	3	13	9	-	7	1900 1930	25	5-9	
Highland Hotel Tel. Strathpeffer 457 Telex 75160	4	5	5	16.00 -	32.00 -	- -	- -	52	98	2	118	11	1930 2130	50	1-12	
Hollylodge Hotel Tel. Strathpeffer 254	4	4	4	10.00 15.00	24.00 30.00	17.00 22.00	133.00 133.00	2	5	-	5	1	1900 2030	13	1-12	

Cairngorm Spey Valley, Glenshee, Glencoe, Lecht

Inclusive holidays and details of hotels, facilities and apres-ski in Scotland's major ski-ing centres.

FREE FROM

Scottish Tourist Board, PO Box 15, EDINBURGH EH1 1UY

VAT is shown at 15%: changes in this rate may affect prices.

Name and Address	Map Ref	Bedrooms	Services	Meals	Prices				Rooms							Facilities		
TOWN County, Establishment, Address, Telephone, Telex					Bed and Breakfast — Single room overnight	Double/twin room overnight	Per person daily	B & B and evening meal — Per person weekly	No. of bedrooms — Single	Double/twin	Family	Private	No. of bath/shower rooms — Public	Evening meals	Parking (no. of cars)	Months open (1-12)	Symbols
STRATHPEFFER continued	4 A8				£min £max	£min £max	£min £max	£min £max					From Last order				Key on back fold-out

THE SQUARE, STRATHPEFFER
Telephone: 09972 542

Set in the centre of this delightful spa village, Mackay's Hotel is a modernised family run hotel. All rooms with radio and tea making facilities, most with private bathroom.

5 day packaged family holidays arranged, golf, fishing, or pony trekking.

Also Strathpeffer is an ideal base for touring the North West Highlands.

Please write for a Colour Brochure, Tariff and Activity Leaflet.

Name and Address	Bedrooms	Services	Meals	Single room overnight	Double/twin room overnight	Per person daily	Per person weekly	Single	Double/twin	Family	Private	Public	Evening meals Last order	Parking	Months open	Symbols
MacKays Hotel, Tel. Strathpeffer 237/542	3	3	4	12.00 –	24.00 –	18.50 –	– –	7	10	1	10	3	1900 2100	30	1-12	
Strathpeffer Hotel, IV14 9DF, Tel. Strathpeffer 200 **(See ad. p. 278)**	3	4	4	9.00 11.00	18.00 22.00	15.00 17.00	92.50 100.00	7	24	3	12	6	1900 2000	35	4-10	
Kilvannie Manor Guest House, Fodderty, IV14 9AD, Tel. Strathpeffer 389	3	3	5	9.00 10.00	18.00 20.00	15.00 16.00	100.00 110.00	2	3	3	–	2	1900 2130	10	1-12	
STRATHTAY, Pitlochry Perthshire															2 B1	
Grandtully Hotel, Grandtully, PH9 0PL, Tel. Strathtay 207	3	4	4	9.50 10.50	19.00 21.00	19.50 20.50	– –	2	7	–	2	2	1930 2030	40	1-12	
STRATHTUMMEL Perthshire															2 A1	
Loch Tummel Hotel, PH16 5RP, Tel. Tummel Bridge 272	–	–	–	11.95 –	19.90 –	– –	– –	–	6	2	3	3	1800 2100	42	1-12	
Port-an-Eilean Hotel, PH16 5RU, Tel. Tummel Bridge 233	4	4	4	14.00 –	28.00 –	21.50 –	133.00 –	2	9	1	5	3	1930 2100	20	4-10	
Queens View Hotel, PH16 5NR, Tel. Pitlochry 3291	4	4	6	12.65 17.55	25.30 30.20	20.40 25.30	135.00 170.00	1	10	1	5	2	1900 2130	25	1-12	

STRATHPEFFER
Ross-shire

Why Strathpeffer?

With the opening of the new Kessock Bridge, Strathpeffer commands a peerless position from which to enjoy contrastive trips covering the whole of the N&W Highlands, Morayshire, Spey Valley. Choice of daily tours encompassing Skye, John o' Groats, Inverewe Gardens, Aviemore, Loch Ness and many other legendary beauty spots.

Village facilities include 18-hole golf course, fishing (salmon or trout), pony trekking, bowling, climbing or relaxing at nearby sandy beaches.

Why Strathpeffer Hotel?

Privately owned and managed imparting that much sought after personal touch. Realistically and competitively priced. Fully licensed. Sauna, Games Room, Separate TV and Residents' lounges. All rooms hot and cold (many with private facilities), electric fires, shaver point, large car park.

Send for illustrated brochure.

THE STRATHPEFFER HOTEL

Strathpeffer, Ross-shire IV14 9DF
Resident Proprietors: Mrs and Mrs T. Kennedy
Telephone: Strathpeffer (099 72) 200

Name and Address	Map Ref	Bedrooms	Services	Meals	Single room overnight £min/£max	Double/twin room overnight £min/£max	Per person daily £min/£max	Per person weekly £min/£max	Single	Double/twin	Family	Private	Public	No. of bedrooms From/Last order	No. of bath/shower rooms	Evening meals	Parking	Months open	Symbols
STRATHYRE **Perthshire**	1 H3																		
Creagan Guest House FK18 8ND Tel. Strathyre 638		3	3	2	- / -	14.00 / -	12.00 / -	84.00 / -	-	4	3	-	2	1830 / 1930	8			1-12	Key on back fold-out
Dochfour Guest House Tel. Strathyre 256		-	-	-	6.00 / 7.00	12.00 / 14.00	9.50 / 10.50	63.00 / 65.00	-	3	1	-	1	1900 / 2000	4			1-12	
STROMNESS **Orkney**	5 A11																		
Braes Hotel Tel. Stromness 850495		3	2	2	10.35 / 10.35	20.70 / 20.70	- / -	- / -	-	6	-	-	3	1800 / 1930	10			1-12	

FERRY INN
Stromness, Orkney Isles
Telephone: 0856 850 280

Fully modernised Inn with strong nautical flavour. Fully licensed. All 15 bedrooms have television, coffee makers, and most have shower or private bath. The dining room provides home-cooked fare to a high standard with many seafood specialities.
Package holidays can be arranged for sea/loch fishing, golf, sub-aqua, archaeology or self-drive. Reasonable rates.
Write or phone resident proprietors.

Name and Address	Map Ref	Bedrooms	Services	Meals	Single room overnight £min/£max	Double/twin room overnight £min/£max	Per person daily £min/£max	Per person weekly £min/£max	Single	Double/twin	Family	Private	Public	No. of bedrooms From/Last order	No. of bath/shower rooms	Evening meals	Parking	Months open	Symbols
Ferry Inn Tel. Stromness 850280		5	4	5	9.50 / -	19.00 / -	14.00 / -	98.00 / -	3	12	-	6	2	2230 / 2230	36			1-12	
Royal Hotel Tel. Stromness 850342		3	4	4	11.30 / -	20.70 / -	14.80 / -	98.00 / -	2	2	-	-	1	1900 / 1900	-			1-12	
STRONE **Argyll**	1 G4																		
Argyll Hotel PA23 8TA Tel. Kilmun 227		3	2	3	9.50 / 10.00	17.00 / 18.00	12.50 / 13.00	87.50 / 91.00	-	2	1	-	2	1900 / 2100	4			1-12	
STRONTIAN **Argyll**	1 E1																		
Kilcamb Lodge Hotel PH36 4HY Tel. Strontian 2257		4	5	5	12.00 / 12.00	24.00 / 24.00	23.00 / 23.00	84.00 / 84.00	3	7	1	3	3	1900 / 2130	50			12-10	

Name and Address	Map Ref	Bedrooms	Services	Meals	Single room overnight (£min / £max)	Double/twin room overnight (£min / £max)	Per person daily (£min / £max)	Per person weekly (£min / £max)	Single	Double/twin	Family	Private	Public	Evening meals (From / Last order)	Parking (no. of cars)	Months open (1-12)	Symbols
STRUAN Isle of Skye, Inverness-shire	3 C9																
Ullinish Lodge Hotel Tel. Struan 214		3	3	4	12.50 / –	25.00 / –	– / –	132.00 / –	1	6	2	–	3	1900 / 2100	12	4-10	Key on back fold-out
STRUY, by Beauly Inverness-shire	4 A9																
Cnoc Hotel Tel. Struy 264		3	3	4	11.00 / 13.00	18.00 / 22.00	18.00 / 20.00	– / –	–	7	1	4	2	1830 / 2030	24	1-12	
Mauld Bridge Hotel Tel. Struy 222		4	4	3	10.50 / –	21.00 / –	17.50 / –	120.50 / –	–	3	1	4	–	1900 / 2200	20	1-12	
SYMINGTON Lanarkshire	2 B6																
Tinto Hotel Tel. Tinto 454		4	4	4	16.50 / –	25.75 / –	– / –	– / –	6	24	4	3	7	1900 / 2030	82	1-12	
TAIN Ross-shire	4 B7																
Mansfield Hotel Scotsburn Road Tel. Tain 2052		3	3	4	15.00 / 19.75	26.00 / 34.25	21.50 / 26.25	150.50 / 183.75	1	18	1	13	1	1830 / 2045	48	1-12	
Royal Hotel IV19 1AB Tel. Tain 2013		5	5	5	19.00 / 25.00	32.00 / 40.00	27.00 / 40.00	140.00 / 280.00	6	19	–	22	2	1900 / 2130	60	1-12	
TANGUSDALE Isle of Barra, Western Isles	3 A11																
Isle of Barra Hotel PA80 5XW Tel. Castlebay 383 Telex 778215		5	5	4	14.50 / 19.00	29.00 / 31.00	21.00 / 26.50	135.00 / –	–	19	11	30	–	1900 / 2030	40	4-10	

Try a Taste of Scotland

Ask the Scottish Tourist Board for the colourful free booklet *A Taste of Scotland*. It lists around 200 places offering fine Scottish cooking, along with notes on regional specialities and recipes which you can try out at home.

While you're on holiday in Scotland, look for the Stockpot sign outside hotels and restaurants. It tells you that the menu offers not only traditional Scottish fare, but also examples of the creative skills of our chefs, using the best Scottish produce.

VAT is shown at 15%: changes in this rate may affect prices.

Name and Address		Prices					Rooms					Facilities		
TOWN / County / Establishment Address Telephone Telex	Map Ref / Bedrooms / Services / Meals	Bed and Breakfast: Single room overnight	Double/twin room overnight	Per person daily	B & B and evening meal: Per person weekly	Single	Double/twin	Family	Private	Public	Evening meals (Last order)	Parking (no. of cars)	Months open (1-12)	Symbols
		£min / £max	£min / £max	£min / £max	£min / £max				From	Last order			Key on back fold-out	
TARBERT Harris, Western Isles	3 C6													

Establishment	Map Ref / Bedrooms / Services / Meals	Single room overnight	Double/twin room overnight	Per person daily	Per person weekly	Single	Double/twin	Family	Private	Public	Evening meals (Last order)	Parking	Months open	Symbols
Harris Hotel Tel. Harris 2154	3 / 4 / 4	13.50 / 16.50	26.00 / 30.00	20.00 / 23.00	123.00 / 145.00	6	12	2	14	3	1930 / 1945	-	3-11	
Macleods Motel The Pier Road PA85 3DG Tel. Harris 2364	- / - / -	12.50 / -	20.90 / -	18.50 / -	124.60 / -	4	16	1	-	2	1900 / 2100	10	4-10	
TARBERT, Loch Fyne Argyll	1 E5													
Bruce Hotel Tel. Tarbert 577	4 / 4 / 5	13.50 / -	25.00 / -	21.50 / -	129.50 / -	2	10	1	12	1	1900 / 2130	5	1-12	
Columba Hotel Tel. Tarbert 241	3 / 3 / 3	8.50 / 8.50	17.00 / 17.00	- / -	- / -	2	7	4	-	3	1800 / 2200	12	1-12	
Skipness Castle Tel. Skipness 207/8	3 / 5 / 3	- / -	- / -	35.00 / 40.00	- / -	3	4	-	1	4	- / -	7	1-12	
Tarbert Hotel Tel. Tarbert 264	3 / 3 / 4	- / 13.50	- / 26.00	- / 22.00	- / 135.00	4	14	4	-	3	1700 / 2100	-	1-12	
West Loch Hotel PA29 6YF Tel. Tarbert 283	3 / 4 / 4	17.00 / 17.00	25.00 / 25.00	23.50 / 23.50	155.75 / 155.75	1	3	2	-	2	1900 / 2030	20	12-10	

Name and Address	Map Ref	Bedrooms	Services	Meals	Bed and Breakfast Single room overnight £min £max	Bed and Breakfast Double/twin room overnight £min £max	Bed and Breakfast Per person daily £min £max	B & B and evening meal Per person weekly £min £max	Single	Double/twin	Family	Private	Public	Evening meals From Last order	Parking (no. of cars)	Months open (1-12)	Symbols
TARBET, Arrochar **Dunbartonshire** Stuckgowan House Tel. Arrochar 262	1 G3	3	3	2	- -	27.00 28.00	39.00 42.00	- -	-	3	-	3	-	1930 2030	4	3-9	

Tarbet Hotel

Loch Lomond, Arrochar, Dunbartonshire. Telephone: 030 12 228.

Standing impressively on the banks of Loch Lomond, this modernised Hotel in Scottish Baronial style offers 85 bedrooms (59 with private bath/shower), Restaurant, and Buttery, with entertainment most evenings during season. Full central heating; lift.

Name and Address	Map Ref	Bedrooms	Services	Meals	Single room overnight £min £max	Double/twin room overnight £min £max	Per person daily £min £max	Per person weekly £min £max	Single	Double/twin	Family	Private	Public	Evening meals From Last order	Parking	Months open	Symbols
Tarbet Hotel Loch Lomond G83 7DE Tel. Arrochar 228		4	5	5	11.00 20.00	22.00 34.00	18.75 24.75	119.00 161.00	20	57	8	55	10	1900 2045	120	1-12	
TARLAND **Aberdeenshire** Aberdeen Arms Hotel Tel. Tarland 225	4 F10	3	3	5	8.00 -	16.00 -	13.00 -	- -	1	1	2	-	1	1700 2200	12	1-12	

TOURIST INFORMATION CENTRES

All over Scotland there are Tourist Information Centres where friendly, well-informed staff will be pleased to give you information about:

PLACES TO STAY • PLACES TO VISIT • ROUTES TO TAKE • LOCAL EVENTS

There will be lots of helpful literature, some free and some saleable, and many Centres can help you book accommodation.

Look for the information symbol

Name and Address		Prices				Rooms				Facilities
TOWN / **County**	**Map Ref**		**Bed and Breakfast**		**B & B and evening meal**		**No. of bedrooms**	**No. of bath/shower rooms**		**Facilities**
Establishment / Address / Telephone / Telex	Bedrooms / Services / Meals	Single room overnight	Double/twin room overnight	Per person daily	Per person weekly	Single / Double/twin / Family / Private	Public	Evening meals	Parking (no. of cars)	Months open (1-12) / Symbols
		£min / £max	£min / £max	£min / £max	£min / £max		From / Last order			Key on back fold-out

TAYNUILT — Argyll — 1 — F2

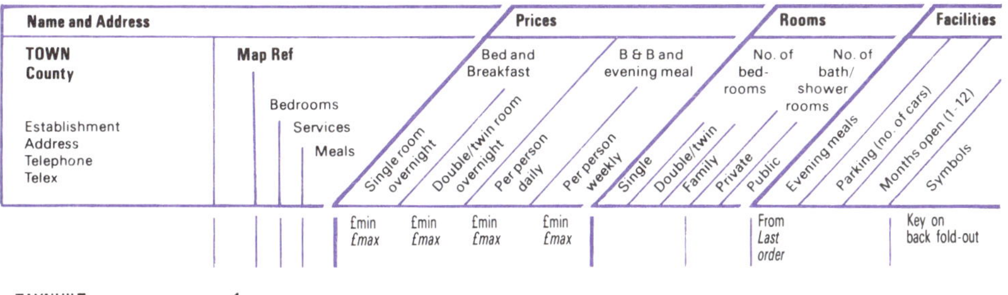

Town / County / Establishment	Map Ref	Bedrooms	Services	Meals	Single room overnight £min/£max	Double/twin room overnight £min/£max	Per person daily £min/£max	Per person weekly £min/£max	Single	Double/twin	Family	Private	Public	Evening meals From/Last order	Parking	Months open	Symbols
Polfearn Hotel / Tel. Taynuilt 251		3	3	5	10.00 / -	20.00 / -	16.00 / -	96.00 / -	3	9	2	-	4	1900 / 2150	20	4-10	
TEANGUE / Isle of Skye, Inverness-shire / Toravaig House Hotel / Knock Bay / IV44 8RJ / Tel. Isle Ornsay 231	3 / E10	4	4	4	12.00 / 15.00	24.00 / 28.00	20.50 / 22.50	130.00 / 136.00	2	8	-	4	2	1900 / 2000	22	3-10	
THORNHILL / Dumfriesshire / Buccleuch and Queensberry Hotel / DG3 5LU / Tel. Thornhill 30215	2 / B8	3	3	4	11.75 / 15.00	21.75 / 25.00	- / -	- / -	3	6	2	4	2	1700 / 2000	44	1-12	
THORNTON / Fife / The Crown Hotel / 7 Main Street / KY1 4AF / Tel. Glenrothes 774416	2 / D4	3	4	4	15.00 / 17.00	24.00 / 28.00	18.50 / -	114.50 / -	2	9	-	3	2	1700 / 2330	100	1-12	
THURSO / Caithness / Central Hotel / Tel. Thurso 63100	4 / C3	3	2	3	9.95 / 11.50	17.50 / 19.50	12.75 / 14.50	75.00 / 85.00	3	7	2	1	3	1700 / 1930	-	1-12	
Holborn Hotel / 16 Princes Street / Tel. Thurso 62771		-	-	-	9.78 / 10.35	19.56 / 20.70	12.28 / 14.13	85.96 / 98.91	3	7	1	-	3	1700 / 1900	4	1-12	

Name and Address	Map Ref	Bedrooms	Services	Meals	Single room overnight £min £max	Double/twin room overnight £min £max	Per person daily £min £max	Per person weekly £min £max	Single	Double/twin	Family	Private	Public	From Last order	Evening meals	Parking (no. of cars)	Months open (1-12)	Symbols (Key on back fold-out)
THURSO continued	4 C3																	
Ormlie House Hotel, Ormlie Road, Tel. Thurso 62733		3	3	3	11.00 / -	22.00 / -	15.00 / -	- / -	2	4	-	2	1	1700 1900	16		1-12	
Park Hotel, KW14 8RE, Tel. Thurso 63251		3	3	3	13.27 / -	24.02 / 24.66	- / -	- / -	1	15	-	-	3	1730 1930	2		1-12	
Pentland Hotel, Tel. Thurso 63202		3	5	4	11.00 / -	22.00 / -	- / -	- / -	29	25	3	11	16	1700 2030	-		1-12	
Royal Hotel, Traill Street, Tel. Thurso 63191		3	5	5	10.90 / 14.90	21.80 / 29.80	14.90 / 20.90	89.40 / 125.40	31	54	3	35	10	1900 2100	30		1-12	
TIGHNABRUAICH Argyll	1 F5																	
Kyles of Bute Hotel, Tel. Tighnabruaich 350/674		-	-	-	10.00 / -	20.00 / -	- / -	- / -	1	3	1	-	1	1900 2030	40		1-12	
Royal Hotel, Tel. Tighnabruaich 239		4	5	5	12.50 / -	25.00 / -	19.00 / -	120.00 / -	2	8	-	-	10	1900 2030	-		4-10	
Kames Cottage, Kames, PA21 2AD, Tel. Tighnabruaich 811259		4	4	4	9.50 / 10.50	16.00 / 18.00	15.00 / 17.50	90.00 / 105.00	-	2	1	-	1	1800 2100	3		3-10	
TILLICOULTRY Clackmannanshire	2 B4																	
Bridge Hotel, 1 High Street, Tel. Tillicoultry 50252		3	4	5	9.00 / 9.00	18.00 / 18.00	11.00 / 11.50	66.00 / 66.00	2	6	1	-	2	1700 2000	5		1-12	
TIMSGARRY, Uig Lewis, Western Isles	3 B4																	
Baile-na-Cille, Tel. Timsgarry 242		3	3	2	11.00 / -	- / -	19.00 / -	- / -	2	2	-	1	2	2000 2300	-		1-12	

TOURING AROUND?

It's easy to make your accommodation arrangements when you use the wide network of Tourist Information Centres in Scotland.

If you plan to stay in a certain area, call in at the Tourist Information Centre, where a **LOCAL BOOKING** will be made for you. Look for centres showing the **BLUE** bed symbols.

If you prefer to keep on the move, many Centres also operate the Book-a-Bed-Ahead scheme, through which you can make a booking anywhere in Scotland for the same night and subsequent nights—and at some Centres, for the next night and subsequent nights. Look for the **RED** bed symbol.

Name and Address	Map Ref			Prices								Rooms				Facilities		
TOWN County — Establishment Address Telephone Telex		Bedrooms Services Meals		Bed and Breakfast — Single room overnight	Double/twin room overnight	Per person daily	B & B and evening meal — Per person weekly	Single	Double/twin	Family	Private	No. of bedrooms — Public	No. of bath/shower rooms	Evening meals	Parking (no. of cars)	Months open (1-12)	Symbols
				£min £max	£min £max	£min £max	£min £max					From Last order			Key on back fold-out		
TIRORAN Isle of Mull, Argyll	1 C2																

Tiroran House
Isle of Mull
Tel: 068-15-232

A remote and enchanting Country House Hotel, beautifully situated on Loch Scridain, renowned for its good food, offers the highest standards of comfort for those seeking to explore the lovely islands of Mull, Iona and Staffa.

Private bathrooms, games room and croquet. Geophysically central for all places of interest. Own garden produce and fresh Jersey cream. Locally caught seafood and Mull meats a speciality.

Special inclusive holidays allowing for free ferry. Egon Ronay; Good Food Guide; BTA Commended Country House Hotel.

Establishment	Bedrooms	Services	Meals	Single overnight	Double overnight	Per person daily	Per person weekly	Single	Double/twin	Family	Private	Public	Last order	Evening meals	Parking	Months open	Symbols
Tiroran House Tel. Tiroran 232	4	4	3	26.50 26.50	50.00 60.00	40.00 44.00	230.00 240.00	2	6	-	6	1	1930 1930	20	5-10	
TOBERMORY Isle of Mull, Argyll	1 C1															
Suidhe Hotel Tel. Tobermory 2209	3	3	4	10.00 -	20.00 -	16.00 -	103.60 -	2	5	2	1	3	1900 -	-	3-11	
Ulva House Hotel Strongarbh PA75 6PR Tel. Tobermory 2044	3	3	5	12.50 12.50	25.00 25.00	19.25 19.25	122.00 129.00	-	1	3	-	2	1900 2000	8	3-11	

Western Isles Hotel

The Western Isles Hotel holds a number of specialised weekends throughout the year at all-inclusive rates. Choose from whatever interests you most.

Golfing Weekend
A heaven on earth for any golfer.

Bird Watching Weekend
A must for anyone with an interest in bird life.

Sea Food Festival Weekend
Superb locally caught delicacies

Ceilidh Weekend
A riotous weekend of music and song.

Photographic Weekend
Scenery to delight the photographer

Gastronomic Weekend
A palate tickling taste bud extravaganza.

Rally Weekend
A spectacular night rally.

Western Isles Hotel
Tobermory, Isle of Mull, Scotland.
Tel: Tobermory 2012.

Establishment	Bedrooms	Services	Meals	Single overnight	Double overnight	Per person daily	Per person weekly	Single	Double/twin	Family	Private	Public	Last order	Evening meals	Parking	Months open	Symbols
Western Isles Hotel PA75 6PR Tel. Tobermory 2012	4	5	5	18.00 19.50	32.00 35.00	27.00 28.50	145.00 165.00	6	14	9	15	5	1900 2045	20	3-10	
Ach-Na-Craoibh Guest House Tel. Tobermory 2301	3	2	1	6.90 14.38	13.80 19.56	- -	- -	-	3	1	-	2	- -	6	4-10	

Name and Address	Map Ref	Bedrooms	Services	Meals	Bed and Breakfast Single room overnight £min £max	Double/twin room overnight £min £max	Per person daily £min £max	B & B and evening meal Per person weekly £min £max	Single	Double/twin	Family	Private	No. of bedrooms From Last order	No. of bath/shower rooms Public	Evening meals	Parking (no. of cars)	Months open (1-12)	Facilities Symbols
TOBERMORY continued	1 C1															Key on back fold-out	
Staffa Cottages Guest House Tel. Tobermory 2464		3	3	2	-	-	15.80 -	100.00 -	-	4	1	-	1	- 1900	6	3-10	🐕 🏠 💻 ♿ Ⓒ ✷ Ⓥ ♺

The Tobermory Guest House

Tobermory, Isle of Mull. Telephone (0688) 2091

Delightfully situated right on the waterfront, with all double, twin, and family bedrooms overlooking the beautiful Tobermory Bay. Tea/Coffee making facilities in all rooms. Two lounges. Licensed. AA Listed. Special Motorist Package includes ferry from Oban, visits to Iona and Fingal's cave, Duart and Torasay Castles and the Old Byre museum. Fishing, sea angling, bird watching, all arranged. Brochure and tariff on request.

Name and Address	Map Ref	Bedrooms	Services	Meals	Single room overnight	Double/twin room overnight	Per person daily	Per person weekly	Single	Double/twin	Family	Private	No. of bedrooms	Public	Evening meals	Parking	Months open	Facilities
Tobermory Guest House 53 Main Street Tel. Tobermory 2091		3	4	3	11.50 12.00	23.00 24.00	16.50 18.00	110.00 120.00	3	8	2	-	5	1930 1930	-	3-11	Ⓣ ♀ 🐕 🏠 💻 ♿ 🏠 ✦ Ⓒ Ⓥ ♺ ✦ ⛷
TOMATIN Inverness-shire	4 B9																

Freeburn Inn Fully Licensed Hotel.

Tomatin, Inverness-shire. Tel: 08082 205.

Enjoy a holiday here with a fund of activities within easy reach e.g. fishing, hill-walking, golf, touring etc. Or use us as a convenient stopping place as you journey through the Highlands.

We are a family run Country Hotel centrally placed between Inverness and Aviemore and we offer spacious accommodation, with a reputation for good service and excellent food.

Name and Address	Map Ref	Bedrooms	Services	Meals	Single room overnight	Double/twin room overnight	Per person daily	Per person weekly	Single	Double/twin	Family	Private	No. of bedrooms	Public	Evening meals	Parking	Months open	Facilities
Freeburn Inn Tel. Tomatin 205		3	4	4	9.00 -	18.00 -	15.00 -	90.00 -	1	5	2	-	2	1915 2015	50	1-12	Ⓣ ♀ 🐕 🏠 ♿ 🏠 ✦ ✷ 🏠 Ⓥ ♺ ✦ ⛷
Glenan Lodge Guest House IV13 7YT Tel. Tomatin 217		1	2	2	6.50 -	-	10.50 -	-	3	6	1	-	3	1830 1930	10	1-12	🐕 ✿ 💻 ♿ Ⓒ Ⓥ ♺ ✦
TOMINTOUL, Ballindalloch **Banffshire**	4 D10																
Gordon Arms Hotel The Square AB3 9ET Tel. Tomintoul 206		3	3	4	11.00 -	22.00 -	-	-	15	15	5	6	10	1930 2000	20	1-12	Ⓣ ⛟ ♀ 🐕 💻 ♿ 🏠 ✦ ✷ Ⓥ ♺ ✦ ⛷
Richmond Arms Hotel The Square AB3 9ET Tel. Tomintoul 209		4	3	4	10.60 -	21.20 -	-	-	7	14	6	8	4	1930 2030	28	1-12	💷 ⛟ ♀ 🐕 ✿ 💻 ♿ 💻 🏠 ✦ Ⓒ Ⓥ ♺ ✦ ⛷
Argyle Guest House AB3 9EX Tel. Tomintoul 223		3	2	2	7.50 -	15.00 -	12.50 -	80.00 -	-	3	3	-	2	1900 2000	12	1-12	Ⓣ 🐕 💻 ♿ 🏠 ✦ Ⓒ 🏠 Ⓥ ♺ ✦ ⛷

VAT is shown at 15%: changes in this rate may affect prices.

Name and Address				Prices									Rooms				Facilities
TOWN / County / Establishment / Address / Telephone / Telex	Map Ref	Bedrooms	Services	Meals	Bed and Breakfast — Single room overnight (£min £max)	Double/twin room overnight (£min £max)	Per person daily (£min £max)	Per person weekly (£min £max)	B & B and evening meal — Single	Double/twin	Family	Private	Public	No. of bedrooms	No. of bath/shower rooms	Evening meals (From / Last order)	Parking (no. of cars) / Months open (1-12) / Symbols (Key on back fold-out)

TONGUE — Sutherland — Map Ref 4 / A3

AA.** R.S.A.C. ** R.A.C.
Ben Loyal Hotel
Tongue, Sutherland IV27 4XE

FULLY LICENSED. The hotel is situated on the north coast overlooking the Kyle of Tongue and Ben Loyal. H. & C. water, electric shaver points and electric blankets in all bedrooms with central heating throughout.

Brown Trout Fishing, Hill Climbing, Hind Stalking by arrangement. Lovely beaches and safe sea bathing. An ideal centre for touring the whole north coast.

Enjoy the friendly atmosphere and good table, under the personal supervision of the proprietors.

Tel: Tongue (080 05) 216

Establishment	Map Ref	Bedrooms	Services	Meals	Single room overnight	Double/twin room overnight	Per person daily	Per person weekly	Single	Double/twin	Family	Private	Public	No. of bedrooms	No. of bath/shower rooms	Evening meals	Parking	Months open	Symbols
Ben Loyal Hotel / IV27 4XE / Tel. Tongue 216		3	4	4	12.50 / 14.50	20.00 / 33.00	19.00 / 21.00	- / -	4	15	-	5	4	1900 / 2000	18	1-12			[symbols]
Tongue Hotel / IV27 4XD / Tel. Tongue 206/7 / Telex 778215		3	4	4	16.65 / 19.95	35.40 / 39.90	23.70 / 28.70	186.55 / 196.35	5	18	-	14	4	1900 / 2045	20	1-12			[symbols]
TORLUNDY, by Fort William / Inverness-shire	3 / G12																		
Inverlochy Castle Hotel / PH33 68N / Tel. Fort William 2177		6	6	6	- / 70.00	98.00 / 120.00	70.00 / 85.00	- / -	1	13	-	13	2	2000 / 2200	2	4-11			[symbols]
TORPHINS / Aberdeenshire	4 / F10																		
Learney Arms Hotel / Tel. Torphins 202		4	3	4	10.50 / 20.00	21.00 / 25.00	16.25 / -	98.00 / -	1	9	1	4	3	1700 / 2045	25	1-12			[symbols]
TORRIDON, by Achnasheen / Ross-shire	3 / F8																		
Loch Torridon Hotel / Tel. Torridon 242		3	3	3	17.00 / 19.00	31.55 / 40.40	26.00 / 28.00	- / -	6	12	1	12	6	1900 / 2100	30	5-10			[symbols]
Annat Lodge / Tel. Torridon 200		3	3	2	9.50 / 9.50	15.00 / -	12.00 / -	75.00 / -	1	2	1	1	1	1900 / -	6	4-10			[symbols]
TOWARD, by Dunoon / Argyll	1 / F5																		
Tollard House Hotel / Tel. Toward 219		3	4	2	9.25 / 10.25	17.50 / 19.50	13.00 / 14.00	80.00 / 90.00	-	9	1	2	2	1900 / 1930	15	1-12			[symbols]

Name and Address	Map Ref			Bed and Breakfast			B & B and evening meal						No. of bed-rooms	No. of bath/ shower rooms			Facilities
	Bedrooms	Services	Meals	Single room overnight	Double/twin room overnight	Per person daily	Per person weekly	Single	Double/twin	Family	Private	Public			Evening meals	Parking (no. of cars)	Months open (1-12) / Symbols
				£min £max	£min £max	£min £max	£min £max								From Last order		Key on back fold-out
TROON **Ayrshire**	**1** **G7**																
Ardneil Hotel St Meddans Street KA10 6NU Tel. Troon 311611	3	3	4	13.00 15.50	26.00 30.00	17.00 18.50	- -	3	5	1	3	3			1700 2100	45	1-12
Craiglea Hotel South Beach KA10 6EG Tel. Troon 311366	-	-	:	17.50 20.00	30.00 34.00	25.00 28.50	175.00 199.50	5	15	2	12	4			1900 2045	17	1-12
Knowe Hotel Templehill KA10 6BH Tel. Troon 311223	-	-	-	13.00 16.00	24.00 28.00	20.50 23.50	143.50 164.50	1	4	2	1	1			1800 -	30	1-12

Marine Hotel, Troon, Ayrshire. Tel. 0292-314444

This luxury hotel with its superb French Restaurant, Hairdressing Salon and Boutique stands overlooking Royal Troon championship golf course in the centre of Ayrshire's many golf courses and Robert Burns homeland. Nearby the Magnum Leisure Centre offers a vast array of indoor sports and the Troon Marina an opportunity for sailing and boating. 70 bedrooms with Private Bath, Tea and Coffee making facilities, colour T.V., Telephone and Radio Intercom.

Name and Address	Bedrooms	Services	Meals	Single room overnight	Double/twin room overnight	Per person daily	Per person weekly	Single	Double/twin	Family	Private	Public	No. of bed-rooms	No. of bath/ shower rooms	Evening meals	Parking	Months open
Marine Hotel Crosbie Road KA10 6HG Tel. Troon 314444 ' Telex 778215	6	6	6	35.00 35.00	54.00 54.00	35.00 35.00	189.00 189.00	26	44	-	70	-			1930 2215	146	1-12
Piersland Lodge Hotel Craigend Road Tel. Troon 314747	5	3	5	14.50 17.50	25.00 28.00	20.50 23.50	- -	-	9	3	12	-			1700 2100	100	1-12
South Beach Hotel South Beach KA10 6EG Tel. Troon 312033	3	4	4	12.00 15.50	21.00 29.50	17.45 22.95	120.00 120.00	2	21	2	6	5			1700 2030	40	1-12

DON'T KNOW SCOTLAND TOO WELL?

You probably know whether you want to stay in the north-east, the south-west, or some other part of the country—but you may not know all the little towns and villages in that area.

That's where the MAPS in this book can help you.

Simply look at the page showing the area you have chosen, then check the names marked on that part of the map. Each name has a corresponding entry in the text, with a list of accommodation which you can contact.

It's easy!

VAT is shown at 15%: changes in this rate may affect prices.

Name and Address	Map Ref				Prices				Rooms						Facilities	
TOWN County Establishment Address Telephone Telex		Bedrooms	Services	Meals	Bed and Breakfast			B & B and evening meal	No. of bedrooms			No. of bath/shower rooms		Evening meals	Parking (no. of cars)	Months open (1-12)
					Single room overnight	Double/twin room overnight	Per person daily	Per person weekly	Single	Double/twin	Family	Private	Public			Symbols
TROON continued	1 G7				£min £max	£min £max	£min £max	£min £max						From Last order		Key on back fold-out

Sun Court Hotel

19 Crosbie Road, Troon.
Tel: (0292) 312727

Popular with local people for Good Food and Sports Facilities. (Real tennis, Squash and Lawn Tennis.) Personally owned and managed. Overlooks Royal Troon Golf Course and the Sea. B.T.A. Commended.

Name and Address	Bed	Serv	Meal	Single overnight	Double overnight	Per person daily	Per person weekly	Single	Double/twin	Family	Private	Public	Evening meals	Parking	Months
Sun Court Hotel 19 Crosbie Road KA10 6HF Tel. Troon 312727	5	5	5	26.00 29.00	42.00 46.00	36.50 39.50	-	7	9	5	18	1	1930 2130	70	1-12
Glenside Guest House 2 Darley Place KA10 6JQ Tel. Troon 313677	3	3	1	- -	14.00 -	- -	- -	-	4	2	-	2	-	6	1-12
TURNBERRY **Ayrshire** (1 G8)															
Turnberry Hotel & Golf Courses KA26 9LT Tel. Turnberry 202	6	6	6	45.00 65.00	70.00 95.00	- -	- -	37	87	-	124	-	2000 2145	250	1-12
TWEEDSMUIR, Biggar **Lanarkshire** (2 C7)															

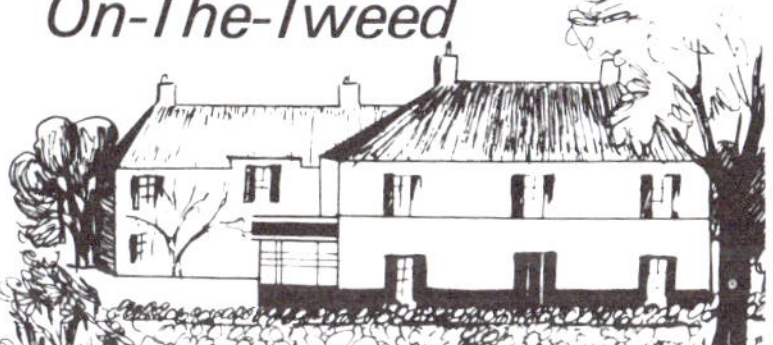

The Crook Inn
On-The-Tweed
Tweedsmuir, Biggar, Lanarkshire. Tel. 08997-272.

The Crook Inn has been a landmark of the Borders since 1604. Set in the heart of the beautiful Tweedsmuir hills it has 8 comfortable bedrooms, most with private bathrooms.

The surrounding area is steeped in history and the Inn is an ideal centre for walking, touring, golf, fishing or just relaxing, while enjoying superb food and the warmth of local hospitality.

Mini breaks and bargain weeks available.

Resident Owners: Charles and Debbie Masraff.

Name and Address	Bed	Serv	Meal	Single overnight	Double overnight	Per person daily	Per person weekly	Single	Double/twin	Family	Private	Public	Evening meals	Parking	Months
Crook Inn Tel. Tweedsmuir 272	4	4	5	17.00 19.00	30.00 34.00	25.00 27.00	144.00 158.00	1	7	-	6	1	1930 2130	53	1-12

| Name and Address | | | Prices | | | | | B & B and evening meal | | | | Rooms | | Facilities |
TOWN County / Establishment Address Telephone Telex	Map Ref	Bedrooms / Services / Meals	Bed and Breakfast				Single room overnight	Double/twin room overnight	Per person daily	Per person weekly	Single	Double/twin	Family	Private	No. of bedrooms	No. of bath/ shower rooms	Symbols
			£min £max	£min £max	£min £max	£min £max								From Last order	Key on back fold-out	
TWYNHOLM Kirkcudbrightshire	2 A10															
Burnbank Hotel DG6 4NX Tel. Twynholm 244		3 4 5	7.50 7.50	15.00 15.00	10.50 10.50	66.50 66.50	2	4	-	-	2	1800 2215	12	1-12	
Star Hotel Tel. Twynholm 279		3 4 4	7.00 8.00	14.00 16.00	- -	- -	-	2	1	-	1	1900 2130	2	1-12	
TYNDRUM, by Crianlarich Perthshire	1 G2															

Family run hotel/free house. Set in beautiful Highland scenery on the new West Highland Way at the junction of the A82 and A85 to Fort William and Oban. Prime area for walking and skiing etc. Packed lunches, drying facilities, central heating, colour TV/video, children and dogs welcome.
Special terms available for parties.
Proprietors: John & Barbara Riley.
Tel: Tyndrum (08384) 219.

Name and Address	Bedrooms Services Meals	Single room overnight	Double/twin room overnight	Per person daily	Per person weekly	Single	Double/twin	Family	Private	Public	No. of bedrooms / Last order	Bath/shower	Months open	Symbols
Invervey Hotel FK20 8RY Tel. Tyndrum 219	3 3 4	8.50 8.50	17.00 17.00	12.00 12.00	75.00 75.00	3	10	2	-	4	1700 2100	50	1-12	
Royal Hotel FK20 8RZ Tel. Tyndrum 272	3 3 2	- 9.00	- 18.00	- 11.50	- -	25	51	8	20	11	1830 2000	200	4-10	
TYNET, Buckie Moray	4 E8													
The Mill Motel AB5 2HJ Tel. Clochan 233	4 3 4	- 15.75	- 30.00	- 23.25	- 139.50	9	5	1	15	-	1930 2030	200	1-12	
UDDINGSTON Lanarkshire	2 A5													
Red Stones Hotel 8 Glasgow Road Tel. Uddingston 813774	- - -	25.00 25.00	34.00 34.00	41.50 51.50	- -	5	8	-	13	-	1830 2130	45	1-12	
Northcote Guest House 2 Holmbrae Avenue Tel. Uddingston 813319	3 3 2	7.00 7.00	12.00 14.00	11.00 11.00	66.00 77.00	1	1	1	-	1	1800 2000	3	1-12	
UIG Isle of Skye, Inverness-shire	3 D8													
Ferry Inn Hotel Tel. Uig 242	3 3 3	15.00 18.00	20.00 26.00	16.00 20.00	- -	-	4	2	1	2	1800 2100	12	1-12	

VAT is shown at 15%: changes in this rate may affect prices.

Name and Address				Prices					Rooms						Facilities		
TOWN / County / Establishment / Address / Telephone / Telex	Map Ref / Bedrooms / Services / Meals			Bed and Breakfast			B & B and evening meal	No. of bedrooms			No. of bath/shower rooms						
				Single room overnight	Double/twin room overnight	Per person daily	Per person weekly	Single	Double/twin	Family	Private	Public	Evening meals	Parking (no. of cars)	Months open (1-12)	Symbols
UIG continued — 3 D8				£min £max	£min £max	£min £max	£min £max				From		Last order			Key on back fold-out

UIG HOTEL ISLE OF SKYE IV51 9YE

Telephone: Uig (047-042) 205   *Telegrams:* Uigotel Portree

A COMFORTABLE COUNTRY HOTEL

In Prince Charlie and Flora Macdonald country on a hillside overlooking Uig Bay and Loch Snizort. Old Coaching Inn with converted steading. Twenty five bedrooms all with private bath or shower. Central heating throughout. Garden produce and good home cooking. Walking, river, loch fishing and pony trekking. Car ferry daily (except Sundays) to and from Tarbert and Lochmaddy in the Outer Hebrides.

Proprietors: **Grace M. Graham and David Taylor**

Establishment	Map Ref	Bedrooms	Services	Meals	Single room overnight	Double/twin room overnight	Per person daily	Per person weekly	Single	Double/twin	Family	Private	Public	Evening meals (last order)	Parking	Months open	Symbols
Uig Hotel, 1V51 9YE, Tel. Uig 205/367 (Guests)	3 D8	4	5	3	15.00 / 24.00	30.00 / 48.00	23.00 / 33.00	180.00 / 195.00	6	18	1	25	-	1900 / 2000	25	4-9	(symbols)
Caberfeidh Guest House, Sheader, Tel. Uig 342		-	-	-	-	13.00	-	-	-	2	1	-	2	-	6	4-10	(symbols)
Uig Guest House, 7 Idrigill, Tel. Uig 269		-	-	-	7.00 / 7.00	14.00 / 14.00	-	-	2	5	-	-	2	-	10	1-12	(symbols)

ULLAPOOL Ross-shire	3 G6

Altnaharrie Inn West Highlands of Scotland

Offers you a romantic secluded setting by the water's edge, a friendly informal atmosphere, excellent food and fine wines.

We have only three bedrooms and access to the inn is by our private launch (the crossing from Ullapool takes only a few minutes).

Tel: or write for brochure: Altnaharrie Inn, Ullapool, Wester Ross. Tel: Dundonnell 230.

Establishment	Map Ref	Bedrooms	Services	Meals	Single room overnight	Double/twin room overnight	Per person daily	Per person weekly	Single	Double/twin	Family	Private	Public	Evening meals (last order)	Parking	Months open	Symbols
Altnaharrie Inn, IV26 2SS, Tel. Dundonnell 230		3	3	4	15.00	30.00	-	-	-	3	-	3	1	1930	-	3-10	(symbols)
Arch Inn, 11 West Shore Street, IV26 2UR, Tel. Ullapool 2454		3	3	4	11.00	20.00	18.00	-	-	7	1	3	2	1845 / 2015	11	3-11	(symbols)
Argyll Hotel, Argyle Street, IV26 2UB, Tel. Ullapool 2422		-	-	-	10.50 / 14.00	21.00 / 28.00	-	-	-	6	2	-	3	1900 / 2030	12	1-12	(symbols)
Caledonian Hotel, IV26 2UG, Tel. Ullapool 2306		3	3	4	8.00	16.00	13.00	84.00	27	75	-	57	15	1830 / 2000	10	4-10	(symbols)

Name and Address	Map Ref	Bedrooms	Services	Meals	Single room overnight (£min/£max)	Double/twin room overnight (£min/£max)	Per person daily (£min/£max)	Per person weekly (£min/£max)	Single	Double/twin	Family	Private	Public	Evening meals (Last order)	Parking (no. of cars)	Months open (1-12)	Symbols
ULLAPOOL continued	3 G6													From			Key on back fold-out
The Ceilidh Place, West Argyle Street, IV26 2TY, Tel. Ullapool 2103		4	5	6	17.00 / 20.00	32.00 / 40.00	25.00 / 28.00	126.00 / 150.00	2	13	-	8	3	1700 / 2100	30	4-10	(facility symbols)
The Ceilidh Place Clubhouse, West Argyle Street, IV26 2TY, Tel. Ullapool 2103		3	2	4	9.85 / 13.50	16.70 / 23.00	12.50 / 15.00	- / -	4	5	2	-	10	1700 / 2100	30	4-10	(facility symbols)
Ladbroke Hotel, Tel. Ullapool 2314		-	-	-	26.50 / -	40.00 / -	- / -	- / -	15	21	24	60	-	1830 / 2100	100	4-10	(facility symbols)
Morefield Motel, Tel. Ullapool 2161		3	3	5	15.00 / -	21.00 / 25.00	- / -	- / -	-	10	2	12	-	1800 / 2100	12	4-10	(facility symbols)
Royal Hotel, IV26 2SY, Tel. Ullapool 2181		5	6	5	16.00 / 23.50	30.00 / 45.00	25.00 / 32.50	150.00 / 200.00	11	41	8	45	5	1900 / 2130	200	1-12	(facility symbols)
Brae Guest House, Shore Street, IV26 2UJ, Tel. Ullapool 2421		3	3	2	9.00 / -	16.00 / -	12.50 / -	- / -	1	8	3	-	3	1700 / 2000	12	5-10	(facility symbols)
Eilean Donan House, 14 Market Street, Tel. Ullapool 2012/2612		3	3	2	- / -	14.00 / 14.00	- / -	- / -	-	7	1	-	3	1900 / 1930	20	4-10	(facility symbols)
Point Guest House, 26 West Shore Street, IV26 2UR, Tel. Ullapool 2080		4	3	2	7.50 / 7.50	15.00 / 15.00	12.00 / 12.00	- / -	-	4	-	1	1	1800 / 1900	6	1-12	(facility symbols)

LADBROKE HOTEL ULLAPOOL

From check-in to check-out you will enjoy the warm hospitality of our Ullapool Hotel.

A drink, a meal and a good nights rest in a room with private bath and colour T.V. It's well worth stopping for.

♦ Ladbroke Hotels

Ladbroke Hotel, Ullapool, Ross and Cromarty, IV26 2UD. Tel: (0854) 2314.

Name and Address	Map Ref	Bedrooms	Services	Meals	Single room overnight £min £max	Double/twin room overnight £min £max	Per person daily £min £max	Per person weekly £min £max	Single	Double/twin	Family	Private	Public	Evening meals From Last order	Parking (no. of cars)	Months open (1-12)	Symbols Key on back fold-out
UPHALL West Lothian	2 C5																
Houstoun House Tel. Broxburn 853831 Telex 727148		5	5	4	38.00 46.00	54.00 64.00	52.00 60.00	- -	6	23	1	30	-	1930 2130	100	1-12	T £ ♀ ♘ ✂ ♘ ▦ ⚲ ◗ ☎ ⌨ ☐ ⌂ ⚮ C ✳ ⌂ V ◡
UPPER LARGO Fife	2 D3																
The Largo Hotel 4 Main Street Tel. Upper Largo 236		3	3	5	10.00 -	20.00 -	12.50 17.00	87.50 119.00	1	5	-	1	1	1900 2100	60	1-12	⚮ ♀ ♘ ♘ ⌂ ⚡ ⌂ V
VIDLIN, North Mainland Shetland	5 G3																
Lunna House Hotel Tel. Vidlin 237		-	-	-	10.00 10.00	20.00 20.00	14.00 14.00	98.00 98.00	2	7	-	2	2	- -	9	5-9	♘ ♞ ⌂ ⚡ ✳ ⌂ V
WALKERBURN Peeblesshire	2 D6																

TWEED VALLEY HOTEL
On the Tweed – 32 miles South of Edinburgh
Walkerburn   Peeblesshire
R.A.C.**   Tel: 089687-220

SPECIAL BREAK RATES
Bedrooms with private bath & toilet en suite.

Privately owned country house hotel in beautiful hill country.

**10% Mill Shop Discount for Guests ·
Car Touring Centre · Shopping ·
Walking · Fishing · Rod hire and
Tuition · Shooting holidays**

Fully Licensed   14 Bedrooms
Central Heating throughout   Bar Meals
Easy reach from England
Proprietors: Charles and Joyce Miller

Ashley Courtenay Recommended

Name and Address	Bedrooms	Services	Meals	Single room overnight £min £max	Double/twin room overnight £min £max	Per person daily £min £max	Per person weekly £min £max	Single	Double/twin	Family	Private	Public	Evening meals From Last order	Parking	Months open	Symbols
Tweed Valley Hotel Galashiels Road Tel. Walkerburn 220	4	4	5	22.50 27.00	37.00 45.00	31.00 36.50	204.00 226.00	4	9	2	14	3	1900 2100	40	1-12	T £ ⚮ ♀ ♘ ✂ ♘ ▦ ⚲ ⌂ ⚡ C ✳ V ◡ ♪ ⚑
WALLS Shetland	5 F4															
Burrastow House	3	4	3	22.50 22.50	45.00 45.00	30.00 35.00	175.00 183.00	-	3	-	-	2	1900 2100	8	1-12	⚮ ♀ ♘ ✂ ♘ ▦ ⚲ ☐ ⌂ ⚡ C ✳ V

Name and Address (Town / County / Establishment, Address, Telephone, Telex)	Map Ref	Bedrooms	Services	Meals	Single room overnight £min/£max	Double/twin room overnight £min/£max	Per person daily £min/£max	Per person weekly £min/£max	Single	Double/twin	Family	Private	Public	Evening meals (From / Last order)	Parking (no. of cars)	Months open (1-12)	Symbols
WATERNISH Isle of Skye, Inverness-shire	3 C8																
Stein Inn, Stein, IV51 9QA, Tel. Waternish 208		3	3	5	9.50 / 9.50	19.00 / 19.00	- / -	- / -	1	4	1	-	2	1900 / 2130	-	1-12	Key on back fold-out
WATTEN, by Wick Caithness	4 D3																
Loch Watten Hotel, Tel. Watten 232		3	3	3	8.50 / -	16.00 / -	14.00 / -	95.00 / -	-	5	1	-	2	1730 / 2100	40	1-12	
WEST LINTON Peeblesshire	2 C6																
Gordon Arms Hotel, Dolphinton Road, Tel. West Linton 60208		3	3	3	6.50 / 8.50	13.00 / 17.00	9.00 / 11.00	- / -	1	4	-	-	1	1800 / 2200	12	1-12	
Cottage Guest House, Mountain Cross, Tel. West Linton 60329		1	2	2	8.00 / -	14.00 / -	10.00 / -	- / -	-	2	2	-	1	1600 / 1830	6	5-10	
Medwyn House Guest House, Medwyn Road, Tel. West Linton 60542		-	-	-	10.00 / -	22.00 / -	16.00 / -	100.00 / -	-	2	1	3	-	1800 / 2100	14	4-10	
Rutherford Guest House, Tel. West Linton 60716		3	3	4	7.50 / -	15.00 / -	- / -	- / -	-	2	2	-	1	1830 / 2030	12	1-12	
Broomlee Outdoor Centre & School Camp, Tel. West Linton 60259		-	-	3	5.70 / 5.70	- / -	6.70 / 8.20	39.35 / 48.65	24	-	-	-	2	1700 / -	50	4-10	Dormitories for Group Bookings
WHITBURN West Lothian	2 B5																
Whitedale Hotel, Main Street, Tel. Whitburn 40818		3	3	4	18.50 / -	28.00 / -	- / -	- / -	2	10	-	3	3	1900 / 2130	50	1-12	

COMPLAINTS

Any complaints or criticisms about individual establishments should where possible be taken up immediately with the management. In many cases the problems can be dealt with satisfactorily, thus avoiding any prolonged unhappiness during your stay.

If this procedure fails to remedy the grievance to your satisfaction, and particularly where serious complaints are concerned, please write to the local Tourist Organisation.

VAT is shown at 15%: changes in this rate may affect prices.

Name and Address		Prices					Rooms			Facilities	
TOWN County / Establishment Address Telephone Telex	Map Ref / Bedrooms Services Meals	Single room overnight £min £max	Double/twin room overnight £min £max	Per person daily £min £max	Per person weekly £min £max	B & B and evening meal (Single, Double/twin, Family, Private)	No. of bedrooms (Public)	No. of bath/shower rooms (Evening meals) From Last order	Parking (no. of cars)	Months open (1-12) Key on back fold-out	Symbols
WHITEBRIDGE Inverness-shire	4 A10										

WHITEBRIDGE HOTEL
WHITEBRIDGE · INVERNESS-SHIRE

The Hotel is situated 600ft high in magnificent un-spoilt country to the south of Loch Ness, ideal for the naturalist and bird watcher. Centrally placed making a convenient and popular centre for touring by car. Also, a friendly atmosphere which is created by guests who return year after year.

Comfortably equipped all bedrooms are centrally heated, have T.V., and tea making facilities, most with private bath/shower and WC.

Fully licensed with popular lounge bar and cocktail bar offering a high standard of comfort and catering.

Excellent trout fishing is available on several easily accessible Hotel Lochs. Fishing for salmon and sea trout can be arranged.

Resident Prop: Mr and Mrs D. F. Bailey
Telephone Nos: Hotel Gorthleck 226
STD 045-63 226
R.A.C.**   R.S.P.B.   A.A.**   EXECHOTELS   R.S.A.C.

Name and Address	Map Ref	Bed	Svc	Meals	Single room o/n	Double/twin o/n	Per person daily	Per person weekly	Single	Double/twin	Family	Private	No. of bedrooms	Public/Last order	Evening meals	Parking	Months open	Symbols
Whitebridge Hotel IV1 2UN Tel. Gorthleck 226		4	4	4	11.00 -	13.25 -	18.00 -	110.00 125.00	1	8	3	8	2	1900 2000	40	2-10	
WHITENESS Shetland	5 G4																	
Westlings Hotel Wormadale Tel. Gott 242		4	4	5	18.50 -	28.00 -	21.00 -	120.75	4	5	-	9	1	1845 2200	20	1-12	
WHITHORN Wigtownshire	1 H11																	
Black Hawk Inn 2 St John Street Tel. Whithorn 231		3	4	4	6.50 -	13.00 -	-	-	1	3	-	-	1	-	10	1-12	
WHITING BAY Isle of Arran	1 F7																	
Burlington Private Hotel Tel. Whiting Bay 255		2	2	2	7.00 7.25	14.00 14.50	10.00 10.50	66.50 70.00	4	7	3	-	3	- 1800	10	3-10	
Cameronia Hotel Tel. Whiting Bay 254		3	4	4	11.50 -	23.00 -	16.10 -	103.00	1	4	2	-	2	1800 2200	13	1-12	
Craigielea Hotel Tel. Whiting Bay 245		2	3	2	6.50 8.50	13.00 17.00	8.50 11.50	59.50 80.50	1	4	3	-	1	1800 1800	10	4-10	

Name and Address — TOWN / County / Establishment / Address / Telephone / Telex	Map Ref	Bedrooms	Services	Meals	Single room overnight £min/£max	Double/twin room overnight £min/£max	Per person daily £min/£max	Per person weekly £min/£max	Single	Double/twin	Family	Private	Public	Evening meals (From / Last order)	No. of bedrooms	No. of bath/shower rooms	Parking (no. of cars)	Months open (1-12)	Symbols (Key on back fold-out)
WHITING BAY continued	1 / F7																		
Invermay Hotel Tel. Whiting Bay 431		3	2	2	6.50 / 7.00	13.00 / 14.00	12.00 / 13.00	84.00 / 91.00	5	4	3	-	2	1800 / -	8		4-10		(symbols)
Royal Hotel Tel. Whiting Bay 286		3	3	2	9.00 / -	18.00 / -	13.00 / -	- / -	3	5	2	1	1	1800 / 1830	20		3-10		(symbols)
Stanford Guest House Tel. Whiting Bay 313		3	2	2	7.00 / -	14.00 / -	11.00 / -	77.00 / -	3	1	2	-	1	1800 / 1200	6		4-9		(symbols)
Trafalgar Guest House Tel. Whiting Bay 396		3	2	5	7.00 / 7.50	14.00 / 15.00	10.00 / 11.00	70.00 / 77.00	-	2	1	-	2	1700 / 2130	5		1-12		(symbols)
WICK **Caithness**	4 / E3																		

Name and Address	Map Ref	Bedrooms	Services	Meals	Single room overnight £min/£max	Double/twin room overnight £min/£max	Per person daily £min/£max	Per person weekly £min/£max	Single	Double/twin	Family	Private	Public	Evening meals (From / Last order)	No. of bedrooms	No. of bath/shower rooms	Parking (no. of cars)	Months open (1-12)	Symbols
Ladbroke Hotel Riverside Tel. Wick 3344		5	5	5	29.50 / -	45.00 / -	- / -	- / -	1	42	5	48	-	1830 / 2100	30		1-12		(symbols)
Mackays Hotel Tel. Wick 2323		2	2	3	15.00 / -	29.00 / -	- / -	- / -	11	17	2	3	10	1730 / 2200	14		1-12		(symbols)
Nethercliffe Hotel Tel. Wick 2044		3	3	2	8.00 / -	16.00 / -	10.00 / -	70.00 / -	-	5	2	1	3	1800 / 1900	-		1-12		(symbols)
Queens Hotel Francis Street Tel. Wick 2992		4	4	5	11.90 / 12.50	22.00 / 24.50	- / -	- / -	4	6	-	-	3	1900 / 2130	20		1-12		(symbols)
Rosebank Hotel Thurso Street KW1 5LF Tel. Wick 3244		4	4	5	11.50 / 15.00	23.00 / 30.00	18.00 / 21.50	126.00 / 150.00	13	14	1	10	3	1730 / 2200	18		1-12		(symbols)
County Guest House 101 High Street Tel. Wick 2911		3	3	1	6.50 / -	12.00 / -	- / -	- / -	-	2	4	-	2	- / -	-		1-12		(symbols)
Harbour Guest House 6 Rose Street Tel. Wick 3276		3	3	2	6.50 / -	13.00 / -	10.00 / -	- / -	1	9	-	-	2	- / 1830	-		1-12		(symbols)

VAT is shown at 15%: changes in this rate may affect prices.

Name and Address	Map Ref	Bedrooms	Services	Meals	Single room overnight £min £max	Double/twin room overnight £min £max	Per person daily £min £max	Per person weekly £min £max	Single	Double/twin	Family	Private	Public	Evening meals (From Last order)	Parking (no. of cars)	Months open (1-12)	Symbols
WIGTOWN	1 H11																
Fordbank Country House Hotel DG8 9BT Tel. Wigtown 2346		4	3	5	12.00 -	20.00 -	16.00 -	100.00 -	1	5	-	3	1	1900 2200	50	1-12	
Craigmount Guest House DG8 9EQ Tel. Wigtown 2291		3	3	2	8.00 -	16.00 -	12.00 -	75.60 -	1	4	-	-	3	- 1900	-	1-12	
Laigh House Church Lane Tel. Wigtown 2375		3	2	2	10.00 12.00	16.00 20.00	12.00 15.00	75.00 95.00	-	4	-	-	1	1800 -	6	1-12	
WINCHBURGH West Lothian	2 C5																
Newton Guest House Newton Tel. 031 331 3298		3	1	2	9.00 -	18.00 -	-	-	1	1	1	-	1	1700 1830	9	1-12	
WISHAW Lanarkshire	2 A6																
Coltness Hotel Coltness Road ML2 7EX Tel. Cambusnethan 381616		3	3	4	- 15.68	- 25.30	-	-	-	12	-	-	4	1900 2100	100	1-12	
YARROW Selkirkshire	2 D7																
Gordon Arms Hotel Tel. Yarrow 222/232		3	3	4	10.50 11.50	20.00 22.00	14.50 18.50	90.00 110.00	-	6	-	-	2	1900 2030	18	1-12	
YETHOLM Roxburghshire	2 F7																
Plough Hotel Main Street Tel. Yetholm 215		-	-	-	9.00 -	18.00 -	12.00 -	-	1	3	-	-	1	1900 2100	7	1-12	
Bowmount Centre & Guest House Belford-on-Bowmont Tel. Yetholm 362 Telex 537174		1	2	3	6.50 -	13.00 -	10.50 -	65.00 -	-	2	1	-	2	1900 -	10	4-10	

The Scottish Tourist Guides Association offers the services of trained guides at reasonable prices. Many are fluent in foreign languages.
UK bookings (during office hours) **031-229 3032.**

Details and charges from:
Mrs Jean Duncan, STGA Publicity Officer, 133 Hillhouse Road, Edinburgh EH4 7AF, or from the Scottish Tourist Board, **23 Ravelston Terrace, Edinburgh EH4 3EU.**

Entries in this guide carry a classification number (on a scale of 1 to 6) for **Bedrooms, Services** and **Meals.** The facilities offered within each category are indicated below.

BEDROOMS

CATEGORY 

Bedrooms. Reasonable free space for movement and for easy access to beds, doors and drawers. Minimum floor areas, excluding private bath or shower areas: single bedrooms 60sq ft (5.60sq metres); double bedrooms 90sq ft (8.40sq metres); twin bedded rooms 110sq ft (10.20sq metres); family rooms 30sq ft (2.80sq metres) plus 60sq ft (5.60sq metres) for each double bed, and/or 40sq ft (3.70 metres) for each single adult bed, and/or 20sq ft (1.85sq metres) for each cot.

Minimum bed sizes (except children's beds): single beds 6ft × 2ft 6ins) (183 × 76cm); double beds 6ft × 4ft (183 × 122cm) spring interior, foam or similar quality mattresses in sound condition; bedding clean and in sufficient quantity.

Beds made daily. Linen changed at least weekly and for every new guest. Soap and clean towel for every new guest, replenished or changed as required. All bedrooms to have: one drinking vessel per person (minimum of two in family rooms); dressing table or equivalent and mirror; wardrobe or clothes hanging space with four hangers per person; adequate drawer space; bedside table or equivalent; one chair or equivalent; wastepaper container; ashtray; bedside rugs or mats where no carpet; at least one window and adequate ventilation; opaque curtains or blinds on all windows; adequate heating according to season. Minimum lighting levels; single bedrooms 100 watts or equivalent; double bedrooms 150 watts or equivalent.
Bathrooms. At least one bathroom, with bath or shower, available for guests at all reasonable times. Hot water at all reasonable times. No extra charge for baths or showers.
WCs. At least one WC equipped with toilet paper and disposal bin for guests' use.
General. Establishment clean throughout; all decorations, furnishings, floor coverings and fittings in good condition.

CATEGORY 

All the above facilities, plus—
Bedrooms. Washbasin, with hot and cold running water, at all times, either in the bedroom or in a private bathroom. Mirror above, or adjacent to, washbasin. One chair, or equivalent, per person (minimum of two in family rooms). One drinking vessel per person (minimum of two in family rooms). All bedrooms must be fitted with a lock that will ensure privacy for guests and security for their property. Guests must be provided with a key to their bedrooms, duplicate or master keys being kept by the management. Resident guests permitted access to their bedrooms at all times.
Bathrooms. At least one bathroom, equipped with a bath or shower, for every 15 resident guests (other than guests in bedrooms with private bathrooms). The bathroom(s) must be for the sole use of guests.
WCs. At least one WC for every 10 resident guests (other than guests in bedrooms with private bathrooms). Where there is only one WC, it must not be in a bathroom. The WC(s) must be for the sole use of guests.

CATEGORY 

All the above facilities, plus—
All bedrooms have: heating without extra charge; electric shaver point; bedside light or equivalent, as well as light controlled from the door.

CATEGORY 

All the above facilities plus—
At least 90% of bedrooms have: single beds minimum size 6ft 3ins × 3ft (190 × 90cm); double beds minimum size 6ft 3ins × 4ft 6ins (190 × 137cm), neither side of a double bed should be against a wall; full length mirror; easy chair; luggage stand(s); central heating. At least 35% of bedrooms have private bath/shower and WC en suite.

CATEGORY 5

All the above facilities plus—
At least 90% of bedrooms have: Post Office telephone connection; radio or TV, if TV reception is available; easy chair per person; heated towel rail or other adequate heating in private bathroom. At least 75% of bedrooms have private bath/shower and WC ensuite.

CATEGORY 6

All the above facilities plus—
All bedrooms to have all the facilities listed in Categories 1-5 above and writing table or equivalent. All bedrooms with private bath, shower attachment and WC en suite. Some suites available.

SERVICES
CATEGORY 

Bed-making and room cleaning service. Breakfast room (unless served in bedrooms). Public areas adequately lit for safety and comfort.
Guests informed when booking if access to establishment restricted during day. Adequate heating according to season.

CATEGORY 

All the above facilities plus—
Lounge area with adequate seating. Use of the telephone.

CATEGORY 

All the above facilities plus—
Early morning call and tea (or tea making facilities in bedroom or nearby). Assistance with luggage on request. Reception facilities. Dining/breakfast room separate from lounge.

CATEGORY 

All the above facilities plus—
Porterage. Shoe cleaning facilities. A separate TV lounge (if no TV in bedrooms), if TV reception is available. Central heating. Public telephone.

**REMEMBER—THE HIGHER THE NUMBER
THE GREATER THE RANGE OF FACILITIES**

CATEGORY  5

All the above facilities plus—
Night porter on duty. Shoe cleaning service on request. Lounge service until 2300. Writing tables if no facilities in bedrooms.

CATEGORY  6

All the above facilities plus—
Valet service. 24-hr. laundry service, except at weekends. All night lounge service.
Two or more lounges (including bar lounge).
Bookstall.
Personal hairdressing arrangements for guests.

MEALS

CATEGORY  1

Breakfast.

CATEGORY 2

Breakfast and evening meal (high tea or dinner).

CATEGORY 3

Breakfast, lunch (bar **meals** acceptable) and evening meal (high tea or dinner).

CATEGORY  4

Breakfast, lunch and dinner. Choice of dishes at all meals.

CATEGORY  5

All the above facilities plus—
Choice of Scottish or Continental breakfast. Continental breakfast available in rooms on request. A la carte menu. Meal can be ordered until at least 2130 (Sunday or off-season 2030).

CATEGORY  6

All the above facilities plus—
Coffee shop/buttery/grill room or a second restaurant. Meal can be ordered until at least 2230 (Sunday or off-season 2130). All meals served in bedrooms on request.

**REMEMBER—THE HIGHER THE NUMBER
THE GREATER THE RANGE OF FACILITIES**

CODE OF CONDUCT

In addition to fulfilling its statutory obligations, the Management undertakes to observe the following Code of Conduct:

1. To ensure high standards of courtesy, cleanliness, catering and service appropriate to the type of establishment.
2. To describe fairly to all visitors and prospective visitors the amenities, facilities and services provided by the establishment, whether by advertisement, brochure, word of mouth or any other means. To allow visitors to see accommodation, if requested, before booking.
3. To make clear to visitors exactly what is included in all prices quoted for accommodation, meals and refreshments, including service charges, taxes and other surcharges. To comply with the requirements of the Hotel Industry Voluntary Code of Booking Practice, where applicable. Details of charges for additional services or facilities available should also be made clear.
4. Adhere to, and not to exceed, prices current at time of occupation, for accommodation or other services.
5. To advise visitors at the time of booking, and subsequent to any change, if the accommodation offered is in an unconnected annexe, or similar, or by boarding out and to indicate the location of such accommodation and any difference in comfort and amenities from accommodation in the main establishment.
6. To give each visitor, on request, details of payment due, and a receipt, if required.
7. To deal promptly and courteously with all enquiries, requests, reservations, correspondence and complaints from visitors.

Isle of Skye (continued)

3D8 UIG
3C8 WATERNISH

Isle of Tiree
1A2 BALEPHETRISH
1A2 SCARNISH

Isle of North Uist
3A8 LOCHEPORT
3A8 LOCHMADDY

Isle of South Uist
3A10 DALIBURGH
3A10 LOCHBOISDALE

SEE SCOTLAND WITH A SCOTTISH TOURIST GUIDE

The Scottish Tourist Guides Association offers the services of trained guides, at reasonable prices.

Many are fluent in foreign languages.

UK bookings can be made by ringing
031-229 3032 *during office hours.*

Ask for full details of guides' services and charges from:
Mrs Jean Duncan
STGA Publicity Officer
133 Hillhouse Road
Edinburgh EH4 7AF
or from the Scottish Tourist Board

Make The Most Of Scotland

If a holiday in Scotland is top of your list this year, you couldn't have made a better choice. There's a wealth of breathtaking scenery, historic towns and points of interest to be explored — and no better way of seeing them than by train.

Getting to Scotland couldn't be easier. Our InterCity services will speed you along the East Coast between London Kings Cross, Newcastle, Edinburgh, Dundee and Aberdeen. Or you can step aboard an Electric Scot, serving the West Coast between London Euston, the Midlands, North West England and Glasgow.

Our range of bargain fares can make it easy on your pocket too — both for travelling to Scotland and after you arrive.

Try our Freedom of Scotland or Travelpass tickets, two very special ways to taste the real Scotland at remarkably low prices.

Our Railcards, for Families, Senior Citizens, Young Persons or Disabled Passengers are another way to cut the cost of travelling. Half-price travel — and sometimes less — can be a terrific help to your budget, allowing you to explore the West Highlands, the Ayrshire and Clyde Coast resorts or the Central Scottish belt without breaking the bank.

Travel to Scotland — and explore it — the sensible way, with British Rail. For more details, contact your British Rail station or rail appointed travel agent.

This is the age of the train ⚡

CLASSIFICATION

The Scottish Tourist Board has established a voluntary classification system for hotels, guest houses and bed and breakfast places in Scotland. It's designed to tell you exactly what facilities you can expect from the accommodation you select.

There are three categories in the scheme:

BEDROOMS  SERVICES  and MEALS 

You'll see them mentioned at the top of each page of entries. Each category has a number, from 1 to 6, showing the range of facilities available.

The higher the number the greater the range of facilities

If an establishment shows **1** in the Meals section, for example, it offers only breakfast—another showing **4** would offer breakfast, lunch and dinner, with a choice of dishes at all meals.

Full details of what each category includes are given in a special section immediately following the entries.

Remember this is a voluntary scheme—the establishments classify their own facilities and the Scottish Tourist Board does NOT inspect them.

TOUR SCOTLAND BY CAR

Fixed itinerary or "Go as You Please" Car Touring Holidays — using selected privately owned hotels throughout Scotland.

See and enjoy the best of Scotland from only £20 per day — dinner, bed and breakfast, in room with private bathroom.

Send for a colour brochure to:

Mhairi Stewart,
Tour Scotland,
14 Crown Street,
Inverness.

or telephone:
085 483 204.

Touring around?

It's easy to make your accommodation arrangements when you use the wide network of Tourist Information Centres in Scotland.

If you plan to stay in a certain area, call in at the Tourist Information Centre, where a **LOCAL BOOKING** will be made for you.

Look for centres showing the **BLUE** bed symbols.

If you prefer to keep on the move, many Centres also operate the Book-a-Bed-Ahead scheme, through which you can make a booking anywhere in Scotland for the same night and subsequent nights—and at some Centres, for the next night and subsequent nights.

Look for the **RED** bed symbol.

McTAVISH'S KITCHENS

Oban and Fort William

For Scottish Food and Entertainment with Singing, Piping and Dancing.

Licensed Restaurants—Centrally situated. Open 12 noon—2.30 p.m. and 6—10.30 p.m. late May/end September. A la carte and set price Table d'Hote Lunch and Evening Meal menus, Daily Chef's Specials, Scottish Specialities including Haggis, Steaks, Salmon, Kippers, Venison and Seafood.
Children's Menu.

Self Service Restaurants—Open all the year round 9.00 a.m.—9.00 p.m. in Summer. Daily Chef's Specials, Main Meals, Snacks, Teas, Coffees and quality Bakery Goods.

Entertainment—"McTavish's Scottish Evenings" 8.30 p.m.— 10.30 p.m. nightly throughout the Season. Scottish and Highland Dancing, Piping and Singing.
Reduced admission for children and parties.

McTavish's Kitchen, George Street, Oban, Argyll   Tel. 0631-63604

McTavish's Kitchen, High Street, Fort William, Inverness-shire Tel. 0397-2406

NEWMILL ELGIN

Opening hours 9.00 a.m. to 5.30 p.m. Monday to Saturday

Barclaycard/VISA and Access credit cards accepted.

KNITWEAR IN CASHMERE, WOOL AND SHETLAND	FABRICS
KILTS, SKIRTS AND JACKETS	KNITTING WOOL
SCOTTISH CRAFTS AND SOUVENIRS	TIES, SCARVES AND RUGS

MUSEUMS

AND

GALLERIES

IN

SCOTLAND

An illustrated guide to over 300 museums and art galleries in Scotland, with details of their collections and facilities. Produced with the Council for Museums and Galleries in Scotland.

ORDER FORM ON PAGE XXVI

Stakis Hotels

Your guarantee of Stakisfaction

Stakis Hotels each with its own distinctive style and character offer attractive Holiday Bargains throughout the year for ail the family.

For example, bring the children to the fabulous Stakis Coylumbridge Hotel near Aviemore or spend a holiday break at the majestic Stakis Dunblane Hydro in Perthshire. These being just two of the many distinguished hotels in the Stakis Group in Scotland.

Choose from over a dozen luxury hotels throughout Scotland. All hotel bedrooms have private bathroom, colour T.V., radio, telephone, tea and coffee makers.

Stakis Hotels are your guarantee of Stakisfaction. For further information on Stakis Holidays please send off the coupon.

To Sales and Reservation Dept., Stakis Hotels, 244 Buchanan Street, Glasgow G1 2NB. Telephone: 041-332 4343

Name ....

Address ....

....WSG

WALKS AND TRAILS IN SCOTLAND

A selection of walks over a wide variety of terrain, most of which do not require specialist equipment and are suitable for children.
Completely revised for 1984.

£1.70 (INC P&P)

ORDER FORM ON PAGE XXVI

SCOTLAND

...for the Independent Traveller.

Inter-Hotel (Scotland) offers you a choice of 24 privately owned hotels all situated at prime tourist locations throughout Scotland.

TOURING SCOTLAND BY CAR

Look out for the Inter-Hotel sign. Wide choice of plan your route tours and go as you please tours available.

CENTRED HOLIDAYS

During Heritage '84, why not relax and discover more about one area of Scotland by visiting our Castles and Historic Battlefields, enjoy the beautiful surroundings and traditional Scottish hospitality.

For **FREE** touring map and hotel list contact: **Inter-Hotel (Scotland), Dept WTS, Suite 2d, Churchill Way, Bishopbriggs, Glasgow G64 2RH. Tel: 041-762 0838. Telex: 777205 INSCOT.** For individual bookings you may contact the hotel of your choice direct.

Have a great day out in
ST. ANDREWS!!

Enjoy a wander round this Historic Wee Town! Visit the **CASTLE**, with its unique, creepy **BOTTLE DUNGEON** (no one ever escaped unaided!). **CATHEDRAL** ruins, picturesque **HARBOUR**. Scotland's oldest (1411) **UNIVERSITY** with its lovely quadrangles, the miles of **BEACHES** and the world-famous **'OLD' GOLF COURSE**.

Scotland's Treasures Assembled for Your Delight in the Woollen Mill!!

Bargain Wools — Tweeds — Tartans — Shetlands — Fair Isles — Lambswools — Cashmeres — Mohairs — Sheepskins — Travel Rugs — Ladies' Kilted Skirts — Ties — Scarves — Stoles — Capes — Arans — Harris Tweed Jackets — Bothy Blankets — Scottish Jewellery!!

WE PACK AND POST FOR YOU—ALL OVER THE WORLD!

Details, Brochure and Golf Tee free—Personal Cheques and all currencies accepted. Also Barclaycard, Visa, Access. N.B. it's easy to get here—Edinburgh 50 miles, Dundee 11 miles. Good Train and Bus services. Plenty of parking.

OPEN MONDAY TO SATURDAY 9 a.m.-1 p.m. and 2 p.m.-5 p.m.

ST. ANDREWS WOOLLEN MILL
The Golf Links, St. Andrews, Scotland

Telephone: St. Andrews (0334) 72366 (24-hour answering service)

SCOTLAND FOR HILLWALKING

Over 60 more difficult walks and scrambles on hills in different parts of Scotland, written by an expert.

£1.00
(INC P&P)

ORDER FORM ON PAGE XXVI

POSTERS

A series of colourful posters is available, illustrating a wide range of Scotland's attractions for visitors. Some show well-known Scottish scenes, such as Edinburgh Castle, the Five Sisters of Kintail or the wild landscape of Skye. Others follow popular holiday themes: the life of Robert Burns and Scotland's traditional winter sport of Curling.

A fine looking piper and some magnificent Highland cattle by Loch Lomond are reminders of particularly Scottish attractions, while a colourful wall map of Scotland and a poster of some unusual Scottish post boxes also make excellent souvenirs.

ORDER FORM ON PAGE XXVI

OSPREY HOTELS WHILEAWAY BREAKS

How about a few days away? Osprey's economical Whileaway tariff includes dinner, bed and breakfast, per person per night (min. stay 2 nights, sharing twin room without bath). **£14.00** bunk rooms **£19.00** rooms with bath. Queensberry Arms Hotel, Annan from **£15.00**.

1. Badenoch Hotel, Aviemore.
   Tel: Aviemore 810261.

2. Carlton Hotel, Prestwick.
   Tel: Prestwick 76811.

3. Isle of Skye Hotel, Perth.
   Tel: Perth 24471/4.

4. Commodore Hotel, Helensburgh.
   Tel: Helensburgh 6924.

5. Queensberry Arms Hotel,
   Annan. Tel: Annan 2024.

6. Harp Hotel, Edinburgh.
   Tel: 031-334 4750.

**Central Reservations Office,
Elmbank Chambers, 289 Bath Street,
GLASGOW. G2. Tel: 041-552 7788.
Telex: BASSEX G 778278.**

OSPREY HOTELS

A welcome across Scotland

PAY A VISIT TO ROBERT BURNS' COUNTRY

Travel through some of Scotland's most attractive countryside, in the south west, and follow The Burns Heritage Trail. Easy to get to, it has something to interest everyone.

Send today for your free leaflet with map.

Scotland's Fishing Heritage

The sea has always played a vital part in the heritage of Scotland, this country with its wandering coastline and hundreds of islands. Today, for holidaymakers it means golden beaches, boat trips and birdwatching; for those who live on the coast it means a hard tradition of gaining a living from the sea.

You can learn about this tradition in the charming fishing villages on the coast, and in the fascinating museums which preserve it.

Write to the Scottish Tourist Board for a FREE pack telling you how to follow **SCOTLAND'S FISHING HERITAGE TRAIL.**

ENJOY SCOTLAND PACK

A handy plastic wallet which contains the Scottish Tourist Board's Touring Map of Scotland (5 miles to the inch) showing beaches, historic sites, gardens, walks, museums, fully updated for 1984; together with *Scotland: 1001 Things to See,* which describes the locates these places with details of opening times and admission charges. Completely revised and updated for 1984.

ORDER FORM ON PAGE XXVI

£3.90 (INC P&P)

GLEN SPEAN HOLIDAYS

A picturesque glen, 13 miles long, nestling between the Ben Nevis and Monadhliath Mountain Ranges. A favourite haunt of the visitor who wishes tranquillity in the beautiful Scottish countryside and for those with an interest in fishing, hill-walking, stalking, climbing, golf, pony trekking or wild life. An ideal touring centre with many interesting towns and villages within easy drive. A holiday to remember!

Hotels & Guest Houses

Kinchellie Croft Motel
Tel: (039781) 265
DBB 3 Day **£36** 7 Day **£83** (inc. of VAT)

Glen Spean Lodge Hotel
Tel: (039781) 224
DBB 3 Day **£55-£65** 7 Day **£120-£140** (inc. of VAT)

Stronlossit 'Family' Hotel
Tel: (039781) 253
DBB 3 Day **£41** 7 Day **£95** (inc. of VAT)

Roybridge Hotel
Tel: (039781) 236
DBB 3 Day **£41** 7 Day **£95** (inc. of VAT)

Spean Bridge Hotel
Tel: (039781) 250
DBB 3 Day **£55-£65** 7 Day **£120-£140** (inc. of VAT)

Coire Glas Guest House
Tel: (039781) 272
DBB 3 Day **£32** 7 Day **£75** (inc. of VAT)

Villa Barbagianni
Tel: (039781) 437
DBB 3 Day **£33** 7 Day **£77** (inc. of VAT)

Also Available: Special Adventure and Activity Holiday Packages.

Post coupon or write today to:
Glen Spean Holidays, Box 1 W/H Spean Bridge, Inverness-shire or Telephone: (039781) 250.

Details of accommodation offered will be found in this publication under 'Spean Bridge' and 'Roy Bridge'.

Send for your free full colour brochure and details to **Glen Spean Holidays, Box 1 W/H, Spean Bridge, Inverness-shire or Telephone: (039781) 250.**

Name . . . .

Address . . . .

Town . . . . Post Code . . . .

Telephone . . . .

Discover Scotland

with the friendly world of Best Western

Discover Scotland's Heritage this year with Best Western hotels and make the most of your holiday.

Best Western is as choosy about hotels as you are: each one meets the highest standards yet retains its own individuality and style. Some Best Westerns have their own leisure facilities — golfing, watersports, fishing — even curling: and they've got Scotland neatly packaged for you so you can enjoy, at your own pace — and the right price — all that Scotland's famous for — and the finest Scottish hospitality on a Discover Scotland's Heritage Tour.

Best Western is a group of 170 fine independent hotels all over Britain — with more than a score in Scotland. Let us show you around with our brand new brochures, brimming with great ideas for the best of British holidays. Booking is as easy as clipping the coupon below.

To: Best Western Hotels, Gordon Chambers, 90 Mitchell Street, Glasgow G1 3NQ. Tel. 041-204 1794

Please send me — free — the brochures I have ticked:—

Discover Scotland's Heritage 1984 ☐ Getaway Holiday Packages ☐ Map and Guide to 170 Best Western Hotels ☐

Name _______________________________

Address _____________________________

____

___________________ Post code __________

WTS84

"